Representing Youth

Representing Youth

Telling Stories, Imagining Change

Lisa Kelly

BOBBE AND JON BRIDGE PROFESSOR OF CHILD ADVOCACY
DIRECTOR, CHILDREN AND YOUTH ADVOCACY CLINIC
UNIVERSITY OF WASHINGTON SCHOOL OF LAW

Kimberly Ambrose

SENIOR LAW LECTURER
DIRECTOR, TOOLS FOR SOCIAL CHANGE: RACE AND JUSTICE CLINIC
UNIVERSITY OF WASHINGTON SCHOOL OF LAW

CAROLINA ACADEMIC PRESS

Durham, North Carolina

Library of Congress Cataloging-in-Publication Data

Names: Kelly, Lisa, author. | Ambrose, Kimberly D., author.
Title: Representing youth : telling stories, imagining change / Lisa Kelly
    and Kimberly Ambrose.
Description: Durham, North Carolina : Carolina Academic Press, 2017. |
    Includes bibliographical references and index.
Identifiers: LCCN 2017022433 | ISBN 9781611630077 (alk. paper)
Subjects: LCSH: Juvenile delinquents--United States--Case studies. | Problem
    youth--United States--Case studies. | Youth--Legal status, laws,
    etc.--United States. | Juvenile justice, Administration of--United
    States--Case studies. | Child welfare--United States--Case studies.
Classification: LCC HV9104 .K425 2017 | DDC 364.360973--dc23
LC record available at https://lccn.loc.gov/2017022433

eISBN 978-1-53100-564-1

Cover photograph: *So Many Journeys II #9* by Linda Sandow
www.lindasandow.com

Carolina Academic Press, LLC
700 Kent Street
Durham, North Carolina 27701
Telephone (919) 489-7486
Fax (919) 493-5668
www.cap-press.com

Printed in the United States of America

*This book is dedicated to the young people
whose stories continue to challenge and inspire us.*

Contents

Table of Cases

How to Use this Book

This book invites you to explore the child welfare and delinquency systems through the eyes of Michael and Maya, their families and the professionals with whom they interact. All of these characters are fictional and represent the drawing together of over fifty years of combined practice experience. You will be asked to reflect upon and respond to the representation of their experiences.

Please don't skip the Preface. It is a critical introduction to the intentions and challenges of writing a narrative text that seeks to simultaneously provide instruction and deconstruction.

The first chapter provides you with the general legal and social science context in which the stories are situated. Federal law dictates the basic structure of state child welfare systems; however, states may differ in the vocabulary and ways in which they implement federal mandates. The jurisdiction in which the stories take place is loosely based on Washington State, but efforts are made throughout to provide you with other approaches. For more nuanced and specific understandings of the law and social science, you should delve into the footnotes that support the narrative. Break-out boxes are intended to address skills and ethics issues relevant to the practice, as well as to assist you in applying the material to your local system. At the conclusion of each chapter, we ask you to take a critical look at the systems and how Michael and Maya's stories may impact what you will do to change them.

Writing this book was intended to be a rebellious act, and we hope that it will inspire more rebellious acts. This is not your usual casebook. This is not your "how-to practice" manual. Instead, this book provides a context to examine the systems that are at play, what it means to be a lawyer in these systems, and how these systems do or do not work for the people they claim to benefit. These footnoted stories, the questions posed, and the exercises provided are intended to prod you to learn more about how your state's systems function, how you can maneuver through them, and what you must do to change them.

Preface

Represent: to act or speak officially for someone or something; to bring clearly before the mind; to serve as a sign or symbol of; to portray or exhibit in art, as in "to depict"; to produce on the stage or to act the part or role of; to take the place of in some respect, usually by legal right; to give one's impression and judgment of or state in a manner intended to affect action or judgment; to serve as a specimen, example, or instance of; to form an image or representation of in the mind; to correspond to in essence.

Merriam-Webster

Lawyers are storytellers. We tell the bits and pieces of our clients' lives in pleadings, in negotiations, to other professionals and to the court. In the context of lawyering for youth, we are constantly presenting and re-presenting our clients to the various state-created systems with which they must interact—the child welfare system, the juvenile delinquency system, the educational system, the mental health system, and a myriad of other social service agencies. We re-tell their stories to a variety of participants—other lawyers and judges, professionals in other disciplines, their families and caregivers, and yes, even to themselves. They hear their own stories retold by us in our interviewing and counseling sessions, in the declarations we craft for them, in the reports we gather and generate, and in the arguments we make in hallways and courtrooms.

Using the classic dictionary definition, we "represent" our clients in virtually every sense of the word. We "speak officially" for them. We hopefully "bring their stories clearly before the minds" of our multiple audiences. We "depict" them in stories that are carefully crafted and produced on the legal stage. We "take the place of" their voices and seek to "affect action" in service of their goals. Often, our clients "serve as an example," as placeholders, for all other youth in their positions. How we depict our clients not only matters to their cases but also to other cases involving youth in foster care or youth in the juvenile delinquency system. The stories we tell "form an image" that builds upon itself as we educate our audiences who often are repeat decision-makers for other youth in similar circumstances.

But in so doing, can it be said that we "capture the essence" of our client's stories? Can we ever authentically represent our clients' lives? Here is where the fault lines in the writing of this book emerge, just as they do in practice. Given that we are limited by our own understandings of how our clients' worlds actually work, what they experience, and how they are impacted by the ways in which the world sees or refuses to see them, our ability to "represent" is undeniably curtailed.

And yet, we are appointed to engage in this representation and to seek the best solutions that our flawed and oppressive systems have to offer.

This is a book that is honest about what we presume to do every day—tell the stories of youth and their families. And like that representation, the writing of this book is indeed a presumptuous act. Presumptuous because we, as authors, dared to tell these stories not just from the perspectives of the lawyers, but also from the points of view of the youth, their families, and the other professionals who hold power over their circumstances. We chose to do this because we believe that the stories of the youth and their families ought to be at the center of this practice and at the center of any narrative for why the systems need to change.

Too often, legal systems are seen only through the eyes of the professionals who have the privilege to describe them. The professionals get to ascribe institutional intent and meaning. We get to say how and why they work the way they do. We even get to define and tally "outcomes" and call out "best practices." And yet, we are the ones whose lives are the least impacted by the consequences of the institutions within which we work. We firmly believe that this is why well-intentioned attempts to "reform the system" so often fail. It is because they continue to operate in the dark and they begin with the system as it is. Our clients, their families, and their communities are the experts on their own lives and yet when it comes to "systems change" the actual "stakeholders" at the table are the professionals who are blind to the ways in which the system is lived. The young people who have experienced foster care and who helped us by reading this book have a saying: "Nothing about us without us." It is this motto that we sought to uphold as best we could, given our own vista from our limited perch.

Meanwhile, we know that tomorrow the child welfare system will likely still be here. The juvenile delinquency system will likely still be here. How do we prepare you to do your best work within it and how do we inspire you to be subversive when you can be? These were the two tensions that we constantly fought in the writing of this book. Because, quite honestly, as we imagined living through this system we wanted at times to say, "Stop! Lay down your legal weapons! Boycott it! Starve it! Make them take the money they spend on all of us and give it to the people who need it instead." Ultimately, we believe in the power of story to change perspectives. Shifting the way a culture sees what its institutions are up to is the first step towards major change in what those institutions do.

Even though we, the authors, have represented numerous youth in these circumstances and have been privileged to hear many of their stories, we know that we have only caught brief glimpses of our clients' complex lives and what we have seen has been reshaped by the filters of our own backgrounds and experiences. Lisa Kelly is a white, cisgender[1] female, queer adult who grew up in a working class, Hungarian immigrant, Catholic family in Pittsburgh, Pennsylvania. Before entering teaching Lisa

---

1. "Cisgender": Denoting or relating to a person whose self-identity conforms with the gender identity that corresponds to the biological sex; not transgender. Oxford Dictionary, [https://perma.cc/CW66-27VY].

practiced civil rights law in Pine Bluff, Arkansas, for ten years where she learned a lot, but never enough, from the black community there. She began her clinical practice in West Virginia where she ran a clinic focused on domestic violence, family law and social security disability. She is now the director of a clinic in Washington state that represents children and youth who are in the child welfare system or are experiencing homelessness.

Kimberly Ambrose is the daughter of Judy Yoshida, a Japanese American woman who spent her early teenage years in a concentration camp in Poston, Arizona, and later raised three children, mostly as a single mother in Tacoma, Washington. Before entering teaching, Kim was a public defender representing children, parents, and others—people accused of committing crimes and people accused of being unfit parents or being the children of unfit parents. She now directs the Tools for Social Change: Race and Justice Clinic, a multi-forum advocacy clinic created to focus on the over-representation of youth of color in the juvenile and adult criminal justice system.

We both have our family secrets and experiences that inform for us what it means to be a daughter, a sister, an aunt, a mother, a grandmother. Our identities have enabled us to experience both oppression and privilege. However, we are now members of an academy from which people of color are largely excluded both as students and teachers. Neither of us has ever experienced what it means to be a teen-aged African American boy, or an African American mother with a drug problem or a father who is incarcerated, or a homeless pregnant white girl surviving a complex trauma history. We like to think we have listened well; we like to think that we have sometimes fully heard what was being communicated. But at the end of the day, we know that empathy has its limits and that "knowing" has its bounds.

The writing of this book has been humbling. It has made us keenly aware of everything we don't know even after all of these years.

It is for this reason that we have sought readers and reviewers who have experienced similar lives and who are in a better position to judge whether we have created good examples. We thank those early readers with relevant life experiences who have helped to provide insight into whether these stories are "representative." In particular, we want to thank Violet C. Banks, Deonate Cruz, Mandy Urwiler and Trai Williams, Network Representatives of the Mockingbird Society.[2] Their comments, critiques and rousing discussion helped to make this book more honest and alive.

Even with this feedback, we remain open to further critique and we anticipate that there will be more from you, the readers. We know this because our early readers had a variety of responses which required us to decide whether and how to edit.

---

2. Learn about the great work of The Mockingbird Society, [https://perma.cc/H7XS-JRNU].

We wrote this book mindful of what Nigerian author Chimamanda Ngozi Adichie has called "the danger of a single story."[3] Most of us carry with us a socially constructed story of identity. Our "single story" may be read from multiple identities. A young black male's single story, for example, is different from a young black female's single story, or an older black male's single story, or an older white female's single story. Our single story is attached to our age, our race, our class, our gender identity, our language, and our cultural expressions which all operate together to telegraph how we will be read by those around us. The more "other" we are in the society in which we operate, the more crystallized and singular our story becomes. This is so despite the reality of our hidden, less obvious, identities. These more surprising and subversive identities, once surfaced, help to disrupt the singularity of the story that society wishes to place upon us.

We take the danger of the single story to heart and realize that offering any one story—whether of a young systems-involved person, his or her family members, his case worker, lawyer or judge—as "representative" carries with it the danger of the single story. We hope that by getting to know our characters you see the disruptive aspects of their identities. We want you to see that, yes, they suffer from common external perceptions that seek to define them, but nonetheless they are more than how the dominant culture sees them; each one embodies something unique and unexpected. We hope that discovering these aspects of our characters will make you look for that disruptive power in your clients and the members of their families.

This narrative approach is intended to lead you to ask yourself about the relevance of your own lived experience to your legal practice. Lawyers are just as much shaped by our lived experience as our clients are. The differences and similarities we share with our clients can both get in the way and be fruitful ground for growing competencies, compassion and understanding. Learning how to detect whether our own stories are becoming barriers or whether they are helping us do our work better is perhaps one of the most critical and yet overlooked lawyering skills, especially in a field which is all about what it means to be human and connected to others. A failure to reflect upon what brings you to this work can unwittingly grease the wheels of an already oppressive system. Mindfulness of your own perspective and how it is shaping your reactions to your clients and their families is critical if you are going to be able to hear what your client is telling you. And humility is a must if you are going to remain open to changing both yourself and the systems in which you work.

So what's your story?

---

3. Watch her wonderful TED talk, Chimamanda Ngozi Adichie: *The Danger of a Single Story*, TED .com, [https://perma.cc/5KPZ-RGXB].

Acknowledgments

Without the financial support of The Bobbe and Jon Bridge Professorship of Child Advocacy and the University of Washington School of Law, we would not have been able to employ the village of research assistants who have contributed to this book. Those research assistants included Bonnie Aslagson, Katherine Brennan, Mark Giuliano, Anna Rae Goethe, Mariah Hanley, Nikkita Oliver, Danielle Ollero, Derek Peterson, Brandon Reeves, Suzy Ruiz, Alex Witenberg, and Kathryn Witmer. All, including the authors, were ably assisted by the expert librarians of the University of Washington's Gallagher Law Library, who provided us with the dedicated support of Maya Swanes in the final weeks of this project. Cynthia Fester, editor-research publications, provided indispensable professional staff assistance.

We also relied heavily on the feedback of others. Our partners at the Mockingbird Society provided us with an engaged focus group of former and current foster youth readers—Violet C. Banks, Deonate Cruz, Mandy Urwiler and Trai Williams—all of whom challenged us to keep their lived experience at the heart of what we do. We also want to thank the readers from practice who provided insight: Hillary Behrman, Jana Heyd and Alicia LeVezu. Finally, the students of Lisa Kelly's Child Advocacy Seminar were the earliest adopters of this book, and we appreciate their candid evaluations from the student perspective.

Representing Youth

Chapter One

State Intervention in the Lives of Youth: Foundational Considerations

The young people in this book are under one or more systems of state control. While systems and terminology may vary from state to state, this chapter aims to give you a basic understanding of how these legal and social service systems typically flow, some of the constitutional and statutory rights at stake, and some of the interdisciplinary knowledge necessary to work within the child welfare and delinquency systems.

Both Michael and Maya, the two main characters in the chapters that follow, have been removed from their homes due to allegations of abuse or neglect. There are many popular names for this system — foster care, "CPS," or the child welfare system among them. State statutes may also use different legal terminology for their child welfare systems, but the most common parlance for the legal action allowing the removal of a child from his or her parent is termed a "dependency proceeding." This proceeding is not to be confused with a proceeding which seeks to terminate parental rights. This more drastic action can sometimes occur as the result of a dependency proceeding, but the first step in any process is most often the removal of the child and a subsequent finding that the child is dependent upon the state for his or her care.

Michael and Maya also have interactions with the delinquency system of their state — another system that can separate youth from their homes and communities. Similar to abuse and neglect cases, states use different terms to describe these proceedings. A common, but not universal, label for a case in which a child is accused of criminal behavior is a "delinquency proceeding." Michael's system involvement revolves around behavior that could be criminalized if he were either an adult or a juvenile. The law's preoccupation with Maya, on the other hand, focuses on conduct that makes her a "status offender."

Status offenses are those offenses that arise out of the young person's "status" as a minor. While Maya may have committed actions that could have been charged no matter her age (shoplifting and prostitution, for example), her story focuses upon how the law responds to her in her dependency proceeding as a runaway. For youth in dependency proceedings, running away from a court-ordered placement may be treated, in some states, as a status offense. While not addressed in her chapters, Maya also could be in trouble for committing the status offense of truancy due to her failure to attend school during her episodes of running away.

In addition, young people's lives in general are impacted by the law's guarantee of a free and appropriate education, and by the extent to which they do or do not have the right to refuse or consent to medical, mental and reproductive health care. The law that governs these areas for minors becomes even more complicated and crucial for children and youth who are in state custody. So much of what it means to be a minor legally revolves around the decision-making authority of one's parent.[1] For example, parents typically consent to medical treatment for their children. Who holds that authority when a child has been removed from those default decision-makers? Who works with the doctor to decide whether a child needs medication? Or, in those states that require parental consent for abortion,[2] with whom must the minor consult? Parents also often hold the power to exercise a child's rights as against government institutions. So, for example, who is expected to participate in or even request an individualized education program for a foster child with a disability?[3] These issues arise in varying degrees for both Michael and Maya, and the legal considerations surrounding them will be addressed within their chapters.

It is challenging to describe the children and families who become subject to state intervention without falling prey to the usual labels that we have devised to sort them into either victims or perpetrators. In fact, the children and families that are processed by these systems share many of the same characteristics even though they are often studied separately. This book seeks to provide a more holistic view, while

---

1. For detailed analyses of the ability of a minor versus the ability of a parent to make legally binding decisions, see B. Jessie Hill, *Medical Decision Making By and On Behalf of Adolescents*, 15 J. HEALTH CARE L. & POL'Y 37 (2012); Yael Zakai Cannon, *Who's the Boss?: The Need for Thoughtful Identification of the Client(s) in Special Education*, 20 AM. U. J. GENDER SOC. POL'Y & L. 1 (2011).

2. Minors' access to abortion varies from state to state. In *Belloti v. Baird*, 443 U.S. 622 (1979), the Supreme Court held that when a state requires a pregnant minor to obtain parental consent to an abortion, it must also provide an alternative procedure whereby an abortion can be obtained. State approaches vary. A 2011 report found that 36 states require some form of parental involvement, and 35 of them have a judicial bypass method for cases in which the youth may petition for waiver of a parental consent or notification requirement. FAMILY PLANNING & CONTRACEPTIVE RESEARCH, UNIV. OF CHI. MED. CTR., YOUTH AWARENESS OF A MINOR'S RIGHT TO ACCESS REPRODUCTIVE HEALTH SERVICES INDEPENDENTLY 2 (2011), [https://perma.cc/9YEH-ACS7]. What this means for young women in foster care is not always clear. Whether the state, their biological parents, their foster parents, or a court appointed guardian ad litem is considered their "parent" for purposes of consent or notification under such statutes is uncertain. In a *per curiam* opinion of the Nebraska Supreme Court, the decision of a lower court that a pregnant 16-and-a-half-year-old girl in foster care was not sufficiently mature to make the decision to have an abortion on her own without the notification and consent of her foster parents was affirmed by the Nebraska Supreme Court. *See In re* Petition of Anonymous 5, 838 N.W.2d 226 (Neb. 2013). In *Ex parte Anonymous*, 531 So. 2d 901 (Ala. 1988), the Supreme Court of Alabama upheld a law requiring that a ward of the state not sufficiently mature and well-informed to make her own decision, in this case, twelve years old, obtain a waiver of parental consent for an abortion through a trial court. In *In re P.R.*, 497 N.E. 2d 1070 (Ind. 1986), the Indiana Supreme Court held that the fact that a minor was a ward of the county did not terminate the parental consent requirement when the mother's parental rights were not terminated by court order.

3. *See* 20 U.S.C. § 1414(B) ("either a parent of a child, or a state educational agency, other state agency, or local agency may initiate a request for an initial evaluation to determine if the child is a child with a disability").

struggling within the confines of existing legal and social constructs. For now, as you enter into the lives of these young people, their families, caregivers and professionals, it is important that you understand: (1) a history of how we got to where we are; (2) the demographics of the children and youth involved; (3) the basic contours of the two main legal and social service systems in which they have become immersed: child welfare and delinquency; and (4) what legal representation looks like for youth in both of these systems.

I. A Brief History of State Intervention

From the start, the state's interest in children has primarily focused upon the children of the poor. On the one hand, it is probably too rosy a view to characterize this interest as emanating solely from a charitable impulse to help poor children overcome their circumstances. On the other, it may be too cynical to theorize that such efforts were undertaken purely to protect society from the ills that befall it when the children of poor and marginalized populations test the limits of the dominant society's tolerance. Nonetheless, what we think of today as the child welfare and delinquency systems have their roots in both of these impulses—the impulse to protect and the impulse to control and punish.

Poor houses, hospitals and "foundling homes" have a long and storied history dating back to at least as early as the thirteenth century's *Conservatoria della Ruota* in Rome established by Pope Innocent III. By the sixteenth century, England too had begun to care for the children of the poor at the Christ's Hospital of London.[4] By the eighteenth century, England had established a network of hospitals intended to address the social ills that had befallen society as a result of the Gin Craze and a series of epidemics that had culminated in extremely high infant mortality rates. These hospitals included The Foundling Hospital, the Magdalen Hospital "to rescue penitent prostitutes," and the Marine Society for Educating Poor Destitute Boys. These institutions were founded in part to provide a better alternative to the workhouses for the poor which were often more unhealthy and dangerous than the streets from which the children came.[5]

As for the role of parents, according to English common law, much hinged on whether the child was born of a marriage or was "illegitimate." Another important distinction, even for marital children, was whether the child was born to parents of means or to poor parents. Those born to poor parents were removed from their parents once they were "past the age of nurture" and apprenticed to ensure "breeding up the rising generation" and that they serve the "greatest advantage of the

---

4. *See* Rhian Harris, *The Foundling Hospital*, BBC (Oct. 5, 2005), [https://perma.cc/5FK4-PB3B]. For more on the history of foundling home practices dating back as early as 1198, *see* Susan Ayres, *Kairos and Safe Havens: The Timing and Calamity of Unwanted Birth*, 15 Wm. & Mary J. Women & L. 227, 239–242 (2009).

5. Harris, *supra* note 4.

commonwealth." Children of parents with means, on the other hand, were to be educated as their parents saw fit. Children born outside of marriage were possessed of very few rights, and the law made provision for the possibility that such a child would be abandoned. The law also made clear that, at least in theory, putative fathers and mothers who abandoned such children continued to bear a duty of support for them. The enforcement of this duty, by the parish, was intended to compensate the public purse for its care expenses.[6]

Much of the common law of England sailed to what would become American shores with the earliest colonists. However, the colonies lacked the infrastructure of London's hospitals, poor houses and foundling homes. Puritan values led to increased efforts to address the problem at its source through the institution of harsh criminal penalties directed at eliminating sexual misconduct and the resulting children, by imposing fines, public whippings, and the wearing of the "scarlet letter" much as depicted in Nathaniel Hawthorne's classic.[7] In keeping with common law traditions, illegitimate children born of these relationships were often "bound out" to provide labor.[8]

The influence of the church in American child welfare continued into the nineteenth century. Quaker reformers were responsible for what has been called "the first great event in child welfare"—the establishment of the House of Refuge in New York in 1825.[9] The New York legislature gave discretion to the Society for the Reformation of Juvenile Delinquents to receive and house children who were vagrants or convicted of crimes. The nineteenth century approach to child welfare in America drew no distinction between children who committed crimes and those who were neglected or needed protection from their parents. Reformers viewed children as a social problem for which the solution was placement outside of their homes and communities. Even when they were convicted of crimes, the reformers understood these children to be victims of poverty and neglect rather than criminals.[10]

The House of Refuge movement spread to other major cities and was eventually upheld against a father's challenge by a Pennsylvania court which relied upon the doctrine of *parens patriae* to hold that the state, acting as the "common guardian of the community," had the authority to intervene in the parent-child relationship when the parents were "unequal to the task of education, or unworthy of it."[11]

Another religiously motivated reformer, considered by many to be the father of the American foster care movement, Charles Loring Brace was trained as a minister. Brace

---

6. 1 William Blackstone, Commentaries *446–59.

7. *See* Lisa Lauria, *Sexual Misconduct in Plymouth Colony*, The Plymouth Colony Archive Project, [https://perma.cc/6K9U-VYRD].

8. During the American Colonial period, "[c]hildren born out of wedlock were routinely separated from their mothers upon weaning and 'bound out' to a master." Mary Ann Mason, From Father's Property to Children's Rights: A History of Child Custody in America 2 (1994).

9. Sanford J. Fox, *Juvenile Justice Reform: An Historical Perspective*, 22 Stan. L. Rev. 1187 (1970).

10. *Id.* at 1191.

11. *Ex parte* Crouse, 4 Whart. 9 (Pa. 1839).

felt called to care for the thousands of homeless or poor children roaming the streets of New York City in the mid-nineteenth century. He founded the Children's Aid Society, which became the first agency of its kind to recruit families to take in children who were homeless or simply living in squalid conditions. While Brace is known for the "orphan trains"—taking poor "vagrant" children from New York City to be placed in "good Christian homes" in the Midwest and West—the Children's Aid Society also placed children in homes in and around New York.[12]

The rise of industrialization in urban areas and the immigrant populations that came to the United States in response to labor demands resulted in overcrowded tenements. Concern arose over street crime caused by vagrant children.[13] While Charles Loring Brace was sending children out of New York City to meet the agricultural demands of an expanding frontier, the children in Chicago who lacked parental care or had been convicted of petty crimes were housed in the Chicago Asylum and Reform School. The failure of this institution in 1872 and the practice of placing children in adult jails and poorhouses eventually led progressive reformers to establish the first juvenile court in Cook County, Illinois in 1899.[14]

The more visible problem of vagrant children may have been the preoccupation of local governments and charities like the Children's Aid Society, the House of Refuge and the Chicago Asylum and Reform School. However, reformers also initiated efforts on behalf of children against their parents and caretakers for private acts of physical abuse in the home. Common law doctrines prohibiting a minor child from suing parents in tort and sanctioning corporal punishment were substantial barriers to actions brought on behalf of children by early advocates of the late nineteenth century. To the extent that parents exceeded the bounds of proper discipline, the child's only protection was in the possible criminal prosecution of the parent.[15]

However, two cases brought in the 1870s by the founder of the Society for Prevention of Cruelty to Animals, against the abusive caretakers of children, resulted in writs to bring the children before the court for protection. Ironically, the most famous of these two children, Mary Ellen, whose story is often erroneously touted as the first case of removal of a child from his or her home for protection, was actually removed from the care of her non-biological parents with whom she had been placed by New York's Superintendent of the Outdoor Poor. Similarly, an even earlier case involved a

---

12. *See* Stephen O'Connor, Orphan Trains: The Story of Charles Loring Brace and the Children He Saved and Failed (2001). Many of the children that Loring Brace transported from New York City to farm families in the Midwest and the West were the children of the large influx of Catholic immigrants. For a documentary featuring adults who were once the children who rode the "Orphan Trains," see *American Experience: The Orphan Trains* (PBS 1995); *see also,* Rebecca S. Trammell, *Orphan Train Myths and Legal Reality*, 5 Mod. Am. 3 (2009).

13. The early child welfare movement dealt largely with children of immigrants who made up over half of the population of the New York House of Refuge by 1829. Fox, *supra* note 9, at 1201. *See also,* Anita Ortiz Maddali, *The Immigrant "Other": Racialized Identity and the Devaluation of Immigrant Family Relations,* 89 Ind. L.J. 643 (2014).

14. *Id.* at 1220–22.

15. *See* Hewlett v. George, 9 So. 885 (Miss. 1891); Johnson v. State, 21 Tenn. 703 (1840).

child named Emily who was visibly battered by her non-biological caretaker. Guarding against abusive treatment in government-sanctioned foster care has been a thread running throughout the history of child welfare in the United States. Cases continue to be brought against child welfare systems for their own failures to protect the children they removed from their parents.[16]

Even though the cases of Emily and Mary Ellen did not involve the removal of children from their biological parents, they are historically significant because they both resulted not only in the criminal prosecution of their caretakers but also in their court-ordered removal and placement outside of what had been their private caretakers. In the case of Emily, her grandmother came forward to claim her. Mary Ellen was sent to an orphanage, The Sheltering Arms.

Mary Ellen's case achieved a great deal of media attention. Undoubtedly the publicity surrounding her situation buoyed the popularity of the nascent New York Society for Prevention of Cruelty to Children (NYSPCC), which eventually was vested with police power in New York City, which allowed it to remove children from abusive and neglectful households. Societies modeled after the NYSPCC sprung up in nearly two hundred cities and towns in the United States by the turn of the century.[17]

Today's court-based dependency and delinquency proceedings sprung from the 1899 legislation creating the Cook County Juvenile Court: "An Act to regulate the treatment and control of dependent, neglected and delinquent children."[18] This Act was spearheaded by a group of wealthy women in Chicago who believed poor children who broke the law or lacked parental supervision were victims of their environment and could be saved from future offending behavior through the court's intervention.[19] The Act codified the *parens patriae* powers of the state giving the new juvenile court broad authority to place children not only in government institutions, but also in privately run institutions and family placement agencies. Under the court's "child saving" philosophy, dependent and delinquent children were commingled in a single system where placement options did not necessarily improve and dependent children could find themselves placed on probation.[20] From the outset, serious

---

16. For cases setting forth constitutional protection for children in the foster care system against the risk of substantial harm, see Braam v. State, 81 P.3d 851 (Wash. 2003); Yvonne L. v. New Mexico Dept. of Human Servs., 959 F.2d 883 (10th Cir. 1992); K.S.S. v. Montgomery County Bd. of Comm'rs, 871 F. Supp. 2d 389 (E.D. Pa. 2012). Children have also successfully brought actions in tort for harms they have experienced while in state care. *See, e.g.*, Miller v. Martin, 838 So.2d 761 (La. 2012); Sean M. v. City of New York, 795 N.Y.S.2d 539 (N.Y. App. Div. 2005). *See also,* Mark Strasser, *Deliberate Indifference, Professional Judgment and the Constitution: On Liberty Interests in the Child Placement Context,* 15 Duke J. Gender L & Pol'y 223 (2008).

17. Child Welfare Law and Practice: Representing Children, Parents and State in Abuse, Neglect and Dependency Cases 128–32 (Marvin Ventrell & Donald N. Duquette eds., 2005).

18. Fox, *supra* note 9, at 1230.

19. Tamar R. Birckhead, *Delinquent by Reason of Poverty*, 38 Wash. U. J.L. & Pol'y 53, 63–64 (2012).

20. Child Welfare Law and Practice, *supra* note 17, at 134.

offenders continued to be processed in the adult criminal justice system and the focus of the juvenile court remained on poor children. These courts caught on quickly and by 1925, all but two states had a juvenile court.[21]

The history of child welfare and juvenile justice cannot be retold without mentioning the racial disparities that existed in these systems from the outset. Houses of Refuge in the north targeted immigrant groups, but initially excluded black children. Eventually, inferior segregated facilities were provided to black children offering fewer rehabilitative services and job training opportunities.[22] Once placed in Houses of Refuge, black children remained there longer than their white counterparts who were often placed in apprenticeships or foster homes.[23] Unsurprisingly, the south, where most blacks lived prior to the great migration of the 1920s, subjected black children, like adults, to post-emancipation Black Codes and convict leases which sent them to adult prisons and subjected them to brutal working conditions.[24] When the first juvenile court emerged in Chicago, black children were initially represented in the court's caseload fairly proportionate to their representation in the population. By 1927, however, black children made up 22% of the court's caseload but only 7% of the city's population.[25] Resources were sorely lacking for black children. Chicago and other cities placed black children in jails and adult prisons at significantly higher rates than whites.[26] Sadly, almost a century later, dependency and juvenile justice systems continue to take in disproportionate numbers of black children.[27]

---

21. Birckhead, *supra* note 19, at 64–65.

22. Geoff K. Ward, The Black Child-Savers: Racial Democracy and Juvenile Justice 52–54 (2012).

23. *Id.* at 57–58.

24. *Id.* at 66–68.

25. *Id.* at 84.

26. *Id.* at 84–85. A 1925 Urban League study in New York found white youth were rarely detained for more than twenty-four hours while black youth could remain in detention for weeks and months. In Chicago, black girls fared the worst — spending the longest time in detention and having virtually no access to rehabilitative services.

27. Robin Walker Sterling, *Fundamental Unfairness:* In re Gault *and the Road Not Taken*, 72 Md. L. Rev. 607 (2013). African Americans make up only 15.4% of Illinois' total population. Sonya Rastorgi et al., U.S. Census Bureau, The Black Population 8 (2011). Despite this, African American youths make up 33.6% of all children in the state dependency system, Ill. Dep't of Children & Family Servs., Child Abuse and Neglect Statistics 7 (2015), [https://perma.cc/RZV9-6BB2], and a shocking 65% of youth in the juvenile justice system, Ill. Dep't of Juvenile Justice, Annual Report 5–6 (2014), [https://perma.cc/RA5E-UARE].

New York State presents similar racial discrepancies. African Americans make up only 15.9% of the population of the state of New York. U.S. Census Bureau, U.S. Dep't of Commerce, 2010 Census: New York Profile, [https://perma.cc/R4GM-GQ26]. And yet 53.5% of New York children in foster care, N.Y. State Office of Children & Family Servs., 2014 Monitoring and Analysis Profiles with Selected Trend Data 7 (2015), [https://perma.cc/X9PC-5H8L] [hereinafter N.Y. Foster Care], and 52.8% of the youth in the state juvenile justice system are African Americans, *see* N.Y. State Office of Children & Family Servcs., 2012 Annual Report 1 tbl.1 (2013), [https://perma.cc/U2KU-R4VZ] [hereinafter N.Y. Delinquency]. New York State is 65.7% white, U.S. Census Bureau, *supra*, but white children make up only 4.4% of the youth in foster care, N.Y. Foster

II. The Children and Youth Who Experience State Intervention

Child Maltreatment Statistics and Demographics

In 2015, more than 4 million referrals alleging child maltreatment were made to CPS, involving 7.2 million children. However, the number of confirmed victims of maltreatment shrinks to 683,000 after screening and investigation.[28] Among these children experiencing substantiated maltreatment, only 148,262 received foster care services. The remainder received services designed to assist the family and maintain the child in the home.[29]

For reporting purposes, child maltreatment data is gathered based on the following broad maltreatment types: neglect, physical abuse, sexual abuse, and other. While the rates of child maltreatment generally may go up or down over the years, one fact has remained constant among the states and throughout recent history: child neglect is by far the most common form of substantiated child maltreatment.[30]

The pie chart below shows the distribution for the most recently published data:[31]

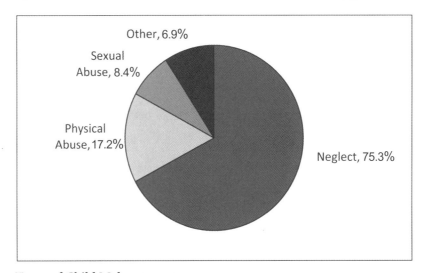

Types of Child Maltreatment

CARE, *supra*, and just 10.2% of the youth admitted to the juvenile justice system, *see* N.Y. DELINQUENCY, *supra*.

28. *See* CHILDREN'S BUREAU, U.S. DEP'T OF HEALTH & HUMAN SERVS., CHILD MALTREATMENT 2015 xii (2017), [https://perma.cc/TL4E-DKV6].

29. *Id.* at x.

30. The pie chart, "Types of Child Maltreatment," is found *id.* at xii.

31. The majority of child victims suffer from a single type of maltreatment. *Id.* at 46.

The largest percentage of all children with substantiated maltreatment claims (27.7%) are between the ages of zero to three. Victimization rates tend to decline as child age rises.[32]

The subject of racial disproportionality and child maltreatment findings has been debated for decades.[33] The stories that follow will provide an opportunity to delve more deeply into this subject. Most recent CAPTA-reported data show that while White children comprise the highest percentage of the substantiated reports (43.2%), with Hispanic children next at 23.6%,[34] followed by African American children at 21.4%, the rate of victimization of African Americans is the highest. The victimization rate for African American children is 14.5 per 1,000 children compared with a White child victimization rate of 8.1. American Indian/Alaska Native children have the next highest rate at 13.8%.[35] The data tells a story of disproportionality not only among substantiated cases, but of a deepening disparity the further one looks into the child welfare system. African American children remain out of home longer than White children and the disparity between Whites and African Americans grows wider on virtually every measure.[36] Of course, these facts only raise more questions as to the causes of disproportionality and what can be done to reverse the trend.

---

32. The rate of victimization for infants less than one year old is 24.2 per 1,000; whereas the rate of victimization for 17-year-olds is only 3.5 per 1,000. *Id* at 20.

33. *See generally* Dorothy Roberts, Shattered Bonds: The Color of Child Welfare (2002); Elizabeth Bartholet, *The Racial Disproportionality Movement in Child Welfare: False Facts and Dangerous Directions*, 51 Ariz. L. Rev. 871 (2009); Elizabeth Bartholet et al., *Race and Child Welfare*, Chapin Hall Issue Brief (2011).

34. See Children's Bureau, U.S. Dep't of Health & Human Servs., Child Maltreatment 2015, *supra* note 28, at 20.

35. *Id.* at 40.

36. John Fluke et al., *A Research Synthesis on Child Welfare Disproportionality and Disparities in* Disparities and Disproportionality in Child Welfare: Analysis of the Research 43 (2011), [https://perma.cc/6HYB-8XV6]. *See also* Washington State Racial Disproportionality Advisory Committee, Washington State Department of Social and Health Services, Racial Disproportionality in Washington State (2d ed. 2008) [https://perma.cc/9DJL-TPRT] ("Children of color generally have longer lengths of stay and are slower to exit the system than white children."); Robert B. Hill, Synthesis of Research on Disproportionality in Child Welfare: An Update 24 (2006), [https://perma.cc/R4R4-8LGH] (more black children exit care through adoption than other ethnic groups, but adoptions of black children take longer to be completed). Children's Bureau, U.S. Dep't of Health & Human Servs., Addressing Racial Disproportionality in Child Welfare (2011) [https://perma.cc/TK9H-SLUG]. In Washington State, the legislature required the study of racial disproportionality in its child welfare system. It also required the state agency to engage in efforts to reduce disproportionality and to report the outcomes of those efforts. To review progress made *see* Children's Admin., Wash. State Dep't of Social & Health Services, Report to the Legislature: Racial Disproportionality and Disparity in Washington State (2015), [https://perma.cc/Z5ZV-JKPA].

> ### *Racial Disproportionality in Your State's Child Welfare System*
> * *What are the rates of CPS referrals and out of home placement for children of color and for white children in your state?*
> * *What is the average length of stay in the system for children of color and for white children?*

The vast majority of children in the child welfare system have parents who are poor. Similarly, most families have members who have experienced mental illness, addiction or domestic violence, and yet, as the statistics above show, relatively few children actually enter out-of-home care, even among those who have substantiated cases of reported maltreatment. One need only look at adult reports of childhood maltreatment[37] to realize very quickly that a very small fraction of those who have experienced abuse or neglect as children ever come to the attention of CPS, much less enter out-of-home care.[38]

The narratives of the children and families who are in the system bear some common themes. As previously stated, neglect is involved in the vast majority of cases entering the system. Neglect is often defined as a parent's knowing or negligent deprivation of a child from shelter, clothing, food or care. Poverty is also characterized by these same deprivations. Neglect findings attribute fault to the parent.[39]

National studies have found that poverty is the single best predictor of child abuse and neglect. The data indicate that children of families with low socioeconomic status (SES) were 3–5 times more likely to experience maltreatment than children from families who were not low SES.[40]

Mental health challenges are also connected to the stress of poverty. For example, one study found that 66% of infants living in poverty have a mother who is suffering from some form of depression. Mothers suffering from severe depression are also more likely to struggle with substance abuse and domestic violence. The quality of the mother-infant interactions among low-income, severely depressed mothers was also found to be diminished in comparison to non-depressed mothers of the same low

---

37. For a look at levels of self-reported abuse, neglect, and household dysfunction by adults reflecting upon their childhoods, *see* CENTERS FOR DISEASE CONTROL AND PREVENTION, THE ADVERSE CHILDHOOD EVENTS STUDY, available at: [https://perma.cc/VG5R-PYGR].

38. Ruth Gilbert et al., *Child Maltreatment 1: Burden and Consequences of Child Maltreatment in High-Income Countries*, THE LANCET, Jan. 3, 2009, at 68, 68–73.

39. Joy Duva & Sania Metzger, *Addressing Poverty as a Major Risk Factor in Child Neglect: Promising Policy and Practice,* 25(1) PROTECTING CHILDREN 63, 65 (2010).

40. Low SES families were defined as those meeting one of three criteria: an annual income less than $15,000, parents who had not completed high school, or including a household member who participated in a poverty-related program. ANDREA J. SEDLAK ET AL., U.S. DEP'T OF HEALTH & HUMAN SERVS., FOURTH NATIONAL INCIDENCE STUDY OF CHILD ABUSE AND NEGLECT (NIS-4) § 5-10 (2010), [https://perma.cc/E8C6-NLD9].

socioeconomic status.[41] Whether poverty results in depression and substance abuse or substance abuse and depression deepen poverty, the mix of all of these factors increases the likelihood of interaction with the child welfare system.[42]

Parental arrest and incarceration also lead to increased likelihood of involvement with the child welfare system.[43] The incarceration rate for women is increasing at a rate even faster than that of the incarceration rates for men.[44] Most children are removed from their mothers' care.[45] Hence, an increasing number of children are entering out-of-home care because their mothers are incarcerated. The criminal justice system disproportionately impacts communities of color,[46] particularly African American communities, which undoubtedly contributes to racial disproportionality in the child welfare system.

Research shows some connection between child maltreatment, the child welfare system and delinquency.[47] A study in Washington State found that 59% of children referred to juvenile court for an offense for the first time had some contact with the state's child protection agency.[48] The percentage went up to 89% for children with more than one referral to the juvenile justice system. The study showed that children

41. Eleven percent of these mothers suffered from severe depression; fifty-five percent suffered from mild to moderate depression. The Urban Institute, *Infants of Depressed Mothers Living in Poverty: Opportunities to Identify and Serve, Brief 1* (Aug. 2010), [https://perma.cc/VS7N-KZNM].

42. Studies indicate that between one-third and two-thirds of child maltreatment cases involve parental substance abuse. Child Welfare Information Gateway, *Parental Substance Use and the Child Welfare System* 2 (2009), *available at* [https://perma.cc/N5L2-G4N2] (last viewed 08/26/2014).

43. In 2009, the General Accounting Office (GAO) was asked to determine the number of foster children with incarcerated parents. After two years of study, the report concluded that "children in foster care with parents who are incarcerated" is not a well-defined population. However, state data revealed that in 2009 over 14,000 children entered foster care because of a parent's incarceration. This number does not answer the charge that the GAO was given, and the report notes that this figure undercounts the population because it does not include those children whose parents are incarcerated after their removal or sometime before. It also does not count the large number of noncustodial fathers who are in prison when their children are removed from their mothers' care. *See* GAO, More Information and Collaboration Could Promote Ties Between Foster Care Children and Their Incarcerated Parents 10–12 (September 2011), [https://perma.cc/7CFA-CYTA].

44. From 1980 to 2010, the incarceration rates for women increased by 646%, nearly 1.5 times the rate of men. *See* The Sentencing Project: Incarcerated Women, available at: [https://perma.cc/LG2J-MQ53].

45. *See* Children's Bureau, U.S. Dep't of Health & Human Servs., Child Maltreatment Report 2015, supra note 28, at 46 [https://perma.cc/TL4E-DKV6]. For a qualitative study of incarcerated mothers detailing the stories of twenty-six women characterized by poverty, victimization, chronic substance addiction, recovery and relapse, *see* Suzanne Allen, Chris Flaherty, & Gretchen Ely, *Throwaway Moms: Maternal Incarceration and the Criminalization on Female Poverty*, 25(2) J. Women and Soc. Work 160 (2010), [https://perma.cc/3DXT-W7DC].

46. *See* Michelle Alexander, The New Jim Crow: Mass Incarceration in the Age of Colorblindness (2010).

47. Janet Wiig & Cathy Spatz Widom with John A. Tuell, Understanding Child Maltreatment & Juvenile Delinquency ix–xi (2003), [https://perma.cc/4DSM-REC8].

48. *See* Gregory Halemba & Gene Siegel, National Center for Juvenile Justice, Doorways to Delinquency: Multi-System Involvement of Delinquent Youth in King County, (2011) [https://perma.cc/MFZ2-3SSH].

who had a history of child welfare legal activity or placement started their delinquent careers a year or more earlier than youth with no involvement, were first detained at an earlier age, detained far more frequently, and spent substantially more time in detention compared to youth with no multi-system involvement.[49]

Although there is a connection between child maltreatment, the child welfare system and delinquency, not all maltreated children end up in the juvenile justice system. All adolescents are vulnerable to doing things that could lead to juvenile justice involvement based on what we know about the adolescent brain.

The Adolescent Brain and the Impact of Child Maltreatment

Without regard to whether they have experienced maltreatment, adolescents are prone to impulsivity, risk taking and sensation seeking behavior, peer influence and a diminished ability to perceive future consequences—all of which can contribute to delinquent behavior. These characteristics have been confirmed by brain imagery, social science, self-report studies and recognized by the U.S. Supreme Court.[50] It is unsurprising, then, that criminal activity typically peaks during the teenage years, from fifteen to nineteen, followed by a decline in the early twenties.[51] This rise-and-fall of criminal activity is known as the age-crime curve, and has been observed universally across Western populations. Even the most serious juvenile offenders have been shown to decrease illegal activity over time regardless of what type of intervention is imposed.[52]

Not all adolescents engage in delinquent behavior and researchers have spent decades searching for other explanations or contributors to delinquency. Offending behavior has been attributed to a complex interaction of individual, social and community risk factors. These include, among others, poverty, community disorganization, exposure to violence, residential mobility, school performance, peer association, parental attitudes and parental criminality.[53]

The adolescent brain is also impacted by neglect experienced at earlier developmental stages. Children who are chronically neglected "experience more severe cognitive and academic deficits, social withdrawal and internalizing behaviors"[54] than

---

49. *Id.* For an overview of other studies that have documented a connection between the child welfare system and delinquency, see Janet K. Wiig & John A. Tuell with Jessica K. Heldman, Robert F. Kennedy Children's Action Corps, Guidebook for Juvenile Justice & Child Welfare System Coordination and Integration xiii–xviii, (3d ed. 2014), [https://perma.cc/U7Q4-NWQX].

50. *See Miller v. Alabama,* 132 S. Ct. 2455 (2012); *Graham v. Florida,* 560 U.S. 48 (2010); *Roper v. Simmons,* 543 U.S. 551 (2005).

51. Rolf Loeber et al., From Juvenile Delinquency to Young Adult Offending 3 (2013), [https://perma.cc/3528-KRN5].

52. Melissa Sickmund and Charles Puzzanchera, Nat'l Ctr. for Juvenile Justice, Juvenile Offenders and Victims: 2014 National Report 71 [https://perma.cc/9835-5476].

53. J. David Hawkins et al., Office of Juvenile Justice and Delinquency Prevention, Predictors of Youth Violence (2000), [https://perma.cc/694L-XN9A]; Kristin Henning, *Criminalizing Normal Adolescent Behavior in Communities of Color,* 98 Cornell L. Rev. 383, 416–17 (2013).

54. *See* Children's Bureau, Chronic Child Neglect (2013), [https://perma.cc/5EBT-MVWT].

children who have suffered other forms of maltreatment. Children who have suffered chronic neglect also often have "problems with attachment, cognitive development, emotional self-regulation, social self-confidence, social competence, perseverance in problem solving, and empathy and social conscience. They may experience language delay, as well as conduct disorders."[55]

The younger the child is when she or he experiences neglect and the more prevalent the neglect, the greater the harm.[56] Infants may experience this neglect as a failure to thrive.[57] Children who have been physically abused may have disabilities and health problems directly resulting from abuse. They also may experience a host of physical and mental health issues flowing from the trauma and disruption in development that physical abuse causes.[58]

The dynamic between abuse, neglect, brain development and disability is complex. Abuse may cause disabilities that impair cognitive functioning. Research also shows that children born with disabilities are more often abused, and are also more often relinquished to the child welfare system, either by force or by choice.[59] Some disabilities or medical conditions that present at birth or shortly thereafter are the result of parental substance abuse.[60]

For the older child, mental health issues such as post-traumatic stress disorder, depression, self-injurious behavior and low self-esteem may also develop as a result

---

55. *Id.*

56. *Id. See also* Arthur Becker-Weidman, *Effects of Early Maltreatment on Development: A Descriptive Study Using the Vineland Adaptive Behavior Scales-II,* Child Welfare, Mar.-Apr. 2009, at 137 (finding that children with histories of chronic early maltreatment resulting in reactive attachment disorder yielded a developmental age of 4.4. years while the average chronological age was 9.9 years).

57. American Academy of Pediatrics Committee on Child Abuse and Neglect, *Failure to Thrive as a Manifestation of Child Neglect*, 116(5) Pediatrics e608–612 (2005).

58. Jill Goldman, et al., A Coordinated Response to Child Abuse and Neglect: The Foundation for Practice, 35–38, Office of Child Abuse and Neglect, U.S. Dept. of Health and Human Services, (2003) [https://perma.cc/QJ9S-46WV].

59. Youth with Disabilities in the Foster Care System: Barriers to Success and Proposed Policy Solutions 8, National Council on Disability [https://perma.cc/76Z9-555V].

60. It is widely recognized by the scientific community that consumption of drugs and alcohol during pregnancy may result in disability and health problems to the child. Alcohol consumption during pregnancy can cause fetal alcohol syndrome or other alcohol related birth defects, which include physical abnormalities, slowed growth, central nervous system damage, and even death. Fetal Alcohol Spectrum Disorders: Competency- Based Curriculum Development Guide 3, U.S. Dept. of Health and Human Services, (2008), [https://perma.cc/9BNH-UAAQ]. Children born to mothers who use illicit drugs during pregnancy face similar risks. For example, children born to mothers addicted to heroin are at risk for premature birth, breathing difficulties, bleeding in the brain, and low blood sugar as well as low birth weight. If a mother is using addictive drugs during pregnancy, the drugs can pass through the placenta to the child, causing the infant to be addicted to the drugs as well (neonatal abstinence syndrome). Babies born with neonatal abstinence syndrome can spend months going through withdrawals, and suffer from irritability, gastrointestinal issues, sleep and feeding disturbances, and a disruption in mother-child bonding. Rajashekhar Moorthy Madgula et al., *Illicit Drug Use During Pregnancy: Effects and Management*, Expert Rev. of Obstetrics and Gynecology, Mar. 2011 at 179.

of early neglect and/or abuse.[61] A young person's mental health issues can lead to behavioral problems that garner the attention of both systems.

Behavior alone, however, does not explain who enters the juvenile justice system. Many adolescents engage in illegal behavior and never get arrested or otherwise have contact with the juvenile justice system. This is significant because, paradoxically, several studies have shown that a juvenile arrest predicts increased future delinquent behavior — resulting in what would appear to be for some youth a cycle of juvenile justice involvement undeterred by the sanctions and services the system offers.[62]

So what explains who comes under the control of the juvenile justice system? Recently, the "school-to-prison-pipeline" has garnered a great deal of attention after schools adopted "zero tolerance" policies resulting in referrals to law enforcement for behaviors that may have previously been handled by teachers and school administrators. School expulsions and suspensions have been shown to predict juvenile justice involvement.[63] In Michael's story, you will see an example of how this pipeline works particularly efficiently for youth who are in the dependency system.

Mental health disorders, substance abuse and traumatic victimization also play a significant role in who becomes involved in the juvenile justice system. Sixty to seventy percent of youth in contact with the juvenile justice system have a diagnosable mental health disorder and of those, 60% also have a co-occurring substance abuse disorder.[64] A large study of youth in juvenile detention revealed that 75% had experienced traumatic victimization — having seen or heard someone being seriously injured or killed.[65] For youth who commit serious violent offenses or chronically offend, trauma and a high number of "adverse childhood experiences" ("ACES") are an ordinary part of their lives.[66]

But not all youth who misbehave in school or struggle with behavioral health or trauma come into contact with the juvenile justice system. The answer to why certain youth come into the juvenile justice system lies squarely in the structures we have created which place discretion with police and prosecutors as the gatekeepers to that system. This is not to "blame" those state actors, but rather to explain how they play

---

61. GOLDMAN, *supra* note 58, at 37.

62. Terence P. Thornberry et al., *The Causes and Correlates*, 9 Juv. Just. 3, 12 (2004); *Article 3*, 3 CRIM. HIGHLIGHTS: CHILD. & YOUTH 6 (2015).

63. *See* TONY FABELO ET AL., COUNCIL OF STATE GOV'TS JUSTICE CTR., BREAKING SCHOOLS' RULES (2011), [https://perma.cc/NE3R-ZQJJ].

64. JENNIE L. SHUFELT & JOSEPH J. COCOZZA, NAT'L CTR. FOR MENTAL HEALTH AND JUVENILE JUSTICE, YOUTH WITH MENTAL HEALTH DISORDERS IN THE JUVENILE JUSTICE SYSTEM (2006), [https://perma.cc/PD9G-YRDF].

65. Karen M. Abram et al., *Posttraumatic Stress Disorder and Trauma in Youth in Juvenile Detention*, 61(4) ARCH. GEN. PSYCHIATRY 403–410 (2004).

66. *See* Bryanna Hahn Fox et al., *Trauma Changes Everything: Examining the Relationship between Adverse Childhood Experiences and Serious, Violent and Chronic Juvenile Offenders*. 46 CHILD ABUSE & NEGLECT 163–73 (2015).

a critical and assigned role in funneling youth into juvenile court.[67] They operate within a variety of state and local legal frameworks, some of which will be discussed below. They are charged with responding to distinct and often challenged communities that demand public safety. They have limited resources. They are human and subject to implicit bias. They are feeding a system that has struggled from the outset to treat children and families equally.

So who are the youth that find themselves in the juvenile offender (delinquency) system?

Delinquency System Statistics and Demographics

Racial and ethnic disparity persists in the juvenile justice system, as it has since its inception.[68] In 1919, two decades after the creation of the first juvenile court, racism was found to be a contributor to delinquency by the Chicago Commission on Race Relations, a commission appointed by the governor of Illinois following the Chicago race riots.[69] A century later, in 2015, the U.S. Department of Justice Civil Rights Division found that race had a "significant and substantial impact" on pretrial detention in the St. Louis Family Court, a juvenile court located where protests had recently erupted in response to the killing of an unarmed black teenager, Michael Brown, by a white police officer. After examining the patterns of detaining youth pre- and

---

67. Professor Henning suggests that police, prosecutors and other state actors bear responsibility for addressing the racial disparities that exist in the juvenile justice system regardless of whether they are a product of intentional racism. Henning, *supra* note 53, at 417. Examples of law enforcement leading on juvenile justice reform can be found in places such as Richmond, Virginia, where the police chief adopted a policy to dramatically reduce the number of juvenile arrests. *See* Ted Strong, *Henrico's New Juvenile Arrest Policy Took Effect Wednesday*, Richmond Times-Dispatch, (July 1, 2015), [https://perma.cc/3WFX-6U5W].

68. Although only 15% of the youth population aged 10–17 are African American, they make up 40% of juveniles in long-term public detention nationally. Jessica Short & Christy Sharp, Disproportionate Minority Contact in the Juvenile Justice System 3, Child Welfare League of America, (2005), [https://perma.cc/G5JC-M98T]. Two-thirds of the girls were youth of color, primarily African American and Latina. *Id.* at 6. Disparities have persisted, even as the overall rate of juvenile confinement has declined. African American youth remain five times more likely than their white peers to be confined. The Annie E. Casey Foundation, Reducing Youth Incarceration in the United States 2 (2013), [https://perma.cc/67V4-GFG7]. *Accord*, National Center for Juvenile Justice & Office of Juvenile Justice & Delinquency Prevention, Juvenile Offenders and Victims: 2014 National Report 197, [https://perma.cc/9385-5U76] (In 2010, the rates of incarceration for black youth were between 5 and 6 times higher than the rate for white youth and almost twice as high as the rate for Hispanic youth). Looking at the problem on a state-by-state basis, yields even greater understanding and reveals that in many places, African American youth far outstrip white youth in percentage of population being incarcerated on any given day. For example, in Illinois and New York, there are 3.5–4 times more African American youth incarcerated than white youth, a disproportionality rate that has increased over time, even though the overall numbers incarcerated have dropped. Explore the interactive state-by-state map, at *Unbalanced Juvenile Justice*, Haywood Burns Institute, http://data.burnsinstitute.org/.

69. Cheryl Nelson Butler, *Blackness as Delinquency*, 90 Wash. U. L. Rev. 1335, 1372 (2013).

post-adjudication, the Department of Justice found that the St. Louis Family Court violated the Equal Protection rights of black youth.[70]

> ### *Racial Disproportionality in Your State's Delinquency System*
> - *What are the differences in the arrest and detention rates for youth of color and white youth in your state?*
> - *What other decision points in the juvenile justice system produce disparities in your state?*
> - *Has your state conducted an assessment into the causes of these disparities and what have they found?*

Since the early 1990s, states have been collecting data on racial disproportionality in juvenile incarceration rates and other decision points in the juvenile justice system in order to comply with one of the core mandates of the Juvenile Justice and Delinquency Prevention Act (JJDPA).[71] Little progress has been made in reducing it.[72] Although the number of youth arrested, adjudicated and detained has dropped significantly nationwide, disproportionality between white youth and youth of color has stayed consistent for the most part, and gotten worse in some places.[73] These disparities exist despite data showing youth of color self-report engaging in illegal behavior at similar or lower rates than white youth.[74] Despite federal oversight and dedicated public and private resources, racial and ethnic disparity remains one of the most persistent challenges facing the juvenile justice system today.

Girls are underrepresented in the juvenile justice system; however, their numbers have increased 69% from 1985–2010, a period during which the number of boys increased by 5%.[75] The increase in arrests for girls has been driven largely by arrests for assault, which scholars associate with the proliferation of mandatory arrest policies for domestic violence.[76] Girls who engage in fighting in their home are now more likely to be swept into the juvenile justice system for intra-family violence.[77]

---

70. *See* U.S. Dep't of Justice, Investigation of the St. Louis County Family Court 34 (2015), [https://perma.cc/F4MP-AV3N].

71. 42 U.S.C. § 5633(a)(22). *See* Elizabeth N. Jones, *Disproportionate Representation of Minority Youth in the Juvenile Justice System: A Lack of Clarity and Too Much Disparity Among States "Addressing" the Issue*, 16 U.C. Davis J. Juv. L. & Pol'y 155, 165 (2012); James Bell & Laura John Ridolfi, W. Haywood Burns Inst., Adoration of the Question: Reflections on the Failure to Reduce Racial & Ethnic Disparities in the Juvenile Justice System (Shadi Rahimi ed., 2008), [https://perma.cc/LX8Q-ER77].

72. *See generally* Bell & Ridolfi, *supra* note 71.

73. Nat'l Ctr. for Juvenile Justice, *supra* note 52, at 157–58.

74. Henning, *supra* note 53, at 413.

75. Nat'l Ctr. For Juvenile Justice, *supra* note 52, at 154.

76. Francine T. Sherman, *Justice for Girls: Are We Making Progress?*, 59 UCLA L. Rev. 1584, 1602–1605 (2012).

77. *Id.; see also*, Darrell Steffensmeier & Jennifer Schwartz, *Trends in Girls' Delinquency and the Gender Gap: Statistical Assessment of Diverse Sources* in The Delinquent Girl 53 (Margaret A Zahn

Girls are overrepresented in the status offender population.[78] This phenomenon is rooted in society's historical desire to protect "wayward girls" as well as to control their "misbehavior," i.e., their failure to conform to societal norms.[79] Girls are particularly at risk for being arrested for running away, which often drives them further into the juvenile system.[80]

As previously discussed, there are many factors that contribute to or correlate with delinquent behavior and juvenile justice involvement. Girls, however, report being sexually abused at significantly higher rates than their male counterparts in the juvenile justice system.[81] In addition, girls report suffering significantly more adverse childhood experiences than boys—they are twice as likely as boys to report five or more ACES.[82] Research also reveals higher rates of mental health disorders among girls in the juvenile justice system, including depression, anxiety and PTSD.[83]

The intersectionality of race and gender plays a significant role for girls in the juvenile justice system. While the overall number of girls being detained has dropped, the proportion of black girls detained has increased.[84] Black girls are also disproportionately impacted by the "school to prison pipeline"—they are suspended at significantly higher rates than girls of any other race or ethnicity and at higher rates than most boys.[85] The institutional racism and implicit bias that undergirds decision-making in

---

ed., 2009) (discussing the Policy Change Hypothesis: "The criminalization of violence occurring between intimates and in private settings such as at home or school will portray levels of female violence that more closely approximate levels of male violence because girls' violence is more likely to take place in this context than in public settings against strangers.")

78. Nat'l Ctr. For Juvenile Justice, *supra* note 52, at 154 ("Although females were charged in only 28% of the delinquency cases formally processed in 2010, they were involved in 43% of status offense cases.").

79. Sherman, *supra* note 76, at 1589.

80. *Id.* at 1599–1600.

81. Michael T. Baglivio et al., US Dep't of Justice, Office of Justice Programs, Office of Juvenile Justice & Delinquency Prevention, *The Prevalence of Adverse Childhood Experiences (ACE) in the Lives of Juvenile Offenders*, 3 J. Juv. Justice 1, 9 (Spring 2014) (Girls were 4.4 times more likely to report being sexually abused than boys.)

82. *Id.*

83. Candice L. Odgers et al., *Misdiagnosing the Problem: Mental Health Profiles of Incarcerated Juveniles*, 14(1) Can. Child & Adolesc. Psychiatry Rev. 26–29 (Feb. 2005) (finding that these gender disparities also found in the normative population increase exponentially for girls in the juvenile justice system).

84. Francine T. Sherman et al., Making Juvenile Detention Work for Girls: A Guide to Juvenile Detention Reform, at 9, at [https://perma.cc/3FLQ-J89X].

85. Data Snapshot: School Discipline, Issue Brief No. 1, 3 (Mar. 2014), Civil Rights Data Collection, U.S. Dept. of Educ. for Civil Rights, available at [https://perma.cc/9KEN-GCQY]; *see also*, Edward J. Smith & Shaun R. Harper, *Disproportionate Impact of K-12 School Suspension and Expulsion on Black Students in Southern States*, 1 Philadelphia, PA: Univ. of Penn. Center for the Study of Race & Equity in Educ. (2015) at [https://perma.cc/Y3KC-S3XB] ("Across the Southern states, Black girls comprised 56% of suspensions and 45% of expulsions, both of which were also highest among all girls. In 10 Southern states, Blacks were suspended most often among girls.").

the school discipline context undoubtedly impact decision-making in the juvenile justice system as well.[86]

Finally, it is difficult to collect data on lesbian, gay, bisexual, questioning, transgender and gender non-conforming youth in the juvenile justice system. Youth may be reluctant to disclose their sexual orientation or gender identity for fear of victimization or other negative responses from peers, parents, and juvenile justice professionals. One national study used a survey implemented in six jurisdictions to estimate that 15% of juvenile justice involved youth identify in one or more of these ways.[87] Lesbian, gay, bisexual and gender non-conforming youth in the study were also found to be more likely than their heterosexual and gender-conforming peers to be homeless, placed in foster care, detained for running away, and detained for prostitution.[88]

The Effect of the Child Welfare and Delinquency Systems

While the delinquency and child welfare systems are intended to be rehabilitative or protective, these systems also carry with them a host of dangers that expose children and youth to new harms.

The Effect of the Child Welfare System

A growing body of research seeks to discover whether the child welfare system has a positive, negative or neutral impact on the well-being of children. One prominent study found that in "close cases," where the decision to remove is uncertain, children have better employment, delinquency and teen motherhood outcomes when they remain in their homes.[89]

The poorer outcomes of foster youth when compared to their in-home peers is likely due to the trauma of removal, the resulting disruption of attachments, and the lack of permanency. Children in state care may be moved frequently from one home to another. This instability can lead to educational disruptions, an inability to form consistent caregiver and peer relationships and the deepening of the negative mental health impacts of maltreatment.[90]

---

86. *See* Janel A. George, *Sterotype and School Pushout: Race, Gender, and Discipline Disparities*, 68 Ark. L. Rev. 101 (2015) and Jyoti Nanda, *Blind Discretion: Girls of Color & Delinquency in the Juvenile Justice System*, 59 UCLA L. Rev. 1502, 1530–1531 (2012).

87. Angela Irvine, *"We've Had Three of Them": Addressing the Invisibility of Lesbian, Gay, Bisexual and Gender Non-Conforming Youths in the Juvenile Justice System*, 19 Colum. J. Gender & L. 675 (2010).

88. *Id.* at 694.

89. Joseph J. Doyle, Jr., *Child Protection and Child Outcomes: Measuring the Effects of Foster Care*, 97 The Am. Econ. Rev. 1583 (Dec. 2007) [https://perma.cc/TR9T-ANSL].

90. *See Braam v. State of Washington*, 81 P.3d 851 (Wash. 2003); Research indicates that roughly half of children entering the system achieve early placement; almost 20% achieve later stability; and nearly 30% never achieve stability. David M. Rubin et al., *The Impact of Placement Stability on Behavioral Well-being for Children in Foster Care*, 110:2 Pediatrics 336 (2007), [https://perma.cc/GE6B -SRHG].

Some children who are removed from their homes never find a permanent home. For those young people who don't, outcomes are not good. Studies looking at foster care alumni indicate that youth who "age out" of the system have lower high school graduation rates,[91] higher rates of homelessness, unemployment,[92] mental health issues,[93] and teen parenthood[94] than their in-home peers.

The Effect of the Juvenile Justice System

Measuring the impact of the juvenile justice system is challenging due to the lack of consistent data on recidivism.[95] In addition, it is difficult to quantify other objectives of the system such as deterrence and holding youth accountable. If the system's primary purpose is rehabilitation, then persistently high recidivism rates for youth who are involved in the juvenile system indicate it is not working.[96] Some research suggests that confining youth in secure detention may actually increase recidivism rates.[97] Detention has been shown to predict future delinquency amongst serious adolescent offenders more significantly than gang membership, parental abuse or neglect, having single parents or carrying weapons.[98] As mentioned previously, studies have also consistently shown that a juvenile arrest will predict future delinquent behavior regardless of the interventions imposed.[99] Finally, research also has found

---

91. Washington State Institute for Public Policy, Mason Burley & Mina Halpern, EDUCATIONAL ATTAINMENT AND FOSTER YOUTH: ACHIEVEMENT AND GRADUATION OUTCOMES FOR CHILDREN IN STATE CARE (Nov. 2001), [https://perma.cc/W6RA-CMC6]. Frank W. Putnam, *The Impact of Trauma on Childhood Development*, 57:1 JUV. AND FAM. CT. J. 1–11 (2006), at 1, 2.

92. Peter J. Pecora, et al., *Educational and Employment Outcomes of Adults Formerly Placed in Foster Care: Results from the Northwest Foster Care Alumni Study*, 28 CHILD. AND YOUTH SERVICES REV. 1459–1481(2006).

93. CASEY FAMILY PROGRAMS, ASSESSING THE EFFECTS OF FOSTER CARE: MENTAL HEALTH OUTCOMES FROM THE CASEY NATIONAL ALUMNI STUDY 1–2 (2003), [https://perma.cc/46QT-Y67H].

94. Heather D. Boonstra, *Teen Pregnancy Among Young Women in Foster Care: A Primer, Guttmacher Policy Review*, GUTTMACHER INSTITUTE, Spring 2011, at 8, [https://perma.cc/G3HT-PLH7]. Amy Dworsky & Mark Courtney, *The Risk of Teenage Pregnancy among Transitioning Foster Youth: Implications for Extending State Care Beyond Age 18*, 32 CHILDREN AND YOUTH SERV. REV. 1351, 1351–1356 (2010).

95. According to the Pew Charitable Trust's public safety project, one third of states do not collect or report juvenile recidivism data and fewer than half use comprehensive measures that can provide a full picture of juvenile re-offense behavior. *See* PEW CHARITABLE TRUSTS, 50-STATE TABLE: DATA COLLECTION AND REPORTING IN JUVENILE CORRECTIONS (2014), [https://perma.cc/K3UZ -Z7CF].

96. *See* Thornberry et al., *supra* note 62.

97. AMANDA PETTERUTI ET AL., JUSTICE POLICY INSTITUTE, STICKER SHOCK: CALCULATING THE FULL PRICE TAG FOR YOUTH INCARCERATION 22 (2014), [https://perma.cc/6PL5-YDM4].

98. Brent B. Benda & Connie L. Tollet, *A Study of Recidivism of Serious and Persistent Offenders Among Adolescents*, 27:2 J. OF CRIM. JUST. 111–126 (1999). Barry Holman & Jason Ziedenberg, *The Dangers of Detention: The Impact of Incarcerating Youth in Detention and Other Secure Facilities*, JUSTICE POLICY INSTITUTE, [https://perma.cc/HAP6-SVHQ].

99. *See* sources cited *supra* note 53.

that Juvenile Court involvement may increase the likelihood of involvement with the adult criminal justice system.[100]

While the research is clear that mental health disorders are pervasive amongst incarcerated youth, there is less research on how incarceration impacts young inmates' mental health. The stressors associated with an incarceration environment, such as isolation, bullying, and victimization as well as the loss of their lives outside may contribute to exacerbating youth's mental health issues and feelings of self-worth.[101]

Other impacts of incarcerating and processing youth in the juvenile justice system include lower employability, lower educational attainment, and lower wages.[102] This makes sense when one considers how incarceration disrupts regular school attendance and participation in the job market. But some of these negative outcomes are also the result of the collateral consequences of a juvenile record, which vary state to state depending on policies for releasing juvenile arrest and adjudication information.[103]

Collateral Consequences

- *What are the collateral consequences of a juvenile adjudication in your state?*

- *Are juvenile delinquency records available to the public, employers or landlords and, if so, for how long?*

Research has shown youth involved in both the child welfare and juvenile justice systems have particularly bleak outcomes. Studies in Washington, Arizona, and California reveal high rates of recidivism for crossover youth and a higher number of placements, as well as a higher percentage of placements in residential centers or group homes rather than foster homes.[104] One suggested contributor to this problem is the lack of interagency coordination. States vary widely with respect to how services are

---

100. Uberto Gatti et al., *Iatrogenic Effect of Juvenile Justice.* 50:8 J. OF CHILD PSYCH. PSYCHIATRY 991–998 (2009).

101. Ian Lambie & Isabel Randell, *The Impact of Incarceration on Juvenile Offenders*, 33 CLIN. PSYCHOL. REV. 448, 453 (2013). There is more research supporting the negative effects of adult prisons on youth's mental health. Irene Y.H. Ng, *Incarcerating Juveniles in Adult Prisons as a Factor in Depression*, 21 CRIM. BEHAV. & MENTAL HEALTH 21 (2011).

102. PETTERUTI ET AL., *supra* note 97, at 28–29.

103. While many states keep juvenile offender records confidential, many states have open records available to prospective employers, landlords and even the general public. NAT'L CTR. FOR JUVENILE JUSTICE, *supra* note 52, at 98.

104. Gary Gately, *'Dual-Status' Kids Endure Another Kind of Double Jeopardy*, JUV. JUST. INFO. EXCHANGE (Jan. 18, 2015), [https://perma.cc/EWZ7-PEXT]. A Los Angeles study found that crossover youth are on average six months younger than non-crossover youth in the juvenile offender population; a high proportion of them are girls; African American youth are overrepresented in this population; and cross-over youth are more likely to be given restrictive placements as first time offenders. A contributing factor for youth crossing over from the dependency side to the juvenile offender side is placement instability. Joseph P. Ryan & Denise C. Herz, CROSSOVER YOUTH AND JUVENILE JUSTICE PROCESSING IN LOS ANGELES COUNTY (2008) [https://perma.cc/5MEB-7K2N].

provided to children who are in both systems, with very few states centralizing administration of services to youth in a single state agency.[105] This lack of coordination can sometimes result in the systems fighting over who should have responsibility for the youth — child welfare social workers may be incentivized to seek secure confinement in detention for youth who are difficult to place while juvenile probation officers may see children who have been victimized as inappropriate for the more punitive delinquency system that comes with additional stigma and collateral consequences that can limit the youth's opportunities.[106]

III. State Intervention Systems

Constitutional Considerations

State intervention in the lives of youth and their families implicates constitutional considerations. Whether youth are removed for protection from their parents or are incarcerated for offending, constitutional doctrines are invoked.

The Fundamental Rights of Parents

While the nineteenth century may have seen the articulation of the *parens patriae* doctrine in the context of an industrializing society, the early twentieth century brought with it a recognition of parents' fundamental constitutional rights. Ever since then, two principles have been in tension in every dependency proceeding: 1) parents' fundamental, constitutionally protected rights to raise their children,[107] and 2) the state's interest in protecting children from harm.[108]

While Supreme Court case law defining the contours of these competing principles is sparse and not always as illuminating as one might wish when applied to the dependency context, it is clear that the state is not free to remove children from their parents' care without due process.

The Supreme Court has held, for example, that a case-by-case due process analysis must be applied to the question of whether parents are entitled to appointment of

---

105. Only seven states centralize child welfare and juvenile justice (inclusive of community supervision or juvenile probation) through a single state-level department: Alaska, Delaware, Mississippi, New Hampshire, New Mexico, Rhode Island, and Vermont. Nat'l Ctr. for Juvenile Justice, *supra* note 52, at 2.

106. Gately, *supra* note 104.

107. *See* Meyer v. Nebraska, 262 U.S. 390 (1923) (holding that the Fourteenth Amendment's protected liberty interests include the right to raise children); Pierce v. Society of Sisters, 268 U.S. 510 (1925) (holding that Oregon's Compulsory Education Act violated parents' Fourteenth Amendment rights to direct the upbringing and education of their children); Prince v. Massachusetts, 321 U.S. 158 (1944) ("It is cardinal with us that the custody, care and nurture of the child reside first in the parents, whose primary function and freedom include the preparation for obligations the state can neither supply nor hinder.").

108. *Prince*, 321 U.S. at 166 (holding that the family is not beyond regulation in the public interest and that the state has a general interest to guard the youth's well-being as *parens patriae*).

counsel in termination of parental rights proceedings.[109] Indeed, most states have recognized even broader and more automatic rights to counsel for parents, not just in termination, but in dependency proceedings more generally. This state-vested right to counsel may arise by statute, or under a state constitutional analysis.[110]

In addition to appointment of counsel concerns, the Supreme Court has also addressed the state's burden of proof in termination matters. In *Santosky v. Kramer*, the Court held that due process requires the state to meet its burden of proof by clear and convincing evidence in order to terminate parental rights.[111] The Court has also held that a statute conditioning appeal of a termination decision on the payment of record preparation fees violates Due Process and Equal Protection guarantees.[112]

Who Is a "Parent" for Constitutional Purposes?

Who qualifies as a parent for constitutional purposes is not always clear. In the typical dependency case, there is rarely controversy over the mother's right to notice and hearing.[113] Similarly, fathers who are married to the mothers of their children are typically included as parents for purposes of due process protections.[114] Consistent with the traditional presumption of paternity in favor of marital fathers, the Supreme Court has held that men outside the marriage have no constitutional right to establish paternity for children born during the marriage of the mother to another.[115]

---

109. *See* Lassiter v. Dep't. of Soc. Servs. of Durham Cnty., 452 U.S. 18, 31 (1981) (applying the *Mathews v. Eldridge* due process balancing test to hold that in this case the mother's due process rights were not violated by not having appointed counsel prior to the termination of her parental rights, but that "[i]f, in a given case, the parent's interests were at their strongest, the State's interests were at their weakest, and the risks of error were at their peak, it could not be said that the *Eldridge* . . . [would] not therefore require the appointment of counsel.").

110. *See* Vivek Sankaran, *Protecting a Parent's Right to Counsel in Child Welfare Cases*, 28 Child L. Prac. 97, 103 (2009) ("At least 38 states have enacted statutes that provide attorneys for parents in every dependency case, and all but five states provide counsel in every termination of parental rights case. A number of state supreme courts have also interpreted their state constitutions to mandate appointing counsel in these cases.").

111. Santosky v. Kramer, 455 U.S. 380 (1979).

112. M.L.B. v. S.L.J., 519 U.S. 102 (1996).

113. In cases of infant abandonment, there may be a question as to the identity of the child's mother, but the underlying principle that the mother is entitled to notice if known is typically not at issue. This assumption of an easily identifiable mother is implicit in the typical way most statutes are constructed. Statutes may require that notice be provided to the mother and then list the types of fathers that must be served. Different mother categories or multiple mothers are not usually described. For example, California provides that notice should be given to the mother, and then "father or fathers, presumed and alleged." *See* Cal. Welf. & Inst. Code § 290.1.

114. The presumption of paternity for marital children is engrained in our common law. This presumption is referred to as "Lord Mansfield's Rule" for the judge who rendered the decision. *See* Goodright v. Moss (1777), 98 Eng. Rep. 1257, 1258, 2 Cowp. 591 ("[T]he law of England is clear, that the declarations of a mother or father cannot be admitted to bastardize the issue born after marriage.").

115. *See* Michael H. v. Gerald D., 491 U.S. 110 (1989).

> ### *Non-Marital Fathers*
> * *Who is a parent for purposes of dependency in your state?*
> * *How are non-marital fathers treated?*

Despite the strong presumption that children born during a marriage are the children of the husband and wife, some states nevertheless have enacted statutes that allow marital fathers to contest the paternity of children born during their marriages. Some states also allow men outside the marriage to claim paternity of children born during the mother's marriage to another.[116] However, when a marital child is removed from his or her parent's home, notice typically will be provided to the husband and wife, unless there are orders in place that disestablish the husband's paternity and/or establish paternity in another.

When the mother is not married, the law is less clear. The Supreme Court has produced a body of decisions that address whether and when a non-marital father should be considered a parent for purposes of constitutional protection. These cases all involved children at least two years old, and all but one arose in the context of a step-parent adoption.[117] When read together, they reflect an evolving recognition that non-marital fathers who "seize the opportunity" to act as fathers to their children are entitled to some constitutional protection.[118]

---

116. The Uniform Law Commission has proposed that states adopt the Uniform Parentage Act (UPA), which does allow for a marital father to disprove paternity of a child during a marriage. It also allows for men to seek to establish paternity of a child born of the mother's marriage to another. However, generally these actions must be brought within two years of the child's birth unless the husband and wife never cohabited, never had sexual intercourse, and the husband never held the child out as his own. *See* Unif. Parentage Act §607 (Unif. Law Comm'n 2002). As of February 2016, eleven states have adopted the Act. *Legislative Fact Sheet: Parentage Act*, Unif. Law Comm'n, [https://perma.cc/TWR6-UYQ5]. However, with the rise and increasing availability of genetic testing, even states that have not adopted the UPA in its totality have allowed similar challenges to the marital paternity presumption. *See* Theresa Glennon, *Somebody's Child: Evaluating the Erosion of the Marital Presumption of Paternity*, 102 W. Va. L. Rev. 547 (2000); Melanie B. Jacobs, *When Daddy Doesn't Want to Be Daddy Anymore: An Argument Against Paternity Fraud Claims*, 16 Yale J.L. & Feminism 193 (2004).

117. The Court most recently decided the case of *Adoptive Couple v. Baby Girl*, 133 S. Ct. 2552 (2013) which did involve a non-marital father's effort to claim his interest in a baby girl adopted at birth. This case, however, raised issues under the Indian Child Welfare Act. Any insight that can be gleaned from this decision into the Court's views on non-marital fathers' rights at the moment of a child's birth would be speculative. The father's constitutional interests were mentioned only in Justice Sotomayor's dissent.

118. *See* Stanley v. Illinois, 405 U.S. 645 (1972) (finding Illinois' statute that did not provide for any notice to non-marital fathers before their children were taken into state care violated due process in the case of a non-marital father who had been an active father in his children's lives); Quilloin v. Walcott, 434 U.S. 246 (1978) (upholding a Georgia statute that allowed for the adoption of a child without the consent of the nonmarital father unless he had "legitimated" the child by a paternity adjudication or by marrying the child's mother and holding the child out as his own in the case of a nonmarital father who did not meet the statute's requirements but who had visited the child

It is unclear from these decisions exactly how a non-marital father is to crystallize his inchoate right. The Court in *Lehr* held "when a father demonstrates a full commitment to the responsibilities of parenthood by coming forward to participate in the rearing of his child, his interest in personal contact with his child acquires substantial protection under the Due Process Clause."[119]

Despite this emphasis on active involvement in a child's life, in the end, the Court has upheld state statutes that qualify fathers based upon more formalistic demonstrations of relationship. For example, in *Lehr*, the Court upheld the New York statute at issue which provided several legal processes for the father to have claimed his rights, including completing a post card and mailing it into the state's "putative father registry." The fact that the father had not taken any of these actions justified the adoption proceeding without notice to him.[120]

In short, the Court's decisions have looked closely at the facts and in some ways these facts have helped to shape the doctrine,[121] but often what is required of states is that they have in place some formalistic mechanism that would allow a father to claim an interest in a child any time after the child's birth.

Because of the limited factual contexts under consideration in the U.S. Supreme Court cases, state courts have been left to apply the *Lehr* holding to cases involving newborns as well as cases outside of the step-parent adoption context.[122] State courts also have, on occasion, considered the non-marital father's rights under state constitutional provisions.[123] These cases have led to a variety of approaches to nonmarital fathers' rights throughout the country. This means that states may treat nonmarital

---

sporadically); Caban v. Mohammed, 441 U.S. 380 (1979) (holding that the New York statute violated the Equal Protection clause by treating nonmarital fathers differently than nonmarital mothers by not requiring the consent of nonmarital fathers in a step-parent adoption case involving a father who had lived with the mother and children for five years and had maintained relationships with them); Lehr v. Robertson, 463 U.S. 248 (1983) (finding that the interest of nonmarital father who has not established a relationship with his child is adequately protected by New York's statute which provides for a number of ways that the father can qualify for notice and hearing prior to the adoption of his child, none of which this father acted to effectuate in a timely way.).

    119. *Lehr*, 463 U.S. at 261.

    120. *Id.*

    121. The father who has cohabited with the mother and helped to parent the child seems to have a better chance of prevailing in his challenge to the statute, while the fathers who have had little opportunity to engage in parenting have been unsuccessful in challenging statutes so long as those statutes have given them the opportunity to establish their interests in more legal or bureaucratic ways. *See text accompanying* note 118, *supra*.

    122. For discussion of state court decisions applying *Lehr* to the newborn adoption context, see Laura Oren, *Thwarted Fathers or Pop-up Pops?: How to Determine When Putative Fathers Can Block the Adoption of Their Newborn Children*, 40 Fam. L. Q. 153 (2006). For a discussion of the treatment of non-marital fathers in the dependency context among various states, see Leslie Joan Harris, *Involving Non-Resident Fathers in Dependency Cases: New Efforts, New Problems, New Solutions*, 9 J. L. & Fam. Stud. 281 (2007).

    123. For a discussion of how non-marital fathers fare under state constitutional analyses, see Mark Strasser, *The Often Illusory Protections of "Biology Plus": On the Supreme Court's Parental Rights Jurisprudence*, 13 Tex. J. C.L. & C.R. 31 (2007).

fathers differently for purposes of when and whether they receive notice of and the right to participate in dependency proceedings.[124]

The Rights of Non-Parental Caregivers

Children and youth may form attachments to caregivers who are not their legal parents. Neither foster parents nor relatives have been afforded the same level of constitutional protection as the child's legal parents.[125]

This is not to say that non-parents always are without rights in the dependency system. For example, if a relative has been awarded custodial rights prior to removal of the child, many states may provide for notice to that relative or other non-parental custodian.[126] In addition, once a child has been removed from his or her parents, federal legislation requires that relatives be considered as placement options.[127]

Another avenue for recognition of non-parents' rights involves the emerging doctrine of *de facto* parenthood.[128] This doctrine typically requires proof that: 1) the adult has acted as a child's parent; 2) the child and adult have formed a parent-child bond; 3) the child's parent has consented to the formation of the relationship; and 4) that

---

124. For example, in Ohio the court has upheld departmental policies permitting courts to deprive nonmarital fathers of custodial rights to their children immediately upon an adjudication finding that the mother abused or neglected them, allowing the court to obtain custody over the child in order to determine the child's best interests for placement purposes. This effectively places the burden on fathers to prove that it is in the child's best interest to be placed with them. *See In re* C.R., 843 N.E.2d 1188 (Ohio 2006); *In re* Russel, No. 06-CA-12, 2006 WL 3692409 (Ohio Ct. App. Nov. 27, 2006); *In re* Osberry, No. 1-03-26, 2003 WL 22336115 (Ohio Ct. App. Oct. 14, 2003). By contrast, Maryland and Pennsylvania do not permit the court to exercise jurisdiction over a child removed from his or her mother's care if a nonmarital father is willing to assume custody and is not unfit. *See In re* M.L., 757 A.2d 849 (Pa. 2000); *In re* Russell G., 672 A.2d 109 (Md. Ct. Spec. App. 1996).

125. *See* Smith v. Org. of Foster Families for Equal. & Reform, 431 U.S. 816, 844–45 (1977) (finding that while it would be improper to consider a foster family to be nothing more than "a mere collection of unrelated individuals," the nature of the interest at stake is not the same as the interests of parents as against state intrusion because "the State here seeks to interfere, not with a relationship having its origins entirely apart from the power of the State, but rather with a foster family which has its source in state law and contractual arrangements"); Troxel v. Granville, 530 U.S. 57 (2000) (finding Washington's third-party visitation statute unconstitutional in that it violates the rights of fit parents to decide with whom their children should visit in the context of grandparents who had been awarded visitation).

126. Relevant federal law provides that "[t]he term 'parents' means biological or adoptive parents or legal guardians, as determined by applicable State law." 42 U.S.C. § 675(2). States typically attempt to bring their definitions into line with federal requirements. *See, e.g.,* Ariz. Rev. Stat. § 8-823; Cal. Welf. & Inst. Code § 308; Tex. Fam. Code § 262.1095; Wash. Rev. Code § 13.34.062.

127. 42 U.S.C § 671(a)(19) (providing that states consider giving preference to relative placement over a non-related caregiver, so long as the relative meets the relevant state protection standards).

128. *See, e.g., In re* Custody of H.S.H.-K, 533 N.W.2d 419 (Wis. 1994); Youmans v. Ramos, 711 N.E.2d 165 (Mass. 1999); V.C. v. M.J.B., 748 A.2d 539 (N.J. 1999); Rubano v. DiCenzo, 759 A.2d 959 (R.I. 2000); T.B. v. L.R.M., 786 A.2d 913 (Pa. 2001); *In re* Bonfield, 780 N.E.2d 241 (Ohio 2002); C.E.W. v. D.E.W., 845 A.2d 1146 (Me. 2003); *In re* Parentage of A.B., 818 N.E.2d 126 (Ind. Ct. App. 2004); *In re* Interest of E.L.M.C., 100 P.3d 546 (Colo. Ct. App. 2004); *In re* Parentage of L.B., 122 P.3d 161 (Wash. 2005).

the adult was not compensated for caregiving.[129] *De facto parentage* is a common law doctrine that requires legal action to be established. In the event that a child has a legally established *de facto* parent at the time of removal, it is likely that such a parent would be entitled to participate in the proceedings as a parent.

Because the foster parent and child relationship is characterized as state-created for the purpose of temporarily caring for children who may be returned to their parents, the foster parent-foster child relationship typically receives very limited constitutional protection.[130]

Emerging Theories of Constitutional Rights for Dependent Children

Traditionally, parents are the holders of substantive and procedural due process rights as against the state in the dependency proceedings that seek to impact their relationships with their children. However, children are beginning to see advances in their constitutional rights *vis a vis* the state in the dependency context.

The Supreme Court has held that a state cannot be held liable for failing to protect a child from the actions of a parent or caregiver, even when the state has knowledge that the parent or caregiver is abusive. The seminal case establishing this principle arose in the context of the state's failure to remove a child from his father's care even though there had been several complaints and reason to believe that the child was being beaten. The child sustained permanent brain damage as a result. Although the Court held that the state has no responsibility to protect a child from a private actor's violence, the court did hold open the possibility that a child already in state custody would have due process rights to be free from harm.[131]

Although children outside of the dependency system have no right to state protection as against the actions of their parents, some state and federal courts have gone on to find that once children are removed from their parent's care, children do have a substantive due process right to be free from harm while in the state's care.[132] Others have held that children have a procedural due process right to counsel in dependency

---

129. For a discussion of the doctrine as it has evolved among states by comparison to the American Law Institute's recommended standards, see Robin Fretwell Wilson, *Limiting the Prerogatives of Legal Parents: Judicial Skepticism of the American Law Institute's Treatment of De Facto Parents*, 25 J. Am. Acad. Matrimonial Laws 477 (2013).

130. *See Smith*, 431 U.S. at 844–45. California is an outlier in allowing foster parents *de facto* parent status. Thus, in those cases where the status has been achieved, foster parents may be accorded greater rights and protections. *See, In re* Matthew P., 84 Cal. Rptr. 2d 269 (Ct. App. 1999).

131. Deshaney v. Winnebago Cty., 489 U.S. 189 (1989).

132. *See, e.g.*, Braam v. State, 81 P.3d 851 (Wash. 2003); Whitley v. N.M. Children, Youth & Family Dep't., 184 F. Supp. 2d 1146 (D.N.M. 2001); Nicini v. Morra, 212 F.3d 798 (3d Cir. 2000); Kitzman-Kelley v. Warner, 203 F.3d 454 (7th Cir. 2000); Charlie H. v. Whitman, 83 F. Supp. 476, 507 (D.N.J. 2000); Jordan v. City of Philadelphia, 66 F. Supp.2d 638 (E.D. Pa. 1999); White v. Chambliss, 112 F.3d 731 (4th Cir. 1997); Kara B. v. Dane County, 555 N.W.2d. 630 (Wis. 1996); Yvonne L. v. N.M. Dep't. of Human Servs., 959 F.2d 883 (10th Cir. 1992); Taylor v. Ledbetter, 818 F.2d 791 (11th Cir. 1987); Doe v. New York City Dep't of Social Servs., 649 F.2d 134 (2d Cir. 1981).

proceedings under the case-by-case balancing test of *Mathews v. Eldridge*.[133] Some state courts have noted that a statutory requirement for the appointment of counsel is a due process requirement.[134] Some have gone so far as to find that children have a constitutional right to effective counsel while in the dependency process.[135]

The importance of children's family relationships is sometimes discussed in cases establishing due process rights.[136] Generally, however, children's constitutional rights seem to be emerging more from a recognition that they are in the custody of the state and less from the proposition that they share a concomitant right to family integrity equal to that held by their parents.[137]

The Rights of Accused Children in Juvenile Court

The original intent of the juvenile court was to treat children, whether dependent or delinquent, as children in need of the state's care. This gave rise to a non-adversarial system designed, ideally, to provide care and services to promote the child's positive development. For children accused of breaking the law, the juvenile court abandoned the procedural formalities that characterized the punitive adult criminal system and fashioned itself as a place where a "fatherly judge touched the heart and conscience of the erring youth by talking over his problems, by paternal advice and admonition, and in which, in extreme situations, benevolent and wise institutions of the State provided guidance and help 'to save him from downward career.'"[138] This "peculiar system for juveniles" carried on for more than sixty years until the U.S. Supreme Court weighed in.[139]

The U.S. Supreme Court first addressed the *parens patriae* power of the juvenile court in its 1966 decision, *Kent v. United States*.[140] The Court condemned the manner in which a juvenile court transferred a sixteen-year-old to the adult criminal justice system — exposing the lack of due process in the juvenile court system as well as noting the critical nature of the decision to try a youth as an adult.[141] One year later, the

---

133. *See, e.g., In re* M.S.R., 271 P.3d 234, 245 (Wash. 2012); *In re* Jaime TT, 191 A.D.2d 132 (N.Y. App. Div. 1993), relying on Mathews v. Eldridge, 424 U.S. 319 (1976).

134. *See, e.g., In re* Interest of Von Rossum, 515 So.2d 582 (La. Ct. App. 1987) (noting that a statutory requirement for the appointment of counsel is a due process requirement).

135. *See, e.g.,* Kenny A. v. Perdue, 356 F. Supp. 2d 1353 (N.D. Ga. 2005); *In re* Jamie TT, 191 A.D.2d 132 (N.Y. App. Div. 1993).

136. *See In re* M.S.R., 271 P.3d, *supra* note 133, at 242.

137. *See* Strasser, *supra* note 16.

138. *In re* Gault, 387 U.S. 1, 26 (1967) (quoting Julian W. Mack, *The Juvenile Court*, 23 Harv. L. Rev. 104, 120 (1909)).

139. *Id.* at 17.

140. 383 U.S. 541.

141. The Court, in an appendix to the decision, indicated its approval of the D.C. juvenile court's list of factors to consider in deciding whether to transfer children to the adult criminal justice system: 1) the seriousness of the offense; 2) the level of violence and premeditation; 3) whether it was committed against persons or property; 4) the prosecutive merit of the complaint; 5) whether the juvenile's co-defendants are adults; 6) the juvenile's sophistication and maturity; 7) the juvenile's record and previous history; and 8) the juvenile's likelihood of rehabilitation. *Id.* at 566–67. These "*Kent*

Court decided *In re Gault*, dramatically changing the way juvenile courts function by establishing minimal procedural due process protections for children accused of criminal behavior. This landmark case gave children accused of breaking the law certain procedural due process rights, including the right to counsel, the right to notice of charges, the right to confrontation and cross-examination of witnesses, and the right against self-incrimination.[142]

Some hailed *Gault* as a triumph for children's rights while others saw it as the end of treating children differently from adults in a rehabilitative setting that would address the child's needs rather than punish.[143] Not long after the *Gault* decision, the Supreme Court continued to expand the due process rights of accused children to include the right to proof beyond a reasonable doubt,[144] but later stopped short of giving children the right to a jury trial.[145]

As more formal and costly procedures were put into place for children alleged to be delinquent, dependent children were separated into a different system and a line was drawn between "victims" of abusive and neglectful parents and children who committed crimes. This dichotomy exists today and has created systems that often run parallel to each other giving rise to a category of youth that would not have existed prior to *Gault,* known as "crossover youth."[146] Crossover or "dual jurisdiction" youth are those who find themselves in both the child welfare and juvenile justice systems — two systems that have evolved to have different goals.[147] While the child welfare system focuses on family integrity and permanence, juvenile justice systems emphasize youth accountability and rehabilitation. In dependency proceedings, the state is concerned primarily with providing and mandating services to parents to enable them to regain custody or control over their children. In delinquency proceedings, the state takes custody or control over children in order to change their behavior through punishment and rehabilitation — to protect the public from the child — with almost no focus on the parents' behavior.

In following the minimum due process requirements established by the Supreme Court, most states' juvenile delinquency proceedings proceed in a fashion that mimics an adult criminal proceeding: beginning with an arrest, followed by a referral to

---

factors" are now adhered to by many states whose courts make discretionary decisions to waive juvenile court jurisdiction. *See, e.g.,* In the Matter of J.C.N.-V, 380 P.3d 248, 260 (Or. 2016); Moon v. State, 451 S.W.3d 28 (Tex. Crim. App. 2014); State v. Childress, 280 P.3d 1144 (Wash. Ct. App. 2012).

142. *See Gault*, 387 U.S. at 1.

143. The *Gault* court appeared to reject the notion that juvenile courts were meeting the needs of children, citing to national reports exposing the shortcomings in the juvenile court system and expressing concern that children were actually receiving the "worst of both worlds" — neither the protections given adults or the care and treatment imagined by the juvenile court's founders. *See id.* at 18 n.23. The dissent, however, insisted that majority's decision was a major step backward in the legal system's treatment of children. *Id.* at 79 (Harlan, J., concurring and dissenting).

144. *See In re* Winship, 397 U.S. 358 (1970).

145. *See* McKeiver v. Pennsylvania, 403 U.S. 528 (1971).

146. Denise C. Herz et al., *Challenges Facing Crossover Youth*, 48 Fam. Ct. Rev. 305 (2010).

147. *Id.*

the prosecutor for a charging decision, the formal filing of charges, the appointment of counsel, an arraignment hearing, a judicial decision whether to hold the accused in secure detention pending adjudication, an opportunity to plead guilty or go to trial and, if found guilty, a sentencing hearing. At trial, the state has the burden of proof and juveniles have the right to confront witnesses and can move to exclude unconstitutionally obtained confessions or other evidence. Most states provide only for bench trials in juvenile court, but a few states allow for jury trials.[148] Steps in the juvenile court process usually have different labels than those found in adult criminal court, for example "disposition" instead of "sentencing," and "adjudicated" instead of "convicted."

States vary widely on sentencing options for youth; however, most states have detention facilities that serve the same function as an adult jail (detaining youth pre-trial or for short sentences) and institutions that serve the same function as adult prisons (longer sentences, usually farther from the youth's community). The U.S. Supreme Court has placed some limits on sentencing juveniles through the Eighth Amendment's ban on cruel and unusual punishment. Children under eighteen may not be executed,[149] sentenced to life without the possibility of parole for a non-homicide offense,[150] or sentenced to a mandatory life without parole sentence without consideration of the youth's individual circumstances.[151]

Because the consequences in juvenile court are generally lower than the consequences individuals face in the adult criminal justice system, who is a "juvenile" for purposes of juvenile court jurisdiction is a widely debated topic and depends on the state and often the charged offense.

States differ on the minimum and maximum ages for juvenile court jurisdiction — ranging from no minimum age limit up to 17 years of age.[152] Many states set a minimum age of seven or eight for criminal responsibility and a maximum age that changes

148. *See, e.g.*, Alaska Stat. § 47.12.110(a); Mass. Gen. Laws ch. 119, § 56(c); Mont. Code Ann. § 41-5-1502(1).

149. Roper v. Simmons, 543 U.S. 551 (2005).

150. Graham v. Florida, 560 U.S. 48 (2010).

151. Miller v. Alabama, 132 S. Ct. 2455 (2012).

152. As of the end of the 2015 legislative session, forty-two states set the oldest age at which a juvenile court has original jurisdiction, subject to statutory exclusions, at seventeen. *Statistical Briefing Book: Upper Age of Original Juvenile Court Jurisdiction 2016*, Office of Justice Programs, U.S. Dep't of Justice (March 27, 2017), [https://perma.cc/KH4W-MPMZ]. The UN Convention on the Rights of the Child, which the U.S. has not ratified, requires governments to set a minimum age of criminal responsibility. Convention on the Rights of the Child, art. 40, ¶ 3, Nov. 20, 1989, 1577 U.N.T.S. 3. The United Nations' Committee on the Rights of the Child considers a minimum age below twelve to be internationally unacceptable. Committee on the Rights of the Child, *General Comment No. 10 (2007): Children's Rights in Juvenile Justice*, ¶ 32, U.N. Doc. CRC /C /GC /10 (Apr . 25, 2007), [https://perma .cc /DD3X-5ZUU] . There has been some movement to increase the age of juvenile court jurisdiction in the U.S. For example, in New York, sixteen-year-olds have been considered adults and adjudicated in adult court; however, pursuant to "Raise the Age" legislation passed in 2017, effective October 1, 2018, sixteen-year olds charged with misdemeanors will be prosecuted in Family Court and seventeen-year-olds charged with misdemeanors will be prosecuted in Family Court effective October 1,

depending on the offense. For example, in California, if you commit certain serious crimes at the age of 14 you will be charged as an adult.[153]

Juvenile Justice in Your State

- *Find and review the statutes that govern your juvenile offender or delinquency process.*
- *What are the ages of juvenile court jurisdiction in your state?*

A trend toward processing more juveniles in the adult criminal justice system began in the 1990s as a response to high juvenile crime rates. This resulted in states adopting a variety of mechanisms for determining who is a juvenile or who is an adult for purposes of criminal prosecution. Most states still give judges some discretion to determine whether a juvenile should be treated as an adult (these decision points are sometimes called "transfer" or "waiver"). This decision may be made by a juvenile court judge, although some jurisdictions have a "reverse waiver" or "reverse transfer" mechanism that allows the adult criminal justice system to return the child to juvenile court.[154] Some states give prosecutors discretion to "direct file" in adult or juvenile court;[155] some states, on the other hand, have attempted to remove discretion by statutorily excluding certain types of offenses from juvenile court.[156]

Arrests per 100,000 juveniles ages 10–17, 1980–2014[157]

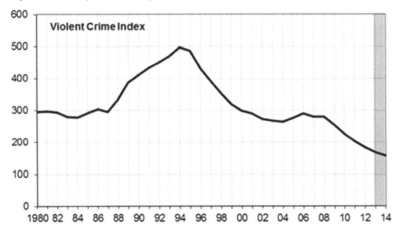

2019. Act of Apr. 10, 2017, ch. 59, pt. WWW, 2017 N.Y. Sess. Laws (McKinney) (to be codified at N.Y. Crim. Proc. art. 722).

153. Cal. Welf. & Inst. Code § 602(b).

154. *See* Nat'l Ctr. for Juvenile Justice, *supra* note 52, at 99 (thirty-six states had such provisions at the end of the 2011 legislative session).

155. *See, e.g.*, Neb. Rev. Stat. § 43-276; Colo. Rev. Stat. § 19-2-517.

156. *See, e.g.*, Wash. Rev. Code § 13.04.030(1)(e)(v). Conversely, some states limit transfers of juveniles to those who are above fourteen years of age. *See, e.g.*, Cal. Welf. & Inst. Code § 602(b); Tex. Fam. Code Ann. § 54.02(a)(2)(A).

157. *Statistical Briefing Book, Law Enforcement and Juvenile Crime: Juvenile Arrest Trends*, Office of Justice Programs, U.S. Dep't of Justice (1980–2014), [https://perma.cc/8DD3-JHCZ].

Research suggests that the transfer of juveniles to the adult system can actually increase recidivism.[158] This evidence, combined with the fact that the juvenile arrest rate has decreased by more than 68% since reaching its highest level in 1996, may be driving some states to rethink how they adjudicate youth crime.[159] A few states are reverting toward a less punitive approach by keeping more young people in the juvenile system.[160]

The Federal Statutes That Drive the State Systems

While variations exist among the states as to terminology and the details of their processes, dependency and delinquency systems are similar from state to state. In the dependency context, common systems are largely due the requirements of federal statutes that help fund them. Evolving constitutional law is the primary driver for similarities in the delinquency context. Nonetheless, even in delinquency, state systems receive encouragement from the federal government to reflect desired federal goals.

Federal Requirements in the Dependency Context

As described in the history above, the earliest child welfare practices and systems emerged from a combination of private charities, religious institutions, and state actors. Charitable and religious institutions continue to play a large role in the provision of child welfare and adoption services today.[161] However, starting in the 1930's with the emergence of the New Deal's social safety net programming, the federal government has become an increasingly bigger player in the field of child welfare, influencing the way that states conduct themselves through federal funding incentives.

By the 1940s, agencies like the NYSPCC had spread across the country and federal support for state Children's Bureaus had grown. A developing body of medical research documenting the battered child syndrome was also becoming more widely known.

---

158. Angela McGowan et al., *Effects on Violence of Laws and Policies Facilitating the Transfer of Youth from the Juvenile to the Adult Justice System*, 32 Am. J. Preventive Med. S7 (2007).

159. *Juvenile Arrest Rate Trends*, OJJDP Statistical Briefing Book (Mar. 27, 2017), [https://perma.cc/B4FM-PCUY].

160. In 2012, Connecticut increased the upper age that juvenile courts retain original jurisdiction to seventeen, after having raised it to sixteen in 2010. *Upper Age of Original Juvenile Court Jurisdiction 2015*, *supra* note 152. Massachusetts raised its upper age from sixteen to seventeen in 2013, Illinois raised its upper age for most felonies from sixteen to seventeen in 2014; and New Hampshire raised its upper age from sixteen back to seventeen in 2015 and New York passed legislation in 2017 that will raise the age for misdemeanors to age 17 by 2019. *See supra* note 152. *Id. See also* Sarah Childress, *Why States are Changing Course on Juvenile Crime*, PBS: Frontline (Dec. 17, 2014), [https://perma.cc/SLZ4-XB4Q].

161. Examples of common long-standing non-governmental service providers in the child welfare field are Casey Family Programs, [https://perma.cc/WR4C-2EJZ], and Children's Aid Society [https://perma.cc/9CSU-UW7T].

These developments led states to act with greater frequency under the *parens patriae* doctrine to remove children from their parents' care.[162]

The federal government provided its first grants to states for programs designed to prevent and protect children from abuse and neglect and to support foster care in 1935 under Title IV-B of the Social Security Act. Eventually, Title IV-E of the Social Security Act was established to provide federal funds to states with qualifying foster care systems. The Adoption Assistance and Child Welfare Act of 1980 later amended Title IV programs further requiring that states engage in reasonable efforts to prevent children from being removed and to reunify children with parents after removal.[163] "Reasonable efforts" became the linchpin requirement imposed upon states in an effort to balance the state's interest in protecting children with parents' fundamental rights to raise their children.

States continue to develop distinct vocabularies to describe the legal processes in place to handle the removal of children from their parents' care. However, because federal funds are conditioned upon state systems submitting plans that comport with federal law, federal law has had a standardizing effect nationally. Catch phrases, like "reasonable efforts," and other federal mandates appear in state statutes across the country.

The two major statutes that drive today's state practices are the Child Abuse Prevention and Treatment Act (CAPTA)[164] and the Adoption and Safe Families Act (ASFA),[165] which further amended Title IV-B and Title IV-E of the Social Security Act. In broad strokes, CAPTA requires states to develop systems of reporting, investigating, and treating child abuse and neglect, while ASFA sets forth requirements for the legal systems' handling of matters once the child is removed.

In addition to these two major pieces of legislation, Congress has also addressed how children of various communities of color should be treated within the system. In passing the Indian Child Welfare Act (ICWA),[166] Congress required states to apply different practices and standards in cases involving children who are enrolled or are enroll-able in federally recognized tribes. Congress has also addressed the question of whether race can be considered in the placement of children once removed from their parents in the Multi-Ethnic Placement Act/Inter Ethnic Placement Act (MEPA/IEPA).[167]

---

162. *See* CHILD WELFARE LAW AND PRACTICE, *supra* note 17, at 135–36.
163. *See* CHILDREN'S BUREAU, MAJOR FEDERAL LEGISLATION CONCERNED WITH CHILD PROTECTION, WELFARE, AND ADOPTION 2 n.1 (2012), [https://perma.cc/5LTZ-7JRD].
164. Pub. L. No. 93-247, 88 Stat. 4 (codified as amended at 42 U.S.C. §§ 5101–5107).
165. Pub. L. No. 105-89, 111 Stat. 2115 (codified as amended at 42 U.S.C. §§ 620–628, 670–679a).
166. Pub. L. No. 95-608, 92 Stat. 3069 (codified at 25 U.S.C. §§ 1901–1963).
167. Pub. L. No. 103-382, 108 Stat. 4056 (codified at 42 U.S.C. § 5115a), *amended by* Pub. L. No. 104-188, 110 Stat. 1904 (codified at 42 U.S.C. § 622).

CAPTA: Child Protective Services

Within some state systems, one might hear the terms "child protective services" (CPS) in reference to those systems that investigate complaints and work with families prior to any court filing, and "child welfare services" (CWS) to refer to those systems that work with families post-filing. In the narratives that follow, you will see this terminology used by both the attorneys and the social workers. However, often families, teachers, and other professionals working outside of both systems will use the term "CPS" more broadly. Likely, this is because CPS has more visibility within the larger community. Not all families who are investigated by CPS wind up in the child welfare system, but nearly all children who are removed were at some point in contact with CPS.

CAPTA is a fairly lengthy statute that allows states to request federal funding for a number of initiatives. Not all of these initiatives will be described here. However, in general, CAPTA is responsible for the common systems of mandatory reporting of child abuse and neglect,[168] for investigation of those claims,[169] for multidisciplinary teams and citizen panels to assist in investigation,[170] for cooperation with law enforcement,[171] for record-keeping and reporting concerning findings of abuse and neglect[172] and for coordination with those service providers authorized by other statutes to engage in family preservation services.[173]

All states have mandatory reporter statutes. Two states, New Jersey and Wyoming, require that all persons with reasonable cause to believe that child abuse or neglect has occurred have a mandatory duty to report. The remaining states, the District of Columbia, and several territories require that certain professionals report. All jurisdictions accept reports from non-professionals as well. The specific details of these mandatory reporting statutes vary and each state's laws should be reviewed carefully to understand who must report. Typically, mandatory reporters include teachers, medical professionals, childcare providers, law enforcement officers, social workers and mental health providers.[174]

Reporters are protected in a couple of key ways. First, their identities remain confidential. While a parent may receive the records of an investigation, the identities of reporters are usually expunged.[175] In addition, mandatory reporters are immune from prosecution so long as they act in good faith to fulfill their duty.[176]

---

168. 42 U.S.C. § 5106a(b)(2)(B)(i).

169. *Id.* § 5106a(b)(2)(B)(iv).

170. *Id.* § 5106a(a)(2)(A)-(B).

171. *Id.* § 5106a(a)(2)(B)(xi).

172. *Id.* § 5106a(d).

173. *Id.* § 5106a(b)(2)(A).

174. For a review of mandatory reporting statutes, see CHILDREN's BUREAU, MANDATORY REPORTERS OF CHILD ABUSE AND NEGLECT (2013), [https://perma.cc/ATP3-WRWS].

175. *Id.* at 4. *See also* 42 U.S.C. § 5106a(b)(2)(B)(xviii).

176. 42 U.S.C. § 5106a(b)(2)(B)(vii).

After a report has been made, CAPTA requires that states have in place a system for "screening, risk and safety assessments, and prompt investigation."[177] The specific screening criteria, methods of assessing risk and the meaning of "prompt" is not defined federally. Accordingly, states approach the handling of reported child abuse and neglect differently. State statutes, regulations and policy should be consulted to learn how an individual state agency determines if a report of abuse and neglect is investigated and if so, how quickly action must be taken.

Not all reports will be investigated, but those that are may result in findings such as substantiated or unsubstantiated. Sometimes states use "founded" or "unfounded" to refer to the results of a CPS investigation. It is important to look at the definitions associated with the outcomes of a CPS investigation. Nomenclature varies and some states include categories of findings that others do not. For example, "unsubstantiated" may be used to mean that not enough proof existed to find abuse, while a finding of a "false" report of abuse means that the allegations were found to be untrue.[178] Because the finding of abuse or neglect may have far-reaching personal, familial and employment consequences,[179] most states do have administrative proceedings in place that can be used to appeal an agency finding. Any such administrative proceedings usually run parallel to any dependency proceedings that may take place upon the removal of the child from the home.[180]

A finding of abuse or neglect does not necessarily mean that the child is removed from the parents' care. CAPTA allows for and encourages the offering of family preservation services, which will enable the family to remain together. Sometimes these interventions will be documented by voluntary service agreements in which the parent agrees to participate in certain services in order to avoid removal of the child from the home.[181] These types of services fall within the state's ongoing duty to engage in "reasonable efforts" before removal of a child from his or her home.

While it is expected that the states will seek to work with parents to avoid removal of a child from his or her home, CAPTA provides that in certain circumstances a child may be removed without having to engage in these reasonable efforts. These

---

177. *Id.* § 5106a(b)(2)(B)(iv).

178. This distinction is alluded to in CAPTA itself when it finds that agencies may seek to keep records with respect to unsubstantiated cases for future risk and safety assessments, while requiring the prompt expungement of false findings from records that could surface during background checks. *Id.* § 5106a(b)(2)(B)(xii). For a discussion of the various terms states used in reporting data to the federal government, see CHILDREN'S BUREAU, U.S. DEP'T OF HEALTH & HUMAN SERVS., CHILD MAL-TREATMENT 2015 17 (2017), [https://perma.cc/TL4E-DKV6].

179. The fact that findings of child abuse or neglect may be maintained in databases relied upon for employment and other background checks is referenced in CAPTA. 42 U.S.C. § 5106a(b)(2)(B)(xii).

180. *See id.* § 5106a(a)(2)(B)(i).

181. *Id.* § 5106a(b)(2)(B)(v).

circumstances are among the most dangerous and include parents who have killed or committed felonious assault, or sexual assault against another child in their care.[182]

Finally, of particular interest to legal representatives of children, CAPTA also requires that the states appoint a specially trained guardian ad litem (GAL) in all cases in which court proceedings are undertaken. The role of this GAL is:

(I) to obtain first-hand, a clear understanding of the situation and needs of the child, and

(II) to make recommendations to the court concerning the best interests of the child.[183]

This GAL may be either a court-appointed special advocate (CASA) or a lawyer. CASA is a volunteer organization that operates in 49 states.[184] It is important to note that the GAL engages in "best interest" representation and has no duty to adhere to the child's stated interest.

> ### CAPTA in Your State
>
> - *Find the statutes that govern mandatory reporters.*
> - *Find the statutes defining abuse and neglect.*
> - *Find the statutes, regulations and departmental policies describing the screening, assessment and investigation process of reports of child abuse or neglect.*
> - *Draw a flowchart of the decision points and time lines involved in the CPS investigation.*

The Role of Risk Aversion in Social Worker Decision-Making

Social workers decide how to handle reports of child abuse and neglect. Protocols are often put into place to direct the discretion of social workers. However, each state actor is still a human being with his or her own natural level of risk aversion or risk tolerance. Child protection service agencies typically develop their own risk assessment tools that are designed to mitigate the level of discretion that a social worker has. However, it is impossible to eliminate completely the impact of subjective assessment on the part of social workers in the field. Research has shown the extent to which, in close cases with very similar facts, some social workers won't remove children and others will, demonstrating the influence that individual levels of risk tolerance dictate the trajectory of a child's experience with the child welfare system.[185]

---

182. *Id.* § 5106a(b)(2)(B)(xvi).

183. *Id.* § 5106a(b)(2)(B)(xii).

184. For more information about the history of the CASA movement, see *CASA Facts*, THE CONNECTION, Spring 2007, at 5, [https://perma.cc/A3XF-T2YP].

185. Doyle, *supra* note 89.

ASFA: Seeking to Balance Permanence and Reunification

Once a child is removed from their home, due process requires that a court proceeding be launched. For the purposes of this book, we refer to these court actions as "dependency proceedings." Different states may use different terminology.

The Adoption and Safe Families Act of 1997 was passed in reaction to "foster care drift." It was believed that children were spending too much time in foster care without a permanent home as they waited to be reunified with their parents. Congress had come to believe that their earlier "reasonable efforts" requirement needed to be balanced against the child's need for permanency. Many legislators believed that the states had gone too far in seeking reunification at all costs, putting children at risk of spending their childhoods in foster care or being returned to unsafe homes.

ASFA was enacted in response to these concerns. While the "reasonable efforts" requirement remains, ASFA amended the law to create timelines that would place pressure upon parents to remedy their problems or face the possible termination of their parental rights. Termination of parental rights or parental consent is required for adoption, and it was thought that if parents were unable to be reunified with their children in a timely way, the children should be made free for adoption so that they could exit the foster care system with newly formed legal families.

In addition to putting pressure on states to adopt federal timelines for dependency cases, ASFA also provided additional funding to states in the form of adoption incentives. These incentives meant that states would receive additional federal dollars upon hitting certain benchmarks in the numbers of children adopted each year.[186] Like CAPTA, ASFA also requires states to report data concerning the time children have spent in state care and permanency outcomes.[187]

Whether ASFA is actually responsible for an increase in adoptions or an increase in "legally free" children who remain orphaned by its requirements is a matter of controversy.[188] Research suggests that, contrary to the rhetoric that spurred the passage of ASFA, adoptions were actually on the rise in the years leading up to its passage, ASFA's greatest impact was on hastening the adoption of children who had been caught in a pre-existing cresting wave of removals, and in the years that followed the pace of adoption, as well as the rate of reunification, slowed.[189] Regardless of whether ASFA has

---

186. *See* KAREN SPAR & MATTHEW SHUMAN, CONG. RESEARCH SERV., CHILD WELFARE: IMPLEMENTATION OF THE ADOPTION AND SAFE FAMILIES ACT (2004), [https://perma.cc/JL88-CEZB].

187. 42 U.S.C. § 679.

188. *See, e.g.,* Jean C. Lawrence, *ASFA in the Age of Mass Incarceration: Go to Prison — Lose Your Child?*, 40 WM. MITCHELL L. REV. 990 (2014) (suggesting that portions of ASFA regarding termination of parental rights proceedings apply too harshly to incarcerated parents, resulting in more legally free children); Marcia Robinson Lowry, *Putting Teeth into ASFA: The Need for Statutory Minimum Standards*, 26 CHILD. & YOUTH SERVS. REV. 1021 (2004) (noting conflicting research on ASFA's effect on adoption rates).

189. FRED WULCZYN ET AL., ADOPTION DYNAMICS: AN UPDATE ON THE IMPACT OF THE ADOPTION AND SAFE FAMILIES ACT 19–24 (2005), [https://perma.cc/K6CD-RT7S].

achieved its intended purposes, all states have enacted laws to comply with it.[190] For most states, ASFA bolstered judicial oversight by requiring that at least once annually the child's permanency plan would be reviewed.

> ### *ASFA in Your State*
>
> * *Find the statutes that govern the dependency process.*
> * *Draw a flowchart depicting the hearings, the issues determined, the standards used, and the statutes referenced as a child moves through the dependency system in your state.*

State processes still vary widely in terms of the vocabulary and the timing of some hearings; however most state systems will involve at least the following steps and hearings after removal of a child:[191]

- Filing of a dependency petition alleging the facts that support why the child can no longer live with his or her parents.

- A hearing to follow quickly thereafter to which the parents receive notice and an opportunity to contest the child's removal from their care. This hearing is sometimes referred to as a "shelter care hearing."[192]

- A fact-finding hearing/trial on the allegations of the petition.[193]

- A six-month case review that may be heard by a judge or an administrative officer to check in on the status of the child. These review hearings must continue every six months until the child exits care.[194]

- A twelve-month permanency planning hearing before the court to review and approve the child's permanency plan, which sets forth the goal for how the child will exit the system and the timeframe for achieving that goal. These hearings also occur every twelve months until the child exits the system. The typical permanency planning goals are: reunification; adoption; relative guardianship

---

190. *See* SPAR & SHUMAN, *supra* note 186.

191. For a description of the permanency planning hearing process mandated by ASFA with some discussion of how states have implemented them, see CHILDREN'S BUREAU, U.S. DEP'T OF HEALTH & HUMAN SERVS., COURT HEARINGS FOR THE PERMANENT PLACEMENT OF CHILDREN (2012), [https://perma.cc/7NR8-TAJE].

192. Some states require that this hearing happen as quickly as within twenty-four hours. *Compare* FLA. STAT. § 39.402 (24 hours), *and* MICH. CT. R. 3.965(A)(1) (24 hours), *and* CAL. WELF. & INST. CODE § 315 (before the end of the next judicial day), *with* WASH. REV. CODE § 13.34.065 (72 hours), *and* MASS. GEN. LAWS ch. 119 § 24 (72 hours).

193. Most states attempt to hold this hearing in sufficient time to comply with other ASFA requirements. This generally means that the issue of dependency will be decided anywhere from 15 to 75 days after the filing of the petition. *See, e.g.,* WASH. REV. CODE § 13.34.070 (no later than 75 days); CAL. WELF. & INST. CODE § 334 (within 30 days, unless the minor is already detained in custody, in which case the hearing must occur within 15 days); *and* 705 ILL. COMP. STAT. 405/2-21 (no later than 30 days).

194. 42 U.S.C. § 675(5)(B).

or placement; legal guardianship or custody with another adult; or other planned permanent living arrangement.[195]

If the child remains in an out-of-home placement for 15 of the most recent 22 months, ASFA requires states to file a petition to terminate parental rights. The state may choose not to file the petition only if: 1) the child is in a relative's care; 2) the state has not engaged in reasonable efforts to reunify the family; or 3) if the state can document a compelling reason as to why termination would be contrary to the child's best interests. The state is required to file a termination petition without waiting in any case that exempts the state from engaging in reasonable efforts.[196]

The Indian Child Welfare Act

Congress passed the Indian Child Welfare Act (ICWA)[197] in 1978 in response to the wholesale removal of Indian children from their homes and tribes. These removals were part of a long history of intentional cultural annihilation supported by the Bureau of Indian Affairs, religious organizations, and eventually the child welfare system. The removal of Indian children took many forms — from actual military raids, to forced enrollment in religious boarding schools, to widespread removal of Indian children for adoption by white families. The impact on the mental and physical health and survival of Indian tribes and families is well documented in the testimony that supported the passage of the ICWA.[198]

ICWA recognizes the special rights that an Indian child and his/her tribe have as a result of a child's membership potential in a federally recognized tribe. ICWA is based on a legal understanding that tribes have sovereignty when it comes to Indian children. When a state child welfare system comes into contact with a child who meets the ICWA definition of an "Indian child,"[199] the tribe must be provided notice of the proceedings.[200] At that point, the tribe has the right to transfer jurisdiction of the matter to its own tribal court and social services system. Parents too may seek to transfer jurisdiction to the tribe, with the tribal court having the right to decline such transfer.[201] Not all tribes have courts and child welfare systems in place, but even if they don't have court systems of their own, tribes are permitted to intervene in the state court proceedings to ensure that the other provisions of ICWA are followed in state court.[202]

---

195. *Id.* § 675(5)(C).

196. *Id.* § 675(5)(E).

197. Pub. L. No. 95-608, 92 Stat. 3069 (codified at 25 U.S.C. §§ 1901–1963).

198. *See* Lorie Graham, *The Past Never Vanishes: A Contextual Critique of the Existing Indian Family Doctrine*, 23 Am. Indian L. Rev. 1 (1999). For a personal telling of the intergenerational harm caused by "the scoop" in which Indian children were snatched from reservations by child welfare workers, *see* National Indian Child Welfare Association, *The Heart of ICWA: Becky*, YouTube (Dec. 7, 2016), [https://perma.cc/2QWZ-A6EH].

199. 25 U.S.C. § 1903(4).

200. *Id.* § 1912(a).

201. *Id.* § 1911(b).

202. *Id.* § 1911(c).

ICWA requirements for state court proceedings place higher burdens of proof on the state,[203] impose heightened duties on the state to guard against unnecessary removal[204] and termination,[205] and establish placement preferences that favor Indian families and tribes over stranger foster care.[206] Failure to follow all of the ICWA requirements can result in disruptions of state established placements and adoptions.[207] Therefore, state agencies are well-advised to be aware of and strictly adhere to ICWA requirements

The recent United States Supreme Court decision in *Adoptive Couple v. Baby Girl*[208] has been read to signal a retreat from the Supreme Court's prior strict reading of ICWA.[209] This case held that some of ICWA's more stringent requirements surrounding involuntary termination of parental rights do not apply when the Indian parent never had custody of the child. The Court ultimately upheld the adoption of

---

203. *Id.* § 1912(e) (establishing the burden of proof for foster care placement orders at "clear and convincing evidence"); *id.* § 1912(f) (establishing the burden of proof for parental rights termination orders at "evidence beyond a reasonable doubt").

204. *Id.* § 1912(d) (requiring "active" as opposed to "reasonable" efforts to justify removal); *see also* Bureau of Indian Affairs, Guidelines for State Courts and Agencies in Indian Child Custody Proceedings, 80 Fed. Reg. 10,146, *challenged* National Council for Adoption Et Al v. Jewell, No. 1:15-CV-00675 (E. D. Va.), *motion dismissed* December 9, 2015.

205. 25 U.S.C. § 1912(e) (requiring a determination "supported by clear and convincing evidence, including testimony of a qualified expert witness" to order a foster care placement); *id.* § 1912(f) (requiring a determination "supported by evidence beyond a reasonable doubt, including testimony of a qualified expert witness" to order termination of parental rights).

206. 25 U.S.C. § 1915 establishes placement preferences for Indian children in both adoptive and foster placements. In adoptive placements, the preferred placement is with a member of the child's extended family, then other members of the child's tribe, and then other Indian families. In foster placements, the preferred placement is with a member of the Indian child's extended family, and then a foster home licensed, approved, or specified by the Indian child's tribe, and then an Indian foster home licensed or approved by an authorized non-Indian licensing authority, and then an institution which is approved by an Indian tribe or operated by an Indian organization which can meet the child's needs. Tribes may establish different preferences, and an Indian child or parent may express preferences.

207. 25 U.S.C. § 1914 allows an Indian child who was placed in foster care or who had their parent or parents' rights terminated, a parent, an Indian custodian who had a child removed from their custody, or the child's tribe to petition "any court of competent jurisdiction" to invalidate the termination of parental rights, removal, or foster care placement if the action violated any provision of §§ 1911, 1912, or 1913.

208. 133 S. Ct. 2552 (2013).

209. Bethany R. Berger, *In the Name of the Child: Race, Gender and Economics in* Adoptive Couple v. Baby Girl, 67 Fla. L. Rev. 295 (2015); Barbara Atwood, *A Response to Professor Berger's 'In the Name of the Child: Race, Gender and Economics in* Adoptive Couple v. Baby Girl,' 67 Fla. L. Rev. 1 (2015); Allison E. Burke, Adoptive Couple v. Baby Girl: *From Strict Construction to Serious Confusion*, 43 Hofstra L. Rev. 139 (Fall 2014); Marcia A. Zug, *The Real Impact of* Adoptive Couple v. Baby Girl: *The Existing Indian Family is Not Affirmed But the Future of the ICWA's Placement Preferences is Jeopardized*, 42 Cap. U. L. Rev. 327 (Spring 2014); *But see*, Jack Trope & Adrian Smith, *The Continued Protection of Indian Children and Families After* Adoptive Couple v. Baby Girl: *What the Case Means and How to Respond*, 2 Seattle U. Am. Indian Law. J. 2, 434–483 (Fall 2014) (urging a limited reading of the decision to apply only to private voluntary adoptions consistent with the factual circumstances presented in the case).

an undisputed Indian child by a non-Indian family in the face of the Indian father's challenge. It is not yet known just how far the holding in *Adoptive Couple* will reach when it comes to newborn infants and other very young children who have been placed before their fathers become aware of their existence.

While Indian children comprise a small number of children in the system as a whole, they continue to be disproportionately represented in child welfare proceedings,[210] and in certain states they comprise the majority of children entering care.[211] However, no matter the size of the Indian population, all states are required to abide by ICWA, and so it is not unusual for form pleadings throughout the country to address the question of whether the child who is the subject of the proceedings qualifies as an "Indian child."[212]

Multi-Ethnic Placement Act/Inter-Ethnic Placement Act

Shortly before passing ASFA, Congress enacted the Multi-Ethnic Placement Act (MEPA),[213] which was subsequently amended by the Inter-Ethnic Placement Act (IEPA). MEPA/IEPA was passed in response to criticism that efforts to match children to families by race had exacerbated racial disproportionality by slowing the adoption of black children.[214] Despite opposition by the National Association of

---

210. In 2013, American Indian and Alaska Native children were represented two-and-a-half times as often in the foster care system as they were in the general population in the United States, with disproportionality rates ranging from 0 in Delaware and Vermont to 14.8 in Minnesota. Alicia Summers, *Disproportionality Rates for Children of Color In Foster Care (Fiscal Year 2013): Technical Assistance Bulletin*, NATIONAL COUNCIL OF JUVENILE AND FAMILY COURT JUDGES, Table 1, p. 3 (June 2015), [https://perma.cc/66PW-TMZS].

211. In 2013, Native children comprised 50.4% of children in care in South Dakota, but only 13.1% of the general child population. Similarly, in Alaska, Native children comprise 50.4% of the children in care, and only 17.8% of children in the state. U.S. DEPARTMENT OF HEALTH AND HUMAN SERVICES, CHILD WELFARE OUTCOMES: 2010–2013, REPORT TO CONGRESS, 42–43, 303–304 (2013), available at [https://perma.cc/ATG5-AELM].

212. In February 2015, the Bureau of Indian Affairs released updated guidelines which clarify that in "every child custody proceeding," agencies and state courts must "ask whether the child is or could be an Indian child and conduct an investigation into whether the child is an Indian child," regardless of whether the child is removed from the home. It also clarified that ICWA applies in any case in which there is "reason to believe the child is an Indian child." It further clarifies that "State courts must ask, as a threshold question at the start of any State court child custody proceeding, whether there is reason to believe the child who is the subject of the proceeding is an Indian child by asking each party to the case, including the guardian ad litem and the agency representative, to certify on the record whether they have discovered or know of any information that suggests or indicates the child is an Indian child." Bureau of Indian Affairs, Guidelines for State Courts and Agencies in Indian Child Custody Proceedings, 80 Fed. Reg. 10,146, 10,152, *challenged National Council for Adoption Et Al v. Jewell*, No. 1:15-CV-00675 (E. D. Va.), *motion dismissed* December 9, 2015, available at: [https://perma.cc/BBK6-WT9S].

213. *See* Ralph Richard Banks, *The Multiethnic Placement Act and the Troubling Persistence of Race Matching*, 38 CAP. U. L. REV. 271, 272 (2009).

214. The passage of MEPA in 1994 and its amendment in 1996 preceded ASFA. This chronology of events has confounded researchers seeking to tease out the impact that ASFA may have had on the rate of adoptions. It could be that at least part of the rise in adoptions prior to and during the early years post-ASFA were caused by social workers allowing transracial adoptions to proceed. et al., *supra*

Black Social Workers,[215] Congress conditioned ongoing foster care funding to the states on compliance with the prohibition against using race, culture, or ethnicity as the basis for denying or delaying placement or adoption.[216] MEPA/IEPA also requires state agencies to engage in diligent recruitment of foster and potential adoptive parents reflective of the ethnic and racial diversity of the communities from which the children and families come.[217] "Indian children," as defined by ICWA, are exempt from the prohibitions found in MEPA/IEPA.[218]

Critics of MEPA/IEPA argue that more resources and effort have been spent enforcing the prohibitions against considering race in placement/adoption than in recruiting and supporting families of color who might want to serve as foster and/or adoptive parents.[219] Some assert that MEPA/IEPA's prohibitions against considering race have had a chilling effect on both recruitment efforts in the minority community and on providing white prospective adoptive parents with the information they need to parent the children of color in their care.[220] The fact remains that children of color continue to enter the child welfare system at rates disproportionate to their white peers and continue to remain in the system longer, while the promise of a licensed foster parent pool reflective of the communities from which they came has yet to be realized.[221]

Federal Requirements in the Juvenile Justice Context

The federal government has exerted less influence over states in the delinquency arena as compared to child welfare. The Juvenile Justice and Delinquency Prevention Act (JJDPA) provides fewer significant financial incentives. Unlike the Title IV funding which states rely heavily on to fund foster care and related child protection services, the JJDPA provides more modest incentives and requires less from states to receive the funding. The JJDPA provides funding for state advisory groups, delinquency prevention programs, programs to improve juvenile justice practices and the Office of Juvenile Justice and Delinquency Programs (OJJDP) which is a federal agency dedicated to providing training, technical assistance, research and evaluation to support state and local efforts.[222]

---

note 188, at 24. *See*, 42 U.S.C. § 671; Pub.L. 104-188 Sec. 1808(a)(3)(18)(A-B) (repealed language in MEPA that allowed States and other entities to consider the cultural, ethnic, or racial background of a child, as well as the capacity of the prospective parent to meet the needs of such a child).

215. *See* Nat'l Ass'n of Black Soc. Workers, Position Statement on Trans-Racial Adoptions (1972), [https://perma.cc/K38E-LBRJ].

216. *See* 42 U.S.C. § 671(a)(18).

217. *See* 42 U.S.C. § 622(b)(7).

218. Pub.L. 103-382 Sec. 553(f); Pub.L. 104-188 Sec. 1808(b)(4).

219. *See* WESTAT, Race Matters Consortium: MEPA/IEPA Overview, [https://perma.cc /H22H-4294].

220. U.S. Comm'n on Civil Rights, The Multi-Ethnic Placement Act 65–76 (2010) [https:// perma.cc/S7DS-L9XK].

221. *See* Evan B. Donaldson Adoption Inst., Finding Families for African American Children 40 (2008), [https://perma.cc/SE3X-JLFH].

222. 42 U.S.C. § 5601 *et seq.*

In order to receive federal funding through the JJDPA, states must comply with four core requirements designed to set standards for state juvenile justice systems: (1) the deinstitutionalization of status offenders; (2) the removal of juveniles from adult jails; (3) the sight and sound separation of juveniles and adults when held temporarily in the same facility; and (4) plans to measure and address Disproportionate Minority Contact ("DMC").[223]

Despite the JJDPA's requirement that status offenders not be incarcerated, youth who run away from foster care sometimes are picked up and placed in detention. States that engage in this practice do so under the JJDPA's "valid court order" exception,[224] which allows a youth to be held in detention for violating a valid court order even if the underlying infraction would be considered a status offense. For youth in dependency proceedings, they are placed in their "homes" by court order; therefore, running away from "home" can be seen as a violation of a "valid court order." Given the disparate impact that this loophole has upon youth in the dependency system, a coalition of local and national advocacy groups have been pressing Congress to amend or repeal the "valid court order" exception.[225]

Although the JJDPA is credited with transforming many states' juvenile justice systems, particularly with respect to reducing the incarceration of status offenders and discouraging the jailing of juveniles together with adults, its initial influence has waned as congress has decreased funding and postponed the Act's reauthorization.[226] Also, there is little evidence that the JJDPA has led to a significant reduction of DMC, the overrepresentation of youth of color, which continues to exist at every stage of the juvenile justice process.[227]

---

223. 42 U.S.C. § 5633(a)(11)–(13), (22). In this context, a status offense is applied to juveniles but not adults, such as truancy or running away.

224. *Id.* § 5633(a)(11)(A)(ii).

225. *See Valid Court Order (VCO) Exception*, Coalition for Juvenile Justice (the Coalition for Juvenile Justice's SOS Project advocates for amending the JJDPA to prohibit the use of the Valid Court Order exception for securely confining youth with status offenses [https://perma.cc/BQ2J-P8BW]. *See also* Status Offense Reform Center (For the work of the Status Offense Reform Center (SORC), a project of the Vera Institute of Justice, which works with policy makers and practitioners to keep juveniles who commit status offenses out of the justice system), [https://perma.cc/F69C-XGCE].

226. Between 2002 and 2015, federal funding to states through the JJDPA decreased by over one half, lowering states' incentives to comply with the federal standards. Gary Gately, *Federal Juvenile Justice Funding Declines Precipitously*, Juv. Just. Info. Exchange (Feb. 12, 2015), [https://perma.cc/7UUD -D7CN]. Senators Chuck Grassley and Sheldon Whitehouse introduced a reauthorization bill at the end of the 113th Congress. *See* S. 2999, 113th Cong. (2014). They re-introduced a similar version of the bill on April 30, 2015. *See* S. 1169, 114th Cong. (2015).

227. *See* Jones *supra* note 71 at 192.

IV. Legal Representation For Youth When the State Intervenes

Counsel for Youth in the Delinquency System

For more than fifty years, young people in the delinquency system have had a constitutional right to counsel under the *Gault* decision.[228] Unlike the Sixth Amendment right to counsel in adult proceedings, the right in *Gault* was established under the Fourteenth Amendment; however, many state courts incorporated the Sixth Amendment right to juveniles, which included the right to effective assistance of counsel at "critical stages" of the proceedings. *Gault*, like its adult predecessor *Gideon v. Wainwright,* has been derided by critics as a disappointment. The implementation of adversarial protections in juvenile court were slow to take hold and continue to face significant obstacles due to a variety of factors including inadequate resources, inattention to the complexities of representing youth, and a juvenile court culture that minimizes the role of counsel.[229]

> ### Appointment of Counsel in Delinquency Proceedings in Your State
>
> • *At what stages in delinquency proceedings do youth have counsel appointed?*
>
> • *How do they interact with dependency counsel when the youth is also in dependency?*
>
> • *At what stages do youth accused of status offenses have counsel appointed?*

Because every state has a different system for delivering juvenile indigent defense services, it is difficult to get a comprehensive picture of the state of juvenile defense. Disparities exist not only from state to state, but also from county to county. After an initial national assessment of juvenile defense counsel commissioned by OJJDP in the early 1990s revealed significant gaps in consistent juvenile defense representation,[230] the National Juvenile Defender Center (NJDC), an organization focusing on improving juvenile indigent defense, sent teams of experts to more than 20 states to observe juvenile court practices and interview system stakeholders. While there exist bright spots where well-trained juvenile defenders zealously advocate on behalf of their clients, concerning themes emerge.

---

228. *In re* Gault, 387 U.S. 1, 4 (1967).

229. Mae C. Quinn, *Giving Kids Their Due: Theorizing A Modern Fourteenth Amendment Framework for Juvenile Defense Representation*, 99 Iowa L. Rev. 2185 (2014).

230. Patricia Puritz, Am. Bar Ass'n Juvenile Justice Ctr., A Call for Justice (2002), [https://perma.cc/8LW9-PWJ5].

In Missouri, for example, NJDC's assessment found youth were frequently encouraged to waive counsel and more than 60% of youth were not represented by the state's designated system of indigent defense. In cases where counsel was appointed, it was often late in the proceeding, such as after an initial detention decision had been made.[231] These findings were later confirmed and cited in an investigation of the St. Louis County Family Court by the Department of Justice Office of Civil Rights. The Department of Justice (DOJ) found that the State violated the due process rights of juvenile defendants by failing to provide meaningful access to counsel. In addition to the statewide concerns raised by NJDC, the DOJ found that in St. Louis County in 2014 only four contested adjudicatory hearings occurred out of 277 delinquency cases; no defense challenges to probable cause at any stage occurred; no evidence was presented by defense counsel during disposition (sentencing) hearings, no expert witnesses were hired by the public defender and no appeals were taken.[232]

The problems of frequent waiver of counsel, lack of practice standards and excessive caseloads were themes that came up in a number of the juvenile court systems assessed by NJDC.[233] Responding to concerns about the role and duties of indigent juvenile defense counsel, NJDC developed the National Juvenile Defense Standards to provide guidance to states and local jurisdictions to improve and develop this specialized practice area.[234]

The National Juvenile Defense Standards begin with the ethical obligations of juvenile defense counsel, including the obligation to follow the client's expressed interests under the Rules of Professional Conduct.[235] By beginning with this particular obligation, the Standards address a common struggle that many attorneys representing youth confront: the desire to substitute their judgment for their client's or to advocate for their "best interest" rather than their stated interest. It was this "best interest" culture that *Gault* confronted in imposing due process protections and it is this same culture, which continues to create challenges for providing competent, and zealous, representation for youth accused of criminal behavior.

When it comes to status offenses, the appointment of counsel has not been uniform across the states.[236] According to regulations promulgated under the JJDPA, status offenders who are alleged to have violated a valid court order are entitled to appointed counsel if they are found to be indigent.[237] This is because, under the JJDPA,

---

231. MARY ANN SCALI ET AL., NAT'L JUVENILE DEFENDER CTR., MISSOURI: JUSTICE RATIONED (2013), [https://perma.cc/ZK6B-HC7G].

232. U.S. DEP'T OF JUSTICE, *supra* note 152, at 15–17.

233. *See, e.g.*, PATRICIA PURITZ ET AL., NAT'L JUVENILE DEF. CTR., FLORIDA 55 (2006) (high caseloads), [https://perma.cc/7RS4-LNKM]; PATRICIA PURITZ ET AL., NAT'L JUVENILE DEF. CTR., COLORADO 40 (2012) (waiver of counsel), [https://perma.cc/EKX2-Y6LN].

234. *See* NAT'L JUVENILE DEF. CTR., NATIONAL JUVENILE DEFENSE STANDARDS (2012), [https://perma.cc/3LAH-BAFT].

235. *See id.* at 18.

236. N. Lee Cooper et al., *Fulfilling the Promise of In Re Gault: Advancing the Role of Lawyers for Children*, 33 WAKE FOREST L. REV. 651, 655–64 (1998).

237. 28 C.F.R. § 31.303(f)(3)(v)(D).

such status offenders are at risk of incarceration.[238] However, states vary as to whether youth charged with status offenses generally are entitled to counsel.[239]

Counsel for Youth in Dependency

While youth in delinquency proceedings have a constitutional right to appointed counsel, young people in child abuse and neglect proceedings may or may not have access to appointed counsel depending upon the state or even the county in which they live.

> ### Appointment of Counsel for Children in Dependency Proceedings in Your State
>
> - *Find the statutes and rules governing appointment of counsel.*
> - *Do parents receive appointed counsel? At what stage?*
> - *Do children receive appointed counsel? At what stage?*
> - *If so, what model of representation is employed for children?*

This lack of uniformity in representation arises from both the absence of a clear constitutional mandate and the fact that states respond to federal statutory requirements differently. As discussed above, CAPTA requires the appointment of a guardian ad litem (GAL) in each case involving an abused or neglected child. CAPTA permits the GAL to be an attorney or a lay advocate. However, under federal law, the advocate's duty is to make a recommendation to the court concerning the child's best interest.[240]

This mandate has led to a proliferation of systems throughout the country. Some states have lawyer GALs; some states have non-lawyer GALs. Some GALs are paid; some are volunteers. In addition to GALs, an increasing number of states have also provided young people with court-appointed attorneys whose duty it is to represent the young person's position and interests. These attorneys operate using a "stated interest" model, as opposed to the "best interest" model required of GALs.[241]

---

238. 42 U.S.C. § 5633(a)(11)(A)(ii) (2006).

239. *See* Bellevue School District v. E.S., 171 Wash.2d 695 (Wash. 2011) (holding that due process does not require appointment of counsel at initial truancy hearing); Lana A. v. Woodburn, 116 P.3d 1222 (Ariz. App. Div. 1 2005) (holding that juveniles have a statutory right to counsel at incorrigibility hearings and any other hearings that might result in their detention); *In re* B.A.T., 174 N.C.App.365 (N.C. App. 2005) (holding that counsel is not required at hearings on undisciplined child petitions).

240. *See* 42 U.S.C. § 5106a(b)(A)(xiii). Nonetheless, the federal Administration for Children and Families has issued guidance emphasizing the importance of legal representation for children in dependency proceedings. The guidance highlights the empirical research that links quality legal representation to "improved case planning, expedited permanency and cost savings to state government." CHILDREN'S BUREAU, U.S. DEP'T OF HEALTH & HUMAN SERVS., *Log No. ACYF-CB-IM-17-02* (2017).

241. For an overview of the different models states use to satisfy the CAPTA requirement of providing representation *see* CHILD WELFARE INFORMATION GATEWAY, U.S. DEP'T OF HEALTH & HUMAN SERVS., REPRESENTATION OF CHILDREN IN CHILD ABUSE AND NEGLECT PROCEEDINGS (2014),

A survey of state statutes shows that 61% of all states require appointment of attorneys for children in child welfare proceedings. This means that 39% of states may rely exclusively on non-lawyer GALs to advocate for the child's best interest in court. This 61% figure, however, does not mean that the children in all of these states have stated-interest counsel. Many have attorney GALs. Only 31% of states require the appointment of stated-interest attorneys for children in dependency proceedings.[242] Many states requiring attorney appointment have mixed models — allowing for best-interest GAL representation when the child is too young to express a stated interest and eventually allowing for more traditional lawyer-client representation as the child matures.[243]

Stated-interest attorneys, unlike a GAL, owe a duty of confidentiality to their minor client and are otherwise bound by the Rules of Professional Conduct.[244] In addition to the Rules of Professional Conduct, two major national organizations have developed standards intended to guide attorneys who represent children and youth in child abuse and neglect proceedings. The American Bar Association (ABA) recommends that all children be appointed stated-interest attorneys, and in 1996 promulgated standards describing the duties of attorneys in this context.[245] The National Association of Counsel for Children's (NACC) standards are closely aligned with the ABA's but at points diverge, particularly around when it might be appropriate for an attorney for a child to engage in a substitution of judgment.[246]

The ABA Standards provide additional insight for attorneys who may find themselves representing pre- or non-verbal children. While not advocating for a best interest model, the ABA standards urge a third model of representation which some have termed a "legal interest" model. Under this model, the attorney seeks to protect the child's legal interests as expressed under case or statutory law.[247] For example, if a child

---

[https://perma.cc/Q76D-NALM]. *See also Legal Research: Public Access to Abuse/Neglect Proceedings*, First Star, Putting Children First, [https://perma.cc/V2ED-KES7] (last updated June 2010).

242. *See* First Star, A Child's Right to Counsel (3d ed. 2012), [https://perma.cc/QP2F-NESR]. This report grades each state individually on whether it provides for well-trained, stated interest legal representation for children involved in the child welfare system's court proceedings.

243. *See* Minn. Stat. § 260C.163(3)(a)-(b) (Minnesota law requires appointment of counsel only for children ages ten and above); Wis. Stat. § 48.23(1m)(b)(2013) (Wisconsin law requires appointment of counsel for children in dependency proceedings who are 12 years old or older).

244. While all of the Rules of Professional Conduct apply to the attorney who undertakes stated representation of his or her minor client, Rule 1.14 dealing with clients with diminished capacity does have special relevance to the representation of children. *See* Model Code of Prof'l Responsibility R. 1.14 (2013) [https://perma.cc/C33T-429A].

245. *See* Am. Bar Ass'n, Standards of Practice for Lawyers Who Represent Children in Abuse and Neglect Cases (1996), [https://perma.cc/AQ8A-WP9S].

246. The NACC maintains current recommendations on practice standards for representing children in abuse and neglect cases. *See Standards of Practice*, Nat'l Ass'n of Counsel for Children, [https://perma.cc/KHA3-TJWM]. The association makes explicit for practitioners where their standards differ with those of the ABA.

247. Standards of Practice for Lawyers Who Represent Children in Abuse and Neglect Cases, *B-4 Client Preferences Commentary* (ABA 1996), [https://perma.cc/6U3C-U73H].; see also

has a right to visitation with siblings under a statute, it is the attorney's duty to ensure that this right is brought before the court. This model would also necessitate efforts to enforce ASFA deadlines incorporated into state statutes.

Because CAPTA does not provide funding for stated interest attorneys, those states that do appoint counsel for children under a pure stated-interest model must seek out other funding sources. Counsel may be paid for by the state, by the county or even by the city.[248] Different states and counties also may draw their appointed counsel from a variety of sources. In some locales, attorneys for children may be employed by government agencies; in others, they may work for non-profit organizations or they may be self-employed. Attorneys serving children may also represent parents (not in the same cases) and may also cycle through other types of court appointed representation during the course of their careers. Some courts may appoint from a mixture of all or some of these models.[249] Financial constraints may result in low pay and high caseloads or caps on the number of hours that an attorney may spend on a case.[250] These limits strain against the demands of the Rules of Professional Conduct and other governing standards.

Delivering on the Right to Counsel

- *How is children's representation funded in your state?*
- *What agency is responsible for children's representation?*
- *Does your state have practice standards for children's attorneys?*
- *What are the training requirements for GALs and/or attorneys for children in your state?*

This book focuses on lawyers as advocates for youth, who follow a "stated-interest" model of advocacy. These lawyers also work in the context of an evolving delivery system of representation. Katie, the lawyer for Michael, is a recent graduate employed by a public defender agency, in which she is starting "in the dependency division," representing children. Julia, Maya's lawyer, started her career in the same public defender system and has cycled through all of its divisions. She is now a private attorney participating in a pilot project in which she confines her representation to children and

---

Lisa Kelly and Alicia LeVezu, *Until the Client Speaks: Reviving the Legal-Interest Model for Preverbal Children*, 50 Fam. L. Q. 38 (2016).

248. *See* Jean Koh Peters, *How Children Are Heard in Child Protective Proceedings, in the United States and Around the World in 2005: Survey Findings, Initial Observations, and Areas for Further Study*, 6 Nev. L.J. 966, 1001–28 (2006); Children's Bureau, U.S. Dep't of Health & Human Servs., Representation of Children in Child Abuse and Neglect Proceedings 4 (2014).

249. *See* First Star, *supra* note 240; *see also* William W. Patton, *Searching for the Proper Role of Children's Counsel in California Dependency Cases; Or the Answer to the Riddle of the Dependency Sphinx*, 1 J. Center For Children & Cts. 21, 31 (1999).

250. Peters, *supra* note 247, at 1026–28.

youth in dependency, with a lower caseload than Katie. Nevertheless, both continue to grapple with the limits imposed upon them by a strained system.

In addition to a close examination of stated-interest advocacy, you will also catch glimpses of the GAL model. One of the big players in the non-lawyer GAL field is the nonprofit organization, Court Appointed Special Advocates (CASA). CASAs are lay volunteers who have received training to serve as GALs in child abuse and neglect proceedings.[251] In some cases, a youth may have both a lawyer and a GAL.

Reflections and Exercises

1. *What? So What? Now What? A Five-Minute Reflection Opportunity.* Take just five minutes to write and reflect on the following questions:

   a. What are your initial thoughts on how the state gets involved in the lives of youth and their families?

   b. Now that you are aware of the significant racial disparities in the child welfare and juvenile justice systems, does this affect your desire to work within those systems? How?

2. *Imagining a Different World:* Throughout this book we will be asking you to think critically about the systems at work in the lives of Maya and Michael. Now that you have learned of the perceived need for intervention and the deleterious effects that the child welfare and delinquency systems generate, consider the following:

   a. What are the stated purposes of the child welfare system?

   b. What are the stated purposes of the delinquency system?

   c. Critics have suggested these systems serve other purposes. Can you imagine what those might be?

   d. Are there purposes that you believe justify the existence of these systems? What are they?

   e. Identify five essential interventions that each system should utilize to achieve the critical purposes you have identified.

---

251. *See* The National CASA Association: Annual State Organization Survey Report 2012, [https://perma.cc/7QZ4-YMHW]. For a report studying the efficacy of CASA, see National Coalition for Child Protection Reform, Evaluation of CASA Representation Final Report, [https://perma.cc/TZ2G-Y5FZ].

Chapter Two

Officially Torn Apart

In this chapter, you will be introduced to Michael, his family, his caretakers, and those whom he encounters in the legal process, including his lawyer. You will follow him as he is removed from his home and taken into foster care. It is the beginning of a journey that will encompass legal and social issues that go beyond the child welfare system.

As you read this chapter, and others, you will be asked to consider the laws that are specific to your jurisdiction. Some of your laws will mirror the laws where Michael lives and some may be different. Understanding the law is important; however, you will see that understanding the law is only the beginning to understanding how the legal system impacts Michael, his family and the broader community. The law provides a framework for the state's intervention, but the legal analysis is just part of what a lawyer does in representing a young person who is removed from his family.

The law has a history. A history, which impacts African American families like the one to which Michael belongs. It is difficult to tell stories of the child welfare system without addressing the overrepresentation of African American children in that system. And it is impossible to understand this phenomenon without understanding the historical context, which begins with our country's shameful history of enslaving black bodies—a topic beyond the reach of this book.

The racial disparities in the dependency system have been researched, debated and written about extensively. African Americans have had higher rates of entry into foster care as well as slower rates of exiting the system. The reasons are complex. As you enter into the story of Michael's family, remember the danger of the "single story" discussed in the preface and be mindful of how race, Michael's and your own, affect the way that we understand how the system operates.

You will enter Michael's life at a crisis point, as lawyers often do when they meet their clients for the first time. Although the legal crisis Michael's family confronts is overwhelming, the story is intended to help you understand that their lives are more than the crisis. The story is told to help you critically consider the legal framework, institutions and individuals that propel the crisis. You will be challenged to rethink the system and imagine another story for Michael.

Michael's Story

It isn't like he isn't used to going to the principal's office. That started in second or third grade. Always something. Late to school too many times. Not wearing the right clothes. Talking too much in class. Disrespecting the teacher.[1] But this time when he showed up it isn't just the principal, Mr. Dixon, or the assistant principal, Ms. Jones. This time it is Mr. Dixon, Ms. Jones, a police officer and some white lady he had never seen before. He walks into the crowded principal's office with all these people staring at him looking serious. Not angry or frustrated—how they usually look. This time they look almost sad. Michael starts thinking that math class is a hundred times better than this and he is about to turn around when Mr. Dixon places his hand on his shoulder and says, "Sit down, son." Michael knows then that it is bad. All bad.

Ms. Jones jumps in quickly, nervously, "Michael, this is Emily Peters from Child Protective Services. She is here with Officer Perez and they would like to speak with you. How are you doin' by the way?" At this point, Michael looks quickly toward the door, wanting nothing more than to run back through it. He nods almost imperceptibly at the two strangers and stares blankly ahead.[2]

"Hi Michael, like Ms. Jones said, my name is Emily and I am a social worker. I work for Child Protective Services, you probably have heard of CPS? How are you doing today?" Blank stare. "I am here because we are concerned about you and your sisters. We want to make sure that you and your sisters are safe." Blank stare.

At this point, the words start to mash together and there are just faces and sounds. Strange adults with serious faces trying to look trustworthy, like they just want to help but really they just want to get into other people's business. Michael notes the police officer is standing back a bit, trying to be inconspicuous. He looks pretty cool. A stocky Latino guy, maybe the same age as one of his uncles. He reminds him of a boxer that he has seen on television. He'd be the one Michael would talk to if he wasn't wearing that uniform.

---

1. Black boys are disciplined at school at rates three times greater than their white counterparts. U.S. Dep't of Educ. Office for Civil Rights, Civil Rights Data Collection: Data Snapshot (School Discipline) 3 (2014), [https://perma.cc/DQ9M-N3MT]. This pattern begins in pre-school. Scholars have identified numerous factors that contribute to these disparities including implicit bias, individual and institutional racism, the adultification of black boys, deficit perspectives toward black boys, and "cultural collision and collusion," among others. *See, e.g.*, Carlos R. McCray et al., *Saving Our Future by Reducing Suspensions and Expulsions Among African American Males*, 25 J. Sch. Leadership 345 (2015); Tyrone C. Howard, Black Male(d): Peril and Promise in the Education of African American Males (2013).

2. The face-to-face interview of children who are the subject of complaints is one of the steps in the investigative process required by CAPTA. *See* ch. 1, *CAPTA: Child Protective Services*. For a sample CPS investigation protocol, see Wash. Rev. Code §26.44.030(14)(a)(i). State law may also require CPS to report certain types of referrals to law enforcement for investigation. *See, e.g.*, Wash. Rev. Code §26.44.030(4) (incidents that involve death, physical injury, or alleged sexual abuse); Tex. Fam. Code Ann. §261.105(b) (any report that concerns the suspected abuse or neglect of a child or death of a child from abuse or neglect); Conn. Gen. Stat. §17a-101b(c) (a report alleging sexual abuse or serious physical abuse). Law enforcement may independently investigate complaints of abuse or neglect and may accompany CPS workers when they seek to remove children involuntarily from their parents. Law enforcement officers and medical personnel generally have the legal authority to place children in state custody without a court order in emergent situations. *See, e.g.*, Wash. Rev. Code §26.44.050; N.Y. Soc. Serv. Law §417(1)(a); Md. Code Ann., Fam. Law §5-709(c).

He realizes that everyone is looking at him and that there was a question asked which he is now supposed to answer. He shrugs his shoulders. Whatever the question was, he is sure that it is none of their business. His mind starts to wander to earlier in the day, retracing his steps from waking up to arriving at school. Where were his sisters? Did they make it to school? He saw them get on the bus before he caught his own. Did this white lady talk to them already?

Michael sees himself pouring cereal for his sisters that morning and telling them to hurry up because they need to make the bus. Searching for coats for everyone to wear because it is getting cold. He knows that they get in trouble at school when they show up without coats in January. He knocks on his mom's bedroom door to say goodbye. He peeks in quickly to see if she is OK and sees her stretched out sleeping next to a man he has seen a few times before who looks familiar. He wonders where her boyfriend DJ is. He ignores the pipe dangling from her limp hand. He gets his sisters to their bus stop on time and manages to make his own bus today too. What could have gone wrong?

He could have been in the principal's office for minutes or hours, he isn't sure. He asks one question, directed mostly to the cop: "Am I going to juvie?" No, no, a chorus of voices tells him he is not in trouble. He is asked to go with the social worker and the cop follows along. He sees the cop car parked out front and he starts to feel sweat on his palms. Then the social worker asks him to get into her car, a white Ford Taurus parked right in front of the cop car. He is relieved, but he wonders why the cop is there if he isn't in trouble.[3]

> ### *Role of the CPS Worker and the Police*
>
> *CPS workers often assume dual roles of investigating and helping families. As in this case, they sometimes find themselves working with law enforcement to accomplish their goals.*
>
> - *What legal authority do child protection workers, police and others have to remove children in your jurisdiction? How do they work together?*
>
> - *What are the standards for the initial removal and are they adequate to protect children and the rights of parents?*
>
> - *What are the pros and cons of CPS workers working together with law enforcement to remove children?*

At the CPS office, a sterile place with flat gray carpet and people moving slowly about, Michael sees his sisters. Relief. Aliyah is standing up on her tiptoes to look through a window. Angel is pacing with her backpack still on. Michael wonders where Deja is. Did he see her in the bed with his mother this morning? He can't remember. His palms start to feel damp again. He feels something tight in his chest. He is

---

3. *See supra* text accompanying note 2.

hugging his sisters. They hold on to him tightly like they used to when they were really little. At six and nine, they don't seem little to him anymore. They seem almost grown. Except now in this terrible and frightening place.

They hold hands for what seems like hours. The white social worker from the principal's office comes in and out carrying a stack of papers. There is nothing to do in that room but wait. There are a few toys and old books for little kids. He wishes the police officer Perez was there in plain clothes and they could play video games. Why can't they have video games here instead of lame baby toys? He asks the social worker, "Where is the baby, Deja?" She says "Deja is in a safe place and you will get to see her soon."

"When is soon?"

"Well, I don't know for sure, but hopefully tomorrow or the next day." Michael thinks that is definitely not "soon." Soon would be now or in 10 minutes or even 30 minutes. His chest gets tighter.

Finally, the white[4] social worker comes back with a look like she is trying to be really happy and positive. "We are going to take you to Miss Morgan's house and Mr. Jeffries' place. I think you will really like them." Now Emily, the white social worker, has a friend with her, an older stocky black guy who says his name is Reggie. "Michael, you can ride with Reggie." The girls start to cry and ask why they can't go with Michael and go home. Michael asks the social worker where his mom is and why they can't go home. The social worker's voice gets low and she says, "Michael, your mom does not have a safe place for you and your sisters to stay right now. So you need to come with me while your mom gets some help. You need to be strong for your sisters. A judge is going to have to decide this week what will be best for you."[5]

---

4. Data from the National Survey of Child and Adolescent Well-Being (NSCAWII) captured the demographic characteristics of 5,052 investigative caseworkers in that large longitudinal study. 58% were White Non-Hispanic, 24% were Black, 15% were Hispanic and 4% were self-described as other. Off. of Planning, Res. & Evaluation, U.S. Dep't of Health & Human Servs., NSCAW II Baseline Report: Caseworker Characteristics, Child Welfare Services, and Experiences of Children Placed in Out-of-Home Care 6 (2011), [https://perma.cc/4ANZ-V4ZD]. Research regarding whether the caseworker's race affects outcomes for children suggests that it does not. J. Christopher Graham et. al., *The Decision Making Ecology of Placing a Child into Foster Care: A Structural Equation Model,* 49 Child Abuse & Neglect 12 (2015)(race of the social worker did not affect initial child placement decision); Joseph P. Ryan et. al., *Investigating the Effects of Caseworker Characteristics in Child Welfare*, 28 Child. & Youth Servs. 993 (2006) (African American youth experienced significantly longer stays in foster care and were less likely to reunify than white children regardless of the race of caseworker).

5. Before children are removed from their homes by state action, certain steps must be taken. The Adoption and Safe Families Act of 1997 (ASFA) requires states receiving federal funding for their child welfare systems to operate those systems in certain ways. For instance, they must make "reasonable efforts . . . to preserve and reunify families" prior to placing the child in foster care. 42 U.S.C. §671(a)(15)(B). There are limited exceptions to the reasonable efforts requirement, for example where a parent has subjected the child to "aggravated circumstances"—as defined by state law. *Id.* §671(a)(15)(D)(i). In addition to the reasonable efforts requirement, parents have due process protections prior to the state's removal of their children, which include notice and an

Michael hates this woman.[6] She doesn't know anything about his family and now she is treating him like a little kid. Now he feels his throat tighten but he won't cry. Thirteen-year-old boys don't cry. But he won't speak either, just in case. He feels trapped like his only option is to go along.

Reggie has an old Toyota Corolla. He has trouble getting into it. He asks Michael what he wants to listen to on the radio. Michael ignores him. Emily the white social worker follows in the Ford Taurus with the girls in the back seat. Michael thinks maybe there is some rule about riding in cars with people of the same sex so you don't get molested. The cars stop in front of a box-shaped yellow house with a chain link fence and two small dogs barking. The white social worker and the girls get out of the Ford Taurus. Michael starts to get out of the Toyota, but Reggie says, "Wait here." Reggie gets out and talks to Emily the white social worker and then returns to the car. The girls follow Emily into the yellow house. Reggie says, "We are going to Mr. Jeffries' house now." He starts to pull away and Michael can see Aliyah's eyes widen as the door to the yellow house closes. Panic starts to set in, but Michael spends every ounce of energy he has trying not to cry, trying to manage his anger and confusion. Reggie starts to say something, but stops. Michael wants to ask why this is happening, what is this bullshit that he can't be with his sisters? But he can't find his voice. He can't find the words. Reggie and Michael look straight ahead as the Toyota picks up speed.[7]

---

opportunity to be heard. A court order for removal is generally required. Most states have procedures for obtaining placement orders from the court on an emergent basis without notice to the parents so long as a court hearing is provided to the parents within 1–3 days. *See, e.g.*, Wash. Rev. Code § 13.34.050; Cal. Welf. & Inst. Code § 305; N.J. Stat. Ann. § 30:4C-12. The first hearing on a child's placement may be called a "Shelter Care Hearing," but states differ on the names and types of hearings.

6. "Legal socialization" refers to the process by which youth develop beliefs in the legitimacy of the law and legal system. Unsurprisingly, youth's perception of their child welfare caseworker has been associated with their subsequent perceptions of legitimacy of the courts and police generally. Karen M. Kolivoski et al., *Applying Legal Socialization to the Child Welfare System: Do Youths' Perceptions of Caseworkers Matter?* 45 Child & Youth Care Forum 65 (2016).

7. A more recent amendment to the Social Security Act—the Fostering Connections to Success and Increasing Adoptions Act of 2008—requires states receiving federal funding to make "reasonable efforts" to place together siblings removed from their home unless a joint placement would be unsafe, in which case states should make reasonable efforts to provide for "frequent visitation" when doing so does not interfere with the siblings' safety or well-being. Pub. L. No. 110-351, 122 Stat. 3949 (codified as amended at 42 U.S.C. § 671(a)(31)). Some states have included sibling placement preferences and visitation requirements in their child welfare statutes. *See, e.g.*, Wash. Rev. Code § 13.34.130(6); Cal. Welf. & Inst. Code § 16002; Md. Code Ann., Fam. Law § 5-525(e.).

> **Race of the Social Worker**
>
> *Michael repeatedly notes the race of his social worker as white.*
>
> - *In your jurisdiction, what are the racial demographics of CPS workers?*
> - *Does it matter?*

Michael tries to memorize where the Toyota is turning, how far away he is being taken from his sisters. It is almost dark now. He searches for buses and strains to read street signs so he can come back and get Aliyah and Angel later. He is trying to remember how much money he has in his backpack. He thinks he has somewhere between five and eight dollars. He thinks of Deja and that ache in his chest returns. He blinks back tears. A flash of anger passes through him as he recalls arguing with his mom just last week about how he needs a cell phone. Now she's sorry. If only he could call her right now.

Mr. Jeffries lives in a two-story brown house with three cars parked in front. One of the cars is an old Chevy Camaro in perfect condition, which offers Michael a tiny glimmer of hope before his chest tightens again thinking about Aliyah's face when she saw him pulling away. Michael also sees a black BMW. Mr. Jeffries must be rich. Being a foster parent must be a good gig.[8]

Mr. Jeffries greets them at the front door. He is a tall black man in his late fifties or early sixties. He is bald and looks like he was in good shape at one time. Maybe an athlete. He says "Hello, Michael" like he already knows him. "Welcome to my humble home." Michael thinks this is kind of a put on, but has to admit that the old guy seems nice enough. Mr. Jeffries and Reggie talk and laugh like old friends. Words about the expensive looking cars out front are exchanged. Mr. Jeffries asks Reggie about how his college classes are coming along. Michael stands uncomfortably in the entryway while the two men talk to each other and then lower their voices and obviously talk about him. The house smells like someone just cooked some kind of meat. Michael feels his stomach growl.

Reggie speaks quietly, "Michael, you are in good hands. I will be back to pick you up tomorrow morning for court and I will bring some of your things from your mom's house, too." He reaches out to shake Michael's hand, like he was congratulating Michael on his new home.

Michael lies in a strange bed that night with a full stomach and a persistent dull ache in his chest. He wasn't going to eat any of the ribs that Mr. Jeffries served him. He wasn't going to eat any of the potatoes either. But then when Mr. Jeffries' grown

---

8. Payments to foster families vary widely among states, and are often based on classifications such as a child's age. No matter the size of the payments, though, they are often not high enough to cover the full cost of caring for a child. For a summary of states' family foster care rates and policies, see Kerry DeVooght et al., Family Foster Care Reimbursement Rates in the U.S. 9–18 (2013), [https://perma.cc/Y28F-FDWP].

son James came in and made such a big deal about his dad's ribs and started shoving them down like he hadn't eaten for days, Michael found himself slowly succumb to his growling stomach and he accidentally cleaned his plate. From his strange bed, he hears the TV blasting downstairs. Mr. Jeffries and James are shouting like they are actually at the basketball game instead of watching it on television. He wonders how they can watch basketball when the world is caving in. He pulls the covers over his head and squeezes his eyes tightly shut hoping that when he opens them again he will wake up from this terrible dream. Where is Deja?

Michael wakes up at 7:15 a.m. completely disoriented, alone in a room he shares with no one — something he had never experienced in his 13 years. It smells different, nothing familiar. Where were Aliyah and Angel? Did they have their own rooms or did they sleep together? Michael hopes they had shared a room so they wouldn't wake up as confused as he had. Did they have ribs for dinner last night? Maybe all foster children get ribs on their first night. And where is Deja? Will he see any of them today? The tightness in his chest comes on in full force. He tries to take a deep breath and act like a man.

Reggie and the old Toyota show up at 8:00 a.m. Reggie nods at Michael as he gets in the car wearing the same clothes from the day before and the same determined, blank expression. They head to the courthouse.

Michael's Mother's Story: Michelle Griffith

She is doing so well until her 30th birthday came along and DJ says that they should celebrate. She knows this means trouble and that she needs to stay strong. She needs to keep focused on her children. During her last pregnancy she made a decision that she would not use, not even weed or alcohol — she is determined to not let CPS get in her business this time.[9] She knows she probably doesn't have many more chances left — either with CPS or her own mother who told her in no uncertain terms when she got pregnant last year with Deja that she would not take care of her children again and she would call CPS the first chance she got.[10] She also can't let Michael down again. He is almost grown now, or at least he acts like he is. She doesn't

---

9. Studies have found that parental substance abuse is a contributing factor to maltreatment in one-third to two-thirds of all cases in the child welfare system. JILL GOLDMAN & MARSHA K. SALUS WITH DEBORAH WOLCOTT & KRISTIE Y. KENNEDY, U.S. DEP'T OF HEALTH AND HUMAN SERVS., A COORDINATED RESPONSE TO CHILD ABUSE AND NEGLECT: THE FOUNDATION FOR PRACTICE 28 (2003), [https://perma.cc/V6E8-BM8G]. The perception of the prevalence of abuse in child maltreatment among state child welfare agencies is even greater, with 85% of state child welfare agencies identifying poverty and substance abuse as the top two problems for families reported to child maltreatment. *Id.* at 33. In 2012, adult alcohol or drug use was the documented reason that 30% of children placed in foster care were removed from their homes, and the number was over 60% in some states. CHILD WELFARE INFORMATION GATEWAY, U.S. DEP'T OF HEALTH & HUMAN SERVS., PARENTAL SUBSTANCE USE AND THE CHILD WELFARE SYSTEM 2–3 (2014), [https://perma.cc/NU7W-7KZS].

10. ASFA provides that when a child is removed from his or her home, preference must be given to an adult relative over a non-relative for placement purposes, provided that the adult caregiver meets the state's child protection standards. *See* 42 U.S.C. § 671(a)(19). In the event that Michael and

know what he will do if he feels like he needs to protect his sisters—and she doesn't want to find out.

Michelle can't really remember a time in her life when she didn't want to get high. Growing up with two parents and three siblings in a cramped two-bedroom apartment—there was always something to fight about. Those fights could quickly turn ugly. Police would often show up and everyone would find some way to disappear—physically or at least mentally. Michelle smoked marijuana for the first time at the age of 10 and loved it. She loved the way it made her feel relaxed, like everything would be alright, just like Bob Marley said it would be. *Every little thing, is gonna be alright.* It dulled the sound of her parents (who were big Bob Marley fans) hollering at each other when the rent was due. Weed made school bearable and the teachers' constant nagging at her for "not working up to her potential" less irritating. It made her feel grown, like her older sister who started smoking pot way before Michelle did with the boys in the apartment down the hall. Most of all, it made her funny—and she loved making people laugh. She really was hilarious.[11]

Weed helped Michelle manage her young life—but crack eventually made it fall apart. Where weed was a comfort and a companion, crack quickly became an affliction and an oppressor. The drug took over her life and drove her to do things she never imagined she would do.[12]

Crack played a part in Michelle having her first baby at the age of 17. Her baby's father Eric Grayson was a few years older, tall, good-looking, with a generous smile and a shiny BMW that was the most expensive thing that anyone she knew owned. He had a crew of teenagers that sold crack in the neighborhood. Michelle's brother worked for him. She met Eric at a party and fell hard. They spent hours together laughing and riding around in the shiny BMW. Eric bought her beautiful things—that made her feel beautiful. She didn't mind that he had other girls, but she thought when she got pregnant he would lose the urge to roam and focus on their family. Now, at

---

his siblings are removed from his mother, the state agency should consider placing the children with their grandmother, if she is willing and otherwise qualified, or with other qualified relatives.

11. Marijuana is the most common illicit drug used in the United States. Substance Abuse and Mental Health Servs. Admin., U.S. Dep't of Health and Human Servs., Administration Results from the 2012 National Survey on Drug Use and Health: Summary of National Findings 13 (2013), [https://perma.cc/4L56-K84M]. Age at first use of marijuana is associated with illicit drug dependence or abuse. *Id.* at 79.

12. Crack is a form of cocaine processed into rock crystal and smoked to produce a quick high by flooding the brain with dopamine, making its users highly susceptible to addiction. In 2012, 1.6 million Americans aged 12 or older reported using cocaine in the past month, down from 2.4 million in 2006. *Id.* at 1. Over 1 million Americans in 2012 were classified as having cocaine dependence or abuse. *Id.* at 6. Crack cocaine use by women has been associated with risky sexual behaviors, including prostitution. Jeffrey A. Hoffman et al., *Frequency and Intensity of Crack Use as Predictors of Women's Involvement in HIV-Related Sexual Risk Behaviors*, 58 Drug & Alcohol Dependence 227 (2000).

30, she laughs at her naïve younger self and wonders when Eric will get out of prison.[13]

Michelle didn't use crack herself until her firstborn Michael was almost two years old. The weed didn't seem to be doing the trick anymore. She wasn't as hilarious. She was angry a lot of the time. She was mad at Eric who never did get them an apartment but instead bounced in and out of jail and was laying low because he was looking at real time in the penitentiary. She was mad at her mom for wanting her to get an abortion and being right when she said "that boy Eric won't ever take care of you." She was mad at her case manager at social services who told her she was going to have to find a better job soon because she can't stay on public assistance forever.[14] She was mad at Nike for charging so much for Baby Jordans. She was mad at the lady at the day care for threatening to call CPS when she showed up late to get Michael because the bus broke down.[15] She was mad at herself, because she knew she wasn't living up to her "potential" just like her teachers predicted.

One night, a few months before Michael's second birthday, an old friend Porsche called and begged Michelle to come out with the girls. Porsche said, "What's the matter with you? You are no fun anymore. Just cuz you have a baby doesn't mean you gotta live like you dead. C'mon it'll be good for you." It had been at least six months since Michelle had hung out with her friends and she really needed a break. She jumped at the chance to be a carefree 19-year-old and left Michael at home with her mother. She didn't do that very often because when she did she wouldn't hear the end of it. Her mother could get real mean real fast about her "lack of parenting skills." This was the type of language Michelle's mother would use when she wanted to sound like a state social worker and remind Michelle that she would not hesitate to call CPS. But Porsche was right—she was no fun anymore, and what good was she if she was angry all the time? If she couldn't make someone laugh every now and then? That night out with the girls changed her life forever.

---

13. Federal and state drug enforcement response to crack cocaine beginning in the 1980s has contributed to what many scholars today are calling "mass incarceration." Incarceration rates in the United States are some of the highest in the world. For a discussion of the intersection between crack cocaine and the imprisonment of African Americans, see MICHELLE ALEXANDER, THE NEW JIM CROW: MASS INCARCERATION IN THE AGE OF COLORBLINDNESS (2010).

14. The Personal Responsibility and Work Opportunity Reconciliation Act of 1996 (PRWORA), which instituted the Temporary Assistance for Needy Families (TANF) program, provides money to states that adopt certain restrictions on who can receive aid. Under PRWORA, families can only receive aid for a cumulative period of up to five years, except for under very narrow exceptions. 42 U.S.C. § 608(a)(7). Adults receiving aid are subject to "[i]ndividual responsibility plans" that require them to participate in education, training, and other activities designed to facilitate gainful employment. *Id.* § 608(b).

15. Every state has a mandatory reporting scheme that requires certain people, such as teachers, doctors, and licensed day care providers, to report suspected child abuse to child protection authorities. Such a scheme is required by CAPTA in order to receive federal support for child protection services. 42 U.S.C. § 5106a(b)(2)(B)(i).

It was a warm summer evening and Michelle just wanted to go get take-out food, a six-pack of beer and some weed and go sit down by the lake and chill with her friends. Porsche and Imani had something else in mind. They wanted to meet boys. According to them, Porsche's cousin's party in the south end was the place to be that night. Desperate to be anywhere away from her demanding toddler, Michelle was happy to go along.

The house party was cool from the start; Michelle knew some of the guys there because of Eric. They weren't his associates, more like acquaintances. Most of the partygoers were smoking weed or drinking beer. Ludacris was blaring from two huge speakers in the living room and a handful of people were dancing. Michelle was immediately drawn in by the comforting smell of marijuana and went straight for some guys passing a blunt. She fell in and quickly became her old funny self. Before she knew it, she was making the guys laugh really hard and that made her even higher. One guy, Tommy, was interested and interesting. He had a deep, warm laugh and the gold chains around his neck signaled success. After a few beers and some successful flirting, Tommy pulled Michelle toward a backroom where they could "get to know each other better." Michelle was more than willing and disappointed when the room they found was already taken by a small group of partiers smoking crack. She tugged at Tommy and said let's keep looking but he paused to joke with one of the guys. Michelle noticed Porsche was in there and she was actually smoking crack. Michelle was irritated. Michelle never wanted to touch the stuff. She had enough cousins, aunts and uncles who wore the title "crack head" and she had no interest in going down that path. She was happy just smoking weed and drinking when she needed to take the edge off of life. In fact, she and Porsche used to entertain each other by trying to do the best imitation of Lips (that's what they called her because of her big cracked lips), a crack head that always hung outside the Safeway begging for change.

As Michelle's stoned brain tried to process the idea of Porsche smoking crack, Tommy's friend handed him the pipe. Michelle's heart sank and she blurted "Shit, you ain't gonna tell me you a crack head?" Tommy flashed that million dollar smile and said "Baby, you *crack* me up. Don't worry, it's not a problem." He chuckled, shook his head, wrapped his arms around her waist and looked at her straight on: "You really gotta try it, you would be *so fucking hilarious* if you just smoked a little. I might die laughin.'" Porsche looked over at her with glazed eyes and a genuine smile. "Mich, it won't hurt. It don't turn you instantly into a crack head. This is my third time now, it's cool."[16] Tommy leans in and kisses her hard and long while the small crack smoking crowd hoots and hollers and laughs. Michelle leans in and lets herself believe that this guy is for real. She pulls him closer and wraps both legs around him as the crowd

---

16. Research has shown that only 5% of cocaine users become dependent within 24 months of first use. Females, however, are 3–4 times more likely to become dependent within 24 months of first use, and African Americans are 9 times more likely than whites to become dependent on cocaine within 24 months of first use. Megan S. O'Brien & James C. Anthony, *Risk of Becoming Cocaine Dependent: Epidemiological Estimates for the United States, 2000–2001*, 30 NEUROPSYCHOPHARMACOLOGY 1006 (2005).

continues to egg them on. The laughter and the kissing and the marijuana and beer all mix together. Her life as the teenage mother of Michael fades away like a dream. "Fuck it" Michelle says and grabs the pipe from Tommy and takes her first hit.

The feeling was amazing. The next two days were amazing. She stayed with Tommy and smoked and laughed and loved until finally Porsche showed up at Tommy's apartment that he shared with his brother and said "Where the hell you been? Momma J.'s head is about to blow off she is so pissed at you. You are fucking in deep shit right now. You better get home before CPS snatches Michael and you are out on the street. Not to mention you gotta deal with Eric because people been talkin' . . . ." It was like a blast of cold water. Michelle told Tommy she loved him but she had to go. She ran out of the apartment and jumped in Porsche's car, while Porsche peeled away shouting expletives and shaking her head.

So began Michelle's journey into drug addiction. Shortly after that first crack experience, she and Michael moved in with Tommy. He became the father of Aliyah and he told her he would die laughing with her. He was probably one of her better choices; he never hit her or spent time in prison and he was fantastic with Michael and their daughter. But like the others who would follow, he grew weary of the drugs and all the ways the drug came first and drove Michelle to the ugliest of places time and time again.

For the next 10 years, Michelle battled her dependence on crack.[17] She had two more children — four precious beings she swore she loved more than the drug.[18] When she was clean she would shine — she earned her GED and got an associates' degree to become a nurse's assistant. She loved her children. She lived to make them happy and follow her rules: respect adults, do your dishes, always say thank you and do your best at school no matter what. Oh, and always laugh at your momma's jokes.

Michelle could get anyone to like her given the chance. At inpatient and outpatient treatment programs her counselors loved her. She was honest about her shortcomings and she used self-deprecating humor artfully, in a way that made everyone laugh in a good way — even during the most tense group session. Apart from crack, she was delightful. But she was rarely apart from crack. She also dabbled in meth, but preferred crack even when it became more expensive.[19] Sadly, from that first hit she never

---

17. For further explanation of the way that addiction alters the brain at the molecular and cellular levels, see Alan I. Leshner, *Addiction Is a Brain Disease*, 17 Issues Sci. & Tech. 75 (2001) (updated availability in 2016, [https://perma.cc/L2AR-2BK5]).

18. Although prenatal exposure to cocaine may result in premature delivery and lower birth weight, the prediction that "crack babies" would suffer severe and lifelong damage was grossly exaggerated. Nat'l Inst. on Drug Abuse, U.S. Dep't of Health and Human Servs., Pub. No. 10-4166, Research Report Series: Cocaine 6 (rev. 2010), [https://perma.cc/NXB2-5HQV].

19. The effects of methamphetamine are similar to crack; however, meth produces a longer lasting high. Nat'l Inst. on Drug Abuse, U.S. Dep't of Health and Human Servs., Pub. No. 13-4210, Research Report Series: Methamphetamine 3 (rev. 2013), [https://perma.cc/P29B-4HCM]. As is the case with crack cocaine, use of methamphetamine is down since the mid-2000s. Substance Abuse and Mental Health Servs. Admin., *supra* note 11, at 15.

made it longer than nine months clean.[20] Short binges wouldn't interfere much with her responsibilities. But there were stretches of consistent use when the nagging threat of losing her children would be the only thing that could tear her away from the pipe.

She was nine months clean when she turned 30. Damn DJ and his thinly veiled excuse to go back to the pipe and violate his probation so he could clear his head in jail and get away from his creditors for a while. Michelle had spent time in jail, not usually more than a week or two, but she hated it. The women in lock up were mean and would steal anything they could get their hands on — constantly threatening violence to extort money or favors. There was nothing funny about jail — what little humor she could muster was lost on the guards and other inmates. DJ, on the other hand, could "do time standing on his head."[21]

Michelle knew DJ was not good for her, but she was so alone when she met him. She dreamed of having a man around to be a father to her children. When he was clean, he was great with the kids. The two of them would dance in the kitchen until the kids would join them and they would all laugh until they cried. DJ could even make Michael chuckle with his outrageous hip-hop impersonations. Michelle was usually the only one who could get her eldest son to laugh. But when Michelle and DJ used, their world got twice as ugly twice as fast. The depth of her shame could only be drowned out, temporarily, when she lost herself in her pipe.

So when DJ brought home a gram for her on her 30th birthday — which he told her she could share with him if she was feeling generous — Michelle was outraged. "You broke ass mother fucker, you wanna ruin everything I've worked for? You don't give a shit about your baby girl? You think we are playin'? You think being a parent is some kind of game?" She screamed and swore until she broke down in tears. And when she cried it was like falling into a deep swimming hole and being sucked down, down, down. DJ could sometimes comfort her with sex, but this time sex was not going to cut it. Michael tried to help, "Momma, stop, we love you, let me help you." Over and over again which just made her cry harder. "Take your sisters away Michael. I am a bad, bad momma. I don't deserve you. I don't deserve any of you. I shouldn't even be alive for all the things I've done."[22] Michael gave up and went into parent mode — making peanut butter sandwiches for Aliyah and Angel and shuffling them into the back bedroom.

---

20. "Addiction should be understood as a chronic and recurring illness. Although some addicts do gain full control over their drug use after a single treatment episode, many have relapses. Repeated treatments become necessary to increase the intervals between and diminish the intensity of relapses, until the individual achieves abstinence." Leshner, *supra* note 17, at 76.

21. While males make up an overwhelming percentage of the jail population, the female jail inmate population increased by 18.1% between 2010 and 2014. Bureau of Justice Statistics, U.S. Dep't of Justice, NCJ 245350, Jail Inmates at Midyear 2014 1 (2015), [https://perma.cc/8TJL -RHHD].

22. Depression and cocaine use are related. Users who seek treatment for addiction have even higher rates of depression, and symptoms of depression can also predict treatment outcomes. *See* Niklaus Stulz et al., *Psychosocial Treatments for Cocaine Dependence*, 114 Drug & Alcohol Dependence 41 (2011).

The crack binge that changed everything lasted about three weeks. The usual pattern: Michelle and DJ burned through all their money, Michael took care of his sisters as best he could and DJ would disappear for a few days at a time while strange men drifted in and out of the apartment to spend time in Michelle's bedroom. As soon as a man would leave the apartment, Michelle would hit the pipe, become animated for a little while and then drift off into a deep sleep. This was, significantly, the first such episode since Deja was born and Michelle had promised her kids again that she was done with drugs. So, when she wasn't experiencing the high, her emotional energy was devoted entirely to self-loathing for what she was doing to her children—which just made her want to get high again.

Michelle barely remembers what happened when CPS arrived with the police on that cold January day. She remembers just wanting to be put out of her misery. She remembers thinking that Michael will take care of things like he always does, he is a good boy and he will watch over his sisters—and they will probably be better off without her.

Michael's Father's Story: Eric Grayson
DOC # 23917 Brannan Hills Correctional Facility

Eric Grayson is known by the Department of Corrections as DOC #23917. In his opinion, doing time isn't that difficult after the first year or so of settling in. Now he is an old timer and others came to him for advice. He made a decision fairly early on that he would do more than spend his free time lifting weights. He took the GED preparation course and earned his GED certificate by passing all five tests in eight months.[23] That felt good so he signed up for the two available vocational training programs: bookkeeping and upholstery, earning certificates for both. He completed a stress and anger management class, joined a weekly bible study and a book group on African American literature sponsored by a volunteer professor from a local college. As it turns out, Eric likes reading and applying himself academically. He likes any setting where he can learn new skills and apply them. This comes as a surprise to him, since he stopped attending school regularly around the eighth grade.[24] He now seeks out any opportunity to learn new skills and apply them. He became a model prisoner.

---

23. General Educational Development (GED) tests are high-school-equivalency exams of four subjects. They were originally created in 1942 to meet the needs of returning war veterans. They are now widely available in correctional facilities. Lois M. Davis et al., RAND Corporation, Evaluating the Effectiveness of Correctional Education 4 (2013), [https://perma.cc/P84N-ZQMP]. Inmates who participate in GED programs have lower recidivism rates. *Id.* at 57. GED participation also probably has a positive impact on post-release employment and earnings, but this connection is less clear. *Id.* at 58.

24. About one in every 10 young male high school dropouts is in jail or juvenile detention, compared with one in 33 young male high school graduates. Among young black male high school dropouts, almost one quarter end up in prison or an institution. Andrew Sum et al., Ctr. for Labor Mkt. Studies, Ne. Univ., The Consequences of Dropping Out of High School 9–11 (2009), [https://perma.cc/4GF4-2RFX].

Eric's transformation is shocking to his fellow inmates as well as to prison staff. He came in as a tough young drug dealer. He spent two lengthy stints in the Intensive Management Unit (a euphemism for solitary confinement): lock-down 23/7, three showers per week and one hour per day in the yard—alone. It is not unusual for someone like Eric to have some issues at the beginning of a lengthy prison term. There are old scores to settle and some jockeying for one's place in the new order. He did, however, stand out as one who radically changed his approach to doing time rather abruptly. Fortunately, his reputation and all the weight lifting he does keeps his skeptical rivals at a distance.

Eric has been in the game since he was 14 years old. He is a third-generation drug dealer. His grandfather, Gerald Grayson, was one of the original dealers when crack first hit the streets in the 1980s.[25] He mentored Eric's father, Gerald, Jr. ("G2") who unfortunately became an addict, breaking a sacred rule for successful dealers.[26] G2's addiction led to carelessness and he was one of the early victims of the harsh penalties ushered in by the War on Drugs.[27] He is still serving a 26-year sentence for drug and weapons charges. Eric was seven years old when his father disappeared into the federal criminal justice system forever.[28]

Eric was raised by his mother Sylvia, a kind, passive woman who feebly attempted to dissuade him from pursuing the family business. After his father went to prison, Eric watched his mother struggle to get by on their monthly welfare check and it was not a difficult decision for him to gravitate toward his uncles and cousins who drove fast cars, wore expensive clothes and got respect.[29]

---

25. Crack cocaine was introduced in the U.S. in the early 1980s, became widespread in 1985, peaked in 1989, and has since been decreasing in use. Its negative impact on the African American community has been significant. *See* Roland G. Fryer Jr. et al., *Measuring Crack Cocaine and Its Impact*, 51 Econ. Inquiry 1651 (2013).

26. "Never get high on your own supply." The Notorious B.I.G., *Ten Crack Commandments, on* Life After Death (Bad Boy Records 1997).

27. Although the phrase "War on Drugs" was originally used by President Richard Nixon in 1971, the "war" took off when President Ronald Reagan signed the Anti-Drug Abuse Act of 1986, which significantly increased penalties for drug crimes and appropriated $1.7 billion to drug enforcement efforts. *See Timeline: America's War on Drugs*, NPR (April 2, 2007), http://www.npr.org/templates/story/story.php?storyId=9252490.

28. Between 1991 and 2007, the number of children with incarcerated parents increased by 80%. Lauren E. Glaze & Laura M. Maruschak, Bureau of Justice Statistics, NCJ 222984, Parents in Prison and Their Minor Children 1 (2008, rev'd Mar. 30, 2010), [https://perma.cc/X83E-SQJR]. In 2007, more than 1.5 million children had a father in prison, and half of them were children of black fathers. *Id.* at 2.

29. In 2010, the average monthly amount of TANF to recipient families was $392. *Characteristics and Financial Circumstances of TANF Recipients: Fiscal Year 2010,* Off. Fam. Assistance (August 8, 2012), [https://perma.cc/YUT8-GLCZ]. Adjusting for inflation, however, the value of cash assistance benefits dropped by more than 20% from 1996–2013. Ife Floyd & Liz Schott, Ctr. on Budget and Policy Priorities, TANF Cash Benefits Continued To Lose Value in 2013 4 (2013), [https://perma.cc/RM83-CNFM]. As of late 2013, "TANF benefit levels are so low that they are not sufficient to provide family income above half of the poverty line in *any* state." *Id.* at 3.

One day when Eric was walking home from elementary school, two 12-year-old boys from the neighborhood stopped him. One of the boys, Tyrone, pulled a handgun from his backpack, pointed it at Eric's face and said, "give us your money." Eric had a twenty-dollar bill that his uncle had given him for his birthday. He was terrified and quickly pulled it from his pocket and handed it over. The boys took off and Eric ran home, his heart almost beating out of his chest. He felt ashamed for being so afraid and giving his money up so quickly. He couldn't wait until he had his own gun. Someday he would take that gun and make Tyrone feel the same way he felt at that moment.[30]

By the time Eric got into dealing crack, meth and other drugs were offering stiff competition. But his family history and connections made business come fairly easy. He really loved the life. He wasn't exactly a big-time drug dealer, but he had his own crew and controlled a respectable piece of real estate. He made a good living. He got the BMW and the beautiful girls. He did finally catch up to Tyrone when they were both in their early twenties. Bullets flew. Both Tyrone and Eric were injured in the exchange, but Tyrone definitely got the worst of it. He spent one month in the hospital and he is confined to a wheelchair. Eric took a bullet to the shoulder and was out of the hospital in three days. It still aches sometimes, but it doesn't really bother him.

Eric found himself in jail on occasion, but he was generally smart and careful when it came to dealing. At 16 he started going to "juvie" which meant 10 days here, 30 days there.[31] The cops rarely caught him with drugs, or if they did it was never enough to prove he was selling. He was put on juvenile probation for nine months and managed to get along well with his probation officer, a likeable guy who would tell him stories about coming back from Vietnam and protesting the war. When he turned 18, the jail stints were longer, 30 days sometimes, but still just a cost of doing business. When Eric was finally charged with his second Possession With Intent to Deliver a Controlled Substance along with Attempted Robbery in the First Degree for trying to take back drugs that a customer had stolen from one of his

---

30. Violent victimization is an important risk factor for subsequent violent offending. Jennifer N. Shaffer & R. Barry Ruback, U.S. Dep't of Justice, OJJDP Juvenile Justice Bulletin: Violent Victimization as a Risk Factor for Violent Offending Among Juveniles 6 (2002), [https://perma.cc/G2VG-HD8T].

31. The differences between juvenile court and adult criminal court are significant: juvenile courts generally emphasize rehabilitation, have shorter sentences, and provide youth with adolescent oriented services. On the other hand, juvenile courts afford fewer due process protections. Many states determine whether to treat youth as juveniles or adults based on the offenses they are charged with. For example, a fourteen-year-old who commits a "class A or B felony" in Connecticut is automatically treated as an adult. Conn. Gen. Stat. §46b-127(a)(1). A handful of states allow juvenile courts to waive jurisdiction for some drug offenses, and two of them—Idaho and West Virginia—do not place an age restriction on these types of waivers. Patrick Griffin et al., Office of Juvenile Justice and Delinquency Prevention, Trying Juveniles as Adults: An Analysis of State Transfer Laws and Reporting 4 (2011), [https://perma.cc/VU5H-9W6E].

crewmembers—he ended up facing prison time. He took a plea deal.[32] He didn't like it and was convinced his public defender didn't care for him and lacked negotiation skills.[33]

Eric fathered four children by three different women: Michael, Tasha and twins Eric, Jr. ("EJ") and Eddy. When he came to prison he was still with the twins' mother, Crystal. She gave birth to EJ and Eddy right before he was sentenced. In three years she had brought the boys to see him twice. It was a six-and-a-half-hour bus ride for them to Brannan Hills Correctional Facility and it wasn't cheap. On the two occasions that they came to visit, Crystal looked tired and angry. She couldn't seem to understand that there wasn't much he could do for her while he was wearing a jumpsuit behind bars. He wrote her letters and tried to explain that he was improving himself and would be a good father when he got out. She didn't write back. He heard from another inmate that she was with another man and she was pregnant.

When he is called into his counselor's office one day in January, Eric assumes that he will be transferred to another facility. He is hoping for a transfer, somewhere he can get more work experience, maybe closer to home. But he is wrong. He is being served with legal papers. His counselor, Officer Jenkins, hands him a lengthy document. Eric scans the papers quickly, he finds the words confusing, much like the other legal documents he has been given to read over the years.

---

32. While there are no exact estimates of the proportion of cases that are resolved through plea bargaining, scholars estimate that between 90 and 95% of both federal and state court cases are resolved this way. Lindsey Devers, Bureau Of Justice Assistance, Plea And Charge Bargaining: Research Summary 1 (2011), [https://perma.cc/BPL9-3V64]. Studies have found that blacks are less likely to receive a reduced charge compared with whites, and that blacks are also less likely to receive the benefits of shorter or reduced sentences as a result of prosecutors exercising their discretion. Brian D. Johnson, *Racial and Ethnic Disparities in Sentencing Departures Across Modes of Conviction* 41 Criminology 449, 464–65 (2003). *See also,* Crystal S. Yang, *Free At Last? Judicial Discretion and Racial Disparities in Federal Sentencing,* (Coase-Sandor Institute for Law & Economics Working Paper No. 661, 2013) (finding charging and sentencing disparities continue to persist in the federal system after mandatory sentencing guidelines were struck down) [https://perma.cc /LA8S-68JP].

33. Although criminal defendants have had the right to a court appointed attorney since the landmark decision, *Gideon v. Wainwright,* 372 U.S. 335 (1963), there is a growing consensus that the guarantee of a fair trial through adequate representation has not been realized for many indigent defendants who are represented by overworked, underpaid public defenders who lack adequate training. *See e.g.,* Thomas Giovanni and Roopal Patel, Gideon *at 50, Three Reforms to Revive the Right To Counsel,* Brennan Center for Justice (2013) [https://perma.cc/FM7Y-6Q9R]; Eve Brensike Primus, *Culture as a Structural Problem in Indigent Defense,* 100 Minn. L. Rev. 1769 (2016) (Discussing the culture of indifference in public defense delivery systems that results in a lack of zealous advocacy and clients who "feel confused, angry and ignored.").

ઇ ຂ

SUPERIOR COURT OF WASHINGTON COUNTY OF BAKER JUVENILE COURT	No:15-7-0234; 15-7-0235 15-7-0236 15-7-0237
IN RE THE DEPENDENCY OF: **Michael Griffith**, DOB 1/22/02 **Aliyah Griffith**, DOB 7/1/05 **Angel Griffith**, DOB 3/31/08 and **Deja Jones**, DOB 8/3/14	Notice and Summons/Order: [x] **Dependency** [ ] **Termination of Parent-Child Relationship** (NTSM)

State of Washington To:

Name: <u>ERIC GRAYSON</u>

Address: <u>BRANNAN HILLS CORRECTIONAL FACILITY</u>

I. Notice of Hearing

1.1   You are notified that a petition, a copy of which is provided, was filed with this court alleging that:

        [X] <u>Dependency:</u> the above named child is dependent. A Dependency Petition begins a judicial process which, if the court finds the child dependent, could result in substantial restriction or permanent loss of your parental rights.

        [   ] <u>Termination of Parent-Child Relationship:</u> the above named child is dependent and a permanent termination of the parent-child relationship should occur. A termination Petition, if granted, will result in permanent loss of your parental rights.

    Notice: If your child is placed in out-of-home care, you may be held responsible for the support of the child.

1.2   The court has scheduled a shelter care hearing on:

    <u>JANUARY 13, 2015</u> [date] at ____8____ [X] AM [ ] PM

    and a fact-finding hearing on:

    <u>APRIL 1, 2015</u> [date] at ____8____ [X] AM [ ] PM

    At BAKER COUNTY JUVENILE COURT   Room/Department: E905

    Address: Third Ave., Seattle, WA 98001

1.3   The purpose of the fact-finding hearing is to hear and consider evidence relating to the petition. You should be present at this hearing.

1.4   If you do not appear *the court may enter an order in your absence*:

        [X] Establishing dependency.

        [   ] Permanently terminating your parental rights.

II. Summons/Order to Appear

[X] *You are summoned and required* to appear at the hearing on the date, time and place set forth above.

[   ] *You are ordered and required* as the parent, guardian or custodian having custody and control of the child to bring the child to the hearing set forth above.

Notice: Violation of this Order or Summons is Subject to a Proceeding for Contempt of Court Pursuant to RCW 13.34.070.

III. Advice of Rights

- You have important legal rights, and you must take steps to protect your interest.
- You have the right to a fact-finding hearing before a judge. At the hearing, you have the right to speak on your own behalf, to introduce evidence, to examine witnesses, and to receive a decision based solely on the evidence presented to the judge. You should attend this hearing.
- You have the right to be represented by a lawyer. If you cannot afford a lawyer you have the right to request that the court appoint a lawyer to represent you at public expense. If you qualify, a lawyer will be appointed by the court to represent you.
- Your lawyer can look at the social and legal files in your case, talk to the supervising agency or other agencies, tell you about the law, help you understand your rights and help you at hearings.
- If you wish to have a lawyer appointed, contact <u>BAKER COUNTY OFFICE OF PUBLIC DEFENSE</u> [Name].

    Address: <u>BAKER COUNTY ADMINISTRATION BUILDING</u>

    Phone: <u>555-232-1023</u>

You may call <u>EMILY PETERS, CHILD PROTECTIVE SERVICES</u> [Name] for more information about your child. The agency's name and telephone numbers are:

    Address: <u>BAKER COUNTY DCFS OFFICE</u>

    Phone: <u>555-232-6445</u>

Dated: _____1/12/15_____

By direction of:

_____
Judge/Commissioner

_____
                                      Clerk

By:_____
                                    Deputy Clerk

❧ ❧

Eric looks up at Officer Jenkins and says, "It looks like I am supposed to go to court for my son Michael. Can I go?"

"Probably not." Officer Jenkins tells Eric he talked to a CPS social worker and told her his expected release date. She didn't ask to have him transported.[34] He told her he would set up a telephone call with her if Eric wants him to.

---

34. Due process generally requires parents to receive notice of a shelter care hearing and a reasonable opportunity to be heard. It should be noted, however, that courts have held that parents do not have an absolute right to attend judicial proceedings—so courts often apply a balancing test to

"Of course I want you to. Michael is my firstborn. I want to be there for him."

"A little late for that, don't you think?" Officer Jenkins is usually respectful and non-emotional when dealing with inmates, but irritation comes through when the subject of children comes up. As a father of five, he is troubled by the scores of fathers under his charge who have left behind children and poor mothers to struggle on their own. He considers that the worst part of their offense history. He knows that it creates a cycle of poverty and violence that devastates communities and it makes him angry.[35]

Eric does not respond. He knows there is no good response to this question, which is really more of a statement. He asks Officer Jenkins if they could try to contact the social worker right now and they try. She is not available and they leave a message for her to call Officer Jenkins to set up a time to speak with Eric.

> ### *Incarcerated Parents*
>
> *Find the cases, regulations, and agency policies that pertain to incarcerated parents in your jurisdiction.*
>
> * *Are incarcerated parents treated differently?*
> * *Should they be?*

The Shelter Care Hearing date comes and goes and Eric does not hear anything. He asks Officer Jenkins if the social worker had called back, and she had not. A week after the hearing date he receives a typed letter and a "Notice of Appearance" signed by a public defender indicating that he was appointed to represent Eric, "the father" in the *Dependency of Michael Griffin*.

Eric begins writing a letter to the public defender. But he doesn't know what to say. His chest feels tight, like he can't breathe.

---

determine whether holding the hearing without them violates their due process rights. *See, e.g., In re Dependency of J.W.*, 953 P.2d 104 (Wash. Ct. App. 1998); *In re La'Derrick*, 925 N.Y.S.2d 741 (N.Y. App. Div. 2011); *In re Adoption/Guardianship No. 6Z980001*, 748 A.2d 1020 (Md. Ct. Spec. App. 2000). Even when parental rights are terminated, courts have held that proceeding without the physical presence of an incarcerated parent does not violate due process. *See, e.g., In re Rich*, 604 P.2d 1248 (Okla. 1979); *In re Juvenile Appeal*, 446 A.2d 808 (Conn. 1982); *State ex rel. Jeanette H. v. Pancake*, 529 S.E.2d 865 (W. Va. 2000); *In re D.C.S.H.C.*, 733 N.W.2d 902, 905–06 (N.D. 2007) ("[P]risoners do not have a constitutional right to appear in person at a termination-of-parental-rights hearing."). Failure to appear at a shelter care hearing can result in an order being entered without the parents' input. Some states, however, allow for an additional hearing in some circumstances. *See, e.g.,* Wash. Rev. Code § 13.34.065(1)(b) (permitting parents unable to attend hearing "for good cause" to schedule a subsequent hearing); Ohio R. Juv. P. 7(G) ("If a parent . . . did not receive notice of the initial hearing . . . , the court shall rehear the matter promptly.").

35. For an in-depth look at the economic and social impact of incarceration on families and communities, see Mary Pattillo et al., Imprisoning America: The Social Effects of Mass Incarceration (2004).

Michael's Social Worker's Story: Emily Peters, M.S.W., Child Protective Services

Emily Peters has worked for the Department of Children and Family Services for almost nine years, and she still finds going to court distasteful. She is comfortable there—she knows the attorneys, court clerks and judges. She is even on a first-name basis with the security guards who check her purse as she enters the juvenile court building. But to Emily, going to court means she has failed. She much prefers working with families on a voluntary basis and she is usually pretty successful. She learned in social work school that keeping families together is best and the involuntary removal of children from their parents should be a last resort.

Many of the social workers Emily works with share her aversion to the court process. Court means arguing with attorneys, waiting around for hearings, and worrying about whether a judge will make the right decision. She has had a few colleagues over the years who really wanted to be police officers, not CPS workers, and they seem to relish the power and structure that they feel in the courthouse. She tends to stay clear of those types.

Emily has spent her entire career with the Department ("DCFS" as they call it in this field with too many acronyms) working as a Child Protective Services (CPS) worker. This puts her in the trenches every day investigating reports of child abuse and neglect. She thought she would do CPS work for a few years and then move into a less intense division of DCFS, like foster care licensing or adoption services.[36] But as it turns out, she is good at what she does. She likes working with families in crisis. She isn't easily rattled. She usually finds something to like about even the most difficult parent and she feels like she is really making a difference for children. She also finds that she likes the quick pace of the work and that she doesn't work with any one family for too long.

Emily did go through one rough patch in her job a few years ago. She had been with CPS for about five years and she started to feel tired and burned out.[37] She had one case that involved a child fatality and one near child fatality. It shook her.[38] She

---

36. State child welfare systems are organized in many different ways, based on function, geography, and practice models. For a detailed comparison of states' models, See Tarren Bragdon, Which State Child Welfare Systems Are Right for Kids?, Found. for Gov't Accountability, (2012), [https://perma.cc/HY48-KN7R].

37. For an overview of the secondary traumatic stress that child welfare workers and other professional involved in the care of traumatized children can experience, see Nat'l Child Traumatic Stress Network, Secondary Traumatic Stress: A Fact Sheet for Child-Serving Professionals (2011), [https://perma.cc/69WS-P8ZS].

38. The number of child fatalities due to abuse and neglect fluctuated between a low of 1,551 and a high of 1,619 between 2011 and 2015, according to the Child Maltreatment Report published in 2017. Nearly three-fourths of the children who died due to child abuse or neglect in 2015 were under three years old. Children under one year old carry the greatest risk for child death due to child maltreatment. Of the children who died, 72.9% suffered from neglect and 43.9% suffered from physical abuse exclusively or in combination with another maltreatment type. How many of these children

thought she did everything right on that case, but still, to feel like she stood between life and death for a child was overwhelming. She found nothing to like about those parents. She questioned whether the way her agency reacted to reports of abuse was really enough. How could her response, how could any social worker's response really guarantee children wouldn't be harmed? Eventually she decided that these questions were not productive. She would do what she could with what she had and not be debilitated by contemplating the societal ills that she could not fix.

Most of the children Emily works to protect are victims of neglect as opposed to abuse.[39] While neglect sounds less serious, Emily learned in her graduate studies that research shows that neglect results in long-lasting effects that ultimately make it even harder for kids to do well in foster care.[40] The problem, of course, is defining "neglect." It is a spectrum—and despite efforts to define the term in DCFS policy and even by statute—different social workers and judges see things differently.[41] Emily generally feels confident about her judgment. She does not believe she is out to get poor parents.[42] She goes into plenty of homes that she knows most ordinary people would find horrifying. She has long ago moved past the urge to save children from

---

may have been known to CPS before they died? According to the 2015 Child Maltreatment Report, 12.0% of the children died at the hands of caregivers who had received family preservation services within the five years prior to their death, and 2.3% of them had been reunified with a parent following a prior removal. *See* Children's Bureau, U.S. Dep't of Health and Human Servs., Child Maltreatment 2015 52–59 (2017), [https://perma.cc/TL4E-DKV6].

39. Child neglect is by far the most frequent type of founded child maltreatment. In 2014, 75% of founded reports of child maltreatment were categorized as neglect. *Id.* at 46.

40. Neglect can impact children in a variety of ways. Malnutrition particularly in the early years can result in cognitive and motor delays, anxiety, depression, social problems, and problems with attention. A neglected infant may show poor muscle tone, unhappy or minimal facial expressions, decreased vocalizations, and general unresponsiveness. The emotional, psychosocial, and behavioral effects can be profound as well. Repeated studies show that nearly all neglected infants suffer from difficulties in developing secure attachments with others. All is not lost, however, research has also shown that a mitigating factor for neglected infants and children is having at least one other emotionally supportive and caring adult at some point during childhood or even later in life. Diane DePanfilis, Child Neglect: A Guide for Prevention, Assessment, and Intervention 21–29 (2006), U.S. Dep't of Health & Human Servs., [https://perma.cc/FK3B-YUV4].

41. Before it was amended in 2010, CAPTA defined child abuse and neglect as "at a minimum, any recent act or failure to act on the part of a parent or caretaker, which results in death, serious physical or emotional harm, sexual abuse or exploitation, or an act or failure to act which presents an imminent risk of serious harm." Child Abuse Prevention and Treatment Act Amendments of 1996, Pub. L. No. 104–235, § 110, 110 Stat. 3063, 3078 (current version at 42 U.S.C. § 5106g). Since passing the CAPTA Reauthorization Act of 2010, which struck the definition from section 5106, Congress has left it up to the states to define child abuse.

42. A federal study found that neglect was 44 times more prevalent in families with an annual income of under $15,000 compared to families who earned over $30,000 annually. Erica Turcios, *Remaining vs. Removal*, 12 Mich. Child Welfare L.J. 20, 23 (2009). As a result, a child who lives in poverty is 22 to 27 times more likely to be identified as harmed by abuse or neglect. *Id.* Even so, about one-third of states require agencies to consider families' financial means when assessing cases of neglect. *Id.* at 24.

impoverished circumstances. She believes families deserve the chance to be together and she will try to use removal only where she sees a clear risk to the child.

Emily finds many of the attorneys working in child welfare irritating. In her opinion, many of them are incompetent.[43] She attributes this mostly to the poor pay, which also draws incompetent people to her field.[44] She does not know how much they are paid but she figures that the best attorneys work for law firms downtown and make lots of money.[45] Still, it doesn't matter. The competent attorneys at juvenile court can be even more annoying.

First, there are the attorneys assigned to represent her. These are the State's attorneys, known as Assistant Attorneys General or "AAGs" for short.[46] Generally a bossy group, Emily feels they are always second-guessing her actions and have no real understanding of what she actually does as a social worker. Over the years she develops relationships with a few that she likes and will try to avoid the others, but when she appears at juvenile court for an initial removal hearing she is stuck with whoever the "attorney of the day" happens to be. Even more annoying. Not only does this person have little understanding of what social workers do, they have likely just read the petition that morning and know next to nothing about the facts of the case for which she is appearing. She has to spend her time, or rather waste her time, educating them about the family and justifying every decision she makes on the case. Frankly, she thinks it would be a more efficient system if she could just go into court and speak directly to the judge without interference from the AAG.

The other attorneys Emily interacts with are public defenders. These underpaid attorneys are assigned to represent parents or children after a dependency petition is

---

43. Lawyers have an ethical duty to provide competent representation, which necessarily requires legal knowledge, skill, thoroughness, and preparation. MODEL RULES OF PROF'L CONDUCT R. 1.1. Meeting this ethical obligation however, does not necessarily ensure quality representation. The American Bar association has adopted Standards of Practice for Attorneys Representing Parents in Abuse and Neglect Cases (2006), [https://perma.cc/6YCT-8DAF], Child Welfare Agencies (2004), [https://perma.cc/ZKV2-MZY7] and Children (1996), [https://perma.cc/QZ59-74AB]. There is a movement to improve the quality of representation for parents in abuse and neglect cases. *See ABA National Project to Improve Representation of Parents: Investment That Makes Sense*, CENTER ON CHILDREN AND THE LAW [https://perma.cc/W5JP-ERQ6]. Evaluations of pilot projects demonstrate that enhancing the legal representation of parents can reduce the need for foster care placement. *See* Mark E. Courtney & Jennifer L. Hook, *Evaluation of the Impacts of Enhanced Parental Legal Representation on the Timing of Permanency Outcomes for Children in Foster Care*, 34(7) CHILD. AND YOUTH SERV.s REV. 1337–1343 (2012); DETROIT CTR. FOR FAMILY ADVOCACY, UNIV. MICH. L. SCH., PROMOTING SAFE AND STABLE FAMILIES 12 (n.d.), [https://perma.cc/M42A-HXHB].

44. 90% of child welfare agencies have reported difficulty in hiring and retaining qualified workers, with inadequate compensation cited as one of the main causes of this problem. U.S. GEN. ACCOUNTING OFFICE, GAO-03-357, CHILD WELFARE: HHS COULD PLAY A GREATER ROLE IN HELPING CHILD WELFARE AGENCIES RECRUIT AND RETAIN STAFF (2003), [https://perma.cc/4EFH-J4UE].

45. In 2010, the median salary for lawyers with five years of experience at big law firms was $144,000. Public defenders with similar experience earned a median salary of $60,000. Larry Krieger, *What Makes Lawyers Happy?*, 83 GEO. WASH. L. REV. 554 (Feb. 2015).

46. Different states employ different types of counsel to represent the state's interest in dependency matters, including prosecutors and city or county attorneys.

filed.[47] They are notoriously poor dressers compared to the AAGs, but she finds them slightly more interesting because they tend to be quirky and easily worked up. In small doses, she actually enjoys the "true believers"—a term used in her office to describe public defenders who always believe their clients and believe their clients are always victims of an over-reaching state.[48] But, on demanding cases or particularly busy days, she doesn't have any patience with this idealistic bunch. Like the AAGs who represent her, the defenders have no idea what it means to walk into the homes or schools she visits and question children about the most intimate details of their lives, or literally take a child from his mother's arms. They have no idea what it feels like to face angry doctors or teachers who can't believe that she can't always take children immediately from what they believe to be obviously dangerous situations. While she often finds defenders difficult to stomach, whether true believers or not, she understands their role and is generally thankful that she can say to parents and children "you can talk to your attorney" when they fume about their rights and the injustice of the system.

Michelle Griffith's case is not unique. Although crack cocaine is not as common as it used to be, she is a fairly typical substance-abusing mother.[49] Emily believes that she probably does love her children very much but it will take something close to a miracle to get her to kick her decade-long habit.[50] She finds these cases, involving siblings who are close and a loving parent with a long history of drug treatment and relapse, particularly difficult. When it comes to having to file these cases in court, she is glad that she is a CPS worker and can transfer the case to a different social worker after the children are removed. The new social worker will work with Michelle on the service plan to get her children home. Good luck with that.

Michelle's children are also not too different from the many children Emily has worked with over the years. They are guarded and needy at the same time. The oldest

---

47. Almost every state provides for appointment of counsel for parents at the outset of a dependency proceeding in keeping with the spirit of the *Lassiter* decision. *See supra* note 34. States differ on whether children are appointed counsel—in fact, only 61% of states require the appointment of an attorney for abused or neglected children. First Star, A Child's Right to Counsel: A National Report Card On Legal Representation for Abused & Neglected Children 10 (3d ed. 2012), [https://perma.cc/UY2E-B2VC].

48. The term "true believer" originates from Eric Hoffer's 1951 social psychology book, *The True Believer: Thoughts on the Nature of Mass Movements*. Hoffer discusses the different personality types that lead mass movements and the tendencies for adherents to mass movements to "breed fanaticism, enthusiasm, fervent hope, hatred and intolerance; . . . all of them demand blind faith and single hearted allegiance."

49. *Supra* note 9.

50. In 2012, 658,000 persons aged 12 or older reported receiving treatment for cocaine during the past years. Substance Abuse and Mental Health Servs. Admin., *supra* note 11, at 84. Research shows a weak to moderate association between receiving substance abuse treatment and sobriety. Pendergrast, et al., *The Effectiveness of Drug Abuse Treatment: A Meta-analysis of Comparison Group Studies*, 67(1) Drug and Alcohol Dependence 53–72 (June 2002) (finding a 57% success rate for the treatment groups compared with 42% for the comparison groups not receiving treatment.).

boy is sullen and responsible. They are all beautiful, despite the disheveled clothing and lack of hygiene.

Emily arrives at court on time with stacks of discovery for the attorneys.[51] From the get-go, she feels slightly annoyed. She knows that the attorney for Michael, Katie something or another, is young and inexperienced and Emily is in no mood to train a new attorney. Katie will most definitely be a true believer. They usually start out that way. When she finds Katie in the courthouse, she takes her usual approach of keeping contact to a minimum. It is useless to engage much in these situations. They play out the same as they always do and Emily prefers not to waste energy that she will need for the next family.

Michael's Foster Parent (for Now): Mr. Jeffries' Story

Eugene Jeffries always knew that eventually he would become a foster parent. His parents fostered children. He grew up with a house full of siblings and foster siblings. Although he had sometimes resented having to share his parents and his space, particularly during his early teenage years, he was raised to believe that God calls us to love our neighbors. In his neighborhood this means taking care of children whose parents are struggling.[52]

Mr. Jeffries grew up in Baker County and lives in the house where he was born and raised. His father passed on when he was in his early 20s. His aging mother had gone to live down south with his sister, a medical doctor, after she started having trouble getting around and managing her diabetes. Mr. Jeffries has stayed in the neighborhood and raised his own family. He moved back into his mother's home after his divorce about 10 years ago. He promised his mother when she moved out of the family home that he would "use the house to do God's work." He knew exactly what this meant to her and he didn't disagree. It took him close to one year to finish all of the licensing requirements, but he never wavered on the commitment he made to his mother to carry on her legacy of foster parenting.[53]

---

51. "Discovery" refers to agency records concerning the family that are provided to counsel for the parents and children in compliance with a state's rules of civil procedure, local court rules, or patterns of practice.

52. Segregated neighborhoods persist in the U.S. and African Americans continue to be over-represented in poor neighborhoods. Between 2009–2013, 32% of African American children lived in high-poverty neighborhoods, up from 27% in 2006–2010. Annie E. Casey Found., Kids Count Data Book 15 (2015), [https://perma.cc/D95H-2J6G]. There has been a great deal of research dedicated to the relationship between neighborhoods and racial and economic inequality. *See, e.g.*, Patrick Sharkey, Stuck in Place (2013).

53. Of the roughly 400,000 children in foster care, approximately 47% are placed in family homes with non-relatives, as opposed to with relatives other than their parents or in group homes. U.S. Dep't of Health and Human Servs., The AFCARS Report 1 (2014), [https://perma.cc/F9J8 -KNFG]. Licensing regulations for foster homes vary among the states, but they all require applicants to pass criminal background checks and home safety inspections, demonstrate family stability, provide character references, and prove that they have a regular source of income. *Foster Parent Information*, Nat'l Foster Parent Ass'n, [https://perma.cc/4V6J-94W2].

By the time Michael comes to him, Mr. Jeffries has been a foster parent for close to seven years and has taken in more than 20 children. For the first few years he was still working full time for the city and two of his adult sons were also living in the house. They helped out sometimes, but it was a challenge for Mr. Jeffries' to have to come home after a full day of work to face children who were not his own and who were not always willing to listen to him.

Mr. Jeffries had been raised in a strict home and when he became a father he followed in his own parents' tradition: "spare the rod, spoil the child."[54] He believes that his children, mostly doing well as adults now, benefitted from his willingness to physically discipline them. Mr. Jeffries is a little surprised by what he learned in the mandatory foster parent training classes—physical discipline is strictly forbidden. A mistake, he thinks, but complies with what he assumes is a fairly new rule. At his age, he does not have the energy for it anyway. Still, he sometimes thinks that the foster children he takes in would benefit from more discipline. His own parents administered "whoopings" to the deserving, without discrimination between biological and foster children. He hopes that he can still be a positive influence without that tool.

Mr. Jeffries originally overestimated his foster parenting abilities. Although he has been a committed father to his own six children, his ex-wife really had done the heavy lifting of parenting. After their divorce, he took care of two of their teenage boys on his own, but that was the extent of his single-parenting experience. Most of his boys weathered adolescence by being good athletes, which Mr. Jeffries could relate to as a former athlete himself. One son had struggled with school and the law, and was still locked up. Mr. Jeffries vacillates between anger and shame when he thinks about Jerome sitting in the penitentiary—so he does his best not to think about him except when he says his prayers.

Mr. Jeffries prefers housing adolescent boys and will only occasionally agree to take a foster child under the age of 12. He finds that he is much better with older children. He can make a difference with them. And, he knows the Department has a difficult time finding homes for teenage boys, particularly African American boys who may have been in the system for a while.[55] He has kept at least four of his charges until

---

54. *Proverbs* 13:24.

55. Nationally, African American children are overrepresented in the foster care system. In 2015, Black children comprised 14% of the child population in the United States. *Child Population by Race*, KIDS COUNT Data Center, Annie E. Casey Foundation, [https://perma.cc/9MXX-EAH8]. However, Black children made up 24% of the children in foster care in 2015. Child Welfare Information Gateway, U.S. Dep't of Health & Human Servs., Foster Care Statistics 2015 9 (2017), [https://perma.cc/8GRA-ZA2F]. The trend since 2002 has been a reduction in the number of African American children in care; however, African American children still have the highest average length of stay in the foster care system—29 months. *See* Admin. of Children, Youth and Families, U.S. Dep't of Health and Human Servs., Data Brief 2013-1, Recent Demographic Trends in Foster Care 4 fig.3 (2013), [https://perma.cc/GH4U-M69X]. There has been a great deal of research, discussion, and debate around the causes of and solutions to these disparities. *See, e.g.*, Dorothy Roberts, Shattered Bonds: The Color of Child Welfare (2002); Elizabeth Bartholet, *The Racial Disproportionality Movement in Child Welfare: False Facts and Dangerous Directions*, 51 Ariz. L. Rev. 871

they turned 18 years old and "aged out" of the system.[56] For the most part, he remains involved in those boys' lives as they transition to adulthood—understanding from raising his own children how porous the line between adolescence and adulthood is. Nothing makes him quite as proud as watching his foster children graduate from high school. A number of them even went on to college at four-year universities.[57] He is particularly pleased when he thinks about Davonte, who is currently playing college football at a small state college not too far away. Of course, they aren't all happy endings. More than one child he cared for ended up in a group home or even a juvenile institution (prison).[58] There is only so much he can do.

When Michael comes to his home, Mr. Jeffries has just completed almost three full weeks with no foster children—the longest period in his seven years of foster parenting.[59] This does not mean he wasn't parenting during that time. Between his own adult children, grandchildren and former foster children, he still has young people in

---

(2009). The causes are complex and include, to name a few, disparities in risk factors (poverty, incarceration rates), racially-biased decision-making, and a lack of culturally responsive services for families. For many years, the National Incidence Study of Child Abuse and Neglect (NIS) showed no statistically significant differences between black and white rates of child maltreatment. However, the most recent study published in 2010, NIS-4, found that black children experienced maltreatment at significantly higher rates than white children. The authors of the study concluded that this change was a result of "greater precision of the NIS-4 estimates" and "the enlarged gap between Black and White children in economic well-being." ANDREA J. SEDLAK ET AL., U.S. SUPPLEMENTARY ANALYSES OF RACE DIFFERENCES IN CHILD MALTREATMENT RATES IN THE NIS–4 53 (2010), DEP'T OF HEALTH AND HUMAN SERVS., [https://perma.cc/79J3-Z3UA] The authors identified "socioeconomic status," or income, as the strongest predictor of maltreatment, *id.* at 27, and observed that "significantly higher percentages of Black children lived in families of low socioeconomic status." *Id.* at 9.

56. Upon turning eighteen, youths generally cease to be under state courts' jurisdictions for dependency purposes—any involvement from that point forward is based on their voluntary agreement to participate and the availability of foster care resources. The Fostering Connections to Success and Increasing Adoptions Act of 2008 created incentives for states to extend provision of foster care to certain youth up to the age of 21 Pub. L. No. 110-351, 122 Stat. 3949 (codified as amended at 42 U.S.C. §§ 671–679c).

57. National data on educational outcomes for foster youth indicate 50% of foster youth complete high school by age 18 and 2–9% of former foster youth attain a bachelor's degree. NAT'L WORKING GROUP ON FOSTER CARE & EDUC., FOSTERING SUCCESS IN EDUCATION: NATIONAL FACTSHEET ON THE EDUCATIONAL OUTCOMES OF CHILDREN IN FOSTER CARE (2014), [https://perma.cc/VY3N-BGUF].

58. Research shows that youth in foster care are at greater risk of entering the juvenile and adult criminal systems. One study in California found that males with prior foster care placement had a five times greater risk of incarceration than males in the general population and for females the risk was ten times. Melissa Jonson-Reid, Richard P Barth, *From Placement to Prison: The Path to Adolescent Incarceration from Child Welfare Supervised Foster or Group Care*, 22(7) CHILD. & YOUTH SERVS. REV. 508 (July 2000). A study of youth in Los Angeles County found that adolescents from the child welfare system processed in the juvenile justice system were more likely to receive a disposition of a group home or correctional placement rather than probation. Ryan, Herz & Hernandez, Marshall, *Maltreatment and Delinquency: Investigating Child Welfare Bias in Juvenile Justice Processing*, 29(8) CHILD. & YOUTH SERVS. REV. 1046 (Aug. 2007).

59. Research has shown that the median length of service for foster parents in some states ranges from eight to 14 months. Deborah Gibbs & Judith Wildfire, *Length of Service for Foster Parents*, 29 CHILD. & YOUTH SERVS. REV. 588, 597 (2007).

his home almost every day for some reason or another. But he has to admit to himself he enjoyed the break from full time responsibility—he realizes he is getting older and much more tired. He felt some relief when a few weeks ago his last foster child, 18-year-old Jordan, moved out to join his older brother and mother in another state. Although Mr. Jeffries is concerned about Jordan's plan, he knows that he can never get in the way of a grown boy who wants to be with family. He hopes for the best and found himself enjoying his time alone.

The call comes late in the afternoon, as it usually does. He feels a complicated mixture of excitement and dread when he sees that it is the Department on his caller ID. Leslie Turner's voice is as exuberant as ever. "Hello Mr. Jeffries, we have a young man who needs you today—are you ready for the Lord's work?" She always uses this language that makes it impossible for him to say "no."

"Sorry, Leslie. I'm getting ready to leave for a 14-day cruise in the Bahamas. I won it on the radio. Do you wanna join me?"

There is silence on the other end of the phone.

"Hello?"

Leslie breaks the silence, "Well, um, I'm so happy for you but . . . well . . ."

Mr. Jeffries can't hold back and busts out laughing, "Leslie, I'm just messing with you. I'm not going on a cruise. I've just been sitting by my phone waiting for your call." His baritone chuckle sets Leslie at ease and she launches immediately into Michael's story.

"So, Reggie will be by in about an hour with Michael, OK?"

"Of course. I was making ribs tonight anyway." Mr. Jeffries hangs up the phone and heads to the kitchen. He starts to whistle.

Michael's Lawyer's Story: Katie Olson, J.D.

She can't believe she has only been there eight months. It feels like an eternity. Every day packs in a lifetime of heartache. Mental illness. Substance abuse. Domestic violence. Poverty. Poverty. More poverty. She loves her job. She really does. She is grateful to have a job. A *public interest* job. She makes a difference every day. Or so she thinks.

Being the new attorney has its advantages in the office and the courthouse. She gets a lot of breaks. Experienced attorneys, even the most curmudgeonly public defenders, will stop and answer her questions. Some judges will still offer an empathetic look as she stumbles over her words or asks for unrealistic, but legitimate (she thinks) relief for her clients. Nevertheless, she looks forward to the day when the work gets easier, when she feels comfortable speaking in court. She wonders if she will always have to write out every argument and question like she was taught to do in law school. She certainly does not see the other lawyers in court doing it. They seem to be able to argue on the fly. OK, maybe what they say is not particularly brilliant or persuasive, but still. The late nights and early mornings preparing for court are taking their toll—she doesn't think she will be able to work like this forever.

As the newbie, on Fridays she has to cover "the morning calendar" which means shelter care hearings,[60] emergency placement hearings, warrant returns, etc. All of the stuff that gets filed on Thursdays by social workers who did not get around to filing their paperwork earlier in the week and have to save the children before the weekend. Other lawyers do not like this assignment, but she does. It is quite an adrenaline rush having to meet clients, digest pages of discovery, prepare for a hearing and argue a case in a three-hour window. It is exhausting, but exhilarating. Once noon comes around she feels like she has accomplished something: orders signed, clients counseled, lives changed forever. Preparation is over-rated in her opinion. Natural skill, a quick mind and lots of energy can go a long way. Experience wouldn't hurt, she admits, but three out of the four seems to get her through the day.

> ### Reflecting on Professional Identity
> - *How does Katie handle her lack of experience?*
> - *What can new lawyers do to be competent?*

On Thursday afternoons, the firm's paralegal delivers the petitions and motions for the Friday morning calendar to the assigned attorney. Katie usually gets them by 4:00 p.m. She tends to stay in the office and review the paperwork and try to contact the clients or find their files, if any existed, before heading home—unlike the attorneys who grab the petitions on their way out the door or wait until the morning to pick them up on the way to court. She is not exactly sure whether her strategy is the best one or whether it is sustainable in the long run, but she strongly believes she should at least attempt to make contact with the client before meeting them in the chaotic courthouse where they are usually scared out of their minds. True, children and teen-agers do not really shine over the phone when contacted by a complete stranger. But she still likes to at least hear their voice and let them hear hers—which hopefully serves to cushion, ever so slightly, the traumatic experience that is juvenile court.[61]

> ### Initial Removal Hearings/Shelter Care
> - *What are these hearings called in your jurisdiction?*
> - *Find the statutes and Court Rules that govern these hearings.*

---

60. For a discussion of the initial shelter care hearing, see ch. 1, *ASFA: Seeking to Balance Permanence and Reunification.*

61. Rule 1.4 of the ABA Model Rules of Professional Conduct requires lawyers to keep clients "reasonably informed about the status" of their cases, to "reasonably consult" with clients about how to accomplish their objectives, and to "explain a matter to the extent reasonably necessary" to let clients make informed decisions. To effectively communicate with child clients, lawyers should consider where and how to communicate with clients in a developmentally appropriate way and in an environment where rapport can be established to facilitate communication. Suparna Malempati, *Ethics, Advocacy, and the Child Client*, 12 Cardozo Pub. L. Pol'y & Ethics J. 633, 659 (2014).

Friday's petitions looked like others Katie had seen before, but she is still not accustomed to reading line after line of someone's worst moments. If her life were boiled down to two-dozen paragraphs in a dependency petition, what would that look like? If she took her childhood and pulled out her parents' very worst moments — how would it read? Her dad's drinking wasn't that bad. And who could blame her mom for taking breaks occasionally from the chaos and arguing? Well, her dad could, she acknowledges, since he was not very excited about her mom's unilateral decision to make theirs an "open relationship." Katie did not mind her mother's boyfriends. They were usually young and fun, but they sure did piss her dad off. No matter, Katie took good care of her younger brother and sister. She was always mature for her age. No matter how crazy their parents got, Katie managed to keep her siblings together. And look at them now, she thinks. All successful, college graduates with jobs and committed relationships. Of course, she has to credit some of that to their wealthy grandparents — a bonus that is sorely lacking for any of her clients. But now she is determined to apply that same steady-under-pressure attitude she honed throughout her childhood to the Friday morning drama before her.

> ### *Ethical Issues in Sibling Representation*
>
> - *Do attorneys in your jurisdiction represent sibling groups? If they do, how do they comply with Model Rule 1.7?*
>
> - *If an actual conflict arises between the siblings, do they withdraw?*
>
> - *How do they handle confidentiality under Model Rule 1.6?*
>
> - *From the child client's perspective, what are the advantages and disadvantages of sibling group representation?*

Based on her whole eight months of experience, Friday doesn't look too bad: two shelter care hearings and one emergency placement hearing to move a youth to group care. Of course, Katie knows enough to know that "nothing is as it seems." Sure, one of the petitions looks like it will be a breeze — the parents are both in jail so there won't be a lot to argue about — but a lot can happen between the time the petition is drafted and filed and the time of the court hearing.[62] The other shelter care hearing looks like it might be more complicated: Four children and she is assigned to represent the oldest one, Michael.[63] He actually is hardly mentioned in the petition,

---

62. Local rules of procedure will govern the notice and scheduling requirements for initial hearings — but the time frame is generally short, from 24 to 72 hours. *See, e.g.*, Wa. Juv. R. 2.3 (notice shall be given within 24 hours of taking a child into custody, and a hearing shall be held with 72 hours); Id. Juv. R. 32 (notify parents within 48 hours).

63. Lawyers in some jurisdictions represent multiple siblings in a dependency case; however, this can create conflicts of interest that may run afoul of lawyers' ethical obligations. The American Bar Association defines a concurrent conflict of interest as the representation of one client whose interests are directly adverse to another client or where there is a significant risk that the lawyer's representation of one client "will be materially limited" by responsibilities to another client. Model Rules of Prof'l Conduct r. 1.7(a). While siblings may not have adverse interests at the outset of a

it looks like the petition is filed because the sisters disclosed something close to sexual abuse. Katie has seen similar scenarios before. Nothing happens until someone gets "inappropriately touched" and then all of a sudden heaven and hell move to rescue the children from their abusive parents. Katie is repulsed by sexual abuse, but she finds it troubling that sexual abuse gets all the attention while children who are chronically neglected for years are allowed to slowly waste away in the care of their drug-addicted or mentally ill parents.[64]

Michael's Dependency Petition

SUPERIOR COURT OF
  WASHINGTON
COUNTY OF BAKER JUVENILE
  COURT	

IN RE THE DEPENDENCY OF: **Michael Griffith,** DOB 1/22/02 **Aliyah Griffith,** DOB 7/1/05 **Angel Griffith,** DOB 3/31/08 **and Deja Jones,** DOB 8/3/14	No: 15 -7-0234; 15 -7-0235; 15 -7-0236; 15 -7-0237 Dependency Petition

I. Basis

I represent to the court the following:

1.1   **Petitioner**

        ☒   DSHS/Supervising Agency by Emily Peters, MSW. _____

            CPS South Unit _____

---

dependency proceeding, there is always some risk that their interests will diverge over the life of the case. For example, one sibling may want to remain in foster care while another sibling wants to return home. Some courts have rules governing how lawyers handle conflicts of interest in representing sibling groups. *See, e.g.,* Cal. Ct. Fam. Juv. R. 5.660(c)(2) (removal is required when an actual conflict of interest exists but not mandatory if there is merely a reasonable likelihood that one will develop).

    64. Out of all cases meeting the definition of harm, CPS investigates a higher percentage of sexual abuse cases (55%) than those resulting from physical abuse (53%), emotional abuse (36%), or physical neglect (27%). Andrea J. Sedlak et al., Fourth National Incidence Study of Child Abuse and Neglect (NIS-4) § 8-28 tbl.8-1 (2010), U.S. Dep't of Health & Human Servs., [https://perma.cc/E8C6-NLD9]. Although investigation rates might suggest otherwise, three distinct forms of childhood abuse — sexual, emotional, and physical — are all associated with similar negative outcomes that are often indistinguishable in adulthood. P.E. Mullen et al., *The Long-term Impact of the Physical, Emotional, and Sexual Abuse of Children*, 20 Child Abuse & Neglect 7, 18 (1996).

1.2   Child(ren) alleged to be dependent: [x] male [ ] female

Name	Michael Griffith	
Date of Birth	12/22/02	
Home Address		

[ ] male [x] female

Name	Aliyah Griffith	
Date of Birth	7/1/05	
Home Address		

[ ] male [x] female

Name	Angel Griffith	
Date of Birth	3/31/08	
Home Address		

[ ] male [x] female

Name	Deja Jones	
Date of Birth	8/3/14	
Home Address		

1.3   Parent(s) or Legal Guardian(s):

	[x] **Mother**	[x] **Father (Michael)** [ ] presumed [x] alleged
Name	MICHELLE GRIFFITH	ERIC GRAYSON
Date of Birth	12/15/1984	11/5/1983
Marital status	[x] single [ ] married [ ] other	[x] single [ ] married [ ] other
Driver's License or Identicard (# and State)	GRIFMI32IQE	GRAYER534SL
Home Address	1356 -57TH AVE S APT 301	BRANNAN HILLS CORRECTIONAL FACILITY

	[x] **Father (Aliyah)** [ ] presumed [x] alleged	[x] **Father (Deja)** [ ] presumed [x] alleged
Name	THOMAS SYKES	DARRYL JONES
Date of Birth	9/9/1984	6/14/1981
Marital status	[ ] single [x] married [ ] other	[x] single [ ] married [ ] other
Driver's License or Identicard (# and State)		
Home Address	4000 S. Hudson	1356 — 57TH AVE S APT 301

1.4   **Child's Indian Status:**

[x] The petitioner has made the following efforts and cannot determine whether the child is an Indian child as defined in Laws of 2011, ch. 309, § 4:

Reviewed CAMIS database, asked mother and grandmother _____

_____

[   ] Based upon the following, the child is not an Indian child as defined in Laws of 2011, ch. 309, § 4, and the federal and Washington State Indian Child Welfare Acts do not apply to these proceedings:

_____

_____

[   ] Based upon the following, the child is an Indian child as defined in Laws of 2011, ch. 309, § 4 and the federal and Washington State Indian Child Welfare Acts do apply to these proceedings:

_____

_____

[   ] The petitioner has made the following preliminary efforts to provide notice of these proceedings to all tribes to which the petitioner knows or has reason to know the child may be a member or eligible for membership:

_____

_____

1.5   **Dependency:** The children should be declared dependent according to RCW 13.34.030 as follows:

[ ]   (a) the child has been abandoned as defined in RCW 13.34.030;

[x]   (b) the child is abused or neglected as defined in chapter 26.44 RCW;

or

[ ]   (c) the child has no parent, guardian or custodian capable of adequately caring for the child, such that the child is in circumstances which constitute a danger of substantial damage to the child's psychological or physical development.

1.6   **Allegations:** The allegation of Dependency is based on the following facts:

1.   I am a social worker employed by the Child Protective Services Division of the Social and Health Services Department of Baker County.

2.   On September 10, 2008, a teacher at John Muir elementary school reported that Michael Griffith arrived at school 2 hours late. He has lice and reported that he hadn't eaten anything except for some potato chips for two days.

3.   On January 12, 2009, the assistant principal at John Muir elementary school reported that Michael Griffith returned to school after 13 unexcused absences. He reported that he was at home caring for his younger sisters while his mother was working.

4.   On March 17, 2010, at 11:30 p.m. a licensed day care provider reported that Michele Griffith did not pick up her daughters Aliyah (3) and Angel (11 months) from day care. The referrant reported that this is the 3rd time that the mother left her daughters overnight with the daycare provider without calling.

5.   On April 19, 2010, the mother Michele Griffith entered into a voluntary services agreement with CPS social worker Jane Uhlrey. She agreed to enter into outpatient

drug treatment, keep her children Michael, Aliyah and Angel in licensed day care, complete parenting classes, submit to random UA's and cooperate with a family preservation specialist.

6.   The mother completed the Voluntary Services Agreement in October, 2010.

7.   On February 2, 2011, Jacqueline Griffith, the maternal grandmother of Michael, Aliyah and Angel, reported that the mother had left the children with her 2 months earlier and had not seen them since. The mother had called a few times, but she hasn't heard from Michelle for 3 weeks and she needs medical coupons for the children. She also needs food assistance.

8.   On April 25, 2011, Thomas Sykes, the alleged father of Aliyah Griffith (5) reported that the mother, Michele Griffith, came to his apartment "high on crack" and insisted that he take Aliyah. He told her that he cannot take Aliyah because he does not have room in the apartment that he shares with his aunt, his girlfriend and their 3 children. The mother "threw the child" at him and left. 4 hours later she returned and "snatched" the child back, grabbing her roughly and Aliyah was crying and saying that she did not want to go. Thomas Sykes does not know how to reach the mother.

9.   On May 30, 2011, the mother called CPS worker Jane Uhlrey and told her she wanted to get back into treatment and that she left her children with their grandmother.

10. On May 31, 2011, Jane Uhlrey contacted the maternal grandmother, Jacqueline G. and confirmed that the children were with her. The maternal grandmother was very upset and said that she didn't think she could keep the children but agreed to meet with the social worker.

11. On June 6, 2011, the mother entered into voluntary placement and services agreement, placing Michael, Aliyah and Angel with their maternal grandmother while she entered in-patient treatment.

12. On September 20, 2011, the mother completed inpatient treatment and moved in with the maternal grandmother and the children.

13. On October 4, 2012, the principal of Hawthorne elementary school reported that Angel Griffith said she was late to school because her "mommy would not wake up." She reported that there was a man named DJ in the house who was "mean and hit them." She showed the principal bruising on the backs of her thighs.

14. On March 8, 2013, the assistant principal at Westside elementary reported that Michael, Aliyah and Angel had been late to school 48 times since the beginning of the school year and had 22 unexcused absences. She reported that the girls were often dressed inappropriately for the weather, were dirty, covered with head lice and hungry.

15. On July 13, 2014, a public health nurse at Southside Community Health Clinic reported that the mother came in for a pre-natal visit and appeared to be high. She had difficult staying awake and speaking clearly but she denied drug use. She had her daughter Angel with her.

16. On January 12, 2015, the principal of John Muir elementary school reported that Aliyah (9) was sent to his office after getting into a fight with a boy during recess. She kicked the boy in his private parts and said "you better never touch me with that or I will kill you." This was overheard by the playground supervisor who brought Aliyah to the office. When Aliyah was asked by the principal why she kicked the boy, Aliyah stated that "boys are bad and they can do mean things to girls." The principal asked her why she would say that and Aliyah started crying

and screaming "stop touching me, stop touching me!" The nurse was called and Aliyah calmed down and said that her mom has "scary boyfriends" and she "doesn't want them to touch her anymore."

17. On January 12, 2015, CPS worker Emily Peters went to John Muir elementary and interviewed Aliyah (9) and her sister Angel (6) separately. Aliyah said that she didn't want to talk about anymore touching and she didn't want anyone to get in trouble. Angel stated that "mom's boyfriends aren't too bad. They just hit us sometimes when we don't listen." She said "Mom has to take drugs sometimes and fall asleep, but Michael always takes care of us. He never hits us." Angel also reported that "my baby sister hardly ever cries anymore and I help take care of her."

18. On January 12, 2015, CPS worker Emily Peters went to the mother's apartment with a police officer to do a welfare check. A male who identified himself as DJ answered the door and let Ms. Peters and the officer in. He appeared to be intoxicated or high. They found the mother passed out on the couch. She did not respond when DJ tried to wake her. Deja, 5 months old was sleeping in a crib wearing only a dirty diaper. There was no heat in the apartment and it was very cold. There were approximately 20 empty beer cans strewn across the floor. A glass pipe was on kitchen counter. The refrigerator was empty except for a 2 liter bottle of Coke. DJ was identified as Darryl Jones and he said he was the father of Deja. The officer placed Darryl Jones under arrest for an outstanding warrant for a probation violation.

19. The mother finally woke up but appeared to be extremely intoxicated or high. She did not respond to questions. The only thing she said was "Get out of my house. Take the baby, I don't care." She went back to the couch and laid down.

20. Deja, Angel, Aliyah and Michael were taken into protective custody by CPS pending the filing of a dependency petition.

21. Department records show that there have been 23 CPS referrals on these children.

22. The alleged father of Deja is Darryl Jones. He is currently in custody in the Baker County Jail. He has an extensive criminal history that includes Possession of a Firearm (2011); 3 convictions for Possession of a Controlled Substance (2006, 2007, 2012); Driving While License Suspended (2012) and Communicating with a Minor for Immoral Purposes (2000).

23. The alleged father of Aliya is Thomas Sykes. He currently resides with his wife and 3 children in a two-bedroom apartment. He has a drug possession conviction from 2004 and an arrest for Domestic Violence Assault in 2005. When contacted by CPS on January 12, Mr. Sykes reported that he has not seen Aliyah for over one year but that he would like to be considered for custody and he will appear at the hearing.

24. The father of Angel is unknown.

25. The alleged father of Michael is Eric Grayson. He has an extensive criminal history and is currently in custody at the Brannan Hills Correctional Facility.

II. Relief Requested

The petitioner requests that the court find the child dependent, enter an order of dependency, and grant the relief below:

[x]   enter a disposition order that includes placement, parent-child and sibling visitation, and services.

[ ]   order a parent to cooperate with the establishment of paternity.

[ ]   order a parent to sign releases for information.

[ ]   Other:

Dated: **1/12/15**   **Emily Peters**   _____
                                                              Petitioner

_____
Emily Peters/Child Protection Services

    Type or Print Name/Title   WSBA No.

_____   **Ed Williams**   _____
    Petitioner

_____
Ed Williams/Assistant Attorney General   24789

Type or Print Name/Title   WSBA No.

III. Certification

I declare under penalty of perjury under the laws of the State of Washington that the foregoing representations are true and correct.

Signed at   Baker County   1/12/15 (Date).

_____
Emily Peters   Emily Peters, M.S.W.

Signature   Print Name

♀ ♂

Substance Abuse, Parenting and Reasonable Efforts

The "reasonable efforts" requirement places an emphasis on providing services to parents in order to prevent the need for out of home placement, consistent with research showing that keeping families together whenever possible is in the best interest of children.

The cycle of recovery and relapse commonly experienced by chronic substance abusers presents challenges for keeping families together.

- *Based on the allegations in the dependency petition, did the Department satisfy its requirement to make "reasonable efforts" to prevent the need for removal of Michael and his siblings? Why or why not?*

- *What should "reasonable efforts" entail for a mother like Michelle?*

After reviewing the petition, Katie picks up the phone at 4:45 p.m. and tries to reach the social worker to see if she can get in touch with her client before the hearing in the morning. So far, she has been batting about 50-50 on these attempts, but that does not dissuade her true-believer spirit. To her surprise, Emily Peters answers her phone.

"Hi, Emily, my name is Katie Olson and I will be representing Michael Griffith at his shelter care hearing tomorrow."

"Oh. Great, he could use some good counseling." Katie thinks she hears a tinge of sarcasm in Emily's voice, but she can't be sure.

"Well, I'm just here to give him *legal* counsel, but I will do my best. Do you know how I can reach him right now?"

Pause. "Uh, usually we don't give out foster parents' numbers at this stage. I haven't had many attorneys ask for the number *before* the hearing. Michael will be at the courthouse at 8:30 a.m. and you can interview him then in person."

"Oh, I know, I just like to check in before so that I can prepare him a little. It's really helpful for me, because I'm kind of new and I will have other matters tomorrow and might be a little rushed." Katie enjoys playing that newbie card.

"Well, OK. What agency did you say you work for? I will give you the number, but I don't know if you will be able to reach him or not tonight. It is up to Mr. Jeffries the foster parent. Michael may be pretty upset over this whole thing and in no mood to talk."

Katie rings the number Emily gave her. Straight to voicemail: "This is the Jeffries' residence. Sorry we are not able to take your call, but it is important to us. Please leave a message and we will return your call at our earliest convenience. Have a blessed day." Katie hopes Michael Griffith was having a blessed day, but she does not leave a message. She still is not sure what the proper way to handle that situation is under her ethical responsibilities.[65] Should she say, "Hi, I am Michael Griffith's lawyer (that he doesn't even know about yet) please have him call me?" She has tried that a handful of times but so far has been completely unsuccessful. A zero percent return call rate. And, she doesn't feel totally comfortable giving out her mobile number to new clients she has not yet met. At least she tries; she won't stop trying.

Driving home Katie thinks about Michael and his sisters. She imagines the apartment his mother lives in, she pictures him sleeping in a strange bed at Mr. Jeffries' house—maybe with other foster children (her clients?). She wonders if his sisters are with him or if he has any relatives that can take him in. As she walks up the steps to her apartment, lugging her briefcase full of the next day's troubles, dying to take off her shoes, she reminds herself to leave it behind. She tells herself: *Stop being so intense. Let it go until tomorrow.* By the time she reaches her front door, she is almost ready to forget the traumatic world of the child welfare system.

---

65. Rule 1.6 of the ABA Model Rules of Professional Conduct prohibits a lawyer from revealing information relating to the representation of a client without the client's informed consent unless it is "impliedly authorized in order to carry out the representation."

> ### Reflecting on Difference
>
> *You now know more than any one character knows about Michael's situation before he goes to court for the first time.*
>
> - *What do you think Michael will need from his lawyer?*
> - *What do you want Michael's lawyer to know before meeting Michael?*
> - *How should Katie think about or approach the differences she has from her client?*

The apartment smells of garlic. She can see Zach in the kitchen doing his thing — creating incredible food and an even more incredible mess of dirty pots and pans. She feels grateful for a boyfriend who cooks, even if he doesn't clean. He turns around and smiles "Pasta Puttanesca! Thursday night carbo loading for the Friday calendar." He cannot be sweeter. And he wants to hear about her day. She wants to tell him all about Michael and how he has to take care of his siblings and how he is sleeping at a stranger's house tonight probably separated from his siblings and it isn't fair that children have to grow up like that. She wants to tell Zach that she feels rage toward the system and toward crack cocaine that poisons mothers. She wants to tell him how driven she feels to fight for Michael and how she will not stop fighting until he is living safely with his sisters and getting an education. But she cannot talk about all those things with Zach. The Rules of Professional Conduct prohibit her as a lawyer from discussing her clients' lives with others, unless they are lawyers or staff in her office who are also bound by the rules of confidentiality.[66] Besides, he doesn't get it. It isn't that he does not care about poor kids, but he is an environmental engineer. He is busy saving the planet — which frankly seems more pleasant to her on some days and she is envious of the money that he also manages to earn while still doing good in the world. They have been together since they were undergraduates and he was so patient and supportive during those three long years of law school. She believes that law school was responsible for his excellent culinary skills — while she studied late at the library he was busy baking bread and mastering Vietnamese spring rolls.

> ### Reflecting on Ethics
>
> - *Is Katie reading her ethical obligations too conservatively?*
> - *How can lawyers like Katie stay healthy and committed to their work without violating their duty of confidentiality to their clients?*

Zach reads Katie's face across the table as she hungrily devours his Italian creation. "Tough day at the office?"

---

66. *Id.*

"The usual. No big deal."

"More kids getting screwed over by their parents and the state?"

"Yup, pretty much." She does not really like it when he talks about her work that way. She knows that he is just reflecting back what she has dished out to him over the past eight months, but it doesn't seem right to have him sound so flippant when he has no idea how complicated it all is.

"This is delicious. Thanks for cooking, Zach." She tries hard not to think about the empty refrigerator at Michael's apartment. *Lighten up, Katie!* "Let's go out this weekend for Chinese hot pot. My treat."

"Absolutely. I gotta get one of those burners to cook on the table, you know that? We can make hot pot at home all winter. You can be my attractive sous chef."

The rest of the evening was spent with Zach doing on-line research about cooking hot pot at home and Katie catching up on a couple of episodes of her latest TV obsession. She falls asleep during The Daily Show and dreams that her younger brother decided to move in with them because he got kicked out of college. She woke up extremely happy that it is Friday.

Reflections and Exercises

1. *What? So What? Now What? A Five-Minute Reflection Opportunity.* Take just five minutes to write and reflect on the following questions:

   a.   What did you feel as you read the stories of Michael, his family and the other people involved as he enters the child welfare system?

   b.   How is what you recorded feeling relevant to your learning and/or practice?

   c.   Now what do you do with these insights as you move forward in your learning and/or practice?

2. *Racial Disproportionality in the Dependency System:* In footnote 55, some of the explanations for the overrepresentation of African American children in the dependency system are addressed. Explanations include higher risk factors (particularly poverty); greater visibility than white children because of more contact with mandated reporters; and systemic racism and unconscious bias that operate to increase the likelihood that child protection workers investigating or reunifying families will reach racially disparate conclusions. Add to this the historical underpinnings of a system that targets poor, racial minorities and at the same time underserved black children and we have a deeply troubling state of affairs.

   a.   What role do lawyers for African American children have in addressing these disparities?

   b.   Does awareness of these disparities impact how a lawyer advocates for her clients? Do lawyers have an obligation to address the systemic problem, and if so, how?

c. Take a moment to reflect on the role race plays in your own life. How do you identify racially? How might that impact your advocacy? What does it mean to be a white lawyer for African American children in this setting? What does it mean to be a black lawyer for African American children in this setting? If you identify as something other than black or white, how does that impact your advocacy?

3   *Imagining a Different Story for Michael:* Being placed in foster care is a traumatic event for Michael and his siblings, even though it is done for their protection.

a. Could there be a different intervention for Michael and his siblings that could protect them but reduces the negative impacts?

b. Think outside the box: what might that look like? What are the costs and benefits of implementing such an intervention? What are the challenges to changing the way systems respond to abuse and neglect?

Chapter Three

The Deep End of the System

In this chapter, you meet Maya, her family, her former teacher, and her friend Kiki. You will also learn about her relationship with Diamond. Maya has spent most of her childhood under the state's supervision. She has lived in many different kinds of homes—with her grandmother, with foster parents, and in group homes with other young people. We join her after she has run away for the second time. You will see how the child welfare system intersects with the status offender system, and how leaving one's placement without permission may be handled through juvenile detention.

Unlike Michael's story, which unfolds in a more linear fashion as he moves through his journey into foster care, we meet Maya after a long history in the system and with an intricate web of family and friends; this chapter is structured to reflect this more complex and fractured context. Trauma is a recurring theme that unifies these stories. Trauma has a pervasive and yet sometimes invisible impact. It is personal. Given the intimacy of trauma, the stories in Maya's chapters are told in the first person, with each character providing you a unique perspective.

This mosaic of perspectives is intended to remind you that the clients you serve come with lives that exist outside of your limited perceptions of them, and that while the law is a powerful force shaping their experiences, other powerful relationships with family, friends and professionals predate you, coexist with you, and likely will continue long after you are gone.

Some background on trauma and resilience will help you to place this chapter in context.

What Is Trauma?

Everyone experiences stress and challenge in their lives.[1] Traumatic events fall outside the expected range of stressors for the particular individual[2] and generally fall into two different categories: acute and chronic. Acute trauma typically involves a

---

1. The National Scientific Council on the Developing Child has classified stress into three categories: 1) positive stress, which is moderate and brief, and which can lead to healthy growth, such as adjusting to new situations; 2) tolerable stress, which could impact brain development, but which occurs infrequently enough to allow time for recovery; and 3) toxic stress, which is strong, frequent, prolonged and triggers the body's stress response system. *See* Child Welfare Information Gateway, U.S. Dep't of Health & Human Servs., Understanding the Effects of Maltreatment on Brain Development 5 (2015), [https://perma.cc/TJP3-PQD7].

2. "Traumatic experiences typically involve two elements: exposure to a traumatic event that threatens the integrity of the individual (either real or imagined) and intense feelings of helplessness

single event. For example, someone who has survived an earthquake may experience acute trauma as a result. Chronic trauma involves recurrent extraordinary stressors and/or single incidents of physical or sexual abuse.[3]

Rates of trauma exposure are high among children in foster care.[4] The trauma they experience arises from at least four sources: maltreatment suffered in the home; the removal from home and separation from siblings;[5] reunifications that sometimes fail.[6]

Trauma is not only experienced at the individual level. It can occur across generations and can impact entire communities. Historical trauma is experienced by communities that share a common identity and have been subjected to a legacy of state-sanctioned or supported abuses over generations.[7] Communities of color, disproportionately represented in the child welfare system, have been exposed to historical trauma. The separation of families through slavery[8] and the removal of Indian children from their tribes to be educated in religious boarding schools[9] are just two examples of state-sanctioned violence against families of color.

------

and horror." Robyn S. Igelman, et al., *Best Practices for Serving Traumatized Children and Families*, 59 Juv. & Fam. Ct. J. 35, 36 (2008).

3. *See* The National Child Traumatic Stress Network, *Defining Trauma and Child Traumatic Stress*, [https://perma.cc/2C6A-AQD2].

4. Rates of trauma exposure approach 90% among children in foster care. *See*, B.D. Stein, et al., *Violence Exposure Among School-Age Children in Foster Care: Relationship to Distress Symptoms*, 40(5) J. Acad. Child Adolesc. Psychiatry 588–94 (2001 May). *See also*, B. Beyerlein & Ellin Bloch, *Need for Trauma-Informed Care Within the Foster Care System: Policy Issue*, 93(3) Child Welfare 7–21 (2014). For a discussion of the impact of parental separation on children, see The National Child Traumatic Stress Network, *Children with Traumatic Separation: Information for Professionals*, [https://perma.cc/JK78-7YKC].

5. *See* Nancy Boyd Webb, Working With Traumatized Youth In Child Welfare 13 (2006).

6. "The disappearance of a parent who has briefly come back into a child's life is often experienced as a crushing blow, accompanied by much anger, sadness, and depression." David A. Crenshaw & Kenneth V. Hardy, *Understanding and Treating the Aggression of Traumatized Children in Out-of-Home Care*, in Nancy Boyd Webb, Working With Traumatized Youth In Child Welfare 174 (2006).

7. Teresa Evans-Campbell, *Historical Trauma in American Indian/Native Alaska Communities: A Multi-level Framework for Exploring Impacts on Individuals, Families and Communities*, 23 J. Interpers. Violence 316, 320 (2008).

8. Marriages between those who were enslaved were not recognized under American law. Even in the northern states, like New York, marriages between manumitted slaves were not recognized until 1809. *See* A. Leon Higginbotham, In the Matter of Color: Race and the American Legal Process. The Colonial Period 144 (1978). The state-sanctioned callousness embodied in the sale of children away from their parents is evident in the many advertisements of the day. For example, Benjamin Davis of Hamburg, South Carolina, boasted, "the lot now on hand consists of ploughboys, . . . small girls suitable for nurses, and several small boys without their mothers." This type of "marketing" was not unusual; an advertisement in the *New Orleans Bee* advertised the sale of "a Negro woman, 24 years of age, and her two children, one eight and one three years old. Said Negroes will be sold separately or together, as desired." *Id*. at p. 12.

9. Starting as early as the colonial period, attempts were made to separate Indian children from their families in order to remove them from "the evil influence of their parents." *Id*. at p. 31. The U.S. government policy of forcing assimilation through the removal of children from Indian parents persisted into the twentieth century in several forms, including the Indian Boarding school movement,

The Impact of Trauma and Stress

Responses to traumatic events, whether acute or chronic, vary from individual to individual. Some develop mental health conditions that interfere with daily functioning, such as depression, anxiety or post-traumatic stress disorder (PTSD).

Not everyone who experiences a traumatic event will develop PTSD.[10] Mental health professionals diagnose PTSD only if specific criteria are met. The individual with PTSD must have been exposed to an event involving actual or threatened death, serious injury or sexual violation. In order for PTSD to be diagnosed, trauma exposure must lead to significant distress or impairment in daily living. Typical symptoms cluster around four different types of responses: re-experiencing; avoidance; negative cognitions and mood; or arousal.[11]

Tools for diagnosing PTSD in young children under the age of six have been developed.[12] These special diagnostics are attuned to the young child's emerging cognitive abilities and verbal expression and focuses on the child's behavior and development.[13]

Without regard to whether PTSD was diagnosed or diagnosable in childhood, research shows that adverse childhood events have cumulative and long-lasting physical and mental health consequences. The Adverse Childhood Events Study (ACES) examined the long-range impact of abuse, neglect and household dysfunction upon the overall health of adults. Household dysfunction included witnessing intimate partner violence, household substance abuse, parental mental illness, divorce/ separation, and parental incarceration. Many of these conditions are also present in the lives of young people who are removed from the care of their parents. This study found that those experiencing multiple adverse events fared worse as adults than those who were exposed to only one event and that, as the number of adverse events experienced

which was initiated through the Civilization Fund Act of 1819. *See* Medium of Instruction Policies: Which Agenda? Whose Agenda? 80 (James W. Tollefson & Amy B.M. Tsui, eds., 2004). For a telling of the long-reach of state-sponsored historical trauma, *see* National Indian Child Welfare Association, *The Heart of ICWA: Becky*, YouTube (Dec. 7, 2016), [https://perma.cc/2QWZ-A6EH].

10. Between 50 and 60% of individuals experience trauma in their lifetime, but only 7–8% of the U.S. population develops PTSD. *How Common is PTSD?*, National Center for PTSD, Department of Veterans Affairs (May 29, 2015, 7:30 PM), [https://perma.cc/8GV2-MPM5]. "[P]osttraumatic syndrome is the result of a failure of time to heal all wounds. The memory of the trauma is not integrated and accepted as a part of one's personal past; instead, it comes to exist independently of previous schemata (i.e., it is dissociated)." Bessel A. Van Der Kolk & Alexander C. McFarlane, *The Black Hole of Trauma*, in Bessel A. Van der Kolk, Traumatic Stress: The Effects of Overwhelming Experience on Mind, Body and Society 7 (2007).

11. For a discussion of the diagnostic criteria used for PTSD under the DSM-5, comparing it to the earlier DSM-4, see Andrew P. Levin, et al, *DSM-5 and Posttraumatic Stress Disorder*, 42 J. Am. Acad. of Psychiatry Law 146 (2014), [https://perma.cc/5LSH-QWYW].

12. *Id.* at 152; *see also*, American Psychiatric Association. Diagnostic and Statistical Manual of Mental Disorders, Posttraumatic Stress Disorder for Children 6 Years and Younger (5th ed. 2013).

13. *PTSD for Children 6 Years and Younger*, U.S. Department of Veteran Affairs [https://perma.cc/K3ZN-TASP].

during childhood increased, so did the likelihood that the adult would suffer from a greater range of chronic physical and mental health conditions.[14]

> ### Reading the Story through the Trauma Lens
>
> *As you read the stories of Maya, her family, and friends ask yourself:*
>
> * *Are the traumas described acute or chronic, intergenerational or historical?*
>
> * *Has Maya experienced any protective factors?*
>
> * *What do you think a lawyer could do to advocate for conditions that would build upon these protective factors?*

Children whose brain development has been impacted by trauma or toxic levels of stress may manifest behaviors that challenge their caregivers and service providers. They may develop persistent fear responses leading to anxiety disorders, hyperarousal that interferes with their abilities to read verbal and nonverbal cues, and a weakened response to positive feedback.[15] Caregivers and service providers, including lawyers, should understand that young people in the child welfare system may not immediately respond as they expect or hope, and that building trust and establishing relationships will take time.

Resiliency and Growth in the Face of Traumatic or Stressful Events

While it is true that stress and trauma have the very serious potential to impact brain development,[16] not all children who experience adversity are plagued with a lifetime of mental and physical health issues.[17] Many, if not most, survivors of trauma develop adaptive or coping behaviors that help them to function well in the world.[18] In fact, it may be difficult at times to distinguish positive adaptive behaviors from the symptoms of PTSD.[19] In addition, positive growth and resilience may actually arise

---

14. *See Adverse Childhood Experiences Study (ACES),* THE CENTERS FOR DISEASE CONTROL, [https://perma.cc/4TD4-HUNY].

15. *See supra* note 1, at p. 9.

16. *See supra* note 1, at pp. 6–9.

17. "Simply put, highly adverse events that typically fall outside the range of normal everyday experience are 'potentially' traumatic because not everyone experiences them as traumatic. Research on PTEs (Potentially Traumatic Events) has consistently revealed a wide range of reactions; apart from a relatively finite subset of people who experience extreme distress, most people cope with such events extremely well." George A. Bonanno & Anthony D. Mancini, *The Human Capacity to Thrive in the Face of Potential Trauma,* 121 PEDIATRICS 2 (February 2008). [https://perma.cc/WF9E-36MG].

18. Scott D. Landes, et al, *Childhood Adversity, Midlife Generativity and Later Life Well-Being,* 69 J. GERONTOL. B. PSYCHOL. SCI. 942 (Nov. 2014); George A. Bonanno, *Resilience in the Face of Potential Trauma,* 14(3) CURRENT DIRECTIONS IN PSYCHOL. SCI. 135–138 (2005).

19. For example, maladaptive safety-seeking behaviors such as avoidance and disassociation may be difficult to distinguish from more adaptive coping behaviors such as positive distancing in which the survivor determines that focusing on traumatic events does not serve them in their current contexts. *See* Richard Thwaites & Mark H. Freeston, *Safety Seeking Behaviours: Fact or Function? How Can*

out of stressful and traumatic circumstances.[20] Advocates and other service providers bear the difficult task of being alert to evidence of trauma in the behavior of their clients while not immediately assuming that every child or youth in the system is suffering from PTSD or other mental health conditions. Pathologizing positive coping or normal adolescent behaviors will complicate the task of building a supportive and trusting relationship with a young person who has endured and is perhaps overcoming serious challenges.

Studies of resilience and the protective factors that support and nurture an individual's capacity to overcome are flourishing. The concept of "resilience" is distinguishable from the idea of "recovery." Resiliency studies examine how individuals manage to undergo traumatic events without developing a symptomatology from which they need to recover. Such studies look at protective factors that guard against the long-term effects of trauma.[21] An early research review found that "[t]he attributes of social competence, problem-solving skills, autonomy, and sense of purpose appear to be the common threads running through the personalities of resilient children."[22]

The Trauma Resilience Scale for Children is a tool used to identify a similar set of protective factors and its use has been validated in work with children in the foster care system. These factors include: self value; self regulation; optimism/motivating power; supportive belief structure; healthy caregiver/family support; supportive peer relationships; supported academic functioning; activity involvement; community safety/support; and actions taken to increase safety in reaction to a traumatic event.[23] While it may seem that the family circumstances of children in the dependency system are often dire, the strengths-based advocate will look for those relationships in

---

we Clinically Differentiate Adaptive Coping Strategies Across Anxiety Disorders?, 33(2) BEHAVIOURAL AND COGNITIVE PSYCHOTHERAPY 177–188 (April 2005).

20. George A. Bonanno, *Loss, Trauma, and Human Resilience: Have We Underestimated the Human Capacity to Thrive After Extremely Aversive Events?* S(1) PSYCHOL. TRAUMA: THEORY, RES., PRAC. AND POL'Y 101–113 (2008).

21. "The initial pioneering research on resilience in children suggested that there are multiple protective factors that might buffer against adversity, including person-centered variables (e.g. temperament) and sociocontextual factors (e.g. supportive relations, community resources)." Resilience does not result from any 1 dominant factor. George A. Bonanno & Anthony D. Mancini, *The Human Capacity to Thrive in the Face of Potential Trauma*, 121:2 PEDIATRICS 5 (February 2008). [https://perma.cc/V9TW-BWAW]. *See also*, Brian M. Iacoviello & Dennis S. Charney, *Psychosocial Facets of Resilience: Implications for Preventing Posttrauma Psychopathology, Treating Trauma Survivors, and Enhancing Community Resilience*, 5:10 EUROPEAN J. OF PSYCHOTRAUMATOLOGY 3402 (2014); Valerie A. Simon, *Positive and Negative Posttraumatic Change Following Childhood Sexual Abuse Are Associated with Youths' Adjustment*, 20 CHILD MALTREATMENT 278 (Nov. 2015).

22. Bonnie Benard, *Fostering Resiliency in the Family, School and Community,* (1991) [https://perma.cc/2QEX-JL9P].

23. Machelle D. Madson Thompson, Trauma Resilience Scale for Children: Validation of Protective Factors Associated with Positive Adaptation Following Violence, A Dissertation submitted to the College of Social Work in partial fulfillment of the requirements for the degree of Doctor of Philosophy, Fla. St. Univ., Degree Awarded: Fall Semester, 2010, [https://perma.cc/HWT4-P4A8].

the child's family or placement history that have offered the child opportunities for growing resilience in the face of challenge.

Finally, researchers have also identified the phenomenon of Posttraumatic Growth (PTG). PTG recognizes that those who have experienced trauma may actually also come to experience growth as a result of that trauma. PTG has been more robustly studied in the context of adults than children or youth. However, a growing body of literature shows that PTG does occur among adolescents.[24] The positive changes associated with PTG generally are identified as manifesting in perceiving new possibilities, changed relations with others, increased personal strength, enhanced appreciation for life, and spiritual change. The research so far does indicate, however, that the surfacing of PTG is more likely to occur in late adolescence and in those situations in which the trauma severity and symptoms are moderate.[25]

Maya's Story

The last time this happened, I was in Shirley's foster home.

Shirley said that I could stay there forever if I just acted right and at first I tried because the bed was so soft and warm, and Shirley smiled at me with all kinds of do-gooder promises and seemed to care. But then, like it always happens,[26] Shirley started getting all cranky, and bitching about the food that was missing from the refrigerator and asking so damn many questions about where I was all the time and why the school kept calling saying I wasn't there.[27] Shirley accused me of stealing food and said she had another girl like that before who hid food in her room, under the bed, in the drawers and closets[28] and that it just got all nasty and the food was wasted and they didn't pay

---

24. Joel E. Milam, *Posttraumatic Growth Among Adolescents*, 19 J. OF ADOLESC. RES. 192 (March 2004); David A. Meyerson, et al, *Posttraumatic Growth Among Children and Adolescents: A Systematic Review*, 31 CLIN. PSYCH. REV. 949 (Aug. 2011).

25. *Id.* (Meyerson et al.).

26. It is not unusual for a youth in foster care to experience multiple placements. One California study documented a range between one and fifteen placement changes during an 18-month period, with an average of just over four placement changes. The number of placements was found to contribute negatively to both internalizing and externalizing behavior disorders. In turn, these escalating behavior disorders contributed to escalating placement volatility. Rae R. Newton et al., *Children and Youth in Foster Care*, 24 CHILD ABUSE & NEGLECT 1363 (2000). Some advocates have sought to create an actionable substantive due process civil rights claim arising from the deleterious impact of multiple placements on the mental health of children and youth in the child welfare system. *See* Braam v. State of Washington, 81 P.3d 851 (Wash. 2003).

27. Youth entering foster care have significant truancy issues. In addition to school absences resulting from multiple placement moves caused by the foster care system itself, foster youth have higher rates of truancy than non-foster youth. NATIONAL WORKING GROUP ON FOSTER CARE AND EDUCATION, EDUCATION IS THE LIFELINE FOR YOUTH IN FOSTER CARE (2011), [https://perma.cc/AQ5K-YR34].

28. Food hoarding is common in severely neglected children. However, punishing children for this type of behavior or accusing them of stealing is likely to actually increase the sense of anxiety surrounding food and may escalate the behavior. It is important that foster parents be appropriately trained to recognize and understand these behaviors. *See* Bruce D. Perry, *Bonding and Attachment in*

her enough[29] to let all that happen to her food. Shirley used to tell me that I didn't have to do that, that if I didn't waste the food there would be food to eat every day.

But I wasn't hiding food back then. And I wasn't skipping school to do drugs like Shirley accused me of either, although sometimes I did smoke some weed, because well hell if you were me you would too, but still.[30] I was "stealing" the food (so much for "what's yours is mine") after Shirley went off to work. I would wrap it up in paper towels and stick it in my backpack. I had a metro bus pass for school but instead of getting on the bus heading to school, I'd go off in the other direction for downtown where I would go to the square and look for my mom. I would hear from my aunt that my mom was in a bad way and that she was downtown again living near the courthouse, all strung out. I would go find my mom, I would find her and look after her a bit. I would tell my mom, "Mom, it's me Maya, remember?" And then I would give her the food. Sometimes, she would recognize me and sometimes she wouldn't,

---

Maltreated Children: Consequences of Emotional Neglect in Childhood, 1 CTA PARENT AND CAREGIVER EDUC. SERIES (1999); Mark D. Simms, Howard Dubowitz & Moira A. Szilagyi, *Health Care Needs of Children in the Foster Care System*, 106 PEDIATRICS 909 (2000) (noting that the extreme behaviors of severely neglected children too often result in a succession of foster homes due to the challenges they pose to ill-prepared foster parents).

29. Maximum monthly TANF rates for a single parent with two children range from a low of $170.00 in Mississippi to a high of $923.00 in Alaska. All states paid less than half of the federal poverty level. The average monthly payment for all states is roughly $409.00. *See* GENE FAULK, , TEMPORARY ASSISTANCE FOR NEEDY FAMILIES (TANF): ELIGIBILITY AND BENEFIT AMOUNTS IN STATE TANF CASH ASSISTANCE PROGRAMS 7–8 (2014), Congressional Research Service, [https://perma.cc/TVG7 -TLJA]. The amount of TANF per child support declines with the number of children in the household, with the highest payment being made for the first child. By contrast, in foster care, the amount provided per child is unique to that child and is typically based on the child's age and level of special need. To highlight the difference in amounts received under TANF, one need only compare the maximum rate for two children in New Jersey, which is close to the national average, for TANF ($424.00) with the maximum amount received for foster care payments for two children ($2463.60). Even at the lowest level of need (for two healthy children under five years of age), the amount is $1412.40, more than three times that of TANF. *See, New Jersey Profile*, CHILD TRENDS, CASEY CHILD WELFARE FINANCING SURVEY: FAMILY FOSTER CARE PROVIDER CLASSIFICATION AND RATES, [https:// perma.cc/U448-HEX8]. For a more in-depth look at how each state classifies their rates of foster care payments, see KERRY DEVOOGHT & DENNIS BLAZEY, CHILD TRENDS, FAMILY FOSTER CARE REIMBURSEMENT RATES IN THE U.S.: A REPORT FROM A 2012 NATIONAL SURVEY ON FAMILY FOSTER CARE PROVIDER CLASSIFICATIONS AND RATES § 4: Appendix: Attachments to State Profiles (2013), [https:// perma.cc/9LUT-9PD3].

30. A study of 90% of 17-year olds in foster care (406 youth) in Pennsylvania found that 45% had used alcohol or illicit drugs during the 6 months prior to the interview, 49% had tried drugs or alcohol sometime during their lives and 35% met the criteria for a substance abuse disorder. While the rate of overall use did not differ significantly from those in the general population, the rate meeting the substance abuse disorder criteria was significantly higher. Youth in congregate care and other more independent living situations were found to have significantly higher use, and those with a post-traumatic stress disorder were found to have significantly higher rates of poly-substance use. Marijuana was the most prevalent illicit drug to have been reported both in the recent use and lifetime use categories. *See* Michael G. Vaughn et al, *Substance Use and Abuse Among Older Youth in Foster Care*, 32 ADDICTIVE BEHAV. 1929 (2007) [https://perma.cc/VM49-V2BE].

but no matter what I would still give her the food. She was always my mom. No matter what.

It wasn't always like this, living in strangers' homes, chasing my mom down whenever I could find her. There were times way early on with my mom, I think, that were different. I think I remember the smell of her then, clean and fresh, her arms hugging me when I fell down maybe. Grandma used to tell me stories about that different time, before mom went crazy and took too many drugs to make the voices go away. Grandma told me that she knew my mom loved me from the start and for always and that she had tried real hard to be a good mom to me. She said she even tried to do it on her own but she needed help and she wouldn't always let grandma and Aunt Hen help her. I guess this is why for the longest time I kept on looking for her, bringing her food, trying to coax her out of whatever bad place she was stuck in. But I have given up on that. For now anyway. I got my own business to look after.

At first, when they took me and Jazz away from mom, I got to stay with grandma.[31] And that wasn't so bad since we had spent a lot of time with her anyway when we were wee little. But my big sister, Jazz, wasn't with me after they took us[32] and I don't know why. I never saw her again. And then grandma got sick and couldn't take care of me anymore. It was scary when I came home from school and there she was all laid out on the kitchen floor. I thought she was dead but I called 911 because I knew to do that and then they showed up and they said she was alive but she had a stroke and it was a very good thing I came home when I did and called. I felt proud right then, like I had saved her life, but scared too because it didn't look like she was doing too good. Then when I got to the hospital the CPS lady came and then I started all over again in foster care.

I don't even know where my grandma is anymore. I know she made it through the stroke and then she went to a nursing home. Would they let her die and not even tell me? Maybe she died and they forgot to tell me. Maybe they don't even know she's dead. Things get lost. People get lost. A case worker told me once they cut off my mom's rights, just like that. Nobody asked me what I thought about it, but maybe I was too little to have a say.[33] Maybe that means my grandma's rights were cut off too? I don't know how CPS thinks about those things. None of it makes any sense to me. Whether my mom and grandma had rights to me or didn't, CPS took me away from them both

---

31. Relative placements are to be given preference under federal law. *See* 42 U.S.C.A. §671 (19).

32. Despite the fact that most children enter foster care at the same time as their siblings, many siblings are separated from one another once they enter care. This is true, even though the research shows that children placed alone have a higher rate of placement disruption than those placed with their siblings and that those who are placed with their siblings achieve permanency at a higher rate than those placed alone. *See* Sonya J. Leathers, *Separation from Siblings: Associations with Placement Adaptation and Outcomes among Adolescents in Long-term Foster Care*, 27 CHILD. AND YOUTH SERV. REV 793 (2005); Mary Anne Herrick & Wendy Piccus, *Sibling Connections: The Importance of Nurturing Sibling Bonds in the Foster Care System*, 27 CHILD AND YOUTH SERV. REV. 845 (2005).

33. For a discussion of the timing and requirements for terminating parental rights, see ch. 1, *ASFA: Seeking to Balance Permanence and Reunification*.

and CPS got to say whether I saw them or not. Seems like CPS has always had all the rights.

For some reason, they wouldn't let me stay with my aunt either, but Aunt Hen almost always found a way to stay in touch, which was cool. She always seemed to know where my mom was and then she would let me know. Mostly when my mom surfaced, she surfaced downtown at the square. But if I couldn't find her there, I would walk around under the highway overpass and look there too. That was the place where everyone would go to shoot up or sleep; and if I didn't find her there I would come back to the square and sit on a bench keeping a look-out, trying to avoid looking at the crazy guy who shouted shit at me and the slimy guy who told me I could score some if I did him "a favor," and the woman with the meth sores and the wrinkly skin that made her look really old,[34] kinda like my mom looks way old, like she could be my grandma. Sometimes I would look at those faces for Jazz too, just in case. 'Cause she might be there too. She's old enough to be out on her own now. You never know.

I used to sit there on the bench and wait and wait until I got tired enough of waiting and hungry enough myself, and then I would eat some of the food and leave the rest there. The pigeons could eat it then, for all I cared, or the woman in the wheel chair or maybe even that woman's dog, the scraggly one with the American flag bandana tied around its neck.

Anyway, when this happened before, when I was 14 and staying with Shirley, I told Shirley I was pregnant and she had a fit.[35] She hollered and screamed and called me a little whore. She demanded to know who the father was and when I told her that was none of her damn business, the only thing Shirley really wanted to know was how old he was. When I told her he was in high school, Shirley looked all relieved. That's when I realized that Shirley probably thought it was the guy that she had been dating. She probably saw the way he looked at me but didn't want to admit it. Not that he hadn't tried to get with me, but I hated that guy, acting like he was some sort of hero

---

34. To learn more about the physical and mental effects of meth, see *How Meth Destroys the Body*, PBS Frontline, [https://perma.cc/RYF3-RKTB].

35. Sexual abuse histories place adolescents at greater risk of teen pregnancy. In this study, two-thirds of the sample of 535 young women who became pregnant as adolescents had been sexually abused earlier in their history. *See* Debra Boyer & David Fine, *Sexual Abuse as a Factor in Adolescent Pregnancy and Child Maltreatment*, 24 Fam. Plan. Perspectives 4 (1992). For girls in the child welfare system, the risk of teen pregnancy is twice that of girls in in-home care. Girls in state care are three times as likely to carry their pregnancies to term than those in the general population where the abortion rate is over three times higher. *See* Mark E. Courtney et al., *Midwest Evaluation of the Adult Functioning of Former Foster Youth: Outcomes at Ages 23 and 24*, Chapin Hall U. Chi. (2010), [https://perma.cc/FS8W-77KH]. A California study found that for those girls in foster care who gave birth before age eighteen, more than one in three had a second teen birth. This study also found that the first birth rate was twice as high for girls who had runaway than for those who had exited care via adoption or guardianship. *See* Emily Putnam-Hornstein, et al., California's Most Vulnerable Parents: When Maltreated Children Have Children (2013), [https://perma.cc/58GF-JPCH]. For a discussion of the rights of foster youth to reproductive health and prenatal care, see Katherine Moore, *Pregnant in Foster Care: Prenatal Care, Abortion, and the Consequences for Foster Families*, 23 Colum. J. Gender & L. 29 (2012).

around Shirley and then getting all up in my space and weird with his hugs when Shirley wasn't around. At least, back in the day, before they took us away, my mom's boyfriends were always straight up about what they wanted, and didn't pretend to be all about being someone there to help us out. They wanted to sell crank and they wanted to buy crank and they wanted to be cranked, if you know what I mean. Jazz was always in trouble that way because mom wasn't always paying attention and mom could get pretty desperate for the stuff herself and I could see them looking at me like I was next. It's an ugly thing seeing that happen to your mom, your sister, knowing that you're next in line. There weren't enough places to hide.[36] Shirley's boyfriend looked at me sometimes that way too, like he was coming for me eventually. But, no way was I going to let that happen. I was bigger by then, and I would have kicked the shit out of him.

Shirley told me that no matter who the father was — and she really didn't want to know — I still was going to have to get an abortion and she would help me get one and that no one needed to know, not even the caseworker.[37] Shirley told me if I thought I was going to be able to keep that baby I had another think coming, that even if I had that baby they would only take it away and I would wind up living in some group home after the baby was born and the baby would be adopted by somebody else, by good people who wouldn't ever let me see my baby.[38] When I think of it now, I realize that Shirley was just worried about her own reputation. She didn't want to get in trouble for letting me get pregnant. She convinced me not to tell anybody, not even my boyfriend. I broke up with him eventually anyway because he was messing with other girls. I don't think he would have wanted to be a daddy anyway.

---

36. While neglect remains the overall most prevalent form of maltreatment for youth (whether male or female) entering the child welfare system, neglect may also be the underlying condition that allows for abuse to occur, specifically sexual abuse. Girls in the child welfare system are 1.3 times more likely to have been victims of abuse than are boys, primarily because of the higher rate of sexual abuse experienced by girls. If one looks to data outside of the child welfare system, one finds that 59% of juvenile victims of violent offenses are girls, and that of these victims 72% had experienced sexual assaults. These high rates of victimization do not take into account the witnessing of violence against other family members, whether siblings or parents, that many youth who enter into the child welfare system have experienced. These high rates of both experiencing and witnessing violence, particularly sexual violence, lead to concomitantly high rates of depression and post-traumatic stress disorder (PTSD) among girls in the child welfare system. *See* Karen Baynes-Dunning & Karen Worthington, *Responding to the Needs of Adolescent Girls in Foster Care*, 20 GEO. J. ON POVERTY L. & POL'Y 321 (2013).

37. Minors' access to abortion and requirements for a parental figure's involvement varies from state to state. *See supra* ch. 1, n.2.

38. Teens who seek to parent in foster care are met with many challenges. While arguably both constitutional and federal statutes protect their right to parent their children, the challenges of foster care licensing and placement serve as barriers to keeping young mothers in foster care in placements together with their children. The fact that foster youth as teen parents are continually under the supervision of the state also means that they are more vulnerable to being separated from their children due to alleged maltreatment. *See* Eve Stotland & Cynthia Godsoe, *The Legal Status of Pregnant and Parenting Youth in Foster Care*, 17 U. FLA. J.L. & PUB. POL'Y 1 (2006).

I got that abortion, but afterwards I had nightmares and felt scared all the time.[39] Even when I was awake, the dreams stayed with me.[40] The nightmares weren't really about the abortion; I don't even remember the abortion that much. I just remember it was cold. The table was cold and I was cold and I hated the way my legs were up and I was cut off from everything. The nightmares, though, were hot and sweaty; they were about being suffocated by men whose faces I never saw. They were about the tastes and sounds and smell of sex and I kept waking up with cramps. I couldn't tell anybody what I had done or about the nightmares, but I thought that telling my mom would be like telling nobody because she would just sit there and maybe she would be too strung out to say anything and that would be good. I just needed to tell someone and then maybe the nightmares would stop.

I did find my mom that day but of all days for her to be able to hear and understand what I said, it had to be that day and after my mom ate the food I had brought and heard what I had done and about the nightmares, I sat there all wiped out and almost crying, even though crying is not something I do.[41] My mom shook her head at me, the white cream from the Twinkie she had just finished still smeared at the corners of her mouth, the Twinkie that I had given her from Shirley's kitchen cabinet, and then she said, "They say I'm a shitty mother? But I didn't kill you, did I?"

I ran away.[42]

I ran away from my mom. I ran away from Shirley. I went to Aunt Hen's[43] and she was so sweet to me. She let me take a really long bath. She fed me such good food. She even fixed my hair all up in braids just like her little girls. I know it looked kind of funny, a white girl trying to be black or something. But I wanted beaded, braided hair just like theirs that flopped around when they ran. I wanted to be little like them and start all over. My hair wasn't quite long enough; so she did corn rows with little braids

---

39. Many studies have looked at whether teenagers who choose abortion in the face of unwanted pregnancy suffer psychologically as a result of the abortion itself. Most studies show that they do not suffer ill effects and in fact that they fare better than their peers who choose to give birth to a child. However, most of these studies also note that those teens who have access to abortion tend to come from socio-economic classes that already place them on a better position than girls like Maya in the child welfare system. Laurence Steinberg, Adolescence 373–374 (10th ed. 2014). In addition, these studies look at teens who freely choose abortion rather than those, like Maya, who are pressured into it by adults with their own motives of self-protection.

40. Nightmares and intrusive thoughts are characteristic of PTSD. See National Institute of Mental Health, U.S. Dep't of Health and Human Servs., Post-Traumatic Stress Disorder (PTSD) (n.d.), [https://perma.cc/4W5D-66X9].

41. Among the typical avoidance symptoms of PTSD is the feeling of emotional numbness. See id.

42. Children in foster care are twice as likely as children in the general population to run away. The percentage of children in the foster care system who are counted as missing due to run at any given moment is relatively small, around 2%. However, the percentage of youth who are missing from care more than doubles if the teenage population is isolated. The reasons youth run away from care vary greatly but it is often a reaction to feeling angry and upset, and is a way of exerting control over their lives. See Jennifer Michael, Children Missing from Care, Child Welfare League of America (Oct. 10, 2005), [https://perma.cc/T2VN-YCC5].

43. Often, youth running from foster care run to relatives and family. Id.

with one bead where the rows ended. The beads kept wanting to slip off but she fixed them with rubber bands so that they wouldn't. As she fixed my hair, just as I was feeling all of the nightmares fall away from me like I had washed them away in that bubble bath, she told me that we would probably have to tell CPS where I was because I need to go to school and she knew that if she tried to send me to school they would want to know where I came from. Even if she tried to tell them that I was her niece and my mom had asked her to take care of me, they would probably look at her like she was crazy and ask for proof. It's true she is a different color but she is still my aunt. I tried to convince Uncle Marcus when he got home, but he said I had to listen to my aunt, that she was right. The next morning, I got up before everyone else and I disappeared.

I disappeared for two weeks. I liked disappearing. I live on the streets and do what I have to do to survive.[44] I am good at disappearing and surviving.[45] The sidewalks are hard to sleep on though; and so I wound up in a shelter one night; it felt so good just to be able to sleep warm that I stayed two nights and that was my mistake because then they had to report me[46] and so I was found. I was brought back. I did time in juvie and was supposed to be writing a stupid essay about why I ran away and how I would never do it again[47] but I refused because whatever I

---

44. Homeless youth are at substantially higher risk of sexual exploitation, physical abuse, substance abuse, mental illness and death. It is estimated that as many as 5,000 unaccompanied youth die each year while on the streets. In order to survive, youth on streets are at high risk of exchanging sex for food, clothing and shelter. They are also at higher risk of dealing drugs in order to meet basic needs. It is estimated that 75% of runaway youth are girls, and studies report that, of these runaway girls, anywhere from between 6% and 22% are pregnant. *See Homeless and Runaway Youth*, NATIONAL CONFERENCE OF STATE LEGISLATURES (Oct. 1, 2013), [https://perma.cc/79KE-VSPA].

45. For video and written interviews of youth who are surviving and invisible on the streets and parks of our cities, see *Recession Drives Surge in Youth Runaways*, N.Y. TIMES, Oct. 25, 2009), https://www.nytimes.com/2009/10/26/us/26runaway.html?_r=0.

46. In order for programs to seek federal monies to fund shelters and services for homeless youth, federal law requires that such programs have in place "adequate plans for contacting the parents or other relatives of the youth and ensuring the safe return of the youth according to the best interests of the youth, for contacting local government officials pursuant to informal arrangements established with such officials by the runaway and homeless youth center, and for providing for other appropriate alternative living arrangements." 42 U.S.C. §5712. Some states have enacted statutes requiring that shelters notify the youth's parents or custodians within a certain period of time of admission into the shelter. *See, e.g.,* CAL. FAM. CODE §6924(b); COLO. REV. STAT. §26-5.7-106; WASH. REV. CODE 13.32A.082-90; ILL. ADMIN. CODE tit. 89 §410.210. Indeed, some states criminalize providing shelter to a minor without parental consent. *See, e.g.,* FLA. STAT. §984.085; UTAH CODE ANN. §62A-4a-501; WASH. REV. CODE 13.32A.080.

47. Some states use civil contempt proceedings to hold youth accountable for running away from their placements in violation of the court orders that govern where they are to live. *See*, Coalition for Juvenile Justice: SOS Project, *Use of the Valid Court Order*, [https://perma.cc/N73V-B329]. In civil contempt, a motion is typically brought alleging that the respondent has willfully violated the court's order. If the youth is found to be in contempt, the court may order the youth to be held in detention. Research has shown that girls generally are more likely to be held in contempt for violation of court orders than are boys, and that girls who run from foster placements are more likely to enter the juvenile detention system through contempt for running away than are boys. *See*, Francine T. Sherman,

would say would be lies anyway and honestly I don't mind detention. It is better than living with confusing people who are supposed to act like family but they aren't and every one of them has their own set of rules and weird food, and a different kind of bed. After a while, you just don't take your stuff out of the black trash bag they move you with. What's the point? If they would just let me stay with Aunt Hen it might be different.

But then they let me out of juvie, because they couldn't keep me there forever (that's the one thing I remember from what my lawyer said) and they put me in a group home called Phoenix and there were lots of rules there. There was this big board with everyone's name on it and next to everyone's names were the stars that you earned for making your beds and going to meetings. The stars could be taken away for doing bad stuff like getting into fights or screaming at a staff person; and you have to have a certain number of stars for a certain period of time before they let you do just the most simple things like go to the school in the neighborhood instead of the school in the group home. And you had to go to group therapy; you got stars for doing that and more stars were added if you talked about all the bad shit that had happened to you and how it made you do the weird shit you do now and it was all such a big fat crock of shit that when I finally did earn enough stars to step out the door, I left and I promised myself that I was never going back.[48]

I avoid my mom now though; I live on different streets in a different part of the city, away from the old sick crazy people. I don't hate my mom. I get that she's sick, but I've decided I just can't be around her anymore. Sometimes I tell myself that I am through with her, but sometimes I think that she is always my mom, no matter what CPS says, and so I will never really be through with her.

On my streets, everyone creates their own families and, just like in the real world, each family is different. Some of them are mean and some of them are nice. Some of them have no rules and some of them are so straight edge they have almost as many rules as the group home. Most of those strict families didn't want anything to do with me when I first showed up, they avoided me because I was too young, only fifteen, and they didn't want to get in trouble.

My last run taught me what to avoid—Aunt Hen and the shelters. You can stop by at a shelter, get something to eat, maybe some clothes, but you better not stay too long or they have to report you. Not that the shelters really want to get you in trouble; they even say they are sorry when the police show up, but the truth is most people care

---

Justice for Girls: Are We Making Progress?, 59 UCLA L. Rev. 1584, 1600-1602 (2012). In civil contempt proceedings, those found to be in contempt may "purge" themselves of contempt and be released if they satisfy the court's conditions. The terms of the conditions are discretionary with the court, and a common practice for the court described in this narrative is to assign the youth to write an essay addressing the dangers of running away. *See,* Gerard Glynn, *Contempt: The Untapped Power of the Juvenile Court,* 15 Fla. Coastal L. Rev. 197 (2014).

48. One study found that youth who are placed in stable, family-like settings are less likely to run away from placement than those who are placed in group care. Brea L. Perry, *Understanding Social Network Disruption: The Case of Youth in Foster Care* 53 Social Problems 371, 373–374 (2006).

more about their own survival than yours. Sometimes you get a shelter social worker who looks the other way, but that doesn't last for long. No one wants to lose their job for you.

Eventually, this time around I found my family with my boyfriend, Diamond; he says he will always take care of me, but I want to pull my own weight. At first, I did pretty well with the spare-changing and then when that wasn't enough, I started making better cash for us both.[49] I mean, it isn't the first time I thought about doing it. I heard another girl talking about it at my old group home. She said it isn't so bad and you can make some good money. She tried to get me to head out with her, but I wasn't into it then.[50] Turns out she is right about the money though. Diamond and me do pretty good most of the time.

The nightmares have come back again, but as long as I stay awake, I don't have them. When bad shit goes down, I just disappear. It's a magic trick I play with myself. Now *you* see me; now *I* don't. Sometimes, when I come out of it, I realize I am just sucking my thumb like a little baby, but some of the guys, they even seem to like that. They think that's part of my thing. Repeat guys ask me to do it sometimes. That's even weirder, and I really wish I could kick the shit out of them, but I don't.[51]

I haven't told Di what I suspect, that maybe I am pregnant, because I'm pretty sure he will get mad. Lately when he gets mad, he turns nasty. But it's not his fault; he's under a lot of pressure all of the time. He has a lot of promises to keep. So don't get me wrong; he can also be really sweet. Sometimes he will take me out on a special date, just the two of us; he'll get me something really fine at one of the cool vintage stores with some big jewelry and new makeup and once even a wig. I get all dressed up and it's like a costume party almost. I am someone else and he is someone else and we go to a restaurant where people wait on us like they see us for real and then we stay at a pretty nice hotel. But those days are probably gone if I'm right about this. I'm not even sure who the daddy might be. It could be Di. It could be anyone he set me up with. Di will say it's my fault, that I should be more careful. They always

---

49. Prostitution as a gendered survival strategy is discussed at length in Melissa Farley, *Prostitution, Trafficking and Cultural Amnesia: What We Must Know in Order to Keep the Business of Sexual Exploitation Running Smoothly,* 18 Yale J.L. & Feminism 109 (2006).

50. Girls in foster care, especially in group home settings, appear to be at increased risk for recruitment into sex work. The idea is often first introduced by a peer who has had some experience herself. Wendy L. Macias-Konstantopoulos, et al., *The Commercial Sexual Exploitation and Sex Trafficking of Minors in the Boston Metropolitan Area: Experiences and Challenges Faced by Front-Line Providers and Other Stakeholders*, 6:1 J. Of App. Res. On Children: Informing Policy for Children at Risk 9 (2015) [https://perma.cc/XT9M-AHD2].

51. Disassociation while "turning tricks" and other symptoms of PTSD are reportedly common among women and girls engaging in prostitution. *Id* at 116–17. *See also,* Bessel A. van der Kolk, Traumatic stress: The Effects of Overwhelming Experience on Mind, Body and Experience, 191 (2007) ("Many traumatized children, and adults who were traumatized as children, have noted that when they are under stress they can make themselves 'disappear.' That is, they can watch what is going on from a distance while having a sense that what is occurring is not really happening to them, but to someone else.").

promise to use condoms but sometimes they don't and what can you do about that in the moment? Not a whole hell of a lot. He will probably want me to get an abortion too. He will be mad about having to pay for it. I know he doesn't want to be taking care of a baby, especially when it's probably not even his. But I don't want to do that again.

I did tell Kiki. I tell Kiki everything. We go way back. I met her the first time I ran. We met at the drop-in shelter, the one that called me in. She was lucky. When they checked on her, there wasn't anybody looking for her and so she wasn't on the list. So they could just let her stay. She has been on her own for a pretty long time and we both use the drop-in shelter as a place to clean up and check our email. I don't like to write stuff so much but I do email her. Otherwise, I don't pay much attention to it. We stayed friends, even after I was picked up and I was put in the Phoenix. When I ran the second time, she was the only one who knew I was heading out. She tried to warn me off Diamond at first, but then I think even she saw that he isn't so bad. At least she stopped giving me a hard time about him. It's like we both decided that being friends was more important than what goes on with the guys on the street. She has her street family she can't really leave. I have mine now too, but we still stay friends. We watch out for each other.

It's crazy how much Kiki and I have in common, but she's never been in foster care. I don't get how that happens. But even if the staff called CPS on her, she would be gone before they ever showed. She's just that smart. Anyway, when I told her about my situation she said I should go to this clinic and have them test, but it was the same place I went before for the abortion and I just don't want to go there again. Maybe I should listen to her though. I probably should listen to her about a lot of things.

Anyway, I should have been more careful when I walked into the store last week. I could feel the security guy watching me. They always do. They know who the street kids are. They see us on the sidewalk. And even if he hadn't seen me before he would have probably known somehow, maybe by the way I walk or look or the fact that I always pay with change. I don't look like the regular high school kids who come in laughing about whatever happened at school and whip out their parent's credit card to pay. At least, I don't feel like I do. So I knew it would be risky and I went extra careful down the aisles trying to pay attention to when people were watching and trying to look like I wasn't paying any attention at all and was just interested in shopping. It's not easy to pull that off—paying attention and not paying attention all at the same time. I had a basket. I put a few things in it: a pack of gum, a small bag of chips, a can of soda. I had some money. But what I was really there for I slipped in the big front pocket of my hoodie. It wasn't a big thing. No one could see it there. But it cost more money than I had. I went to the counter and paid for the things in my basket. I was walking out the door and the security guy stopped me. I tried to push past him and he stepped out in front of me, blocking me against the store out on the sidewalk.

When he backed me against the wall like that, fast and taking me by surprise, something happened inside me then—I don't know what, but it has happened before that feeling—and I almost blacked out.[52] I felt my fist hit him in the chest before I lost track of where I was. I thought I hit him hard, but it must not have been that bad because when I came back to myself I was inside the store, sitting in a chair in the back office with my head on the desk, and he was there all fine like nothing had happened.

"You a cop?" I ask and when I speak the fog in my head starts to clear away.

"No, store security. Can I see what's in your front pocket, please?"

"If you ain't a cop, I don't need to listen to you, do I?" I was feeling better now, ready to argue, ready to figure a way out of this situation.

He sighs, not looking mad, not looking frustrated, almost looking bored, like he's done this a million times before. "OK, if that's the way you want to do it." He reaches for the phone on the desk.

I try to get up and run but I am slow and he reaches across his desk and grabs the hood of my sweatshirt before I even make it all the way out of the chair. Pretty lame effort, but I'm not quite back to myself yet.

I listen to him call the police; he doesn't mention that I hit him, just that I was shoplifting. He is a softy; maybe I can talk him out of making me wait for the police to come and so I hand him what was in my pocket. And there it is: the pregnancy test. I look him right in his face and say, "Come on, give me a break. You can have the damn thing back. I already know I am anyway."

But he just looks away. Shakes his head. Too late now. He's already called them.

The police arrive; they ask my name. I tell them my name is Blossom. When they ask for my last name, I act like I don't even hear the question. The cop says, "If you let us reach your parents and if they come get you, this could end here. Looks like with what you took there, you might need your parents."

They are so clueless I want to scream. But I don't. I lost my screaming voice a long time ago.

I tell them my mom's name is Chicken and I tell them that I had no idea where she is but that I am pretty sure she doesn't have any phone for them to call. All of that is true but they look at me like I am high or a liar or telling some kind of bad joke because who has a mom named Chicken? Well, I do. At least that's what everybody calls her. There are more big sighs and shrugging, but finally they take me to juvie and

---

52. Freeze, flight, fight, fright are characteristic responses to the hyper-vigilance that often accompanies PTSD symptomatology. During acute experiences, "tonic immobility" or fainting may also result. *See* H. Stefan Bracha, *Freeze, Flight, Fight, Fright, Faint: Adaptationist Perspectives on the Acute Stress Response Spectrum*, 9 CNS Spectrums 679 (2004). *See also*, Bessel van der Kolk, *The Body Keeps the Score: Memory and the Evolving Psychobiology of Post-Traumatic Stress*, Harv. Rev. of Psychiatry 5 (Jan.-Feb. 1994) ("Instead of using feelings as cues to attend to incoming information, in people with PTSD arousal is likely to precipitate flight or fight reactions. Thus, they are prone to go immediately from stimulus to response without first making the necessary psychological assessment of the meaning of what is going on.").

when I show up there, I really just want it all to end and I let the people behind the desk figure out who I am. They tell me I have a pick-up order out on me, which means they have to hold me until I see the judge because I ran away from the group home. I feel a funny moment of something like pride for being WANTED. Not wanted like your grandma wants you or your aunt wants you or even your high, crazy mother wants you, but WANTED like the Top Ten Most Dangerous Criminals are WANTED.

They tell me they are going to call my caseworker and my lawyer to let them know I am here. I think it's kind of weird. Before, when they thought I was a regular kid, the police just wanted to call my parents and send me home. Other kids must get in trouble and have their parents come get them or something.[53] But me, my parents are like my caseworker and my lawyer. And I don't even know their names. It's been awhile since I've seen either of them, and they always seem to be changing. The lawyer I had last time got me out of juvie but I really didn't so much want to get out and go to that group home. So thanks a lot. Honestly, I don't even care who these people are. They all say they are on my side, but it sure doesn't seem like it. I don't think anyone is really on my side. And besides—if they are on my side, who is on the other side? Not my mom, because they kicked her out of my case I think and even if she were on the other side, I think I'd rather be on her side than theirs.[54]At least I know *her* name and I know she *wants* to be a good mother, even if she's not. Right then, I promise myself that this will never happen to my baby. I will be there to bail my baby out.

> ### *Required Lawyering Skills*
> *Now that you have heard Maya's story, you have heard more than her lawyer is likely to learn.*
> - *What do you hope the lawyer will find out?*
> - *Why is it important that the lawyer discover the things you have identified?*
> - *What are the lawyering skills and practice conditions necessary for these things to be learned?*
> - *What does it mean for the way you approach this practice that there are aspects of your client's story that you will never know?*

---

53. Denise C. Herz, et al, *Challenges Facing Crossover Youth: An Examination of Juvenile Justice Decision-Making and Recidivism*, 48 Fam. Ct. Rev. 305 (Apr. 2010) (noting that when young people from the child welfare system cross-over into the delinquency system, they tend to stay longer and penetrate deeper into the juvenile justice system than their non-child welfare involved peers); *Also see supra* ch. 1, n.188.

54. "Another confusing and upsetting experience for children . . . is the legal termination of parental rights. . . . [T]hey are confronted with the full impact of this loss. . . . This is occasion for intense grieving even for the most reluctant grievers among children in placement." Crenshaw & Hardy, *Understanding and Treating, supra* n. 6 at 174.

Maya's Friend: Kiki's Story

I'm Kiki. Just Kiki. And, no, it's not my *real* name, but it's my street name and it's been my name so long now that I don't even think of myself any other way. I took it from this movie I saw when I was little and at a friend's house. It was one of those anime movies where the characters all have big eyes and their expressions are always either really happy or really sad or really shocked. They are always *really* something. Kiki is a witch, but not a bad scary witch; she's a little girl witch with a big red bow in her hair, but before she can become a grown-up witch she has to be on her own for a whole year. She does some pretty cool things to survive, and because she can fly on her broom she starts her own delivery service.

So it was only natural that when I wound up doing what I do and someone asked me my name, Kiki was what came out of my mouth. I don't think the guy got the joke at all; maybe he did, some potheads like that kind of stuff, but anyway it made me smile when I said it and I have been running my own little Kiki's Delivery Service[55] ever since. Kinda funny because I don't look Japanese at all, but then again, neither does the cartoon Kiki.

When I met Maya the first time, we became friends really fast.[56] She reminds me of myself when I first ran away, excited and scared all at the same time. So happy to be free one minute and so miserable the next. It wasn't long, though, before the shelter turned her in. I tried to tell her about how all that worked, that if she showed up when they looked in the computer for her name, she would wind up with a call being made. I told her she should come up with her own name, like I did, and just use that.[57] When I have to use a last name, I come up with different ones, depending on my mood. I have always been good with stuff like that. Making shit up fast. Maya . . . not so much. She is always good with numbers. She remembers shit like addresses and phone numbers and all that. Could be really handy in the delivery service. But she just doesn't have any imagination. She says she has always been Maya and doesn't know how to be anybody else. I asked her whether there was anybody else she ever wanted to be when she was little. She said she wanted to be Hannah Montana[58] because then she could have a secret life that no one knew about and she could be a

---

55. *See* KIKI's DELIVERY SERVICE (Studio Ghibli 1989).

56. For a study of the impact of female friendships on criminal activity, see Bill McCarthy, Diane Felmlee & John Hagan, *Girl Friends are Better: Gender, Friends, and Crime Among School and Street Youth*, 42 CRIMINOLOGY 805 (2004). *Accord*, Dana L. Haynie et al., *Gender, Friendship Networks, and Delinquency: A Dynamic Network Approach*, 52 CRIMINOLOGY 688 (2014).

57. For an example of one shelter's intake procedures and policies with respect to the use of street names, aliases and actual birth names, see *Runaway & Homeless Youth Program Intake Procedures*, ATTENTIONHOMES.COM, [https://perma.cc/6QCZ-W3Z9] (providing that youth may sign in with street names for drop-in but for overnight stays, youth must provide birth names, parent names and contact information).

58. Hannah Montana was a series on the Disney Channel in which Miley Cyrus played a "typical teen" with a secret life as a "world famous pop star." *See Hannah Montana*, DISNEY CHANNEL, [https://perma.cc/ELT8-6X7V].

rich rock star and live in a fancy beach house where it is always sunny. I told her that was pretty lame and they would know that was made up if she signed in as Hannah Montana. I still call her Hannah sometimes when she's doing something dumb. It makes her laugh.

It took us a while to come up with a better idea. I told her she looked like Blossom, the orange-hair Powerpuff[59] girl? She said she hadn't ever seen that show, which I couldn't believe, I mean how could you not know about the Powerpuff Girls? They're so awesome. I guess I spent more time whenever I could at other kid's houses watching TV, trying not to be too much trouble, trying to eat their food and have a pretend normal life. She said her grandma didn't have a TV but she sometimes watched the Disney Channel at her aunt's house because they had cable. I told her she should have watched Powerpuff Girls instead. I told her about how Blossom is the coolest of the three Powerpuff Girls because she is the leader and even though she is "everything nice" she is also really strong and smart and always has her shit together. Maya liked that and she thought the name was pretty cool too. She tries to use it, but she keeps forgetting and saying "Maya" when people ask her.

She isn't like me. We've been through a lot of the same shit, that's for sure, but I so wanted to leave my old life behind when I ran away. Start over. Don't look back. That's what I say. I think foster care fucked Maya up because she is always trying to figure out ways to get back with her family. Me, I *know* my family is messed up. That's why I left. Nobody ever tried to rescue me or put me in foster care. And once I was gone, no one came looking for me. That's fine. I prefer it that way. I have my own life now, and its better here than it was with them. I was pretty much on my own anyway, trying to stay out of sight so as not to get beat or worse. Hell, I'd a starved to death if I didn't figure out how to take care of myself even then. Might as well go my own way.

> ### *Comparing Maya and Kiki*
> *Maya entered the child welfare system while Kiki did not.*
> - *Consider the factors that might lead one child to end up in state-supervised care while the other does not.*
> - *What difference does it make that Maya entered the state system and Kiki did not?*

After they picked her up, Maya wound up in some group home and hated it. Of course. I could have told her that. So then she kept emailing me and I told her she could come out and hang with us for a while if she wanted. She finally worked her way out of there and stayed with us. I tried to get her into my little delivery service. It's no big drug thing. It was just me and a few friends buying and selling weed. But

---

59. *See The Powerpuff Girls*, CARTOON NETWORK, [https://perma.cc/K2TJ-GBSD].

still, she was like, "I'll smoke some if you got it, but I don't want to sell it." She has a thing against "drug dealers." I tell her that the pot people aren't the same as the meth people or the heroin people but she says she doesn't want to have anything to do with any "drug dealers." I know how she feels about that and I don't blame her. I get it, but still you can avoid them if you're careful. Believe me, I have had enough of that shit in my life too. You just have to know who to work with is all. Some people are safer than others.

She wound up taking up with Diamond instead. Now there's a lame street name. If that doesn't shout "PIMP" I don't know what does. Him with his stupid tear drop tats, all trying to look sensitive or like he's the victim of some tragedy. Bull shit. But she can't see it. She thinks he is crushing on her. He is cute though if you look past what he does, younger than most. Not like some of 'em, who are just old, mean and ugly. Diamond's kind of like a wanna-be pimp, just learning the ropes. That's probably why he has such a dumb street name. He hasn't hit his stride yet. She says he never done anything mean to her, except yell. She says he *mostly* treats her nice. I don't know though. I'd rather sell pot any day. Pot don't get you cut or pregnant.

Diamond's Story

I went with "Diamond" because I heard someone say that no one can break a diamond no matter how hard you try. David is the name my mom gave me. But she's dead.

The man my brother says might be my daddy did it. We saw it. Me, fucking hiding under the kitchen table; Douglas, my brother, getting into the middle of it until he got cut and thrown and I saw him sliding down, down, down smearing the blood that was his and my mother's down that old yellow wall. With Douglas out of the way, he was even madder and he kept beating on her, calling her a bitch, kicking her head in, stomping on her ribs, she was screaming until she couldn't anymore and I could see it all happening on the floor right on the other side of the table legs, and I didn't call the police. Even though I saw a cell phone on the chair tucked under the table right in front of me, I couldn't move. I could've called the police but I didn't and that was it. He was mad because he said she had stolen his money. When it was done, and he was heading out the door, he went to grab his phone and he saw me. He asked me what the fuck I was looking at. I couldn't say anything. He shook his head like I wasn't worth the trouble to kill. Then he left.

Like a baby, I think I fainted or something because I don't remember anything after that until I was in some stranger's house.[60] Douglas was there too. He said the neighbors had called the police and he got up and held my mom in his lap until the ambulance came and the people said she was dead. He said she didn't say nothing but

---

60. Disassociation is the more common adaptive response to threat among children than the hyper-arousal responses of fleeing or screaming. See, Bruce D. Perry et al, *Childhood Trauma, the Neurobiology of Adaptation, and "Use-dependent" Devlopment of the Brain: How "States" become "Traits,"* 16(4) INFANT MENTAL HEALTH J. 271–291, 275 (1995).

her eyes opened and saw him before they stopped working. He said the police might want to talk to me but I should probably watch my back and say I was in shock and didn't see shit, which was halfway true. He said he already told them who did it anyway. *What about your back?* I wanted to know. He says he isn't afraid of that mother fucker and he better hope he's arrested because he is going to shoot him dead next time he sees him if he isn't.

The man I learned was named David, just like me, was arrested and the police left me alone, probably because I was only six when it happened. Douglas, who was twelve, gave them the statement they needed. They put that David in prison for thirty-five years, and they put us in foster care.

Foster care was no place for us. We pissed off enough foster parents that they separated us, thinking that would help I guess, but it made me worse.[61] I did shit I wouldn't ever do when I was living at home. I smashed windows. I smeared my shit on walls. I learned that if I didn't want to be where I was, which I never did, I just needed to scare the fuck out of whoever was unlucky enough to get me.[62] I never took stuff out of the trash bags I came with, never got comfortable.[63] I got kicked out of classes and schools and once they made me go to a school where they put me in a "special" class with a bunch of other bad-ass boys who had been expelled from other places, just like me.[64] And they kept putting me in tighter and tighter security.[65] No family could handle me so I wound up in a place for crazy kids where they gave me more and more

---

61. Studies have shown that the likelihood of obtaining permanency increases, and disruptions in placements decline when siblings are placed together. CHILD WELFARE INFORMATION GATEWAY, U.S. DEP'T OF HEALTH & HUMAN SERVS., SIBLING ISSUES IN FOSTER CARE AND ADOPTION 7 (January 2013), [https://perma.cc/7998-SXTN].

62. In a study of 1,084 children involved in foster care, 20% of the placement disruptions that occurred were due, alone or in part, to the child's behavioral issues. Sigrid James, *Why Do Foster Care Placements Disrupt? An Investigation of Reasons for Placement Change in Foster Care,* 78(4) SOC. SERV. REV. 601–627, 614 (Dec. 2004).

63. The use of trash bags to remove and move children in foster care has become so ubiquitous that charitable organizations have been established to provide foster children with luggage when they enter into state care. *See, e.g.,* COMFORT CASES, [https://perma.cc/7SLD-EHX2]; DUFFELS FOR H.O.P.E., [https://perma.cc/H9RU-XBCQ].

64. Under the Individuals with Disabilities Education Act, children with "emotional disturbances" are entitled to a special education plan. Behavioral disorders are included within this category. Children classified as having severe emotional or behavior disorders may be placed with other similarly categorized students in self-contained classrooms or schools. While theoretically the IDEA is intended to ensure that all students receive an appropriate education, research indicates that the self-contained classroom or school for ED/BD students likely serves the general education population more than it does the special education students who are segregated in this way. One study of both self-contained classrooms and self-contained schools revealed "limited academic improvement in either setting." The same study also determined that there was no significant progress for students in either setting in the behavioral and social realms. *See* Kathleen L. Lane, Joseph H. Wehby, M. Annette Little & Cristy Cooley, *Students Educated in Self-Contained Classrooms and Self-Contained Schools: Part II—How Do They Progress Over Time?,* 30(4) BEHAV. DISORDERS 363–74 (Aug. 2004).

65. Children in foster care use residential treatment, emergency room and inpatient mental health treatment more often than children in the overall Medicaid population. Residential treatment/therapeutic group care represents the highest mean annual expense among all behavioral services utilized

meds.[66] Meds for ADHD, meds for anxiety, meds for depression, meds because I couldn't sleep at night, meds because I couldn't wake up in the morning, until I was a fucking zombie and I'm not sure how long I stayed like that. But eventually, they thought I was good enough to leave that place, and put me in with foster parents who supposedly knew what to do with me. That's when I stopped taking the pills and I slowly got back to being me again. I had to go see this counselor who was young and hot and that was OK but she wanted me to draw pictures like I was some kind of baby. I played along, but it was pretty dumb. She wanted me to talk about that day but I didn't want to.[67] So I just scribbled with black and red crayons until her fifty minutes was up.

Those last foster parents, Marnie and Oliver were their names, they were OK. But you know it just wasn't me to start being who they wanted. I thought about busting up their place so I could move on, but by then I was just tired of that and I knew that

---

by children in foster care. *See Medicaid Behavioral Health Care Use Among Children in Foster Care*, CENTER FOR HEALTH CARE STRATEGIES, INC., [https://perma.cc/QFS5-8A7Q].

66. The percentage of children in foster care being prescribed psychotropic drugs is much higher than for children generally in the United States. Cody Dashiell-Earp & Sarah Zlotnik, *Psychotropic Medications and Children in Foster Care*, 69(1) POL'Y AND PRACTICE 27–39 (2011), [https://perma.cc /LL4B-28SF]. Children in foster care are covered by Medicaid. One national study found that while 4.8% of children on private medical insurance were prescribed psychotropic medications, 7.3% of children on Medicaid were prescribed psychotropic medications. Chris Kardish, *How America's Over-medicating Low-Income and Foster Kids*, HEALTH AND HUMAN SERVICES, March 2015, [https://perma .cc/R7V5-KWZB]. Within the Medicaid child population, children in foster care are four times more likely to be prescribed psychotropic medications. Kamala D. Allen, Taylor Hendricks, *Medicaid and Children in Foster Care, Center for Health Care Strategies*, STATE POLICY ADVOCACY AND REFORM CENTER, (March 2013), [https://perma.cc/72EJ-4MJ3]. States differ in the rate of psychiatric medication of their foster children; however, depending on the state, between 13 and 52% of foster youth are pre-scribed at least one. *See*, Christopher Scozzaro & Timothy P. Janikowski, *Mental Health Diagnosis, Medication, Treatment and Placement Milieu of Children in Foster Care*, 24(9) J. CHILD FAM. STUD. 2560 (2015), [https://perma.cc/6DZB-PEUW]. As many as 41% of foster youth take three or more psychotropic medications. *See*, L.F Stambaugh et al. *Psychotropic Medication Use by Children in Child Welfare*, OPRE Report#2012-33, Washington, DC: Office of Planning, Research and Evaluation, Administration for Children and Families, U.S. Department of Health and Human Services, 2012, [https://perma.cc/W3YV-X97X] Concerns about overmedication of children in foster care resulted in a General Accountability Office Study which found that full documentation was lacking to support concurrent use of multiple medications in 75% of the cases studied. See, *Foster Children: Additional Federal Guidance Could Help States Better Plan for Oversight of Psychotropic Medications Administered by Managed-Care Organizations*, GENERAL ACCOUNTABILITY OFFICE, GAC-14-362: Pub-lished Apr. 28, 2014. Publicly Released: May 22, 2014, [https://perma.cc/2D8N-Z6XA] For further critique of the inadequacy of state law when it comes to protecting children in foster care from over-prescription of psychotropic medications, see Matthew M. Cummings, *Sedating Forgotten Children: How Unnecessary Psychotropic Medication Endangers Foster Children's Rights and Health*, 32 B.C. J.L. & SOC. JUST. 357 (Spring 2012).

67. CHILD WELFARE INFORMATION GATEWAY, U.S. DEP'T OF HEALTH & HUMAN SERVS., ISSUE BRIEF: TRAUMA-FOCUSED COGNITIVE BEHAVIORAL THERAPY FOR CHILDREN AFFECTED BY SEXUAL ABUSE OR TRAUMA, CHILDREN'S BUREAU (August 2012), [https://perma.cc/X6PN-HQ7F]. *See also* Anthony P. Mannarino, *Trauma-Focused Cognitive-Behavioral Therapy for Children: Sustained Impact of Treatment 6 and 12 Months Later*, 17(4) CHILD MALTREATMENT 231–241 (August 2012).

wherever I would go, it would not be as nice as that place and I thought they didn't deserve to have their place trashed because they actually were alright.

So I just left.

And I never went back. I was fourteen years old then and honestly I don't think my caseworker looked for me very hard. Most of the time, I was right under their noses. I got arrested a couple of times and I just got released to the guys I hung out with on the streets. Never anything big. Mostly possession. Or shoplifting. And now I'd be too old for that foster care shit and so I'm guessing they already wrote me off their books or whatever.

Maya is actually my first real girl. We have lots in common, what with us both having fucked-up families and hating on foster care. And so we kind of teamed up. She feels safer with me than being on her own. I knew that it was easier to spange[68] with girls doing it for you. People just like them more. Feel sorry for them. But I never really could put up with all the drama that comes with hanging out with a bunch of girls until Maya came along. She is easy. And then one thing led to another and I know that you won't believe me but it isn't like I decided when I met her that I was going to be her pimp or anything like that. But some guy came onto her on the street and he offered her $25.00 for a hand job. And we talked about it and she said she could do that but she didn't want me to be mad and I said I wouldn't be mad. We needed the money. And so that's kind of how it started. She wanted me to be nearby when it goes down, just in case, and so it turned out that we got a rep and before you know it people were coming to me.[69] And so we started and she said that she promised to only love me if I promised to only love her, no matter what. And we both said deal.

And damn, the money is so much better than spange-ing, better than selling weed. And selling drugs is a whole different thing now that I am twenty. No more juvie for me.[70] At first we were going to just keep it to hand jobs and blow jobs and keep sex for

---

68. "Spange" is a street term for asking for spare change.

69. The classic pimp narrative involves the older male who kidnaps or tricks the much younger girl into a life of prostitution, entrapping her through a combination of violence, drugs, and emotional manipulation. This portrayal does capture one slice of the commercial sexual exploitation of children. However, research has uncovered a much more layered and complex reality, particularly when it comes to street or survival sex among young people. This research has revealed a competing narrative, one in which the pimp is a close-in-age peer, who is often the instigator but also may be sought out by the girl. *See*, Anthony Marcus et al., *Conflict and Agency Among Sex Workers and Pimps: A Closer Look at Domestic Minor Sex Trafficking*, 653 ANNALS AM. ACAD. OF POL. & SOC. SCI. 225 (May 2014); Amber Horning, *Peeling the Onion: Domestically Trafficked Minors and Other Sex Work Involved Youth*, 37 DIALECT ANTHROPOL. 299 (2013). Adolescent girls on the street may have no pimp at all, and may independently trade sex for drugs, money or basic necessities. In some cities, gangs may be involved. In some cities, pimps may operate independently or with loose networks of support. *See*, Meredith Dank, et al. *Estimating the Size and Structure of the Underground Commercial Sex Economies in Eight Major US Cities*, THE URB. INST. (March 2014).

70. Research shows that many pimps had engaged in selling drugs prior to becoming involved with sex trafficking, and that while sometimes they continue to do both, it is not unusual for them to

us, but the offers for sex were too good. And so we decided that sex would be OK but she said she won't kiss them or say she loves them.

I'm not a pimp but let's just say I know how it works. And so I offered the same deal to another girl, Hailey, who is like Maya was, fresh out on the street and Maya vouched for me, said I would treat her nice, which I did and then I had two girls working for me. I come on a little to Hailey too, but I had to let her know that Maya is always first. Which means that sometimes I have to be hard on her in front of Maya. I hit her sometimes, but not that bad, and only when she was trying to stir up trouble with Maya, trying to make it seem like she was my favorite.[71] In those moments, when I am hitting on her and she cries, I sometimes feel something else happening and I forget where I am, kind of black out almost, and then I have to say I am sorry. I don't want to be like him because I ain't like him.

Hailey stuck it out with me, forgives me or whatever and before I knew it, I had them both making enough money to move it indoors some of the time and that is better. I was able to get me a cell phone which made everything go big. It's easy to post and we actually had to turn guys away.[72] We were living large, going to restaurants, regular showers, nice clothes. I had another girl lined up because there is enough work to go around.

I learned a few things though about not getting too big. One time I got us all a place down in the International District because it was cheap and there seemed to be business down there. I had my own friends up in our neighborhood but they were just friends, almost like family, but down there in the ID you had to be careful, because there are real gangs down there who have their own shit going on. They aren't just kids either, and some of those people are serious about not letting anybody set up in their area. We pulled three nights of good money before I got the shit kicked out of me and a gun pulled next to my head. They threatened to take Maya and Hailey with them but they took most of my money instead and said we needed to get out. We left in a hurry and I've stayed the hell out of there since then.

It wasn't too long after that, Maya started acting strange. It probably wasn't good for her to see that go down. Maybe she was scared and maybe she just didn't think I could keep her safe anymore. Anyway, she just disappeared. I hear she got arrested for shoplifting but if that's true she should be back on the streets by now. Ain't nobody spends that much time in juvie for something like that.

---

transition to sex trafficking because it is perceived as both safer and more remunerative. *Id.* at 2–3.

71. Pimps do report using coercion and fraud in recruiting and maintaining relationships with girls who do the sex work. Feigning romantic interest and emphasizing mutual dependency are common tactics. *Id.*

72. The proliferation of internet availability through cell phones has been seen as a major factor in the expansion of sex trafficking and the ability to bring what was once a public trade into private spaces. *Id.*

Maya's Aunt's Story: Henrietta (Phillips) Clark

I was the lucky one. Chicken—that's what I always called my sister; she was Chicken and I was Hen—Chicken was not so lucky, but she always protected me and so I stayed safe under her wing. I know our names should be reversed. She should be like the protective mother Hen; and I should be the cowardly Chicken. But the names happened early, before mom took up with Sam who should be in prison but instead just died young of liver poisoning or something like that, which is also what he deserved but it would have been better if he had died old in prison of something even worse, like cancer maybe.

Not that I am bitter, but what he did to wreck my sister's life I can never forgive. And I am not going to talk about it here. You can use your imagination. There are no words.

My mom had bad luck with men. She married Chicken's father and he died in a car accident. To hear her tell it, Chicken's dad was a fine, fine man with a decent job and it was just a shame that he didn't survive. If he had, all of our lives would have been different. But then again, I wouldn't even be here telling this story, unless I would have been his second child. I don't know how all that works—fate and why we are born to who we are born to.

My daddy was not someone who my mom let herself be very serious with and I guess his family wasn't big on him being very serious with her either. He was a handsome man. Tall, dark and handsome. With emphasis on "dark." I think my mom was kind of pretty back then too and so I am sure that after Chicken's dad died she had plenty of guys interested in her. She probably also needed to be distracted from her grief. My daddy was that distraction. I never met him that I remember, although my mom said that I am named after his sister who she met at the one family gathering he had taken her to; she said that his sister was the only person there who treated her nice. His mother hated her and thought it would never work out. Mom said, to be fair, that her family didn't approve of her dating a black man either, but they didn't live nearby so she didn't feel the pressure like my dad did. I like to think that when she got pregnant, he wanted to do the right thing but they decided not to because it just wouldn't work. But I don't really know. My mom didn't talk about that. She said he sent money when he could.

Then my mom had a bit of a dry spell; all work and no play, trying to raise us two little girls. And then came Sam. I think at that point Mom was tired of being lonely and raising two kids on her own and having to spend so much money on babysitters. I am not sure where Sam even came from, how she met him or anything. He just showed up one day in our house. I should have known he was bad news when my mom asked us to give our new daddy a kiss and hug. That felt really uncomfortable. Who was this strange man and why did he want us to be his kids all of a sudden?[73]

---

73. Research shows that there is a higher incidence of childhood sexual abuse perpetrated by stepparents and non-relative acquaintances when compared to biological parent perpetrators. *See* Bill

Mom didn't really know or at least she pretended not to know how bad Sam was. She had a job; sometimes she had two. And Sam, he had nothing but time and drink on his hands. She was glad to have the help at last. She let him watch us, which was her mistake. Chicken was older by three years, which made her more of a target for him.[74] It wasn't that he was nice to me either. He called me names, mostly things like "my little n****r;" I knew by the way he said it that I looked ugly in his eyes, but somehow he both hated me and was curious about me all at the same time and that made me want to stay as far away from him as I could.

Chicken always told me I was a beautiful princess. I was her little Princess Hen and she was Queen Chicken and we played like that all of the time. Queen Chicken would order me to stay away from the evil Sam. And I did. She said she would cast a spell on him that would keep him away from me. And she did. Unfortunately, that meant that she took everything he had to give instead.

Mom was sorry once she found out and put all of the pieces together. It took her a while; it had been almost two years of him watching us. Sometimes mom worked night shift, sometimes days, and so with school there were times when we didn't see her that much and Sam was in charge.

At first when Chicken got pregnant and was only thirteen, Mom thought some boy had done it and she was mad at Chicken for not saying no. It took her a while to believe that it wasn't a boy, but a man that had done that to her. I spoke up for her then. I told mom that Chicken didn't have a boyfriend and that Sam was with her with the door closed a lot.

It was hard to get him out of the house after that. Really hard. Mom didn't want to confront him or make him mad. She was afraid of him. We had to run away. Mom lost her job and we were living for a while on the checks that came in, social security because Chicken's dad was dead and some money from my dad too I think maybe. So even though our daddies were gone, they were kind of still there with us, helping us. Still, it wasn't a lot. We stayed in a shelter once and that was really hard. So many moms and their kids all sad and scared and wanting to go home. Seemed like Mom never once thought to call the police or maybe she did think about it but she was too afraid or ashamed or maybe she thought it would be hard on us to have to be in the middle of a police investigation or maybe she thought that they would take us away from her or maybe she thought no one would believe her or us. He could be very nice when he wanted to be, respectable almost.

Muehlenberg, *Child Abuse and Family Structure*, BILLMUEHLENBERG.COM, [https://perma.cc/C9ZN -5R7R].

74. While it could be that sexual abuse for younger children is undercounted, a literature review in 1994 reported that the peak vulnerability for sexual abuse occurs between the ages of 7 and 13. *See* David Finkelhor, *Current Information on the Scope and Nature of Child Sexual Abuse*, 4 THE FUTURE OF CHILD. 31, 31 (1994). Recent Child Maltreatment data show that the highest number of reported incidents of sexual abuse occur against children between the ages of 12 and 14. CHILDREN'S BUREAU, U.S. DEP'T OF HEALTH AND HUMAN SERVS. CHILD MALTREATMENT 2012, 21 (2012), [https://perma .cc/569L-NKF7].

Anyway, we have never talked about it. That whole time feels like what the earth looks like in cartoons after an earthquake. Lots of deep, jagged cracks and me, my sister and her little baby Jasmine (who we called Jazz), and my mother, we were all on separate little pieces of the earth with cracks so deep between us. But we loved one another across the cracks. We called out each other's names but couldn't really reach each other. And my sister, she was just hanging on, trying not to fall into the hole and be swallowed up by the earth, at the same time she was also trying to decide whether and how to be a mother, whether to take Jazz down with her or throw her off to one of us.

I still reach out to Chicken. She always knows my phone number and sometimes she finds a way to call it. Sometimes she is gone for long stretches and I don't know where she is at all. After they took Maya and Jazz away, she just went missing for over a year. I have no idea where she was then. But she always surfaces. When she seems to be doing better, is more at herself, she even calls and asks, "How is my baby?" I know she means Maya and not Jazz because Jazz seems always to have been lost to her somehow. She was just too young and the way that Jazz came to be was just too hard.

Maya came along after Chicken ran away from home the first time. Chicken was almost 18 and I could tell that she was having problems. Instead of settling down, Chicken was just getting wilder and wilder. She seemed sometime to be talking to herself. But I don't know if it was because of the drugs she was using or whether something inside of her had just snapped.[75] Mom said she had to stop all that nonsense and that she had to do better and go back to school and realize she has a little girl who looks up to her. I think all of that just made Chicken wilder and so she ran and left Jazz behind. Then she came home about a year later pregnant again and little Maya was born.

I don't know who Maya's daddy is. I don't even know if Chicken knows for sure. Sometimes she mentions someone named Luke, but that's been only in the last few years she's brought him up. So who knows? Maybe there's some red-haired man named Luke out there who is Maya's daddy. Maya is the only person in our family I know of with red hair like that.

The one thing I do know for sure is that Chicken loved that baby to death when she was born and Maya inspired her, she did. She inspired her to try to be a good mom and to try to get off drugs and to do better, even with Jazz.

She was doing better when she decided to take off with both of them, which seemed like a bad idea to me even then. I wasn't sure she was ready, and I was right. She wasn't. She needed more help. So mom and me visited her a lot once we found her and we helped to take care of Maya and Jazz as much as we could but she kept getting kicked out of her apartments and we could tell that she was starting to lose it again. She would holler and scream and swat at the air and then she would get high and when mom

---

75. The symptoms of schizophrenia (hallucinations and delusions) typically start between the ages of 16 and 30. Within this age range, the symptoms in males tend to emerge earlier than females. NATIONAL INSTITUTE OF MENTAL HEALTH, SCHIZOPHRENIA, [https://perma.cc/CA3Q-GVZU].

told her that she needed help, really big help, Chicken got mad at her and ran off and took both kids with her. We didn't know where they had gone. We looked and looked in all of the shelters and all of the places where we knew homeless people stayed but we couldn't find them and we were so scared for her and for both of those babies.

I hate to admit it but I was kind of glad when they surfaced again because of CPS. Not that I think CPS should have done what they done and separated those babies from one another and eventually from all of the family they ever had, cutting off all of Chicken's rights to both of those kids, but I was glad to know then that at least they were alive, glad to know where they were. And now I try really hard never to lose track of any of them. I don't know where Jazz is anymore though. She got lost in foster care and I think she is too old for that now. So she is out there somewhere on her own with no family. Poor baby. I wish she knew how often I think of her.

When Chicken asks about Maya, I tell her that I tried to have Maya come stay with me after mom got sick and couldn't keep her, but they wouldn't let that happen. I feel bad because even after I tell her that she says, "But where is my baby?" I feel so bad because if Maya were with me she would know that her baby is safe and with me. I could tell her that and maybe she would have some peace. Sometimes she gets so confused and seems to have forgotten Maya. She says, "Didn't I have a baby? Was it a boy or a girl?" And then I tell her the story of Maya and what a beautiful baby she was and how much she loved her and tried to take care of her. I tell her about how way back, I even tried to have them both stay with me, instead of mom, but they said no to that too. I knew even then that mom was getting old and I also worried just a little bit about letting Maya stay with her because, after all, I hate to say it (and I don't say so to Chicken) but it was mom's mess that started Chicken's problems to begin with. I still have a hard time visiting mom in the nursing home. I haven't been in to see her in a really long time.

Relative Preferences

Federal law requires states to give preference to relative placements, provided that the relative meets with state child protection standards. Locate your statute or regulation that answers the following questions:

- *Who is considered to be a "relative" for purposes of your state's dependency system?*

- *At what points in your state's process must relatives be considered or notified?*

- *How does your state handle the issue of placement of siblings?*

Anyway, I do keep asking CPS if Maya can just come and live with me. The first time she ran off she ran to me at first. I fed her and got her all cleaned up and did her hair just like she wanted it, all in braids, so it looked like her little cousins'. And then I told her we were going to have to get her in school and talk to the CPS people. She nods her head and everything and asks for just one more night with me before we call them and I say OK. When I get up the next morning, she is gone. I call and tell them and I say they should just let her stay with me. If they would just say it's OK, maybe she will come back to stay and stop running off. I don't think that caseworker liked me very much though because she just keeps saying no.

Last time I called CPS to check in on her they wouldn't even tell me where she was. They say it is confidential.[76] I called the last place I knew about, that group home place, and one of the staff let it slip that she had run away. Again. They would rather have her on the streets than with me?

I think it's because I always stick up for my sister too much in those meetings. I think it's because I spoke my mind once to a caseworker way back; I really lit into her in the hallway after one of those hearings when she said I wasn't allowed to take care of Maya; I tried to tell the judge that I should take care of her, but everyone said I didn't have the right to talk. I got pretty mad and she put something nasty about me in a file. I said all kinds of things then that I can't even remember about how dare they keep me from speaking my mind. She says that Maya needs to have no contact with her mother and they don't trust me to make sure that doesn't happen.[77] I pointed my finger in her face and told her that maybe if Maya hadn't been totally cut off from her mom, maybe her mom wouldn't be so messed up now. Maybe her mom needs to see her children in order to *want* to get better.[78] I'm sure I probably did curse her out and raise my voice. She was so high and mighty.

It also could be that they don't want to put a white girl in a black family. They won't say that of course.[79] They would never say that. They say instead that they are afraid I won't "protect" her from her mom; they say she ran away from me too and so I can't

---

76. Federal law requires that states receiving federal money for foster care must have a plan in place that "provides safeguards which restrict the use of or disclosure of information concerning individuals assisted under the plan." 42 U.S.C. §671(a)(8). This requirement means that the states have laws in place prohibiting the sharing of information maintained in child welfare cases.

77. Although relative placement is preferred under federal and consequently state law, the state typically has discretion not to place with relatives if such a placement is not in the best of the interest child. *See*, 42 U.S.C §671(a)(19) (providing that states consider giving preference to relative placement over a non-related caregiver, so long as the relative meets the relevant state protection standards); For a summary of how states have defined "relative" and the various requirements placed on relatives in order to be considered for placement, see CHILD WELFARE INFORMATION GATEWAY, U.S. DEP'T OF HEALTH & HUMAN SERVS., PLACEMENT OF CHILDREN WITH RELATIVES, State Statute Series (Current through 2013), [https://perma.cc/5C63-843E]. For a discussion of the challenges still facing relatives who seek to serve as placements for children, see Judge Leonard Edwards, *Relative Placement in Child Protection Cases: A Judicial Perspective*, 61 JUV. & FAM. CT. J. 1 (2010).

78. Research supports that mothers fare better in substance abuse treatment when their children are a part of the treatment plan and when health and mental health services are also available. *See*, K.L. Osterling & M.J. Austin, *Substance Abuse Interventions for Parents Involved in the Child Welfare System: Evidence and Implications*, 5 J. EVID. BASED SOC. WORK 157 (2008).

79. If the state were to admit that it was not placing a child with a particular family because of race, such a decision would violate the Multiethnic Placement Act/Inter Ethnic Placement Act. *See* 42 U.S.C. §622, discussed *supra* in ch. 1, *Multi-ethnic Placement Act/Inter-Ethnic Placement Act*.

control her either; they say I would have to get licensed; they say I have anger management problems. Damn right, I have anger management problems when I talk about
stuff like this with rude, disrespectful people who don't know anything about who I am
and what Chicken has been through. They won't even listen. They cut me off and say
stupid things like, "We have offered Ms. Phillips numerous services and she has failed
to follow through." Or "Your sister has failed to acknowledge her deficiencies." What
the hell kind of way is that to talk to someone who wants to help? They don't know
us; they don't know why my sister does the things she does. They don't know why
Maya does the things she does. But I do. I get it because I know them both and what
they have been through.

They want to make our story—Maya's story—all about the bad things Chicken
has done and the fact that she hasn't done anything to fix herself. They say things like
"family history of abuse" and try to lump us all together into some big poisonous stew
of misery. And yes, we are all having to put up with all that bad stuff that happened
to us. And yes, I do love my sister. But my life is not all about this. If they would leave
us alone and let us move on, they would see that. I wake up every morning. I go to
work. I have a husband who gets up and goes to work every day and we have two kids
of our own and we are doing just fine. Maya deserves to know her cousins. They are
good kids. We aren't rich or anything, but we have room for one more. There's always
room for Maya.

What really burns me now is that when I ask this new caseworker—Sarah I think
her name is—in the "Behavioral Resources Unit," she says that Maya has mental health
issues and special needs and she needs special care. She sounds nicer, like she cares
about Maya, but it's still offensive that she thinks we can't take care of our own. All I
can say to her then is, "Well, I wonder why *that* is? If she's all crazy, it doesn't seem
like foster care is doing a very good job of anything except making her crazier."

The caseworker didn't say anything then. What could she say? She probably knew
it's true. I think they should let us have a try.

Maya's Sister: Jasmine Phillips' Story

They used to call me Jazz, but I dumped that name once and for all after I found
Grandma Ruth, who is not my "real Grandma" but she is my real family as far as I am
concerned. After I found my place with her finally, I went back to being Jasmine because
I needed a fresh start, one that would smell clean like a flower and was not all chaotic
and crazy like Jazz. It seemed right to just leave all that behind finally. I don't even
like jazz music; it makes me jumpy and anxious. Who needs that?

My "real grandma" has dementia and lots of other health problems and so she
doesn't really remember me. She gets me confused. Right now, though, probably none
of my other "real" family would recognize me either, and that is really ok with me. I
don't really need anything from them anymore and I know I can't fix them. The only
one I care about is my sister, Maya. I worry about Maya. I wish I had not been separated
from her, but I could not really keep her safe and so I had to save us both the only

way I knew how. I didn't know they would put her one place and me another. If I'd have known that then, I might not have done what I did.

I actually turned us in. I turned us all in. I went into that school and I told that principal that it just wasn't right and I couldn't keep it up any more. I am proud of my ten-year-old self now. What ten-year-old has the presence of mind to say that her mom is too sick to take care of her and her baby sister? Maya was only five and it was bad what was beginning to happen. I had already been seeing and doing shit I wasn't supposed to see or do and then there she was, and I was not going to let anything really bad happen to her. I just wasn't. She was such a pretty little girl and mom wasn't paying any attention at all. We had been kicked out of our old apartment and we had moved into this falling down place and grandma and Aunt Hen didn't know where we were. I wanted to go to school and I was missing school a lot. I knew that Maya should have started kindergarten but mom hadn't taken her. I saw a school near where we were staying and so I just wandered off one day, with Maya's hand in mind, and I showed up. I asked to talk to the principal. And I told him that Maya and I wanted to go to school. We must have been a sight. Probably pretty dirty and certainly hungry. He asked us where our parents were and I told him the truth—we don't have any dad and my mom lives in the squat down the street.

He called CPS. A lady came to talk to us. They looked at where I said mom was staying and she wasn't there and they said it wasn't safe for us to live there anyway. They said I was right to do what I had done, to ask for help. At first it was really scary. They put us in this stranger's home. She was a nice enough lady, but we didn't know her. She said we wouldn't be there long, just long enough for them to figure out who we would live with.[80] I had done a big thing. I was sure that my mom was mad at me and that my aunt was mad at me, and that probably my grandma was mad at me too. Maya might have been mad at me too, I think, if she had understood that I was to blame, but she clung to me because I was all she had. But that lady was really pretty good and made sure we both got to school and told us it was OK to cry, that things would get better.

After what was only maybe a week, but felt like a month, they put Maya with our real grandma and me in foster care. Back then, I was sure they put me in foster care because grandma was mad at me for what I had done and didn't want me around.[81] Now that I am older, I don't really know why they did it that way. I don't know

---

80. When children first come into state care, they often spend time in temporary short-term placements prior to the first hearing and while the court and agency determine whether the child is to remain in state care and with whom. These temporary placements may be in group-care facilities or in foster homes typically known as "receiving homes" which are specially licensed to take in children on short-notice and for brief periods of time. For an example of state guidelines governing receiving homes, *see* CHILDREN'S ADMIN., WASH. STATE DEP'T OF SOC. & HEALTH SERV., CHILDREN'S ADMINISTRATION REGION 1 FISCAL GUIDELINE 09-01, (2010), [https://perma.cc/9ERP-YDEA].

81. "In the aftermath of traumatic events, as survivors review and judge their own conduct, feelings of guilt and inferiority are practically universal." JUDITH LEWIS HERMAN, TRAUMA AND RECOVERY: THE AFTERMATH OF VIOLENCE — FROM DOMESTIC ABUSE TO POLITICAL TERROR 53 (1997).

whose decision it was to not let me stay with Maya. Grandma probably couldn't handle two kids, especially two kids like us who had gotten a little bit out of hand; maybe that's why. I do know that I missed Maya really bad and I was always worrying about her. It had been my job to keep her safe. The case workers were always telling me that it was not my job to be Maya's parent; that it was my job to be a kid and let other people take care of me for once.[82] But they didn't seem to understand how important it was to me still to see Maya.[83] We had fun together too. It wasn't all just the hard times.

In the long run, even though Maya was with family, I think I got the better deal. I did move around a lot in the first few years, but finally I wound up with Grandma Ruth, someone whose life had just enough bumps in it. That's how I think of it anyway. Some of the homes I stayed in were homes with foster parents whose lives had been so smooth they didn't seem to understand how mine could be so rocky; they didn't have the patience for the way I acted; and were surprised and offended that I was not grateful. I thought those people would have been better off rescuing a dog from the pound. They would have gotten the kind of appreciation they wanted then.

---

82. The existence and impact of "parentification" among sibling groups is controversial. The concept developed as a descriptor for the phenomenon of role reversals between parent and child, i.e. when a child assumes the role of caring for a parent either emotionally, behaviorally or physically. The concept was broadened to include the notion of one sibling assuming parental responsibility for others in a sibling group. This phenomenon appears frequently among children with a history of parental neglect. During the 1990's, most of the literature sought to document the negative impact of this role reversal. However, subsequent research has revealed that there are protective factors that arise from the "parentified" relationships between siblings and even parents. These studies have shown that behavior previously characterized negatively as "parentification" may actually promote resiliency in that through the establishment of close emotional and instrumental caretaking relationships, children learn about responsibility, empathy, and the importance of caretaking. *See* Lisa M. Hooper, Sylvia A. Marotta & Richard P. Lanthier, *Predictors of Growth and Distress Following Childhood Parentification: A Retrospective Exploratory Study,* 17 J. OF CHILD & FAM. STUDIES, 693 (2008). Despite these controversies, some case workers still seek to separate siblings with a perceived "parentification" dynamic, even though the research regarding sibling placement generally demonstrates that keeping siblings together reduces the level of placement disruption and leads to better mental health outcomes. *See* Sonya J. Leathers, *Separation from Siblings: Associations with Placement Adaptations and Outcomes Among Adolescents in Long-term Foster Care,* 27 CHILD. AND YOUTH SERV. REV. 793 (2005).

83. The research supporting the benefits of sibling co-placement and maintaining a sibling connection is strong. For a summary of this research, *see* CHILD WELFARE INFORMATION GATEWAY, U.S. DEP'T OF HEATH & HUMAN SERV., SIBLING ISSUES IN FOSTER CARE AND ADOPTION (2013), [https://perma.cc/CL3D-CSX2]. In recognition of the importance of these relationships, the Fostering Connections to Success and Increasing Adoptions Act now requires that State agencies make reasonable efforts to place siblings in the same placement, including adoptions, unless placement together would be contrary to the safety or well-being of any of the siblings. If siblings are not placed together, states are required to make reasonable efforts to provide for "frequent visitation or other ongoing interaction" between siblings unless there is documentation that providing this type of interaction would be contrary to the safety or well-being of any of the siblings. 42 U.S.C. § 671(a)(31). For a state-specific listing of statutes requiring reasonable efforts for sibling co-placement and/or visitation when siblings are separated while in foster care, *see* CHILD WELFARE INFORMATION GATEWAY, U.S. DEPT' OF HEALTH & HUMAN SERV., PLACEMENT OF CHILDREN WITH RELATIVES (2013), [http://perma.cc/PYQ9-DBTY].

Then there were other foster parents whose lives had been so bumpy that it seemed like they had no idea how to help me navigate my own drama and trauma. Instead, it felt like my drama and trauma became their drama and trauma. Before long, they were saying I had to go. I pushed all the wrong buttons.

Finally, I found my home. I found Grandma Ruth who is just old enough and has lived through enough challenges of her own to know that my nonsense was not permanent. She had lots of foster kids over the years and she is always bragging on them, what all they have done, how all but one has graduated from high school and nearly half of them have gone on to do some college and a few of them have even finished college and become teachers and one is even a lawyer. She let me know that the person who was brave enough and strong enough to tell that principal that she needed to step out of that squat and go to school is worth letting out again.[84] After some initial testing on my part, I learned she isn't going to give up on me. I was bad, really bad. I did everything I could to see what it would take for her to kick me out.[85] When she didn't and I got tired of trying to piss her off, we settled in together and I became a part of her big loud family and she helped me get caught up in school and figure out what I want to do with the only life I could save — my own.

Part of me always wishes she would adopt me because my mom's rights have been terminated a long time ago, but we decided I should stay in long-term foster care with her instead because that would let me live with her longer and get help with my schooling.[86] I had a lot of catching up to do; so I would be a "super senior" which is a pretty funny way of saying that I would be 19 when I graduated.[87] I wound up going to

---

84. Many studies have sought to discern both the risk and protective factors associated with successful foster care placements. The risk of disruption in placement is generally associated with the age of the child at placement, behavior problems exhibited by the child, and whether the child had been placed in previous residential care. However, factors that protect against disruption, even when the risk is high, rest heavily on the motivations of and supports available for the foster placement. "Foster children in highly motivated, involved and nurturing foster families experienced less breakdown." Mijam Oosterman, et al., *Disruptions in Foster Care: A Review and Meta-Analysis*, 29 CHILD. AND YOUTH SERV. REV. 53, 74 (2007). Some studies have found that non-kinship placements are more likely to disrupt than kinship placements, even with similar rates of problem behaviors exhibited by the child. *See* Patricia Chamberlain, et al., *Who Disrupts from Placement in Foster and Kinship Care?* 30 CHILD ABUSE & NEGLECT 409 (2006).

85. "Frequently a 'crisis of connection' occurs when someone gradually becomes more real to a child and the potential for forming an attachment becomes more real. A dramatic increase in acting-out behavior, running away, or other symptoms may be the outcome. . . . We should never underestimate the degree of anxiety that the prospect of closeness evokes in these children, even though their hunger for connection is intense." Crenshaw & Hardy, *Understanding and Treating, supra* n. 6, at 175.

86. Many states have adopted statutes allowing youth to stay in foster care beyond their eighteenth birthdays in order to finish high school and pursue post-secondary education or vocational training. These statutes have been passed in response to federal legislation appropriating federal funds to support such programs. *See* EMILY TAYLOR, NATIONAL CONFERENCE OF STATE LEGISLATURES, FOSTERING CONNECTIONS TO SUCCESS AND INCREASING ADOPTIONS ACT OF 2008 (2008), [https://perma.cc/L5NV -WLPC].

87. Youth in foster care struggle in school as compared to their in-home peers. Multiple placements can lead to multiple changes in schools, which results in mounting educational losses. Youth in

community college after that and I just got my LPN. I work in an elder care facility now. I hope to go back for my RN someday. I always have a seat at Grandma Ruth's table, just like everybody else, and her family is my family. Right now I am staying in the little apartment above her garage but I am saving my money and once I save enough money, which should be within a year, I will get my own apartment nearby.

I don't know what happened to Maya. I would like to know. I look her up online sometimes but I never find her there. I have thought about trying to find my Aunt Hen. She will probably know. She really wanted us to live with her but the state wouldn't let us. I am not sure why. But I wonder what my life would have been like then. I can't think about that too much because I am just glad it turned out the way it did.

Through one strange coincidence, I did see my real grandma again. It turned out that, as I was finishing up my practicum at my nursing home placement, grandma was admitted to that very same facility. What are the chances? Before I left, I got to visit her. She didn't know it was me. She confused me with my mother. I held her hand; she called me her little Chiclet, and cried. She said she was so, so sorry. She said something about Maya but I couldn't hear her. Her speech was all garbled and confused. I am used to dealing with older people with dementia, but it is a lot harder when it is your own people. I haven't been back.

Maya's Grandma's Story: Katherine Phillips

My little Chiclet came to see me the other day. It was so good just to see her. She looked good. Healthy. Something happened a long time ago. She didn't seem to remember it and neither did I, but I know that whatever it was made it hard for her and I am pretty sure I should have done something about it before now and now it's too late, but whatever it was she must have gotten over it, because she looked like she was taking good care of herself.

She looked at me like she barely remembered me; it made me cry. A child should remember her mother, even when her mother is old. I told her I took care of little Maya for as long as I could. I told her I was sorry I had to give her back. I wanted to ask her if she had Maya back now but the words wouldn't come out. I kept hearing this tinny little buzzing in my ear, like a mosquito or an angry hummingbird.[88] It stops me sometimes from being able to make my own words and it makes me not hear so good. Maybe she will come back again. It would be good to see her. Even just sitting with her would be good. I do have good days when I can hear and talk better.

---

foster care drop out at a rate much higher than their peers and those who do graduate, tend to graduate later. *See* NAT'L WORKING GRP. ON FOSTER CARE AND EDUC., EDUCATION IS THE LIFELINE FOR YOUTH IN FOSTER CARE (2011), [https://perma.cc/AQ5K-YR34].

88. Tinnitus is common in people with a dementia diagnoses. This condition aggravates the ability of patients with dementia to concentrate and communicate. *See* Colin J. Mahoney, et al., *Structural Neuroanatomy of Tinnitus and Hyperacusis in Semantic Dementia*, 82 J. OF NEUROLOGY, NEUROSURGERY & PSYCHIATRY 1274 (2011).

I know I have changed a lot since the last time she saw me. I mostly stay in bed all day now because the stroke did me in and sometimes I fall when I try to get up too fast. My hair is white now, and it sticks up straight this way and that. My mouth is still kind of crooked too on one side. I try not to look in the mirror too much because I don't even recognize that person. I probably looked a fright for poor Chiclet. I wasn't expecting visitors.

The nurses take good care of me but they don't really know me either. One of them reminds me of Hen; she's a pretty light-skinned girl with hazel eyes. Sometimes I look at her and ask, "Do I know you?" She says, "Yes, Ms. Phillips, you know me. I am nurse Marianne, remember?" Most people end their statements with the question "remember?" when they talk to me. It gets annoying. They are just lucky my words get stuck in my head and won't come out. Sometimes I want to shout at them, "No, dummy, of course I don't remember. Isn't that why I am here? I am old and I am sick and I don't remember anything."

Except Chiclet playing in the yard with Hen. I do remember that. How she loved her little sister Henrietta. How they both laughed together when they were wee little. They played princess and queen and they cast spells on each other. Giggling and running and chasing each other in the yard. It was pure joy to watch them while I did dishes in the kitchen. Life was good then. Not like how it is now.

Maya's Third Grade Teacher: Mrs. Brockhaus's Story

I have been a second and third grade teacher a long time, almost thirty years now. So many students, twenty or twenty-five or thirty of them per class. The numbers in my classroom keep growing. So it gets harder and harder to give each child what they need; and at my age, my memories have started to fade. I hate to admit that I can't remember all of my students. Not by a long shot. Sometimes they come back to visit me with their own children and I can't remember who they are, and I am just glad to know that they remember me well enough to want to still stop by and say hello.

There are those who stick with you. They stick with you because they were a challenge you were unable to meet. They stick with you because of something tragic or wonderful that happened for them in that one year that you had them. They stick with you because of a winning smile or a presence that commands the classroom. They use words you don't think a third grader could or should know. They tell a joke that makes you laugh despite yourself.

But the best ones, the ones who stick with you the longest, the ones who keep you going when you feel like maybe it's time to call in sick and get a sub for the day, are the ones who make you feel like maybe you got to see something in them that no one else did, and you saw it at the time they most needed it to be seen, and you hope that maybe, just maybe, the fact that you bore witness to that quality in them made some small but real difference.[89]

Maya Phillips was one of those little girls. It must be at least eight years ago now. Would she be fifteen? Fourteen? Hard to imagine! She was such a tiny one. You would hardly notice her. I had a split classroom that year. I had the second graders who needed to move a little faster and the third graders who needed to move a little slower. Maya was one of the third graders, so I expected that she would need extra help.

Yes, she was slow in her reading. That was true. And she used best-guess spelling still in her writing. She was quiet and hardly ever raised her hand. But when it came time for the Math Bee, I saw something catch hold in her.

The Math Bee was an idea I had come up with several years back. For most of the semester I would have the students work in mixed second- and third-grade teams doing group work to learn their multiplication tables and to be able to show the reasoning behind the work. They would go on "expeditions" in the classroom and on the playground, finding things to count by twos, threes, fours, fives, all the way up to twelves. They would draw pictures of groupings. They would make graphs. They would write reports of their discoveries. But in the end, I hoped they would actually learn their times tables and be able to know the facts, as well as what they meant. Call me old fashioned, but I still think it's good to just automatically know that 12 times 12 is 144 without having to think about its deeper meaning.

When it came time for the Math Bee, the students would participate individually but would also be recognized as members of their team. They designed their own t-shirts for their teams and they wore them in the competition. Their parents were invited to come. Not many made it because it was during the school day and most of the parents worked. But Maya's grandmother came and I can still see her standing there in the back of the classroom, smiling so proudly as Maya got up and answered every question correctly and swiftly. And each time Maya stood up both she and her grandmother smiled a bigger smile. She spoke with more confidence. She said her answers more loudly. When it was just her and a little boy named Aidan and I couldn't stump either one of them, Maya stood up and said, "Anything, Mrs. Brockhaus, you just ask me anything. I can do the thirteens."

She was so proud. I had to be fair to Aidan, but I didn't want her to miss her chance to shine. I told her that they were both winners because clearly they both knew everything that was expected of them, but if she wanted to do the thirteens for good measure she was welcome to go right ahead. And she did, and when she got to 13 times 13 is 169. I said, "Why, Maya, that is excellent!" And all of her team-mates cheered for her, and her grandma cried she was so happy.

---

89. For a study finding that success in school and attachment to teachers are among the strongest protective factors leading to resiliency and avoidance of delinquency and substance abuse for otherwise high-risk youth, *see* Carolyn Smith et al., *Resilient Youth: Identifying Factors that Prevent High-Risk Youth from Engaging in Delinquency and Drug Use, in* CURRENT PERSPECTIVES ON AGING AND THE LIFE CYCLE: DELINQUENCY AND DISREPUTE IN THE LIFE COURSE 217 (Zena S. Blau, ed. 1995).

After that, Maya started to raise her hand more often in class. She spoke up more. Especially in Math, but a little more in Science too. She seemed to have more friends at recess. I hope she kept at it. I know they say that girls don't go into the math and sciences in college,[90] and it is true that if you find a male school teacher, he seems to be teaching Math or Science,[91] but from where I sit, it seems like the girls do just as well, if not better, in the classroom.[92]

That girl knew her numbers. At the end of the year, she gave me a card. It could be that her grandmother made her write it, but I don't think so because the spelling was still hers. I still have it in my teaching scrap book.

It says, "Mrs. B., Thank you for the Math B. You ar my best teetcher. Sinsearly, Maya."

Maya's Mother's Story: Chiquita Phillips

Sometimes I can hear them calling me. Hen calls out, "Chicken, can you hear me? I'm here. Let's get you something to eat alright?" She calls me Chicken; my mom called me her Chiclet. My real name was Chiquita, because my mom thought it was pretty, no other reason. My sister's name was Henrietta, and so it happened my mother had a Chicken and a Hen. I am Chicken, Chiclet, sister, daughter, mother; none of those things; all of those things all at once.

My girl Maya, she comes to me sometimes, she says, "Here you go mom. I brought you a sandwich." She is a sweet one, that girl. I did something good there bringing her into this world. They took her away right when I was just beginning to know that things had gotten too bad, I had hit bottom, right when I was thinking I should turn

---

90. *See* Andresse St. Rose, *STEM Major Choice and the Gender Pay Gap,* 39(1) On Campus with Women (Spring 2010), [https://perma.cc/5FQL-ZP6Y].

91. Only 18% of female teachers teach math as their subject, whereas 24% of male teachers are math teachers. The disproportionality is even greater when it comes to the sciences. There, only 2% of female teachers are assigned to teach physical science, while 8% of men are physical science teachers. *See* C. Emily Feistritzer, National Center for Education Information, Profiles of Teachers in the U.S. 2011, 60 (2011), [https://perma.cc/3UJN-9X4G]. Although the number of men in the teaching profession has increased, women still dominate the teaching profession. Women comprise 70% of the teaching workforce as a whole. While the number of male teachers at the elementary school level did increase by 25% from 2001 to 2006, female teachers continue to be concentrated at the elementary school level, while male teachers tend towards teaching senior high school. Senior high school teachers teach in specific subject matters, and so not surprisingly, male teachers more often than female teachers say they go into teaching because of an interest in their subject matter. *See* National Education Association, Status of the American Public School Teacher 2005–2006 (2010), [https://perma.cc/M9GD-H2C5].

92. Common gender stereotypes often claim that boys perform better than girls in math and science. Meanwhile, recent headlines claim that we are undergoing a sudden "boy crisis" in which girls excel academically. *See* Daniel Voyer & Susan D. Voyer, *Gender Differences in Scholastic Achievement: A Meta-Analysis,* 140 Psychological Bulletin 1174 (2014) (concluding that neither is correct. Instead, girls have consistently outperformed boys when it comes to grades in all subjects. However, if one looks to the results of standardized testing, boys have consistently outperformed girls in math and science while girls outperform boys in reading comprehension. The article explores possible explanations for these differences in light of the data.).

the corner and do something different and start over. But they took her and Jazz away and then I was just too sad, too sad to talk to social workers, to go to appointments, too sad to go to court. My mom used to come and holler at me when they gave her Maya to take care of, and my mom would say, to me "Stop this nonsense!" and then she would say she was sorry, like my nonsense was her nonsense and she knew it but wouldn't say so.

One time, I got this idea to start over, leave Maya and Jasmine and my mom and Hen, all of them behind, and I went off with Luke who had a car and that car worked long enough to take us far enough away that I didn't have to think of social workers or my mother or my missing children. He said he knew all about how it hurt to have your children taken away. He was sweet to me. He was into pain killers because he had a bad back he got from working on the fishing boats and then he switched to heroin, and then he lost his job, and then he wound up at the square downtown with just a car that only worked sometimes. Anyway, he said he wanted to go to his home, which was far away, I don't remember where, a different state, and he asked me to come along. He said we would get clean together. I said sure, but that's when I added heroin to the mix because the meth wasn't doing it for me anymore,[93] and heroin is cheaper and then heroin just took over because that junk is just so much sweeter than anything else.

Somehow though I wound up back here, under this bridge. I can't remember how. Maybe I never really left it, but I think I did. I think Luke brought me back and then he disappeared. But maybe he wasn't real. I still hear his voice sometimes and he is always a good voice, sometimes a sad voice, but he is a voice that says maybe we will get clean together someday.

Jasmine, my Jazzy big girl — I don't hear Jazz, and she doesn't ever come. And the last one, Luke's baby, the one I didn't even get to name? I think he was a boy. They took him right from between my legs and put him somewhere else. He is my secret child. Sometimes I wonder if he is really real. Did I dream him up and Luke too? No one seems to know about him. I ask Hen and she just talks about Maya.

But Maya and Hen are real and here and they are all the time bringing me food and sometimes I don't really want to eat. I am not as hungry as you would think. My teeth aren't so good. I do get thirsty though, really thirsty, even though when I drink anything but soda I feel sick.[94]

---

93. The chemical strength of meth has risen and fallen with the availability of its major ingredient, depending on the region, with the west coast the first to experience the changes followed by a steady march across the country. To learn more about the ebb and flow of meth potency, see *The Meth Epidemic*, PBS FRONTLINE, [https://perma.cc/5UE6-9QBK]. More recently, the use of black-tar heroin, exported from Mexico, is on the rise. Heroin use often follows the abuse of other legal painkillers. *See With Rise of Painkillers, A Closer Look at Heroin*, KUOW.ORG, [https://perma.cc/XY33-S6CN].

94. Both meth and heroin users suffer with very poor dental health. Tooth decay and "cotton mouth" are common. This seems to be true whether the drugs are injected or smoked. *See* Laird Harrison, *Methamphetamine, Heroin Users Both Suffer from 'Meth Mouth,'* MEDSCAPE.COM, (Sept. 14, 2012).

Sometimes I don't hear them but I feel that they are all here, even that baby who just let out one whimper like a sick cat, and I don't know if they are for real or not; but it seems like they are and I just can't tell what they are saying and my voice won't come to say anything back to them. And when I do say something I don't even know for sure it's me talking. Sometimes it's someone else talking. A mean person with a whispering but deep voice. I am not sure if that voice is coming from me or at me. I am not a mean person. But there is a mean person who lives in me sometimes and I have to figure out a way to put that mean person down. I put that person down. I do. That's how I got started taking drugs in the first place. The voices come and they scare me and I have to shut them up.[95]

It isn't hard to find the stuff that helps me; that is everywhere. But it is hard to get it sometimes. There's only one thing left to trade, but sometimes I can't even do that. I am too sick sometimes to do what needs to be done. Luckily, I have friends who don't like to see me sick. I do the same for them when I can. We take care of each other because we know that next time it could be any one of us.[96]

Sometimes Hen begs me to go get help. I can hear that and I know it's her voice, not mine. She says she is sorry and she knows it's not my fault and that I have had a hard life and that it hasn't been fair. She cries. I don't cry. I have gone once or twice for help at the shelter. But the truth is, when I don't score anything, what I am really like underneath all floats up to the surface like a bunch of dead bodies, all decayed and ugly. Chicken is not there anymore. Chicken is dead. Then I hear the voices that don't belong to anyone—not Maya, not Hen, not my mom, not even me. Those voices crawl on me like ants, crawl through me like worms. They start in whispers and then they nag and accuse, and then they shout. I try to stop them before they start screaming. When they start getting loud, that's when I always have to leave.

---

95. It has long been documented that substance abuse and mental illness frequently co-occur. *See, e.g.,* R. Kessler et al., *The Epidemiology of Co-Occurring Addictive and Mental Disorders: Implications for Prevention and Service Utilization,* 66 Am. J. Orthopsychiatry, 17 (1996). The co-occurring nature of the problem is often overlooked for parents with children in the foster care system, despite its prevalence, with case workers more often targeting the substance abuse issue as the problem to be addressed, while the parents themselves often ask for mental health treatment. *See* Layne .K. Stromwall, et al., *Parents with Co-occurring Mental Health and Substance Abuse Conditions Involved in Child Protection Services: Clinical Profiles and Treatment Needs,* 87 Child Welfare 95 (2008). To learn more about the extent of the problem, including the prevalence of psychosis co-occurring with substance abuse, see Co-Occurring Mental Health and Substance Abuse Disorders, The Washington Institute for Mental Illness Research & Training, Wash. St. Univ., Spokane (2003), [https://perma.cc/U8G7-UGS8].

96. To understand more about how addicts maintain their addictions, see Chris Lehman, *Drug Cartels Thrive on Ultimate Consumers: Addicts,* NW News Network, Sept. 13, 2013, [https://perma.cc/88WE-3JQG].

Luke Gordon's Story: Maya's Half-Brother's Father (Unknown to Maya at this Time)

It took me awhile to do right by Lawrence; I first had to do right by myself. I knew when they took him from Chicken, I knew right then, that I would need to get clean for real, no messing around this time, and get back to where I belonged. My mother and father both were taken away from their homes on the reservation when they were just six years old and put in boarding schools where they learned to be good Catholics,[97] but they had a deep sadness to find their mothers again, and they never really could fix it.[98] By the time they got back to the tribe, wanting to share the joy of my birth with them, all of my grandparents were already dead, and my father, he was very sick.

But I grew up here on the Umatilla[99] with other elders who were like my grandparents and they did their best to look after me when my father died. I learned to fish on the Umatilla River, when the salmon were just beginning to come back,[100] but we were very poor and there were no jobs for a young man and so I went further west and got a job on the fishing boats and from there it was all downhill. That one day, when I pulled up the net wrong and I hurt my back, that one God-awful day, started me on painkillers and then heroin and before I knew it I was another homeless Indian in Seattle.[101] But I still had a broken down car that worked sometimes. I lived in that.

---

97. To learn about the use of boarding schools as a government-sanctioned assimilation strategy in the Pacific Northwest, see Carolyn J. Marr, *Assimilation Through Education: Indian Boarding Schools in the Pacific Northwest*, U. Washington Digital Collections, [https://perma.cc/GQX9-G8N5]. You can learn more about the Catholic boarding school era forced specifically upon the Umatilla tribe here: *History of CTUIR*, Confederated Tribes of the Umatilla Indian Reservation, [https://perma.cc/B4WL-3USB].

98. The repeated governmental and private assaults upon Indian culture and families throughout generations have had a cumulative and devastating effect upon the mental health of American Indian people. One study of the intergenerational impact of historical trauma in the reservation context found that tribal elders reported a range of emotional responses to historical loss of culture, language, land and family perpetrated by those outside the tribal community. These reactions included "sadness, depression, anger, anxiety, discomfort around White people, fear of White people. Shame, loss of concentration, feelings of isolation, rage, feelings that more trauma will happen, and avoidance of places or people that are reminders of loss." as reported in Teresa Evans-Campbell, *Historical Trauma in American Indian/Native Alaska Communities: A Multi-level Framework for Exploring Impacts on Individuals, Families and Communities*, 23 J. Interpers. Violence 316 (2008 23). Also see, *The Heart of ICWA: Becky*, *supra* note 9.

99. The Confederated Tribes of the Umatilla Indian Reservation is located in northeastern Oregon in the Columbia River Basin. To learn more about the Confederated Tribes of the Umatilla, see Confederated Tribes of the Umatilla Indian Reservation, [https://perma.cc/5C3M-RABM].

100. Salmon have been an important part of the Umatilla Confederated tribes' traditional way of life. To learn more about the successful efforts of the Umatilla to restore salmon in their traditional waterways, see *Salmon Success in the Umatilla River*, Confederated Tribes of the Umatilla Reservation, [https://perma.cc/M7UE-WZBQ].

101. Seattle has one of the highest homeless urban Indian populations in the country. *See* Paige Cornwell, *Legal Clinic Helps Native Americans Navigate Urban Life*, Seattle Times (Aug. 19, 2013), http://www.seattletimes.com/seattle-news/legal-clinic-helps-native-americans-navigate-urban-life; United Way of King County, Assessment of Assets and Opportunities of the King County Urban

I saw Chicken under the bridge where I went to score. She was miserable and crying. I asked her what was wrong and she cried and cried about her lost children. She wanted them back so bad but knew she was in no shape to take care of them. She said she just needed to say goodbye but her heart wouldn't let her. She said she wanted to give up and die and that her children would be better off without her. I told her no, no that can't be right, all children, they want their mothers.

She was not a beautiful woman. She was sick and the meth had eaten away her face. But I could see in her that familiar sadness and I was crazy to fix it. Her sadness made me want to fix myself too. I could see that we were both in a world of hurt. I told her that we both could get clean and that after she was clean she could get her children back. She didn't need to feel so sad. She didn't need to die. I said we just needed to get back to the reservation, that maybe we could get clean there.

We got in my car and we drove away. I was hard on her, reminding her about her kids, which was pretty hypocritical of me because I wasn't really ready to be clean myself, but when you are using, you never really are. I wouldn't let her take that meth poison. So I thought I was doing her a favor, even though I was still secretly using heroin. She didn't seem too bad at first but then she got even more depressed and one day I found her cutting herself with a piece of broken glass. She said she just wanted to die. I wasn't quite myself and so I let her try some of mine, just this once I thought, so she would feel better and not kill herself, just so that she could calm down. And of course she loved it. Then there was no more meth for her, but she really wanted heroin and so did I. The car broke down in Ellensburg and so did we. We both just started using hard.

The baby came before either of us even really believed she was pregnant.[102] If she knew, she didn't tell me. She was in such pain. A different kind of pain that I had never seen in her before. And when I finally saw what was happening the baby was almost out of her body. I ran around shouting until someone called the police. What a crazy sight we were. The ambulance came. Lawrence almost didn't make it. He was really tiny and premature and he was addicted too[103] but he was a fighter and he kicked the habit better than either of his grown parents. That's what really shamed me into it. If a scrawny little half-made baby can do it, so can I.

INDIAN POPULATION (2014), [https://perma.cc/3CH9-524A]. To learn more about the history of homeless Indians in Seattle, see SEATTLE INDIAN CENTER, [https://perma.cc/R4H8-VTVT].

102. Research has established that both heroin-addicted mothers and their newborns show high levels of infection contributing to high rates of preterm birth. *See* Richard L. Naeye, et al., *Fetal Complications of Maternal Heroin Addiction: Abnormal Growth, Infections, and Episodes of Stress*, 83 J. PEDIATRICS 1055 (1973).

103. Heroin use during pregnancy can lead to a heroin dependency problem in the fetus and newborn. This addiction is known as neonatal abstinence syndrome (NAS) and can be treated with medications to relieve the symptoms of excessive crying, irritability, fever, seizures, slow weight gain, tremors, diarrhea, and vomiting. In fragile untreated infants, NAS can also lead to death. Research suggests that while methadone use by a mother during pregnancy does not increase the harm to the fetus of a heroin-addicted mother, the use of buprenorphine is safe for both the mother and the fetus and lessens the impact of NAS on the newborn. *See How Does Heroin Use Affect Pregnant Women?*, NATIONAL INSTITUTE ON DRUG ABUSE, [https://perma.cc/VJ4Q-38XP] (last updated Nov. 2014).

Still, they never let Chicken have Lawrence. The only thing that stopped him from getting lost in the foster care system like her other children is that I told them I was from Umatilla. I had to prove I was his daddy. Chicken said I was, but that was not enough. They took stuff from my mouth and Chicken's mouth and the baby's mouth and then they tested for paternity[104] and they agreed that he is mine. Then they had to tell the tribe they had one of their babies.[105] The tribe wouldn't let him go into the state system.[106] And that's what saved us both. Lawrence and me, I mean. Chicken seems lost for good.

> ### Read Adoptive Couple v. Baby Girl, *133 S.Ct. 2552 (2013)*
>
> - *Is* Adoptive Couple *relevant to the facts here?*
> - *How might it be distinguished from this case?*
> - *Assuming* Adoptive Couple *had been decided at the time that these events had unfolded and if you were the attorney for the state, how would you have proceeded vis-a-vis the tribe? What rights would Luke have in these proceedings?*

And I got to name him because Chicken didn't care. When they told her they were going to take him she didn't want to have anything to do with him. I know it sounds cold but I know she just didn't want to get attached. She had enough pain. She signed a bunch of papers and she said she didn't want to name him or see him ever again. I call him Lawrence after my father, and I promised her that I would be worthy of him someday.

Chicken didn't look like she believed me. She said she just wanted to go home. I tried to convince her to come back with me to Umatilla. But she was tired of my promises and I don't blame her for that. I hadn't done anything but make her life sadder and harder and drag her out into the middle of nowhere. The social worker said she would help her to get back home. I don't know how that happened. I just know that when they let her out of the hospital she was gone and I have never seen her again.

It's a funny thing. When I left the tribe, I was little more than a boy and there was no work for a young man like me. But when I came back, we were not rich, but you could see that things had gotten better. The salmon are back in greater force and that is good, but really what is even better for the tribe is the Casino.[107] With the Casino, more people have work and the tribe has money to have their own child and family

---

104. For a discussion of paternity establishment and the rights of non-marital fathers, see ch. 1 — *Who is a Parent for Constitutional Purposes?*.

105. 25 U.S.C. § 1912(a).

106. 25 U.S.C. § 1911(b).

107. The Confederated Tribes of the Umatilla Indian Reservation own and operate the Wildhorse Resort and Casino, which generates income for the tribe as well as provides employment opportunities for its members. *See Career Center*, WILDHORSE RESORT & CASINO, [https://perma.cc/LL5Z-V6LT]. In 2001, the Wildhorse Foundation was established to provide grants to support charitable organizations which benefit Native American tribal governments, with a particular focus on those in Oregon and the previously ceded Umatilla territories in Washington. *See The Wildhorse Foundation*, WILDHORSERESORT.COM, [https://perma.cc/3K45-6RRW].

services.[108] When I came back, they put my little boy with another family in the tribe and then I started working on myself. I got to see him all the time though because the tribe is really good about that. They believe in you and everybody knows everybody anyways. And they help you get right not just with yourself but with your people too. And then you find you have a place to be healthy and a way to stay healthy.[109] I got clean. I married a beautiful woman who loves me for how I love and fight for my son. She decided I would be a good father. We have a baby of our own, and so now it is me and my wife, Shannon, and Lawrence who is eight years old, and his little brother, Nolan, who is four. I have been clean and sober for seven years. It hasn't always been easy but I am able to do it because I have a lot of love around me.

Lawrence is growing strong now; he's right on track.[110] He calls my wife "mama." He is as much hers as mine, but there are still times that I think of Chicken, and wonder if those funny things about him that are not like either me or my wife, come from some part of her that I didn't get to know because, when I knew her, too much of what was good and strong in both of us had been lost or at least buried.

Reflections and Exercises

1. *What? So What? Now What? A Five-Minute Reflection Opportunity.* Take just five minutes to write and reflect on the following questions:

    a. What did you feel as you read the stories of Maya and her family?

    b. How is what you recorded feeling relevant to your learning and/or practice?

    c. Now what do you do with these insights as you move forward in your learning and/or practice?

---

108. Tribes may access federal funds to assist in the creation of a child welfare infrastructure and/or they may use their own funding to support services. *See State & Tribal Funding*, Children's Bureau, [https://perma.cc/5836-JNU9]. Accepting federal funding means that the tribe must follow federal guidelines, including data tracking systems that may not be feasible for small, less resourced tribes. Technical assistance is often required when federal funds are accepted. *See American Indian Child Welfare Systems*, National Indian Child Welfare Association, [https://perma.cc/2KVU-4DHN]. Therefore, the use of unfettered tribal income allows for more flexibility in creating culturally appropriate tribal child welfare systems. For a look at the child welfare services in place at Umatilla, see Department of Children and Family Services Resource Manual, Confederated Tribes of the Umatilla Indian Reservation (2013), [https://perma.cc/42VS-SHZ8].

109. Despite the impact of historical trauma, research also indicates that coping strategies and resiliency also exist within tribal communities. Deep emotional attachments, holding traditional values, engaging in traditional practices, helping others, and focusing on future generations all contribute to emotional well-being and healing even in the face of historical trauma. See, Teresa Evans-Campbell, *Historical Trauma in American Indian/Native Alaska Communities: A Multi-level Framework for Exploring Impacts on Individuals, Families and Communities*, 23 J. Interpers. Violence 316, 325 (2008).

110. While it is true that addicted newborns struggle immediately after birth and if their care is not properly managed they are at risk physically, most research has shown that the impacts of in utero addiction are not necessarily long lasting. Research has shown that to the extent that children of heroin addicts show developmental and intellectual delays, these delays are more strongly related to a deprived environment of living with heroin addicted parents than to the actual fact of the child's in utero experience. *See* Asher Ornoy et al., *The Developmental Outcome of Children Born to Heroin Dependent Mothers, Raised at Home or Adopted*, 20 Child Abuse & Neglect 385 (1996).

2. *Mapping Maya's Family:* Create a visual map or diagram of Maya's family. Who are all of these people and how do they relate to one another and to Maya? Think about color-coding the lines that connect them to Maya. Choose colors that you think reflect the emotional nature of the relationship she has with them. Create a key that explains your color choices.

3. *Imagining a Different Story for Maya:*

   a) *Maya and the child welfare system:* The child welfare system is an expensive legal intervention involving courts, lawyers, social service agencies and professionals across many disciplines. Outcomes for children and youth entering the child welfare system are not uniformly positive. With this in mind imagine a different story for Maya by considering other responses that could have been taken:

      i. Create a visual representation that maps out the various points in Maya's family story in which her family began to meet challenges that contributed to Maya and Jasmine's ultimate removal from her mother's care.

      ii. Examine these moments that impacted the trajectory of Maya's family and consider whether some alternative supports or interventions might have ameliorated the crisis. What would a social services system look like that met the needs of Maya's family in a preventative way?

      iii. What are the barriers that stand in the way of establishing your alternative response system?

      iv. Do lawyers have a role in effectuating these alternative response systems that may well arise out of other disciplines? What is that role?

   b) *Maya, Kiki and the law surrounding runaways:* As discussed in footnote 46, shelters and other service providers have a variety of reporting requirements when it comes to young people who run away. On the one hand, service providers may have to notify law enforcement if the child is reported missing. On the other, if they have reasonable grounds to believe that child abuse or neglect has occurred in the home, they are required to make a report to Child Protective Services. These reporting requirements are both intended to protect children from the dangers of the streets as well as the dangers of parents who might have driven them there. These requirements do present challenges for service providers and the youth who might wish to access critical services.

      i. Is the law striking the right balance? If not, how should this balance be struck differently?

      ii. What would need to be changed in order to improve service provision for runaway youth?

Chapter Four

Michael Goes to Court
for the First Time

The initial removal or shelter care hearing is a creature of state statutes, influenced by the federal law and constitutional mandates outlined in Chapter One. The laws seek to balance the rights of children to safety against the rights of parents to raise their children free from state intrusion. The result of this tension between the safety of children and the rights of parents is a court hearing set very quickly to allow a judge to review the State's decision to remove a child. The hearing can be one of the most critical stages in the dependency court process.

Jurisdictions have different procedural rules and cultures that control the initial removal or shelter care hearing. For example, in some jurisdictions children may not attend these hearings, regardless of their age. In Michael's jurisdiction, he appears at the hearing and has counsel (Katie) but his younger sisters do not. Jurisdictions may also vary on how much time children's attorneys and parents' attorneys have to prepare, how much information they have beforehand and what type of evidence they may present during the hearing.

In many juvenile court proceedings, attorneys meet and interview their clients in a very compressed timeframe. Often lawyers may have to go into a court hearing and represent their client immediately after a brief interview. This presents may challenges for both lawyers and clients.

In shelter care or removal hearings, the stakes can be high—whether a child will be ordered to live with a strange foster family or be allowed to remain with or return to her or his family. Other decisions may also be made regarding the availability of relatives, visitation with parents and siblings, services which might be provided to various family members and where the child will attend school. The facts leading up to these critical decisions may span a child's entire lifetime or may have emerged only recently.

The emergent nature of shelter care hearings also means that the youth has recently experienced a traumatic event such as physical or sexual abuse or seeing a parent arrested. Appearing in juvenile court for the first time may in and of itself be a traumatic event for a young person. In addition, within days or hours preceding the hearing, a youth like Michael, who is the subject of a dependency petition, has probably been interviewed by a number of unfamiliar adults: school officials, police and/or CPS workers.

To further complicate this difficult interview scenario, the differences between lawyers and young clients, like Katie and Michael, in terms of age, education, culture, and socio-economic status are often so great that their ability to communicate is impeded from the get-go. Lawyers need to develop trust with their clients in order to obtain accurate information that they can use to represent them. When time is short and the lawyer and client start from such different places — this task can seem almost impossible.

Interviewing young people requires more than building trust. It also requires some understanding of adolescent decision-making. A lawyer representing a young person needs to know whether a client is making his or her own decision. This involves understanding a client's suggestibility, to the lawyer, to his or her family members, to social workers or other adults. It is also related to how much and what kind of information a young client needs to make a decision.

In this chapter, you will learn about the challenges that Michael's lawyer faces meeting and interviewing him for the first time right before court. You will have the opportunity to see how a new attorney approaches this task and reflect on how differences between the attorney and young client impact advocacy. You will also see how trauma, as discussed in the previous chapter, impacts the attorney-client relationship as well as a family's interactions with the court.

You will also learn about the nature of advocacy at initial hearings where attorneys, social workers and judges sift through complicated family histories with limited time to prepare. You will learn about the advocacy skills of theory development and negotiation. In Michael's jurisdiction, lawyers must interview clients, gather facts from the social worker and each other, and, where warranted and time permits, negotiate. All of this must occur before appearing before a juvenile court judge who only has the facts set forth in the dependency petition as a background to the State's decision to seek removal of the children.

You will see in this chapter how a court system processes and legally separates Michael's family in the span of a few hours.

Before the Shelter Care Hearing

Katie meant to get to court by 8:00 a.m. so that she can spend time preparing for the onslaught that will occur around 8:30 when clients, social workers and attorneys fill the courtroom lobby. Unfortunately, she pushed the snooze button one time too many and has to rush to arrive by 8:20.

The Baker County Juvenile and Family Justice Center is a large brick box built in the 1990s on the outskirts of downtown. Behind and connected to the large brick box is a smaller cement box, the juvenile detention center, otherwise known as the "juvie jail" or just "juvie."[1] The buildings are fairly nondescript. A passerby may not suspect

---

1. For a history of juvenile court see *supra* ch. 1, *A Brief History of State Intervention*.

the serious nature of the work within. The first floor of the large brick box is dedicated to juvenile delinquency matters — where detained children are kept in holding cells before appearing before juvenile court judges in Courtrooms 1, 2 and 3. A spacious lobby on the first floor has seating for family members and the youth who are free awaiting their court proceedings. Dependency proceedings take place on the second floor in Courtrooms 4 and 5, which are slightly bigger than Courtrooms 1–3 and do not have adjacent holding cells. Also on the second floor is Courtroom 6, a conference room converted to accommodate different treatment courts — Juvenile Drug Court and whatever other new alternative court might be trending.[2] The third floor of the Family Justice Center is dedicated to the court clerks' office and other administrative offices. The fourth and fifth floors house the juvenile probation department, the offices of the state's attorneys, and some volunteer programs.

Katie gets a parking spot close to the courthouse, files dutifully through security and reports directly to the second floor reception area where clients, social workers and lawyers sign in for their hearings. She rarely even stops on the first floor, where a different set of attorneys and clients mill about waiting for delinquency hearings. Although she knows some of the public defenders that represented youth in the delinquency system, she knows little about how it works and at this early stage in her career she doesn't have the bandwidth to engage meaningfully with what is happening on the first floor. Her office represents only parents and children in dependency proceedings and she has made an intentional choice to avoid representing clients in criminal cases.[3]

Katie manages to arrive before any of her clients. She is mostly concerned with the shelter care hearing for Michael and notes as she signs her name next to "*In re* the Dependency of Michael Griffith" on the court docket sheet that the CPS worker Emily

---

2. Problem-solving courts, beginning with Drug Courts, have been proliferating in the United States since the late 1980s. In the dependency system, "Family Drug Treatment Courts" sprung up in the mid-1990s and exist in a few hundred counties. Although models vary by jurisdiction, defined broadly, "[a] family dependency treatment court is a collaborative effort in which court, treatment, and child welfare practitioners come together in a non-adversarial setting to conduct comprehensive child and parent needs assessments. With these assessments as a base, the team builds workable case plans that give parents a viable chance to achieve sobriety, provide a safe nurturing home, become responsible for themselves and their children, and hold their families together." Bureau of Justice Assistance, U.S. Dep't of Justice, Family Dependency Treatment Courts: Addressing Child Abuse and Neglect Cases Using a Drug Court Model 7 (2004), [https://perma.cc/S8PM-ZCTF].

3. The original juvenile courts treated dependent and delinquent children similarly under the progressive belief that children are a product of their environments. Petitions filed in these courts might allege that a child was "dependent" or "delinquent," but the procedures used and the outcomes would be the same. This practice changed after 1967, when the U.S. Supreme Court in *In re Gault* placed limits on the State's *parens patriae* authority in delinquency matters and applied due process protections to juveniles accused of crimes. Although frequently still housed in the same juvenile court building, the *Gault* case effectively put an end to the comingling of delinquent and dependent children and created two distinct systems to serve children who were once believed to be very similar in their need for state intervention. *See supra* ch. 1.

Peters has already signed in. This means she is somewhere in the courthouse. The second floor waiting area is already fairly full with the usual mix of families and professionals. Katie drops her briefcase and files down on a table in "the attorney room," a crowded space with tables, chairs, a few phones, two computers and a handful of lawyers reviewing files, making phone calls and checking email before and between hearings. Katie isn't a morning person so she avoids eye contact with the attorneys and avoids any possible morning small talk. She heads back out to the lobby area and is immediately stopped in the hallway by a 30-something woman, "Are you Katie Olson?"

"I am."

"Your client is here. I'm Emily Peters and Michael just arrived if you want to talk to him. Here is your discovery." She handed Katie a stack of papers about an inch thick held together by a rubber band.[4] Katie isn't prepared for this interaction and has nothing to say but "Thank you."

Discovery

Preparation for an initial hearing will be driven by what evidence a lawyer is able to use in court.

- *In your jurisdiction, what documentary evidence will be provided by the state prior to the initial hearing?*
- *Can it be introduced as evidence during the hearing or used to cross-examine witnesses?*
- *If discovery is not provided prior to the initial hearing, when and how will it be obtained by counsel?*

"Do you want me to introduce you now?" Emily's tone is brusque. Katie is caught off guard, not sure she is quite ready to meet her new 13-year-old client, but replies "um, sure." Responding to Emily's curtness, Katie tries to come across as very pleasant. She has learned during her short career that CPS workers have a lot of power and it is always best to stay on their good side.

Katie follows Emily across the lobby and sees a slightly built African American boy slouching in a chair against the wall. "Michael, this is Katie Olson. She is your lawyer. She is going to want to talk with you this morning before court." Emily turns and leaves abruptly. It is 8:35 a.m. and Katie is still not ready for this interaction, which feels uncomfortable even in the best of circumstances. It appears that Michael feels the same way.

---

4. "Discovery" is used here to refer to the agency records that serve as the factual basis for the state's dependency petition. Jurisdictions differ by court rule or practice on what evidence is made available to counsel prior to the initial hearing.

"Hi Michael, nice to meet you. I have a few things to take care of before we talk. Can you give me a few minutes? Then I can explain to you what's going on this morning and we can talk about your hearing." He nods once without making a sound—but made good eye contact giving Katie some hope for their looming conversation. Katie checks at the sign-in desk to see whether her other clients have signed in—they have not—so she goes back to the attorney room with her stack of discovery.

Reviewing Discovery

Before a petition is filed, the agency may have had several documented contacts with a family over an extended period of time. These records will include CPS referral history and may also include risk assessments, family assessments, case plans, safety plans, medical records, law enforcement records, school records, criminal background checks, treatment records of parents or children, voluntary service agreements, referrals for services and social worker notes.

- *What documents will be most important for the youth's counsel to review when time is short?*

Having read the petition yesterday, she isn't surprised that the record CPS had on Michael's family filled many pages. She pulls out her yellow highlighter and starts flipping through the stack of paper. She still doesn't really understand everything that she is looking at. There is a copy of the petition, several pages of computer-generated "referral history" that documents phone calls received by CPS from various sources with names of referents redacted. There are several pages of caseworker notes from at least three different social workers, starting with Emily Peters and going in chronological order backwards for several years. The notes document discussions with teachers, day care workers, Michael's mother, other relatives and at least one father. She pages through and notices at least one Voluntary Services Agreement dated April 19, 2010, and a certificate of completion for an inpatient drug treatment program called Genesis House.

Intake Information

DATE: 01/12/15   **SCREENER:** J. Ater

CHILD: ALIYAH G.
DOB:
ADDRESS:

RACE: AA

PARENT/GUARDIAN
MOTHER:
FATHER: unknown

REFERRANT INFORMATION:

XXXXXX
Pinehurst Elementary

NARRATIVE: XXXXXXX, a school administrator at Pinehurst Elementary School reported that 9 year old Aliyah was sent to his office after getting into a fight with a boy during recess. She kicked the boy in his private parts and said "you should never touch me with that or I will kill you." This was overheard by the playground supervisor who brought Aliyah to the office. When Aliyah was asked by the principal why she kicked the boy, Aliyah stated that "boys are bad and they can do mean things to girls." The principal asked her why she would say that and Aliyah started crying and screaming and saying "stop touching me, stop touching me!" The nurse was called and Aliyah calmed down and said that her mom has "scary boyfriends" and she "doesn't want them to touch her anymore."

CPS HISTORY: 9 prior referrals

OPEN CASE? N

RELATED: Michael G., Angel G.

RISK: HIGH

ACCEPTED

Intake Information

DATE: 07/13/14   **SCREENER:** D. Brown

CHILD: ANGEL G.
DOB:
ADDRESS:

RACE: AA

PARENT/GUARDIAN
MOTHER: Michelle G.
FATHER: unknown

REFERRANT INFORMATION:

XXXXXX
Jefferson Community Health Clinic

NARRATIVE: XXXXXXX a public health nurse at Jefferson Community Health Clinic reported that Michelle G. came in for a pre-natal visit and appeared to be high. She had difficulty staying awake and speaking clearly but she denied drug use. She had her daughter Angel with her.

CPS HISTORY: 8 prior referrals

RISK: LOW INFORMATION ONLY

NOT ACCEPTED
REFERRED TO ARS: N

Intake Information

DATE: 03/08/13   **SCREENER:** B. TIPPETT

CHILD: MICHAEL G.
DOB:
ADDRESS:

CHILD: ALIYAH G.
DOB:
ADDRESS:

CHILD: ANGEL G.
DOB:
ADDRESS:

RACE: AA

PARENT/GUARDIAN
MOTHER: Michelle G.
FATHER: unknown

REFERRANT INFORMATION:

XXXXXX
BROADVIEW ELEMENTARY

NARRATIVE: XXXXXXX an administrator at Broadview elementary reported that Michael, Aliyah and Angel had been late to school 48 times since the beginning of the school year and had 22 unexcused absences. He reported that the girls were often dressed inappropriately for the weather, were dirty, covered with head lice and hungry.

CPS HISTORY: 7 prior referrals

RISK: LOW INFORMATION ONLY

NOT ACCEPTED

REFERRED TO ARS: Y

Voluntary Services Agreement

This agreement is entered into between the Department of Social and Health Services, Children's Division (DSHS) and Michelle Griffith.

Michelle Griffith agrees to participate in the following services:
1. Enter into inpatient treatment at Genesis House on or before July 1, 2010.
2. Place Michael, Aliyah and Angel voluntarily in the custody of their maternal grandmother, Jaqueline Griffith.
3. Provide releases of information to DSHS for Genesis House and other mutually agreed upon service providers.
4. Successfully participate in inpatient treatment and follow all treatment recommendations.

DSHS agrees to provide the following services:

After about 10 minutes of flipping through the documents, Katie becomes over-whelmed and decides it is time to talk to Emily to see what she is going to ask the judge to do. When she first started doing these hearings, she began by sitting down with her client after paging through some of the discovery. She wants to be attentive to the client and thinks that getting to know her client first before being colored by the social worker will help her to be a more client-centered advocate. She quickly changed this approach when she realized how pressed she would be for time. Her clients had many questions that she couldn't answer so she spent a lot of time saying "I am not sure, let me find out." Now that she is more familiar with what some of those questions will be, she tries to ask the social worker first about her recommendations before interviewing the client.

Timing

- *When is the appropriate time for counsel to review the discovery, before or after speaking with her client?*

Katie finds Emily leaning against a wall outside of Courtroom 5 talking to another social worker. Keeping her most polite demeanor, she approaches them. "Excuse me. I am sorry for interrupting but, Emily, can I ask you a couple of questions about Michael's case?"[5]

Emily replies, "Sure" and they step a few feet away from the other social worker, not out of earshot, but this is how things worked in a courthouse that has limited space for private conversations.

Emily stares at Katie and waits for her questions.

Access to Social Worker

- *In your jurisdiction, how is the agency social worker represented?*
- *Do youth's counsel have the legal authority to communicate directly with social workers?*

Katie tries to sound bright and deferential, not like an adversary. "So, what are you asking for this morning? Where do you want Michael to be placed?"[6]

---

5. Emily is represented by a lawyer, the Assistant Attorney General (AAG). Pursuant to Model Rules of Prof'l Conduct R. 4.2, lawyers are prohibited from communicating with represented persons about matters that are the subject of that representation, "unless the lawyer has the consent of the other lawyer or is authorized to do so by law or a court order." In many jurisdictions, like this one, state's attorneys in dependency proceedings consent to parents' and children's lawyers communicating directly with state caseworkers.

6. Katie's initial encounter with the social worker can be critical to establishing the optimum environment for negotiating, which she will likely need to do in the very near future. Studies have found that the when parties begin their discussions on a pleasant note, negotiations go more smoothly and more agreements are reached. Also, negotiators who are able to get opposing parties to like them and

"I want him to stay where he is. He is at Mr. Jeffries' home, it's a great placement and I was lucky to get him there. It is a little far from his school, but I think we can get transportation for him set up in the next few days." Emily is all business. Her answers are short—she is making Katie work for everything. She isn't unpleasant, just matter of fact.

So far in her career, Katie finds every social worker to be different. Some go on and on and give you more information than you want—as if they are gossiping about the Kardashians and enjoy sharing every lurid detail without you even asking. Others seem to think interactions with lawyers should be kept at a minimum and will respond to questions succinctly, even defensively, as if they are being deposed. Emily Peters leans toward the latter. She is not particularly defensive—but she clearly doesn't have an interest in friendly chitchat or providing detail.

"What about his sisters, where are they?"

"Two different foster homes. Angel and Aliyah are together. Deja is in a different foster home. We are still looking for relatives." Emily is impressed that Katie is thinking about sibling contact—fairly insightful for an inexperienced attorney.

"Will his mom be here today? Or his dad?"

"Mom—I have no idea. She knows about the hearing. Dad won't be here, he's in prison. I did attempt to serve him through his corrections counselor. Maternal grandma might show up. She has had the kids before and I left her a message yesterday to see if she was interested in taking any of them. She didn't return my call, but she could show up."

> ### Interviewing the Social Worker: Theory Development
> At the shelter care hearing, the CPS worker often acts as a party—with authority to negotiate and settle issues of placement, visitation and services conditional upon court approval. The CPS worker will also be a key witness, perhaps the only witness for the state. In light of these dual roles, the child's attorney must identify where her client's interests align with the state's interests while also preparing for an imminent potentially adversarial hearing. This brief interview of the agency social worker may be the only way the attorney may obtain facts necessary to represent her client at the hearing so she must listen carefully for facts that will support the state's theory as well as any possible countervailing theory that the client or his parents might have.

Katie is surprised by how quickly she got used to the way that all of the professionals in these cases referred to people generically by their roles—"mom," "dad,"

---

who treat them respectfully and professionally are more likely to get good results for their clients. *See* Charles B. Craver, *What Makes a Great Legal Negotiator?*, 56 Loy. L. Rev. 337, 355 (2010).

"kid"—like widgets, not people with names. She realizes that it is just shorthand necessitated by the sheer volume of cases and not meant as disrespect, but she wonders how it might sound to the families who can overhear them discussing their most intimate problems in the juvenile court hallway. These labels are just one of the ways that Katie sees people who work in this business distance themselves from the weighty issues and tragic lives that pour past them every day.

She thanks Emily cheerfully and turns to go find Michael.

The Client Interview

It's 8:55 a.m. and Michael is where she left him, unchanged in his expression except now he is tapping his foot as if to the beat of a song playing in his head. He is looking straight ahead, perhaps trying to pretend he is somewhere else.

"Hey, let's get that empty interview room," Katie says casually, pointing in the direction of a small room with a table and four stackable chairs. She shuts the door behind them. "Thanks for waiting. How are you doing today?" *Really? This seemed to be a ridiculous question.* Katie tries to look kind, interested. Serious, but not worried. Memories of her own adolescence tell her that she needs to act "normal"—as if coming to juvenile court happens to everyone, no big deal. Don't look afraid.

"Alright." Michael is nervous but doing a good job of acting disinterested. The sustained eye contact Katie noted hopefully during their introduction is gone. He glances quickly at her then looks down at the stack of papers that Katie puts on the table that separates them.

"So, you probably want to know what is going on today. Let me start by telling you about who I am. I am a lawyer and I have been appointed to represent you." She slid her business card across the table toward him. He looks down at it but does not move. "Have you ever had a lawyer?"

"Nah."

"OK, do you know what lawyers do?"

"Nah, not really."

"Have you seen one on TV?"

"Nah, not really."

Katie is still working on how to introduce her role to young clients who have never dealt with a lawyer before. She thinks the TV line is a good one, but isn't quite sure what to do with someone like Michael who apparently has never seen an episode of *Law and Order*.

"OK, well, lawyers represent people. Like in court. Court is a place where judges make decisions about cases. So today we will go into court a little bit later and the judge will make a decision about your family and where you should live. And my job as your lawyer is to tell the judge what you want to happen and make sure that your rights are protected."

"I have rights?" Michael makes eye contact.

"Yes, you do." Katie tries to hang on to the eye contact for as long she can.

"Do my sisters have rights too?"

"Um, sure they do." Katie isn't quite sure how to answer this because she knows that Michael's sisters are much younger which means they will be appointed a "guardian ad litem"—a non-lawyer who will represent their "best interests." Katie perceives this role very different from her own—which is to represent her clients' "stated interests"—what they tell her they actually want. Michael's sisters do not have the "right" to counsel because, unlike Michael who is appointed his own lawyer, Aliyah, Angel and Deja have not reached the magic age of twelve. Since their representation depends on the availability of volunteers, who for practical reasons cannot be present on a short timeline, the girls will not have representation at this morning's hearing. This makes Katie think they really do not have many rights, at least not this morning. And if they do, they don't really have anyone whose job it is to protect them. This is much too complicated to explain to Michael during this brief interview, so she goes for the short answer that is, technically, correct.[7]

"So back to what I do as your lawyer. I have certain rules I have to follow. One of the big ones is the rule of confidentiality—that means that what you tell me is a secret. We have a confidential relationship and I can't tell anyone else what you tell me unless you give me permission. That means your social worker, your mom, the judge, your foster parent. Does that make sense?"

Michael nods. He seems to be paying attention now. It seems to Katie he is getting it. Although she has to admit she doesn't completely understand her duty of confidentiality. It isn't accurate to say that *everything* Michael tells her is a secret. After all, she needs him to give her facts she can use to persuade the judge, social worker, or others to take his wishes seriously. This falls under what the rule calls "impliedly authorized" disclosure—but she can't quite figure out how to explain that without complicating things too much and losing his attention entirely.[8]

"I will tell the judge and others what you want, that's my job. You tell me what you want to have happen in this case and I try to make that happen for you. I am on your side. I am not here to be on the side of the social worker or the judge or even your

---

7. As discussed at length in Chapter One, there are numerous models of representation for children in dependency proceedings, including professional or volunteer guardians ad litem, best interest lawyers and stated interest lawyers. State statutes and court rules dictate the type of representation children in dependency proceedings receive. For a state-by-state breakdown, see First Star, A Child's Right to Counsel (3d ed. 2012), [https://perma.cc/QP2F-NESR].

8. *See* Model Rules of Prof'l Conduct R. 1.6. Attorneys acting in a stated interest capacity are not typically mandatory reporters due to the ethical duties of confidentiality. There are a few states that treat attorneys for children as mandatory reporters. For state-by-state compilations of mandatory reporting requirements, see Child Welfare Information Gateway, U.S. Dep't of Health & Human Servs., Mandatory Reporters of Child Abuse and Neglect (2013), [https://perma.cc/ATP3-WRWS]; Commission on Domestic Violence, American Bar Association, Mandatory Reporting of Child Abuse (2009), [https://perma.cc/QZ4Q-WC3F].

mom or dad. I just need to know what you think should happen today."[9] Katie says this knowing that this concept is totally unfamiliar to Michael, a child who under normal circumstances has others making decisions for him. Children don't usually tell adults what to do, especially unfamiliar adults who wear suits. Even an adolescent who cares for his younger siblings and sometimes his mother probably doesn't believe that he has the power to tell anybody in this building what to do. With limited time, Katie's main goal is to convince Michael that she is on his side — that he can trust her and that she isn't part of the state machinery that is tearing his family apart.[10]

Role Explanation and Rapport

Lawyers for youth must explain their role to clients in developmentally appropriate language; however, accessible language alone may not compensate for some of the normal deficits that adolescents have in comprehending their relationship to the many different professionals in the dependency system. The ability of adolescents to understand their lawyer's role and communicate with their lawyer will hinge on the lawyer's ability to develop rapport and build trust.

* *What is the best way to explain a lawyer's role to a young client?*

* *How did Katie do?*

* *How has Katie done so far with establishing rapport with Michael?*

* *Can you think of other ways to build rapport quickly with Michael?*

"I want to know where my sisters are and why we aren't together."

"Good question. I was just told by the social worker that Angel and Aliyah are together in a foster home and Deja is in a different foster home. I don't know exactly where, but I can get some more information for you. Sometimes it is tough for the Department to find a place where you can all be together, but they have a duty to try so I will raise that with the social worker and judge if it is important to you."[11]

---

9. Rule 1.2 requires a lawyer to "abide by a client's decisions concerning the objectives of representation." This is part of the "normal client-lawyer relationship" that is required even where a client is young and may have a diminished capacity to make "adequately considered decisions." *Id.* R. 1.14.

10. Because of their limited life experience, youth may struggle to understand their attorney's role when it is initially introduced to them. Emily Buss, *"You're My What?" The Problem of Children's Misperceptions of Their Lawyers' Roles*, 64 FORDHAM L. REV. 1699, 1761 (1996).

11. A more recent amendment to the Social Security Act — the Fostering Connections to Success and Increasing Adoptions Act of 2008 — requires states receiving federal funding to make "reasonable efforts" to place together siblings removed from their home unless a joint placement would be unsafe, in which case states should make reasonable efforts to provide for "frequent visitation" when doing so does not interfere with the siblings' safety or well-being. Pub. L. No. 110-351, 122 Stat. 3949 (codified as amended at 42 U.S.C. § 671(a)(31)). Some states have included sibling placement preferences and visitation requirements in their child welfare statutes. *See, e.g.*, WASH. REV. CODE § 13.34.130(6); CAL. WELF. & INST. CODE § 16002; MD. CODE ANN., FAM. LAW § 5-525(e.).

"Why can't we just go back to our apartment? There is room for all of us there. All of our stuff is there."

"Well, this is a good time to explain what is happening and why we are here. Did you get a piece of paper from the social worker—that looks like this?" Katie slides a copy of the dependency petition across the table so that it is facing Michael. Michael looks at the paper in front of him and shakes his head.

"This is the paper that was filed by the social worker Emily asking the judge to put you and your sisters into foster care. It lists the reasons." Katie proceeds to read the document out loud, pointing to where she is reading so that Michael can follow along. He reads along with her and it appears to her that he understands the words on the page. It is tedious reading through the whole thing line by line, but she feels like it is necessary so long as her client is interested. She gets to the second paragraph of the allegations and Michael interrupts, "That's a lie. I never said 'all I ate was potato chips.'"

"OK, good to know." Katie underlines the statement about potato chips and writes "not true" in the margin. She keeps going and has a feeling that this is going to take a while. She looks at her watch. When she finally gets through all twenty-five paragraphs of the allegations section of the dependency petition there are several more sentences underlined and more notes scribbled in the margin denying or explaining the "facts" reported by the social worker. Michael gets visibly upset a couple of times and almost doesn't make it through this painstaking process, but he stays with it when Katie asks him to "help her out" and promises him that he will only have to do this once.

Katie is impressed by how much Michael engages with her as she reads the petition to him. He does not have a lot of words, but he has strong opinions and is clearly an expert when it comes to his family. After they read the last line Michael says, "If there are so many lies in there, why can't we just go back with my mom to the apartment?"

> ### *Explaining Legal Documents*
>
> *When reviewing court documents with a client lawyers must check for reading comprehension and assess the client's ability to understand what is on the page. It is important to do this respectfully and without judgment.*

Good question. This time Katie thinks it, but doesn't say it out loud. She is getting to the point where she needs to, as they say in this work, "manage client expectations."

"Unfortunately, judges sometimes believe whatever the social worker says at this stage. We don't have a lot of time today to prove that these things are wrong, but we will have a chance later to really explain the truth about your family." *Hmmm, after this comes out Katie wonders if they really will want to explain "the truth" about his family.* At this point she pulls out her yellow legal pad and starts to draw a diagram for Michael to show him where they are in the proceedings. She thinks that this is a useful tool to show her clients that the first hearing is not the only chance to ask for what they want.

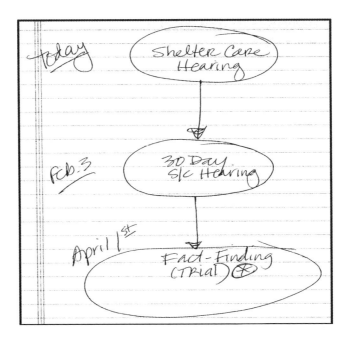

> ### *Explaining Procedure*
>
> *Using visuals can be helpful when explaining court processes.*
>
> * *In your jurisdiction, what and when is the next court hearing following the initial shelter care hearing?*
> * *How might you explain the next steps to a young client?*

"So today we may not get very far at the Shelter Care Hearing, but we will have another chance down here." She points to the diagram where it says "Fact-finding." "Today the judge will make a decision based on very limited information. If you want to talk to the judge today you can, but it isn't always helpful. And we can also come back in 30 days. If there has been any change in circumstances, we can ask the judge to make changes, like to where you are living or how often you see your mom or sisters. Now, if I understand you right, you do not want to be in foster care?"

Michael shakes his head. His expression is blank now. Not angry, not worried, just completely blank.

"OK, well I will definitely ask the judge if you can be returned to your mom. But if the judge disagrees, we should have a backup plan. Do you have any relatives you might like to stay with? I hear you have a grandmother who you stayed with before."

"Yeah. Momma J."

"Would you want to stay with her?"

"I want to stay with my mom."

"Yes. You want to stay with your mom. But what would your second choice be? Momma J. or foster care?"

Long pause. "Momma J."

Active Listening

Active listening is a technique that can help your client feel heard and build trust. Acknowledging and reflecting back facts and emotion can also help young clients make it through lengthier interviews where they need to absorb difficult information. Taking notes appropriately can also help clients feel heard.

- *How did Katie handle the review of the dependency petition with her client?*

- *Are there other effective ways to prepare Michael for the hearing?*

"Do you have any other relatives you might be able to stay with—uncles, aunties, cousins?" Katie becomes self-conscious when the word "auntie" comes out—it sounds like she is trying too hard. She has African American clients and friends who refer to their aunts as "auntie" and so she picked it up. But she realizes when it comes out that it doesn't sound natural coming from her Scandinavian American mouth. She grew up referring to her aunts as aunts not "aunties."

"What about my dad?"

"Is he available? The social worker told me he is in prison." Katie tries to sound neutral, genuinely hopeful. The dependency petition had listed the address for Michael's father as "Brannan Hills Correctional Facility." Katie specifically noted Michael's expression when she read him that section of the petition. In Katie's limited experience, fathers are frequently unavailable but she has had some uncomfortable experiences with clients addressing this issue.[12] A few weeks earlier she found herself in the awkward position of telling a fourteen-year-old client who her father is—or at least who the Department identifies her father to be. When Katie went through the exercise of reading the dependency petition to that client, who had allegedly been sexually abused by her stepfather, the girl said "Who is that?" when Katie read the paragraph identifying her father by name. Katie, caught completely off guard, stammered her way through a confusing explanation of paternity law.

---

12. Several studies have shown that a majority of fathers are uninvolved in their children's dependency proceedings. *See, e.g.*, John M. O'Donnell, *Paternal Involvement in Kinship Foster Care Services in One Father and Multiple Father Families*, 80 CHILD WELFARE 453, 468 (2001) (70% of fathers had never participated in case planning activities); Tanya M. Coakley, *The Influence of Father Involvement On Child Welfare Permanency Outcomes: A Secondary Data Analysis,* 35 CHILD & YOUTH SERVS. REV. 174 (2013). (61.4% of fathers did not sign case plans and fewer than half of those who signed did not comply with them.) For a discussion of possible reasons for fathers' lack on involvement, see Steve M. Wood & Jesse R. Russell, *Effects of Parental and Attorney Involvement on Reunification in Juvenile Dependency Cases,* 33 CHILD. & YOUTH SERVS. REV. 1730, 1732 (2011).

> **Differences**
>
> - *What can a lawyer do to address the differences that exist from the outset between the lawyer and her client?*
> - *How did Katie do?*
> - *What could she have done differently?*
> - *In what ways are you different from your clients and how will that effect how you communicate with them?*

Michael looks blank again. He appears to be shutting down now. The time is 9:30 a.m. Katie sees the court bailiff standing outside of the interview room, peering through the window in the door to get her attention. *Michael and she are both saved.* She opens the door.

The bailiff says, "Excuse me" politely to Michael and turns to Katie. "Can you give me an idea about how much time you will need on Griffith? We have a heavy calendar this morning and I am just trying to figure out what is going to go in first and how much time these hearings will take. You also have the Jimerson case and your client can't be brought over from the jail until this afternoon. You don't have a client yet on the emergency placement hearing—Dawson. The social worker is here, though, and she wants to get the order signed soon."

Katie leads Michael back to his seat against the wall and instructs him to "hang on for a little bit while I go handle a few other things." He looks relieved to be released from the small interview room and all of the questioning.

> **Limited Time**
>
> - *In your jurisdiction, how much time do lawyers have to prepare for shelter care hearings?*
> - *Is this adequate to review discovery and meet with and interview clients?*
> - *How can you structure an interview to make sure that you give and get the information you need to competently and ethically represent your client in a short time period?*
> - *How did Katie do?*
> - *What could she have done differently?*

Katie deals quickly with the Dawson matter by having her client paged in the lobby and placing a call to the last phone number she has in her file. Disconnected. It seems clear that this client is MIA, which is precisely why there is an emergency placement hearing. The social worker wants authority to put the sixteen-year-old dependent girl in a group home once she surfaces after allegedly running away from a relative placement. Katie has no client and no position—she inherited this file from another attorney and has never had contact with this teenager. Feeling there is nothing she can do, and plenty she still needs to do for Michael's case, she shuffles quickly into the courtroom while the social worker asks the judge to sign an order placing the absent Miss Dawson in a group home. Katie says "No position" when the judge looks toward her following the social worker's lengthy explanation of this youth's "out of control" behavior. Katie's statement is understood by everyone in the courtroom as code for "I have no clue where my client is."[13]

Emily Peters is waiting outside of the courtroom when Katie emerges. "Are you ready on Griffith?"

"Well, I have a few questions for you. Did the grandmother ever show up? What about mom? Michael's preference is to be at home with his mom and sisters, but his second choice is grandma."

"Mom is here, she just finished meeting with her attorney. Grandmother did not show, but I am willing to speak with her and consider placement if she is willing. In reviewing the record, I think she probably doesn't have room for all of them. My guess is that she will be willing to take the baby." Again Emily's answers are short and Katie has no idea what she is really thinking about this family and whether to trust her. She shows little emotion—including no evidence of compassion for Michael and his desire to be reunited with his family. Katie wishes she had asked Michael whether he has an opinion about Emily. She figures that he probably doesn't, or at least won't share one with her, but he has spent more time with Emily now than Katie has and he likely has some kind of feel for whether she can be trusted to follow through.

Katie thanks Emily for being willing to explore the grandmother as a placement option and turns around to look for Michael's mom's attorney. Michael's mother's position will be crucial. If she is not going to fight to get her children back, Katie is not going to be able to fight to get Michael returned to his mother's care. Ambivalence on the mother's part will be devastating to Michael's stated desire to return home.

> ### Negotiation Approaches
>
> *Negotiators have different approaches, identified in the literature as either "Cooperative/Problem Solvers" (a "win-win" approach) or "Competitive/Adversarial" (a "win-lose" approach). While most scholars assert that the Cooperative/Problem Solver approach is more effective, research suggests that good negotiators often combine styles and are able to apply different types of approaches to different settings.*
>
> * *What types of negotiators do you think Katie and Emily might be?*

---

13. MODEL RULE 1.6 prohibits an attorney from revealing "information relating to the representation of a client" unless the client gives informed consent or implied authorization to do so. Attorneys may handle the situation of an absent client with whom they have had no contact in different ways; however, the rule is broad and would place limits on what an attorney can say.

George Bowman is appointed to represent Michelle Griffith. He is an older portly white man, whose years of experience do not necessarily translate to more competent representation of his clients. Nevertheless, Katie likes him, in the way that she is fond of most of the public defenders in juvenile court who she finds to be generous and iconoclastic.

"George, I am representing Michael Griffith, the oldest son of Michelle Griffith."

"Who?" George takes a handkerchief from his back pocket and blows his nose. Katie thinks, *Gross. Who uses handkerchiefs anymore?*

"Michelle Griffith is your client, the mom on the shelter care hearing you have this morning."

"Oh, yeah, right. Michelle. Nice lady. Just talked to her. She wants her kids back."

"Great. Michael wants to go back with her. What is she doing about treatment and that boyfriend she supposedly lives with who is causing problems?"

"She's signing up today for an inpatient program. The boyfriend is gone. He is in jail. She wants her kids with her mom while she completes a 30- or 60-day program."[14] George is adept with facts once he focuses.

"Is the grandmother willing? My client is fine with that temporarily but the social worker says she isn't sure the grandmother wants the kids. Is grandma here?"

"She is supposed to be here. Not sure where she is. But my client assures me that she is on board. Of course, the Department will want a home study or at least a criminal background check and that could take a while.[15] Michelle also mentions a cousin that she thought might be interested. Prius? No, wait, Porsche? Yeah, Porsche. Lives on the east side but she is family." George squints to look at his notes.

"OK, I'll run that name by Michael. He is also really worried about his sisters being separated. We will ask for a placement where they can be together. Is Michelle hoping to take the baby to treatment with her? She is less than a year old; mom might be able to take her." *Oh, shoot, there she goes referring to "mom" like she isn't a person with a name just like everyone else around here.*

---

14. Completing substance abuse treatment is associated with significantly fewer days in foster care for dependent children and a greater likelihood of family reunification. Beth L. Green et al., *Does Substance Abuse Treatment Make a Difference for Child Welfare Case Outcomes?*, 29 Child. & Youth Servs. Rev. 460, 467–68 (2007). Unfortunately, less than half of parents referred to substance abuse counseling in dependency cases attend any portion of treatment, and only about 20% of parents fully complete the programs. Arazais Oliveros & Joan Kaufman, *Addressing Substance Abuse Treatment Needs of Parents Involved with the Child Welfare System*, 90 Child Welfare 25, 28 (2011).

15. Federal law that encourages states to consider relative placements allows the states to set their own "child protection standards," which can prevent placement with relatives who would otherwise receive preference over non-relatives. 42 U.S.C § 671(a)(19). As of July 2013, twenty-eight states and the District of Columbia require that potential relative caretakers — and sometimes all adult members of their households — undergo criminal background checks. Child Welfare Information Gateway, U.S. Dep't of Health & Human Servs., Placement of Children with Relatives (2013), [https://perma.cc/AB7L-CB9K].

George is blowing his nose again. "Well, I told her to take the quickest spot she could get, with or without her baby. Of course she'll take her baby if she can. I think we are mostly in agreement with the Department at this point, not much we can fight about."

Katie nods in agreement and turns around to find Michael again. This time she finds him sitting next to a young African American woman dressed in sweat pants and a wool sweater, and they are laughing. Not really laughing, more like a chuckle, as if they have an inside joke. Shoulders going up and down, almost imperceptibly. Michael doesn't have a huge grin, but the corners of his mouth are turned up and he is shaking his head, like he is trying not to laugh. Similarly, the woman, who Katie assumes must be his mother, is shaking her head and smiling sheepishly. They quickly become serious when Katie approaches them.

"You must be Michelle. I'm Katie Olson, Michael's attorney." Katie holds her hand out but Michelle has no intention of shaking her hand. Michelle nods and stares up at Katie from her seat without saying a word. She looks very tired. Michael seems angry, but it is unclear to Katie whether his anger is directed toward her or toward his mother. Katie tries not to skip a beat, "Michael, can we talk for just a few more minutes?"

Michael doesn't look directly at Katie and responds, "Can my mom come?"

"Well, let me talk to her lawyer and see if we can all speak together. But I would first like to have a couple of minutes just with you, if you don't mind." Katie does not have time to explain the ethical rules that prevent her from meeting with a represented person without her lawyer or to discuss the importance of maintaining attorney–client privilege.[16] She just needs to use the few minutes she has left before being hauled into court to let Michael know what is going to happen during the hearing and find out whether he can live with it.

> ### *Parent-Child Privilege*
>
> *States' evidentiary rules differ with respect to whether a child's communications to a parent are privileged.*
>
> - *What are the rules in your jurisdiction?*
>
> - *Are parent witnesses asked to testify about statements their children have made to them?*

---

16. Putting aside the ethical prohibition of communicating with a represented party without that lawyer's permission, an attorney who meets with a client and a third person waives the attorney-client privilege with respect to any statements made by the client during that meeting. A few states have a parent-child privilege created by statute or common law, which may protect statements made by children in front of their parents. *See, e.g.*, RCW 5.60.060 (parent of minor arrested on a criminal charge may not be examined as to a communication between the child and his or her attorney if the communication was made in the presence of the parent or guardian); Idaho Code § 9-203(e) (the limited privilege does not apply to cases between parent or child, criminal cases involving violence between parent and child or to cases where a child has been physically injured by a parent); People v. Fitzgerald, 101 Misc.2d 712, 422 N.Y.S.2d 309 (1979).

Michael slowly gets out of his chair. He exchanges a look with his mom—that almost-smile again—and follows Katie back into the small interview room. Katie shuts the door as she begins talking. "According to your mom's attorney, she wants to get into inpatient treatment and would like you to live with your grandmother while she finishes treatment. What do you think?"

Michael shrugs his shoulders. "OK, I guess." Michael seems more distant now. Is there something about his conversation with his mom that makes him trust Katie less?

"I don't know whether your grandmother is ok with taking you and your sisters because she isn't here this morning. Do you know whether or not you can live with her?"

Michael looks out the window in the door of the interview room as if the answer might be out there. "Nah. Maybe. I mean prob'ly. I don't really know. You'd have to ask her."

Katie wonders if she has time to call the grandmother before the hearing, but knows she should at least try. "Do you have her number?"

"Nah. But my mom does."

"Can you get it from her?" Katie doesn't have time to think whether this is appropriate, whether she should really go through George to get the number or whether she can use her client to get the information.

Michael gets up, slowly again as if he is very old, and goes out to find his mother. Katie waits in the interview room and shuffles through the discovery again. Michael returns with a scrap of paper and a number scribbled on it. He puts it on the table in front of Katie and sits down again. Katie pulls out her phone, but pauses wondering whether she should make this call in front of Michael. He doesn't budge and appears interested in seeing her make the call. She dials and waits. It goes to voicemail. She leaves a message, "Hello, Mrs. Griffith, my name is Katie Olson and I am an attorney in juvenile court representing your grandson Michael. I would like to speak with you as soon as possible; if you can call us back at this number I would really appreciate it. Again, the name is Katie Olson, Michael's attorney." Katie looks at Michael and says, "Well, I wish we knew the answer before we go into court." She looks down at her notes. "Oh, yeah, your mom's attorney mentioned a cousin by the name of Porsche if your grandmother is not available. Do you know her?"

Communicating with Witnesses and Other Third Parties

Prior to hearings, lawyers often need to gather information from potential witnesses quickly.

- *Was voicemail the best method of communication for Katie to use with Michael's grandmother? Should she have texted?*

- *With so little time, what other means could Katie have used in this situation to contact the grandmother?*

- *Are there ethical considerations?*

Michael nods, "Yeah, she's OK."

"What is she like? How well do you know her?"

"She is my mom's cousin. She lives kind of far away. She has like four of her own kids so I don't know if she can take all of us."

"Would you prefer her to foster care?" Katie knows that these questions are unreasonable, almost ridiculous at this stage, but she still needs answers. She knows her client has limited information about his choices or what they mean and that she is putting him on the spot. Still, there seems to be no other way to state Michael's position in court without getting as many definite answers as she can pull out of him.

Michael pauses. He looks to be seriously considering the question. "I guess so. If she will take my sisters too."

"Well, what I can do is ask the social worker to check Porsche out and ask the court to give the social worker permission to place you with her if your grandmother doesn't work out. How does that sound?"

Michael nods.

> ### Client Decision-Making and Direction
>
> *Stated interest lawyers are directed by their clients. This means that lawyers need to be able to understand their client's position and be able to accurately state that position in court.*
>
> - *Does Katie understand Michael's position with respect to placement?*
> - *How can you be sure that you understand your client's position?*
> - *What role does the lawyer have, if any, in formulating that position?*

At this point, Emily is standing outside of the interview room holding a piece of paper. Katie opens the door and Emily hands her a Shelter Care Order. "Here you go. Mom is pretty much in agreement with everything but we might have to argue about visitation."

Behind Katie stood the court bailiff, "We need to get you in right after the morning recess, about 10:30. One of the dads just got here from the jail and this hearing takes priority. Does that work?" She turns and leaves without waiting for an answer.

The Judge's Story: Honorable Dorothy L. Adams

When Judge Adams leaves the bench and enters her office chambers, the first thing she does is pull off her black robe and throw it over a small orange couch that is crammed in the corner. That robe is one of the worst parts of her job. Hot and itchy, no matter the season or what she has on underneath. She keeps meaning to upgrade to a higher quality robe at her own expense. But, frankly, she does not think she is paid enough to have to use her own resources for a work-related purchase.

Dorothy Adams spent the first 20-plus years of her career working for a large private law firm. She made it to managing partner of the firm's litigation section when she realized that she was not particularly happy at work. Although she enjoyed her colleagues and her occasional opportunities to appear in court, these positives were squeezed out as she spent more time doing administrative work. She was paid well, which helped when her children were admitted to expensive private colleges, but she felt less motivated by her paycheck after they graduated. She was able to satisfy her passion for serving the community by volunteering on several boards and teaching occasionally at the local law school. But eventually all of the volunteer work on top of her responsibilities at the firm just wore her out and made her long for a career where she could do something fulfilling during a 40- or 50-hour workweek. She feels almost guilty even thinking this way. She fears that her thirty-something "millennial" children are rubbing off on her — with their craving for purpose and work-life balance. She is a hard-working baby boomer and often thinks her children's desire to "have it all" is unrealistic.[17]

Dorothy Adams inherits her commitment to community service from her parents. Her father was a lawyer, with his own firm in a small suburban town. At various times he served on the town council, the school board and on many non-profit boards. Judge Adams' earliest memories are of attending community meetings with her father, where he always treated people kindly. Judge Adams' mother was a public schoolteacher who received a national award for her work assisting teenage parents to graduate from high school. Judge Adams knew at a young age that she wanted to be a lawyer and would be happy following in her father's footsteps.

When her father passed away after a grueling battle with cancer, Dorothy Adams found herself immobilized by grief. She was surprised by her reaction — a grown woman, successful attorney, unable to take a parents' death in stride. She still remembers having lunch with her close friend and mentor, a few months after her father died. She could barely order from a menu, when her mentor asked, "Have you thought about the bench?" How ridiculous, she thought. She couldn't decide what to eat for lunch, how could she make decisions about people's lives? That turned out to be the beginning of her journey to wearing a black robe and making many difficult decisions about many people's lives.

By the time she was assigned to the Baker County Family Justice Center, Judge Adams had been a judicial officer for four years, mostly sitting on the civil calendar where she felt comfortable after her years as a civil litigator. She often recognized the lawyers who appeared before her and she was unfazed by the huge sums of money at stake. When the presiding judge announced her assignment to juvenile court

---

17. Brigid Schulte, *Millenials Want Work-life Balance: Their Bosses Just Don't Get Why*, Wash. Post, May 5, 2015, [https://perma.cc/YGT5-ERK6].

without even consulting with her, Judge Adams was initially perturbed. But she knew it was inevitable that she would wind up there eventually and she figures that she is probably more suited for the job than many of her colleagues.[18] She heard complaints from other judges that the Family Justice Center was "chaotic" and "heart breaking." The workload was often described as unmanageable and the pace impossible. None of these things really caused her concern.

Juvenile Court Judge Assignment

- *How are juvenile or family court judges selected in your jurisdiction?*

- *Do they specialize or do they rotate amongst different divisions or practice areas?*

- *What are the benefits and challenges of your particular system?*

Judge Adams is not one to back down from a challenge. In fact, she became excited once she got over not being consulted about the transfer. She began reading voraciously everything she could get her hands on to prepare for the new assignment. She read bench books, bench cards and the articles on child welfare and juvenile justice that were cited in them.[19] She read publications from nationally recognized organizations like "Reasonable Efforts: A Judicial Perspective,"[20] "Forever Families: Improving Outcomes by Achieving Permanency for Legal Orphans"[21] and "Racial and Ethnic Disparity and Disproportionality in Child Welfare and Juvenile Justice: A Compendium."[22] She toured the juvenile detention facility, the juvenile prison two hours away and even visited a group home (one that fell under the umbrella of a

---

18. Jurisdictions vary in the structure of their juvenile court systems. While some juvenile courts are independent and have career juvenile court judges, many others are divisions of superior or other courts with broader jurisdiction and judges rotate between different assignments including juvenile, civil, criminal and family court.

19. "Bench books" and "bench cards" are materials, similar to manuals that judges refer to for guidance. *See e.g.* COURT IMPROVEMENT TRAINING ACADEMY, WASHINGTON STATE JUVENILE NON-OFFENDER BENCHBOOK, (2011), [https://perma.cc/YK97-YN2V]; NANCY B. MILLER & CANDICE L. MAZE, JUDICIAL COUNCIL OF CALIFORNIA A DOGBOOK FOR ATTORNEYS REPRESENTING CHILDREN AND PARENTS (2d ed. 2011), [https://perma.cc/H4BQ-NAUG]; NATIONAL COUNCIL OF JUVENILE AND FAMILY COURT JUDGES, RIGHT FROM THE START: CCC [COURTS CATALYZING CHANGE] PRELIMINARY PROTECTIVE HEARING BENCHCARD—A TOOL FOR JUDICIAL DECISION-MAKING (2010), [https://perma.cc/T3N7-9N8U]; AMERICAN BAR ASSOCIATION CENTER ON CHILDREN'S LAW, ENGAGING ADOLESCENTS (AGES 12–15) IN THE COURTROOM, (2009), [https://perma.cc/5TXA-HFWH].

20. NATIONAL COUNCIL OF JUVENILE & FAMILY COURT JUDGES, *Reasonable Efforts: A Judicial Perspective*, (Sept. 23, 2014), [https://perma.cc/VF6E-N96C].

21. NATIONAL COUNCIL OF JUVENILE & FAMILY COURT JUDGES, FOREVER FAMILIES: IMPROVING OUTCOMES BY ACHIEVING PERMANENCY FOR LEGAL ORPHANS, (April 2013), [https://perma.cc/JJ77-A9TU].

22. CENTER FOR JUVENILE JUSTICE REFORM, RACIAL AND ETHNIC DISPARITY AND DISPROPORTIONALITY IN CHILD WELFARE AND JUVENILE JUSTICE: A COMPENDIUM (2009), [https://perma.cc/BRN4-6KS2].

non-profit organization where she had previously served as a board member). She immersed herself in the research and data so that by the time she showed up at the Baker County Family Justice Center, she felt confident she would not completely screw up.

The juvenile court is a new world to her, far from the 40th floor office she once inhabited as a managing partner. But as a mother, particularly as a mother of a child with a disability, she feels it is not entirely foreign terrain. Although she lacks experience in dependency law and juvenile delinquency proceedings, Dorothy Adams is not a stranger to advocating for children. Her youngest child, Jason, was diagnosed with autism in his later years in elementary school. He struggled socially and emotionally for many years before being diagnosed. Back then, "Autism Spectrum Disorder" as it appears now on the DSM-5, was often misdiagnosed or completely overlooked.[23] This leaves parents like the Adams feeling helpless, and to make matters worse, judged. She has vivid memories of sitting in the principal's office at her son's school. She was dressed in a suit, like lawyers often are, and she was taking notes on a yellow pad of paper, as lawyers often do. But she was unprepared for the blank stares when she asked about services that might assist Jason. She was unprepared for educational professionals to ask her what was "going on at home" and suggesting that her "busy career" might be causing her child to act out and behave in ways that drew much needed attention from his teachers and classmates. She remembers the tears that she held back when she sat in a room full of near strangers discussing her son's most recent episode of spreading feces on the walls in the school bathroom. She still cringes at the time she lost it, screaming at the special education specialist who insisted that Jason just needed more attention at home and perhaps some weekly counseling sessions to deal with his issues of abandonment. *Abandonment. Are you f--- ing kidding me?* It was not one of her better moments.

After 18 months in juvenile court, Judge Adams has had countless opportunities to empathize with parents who feel judged. She finds it both exhilarating and exhausting. She wonders if this is her calling.

The Shelter Care Hearing

"All rise." The bailiff is barely able to get the line out before Judge Adams is sitting down saying, "Please be seated."

---

23. In 2013, the fifth edition of the Diagnostic and Statistical Manual of Mental Disorders ("DSM-5") changed the definition of autism, and included autistic disorder, Asperger's Syndrome and other Pervasive Developmental Disorders Not Otherwise Specified ("PDD-NOS") under one umbrella category: Autism Spectrum Disorder ("ASD"). ASD is characterized by impaired social interaction and restricted and repetitive behaviors. Over the past several decades, it has increasingly been accepted as a neurobiological disorder. *See* Catherine Lord & Somer L. Bishop, *Recent Advances in Autism Research as Reflected in DSM-5 Criteria for Autism Spectrum Disorder,* 11 Ann. Rev. of Clinical Psychol. 53 (2015).

Judge Adams is a medium-sized blonde woman who appears to be in her late fifties or early sixties. She wears tortoise shell reading glasses and a frown. It is difficult to tell if it is a real frown or whether her face is permanently set in a scowl she earned through years of making difficult decisions. She sits robed behind a raised desk with the court bailiff seated below to her left and a clerk seated below to her right. There is a nameplate in front of her with her full name and title: "Honorable Dorothy L. Adams."

The bailiff announces, "Before the court are the cases of Michael Griffith, Angel Griffith, Aliyah Griffith and Deja Jones. Cause numbers 15-7-0234, 0235, 0236 and 0237. Will the parties please introduce themselves for the record."

Michael sits next to Katie behind a table about 12 feet away from the judge, right in the middle of the courtroom. There is a microphone on the desk in front of him. To his right sits a large middle-aged white man in a gray suit with a stack of files in front of him on the table. To the white man's right sits Michael's mother, Michelle. To her right sits a white woman with dark wiry hair and next to her a familiar face to Michael, Tommy Sykes, Aliyah's father. Crowded next to Tommy is another older white-haired man in a rumpled suit jacket and next to him is D.J. looking haggard in an orange jumpsuit. His legs are shackled and a uniformed police officer is standing directly behind him. Michael is taken aback by D.J.'s appearance but he is even more surprised to see Tommy. He has not seen Tommy in a couple of years and he wonders what he is doing there. He looks tired. Michael stares at him and thinks about the last time he saw Tommy. Tommy had dropped Aliyah off after taking her out for her birthday. He didn't walk her to the door or come in and say hello. He just sat in his gold Buick while Aliyah got out of the passenger side and then he drove away quickly when she reached the front porch. Aliyah didn't seem to mind; she burst into the apartment cheerfully bragging about being taken out to Chuck E. Cheese and getting birthday cake and fingernail polish.

While Michael is thinking about Tommy and Aliyah, he hears Katie say her name and then, "seated to my right is Michael Griffith." Michael looks up at the judge and is unsure if he is supposed to say anything. She looks at him and appears to smile—at least with her mouth. Then the man next to him says gruffly "George Bowman for the mother, Michelle Griffith," followed by the white wiry haired woman who says "Leslie Spector for Thomas Sykes, father of Aliyah Griffith, who is seated to my right." Finally, the white-haired man says "Adam Cross for Darryl Jones, father of Deja Jones. Mr. Jones is present, transported from the county jail for this hearing." Michael thinks that seems obvious. Why would his attorney point that out?

The judge then looks toward another woman, this one seated behind a table to the far left of Michael. This young woman wears a dark suit and sits up straight with several files in front of her. She is sitting next to Emily Peters, the caseworker. Michael feels his face grow warmer when he sees Emily and is reminded about how much he does not like her. The tightness in his chest returns and he notices that again his palms are feeling sweaty. He sees Emily raise her right hand and say that she would tell the truth to the judge. Michael wonders how she will do that when she does not know the truth about his family and she is reading from a piece of paper that is filled with lies.

Emily talks directly to Judge Adams, who seems to hang on her every word. The woman sitting next to Emily, who identified herself as the Assistant Attorney General, occasionally asks her questions. Emily explains that everything she wrote in the dependency petition was true and she elaborates where she could provide additional facts that generally make Michelle look even worse than she appears on paper.

Emily ends her testimony with "I am asking the court to place all of the children in DCFS-approved care, with the authority to place with relatives should they be available and appropriate." Michael continues to hate her.

Judge Adams appears to be taking notes. She pauses, looks at the computer monitor on her desk, and then turns to look at George Bowman. "Mr. Bowman, would you like to cross-examine the caseworker?"

George Bowman does not look up from his yellow pad of paper but starts talking, "Just briefly, your honor." He then looks at Emily and says, "Ms. Peters, Michelle Griffith's mother, the children's maternal grandmother Jacqueline Griffith, has cared for the children before, correct?"

"That's correct."

"With the Department's approval, correct?"

"Yes."

"And you are willing to place the children with the maternal grandmother if she is willing to have them?"

"Yes, assuming she still has an appropriate home for them and can pass a new criminal history background check for all of the adults living in her house."[24]

"And that determination will take how long?"

"Depends on the maternal grandmother. I can start the process today, but she needs to make herself available."

After a few more questions, George Bowman looks at the judge and says "Nothing further, your honor." Michael thinks that Emily sounds irritated with Mr. Bowman's questions, like they are not very smart questions and he should know the answers already.

Next, the wiry haired Leslie Spector begins to ask Emily questions. "Ms. Peters, the Department has not received any CPS referrals regarding Mr. Sykes, right?"

"That's right, Mr. Sykes has made referrals to CPS regarding the mother but has not been the subject of any referrals."

"So you have no reason to believe that Mr. Sykes is not capable of parenting at this time, correct?"

---

24. *See supra* note 15.

"Mr. Sykes says to me he is unwilling to parent at this time, which seems to make him unavailable. And, he has convictions for drug possession and domestic violence which need to be explored further."

"The convictions are over 10 years old." Leslie Spector says this incredulously as a statement not a question. Ms. Peters does not respond.

"Am I right?" Leslie Spector now sounds a little angry.

"Yes." Emily replies calmly, without apology or defensiveness. Michael is curious about Tommy's criminal history but he wonders what any of this has to do with anything. He is also confused about why the lawyers seem to be asking questions that they already know the answers to.[25]

"Nothing further." Ms. Spector stops speaking and the judge turns her eyes toward the white-haired Mr. Cross sitting next to D.J.

Mr. Cross asks Emily one question about whether she has investigated any of Mr. Jones' relatives, which she has not. D.J. looks bored and weary. It is Katie's turn. Michael is trying to listen carefully to what is happening but he is having trouble understanding the language and why there are so many different people talking. Katie tried to describe to him what would happen in court as they were walking in and as they were sitting in the courtroom waiting for the judge to enter. The proceedings go quickly at first and he can not keep up. He tries, but then as the lawyers keep talking and asking questions things begin to drag on, mind numbingly. He becomes distracted and wants it all to be over with.[26]

Katie asks Emily more questions, using the same tone and sentence structure as the other two lawyers. Her questions are more interesting to Michael—she asks about his sisters and whether they could be placed together; she asks about whether they can visit with each other if they are not placed together and how often.[27] The

---

25. One of the classic rules of cross-examination, famously coined by Professor Irving Younger as the "Ten Commandments of Cross-Examination" and still adhered to today is: "4. Be prepared. Never ask a question to which you do not know the answer." IRVING YOUNGER, THE ART OF CROSS-EXAMINATION, ABA MONOGRAPH SERIES No. 1 (1976) (ABA Section on Litigation).

26. Jurisdictions vary as to whether youth are allowed to attend shelter care and other dependency hearings. Andrea Khoury, *Seen and Heard: Involving Children in Dependency Court*, 25 CHILD L. PRAC. 145, 146 (2006). Some states have adopted language to give foster children certain "rights" including the right to be heard in court. *E.g.*, ARIZ. REV. STAT. §8-529 (child has right to attend hearings and speak to judge); CAL.WELF. & INST.CODE §16001.9(a)(17) (right to "attend hearings and speak to the judge."); FLA. STAT. §39.4085(19) (right "[t]o be heard by the court, if appropriate, at all review hearings."), TEX. FAM. CODE ANN. §263.008(b)(13) (right to "participation in a court hearing that involves the child.") Surveys have shown that youth have a positive experience in court and judges find their presence helpful. *See, Engaging Youth in Court: A National Analysis*, ABA CENTER ON CHILDREN AND THE LAW (2015), pdf [https://perma.cc/J3QL-FTBA]; *Dependent Youth Interviews Pilot Program*, WASHINGTON STATE CENTER FOR COURT RESEARCH, FINAL REPORT TO THE LEGISLATURE (2010), [https://perma.cc/6Z8Y-P3FE].

27. Federal law requires states receiving funding for their foster care systems to make reasonable efforts to place siblings together and if that is not possible to provide for "frequent visitation" when doing so does not interfere with the siblings' safety. 42 U.S.C. §671(a)(31).

answers Emily gives are vague and unhelpful. "The Department will do its best to ensure that the children have regular contact." "The Department will arrange for visits at least once per week between the children and their mother."[28] Michael does not think these are very good answers and he does not trust that Emily cares at all about whether he sees his sisters or his mother. He is glad that Katie is raising these issues and he feels like she really does care if he sees his sisters, although he isn't sure why.[29]

Judge Adams appears to be interested in Emily's answers to the lawyers' questions, but only mildly so. Michael catches the judge looking at him while Emily is talking. He looks away quickly. He is not sure where to look. He does not want to look at Emily when she is talking. He hates her. If he stares at the judge, she might stare back at him. He is afraid to look at his mother, her sorrow and helplessness make his throat tight. He exchanges looks with Tommy but Tommy also looks lost and uncomfortable. Michael decides to just look down at his hands that are sitting on the desk in front of him. He taps one finger nervously.

When Katie is finished asking questions, she uses the same phrase that George Bowman and Leslie Spector used, "No further questions, your honor." Michael is disappointed that Katie did not ask Emily about why she lied in the petition. Katie acted like she believed what he told her about the lies. She took notes and wrote what he said down on paper, but she does not ask about any of it. Even after Emily told the judge that everything in the petition is true. This seems to Michael to be a big mistake on her part and he begins to question Katie's capability.

Michael is surprised when Judge Adams starts asking Emily questions. Michael actually has a fleeting pang of sympathy for Emily. He can't help but think how awful it is to have so many people asking you questions. And then he has a flash of terror wondering if the judge will ask him questions even though Katie has promised him he won't have to talk if he doesn't want to.

Looking over her reading glasses, Judge Adams asks Emily, "Where are these children going to school?"[30] Michael thinks she sounds a little mad. He isn't sure if he is going to be in trouble. His mind races thinking of his school attendance record.

---

28. Studies have consistently found that the frequency of parent-child visitation is a key predictor of reunification. Inger P. Davis et al., *Parental Visiting and Foster Care Reunification*, 18 Child. & Youth Servs. Rev. 363, 377–78 (1996). Unfortunately, many parents fail to visit consistently and it is common for them not to visit at all. Ande Nesmith, *Factors Influencing the Regularity of Parental Visits with Children in Foster Care*, 32 Child & Adoles.t Soc. Work J. 219 (2015). Two factors that often hinder visitation are lack of facilitation by caseworkers and parental substance abuse. *Id.* at 226–27.

29. One argument for youth's court attendance is that it gives young clients the opportunity to observe their attorney in action and thereby understand their attorney's role. Buss, *supra* note 10, at 1756–61.

30. All placements must be made with the child's best interests in mind, which impliedly encompasses schooling. At least seven states require specific consideration as to whether a placement meets the child's educational needs. *See, e.g.*, Md. Code, Fam. Law § 5-525(f)(1)(v); N.Y. Fam. Ct. Act § 1089(c)(2)(iii); Wash. Rev. Code § 13.34.138(2)(c)(viii).

Emily seems a little caught off guard but does not hesitate, "Aliyah and Angel attend John Muir Elementary. Their foster mother will be transferring them to Jane Addams Elementary next week; it is right down the street from where she lives. Michael was attending Stewart Middle School. We will do our best to make sure he stays there." Michael is caught off guard by the term "was attending." As if yesterday was a long time ago and he now does not go to Stewart anymore. Could that be true?[31]

The judge presses further, "Where will they go if they are placed with their grandmother?"

"I am not sure where the grandmother lives or what schools are in her area." Emily answers honestly.

Katie leans over to Michael and whispers, "Do you know what schools are near your grandma's?" Michael tells her that their grandma lives farther from their schools than their mom but she has a car and can probably drive them. Katie frowns. She is irritated with herself for not talking to Michael about school before the hearing. She knows Judge Adams is always going to ask about school; it is her pet issue now.[32] Michael does not understand why they are talking about school or what he said that made his lawyer look cross. The talk of school makes him long to be there, like he was just a few days ago, before all of this happened and his world was torn apart.

> ### *Educational Needs of Foster Youth*
> * *Does your state have specific statutes that address the educational needs of dependent children?*

After the judge questions Emily, she asks the lawyers if they have any more questions for her. Michael is relieved when all the lawyers decline the judge's offer. Judge Adams turns to George Bowman and says "I will hear from you first Mr. Bowman. Do you have any evidence to present?"[33]

---

31. The federal McKinney-Vento Homeless Education Assistance Improvements Act of 2001 encourages states to ensure educational stability for homeless youth. *See* 42 U.S.C. §§ 11431–11432. This is chiefly achieved through assistance that allows students to continue to attend their accustomed schools in spite of a loss of housing. Children in shelter care status or otherwise awaiting placement are considered homeless for purposes of the law. *Id.* § 11434a(2)(B)(i).

32. Because of the poor educational outcomes faced by children in foster care, advocacy organizations have created tools for judges to use to address the educational needs of foster youth in the courtroom. *See, e.g.* National Council of Juvenile and Family Court Judges, Asking the Right Questions II: Judicial Checklists to Meet the Educational Needs of Children and Youth in Foster Care (2008), [https://perma.cc/YNT8-WRAF].

33. The Fourteenth Amendment requires that parents be given a full opportunity — even at an emergency removal hearing — to present witnesses and evidence on their behalf. Doe v. Staples, 706 F.2d 985 (6th Cir. 1983). But procedural due process may be circumscribed in other ways due to the nature of the exigency. For instance, the ordinary rules of evidence typically do not apply. *See, e.g.*, Wash. R. Evid. 1101(c)(3); Mich. Ct. R. 3.965(B)(12).

George Bowman looks up from his papers and pad and strokes his tie. "Your honor, I would like to make an offer of proof on behalf of Ms. Griffith. Ms. Griffith acknowledges her drug problem and intends to enter treatment immediately. She loves her children very much. She wishes for her children to be placed with her mother while she is in treatment. If the program allows, she would like her youngest, Deja, to be placed with her in treatment and she would like to visit all of her children as often as possible. We would ask the court to order visits at least twice per week."[34]

Presentation of Evidence

- *What type of evidence is typically presented in removal hearings in your jurisdiction?*
- *Is this controlled by court rule, statute, common law or culture?*

Michelle sits quietly while her lawyer talks. Tears stream down her cheeks and she gives up trying to brush them away. She looks directly at Judge Adams, but she feels her son's eyes on her. She cannot bear to look at him. She knows how deeply she has hurt her oldest child and the shame is overwhelming. She tries to look strong, sitting up tall and staring ahead despite the tears running down her face and falling on to the desk in front of her. George Bowman moves a box of tissues that are on the desk toward her while he continues to address the court. Michelle does not move, concentrating only on gazing directly at the judge and not turning toward the young boy's eyes that are boring into the side of her head.

Michael cannot sustain the angry stare. His eyes begin to fill and he looks away from his mother, blinks hard and listens to her lawyer. He watches George Bowman's mouth move as he talks about the steps that his mother will take, *again*, to stop using and stop ruining their lives. He tries to imagine what it might be like if he and his mother could just get up and run out of the courtroom, holding hands and laughing. They would run and run until they found Aliyah, Angel and Deja and then they would all keep running until they were far, far away from CPS, judges and lawyers. They would run so long and hard that his mother's drug addiction would be left behind, like tired old clothes that she could step out of and leave crumpled on the floor. Michael's heart is racing when he hears the wiry-haired woman say, "Aliyah should be placed immediately with her father, Thomas Sykes, who is a capable parent." Michael's head turns abruptly to look at Tommy, staring earnestly at the judge while Leslie Spector describes him as a model parent.

Michael is unprepared for this turn of events. He turns to Katie and whispers loudly, "Can he just take Aliyah like that?" Katie leans in and speaks quietly, "Do you think he shouldn't? Do you know if Aliyah wants to live with him?" Michael does not have

---

34. "Offer of proof" is used here imprecisely by Mr. Bowman in an effort to introduce evidence without having his client testify. Since the rules of evidence do not apply to initial removal hearings, the court may allow this in interest of time where the facts are not disputed. Generally, an offer of proof would still need to be followed by admissible evidence.

a response to her exact question but answers, "She should stay with Angel." His chest tightened at the thought of Angel being left alone in a foster home while Aliyah went to Chuck E. Cheese with Tommy. Katie saw the judge scowling at them and scribbled on her yellow pad "Give me reasons why Tommy should not have Aliyah live with him."

Michael takes the pen from Katie and is poised to write. He understands that Katie is asking him to tell her something that would show that Tommy is a bad parent. He turns to her and says, "It's not like he's a bad person, but . . ." Judge Adams interrupts, scowling over her reading glasses.

"Counsel, is there something your client would like to say? Because he will have his turn."

Apparently this is not a real question, because Katie just looks at the judge and does not answer. She puts her hand on Michael's arm to quiet him and Leslie Spector continues with her "offer of proof" about what a great guy Tommy is and how much he loves his daughter and wants her to live with him.

Michelle cannot sustain the stoic tears. Her sobs become audible as Leslie Spector argues indignantly on behalf of Tommy, whose rights are apparently being trampled upon by the state. Michelle remains upright and holds her head high, but her shoulders begin to shake and she cries softly, finally reaching for a tissue. George Bowman stares down at his legal pad and keeps writing.

When it is finally time for Katie to talk, Michael is mentally and emotionally exhausted. He is still alert, worried about what this all means, but he is having trouble staying focused on the words that are tumbling out around him. He hears Katie express his desire to be with his mother and sisters, he hears her say his second choice is residing with his grandmother and he thinks she actually brings up Porsche, who no one else has mentioned. Katie talks about the importance of Michael remaining at Stewart Middle School, which Michael is not completely sure he agrees with, but he figures that Katie is saying what the judge wants to hear. Katie talks for what seems like a very long time. Michael is glad that he declined her offer to allow him to talk to the judge directly. He is in no mood to speak in a room full of strange adults with his mother crying and his sister's dad acting all self-righteous.

After Katie stops talking, Judge Adams looks directly at Michael and says "Hello, Michael. I have listened carefully to what your lawyer has said, but is there anything else you would like me to know?" Her voice is kind even though her forehead still displays the frown. Michael is startled when he hears his name. He looks at Katie and then at the judge and manages to get out, "No. . . . Thank you."

Youth in Court

- *In your jurisdiction, do children regularly attend initial removal or other dependency hearings?*
- *Are they given the opportunity to testify?*

Judge Adams persists, "Well, OK. But I noticed you were talking to your lawyer and you seemed to have some concerns about what was going on during this hearing. I just want you to know that you can tell me if you have any questions or have something that you think I should know that I haven't heard about yet."

Without thinking, Michael blurts, "You should know that my sisters should stay together. If Tommy thinks he's such a good parent then he should take both Aliyah and Angel. That's all." Michael's face gets hot and he looks at Tommy and then his mother. They look surprised.

Judge Adams sits back in her chair. She looks at Tommy and his lawyer. "Ms. Spector, perhaps you should talk to your client about this suggestion. Mr. Sykes, you heard Michael's suggestion. What do you think?"

Leslie Spector turns toward Tommy and begins to converse with him in hushed tones. They go back and forth a few times and then Ms. Spector says, "Your honor, Mr. Sykes has a wife and three other children. He will need to consult with her before agreeing to take Angel, but he will look into it."

At this point, the dark-suited young Assistant Attorney General came to life and asked the judge if she might be heard on this issue. The judge says, "Don't worry, you will get your turn in a minute. Michael, is there anything else you wanted to say this morning?"

"No. . . . Ma'am." Michael looks over at his mother again. She has stopped crying and is looking down at the table.

Judge Adams says warmly, "Thank you, Michael. I appreciate your speaking up. I want you to understand that we are here to help your family. I am sure that it is difficult for you to be separated from your mother and your sisters. But you need to know that none of this is your fault and we want your mother to get the help she needs so that you can be a family again. Your sisters are very lucky to have you here today to speak up for them." Her warm tone does not match her stern face, but Michael feels satisfied that he has said something meaningful and that he is not in trouble for saying it.

Michelle starts to lose it again, sobbing more loudly than before. Her head is down now. Leslie Spector appears to be fighting the urge to put her arm around her. George Bowman looks up, as if he is just rejoining a conversation.

Michael holds the judge's gaze for a moment and then turns to look at Katie as if to say, "Are we done yet?" Katie nods approvingly at Michael, a tight-lipped smile just barely perceptible on her face.

Judge Adams turns to the dark-suited woman, "Alright, Ms. Taylor, would you like to address the placement and visitation issues? Also, I would like to know whether you think this family would be appropriate for the Family Dependency Treatment Court."[35]

---

35. *See supra* note 2.

Ms. Taylor first launches into a legal argument, expressing concerns about whether Thomas Sykes meets the legal definition of a "relative" for Angel and indicating that her client is opposed to any placement of Aliyah or Angel before a thorough home study can be completed, referencing Tommy's past ambivalence and criminal history.[36] She then states that the parties are largely in agreement about out-of-home placement, it is just a matter of timing and figuring out the availability of the grandmother. With respect to visitation, she states that the Department will try to arrange weekly supervised visits for the mother once she enters treatment, so long as it is approved by the treatment program, but she emphasizes that DCFS does not have the resources to provide visits for all four children more than once per week. "As you can imagine, transporting four children from three different homes to attend visits with their mother more than once per week is a huge undertaking." Finally, almost as an afterthought, she responds to the Judge's prompt about Family Dependency Treatment Court: "I doubt that this mother would be eligible for one of the few spots in the Treatment Court. I think they are full, but even so, she has failed treatment more than once before which I believe makes her ineligible."

Judge Adams listens patiently and then allows each attorney to respond. To Michael, it sounds as if the lawyers are all saying the same things in different order or with slightly different words. "Visitation," "placement," and "approved care" are all terms that mean very little to him. What do they mean "supervised visitation" with his mother? Will she come to their foster homes? To their grandmother's house? To school? Does "placement" mean today? For a week? For a month? Forever? Will Michael be able to visit his sisters where they are living? What does "supervision" mean? Will someone always be watching them? Who will do that?

The lawyers talk for what seems to Michael to be a very long time in a language he barely understands—back and forth. It does not seem like they are arguing about anything very important. It is clear he is not going to be going home to his mother today and he probably will not see his sisters. The lawyers seem to be talking about details that make no sense to him but that hopefully will allow him to go to his grandmother's soon. The more they talk the more detached Michael becomes. Finally, Judge Adams says, "Thank you counsel. I am ready to make my ruling."

She begins, "I am finding that the mother and the fathers of Michael, Aliyah, Angel and Deja received proper notice of this hearing. I am finding that the Department has made reasonable efforts to prevent or eliminate the need for out-of-home placement. The children are in need of shelter care. They should remain in DCFS-approved care pending investigation of appropriate relatives. I am ordering the Department to . . . ." At this point, Michael gives up trying to follow the judge's words. He waits to hear Tommy's name.

---

36. State law determines who is a relative for purposes of the placement preferences required under Title IV. In some states, relatives of half siblings may be considered relatives. *See, e.g.*, WASH. REV. CODE § 74.15.020(2)(a); FLA. STAT. § 39.621(6).

"Mr. Sykes." Tommy and Michael sit up. The judge goes on, "I agree with your attorney that there is no reason to keep your daughter Aliyah from you. But I need to know that you are committed to caring for her and that your wife will also support your decision. Also, I know it's a lot to ask, but I would like to see Aliyah and Angel remain together. It is hard to be torn away from your sibling." Tommy nods. He starts to say something, but Leslie Spector cut him off. "Your honor, Mr. Sykes is very committed to his daughter and if you would give the Department authority to place Angel with Mr. Sykes we will discuss this with his wife and work closely with the social worker to ensure that the girls have as much contact as possible even if they are unable to both reside with him." The judge looks disappointed not to hear the words that almost came out of Tommy's mouth directly.

Judge Adams continues, "I will place Aliyah with her father, Tommy Sykes, and give the Department authority to place Angel with Mr. Sykes as a relative. I believe that he is a step-parent under the statute. With respect to visitation, I am ordering weekly supervised visits between the children and their mother. The children should also have weekly visits with each other — this can be satisfied through visits with their mother. The Department may provide more visits if resources allow. The Department should set up supervised visits between Deja and her father when he is released from jail." The judge pauses, looking down at her notes. "Has counsel been assigned to Eric Grayson?" Michael's eyes shot up at the mention of this father. He doesn't know who the judge is directing the question to, but he looks around the room to see who might answer — who might provide a thread of connection to his absent parent.

Ms. Taylor responds, "Your honor, we have not confirmed Mr. Grayson's paternity yet but we believe he is the legal father.[37] You can speed up the process if you write appointment of counsel for Mr. Grayson, upon confirmation of his paternity, in the order. Mr. Grayson is in prison."

For the second time that day, Michael tries to picture his father in prison. He cannot get his face to come into focus — it has been years since he has seen even a photograph. He feels empty. He conjures the image of a generically attractive and well-built black man in a gray prison suit. As these images dart through his brain he hears the bailiff announce, "That concludes this hearing. Parties please remain seated until Mr. Jones has left the courtroom."

DJ leaves the courtroom first, shuffling between two officers, trying to make eye contact with Michelle who is still crying but not audibly. Tommy follows his attorney who is headed in the direction of Emily. Michael does not move until Katie gets up and asks him to wait for her outside the courtroom. Michelle follows her attorney out of the courtroom and does not look at her son.

---

37. See ch. 1, *Who is a Parent for Constitutional Purposes?* for a discussion of the rights of non-marital fathers.

Reflections and Exercises

1. *What? So What? Now What? A Five-Minute Reflection Opportunity.* Take just five minutes to write and reflect on the following questions:

    a. What did you feel as you read the stories of the legal system's interactions with Michael?

    b. How is what you recorded feeling relevant to your learning and/or practice?

    c. Now what do you do with these insights as you move forward in your learning and/or practice?

2. *Mapping Michael's Journey Through the System:*

    In Chapter One you were asked to create a flowchart of your state's dependency system. Locate where Michael is now on that flowchart and note the path that he would have taken in your state's system.

3. *Imagining a Different Story for Michael:* The court experience is challenging and uncomfortable for a child — particularly at the point of initial removal, which is often the first time a child has ever been to court. The initial decision to remove a child from his home can be the most significant decision in a case, yet attorneys often proceed with very little information, inadequate time to review or uncover evidence, and limited time to interview and prepare their clients for what will happen in the courtroom. Different jurisdictions develop different practice norms, which can either set the bar high or low for what is expected from advocates, social workers and courts in the dependency context. Case caps, low hourly rates and high caseloads play a significant role, but other dynamics influence what families experience.

    a. If you could imagine a better court experience for Michael, what would that look like?

    b. What changes would need to be made to improve his experience?

    c. Given the constraints Michael's lawyer appeared to be working under, how did she do explaining the process and helping him to understand what was happening and why?

Chapter Five

Maya in Contempt

In Part 1 of this chapter, you will learn about the major professional players in Maya's life as a child of the state. These players include her lawyer, her social worker, the lawyer for the state, and her judge. Because Maya's mother's rights have been terminated and her father is unknown, the state is the only other party in her case.

Each of the professional players in this system is constrained by their roles, duties and the limitations of the system in which they operate. You will have an opportunity to explore questions of professional responsibility and role, as well as observe how these professionals emotionally respond to the challenges their young clients face. Service providers who work with the stories of the suffering and trauma of others are challenged to find ways to cope with the fatigue that arises as a result. This fatigue is sometimes referred to as "secondary" or "vicarious" trauma, or more broadly as trauma exposure response.[1] Fatigue can arise not only from hearing about clients' traumatic events but also from the frustration and helplessness that results because the larger systems in which service providers work and even the methodologies in which they engage are flawed in such a way that, rather than helping, further harm may result.[2]

In Part 2, you will watch as Maya's attorney, Julia, seeks to prepare herself and Maya for the contempt hearing Maya faces for having run away. Unlike Katie, Michael's attorney in Chapter 2, Julia has more time to spend with Maya the day before her contempt hearing. Nonetheless, the arc of their relationship is new and even with a lengthier first meeting, there is still much trust building left to do.

Trust is particularly challenging to build given Maya's length of time in the system and her chronic and complex trauma history. We have already seen that Maya can be triggered when she feels suddenly trapped, as she was by the security guard that caught her shoplifting, or when she relives certain aspects of prior sexual trauma. When she was trapped, she punched the security guard and blacked out. We also heard about her reaction when she finds herself in sexually unsafe situations—she disassociates or, as she describes it, disappears; sometimes she regresses by reverting to sucking her thumb. She copes with stress through counting and numbers. Each client will have their own cluster of coping strategies, some of which are conscious and deliberate and others, reactive and compulsive.

---

1. "A trauma exposure response has occurred when the external trauma becomes the internal reality." Laura Van Dernoot Lipsky & Connie Burk, Trauma Stewardship: An everyday guide to caring for self while caring for others, 37–38 (2009).

2. *Id.*

What does this trauma history mean for how Maya's attorney should approach the attorney-client relationship? Attorneys who practice trauma-informed interviewing realize that trust may come slowly. Even when the attorney does everything "right," the client may at first be distant, closed off, or hostile. Other clients, who have not learned how to establish safe boundaries, may appear to trust too readily and disclose intimate information in an immediately friendly manner.[3] In either case, attorneys practicing in a trauma-informed way must be prepared to respond to the private logic that uniquely drives each youth's individual trauma response.[4]

In the trauma context, trust can only be established when the client feels safe. An attorney is best positioned to create a zone of emotional safety by approaching the client interview with an attitude of curiosity and respect, free from judgment.[5] Other essential elements of a trauma-informed attorney-client relationship are: 1) transparency; 2) predictability; 3) client control; 4) reliability; 5) proactive support; and 6) patience.[6]

Being aware of the physical aspects of safety are critical as well.[7] For example, given Maya's reactions to feeling trapped, invading her physical space, blocking access to exits, or otherwise physically restraining her likely will impact her ability to attend to the information that her attorney is seeking to convey. Even with a safe emotional and physical space, the trauma-informed attorney realizes that, if a client is struggling with trauma while being interviewed, her ability to process information may be reduced. Simplifying explanations, checking for understanding and being sure not to overload a client with too much information all at once is important.[8]

The client's private logic of trauma and prior interview experience also shapes the client's affect when telling her story. Given the frequent turnover in social workers,

---

3. Disinhibited Social Engagement Disorder (DSED) is a relatively new diagnosis for a cluster of behaviors previously considered to be a variation of Reactive Attachment Disorder (RAD). DSED typically is the result of social neglect but has also ben seen in some children who are struggling with PTSD. While research on DSED in adolescents is nascent, the defining characteristic of DSED is the child's willingness to leave caregivers and "go off" with complete strangers. Children with DSED are often described as being excessively friendly and attention seeking. Adolescents with DSED may show behaviors that extend beyond the caregiver versus adult stranger distinction and into peer relationships. For example, adolescents with DSED may identify newly met peers as "best friends" or they may experience shallow and frequently changing relationships. Charles Zeanah et al., *Practice Parameters for the Assessment and Treatment of Children and Adolescents with Reactive Attachment Disorder and Disinhibited Social Engagement Disorder*, 55(11) J. OF THE AM. ACAD. OF CHILD & ADOLESC. PSYCHIATRY 990 (Nov. 2016), [https://perma.cc/PA7T-SVVB].

4. Each young person who has experienced trauma will have their own "private logic" that dictates the behaviors exhibited as a result of their trauma, including the manner in which they establish relationships with others. "The private logic of traumatized children and adolescents is rooted in terror and the anticipation of pain." WILLIAM STEELE & CATHY A. MALCHIODI, TRAUMA-INFORMED PRACTICES WITH CHILDREN AND ADOLESCENTS 147 (Routledge 2012).

5. STEELE & MALCHIODI, *supra* note 4, at 141–155.

6. Talia Kraemer & Eliza Patten, *Establishing a Trauma-Informed Lawyer-Client Relationship (Part One)*, 33(10) ABA CHILD L. PRACTICE 199–200 (Oct. 2014).

7. Kraemer & Patten, *supra* note 6, at 209.

8. *Id* at 215.

lawyers, and mental health providers, children and youth in dependency proceedings often are asked to tell their trauma stories repeatedly, which can result in a deadpan and scripted telling. Even when clients recount their trauma history for the first time, they may disconnect emotionally from the telling as a way of protectively distancing themselves. Some clients may smile or even laugh while telling their stories. Some will cry. For some, telling their stories can trigger a trauma response, which can be anything from withdrawal to lashing out.[9] For others, telling the story is not nearly as triggering as some embedded sensory experience leftover from the trauma.[10] It is quite possible, for example, that the client can discuss traumatic facts with relative ease, but the sound, smell or taste of something associated with the trauma will cause them to react in ways the attorney may not understand. The attorney has to be prepared to hear whatever the client has to say in whatever manner the client tells it.

For lawyers in the child welfare system, it can be challenging to have the time necessary to build the trust clients need to feel safe. If the lawyer is new to the client and does not need to discuss the details of a traumatic situation in order to represent the client competently on the issue immediately before the court, the attorney has to decide whether delving into the details might be better left to another day after more trust has been built. However, there are times when the lawyer needs to discover facts that surround a likely traumatic experience in order to be prepared for a hearing that has been set on the calendar with little warning. Maya's upcoming hearing has been set with little notice; Maya and Julia barely remember one another. In such situations, the attorney needs to focus on establishing some rapport quickly, demonstrate to the client that she is clearly on her side, and determine what information is most critical to discover for the immediate purposes. As you read the interview between Maya and her attorney, consider whether and how you think Julia practiced in a trauma-informed way.

Finally, this chapter gives you a glimpse into the intersection of status offending and the child welfare system. It is the police who return Maya to the jurisdiction of the child welfare system through the way-station of juvenile detention. Maya's social worker had sought a pick-up order that ultimately resulted in her being held in juvenile detention while awaiting a court hearing for civil contempt. The order that she is alleged to have violated originated in her dependency case and required that she reside in the group home from which she ran. In the hypothetical jurisdiction in which this narrative is set, the court has the authority to hold her in detention for contempt for an additional seven days. Even though the federal Juvenile Justice Delinquency and Prevention Act of 1974 prohibits the placement of status offenders in secure confinement,[11] Congress amended the law in 1980 to provide for the valid court

---

9. Kraemer & Patten, *supra* note 6, at 198–201.

10. When an experience terrifies a person, the memory of that experience is stored "as sensory fragments that have no linguistic components. . . . . In essence, trauma memories are experienced through images and sensations." STEELE & MALCHIODI, *supra* note 4, at 3.

11. *See*, 42 U.S.C. § 5633(a)(11).

order (VCO) exception.[12] States vary as to how long they allow detention for violation of a court order, and some states do not allow the exception at all.[13]

> ### *Legal Responses to Running Away from Placement*
> *States vary in their treatment of runaways.*
> - *Find the law pertaining to youth who run away from their parents in your state.*
> - *Find the law and agency policies pertaining to youth who run away from court-ordered foster care placements in your state.*

Part I: The Professionals

Maya's Lawyer's Story: Julia Yasko

My usual rhythm—removal hearings[14] in the mornings, review and PP[15] on Tuesday afternoons, pre-trials on Wednesday afternoons, Thursdays in the field and Fridays hopefully spent catching up with drafting motions, reports, and responsive pleadings—has been interrupted by a weeklong TPR.[16] I put up the good fight, so good in fact that the judge[17] did not rule from the bench but instead said he would

---

12. 42 U.S.C. § 5633(a)(11). Some states use contempt proceedings to enforce court orders. *See, e.g.,* Ariz. Rev. Stat. Ann. 8-247; La. Child. Code Ann. art.1509.1. *See also* Hannah Benton, et al., Representing Juvenile Status Offenders (2010), [https://perma.cc/6KUY-93N3].

13. According to 2012 data, 27 states made at least some use of the valid court order exception to hold status offenders in detention. Sixteen of those states relied heavily upon the use of the valid court order exception with one hundred or more instances of detention for violations of court orders. Washington and Kentucky make the greatest use of contempt to hold status offenders in detention. *See* Coal. for Juv. Just./SOS Project, Status Offenses: A National Survey (2015) [https://perma.cc/YP6B-HMWD]. Girls make up 61% of those detained, and their time in detention is, on average, twice as long as time served by boys for status offenses. Coal. for Juv. Just., Deinstitutionalization of Status Offenders (DSO): Facts and Resources (2011), [https://perma.cc/KPX3-5KYB].

14. Whether called shelter care, preliminary or removal hearings, most courts have to reserve time on their dockets for hearings that must occur shortly after a child is removed from his or her home. *See, e.g.,* Ohio Rev. Code Ann. § 2151.28; Wash. Rev. code § 13.34.065; Tn. R. Ju. P. 16; Ill. Compiled Stat. 405/3-12; Pa. Code 1242; Cal. Welf. & Inst. Code § 305; N.J. Stat. Ann. § 30:4C-12.

15. "PP" refers to "permanency planning." Under the federal Adoption and Safe Families Act (ASFA), states must conduct periodic review hearings in order to check on the status and safety of the child in his or her current placement and the extent of compliance with the case plan. Such review hearings must occur at least once every six months. Each child must also have his or her permanency plan reviewed annually. 42 U.S.C.A. § 675(5) (Westlaw through Pub. L. No. 114-9). To learn more about recommendations on how courts should handle these complex dockets, see Enhanced Resource Guidelines: Improving Court Practice In Child Abuse And Neglect Cases, National Council Of Juvenile And Family Court Judges (2016) [https://perma.cc/F79F-XAG5].

16. "TPR" refers to "termination of parental rights."

17. In most states, termination of parental rights cases are decided by judges, not juries. Only five states permit or require jury trials for termination of parental rights. Linda A. Szymanski, *Is a Jury*

issue his decision on Monday. So when I come into the office this morning and see that the message light is on, I feel that flutter of excitement and anxiety that I rarely get to feel anymore.

I had forgotten that feeling, from back in the day, when I did adult felonies, when the phone call would come in and—just like in the movies—the voice on the other end of the line would say, "They're back," meaning the jury was ready and somebody's ultimate freedom or incarceration had been decided. It had been a long time since I had done a criminal trial, and at least a year since I had even done a TPR[18]—most of them settled or were defaulted—long enough anyway that I felt nervous thinking for a moment about whether I would get to tell my client good news—that he had gotten what he wanted, and his mother's rights weren't terminated. But then I would have to manage his expectations, letting him know gently that this didn't mean he would get to go home; it just meant his mom would get a second chance.[19] Or would it be bad news, the kind of news that would require me to help talk him through how he was going to handle his anger and grief? One of the casualties of not getting what a child wants in a major hearing like this all too often is that the child winds up in trouble in school or in his placement when he lets loose his anger and disappointment on a teacher or foster parent. If that happens, then he might wind up kicked out of school or having a 911 call made. Then he would be in juvie. Once he is in the offender system, it is like he is just getting conditioned to being incarcerated. I've seen too many of my clients aging out of foster care and into prison.[20] Trying to be

---

Trial Ever Available in a Termination of Parental Rights Case?, NAT. CENTER FOR JUV. JUSTICE (2011), [https://perma.cc/V5HY-QR9G].

18. Under the federal Adoption and Safe Families Act, states desiring federal funding must enact statutes which require the termination of parental rights once a child is in out-of-home care for 15 of the last 22 months, unless exceptional circumstances are shown. These exceptions allow for not terminating parental rights if: 1) the child is placed with a relative; 2) compelling reasons exist as to why termination would not be in the child's best interests; or 3) the state has failed to engage in reasonable efforts to reunify the family. *See* 42 USC § 675(5)(E).

19. Of course, whether a child supports or opposes termination of his or her parents' rights will vary from case to case. In those cases in which termination is being had to facilitate an adoption that the child supports, it is much more likely that the lawyer's role will be to push for termination in order to facilitate that goal. However, not all terminations of parental rights actions are taken with an adoption waiting in the wings. The Adoption and Safe Families Act placed strict timelines on states to move for TPR without respect to whether a permanent home is awaiting. *See* ch. 1, *The Federal Statutes that Drive the State Systems.* According to national statistics, only 12% of the 111,820 legally free children awaiting adoption in 2015 were actually living in pre-adoptive homes. *See,* THE AFCARS REPORT: PRELIMINARY FY 2015 ESTIMATES AS OF JUNE 2016, CHILDREN'S BUREAU, U.S. DEP'T OF HEALTH AND HUMAN SERVICES (2016), [https://perma.cc/BL22-9N7B].

20. The extent of reported foster care involvement among the adult correctional population varies. In one study, "nearly 20% of the U.S. prison population under 30, and 25% of these prisoners with prior convictions, report spending part of their youth in foster care." *See* Joseph J. Doyle, Jr. *Child Protection and Adult Crime: Using Investigator Assignment to Estimate Causal Effects of Foster Care,* 116 J. POL. ECON. 746, 747 (2008). Rates vary based on gender. A Midwest study reported that 44.9% of males and 17.9% of females who had aged out of care stated that they had spent at least one night in a jail or prison. *See* MARK E. COURTNEY ET AL., MIDWEST EVALUATION OF THE ADULT FUNCTIONING OF FORMER FOSTER YOUTH: OUTCOMES AT AGES 23 AND 24, 68 (2010), [https://perma.cc/HW5S

preventative and avoiding the juvenile detention system for my clients is one of the things that keeps me in this practice.

That, and the fact that, quite honestly, these kids are great. Every single one of them has some quality to admire. Even when I don't succeed in getting them what they want, I at least hope they know that I see that they are amazing. We all want to be seen for who we are or can be, our best, most beautiful selves. That is one gift I can give them if nothing else. I've been on a lot of CLE panels because I have been doing this work for so long. Whenever I get asked questions like, "How do you see your role?" I always say what needs to be said, about confidentiality and trust, about knowing when to collaborate and when to advocate, about stated interests and holding the system accountable — that's all true and so important — but I always also say that the most important thing is to allow yourself to like your client and to let that show, to find out what she or he does best and find a way to surface that and make sure that strength is supported, because, in the end, the recognition of that individual's strength will be what supports the resilience that he or she is going to need to survive this often inhumane system. And seeing that beauty, despite all of the tragedy, that is what will make you love your work. And even if you can't stage a revolution and demolish the system, which is what I sometimes dream of doing, at least you can make the child's experience of it better by being more than just an attorney who greases the wheels. When I can remember to do that, I love my work. Sometimes, according to my wife, Jill, I could love it a little less. I could put in fewer evenings and weekends. She teases me about it mostly; she doesn't have much hope of changing me at this point.

But when I get into the office and listen to the voice mail message, it doesn't have anything to do with the termination trial; it isn't the judge's clerk summoning me back to court. It is the social worker in another case I had to struggle to remember. The social worker's voice sounds tired, or perhaps just a little irritated that this challenging case has interrupted her weekend. I know her, have worked with her on a lot of cases. She is a good social worker. But now, she sounds like she is all out of ideas.

So Julia, this is Sarah over at the Adolescent BRS unit. Calling bright and early this Monday morning. It looks like our girl Maya Phillips is back. Case no. 10-7-6581. Remember her? Just turned fifteen? She ran away from her group home about five months ago? We got a pick-up and an order to show cause on her.[21]

-765M]. For a personal account of the foster-care-to-prison-pipeline, see Arthur Longworth, *Raised, and Imprisoned, by the State*, THE MARSHALL PROJECT (2015) [https://perma.cc/SV75-S6ZW].

21. When a child runs away from a court-ordered placement, that child may be held in contempt of the court's order. While states vary in the language that they use to describe the procedure for ordering a child to be returned to care, in this case, the court has ordered that law enforcement find her, return her to the court, and that she should then have to show why she should not be held in contempt of court. These hearings are sometimes called "show cause hearings" because the young person is required to "show cause" why he or she should not be held in contempt for violating the court's order. While statutes vary from state to state, typically a person is in contempt of court, if he or she has willfully refused to obey the court's order. The person may be held in confinement until they "purge" themselves of contempt. WILLIAM G. JONES, WORKING WITH THE COURTS IN CHILD

Anyway, she was picked up Sunday for shoplifting. They have her in detention now and I am going to call the AG to set the contempt hearing, maybe for tomorrow? I am thinking maybe I have to let juvie have her for a while. She's blown through mostly everything I've got for her. Except for maybe Safe Harbors? She might qualify. Not sure. Just giving you a heads up. Not sure whether you will wind up doing this or whether it goes over to the offender side now.[22] Give me a call if she's still yours. Oh . . . and not sure but the arresting officer said she might be pregnant. Thought you might want to know.

I go to the file cabinet. Yes, I still have a file cabinet. I also have electronic files but, personally — call me old-fashioned — I still like the heft and feel of the file itself, even though some of them have multiple volumes. They keep telling me that once the courthouse goes fully electronic, we won't need paper any more, but we aren't there yet. I can tell when I open the drawer that Maya has been in the system for a while. The sight of a full file drawer like that lets you know, in a way that a little file icon in a computer can't, that this girl has had a five-volume childhood spent trudging through the child welfare system.

It looks like she came in first when she and her sister were removed from her mom's care but then that dependency was dismissed as to her after her grandmother became her guardian. Her sister was placed in licensed foster care. So her sister's dependency might still be going on, although it looks like she is old enough to have aged out by now. Anyway, after Maya's first dependency was dismissed, her grandmother had a stroke; and so the second time Maya came into the system she ran through a series of foster homes and group homes, along with two run episodes now. Her mom's rights were terminated in the second dependency. Unknown father. So it is just Maya and the state in this case now.

> ### *Finding Maya on Your Dependency System Map*
>
> *At the end of Chapter 1, you created a map of your state's dependency system.*
>
> * *Locate Maya's approximate present position on your map.*

PROTECTION, U.S. DEP'T OF HEALTH & HUMAN SERVICES, 12 (2006), [https://perma.cc/3SDH -MPY6]. *See, e.g.*, FLA. STAT. § 985.037; WYO. STAT. ANN. § 14-6-438.

22. Originally, juvenile offender matters and what we now think of as dependency or abuse and neglect matters were heard in the same court. With the decision in *In re* Gault, 387 U.S. 1 (1967), the two proceedings were separated and handled differently. Juvenile offender matters, given greater due process protection under *Gault* may result in the restriction of a child's liberty by placement in detention. Accordingly, all children in juvenile offender matters have the right to counsel without respect to their age. The due process right to counsel in the dependency context has not yet been decided by the United States Supreme Court. Most states that have counsel in both proceedings will have separate agencies handling the responsibility for providing counsel for each system. Therefore a child may have two lawyers — one for his dependency matter and one for his juvenile offender matter. Once a child is in detention, some states may allow or require the withdrawal of the attorney in the dependency.

Maya has had more than one attorney too. She didn't have an attorney in the first dependency; she had a GAL, because the court assumed she was too young to direct counsel. Then, in this current dependency, her first attorney left the dependency division during Maya's first run episode. When she came back, I was assigned as her attorney, but I barely got to know her before she ran away again. Her social workers have changed too. She was moved from the Kinship Care unit to the Foster Care unit and then to the Legally Free unit once her mother's rights were terminated, and then from Legally Free[23] to Adolescent BRS[24] when she was placed in the group home.[25] There, she probably had a lot of other service providers she had to answer to. This kid has had a lot of people moving through her life — caseworkers, GALs, attorneys, foster parents, group home staff, counselors — to add to the loss she already had when it came to having to leave her grandmother's care and, before that, separation from her mother and then her sister.

How can I expect her to remember me, much less know what I am supposed to be doing for her, given the array of other adults in her life? Unfortunately, in part because of her run history and probably even more because of our fragmented service delivery system, no one has had the luxury of time to work with her and come up with a plan that meets what she wants and needs. This time maybe I can take enough time and prioritize her case. It will take more time than the county usually approves per case to do that[26] but I can try to ask for an exception; Maya is what everyone would probably agree is a "high-needs" child and, after all, she has banked her time with me while she was on the run; she needs more time now if someone in this system is to do right by her.

I look for the most recent order in the thinnest and most recent volume of her file. It's the pick-up order:

---

23. "Legally free" is a term used to refer to children whose parental rights have been terminated and who are therefore "legally free" to be adopted.

24. "BRS" refers here to "Behavioral Rehabilitation Services," which also is sometimes referred to as therapeutic foster care or a therapeutic group home. BRS services access funding from Medicaid as well as usual federal foster care funding to provide increased mental health services for youth. For a description of BRS or therapeutic group home services examples, see RE-DESIGN OF BEHAVIORAL REHABILITATION SERVICES, WASH. DEP'T OF SOC. & HEALTH SERVICES (2010), [https://perma.cc/F32W-JHQV]; *Therapeutic Group Homes*, DHH.LOUISIANA.GOV, [https://perma.cc/KS9G-TZLW]; Therapeutic Group Homes, YOUTHHOMESMT.ORG, [https://perma.cc/YCC2-TQ2A]; *Therapeutic Group Home*, BRIDGEFAMILYCENTER.ORG, [https://perma.cc/4BWP-AL7F]; *Therapeutic Group Home: Level II*, CGA.CT.GOV, [https://perma.cc/YY8M-FFSW].

25. Child welfare services delivery systems vary in how they resolve the tension between the felt need for specialization and the problems that children and families experience when they have changing social workers and case managers. The types of service delivery units that families experience vary not only across states, but even within states. For an example, see LYNDA ARNOLD, PAT DEVIN & SARAH WEBSTER, TECHNICAL ASSISTANCE REPORT FOR THE STATE OF OREGON DEPARTMENT OF HUMAN SERVICES (2006), [https://perma.cc/8XMS-BTU9].

26. Explanation of the different methods of delivering legal services is explained in greater detail in ch. 1's *Fifty States; Fifty Models* section.

SUPERIOR COURT OF WASHINGTON
BAKER COUNTY
JUVENILE DIVISION

IN RE THE DEPENDENCY OF:	)	NO. *10-7-6581*
Maya Phillips	)	
DOB 2/8/2000	)	ORDER TO SHOW CAUSE
Minor child	)	WHY CHILD SHOULD NOT
	)	BE HELD IN CONTEMPT
_____	)	

This matter comes before the court on behalf of the state, by and through its counsel, Regina Morrison, Assistant Attorney General. The court considered the state's motion for an order to show cause, the response of the child's counsel, and the declarations presented to this Court. The Court makes the following Findings:

1. Pursuant to order dated May 10, 2014, the child Maya Phillips was placed in a licensed therapeutic group home. She was ordered to remain in that placement, comply with all therapies offered, comply with the rules of that group home, and attend school.

2. On October 28, 2014, the child left the group home with permission to go to a local store and failed to return.

3. The group home staff immediately informed the state social worker of the child's failure to return. The state social worker promptly took all appropriate action with respect to notifying law enforcement.

4. This is the second time that the child has left a court-ordered placement and failed to return voluntarily. Maya Phillips also ran away from the foster home in which she was placed prior to this group home. After two weeks, she was picked up by the Baker County sheriff department, brought to juvenile court and found to be in civil contempt of this court's placement order. She spent seven days in juvenile detention, during which time she refused to purge herself of contempt.

5. This court has no evidence at this time as to whether Maya Phillips' failure to return is the result of a willful and intentional action to disobey this court's order.

6. However the court finds sufficient evidence to enter an order requiring Maya Phillips to be brought before this court to show cause why she should not be held in contempt.

WHEREFORE, it is hereby ordered that:

1) The child's social worker shall immediately provide a copy of this order to law enforcement.

2) Should the child come to the attention of law enforcement, she shall be brought to and held in juvenile detention in this county until such time as she can be brought before this court to show cause why she should not be held in contempt.

3) Prior to appearing before this court the child shall be served with a copy of this order to show cause.

4) The child is hereby provided notice that should she be found to be in civil contempt of this court's orders, she shall be subject to a maximum of seven days in juvenile detention unless she purges herself of the same by fulfilling conditions imposed by this court.

5) Further, the child Maya Phillips is provided notice that this court may also refer this matter to the prosecuting attorneys' office for the filing of a complaint for criminal contempt which may subject her to sanctions of up to 30 days in detention for each criminal contempt violation found.

Dated: 10-30-14

Jackson Jamison

Judge

★★★

Slowly, the case is starting to come back to me. I vaguely remember that show cause hearing. Of course, my client wasn't there and I had no idea what had happened to her, but neither did anyone else. I did not know what she wanted, whether she wanted to be found or not, whether she was in danger or with a relative; so I had no idea what position I should take. I had called the phone number she had given the last attorney but it was one of her former foster homes and they had no idea where she was. I sent an email to *BlossomHM@yazoo.com*, the address she had given her last attorney for contact purposes, but she did not reply. I informed the court that I had no position. The judge and the social worker probably looked at me as they always did, wanting to ask me whether I had any idea where my client might be, but I had long ago established that I wasn't going to divulge any of my clients' confidences without client permission, and so they had stopped asking me. The judge likely just looked at me, sighed and signed the pick-up order without much argument.

> ### Professional Responsibility and the Runaway Client
>
> *Review Julia's conduct and the Rules of Professional Conduct in your state and decide whether you agree with her actions:*
>
> * *Which rules apply to her decision not to take a position?*
> * *Which rules apply to her practice of not disclosing her client's whereabouts if known?*

And now Maya has been picked up and is being held in detention and it appears that she was indeed the runaway that the state claimed she was. But still many unanswered questions. What about Sarah's offhand reference to her possibly being pregnant? How did that come about? Kids on the streets can get into a lot of trouble for sure. I've heard so many hard stories — girls pimped out before they even knew what was happening, girls who think why not get paid for the same abuse they endure at home for no compensation,[27] girls who claim being "in the life"[28] is the place to be,

---

27. Seventy percent of adult women engaging in prostitution in one study claimed the childhood sexual abuse paved the way for their entry in prostitution and majority entered into prostitution as adolescents. *See* Mimi H. Silbert & Ayala M. Pines, *Early Sexual Exploitation as an Influence in Prostitution*, 28 Social Work 285 (1983). Histories of child maltreatment, especially sexual abuse, are common among youth and adults who engage in sex work. For example, a study of 47 women engaged in sex work revealed that 91% experienced some form of childhood maltreatment, with 80% reporting childhood sexual abuse. Kendra Nixon et al., *The Everyday Occurrence: Violence in the Lives of Girls Exploited Through Prostitution*, 8 Violence Against Women 1016 (2002). Other research also highlights situations in which family members are sometimes responsible for commercially sexually exploiting their own children. Margaret Ann Kennedy et al., *Routes of Recruitment: Pimps' Techniques and Other Circumstances That Lead to Street Prostitution*, J. of Aggression, Maltreatment and Trauma 1 (2007).

28. "In the life" is a common way of referring to living a life in which ones sexual services are bought and sold. For a description of what that life is like and how it contrasts with societal impressions generated by the entertainment industry, see Phillip Martin, *'Pretty Woman' vs. The Real World of Prostitution*, WGBH News, (Nov. 19, 2013, 8:55 AM), [https://perma.cc/HCL7-K8KC].

girls who seek to create family, girls who trade sex for drugs or food or a place to live,[29] girls who are raped without money changing hands, girls who simply have no access to birth control.[30] So what is Maya's story? How did she become pregnant and what does she want to do about it?

And Sarah's reference to Safe Harbors—isn't that the new program for youth in prostitution?[31] But she was picked up shoplifting? Sarah must really be desperate for options if she's hoping to get Maya in there. Or she knows something I don't know.

I flip to the log section of the most recent file and find my log print-out from the last contacts I had with Maya. I was appointed after they picked her up from her first run and met her at court that day. She told me then she wanted to live with an aunt and an uncle. The judge found her in contempt then and said she could purge it by writing a 300-word essay about why running away was a dangerous thing to do. She never wrote the essay. I met with her again when she was in detention and she said she'd rather be in juvie than a group home or with "two-faced foster parents." She stayed in detention for seven days before the court released her and ordered her to be placed in the Phoenix House.

It's coming back to me. I remember her sitting there in detention, a tiny girl for 14. Even the smallest orange jump suit seemed too big and baggy on her. Even though she was white, she wore her strawberry blond hair in corn rows, thin braids that ran close to her scalp. I wondered whether she always wore her hair that way or if that was something she had picked up in juvie to fit in with all of the African American girls there.[32] Had she made a friend who braided her hair for her? It would have been hard for her to have done that herself. She had a sprinkling of freckles across the bridge

---

29. Nearly a third of children who run away or are kicked out of their homes engage in sex in exchange for shelter, drugs or food. *See* Ian Urbina, *For Runaways, Sex Buys Survival*, NYTIMES.COM (Oct. 26, 2009), [https://perma.cc/XK42-UN27].

30. Runaway/homeless female adolescents are four times as likely to become pregnant as their non-runaway peers. Sanna J. Thompson, Kimberly A. Bender & Rita Watkins, *Runaway and Pregnant: Risk Factors Associated with Pregnancy in a National Sample of Runaway/Homeless Female Adolescents*, 43 J. ADOLESCENT HEALTH 125 (2008). Runaway youth report sexual relationships at earlier ages, have a greater likelihood of multiple partners, inconsistent contraception use, and may trade sex for money, drugs, or shelter—either by choice out of necessity, or by force. *Id.* For an exploration of how and why the sex trade works with respect to societally marginalized and previously abused women and girls, see Melissa Farley, *Prostitution, Trafficking and Cultural Amnesia: What We Must Know in Order to Keep the Business of Sexual Exploitation Running Smoothly*, 18 YALE J.L. & FEMINISM 109 (2006).

31. Some states have begun to move away from treating minors involved in prostitution as offenders and instead have been treating them as victims. Some states, such as New York, engage in a diversion program for girls who would have been prosecuted for prostitution to instead agree to participate in wrap around services that address their experiences as commercially sexually exploited youth. To hear an interview of a young person who took advantage of this program and is now serving as a mentor for others, see *Former Child Trafficking Victim Now Mentors Others*, NPR.ORG (Aug. 4, 2013), [https://perma.cc/U7F3-F9GY].

32. For a discussion of racial disproportionality in the delinquency system, *see* ch. 1, *Delinquency Systems and Demographics*.

of her nose. She looked like a modern-day Pippi Longstocking with her red hair, freckles and braids that ended in wispy curly-cues at the base of her scalp. How ironic it was that today's parentless, truant Pippis — the Pippis portrayed in childhood books and movies as creative and harmless, feisty and strong — in real-life are locked in small rooms with thick doors. The real-life Pippi wears an orange jump suit and a hardened expression while she sullenly refuses to answer her lawyer's questions or do the homework assigned to her by a judge. Maya's Pippi was decidedly not perky.

I knew this work was challenging when I returned to it, and Maya is what some people call a "deep-end" kid, with little hope of finding a permanent home. Kids like Maya are the hardest to establish a working relationship with.

It was a boy named Oscar, though, another "deep-end kid," who made me decide to return to dependency work representing just kids. Not that Oscar was a success story. To the contrary. I first met him after I joined the public defender's office and was a baby lawyer in the dependency rotation; he was only twelve years old. He had been removed from his home after his father murdered his mother right in front of him. When I met him at shelter care, I was surprised to see a smiley-faced boy, giving his little brother piggy-back rides in the courthouse lobby. And because I was new and he was one of my first clients and what had happened to him was so terribly sad, I gave him more of my time than I have given almost any other client since.

I learned more details about him as we traveled through the dependency system for the first time together. I learned that he liked to play football when he was mad (because the coaches like it when you knock people over), that he secretly liked being forced to go to church, that he loved to play hide and seek with his brother as a way of getting to know the new homes they were being placed in all the time. I learned so much from him and about him, and what he learned from me was often so hard. I was the one who told him his brother was going to be placed in an inpatient mental health facility, but that I would ask the court to order visits with him there. I was the one who told him that his father had pled guilty in exchange for a reduced sentence. I was the one who gave him his mother's personal property from the evidence room after the plea was accepted. I was there with him when he opened her purse; he put his face in it and said he could smell her in there. Through it all, he almost cried, but he never did. He always found a way to smile. His bright white smile made me want to take him home with me myself, but I knew that wasn't what lawyers were supposed to do. So he kept moving through the system with the way-too-many placements that followed, and I made sure to keep his case in my caseload.

. . . Until I rotated out. I was given the chance to leave and I took it because I was ready to go. That was back when I represented parents too and I had had another case with a parent that had ended badly and I was running scared and was ready to do something different. I was burning out fast and at that point, I really needed a change. So I moved into the juvenile offender unit. When I told Oscar I was rotating out, he looked surprised for a minute, but just a minute, and then he said, "Hey, it's cool. I know you gotta do what you gotta do." I gave him my card and told him I hoped he would call me because even though I wasn't his lawyer anymore, I still wanted to know how he was doing, which seemed like something I was maybe not supposed to do, but I did it anyway. I wasn't sure what the rules were about boundaries, but I knew I wasn't ready to say goodbye to Oscar.

Ending the Client Relationship

Julia describes her ambivalence over ending her relationship with Oscar. It is important that clients are clear about when your attorney-client relationship ends.

- *Which ethical rules apply?*
- *How well did Julia handle ending this client relationship?*
- *How would you have handled it?*

He never called. I was so busy learning the ropes on the offender side that I was distracted, which was a good thing then because I needed to stop thinking about my dependency cases. Just when I was starting to miss him and was thinking about checking in on him, he popped up. But this time, he was on the offender docket. When I saw him that day in the hall, he smiled that same big bright smile and said, "I'll be alright, just a little bump in the road." I joked with him about how I missed him too, but he didn't need to follow me down to the other floor of the courthouse.

After another couple years, I rotated into adult criminal, first handling misdemeanors, and it wasn't too long before I got to see Oscar yet again. He had aged-out and had gotten into trouble for trespass. Someone else had his case then, but I was in court that day, and I saw him. He looked scruffy, like he'd been on the streets awhile. He told me he hadn't quite found a place to land yet, but not to worry.[33] He'd make it just fine.

I saw Oscar for the last time during my rotation in adult felonies. This time, for aggravated robbery, and apparently it wasn't his first felony offense. This time he was twenty-two years old and when he saw me, he did not smile. He looked away, as though by looking away he gave me permission to look away too. That's when I thought, what happened to Oscar? How had we messed up so badly? Yes, he had a terrible trauma, but what had we done to address it? Did we ignore it because he smiled so winningly? How did we keep hurting him over and over, letting him be moved around like so much furniture? Why? Because we had given up on finding a family for him? Because he had become a teenager and too big and scary? Because we had forgotten that somewhere there might be biological family that might have wanted to help? So many chances missed, so many good things that could have happened but didn't. So many bad things that happened that shouldn't have.

---

33. Homelessness and housing instability are common among youth who have aged out of foster care. Amy Dworsky et al., *Homelessness During the Transition From Foster Care to Adulthood*, 103 AM. J. OF PUBLIC HEALTH 318 (Dec. 2013) (Review of research published between 1990 and 2011 finding that between 11% and 36% of the youths who age out of foster care become homeless during the transition to adulthood).

That's when I decided to come back to dependency and start over, have a do-over and do it right this time. It had taken a long time but I had forgiven myself for the mistakes I had made with Oscar and with the other cases that had pushed me out of the rotation in the first place, and I decided I was ready to try again and just keep getting better at it. When I came back, they had separated parents representation from kids' representation, and I decided to come back to representing just kids. Still, it isn't easy to do it right with one hundred and fifty open files.

I couldn't resist last year when the county received state funds to participate in a pilot project that would require following established practice standards[34] to handle a smaller caseload solely devoted to representing children, and I decided to jump ship from my old agency to take advantage of being a part of that pilot. I went private and decided to take eighty kid cases and have my outcomes tracked. Nevertheless, as so often happens, the money is not completely enough to really do it right and eighty cases is still a lot of cases. I still have caps on the amount of time I can spend on each case and so I have to struggle to meet the standards of the folks who came up with this idea. Jill thinks I am crazy; I could have retired from the county in less than ten years, and it was no time to start my own non-profit with a business plan to expand from a home office to a storefront, but I say what better time to make a difference? It's now or never really. Sure it would have been better if I could have retired first, but the timing just wasn't right for that. It's important that we show that this can be done right so that the legislature more fully funds it.

So here I am trying to get those measurable positive outcomes, which includes decreasing interaction with the offender side. Works for me. Oscar had already inspired me to do that.[35] And the more I do this work, the more I want to get my clients where

---

34. A number of different practice standards applicable to youth have been developed. These standards elaborate upon the special duties of counsel for children and youth. Some also include caseload standards and requirements for social work assistance in the attorney's office. *See See* Am. Bar Ass'n, Standards of Practice for Lawyers Who Represent Children in Abuse and Neglect Cases (1996), [https://perma.cc/AQ8A-WP9S]; The NACC maintains current recommendations on practice standards for representing children in abuse and neglect cases. *See Standards of Practice*, Ass'n of Counsel for Children, [https://perma.cc/KHA3-TJWM]. The association makes explicit for practitioners where their standards differ with those of the ABA.; Standards of Practice for Lawyers Who Represent Children in Abuse and Neglect Cases, *B-4 Client Preferences Commentary* (ABA 1996), [https://perma.cc/6U3C-U73H]. *See also QIC Best Practice Model of Child Representation*, QIC Child Rep, [https://perma.cc/M7HD-8ZRC]; Family Court Advisory Rules Committee, District of Columbia Courts, Super. Ct. of the District of Columbia Child Abuse and Neglect Attorney Practice Standards (2003), [https://perma.cc/8KJY -7HR8]; Statewide Children's Representation Workgroup, Washington Supreme Court Commission on Children in Foster Care, Meaningful Legal Representation for Children and Youth in Washington's Child Welfare System (2010), [https://perma.cc/369Z-MYF6]; Florida Bar Standing Committee on the Legal Needs of Children, Florida Guidelines of Practice For Lawyers Who Represent Children in Abuse and Neglect Cases, June 2014 [https://perma.cc/WM8T-JXRS].

35. A Florida study found that between 60–70% of females in its juvenile offender system have substantiated histories of child maltreatment, and 25–64% of the boys have histories of maltreatment. Child Welfare League of America, Policy Brief: Dual Jurisdiction Youth 2

they want to be and out of the system, somewhere where their childhoods are not state-regulated and micro-managed, where they don't need visitation orders and special transportation to see the people they care about, where they can stay put with the people that matter to them—whether that's their biological family or their foster parent, where they don't need to have a case worker give them permission to go to a slumber party after a background check is completed.[36] Some place where they are not treated like they are either a victim or a perpetrator, and are just allowed to be kids.

> ### *Trauma Exposure Response*
>
> *Julia's work exposes her to her clients' trauma on a regular basis. How do attorneys do this work well and maintain a balanced outlook on their work and the larger world?*
>
> - *What tools have you seen Julia use?*
> - *What tools would work for you?*

I take the most recent pleadings subfolder out of Maya's file and slip it in my old leather brief case. If I am going to have to go to court with her tomorrow, I better try to see her today after I take care of the shelter care hearings this morning. As much as I wish the systems were separate, right now I have to admit I'm glad that juvenile detention is right next door to the dependency court.

Maya's Social Worker's Story: Sarah Prince
Child Welfare Services Worker
Adolescent Behavioral Resources Unit

My brother, the corporate vice president, is in town visiting with me this weekend and, of course, my pager goes off. He looks at me and sighs when I say, "I gotta get

---

(undated), [https://perma.cc/8QYJ-SXZE]. However, it is important to realize the nuances of this issue. Research also has shown that while there is a significant link between childhood maltreatment and adult crime, the link between the two nearly disappears when other life factors are considered. Protective factors such as graduating from high school or earning a GED as well as being married lowered the risk for engaging in adult criminal behavior, while poverty surfaced as the major predictor. Hyunzee Jung, et al., *Does Child Maltreatment Predict Adult Crime? Reexamining the Question in a Prospective Study of Gender Differences, Education, and Marital Status*, 30(13) J. Interpersonal Violence 2238 (2015) (first published Oct. 6, 2014). For a more general discussion of crossover youth, *see* ch. 1, *The Effect of the Juvenile Justice System*.

36. Recent legislation in Washington State, advocated for by foster youth themselves, rolled back the state regulations that required background checks and social worker permission for overnight activities and put in its stead a "prudent parent" standard which allows foster parents and other custodians to make decisions surrounding activities like slumber parties and camping trips. *See* Wash. Rev. Code § 74.13.710; *2014 Post-Session Recap*, The Mockingbird Society, [https://perma.cc/B6GG-BPGY]. Washington modeled its statute on a similar one in California, see Cal. Welf. & Inst. code § 362.04. Additionally, the 2014 Preventing Sex Trafficking and Strengthening Families Act implemented the "reasonable and prudent parent" standard federally. 42 U.S.C. § 675(1)(B).

this; hold on." He doesn't get why I do what I do and why I have been doing it for the last ten years. He knows that social workers don't make much money, and he also knows that social workers working for child welfare are paid less than social workers in other fields. He says his colleague's wife has an MSW and she works for a hospital and probably makes a lot more than what I do *and* she doesn't have a pager that goes off when her brother is in town taking her out to a nice restaurant.[37]

That's probably true. But here's my truth, I started doing this work in this unit because I wanted to see if I could handle it. I had done intake on the CPS side, where they start you out having to discern when a call should be acted on and if so, how quickly. After that, I worked in the Legally Free Unit trying to match children with the right pre-adoptive home and support them as they go through the sometimes rocky transition on the way to becoming a new family; I even spent a few weeks in licensing, which was pretty boring actually. That's when I knew that my strength was not in checking boxes or inspecting houses for switch-plate covers.

When this opportunity came up, I thought I might want to go deeper in the mental health field, maybe even start my own practice, but now I am not sure what will come next for me. I have been talking to my friends who got their degrees when I did, and it's hard to build a practice. Lots of competition. So for now, I have a pretty secure job with benefits that lets me pay down my student loans and also gives me some pretty interesting work to do. Besides, working in a hospital would mean, well, you would have to work in a hospital. I am not a fan of hospitals. Our mom died from cancer when I was in high school and I was so tired of hospitals after that, the sickly sterile smell of them, their buzzing fluorescent lights, their confusing long corridors, the doctors who never had enough time or the right words. One of the many things you learn in graduate school is to examine your limits, to know what work you can do and what you can't, what is just too close to home. Most people would find it odd that I can deal with mentally ill, abused, and neglected teenagers, but I can't work in a hospital where I would be helping people prepare for discharge. But everyone is different; we all have our histories to wrestle with.

> ### *Knowing Your Limits*
>
> *Sarah's choice to work in child welfare as opposed to a hospital is informed by her self-awareness of her limits.*
>
> * *Are there certain practice contexts that you know you should avoid? What are they?*
> * *Why do you believe that avoiding them is best?*

---

37. In 2015, the median annual salary for social workers in the hospital setting was $56,650. By contrast, state and local government social workers median annual salary was $46,940. *Occupational Employment and Wages,* U.S. Bureau of Labor Statistics, Occupational Employment Statistics, (May 2015), [https://perma.cc/G9HR-JU9Y]. *See Social Workers,* U.S. Bureau of Labor Statistics, Occupational Outlook Handbook (Dec. 17, 2015) [https://perma.cc/B4W3-MRCS].

Yes, my job is stressful and the stories are hard. The kids I work with have usually been through some of the worst situations you can imagine and they are at a very critical moment in their adolescence. If they don't get the help they need now, they will likely continue to struggle for the rest of their lives.

The foster care system stops serving youth when they turn eighteen most of the time. We just started offering extended foster care to age twenty-one, but to be eligible, the kids have to be enrolled in a school of some kind.[38] So many of the kids we work with in this unit are so far behind that they become discouraged with school. They don't see college in their future and are lucky to get a GED.[39] If we don't do something to help them when they are teens, they certainly won't be eligible for help at eighteen.

Ironically, the kids who need the most support when they turn eighteen are the ones who are excluded from extended foster care. Crazy if you ask me. I see the kids in my unit leaving foster care with no place to go. They are excited at first to finally be free, to have me off their backs, but then they are homeless with no place to turn.[40] Once in a while, if we have enough time before they are ready to age out, we can turn it around, get a kid the help he or she needs and get them back in school and on track.

This call is about one of those kids at her critical moment. Picked up by the cops for shoplifting a pregnancy test. She's been on the run for a long time. Who knows if

---

38. The Fostering Connections to Success and Increasing Adoptions Act, 42 USC 675(8) provides federal funds to states that elect to extend foster care beyond age eighteen. While states have some leeway to craft their own eligibility requirements, under 42 USC 675(8)(B)(iv), a child is considered eligible if s/he is still in high school or in a GED program, is enrolled in college or a vocational technical school, is participating in a program designed to alleviate the barriers to employment, or is employed for at least 80 hours per month. A youth may also qualify if they have disabling conditions that prevent them from participating in any of these activities, but the evidence supporting such a disability must be in writing and regularly updated. States are not required to extend foster care beyond the eighteenth birthday, and so availability and eligibility requirements vary across states. "Between 2009 and 2014, more than 37 bills have been enacted in 22 states extending foster care or other services and supports to youth aging out of foster care." NATIONAL CONFERENCE OF STATE LEG-ISLATURES, EXTENDING FOSTER CARE BEYOND 18 (2016) [https://perma.cc/TTQ9-MWCL].

39. A 2014 national survey completed by the American Bar Association's Legal Center for Foster Care & Education found that only half of the foster youth surveyed had completed high school by age 18. See NATIONAL WORKING GROUP ON FOSTER CARE AND EDUCATION, FOSTERING SUCCESS IN EDU-CATION: NATIONAL FACTSHEET ON THE EDUCATIONAL OUTCOMES OF CHILDREN IN FOSTER CARE (Jan. 2014), [https://perma.cc/H69T-KEED]. Another study of youth in the Midwest who had aged out of foster care, found a slightly lower overall rate of educational attainment (only 47.3% had a high school diploma) and found that the group least likely to have completed high school or to be enrolled in school were classified as "struggling parents." This group was 75% female and had at least one resident child in their care. See MARK E. COURTNEY ET AL., CHAPIN HALL ISSUE BRIEF, DISTINCT SUBGROUPS OF FORMER FOSTER YOUTH DURING YOUNG ADULTHOOD: IMPLICATIONS FOR POLICY AND PRACTICE 6, 8 (2010), [https://perma.cc/43LW-UFKH].

40. Some states have allowed youth who have aged out and declined extended foster care services to reapply for them within a certain period of time after aging out. See, e.g., ARK CODE. ANN. § 9-27-306; CAL. WELF. & INST. CODE § 391; FLA. STAT. § 39.6521(6); MICH. COMP. LAWS ANN. § 400.647; MINN. STAT. ANN. § 260C.451(6); N.Y. FAM. CT. ACT § 1091; N.C. GEN. STAT. ANN. § 131D-10.2B; TEX. FAM. CODE ANN. § 263.6021; WASH. REV. CODE § 74.13.336.

she's really pregnant and, if she is, how that happened. I hope she's not. For so many reasons. We will need to have the talk about what she wants to do. I take the position that it's up to her obviously, but I try to walk her through the practicalities of being a foster youth with a baby in care. It's not easy being a parent. It's not easy being a teen parent with stresses of her own, including being behind in school and having limited placement options. And that's a fact. She has to understand that there are very few foster parents who are licensed to care both for teenagers in her situation and babies,[41] and that there are fewer teen parent group homes. It used to be that I would have to talk her into letting the baby be dependent too so that whoever takes care of them can have funds for them both, but now the federal law changed or something and at least I don't have to do that anymore.[42] But the eyes and ears of the system still will be watching carefully to see if she can handle a little baby.[43] Of course, there is a third option, she can have the baby and place it for adoption, but fewer and fewer young mothers are choosing that option these days.[44]

So first things first: is she pregnant? I will ask the detention infirmary to offer her a pregnancy test first thing Monday morning and request a rush result. That way, maybe by Tuesday when she has her hearing on contempt, we will know at least whether we are dealing with a pregnant foster youth and what she might want to do about it.

---

41. Foster care licensing typically involves restrictions on the type of license a foster parent may have by the number, age range, or gender of the children in their care. This can lead to challenges when seeking to place a teen parent with his or her infant. *See, e.g.,* Fla. Stat. Ann. §409.175(3)(a); Ill Admin. Code 89, §402.15 (3)(b); Mo. Code Regs. Ann. 13, 35-60.020 (1); WAC 388-148-1385. See also, Amy Dworsky & Jan DeCoursey, Pregnant and Parenting Foster Youth: Their Needs, Their Experiences 40, Chapin Hall (2009), [https://perma.cc/CJ2X-SL4V] (qualitative study of service providers in Illinois noting the lack of appropriate placements for pregnant and parenting foster youth, resulting in three to four month waits to be placed in group homes for parenting foster youth).

42. 42 USC §475(4)(B) now allows for foster care payments for a teen parent in foster care to include payment to support her son or daughter in the same home.

43. The challenges of being pregnant and parenting while being a "child" in foster care are detailed in Tara Grigg Garlinghouse, *Fostering Motherhood: Remedying Violations of Minor Parents' Rights to Family Integrity,* 15 U. Pa. J. Const. L. 1221 (2013); Katherine Moore, *Pregnant in Foster Care: Prenatal Care, Abortion, and the Consequences for Foster Families,* 23 Colum. J. Gender & L. 29 (2012).

44. From 1952–1972, 8.7% of all births outside of marriage resulted in adoption placements. By contrast, from 1982–1988 only 2% of babies born to unwed mothers were placed for adoption. *See* National Committee for Adoption, Adoption Factbook: United States Data, Issues, Regulations and Resources 246 (1989). This downward trend has continued. Only 1% of babies born to never-married women were relinquished for adoption from 1989–1995. Anjani Chandra, Centers for Disease Control and Prevention, Adoption, Adoption Seeking, and Relinquishment for Adoption in the United States 1 (1999), [https://perma.cc/D4MB-XXQ4]. Those who do relinquish tend to be white and some studies suggest that teenagers who relinquish tend to come from intact families with highly educated parents. *See* Child Welfare Information Gateway, U.S. Dep't of Health & Human Servs., Voluntary Relinquishment for Adoption (2005), [https://perma.cc/24CH-Z6VJ].

And the problem is that even without her being pregnant, her placement options are pretty slim. She is now a high-needs child with a high-needs classification,[45] and that means she can only be placed in specially licensed therapeutic foster or group homes. She ran off from one of the best group homes last time. I am not sure how she wound up pregnant—if she is—but I know that it's not unusual for girls who run away to be pimped out, and girls with a history of sexual abuse seem to be the easiest targets of all.[46]

. . . Which leads me to one possibility that can get her the wraparound services she needs—great trauma-based therapy, specially adapted schooling with low teacher-student ratios, great medical care including reproductive health, and really a pretty nice housing situation to boot. It's called "Safe Harbors" and it just opened up for girls who have been subject to "commercial sexual exploitation,"[47] which is one of the new ways of referring to minors who, under our old laws, would have been charged with prostitution.[48]

But in order to get her in there, she will have to admit that that's what happened and she might have to be willing to identify her pimp. That could be a hard sell. Even girls who have experienced prostitution don't immediately identify it as prostitution and instead think of it as a relationship with a guy who takes care of them. If Safe Harbors isn't an option, I may have to let her stay in juvie for as long as possible. At least she couldn't run away.[49] That would give me some time to see what else is out there. We may have to look outside of the county for her, or maybe even the state.

---

45. Children with higher needs result in higher foster care rates. *See* Kerry DeVooght & Dennis Blazey, Child Trends, Family Foster Care Reimbursement Rates in the U.S.: A Report from a 2012 National Survey on Family Foster Care Provider Classifications and Rates § 3 (2013), [https://perma.cc/73BB-X98S].

46. Farley, *supra* note 30, at 110–11.

47. Tessa Dysart, *Child, Victim, or Prostitute? Justice through Immunity for Prostituted Children,* 21 Duke J. Gender L. Pol'y 280–281 (2014). For examples of programs similar to Safe Harbors, see *The Bridge Continuum of Services for Sexually Exploited Youth,* YouthCare [https://perma.cc/J5BJ -MB58]; *Brittany's Place: A Safe and Sound Shelter for Girls,* 180 Degrees [https://perma.cc/F4HP -JJSR]; Home of Hope [https://perma.cc/2UH3-5AHJ]; Rise (Restoring Identities after Sexual Exploitation) [https://perma.cc/X4ET-UNGH].

48. Decisions like *In re* B.W., 313 S.W. 3d 818 (Tex. 2010) (holding that a 13-year-old girl lacked the capacity to consent to sex, and therefore could not be convicted of prostitution) recognize the contradictions between traditional statutory rape laws and the laws that allow for prosecution of minors who engage in prostitution. *See also,* Dysart, *supra* note 47 at 255.

49. That youth who cross-over from child welfare into the juvenile offender system, whether as status offenders or otherwise, spend more time in detention than their in-home peers is not in doubt. *See* Gregory Halemba & Gene Siegel, Doorways to Delinquency: Multi-System Involvement of Delinquent Youth in King County National Center for Juvenile Justice, (2011), [https:// perma.cc/A9JY-D7BJ].

A shortage of placements in the foster care system may contribute to the problem. Advocates challenging conditions in foster care have alleged that "the shortage of homes even causes some children in foster care to be unnecessarily housed in juvenile justice detention facilities. When children in DSS custody are placed in detention or other juvenile justice facilities, DSS has a pattern or practice of recommending that they remain there, without a pending charge or awaiting a hearing or

My brother can see my mind is not on this dessert, as good as it is. He asks me whether it's worth it to be distracted from my flourless chocolate torte. I tell him that even though I can't discuss the details of my job or the call I just took, I can't imagine doing anything more challenging or interesting. He teases me about how my "top secret" attitude makes it sound like I work for the CIA. I say in my best James Bond voice, "Not the CIA, the CWS." He rolls his eyes and asks the waiter for the check.

The Assistant Attorney General's Story: Samuel Green

It seems like they are always doing some reorganization of our division in response to the latest budgetary constraint or best practice report or just some new administrator who perceives some new way to achieve optimal efficiency. This latest reorganization seems like a good idea in theory, but I would hardly call it the most efficient. Now each case is supposed to keep the same AAG,[50] but how to define what we mean by a "case" can even get complicated. Is it based on the parent or the child? Is it based on the case number — dependency or termination? It seems to require that we be in two places at once, when it comes to court, so we wind up having to get others to cover for us on our cases. The great idea behind *this* change is that a family should have the same AAG throughout so that there would be consistency in terms of case planning. Easier said than done. Social workers, who have the most impact on the family anyway, still change, whether because of turnover[51] or the way that the agency is structured.

> ### Lawyers for the State
>
> *Jurisdictions differ as to how the state's interests in dependency proceedings are represented.*
>
> - *In your jurisdiction, what entity represents the state's interests?*

The great idea before this one was to assign us according to agency unit. That made good sense in terms of making sure that the unit as a whole was operating in a way that was consistent with the statutes, regulations and agency policies.

---

determination on their charge beyond the term of their plea or adjudicated sentence specifically because DSS has nowhere else to house them." H et al v. Haley et al, Docket No. 2:15-cv-00134 (D.S.C. Jan 12, 2015), Exhibit A: Settlement Agreement, entered June 3, 2016, [https://perma.cc/92CX-5FZY].

50. "AAG" refers to "assistant attorney general." States and localities differ as to who represents the agency charged with protecting children and offering services to their families. In 2004, the American Bar Association proposed Standards of Practice for Lawyers Representing Child Welfare Agencies, which recognized the varying practices throughout the country but which sought to establish uniform guidelines and principles. *See* American Bar Association, Standards of Practice for Lawyers Representing Child Welfare Agencies (2004), [https://perma.cc/WH7D-5ZVU].

51. *See Worker Turnover*, Child Welfare Information Gateway, [https://perma.cc/2V3J-7YPL]; Diane Riggs, *Workforce Issues Continue to Plague Child Welfare*, Adoptalk (North American Council on Adoptable Children, St. Paul, MN), Summer 2007, [https://perma.cc/Z9HU-PX2G].

Before that, we were assigned according to the day we needed to show up in court. Some of us were shelter care AAGs. Some of us were permanency planning and review AAGs. Some of us just dealt with contested motions. Some of us only did trials — whether TPRs or Dependency Fact-Finding. This was definitely the most efficient from a court and legal expertise perspective, but it left us not knowing much about the cases themselves or how the system worked as a whole.

I started during the era of being assigned according to court proceedings. I did TPRs. I knew that a lot of the defense attorneys called my colleagues and me "The Terminators." At first I found the derisive tone that accompanied that nickname to be offensive because most of the time I was working towards getting kids the permanency they needed with adoptive homes, and often we were able to settle with some form of open adoption[52] that at least allowed the biological parents to receive pictures of their children a couple of times a year. Eventually, though I just rolled with the nickname. If you saw me, you would know the irony of any association with Schwarzenegger. I'm fit, mind you, but more of a flyweight. Running is my thing. Greased bodybuilding — not so much.

Anyway, after they re-orged me out of TPR, I made the natural transition into being counsel for the Legally Free Unit, and that's when I got to see what it was like for the kids who didn't have homes waiting for them after TPR. The social workers try hard to get the ones who are in pre-adoptive homes moving toward adoption, but a lot of the time is spent just trying to find good placements for the long-term kids. My court schedule switched from trials to the six-month alternating permanency planning and review hearings, often involving the legally free kids who had little chance of being adopted.[53]

Then we moved into this new case assignment system based on "one family-one attorney" and I essentially become the lawyer for the cases involving all of the legally free kids. Ironically, there are no "families" anymore in my cases. I am essentially the attorney for the state who is now the only legal parent that a child has. On rare

---

52. "Open adoption" is a form of adoption that allows the birth parents to maintain contact with the adoptive parents and/or the child after the adoption. The level of this contact varies from case to case, ranging from receiving photos or updates about the child to having regular contact with the child. The adoptive parents, however, are the legal parents of the child and retain authority to parent the child as they see fit. *See*, CHILD WELFARE INFORMATION GATEWAY, OPEN ADOPTION [https://perma.cc/L2TK-Z2TW]. In addition to negotiation, mediation is used in some states after the filing of a petition for termination of parental rights to resolve open adoption terms. *See* Nancy Thoennes, *What We Know Now: Findings from Dependency Mediation Research,* 47 FAM. CT. REV 21, 34 (Jan. 2009).

53. Children and youth whose parents' rights have been terminated are often referred to as "legally free." This terminology refers to the fact that the child has no legal parents and therefore is available to be adopted. Once a termination of parental rights has occurred, the dependency proceeding no longer involves the parents. However, the child remains under the jurisdiction of the court in the dependency proceedings. The focus of such a case should be on achieving a permanent placement for the child, whether through adoption, guardianship or some other long-term care arrangement. For more about dependency proceedings, including permanency planning and review hearings, *see* ch. 1, *ASFA: Seeking to Balance Permanence and Reunification.*

occasions, I get to defend against a petition by a child to reinstate his parent's rights.[54] It's a pretty new law that allows that and not many kids use it, but those cases are interesting and sometimes they actually work for the kid and I can agree. It's not because the termination was wrong in the first place; it's just because enough time has passed that the parent has actually gotten her, or his, act together.

There are days I wish I had been more careful about taking some of those cases to TPR, but really the law gave me little choice. If the child was out of the home 15 months I had to file, unless there was an exception that applied.[55] I could have worked harder on making the arguments for those exceptions I guess, but back then it seemed like the social workers often had it right. There were cases in which it seemed that the child needed that closure with the parent or the parent was truly dangerous, and there was always hope that a mythical someone could provide a permanent home when it was clear that the parent never could.

Anyway, my hardest cases are the ones in which the child is now a teenager, a frequent runaway with mental health or drug problems, and who has been through lots of placements. That's when the social worker looks at me with a sigh and a shrug. We have a duty to place the child somewhere safe but where? When they run away, it's tempting to keep them in juvenile detention for as long as possible, but that is not a permanent solution and unless the detention is for violation of a valid court order, it runs afoul of federal law.[56] The beds in good, therapeutic foster or group homes are few and far between. Sometimes we have to look statewide or even out-of-state for appropriate facilities.

This morning I get a call from the Adolescent BRS Unit on one of those cases. Looks like we have a show cause hearing tomorrow on a runaway. Oh yeah, I forgot to mention—what's the only case harder than a legally free teenager with mental health problems who has run away from the last good group home she could have had in the area? A legally free teenager with mental health problems who is back from her run *pregnant*. Thank God this one has Sarah. She is usually pretty creative.

The Judge's Story: The Honorable Esther Goodloe

I know I was blessed, blessed to be raised by both my mother and my father. My father was sometimes a hard man, but he loved us all in the best way he could. He was a military man and so we moved quite a bit. I saw a lot of how the world works, and I do mean the world. We were stationed all over the place—from Guam to Gulfport, from Okinawa to San Diego. Sometimes we stayed behind in the states with our mother but more often than not we were pulling up stakes as soon as we had planted

---

54. Several states allow for a child to petition for reinstatement of parental rights, subject to certain conditions. *See, e.g.,* Cal. Welf. & Inst. § 366.26; Wash. Rev. Code § 13.34.215; *see also,* Reinstatement of Parental Rights: State Statute Summary, National Conference of State Legislatures (Apr. 2016), [https://perma.cc/S4PQ-ADHX].

55. 42 U.S.C. § 675(5)(E).

56. *See* 42 U.S.C. § 5633(a)(11).

them. Having a father who was an officer in the Navy meant we rarely stayed in one place for long. It was sometimes hard leaving friends we had just made, churches we had just joined, but it made us a close family—me and my six brothers and sisters. My mother and father met when he was first stationed in Gulfport. Her people were from Mississippi and his were from Louisiana. So we went to family reunions in both places as often as we could. How I loved those gatherings—getting to play with all of our cousins, at least from one side of the family, all in one place. I envied them because they got to see each other all the time; they envied us because we seemed to have everything they thought they lacked—a nice car, nice clothes, and stories about strange places they never knew existed.

My father was a big success by all accounts.[57] All the parents told their sons to follow in their Uncle Edwin's footsteps and they instructed their daughters to look for a man who would be half as strong and steady. The advice my father always gave in return was to get an education.[58] He got his through the Navy. He didn't expect us girls to do that; but he still thought we should be educated. And so we were. All of us. Boy or girl. Whether we wanted to or not. We were all going to college. And some of us went on further than that. Me, to law school and one of my brothers, to medical school. We all knew we had to be twice as good to go half as far. We pushed ourselves sometimes harder than we thought we could take. We were taught to respect ourselves and to fear and love our God and our elders.

My father was always being asked for his opinion, and yes, his money. My parents were generous so long as my father felt like whoever was asking was actually trying to do something to better their lot in life. My mother had a softer heart; she tried to convince him that sometimes you have to be kind just because there's a need. But he wasn't going to make weak people weaker by giving them too much.

To this day, sitting in this courtroom, I hear both of their voices when a difficult decision awaits my judgment—one saying that when you baby people, they stay babies forever and there's nothing more unbecoming and unsuccessful than a grown-up baby; the other quizzing me on the Bible verses we had to memorize for Sunday School. "Remember Esther, what did Jesus say? 'Blessed are the merciful, for they will be shown mercy.'[59] That's right, and don't forget your Old Testament either . . . 'And what does the Lord require of you? To act justly, to love mercy, and to walk humbly with your God.'"[60]

---

57. For an account of the impact of military participation on upward mobility in the black community, see Andrew Billingsley, Climbing Jacob's Ladder: The Enduring Legacy of African-American Families 185–200 (1994). However, despite their historic and monumental contributions in the military and the relative opportunities provided through it, blacks remain underrepresented at the highest ranks. Even though blacks comprise 17% of the military, only 9% of officers within the military are black. H. Roy Kaplan, The Myth of Post-Racial America: Searching for Equality in the Age of Materialism 176 (2011).

58. To learn more about the long tradition of emphasizing the importance of education within African American families, see Billingsley, supra note 57, at 171–184.

59. Matthew 5:7.

60. Micah 6:8.

Part II: Diving in the Deep End

Maya in Detention

Maya's First Meeting with Her Social Worker

Sometimes, when it gets like this, I just curl up into a little ball and close my eyes. Sometimes I count backwards from 100 until I fall asleep or I count by tens or by twos for as long as I can. I like numbers. They are safe, always the same, always either right or wrong. No in-between. And they don't lie. They don't promise you one thing and give you another. They just are.

My day starts out with a visit to the infirmary to get the pregnancy test done. They wake me up way early and ask if I would like to be tested. I don't think the sun was even up yet and there I am shuffling down the hall in these stupid plastic slippers they give you. They wouldn't let me pee before I left because they said I had to do that for the doctor. I pee in the cup like they say and then shuffle back. Just about when I am about to fall back to sleep, they call me back to the infirmary again and tell me what I already know. The nurse who tells me I am pregnant acts like it didn't matter to her one way or another. No congratulations or anything, that's for sure.

I must have missed breakfast when I was in there and so I just decide to go back to sleep. Then Sarah, my caseworker, shows up before I can fall back to sleep *again*. Now I'm hungry *and* tired. She knows I had taken the test, but doesn't know the result. She asks me what the test said, which just seems wrong to me. I mean really, isn't it my life? Why do I have to tell her anything? So I don't tell her because she pissed me off and it's early and I feel sick anyway because—guess what—I am pregnant.

So she says since I won't tell her she has to assume I am pregnant and that if any of this stuff she's about to tell me isn't important to me I can just tell her to go away.[61]

---

61. The Health Insurance Portability and Accountability Act (HIPAA) is a federal statute that governs when and how medical information can be shared. *See*, Health Insurance Portability and Accountability Act of 1996, Pub. L. No. 104-191, 110 Stat. 1936 (codified as amended in scattered sections of 18, 26, 29, 42, U.S.C.). One of the underlying tenets of the act is that medical information cannot be shared by health care providers without the consent of the individual who must consent to the treatment. When it comes to minors, HIPAA's default position is that the minor's parents, guardian or those acting in loco parentis stand in the minor's stead for purposes of both consenting to treatment and consenting to disclosure. However, the act enunciates specific exceptions to this rule. Among the specifically outlined HIPAA exceptions is the circumstance in which the treatment was provided with the minor's consent. The other circumstance is where the state law specifically provides that the youth has authority to consent to the treatment. *See* Brittany Strandell, *Medical Privacy in Dependency Cases: An Exploration of Medical Information Sharing in the Foster Care System*, 11 J. Health & Biomedical L. 107, 134–137 (2015). Some states allow young people who have reached a certain age to consent to reproductive and/or mental health care. *Id.* at 140. Therefore, assuming that Maya is permitted to consent to the pregnancy test, her health care provider could not disclose that information without her consent. That being said, these privacy protections are often subverted through court orders in dependency cases that provide that social service workers should be granted access to the child's medical records. These orders are not uniformly respected by health care providers if state law does not allow for them. *Id.* at 143–144.

So she starts telling me about how it's my choice what to do about it, but either way I am going to get "proper health care." She says that she can arrange for me to have an abortion if I want to, and it's at that point that I guess I give it all away by telling her that I'm not doing that. Then she says that is my choice but that I will still have some time to think about it if I want to, depending on how far along I am.[62] I say I already know I am keeping this baby, that she is mine and isn't anybody going to take her away from me.

Access to the Medical Records of Foster Youth

In this case, we see that Maya's social worker does not have access to the results of her pregnancy test for reasons discussed in footnote 61.

- *What does state law in your jurisdiction provide as to who would have to consent to the treatment in Maya's case?*

- *Which individuals or agencies would have access to the results?*

I don't know why I start saying "her"; it could be a boy. But I never really had any little boys to think about before. If it's a boy, maybe I'll call him Marcus for my uncle, or Diamond maybe. That would be different. He could be my shiny Diamond, my treasure. If it's a girl though, what then? I don't know, there are so many pretty girls' names. I could name her for family. Or maybe I could name her Blossom. I always liked that name. But anyway, I want to be happy about being pregnant but Sarah starts talking like there is nothing good about the news at all and it almost feels like I am back with Shirley who made me get an abortion that first time and so I just tell myself not to even listen to her, not to be tricked again.

She tries to find out who the daddy is and I tell her I don't know. She asks me to tell her if I have any ideas. I shrug. Then she starts asking me about what happened when I was gone. I tell her I was doing fine until I got pregnant, and then I started thinking I would have to find a better place to be and see a doctor and stuff like that. She asks me about what my plans would have been if I were still on the streets and had found out for sure I was pregnant. I tell her I don't know but that I will take good care of myself for the baby because I know that's an important thing to do. She seems

---

62. Roe v. Wade, 410 U.S. 113 (1973) recognized that the fundamental right to privacy under the Fourteenth Amendment of the Constitution extended to a woman's right to decide whether to have an abortion. Under the framework provided by the decision, during the first trimester of an abortion the state may not restrict the woman's right to choose to have an abortion. The state may regulate abortions in the second trimester in the interest of the health and safety of the woman, and in the third trimester, the state may regulate abortion to protect the potential human life of the fetus. *See also* Whole Women's Health v. Hellerstedt, 2016 WL 3461560, 136 S.Ct. 2292 (decided June 27, 2016) (Texas statute which required abortion providers to have admitting privileges at local hospital located no more than 30 miles from the abortion facility and requiring abortion facilities to meet minimum standards for ambulatory surgical centers held unconstitutional as creating a substantial obstacle to a woman's right to a pre-viability abortion through the enactment of unnecessary health regulations). For a discussion of minor's access to abortion, see ch. 1, n. 2.

a little happier then to hear me say that, like I had offered her some ray of hope that I was a decent, smart person or something. She starts talking to me about what I hope for this baby, and I am careful then because I feel like maybe she is trying to trick me into giving her up for adoption like Shirley told me would happen the first time, and I just snap back at her that I hope that this baby will be raised by her mother, which is me.

Then she launches into this long lecture about how it can be hard to find a place for us both to be — me and my baby — because there aren't a lot of "options," but that she will do her best, even though it is a "difficult case." I just stop listening again and I feel my ears just begin to shut down and I am at about 45 in the backwards counting and starting to get kind of sleepy and before I know it I am curled up on the bed, not asleep, not awake, not crying, just not anything. After I get to zero in the backwards counting, I start counting by fives, and, at 135, I notice she is acting like she is almost ready to go. As she finishes making her notes in what I guess is my file, she asks me what I want. I told her I want my baby and I want her to leave me alone.

She says she knows it is a lot for me to take in, but that she wants me to know that, unless she finds a placement for me today, she is going to ask the judge to keep me in juvie for a while so we could sort all of this out. She says she has to figure out where I can live since I want to keep the baby; not everyone is licensed to have a pregnant girl apparently, and it is even worse to find someone for both a baby and a teenage foster kid.[63] I feel like some sort of dangerous race car or fast motorcycle. Not just anyone is licensed to have me. They have to prove they can handle it first, take some kind of test or something. It will be great if we can go for a test drive first maybe but let me be the one who gets to decide whether they have a chance. But that isn't happening. It isn't up to me. It's never up to me. She wants me to know that she isn't trying to punish me by keeping me in detention, just keep me safe until we can figure out together where I will go next. Yeah, right.

> ### *Agency Use of Contempt to Buy Time*
>
> *Placing a foster youth in detention is not permitted, unless ordered by the court as a consequence of contempt for disobeying a valid court order. In this case, Maya will be brought before the court for contempt because she ran away from her court-ordered placement. Here, her social worker seeks to take advantage of this legal maneuver to buy more time to find a placement.*
>
> - *Does your state use contempt proceedings when a youth has run away from court-ordered placement?*
> - *Should it?*

---

63. For a discussion of the barriers that foster care licensing requirements pose for co-placement of parenting foster youth and their children, *see supra* note 41.

Even though I know what the answer will be, I ask her if I can just go stay with my Aunt Hen and Uncle Marcus because I feel like I want her to know that there are people who don't feel they need a license or money to keep me. And just like I knew she would, she says no, that she wants to be sure I can get the help I need and that I will be safe. She says that I have been through a lot, and before I can be a mom, I need to work with therapists who can help me deal with my own stuff.

I think to myself *if you want to help me, you will let me be. You are the shoveler of the shit I have been through*.

So here I am now still curled up on my little skinny mattress. But, hey, it is a bed. Not as nice a bed as the ones that Diamond would sometimes set us up with at the hotel. They weren't fancy hotels or anything but they were good enough to have cable TV and when we weren't busy, we could watch shows and eat take-out from Chinese restaurants, and we would laugh and joke and have a good time. It wasn't all bad. We made it work, you know.

But those days need to be over if I am going to be a mom for real. I know babies shouldn't be on the streets, with their moms working, but where will we wind up if not at Aunt Hen's?

I hate this shit.

Maya's Social Worker's Search in the Land of Limited Options

I can't say that went well, but I don't expect these conversations to be life altering. I know that building a relationship with a young person in Maya's situation takes time. There may have been a moment, a brief second when her eyes met mine, and a glint of, not of trust, no not that at all, but a flicker of curiosity moved between us. That is the most I can wish for in this situation. And how can it be more when she is in juvenile detention, pregnant, knowing that I am the one who is responsible for where she goes next? I told her that I will look for a placement today and I know the best way to build a relationship that might someday yield trust is to keep my promise. So I start calling.

The Phoenix is where she was last and I always start there. I check first to see if they are licensed for pregnant and parenting. Pregnant yes, parenting no. They will not be my first choice anyway, since she ran from there and won't be able to stay there long. But there aren't many group homes that are both pregnant and parenting and so I call. I know Jacqui, the program manager there, and I might be able to talk her into it. But she says no, for two reasons. First, she doesn't think it's a "good fit" and second they have no room right now. When I ask her to tell me more about why Maya won't fit in there, she says, "Well, obviously she voted with her feet. We thought we were making progress with her, but she chose to leave. Plus, she has too many friends on the street now. I don't need her here destabilizing our kids."

I call the two pregnant and parenting teen group homes in our county. No luck. All full.

I check our therapeutic foster parent list for someone who is licensed and has room for both a teenager and eventually a baby. There's one, Helen, who is very good and it looks like she does have capacity. I call her and tell her Maya's story. I try to make Maya sound as compelling as I can. It's a fine line—telling sufficient facts to create empathy but not so many that I am over-sharing confidential information or scaring the placement away. But Helen has been doing this for a while. She knows what to ask.

"So she's a runner?"

"She has run from the last two group homes, but it could be that she needs more of a family setting. She's your kind of girl, Helen. A challenge—but you could make a huge difference for her. She wants to keep her baby and maybe that will give her the motivation to stay put. She needs someone to believe in her."

"How long was she gone last time?"

"Six months."

"That's a long time. She's probably pretty street by now. The father?"

"She hasn't shared that information yet."

There's a pause. I don't like this pause. There's no sigh in it, no hesitation, no openness. She sounds like she's holding her breath, like she's steeling herself to say no. "Listen Sarah, I have to think about my other kids here. I just got one of my girls to be stable with her treatment."

"I don't have the sense that she's a heavy drug user, Helen. Of course, I don't know but she seems like she hasn't done much self-medicating. Can't say for sure, but that doesn't seem to be her thing."

"What *is* her thing then?"

"Not sure yet, all I can tell is that at this point she's had lots of trauma and instability."

"I don't think I can do this to Janelle, Sarah. We've come a long way, but we aren't all the way to where she won't be triggered by someone with a lot of connections with the street. I'm going to have to say no. I'm sorry. Maybe if she can show that she is making progress somewhere else first, that she's broken away from it all."

I have to give her credit for caring so much about her current foster youth, Janelle. There are some who wouldn't think about that. That's what would make her so good for Maya; it would be great if Maya would be able to get that level of thoughtfulness from an adult in her life.

Finally, with no other option, I research this new place—Safe Harbors. Maya doesn't strictly fit the eligibility requirements and the length of stay is limited to one year. The usual referral source is through the juvenile justice system and the diversion of a prostitution charge. They also take youth who are in need of a safe space in order to be witnesses for the prosecution against their traffickers.[64] On the plus side, they are

---

64. For an overview of the various state responses to create an alternative system for youth who would otherwise be charged with prostitution, see Shared Hope International, JuST Response

licensed for pregnant and parenting teens. I might as well try. She is in detention. She's pregnant and she had to have survived somehow during those six months. Her file indicates that her mother allowed her sister to be sexually abused in exchange for drugs and that her sister "didn't want that to happen to Maya." That kind of childhood puts her at risk for being sexually exploited on the street.[65]

I call and speak to their intake social worker. I give her my best pitch. It turns out that they have an open bed. While technically their funding is only supposed to support juvenile justice referrals, she has one privately funded bed that allows her more flexibility in cases like these when a young person at-risk of juvenile justice involvement presents a need. It's their "prevention against detention" bed. To qualify, the youth has to be willing to participate in the program. The bed is intended for those who come off the street without a charge, asking for help to leave the life, but so far the bed has not had as many takers as they had hoped and those who have come have not stayed long. So she's willing to take the risk. She says that this bed is funded for the next four months and they hope to have funding renewed. They are working with the donor and it would be great to have someone in place. No guarantees though. I thank her and promise to talk to Maya and hopefully tomorrow get the court's approval for her release from juvenile detention. She agrees to hold the bed for me until noon tomorrow.

Considering that the only placement that Maya expressed any interest in is the aunt's, I look in the file and see whether I have authority to explore that placement. The notes from my last contact say that I was told that I was not permitted to share information concerning Maya with her aunt and that before considering relative placement, the unit supervisor would need to pre-clear it. Of course, that unit supervisor is gone; so who knows what my new super will say. It seems likely that a relative placement will not be her first choice given Maya's need for intensive services, but I send her an email anyway, requesting authority to explore the feasibility of placement with the aunt. I get an out-of-office reply saying she is in court today. At least I can say that I looked into it.

I set a reminder to head back to detention after lunch. Promise kept, but not quite sure how Maya will take to the only option I have. In an ideal world, I would have had several meetings over several weeks to get to the point that I could talk to her

STATE SYSTEM MAPPING REPORT: A REVIEW OF CURRENT STATUTES, SYSTEMS, AND SERVICES RESPONSES TO JUVENILE SEX TRAFFICKING (2015), [https://perma.cc/7PXT-SG7U]. For descriptions (and critiques) of the trend toward juvenile offender diversion programs for sexually exploited youth, see Brendan M. Conner, *In Loco Aequitas: The Danger of "Safe Harbor" Laws for Youth in the Sex Trade*, 12 Stan. J.C.R. & C.L. 43 (Feb. 2016), [https://perma.cc/B7VF-WC6F]; Jennifer Musto, *Domestic Minor Sex Trafficking and the Detention-to-Protection Pipeline*, 37 DIALECT. ANTHROPOL. 257 (2013).

65. Some young people who find themselves selling sex either for their own survival or to profit others have a history of being prostituted at a young age by a parent in order support that parent's drug habit. Wendy L. Macias-Konstantopoulos et al., *The Commercial Sexual Exploitation and Sex Trafficking of Minors in the Boston Metropolitan Area: Experiences and Challenges Faced by Front-Line Providers and Other Stakeholders*, 6(1) J. APP. RES. ON CHILD.: INFORMING POL'Y FOR CHILD. AT RISK 8 (2015).

about her experiences on the street and whether this is a program that would work for her. But this is far from an ideal world. And if this placement doesn't work out and her aunt is a no-go, I will need to look for a therapeutic placement in another county and if that doesn't work, I will be forced to look outside of the state. I will need at least the week to figure all of that out.

Lawyer as Counselor: Julia Reconnects

The officer comes and says that I have another visitor. She wakes me up and as I stand up, I feel dizzy and nauseous. I tell her I feel like I'm going to be sick and she helps me over to the toilet so I can throw up my lunch. She says my lawyer is here to see me in the attorney room.

Just once, I wish I had a different kind of visitor. Diamond or KiKi, one of my other friends from the street. Or my sister Jazz or my Aunt Hen — now wouldn't that be something? A visitor who isn't paid to see me.

The attorney room is small with a tiny round table and two black plastic chairs. I sit down in one of them and look at this lady. She looks even older than my caseworker, Sarah. She's dressed really boring but she's ok looking. I think she should work a little harder. Put on some make-up or something. She could look almost pretty, for an old person.

"Hi Maya, my name is Julia Yasko. I don't know if you remember me from before? We met here in detention almost two years ago. I am your lawyer. How are you?" She looks a lot friendlier and less worried to see me than the caseworker. I wonder if she knows about the pregnancy test too. Probably not or else she'd look more mad.

"I kind of remember you." I don't really remember her, but I don't want to piss her off; I don't have the energy right now.

"I know that we really haven't had a chance to work together much before, but I wanted to meet with you today to explain to you what's going on, why you are here in detention and I hope you will let me know what you would like to have happen. If you have any questions about what's going on with your case, I can see what I can do to get answers. Anything we discuss here is private — just between you and me — and I won't tell anyone else anything you say unless you tell me it's OK."

She spends some time talking to me, not about my case or anything, just asking me how I am and stuff, whether they are treating me ok, whether I am getting enough to eat, and I tell her that I am not very hungry but that it's not too bad. It's not like I have anywhere else I can be right now, and it's not like I'm going to tell her I kind of miss Diamond but at the same time I'm glad I don't have to tell him I'm pregnant. Still, she seems kind of nice, but I keep wondering whether there's some kind of trick and what she really cares about. I mean, everyone's got a job to do and I am part of it. And apparently I am "a difficult case." I know most of these people are just trying to game me.

> ### Building Rapport
>
> *Even if time is short, attorneys should spend at least a few moments getting to know their clients and learning how they are doing. Building rapport not only provides important information about the client's personality and how receptive they are to a meeting; it also respects their dignity as a person and not just "a case." How would you build rapport with Maya?*

Eventually, she comes around to talking business.

She asks, "Is it OK if I take notes? I won't scribble the whole time, I hope, but it's important that I get what you tell me down somewhere that I can review later when I am working on your case. It's just for me; I don't share them with anyone else, and if you ever want to see what I am writing, just ask."

I tell her I guess so. And I'm thinking that's a first too. Nobody ever wants me to see what they are saying about me.

> ### Note-Taking
>
> *Young clients may be curious and/or concerned that you are taking notes. Explaining why you are and asking for permission restores some measure of control. How would you explain note-taking to a teenage client?*

She says thanks and keeps talking, "I don't share my file with your social worker, I want you to understand that, although your social worker is supposed to let me see most of her file if I ask her to."

She stops for a second to look at me and then says, "I know you have a lot of people coming in and out of your life — social workers, case managers, judges, correctional officers here in detention. This isn't a test. I just want to make sure I'm doing a good job of explaining why I am here and how I am different from all of the others. Can you tell me something you think might be different about what I do for you compared to what, say your social worker, does?"

> ### Checking for Understanding
>
> *It is important to make sure that your client understands you.*
> - *What do you think of the way Julia has done that here?*
> - *How else could she check for understanding?*

I look at her and shrug. But she just waits smiling at me, and so I figure I better say something, "Well, I guess you are supposed to go to court for me?"

"That's right. My job is different than your social worker's. Or anyone else's. I don't work for the state or the court. I just work for you and so when I go to court I will be trying to convince the judge that she should give you what you want. But my job is bigger than that too. Because I also want to make sure you understand what's going on—you need to know what the judge wants to know about before we go to court and, after court is over, I need to make sure you understand what happened because this is your life everyone is talking about. And sometimes I will try to work behind the scenes with the social worker to get her to agree with what you want before we get to court because if we can get her on our side, the judge is almost always going to give us what you want. But the main point is I work for you, not anybody else."

"Yeah, well, who is paying you then? Because I sure can't." I am so tired of people pretending they care and are on my side when it's just a job. Everyone gets paid to have a piece of me. Talk about being pimped out. How many people make money off me being here and not on the streets? I bet they all get paid way better than Di.

"Fair question. I get paid by the government to be a lawyer for kids. There is a rule that says all kids have to get lawyers when they are your age, which means that it doesn't matter whether the government likes it or not, they have to pay me. But it doesn't matter *who* pays me because I am still on your side. You get to tell me what you want, because as far as I am concerned you're my boss." She smiles at me, like she thinks she's the luckiest person in the world to get to sit here in juvenile detention with me. Is she for real?

Language Choice

Julia uses "kids" to refer to her clients. She also characterizes her role by saying that Maya is the "boss." What do you think of Julia's language choices?

She keeps talking, "Tomorrow morning, we go to court in front of Judge Harris. There is an order that says you have to go to court and explain why you left the group home. I can help you to figure out what you want to say about that. I can talk to the judge for you or if you want to say something to the judge yourself, you can do that too. The judge will probably ask you some questions. If she decides that you left the group home, even though you knew that there was an order that said you had to stay there, then she will say that you are 'in contempt of court.' If you are in contempt, then she can make you stay in detention for up to seven days, unless she gives you a chance to get out sooner by writing an essay or something.[66] I haven't had a chance to talk to your social worker yet, but I think she wants to have you kept here in detention for at least seven days because she seems kind of out of ideas as to where you can go next."

---

66. To learn more about contempt, see ch. 3: *Maya's Story*, n.47.

> ### Explaining Legal Terms Using Simple Language
>
> *If there are legal terms that the client will need to understand to be prepared for court, they should be explained as concretely as possible as applied to their situation.*
>
> - *What do you like about the way Julia has explained the current legal proceedings to her client?*
> - *What would you do differently?*

I tell her that I know that my caseworker wants to keep me here, that she came by this morning already and talked to me about it. When the lawyer asks me to tell her more about that conversation, I just tell her that mostly the social worker tried to talk me into getting an abortion but I am not going to do that. When I told the caseworker that I want to have my baby, she told me about how it was going to make it hard for her to find us a place to live together and that they will be watching me real close to see if I can really handle the baby even if I don't get to keep her with me. My social worker seems pissed I am making her job harder.

> ### Adolescent Perceptions
>
> *Maya recounts the intent of Sarah's conversation differently than Sarah probably would. Julia may suspect that Sarah didn't say or intend to say what the client believes she heard. Julia does not correct or challenge Maya's perceptions.*
>
> - *Should Julia have challenged Maya's perceptions?*
> - *What are the advantages and disadvantages of trying to reframe what Sarah said?*

I guess I just told the lawyer I was pregnant without even saying I'm pregnant. I must be getting used to it being for real already. She doesn't seem surprised or anything.

"It sounds like you were kind of pissed at her too," she says, not like she's mad at me or anything. Just like it's a fact, which it is.

"Yeah. I mean, I didn't tell her I was pissed or anything but I get sick of everybody treating me like the fact that I'm pregnant is some big problem."

"You want to have your baby and raise her, is that right?" She asks, not like she thinks it's the dumbest idea in the world, but like she's curious and wants to make sure that she understands. And she uses the word "her" like I did and like my baby is a real person and like I am a real person. Maybe she is on my side for real, too. But maybe she just has to act that way or something.

> *Active Listening*
> - *What do you like about the way that Julia actively listens?*
> - *What would you do differently?*

"Yes, I do want to have her and keep her. Can I? Or will they take her away?"

"We can talk about that some more later but the short answer is that you have just as much right to be a parent as anyone."

She waits a second, like she's thinking I might say something else about that, but I like that short answer, so I don't. I don't want to hear about all the ways that can maybe go wrong. Not now.

"Well, let me be the first person to congratulate you then, Maya. Having a baby is a really exciting thing I imagine. But I know it can be rough sometimes. How are you feeling? Have you been sick?"

"Man, have I ever. I puke all the frickin' time." I smile a little as I say it because goddamn she is the only person who has congratulated me.

"I have heard that sometimes if you just eat some really plain saltine crackers before you get out of bed that helps sometimes. Maybe we can see about whether they can do that for you here. I can check. Would you like me to?"

"OK, but I doubt they'll do it."

"No harm in asking though, right? So you feel like it's a girl?," she smiles and asks as though she wants to imagine with me what it will be like when this baby is really here and is really mine.

"Yeah, just a feeling. Who knows? If it's a girl, I might call her Jasmine or Blossom. Not sure."

"Both are pretty. Seems like you like flower names. And what if it's a boy?" She talks as though she's interested, as though she gets it, but she might be trying to trick me, because I might name it after the baby's daddy or something. Everybody always wants to know who the daddy is, like it's any of their business even if I knew. Or maybe she's trying to distract me from asking more questions about whether I will really be able to keep her.

"Not sure. I might name him after my Uncle Marcus," and then I add, so she doesn't think I'm some kind of flower freak, "Jasmine is my sister's name but I haven't seen her in forever."

And then we start talking about my Uncle Marcus, how he's such a good daddy to his two little girls. And how I want to be as good of a mom as my Aunt Hen is, and soon we've taken off talking and before I know it I've told her about how my Aunt Hen wants to take me in but the state won't let her and that I just want to go stay with her and I bet she would be excited to help me take care of this baby, but the caseworker won't let me because she thinks I am some kind of crazy person who needs to see a therapist and live with other crazy girls, but what kind of place is that to have a baby?

The lawyer tells me that it sounds like my aunt and uncle are really important people to me. I feel better that she seems to get that we are not all crazy people.

Thinking about how weird it is to have a baby in a group home makes me nervous thinking about whether I will get to keep my baby again and so I decide I want to know, "Are you sure they won't take my baby away from me?"

She says again that I have just as much right to be a parent as anyone, but that it is true that the fact that I am in foster care means that there will be more people paying attention to how well I do and that if they feel the baby is in danger in any way they could complain to CPS. She says that it means that while it may be good that I will have more people wanting to help and teach me what to do, it will also mean that there will be more people paying attention to us.[67]

She probably sees that I am not happy about this because she says she knows it's not fair and then she comes back around again to talking about Aunt Hen and Uncle Marcus because she understands that I would really like to have them be the ones who can help me when I get stressed out. She says it's ok to be stressed out when you have a new baby because all new parents are stressed out but that she understands that I need to have somebody I trust who I can reach out to for help.

> ### *Giving Clear Truthful Information, Even When It's Hard*
> *Young people in the child welfare system have suffered broken promises made by well-intentioned service providers, who don't want to tell them bad news. It's an attorney's duty to provide his or her client with information needed to make informed decisions. Being clear and honest about the reality that a youth faces can build trust. How would you explain to Maya the challenges she will face?*

She says that she wants to see if there is a way to at least get the social worker to consider the possibility of letting me stay with them but she tells me it sounds like the social worker is thinking more about group homes for now. She asks me whether I know why the social worker doesn't want me to be with my aunt and uncle.

I tell her that the social worker thinks my aunt will let me stay with my mom but that's stupid because my mom is homeless and my aunt has a place of her own. I tell her my aunt cares about my mom and that it's only right that she does because they are sisters. I care about my sister even though I haven't seen her since we were kids. She won't sell out her sister just because the social worker doesn't like her, but she also isn't going to have my mom come live with her either because my mom has way too many problems for that and Aunt Hen and Uncle Marcus know that she would be hard to have around their little girls. Not that my mom would do anything bad to

---

67. For an exploration of the challenges parenting foster teens have in retaining custody of the children, see Eve Stotland & Cynthia Godsoe, *The Legal Status of Pregnant and Parenting Youth in Foster Care,* 17 U. Fla. J.L. & Pub. Pol'y. 1 (April 2006); Kara Shelli Wallis, *No Access, No Choice: Foster Care Youth, Abortion, and State Removal of Children,* 18 CUNY L. Rev. 119, 146–149 (Winter 2014).

them or anything like that. She's not a violent person. She's just got problems, and those girls don't know anything about those kinds of problems, and Aunt Hen and Uncle Marcus don't probably want them to.

Theory Development

The lawyer needs to anticipate the opposing side's argument. You will often learn the state's position through discovery and from the social worker or attorney. Still, asking the client what she thinks the opposing side's objections are can often yield important insights into the facts and the way in which the client perceives her reality. These questions also help the client understand the adversarial process—that there will be more than one side presented.

She nods a lot and writes things down on her yellow note pad. She "uh-huhs" and says "tell me more about that" until I have told her everything I know about what my Aunt Hen and Uncle Marcus are like, all the stuff I like about them and all the stuff I don't, because, like she said, no one's perfect.

Passive Listening and General Questions

Passive listening is a helpful technique. Brief acknowledgments let the client know you are tracking without interrupting the flow of information.

Asking general question—"Tell me more about that"—may yield more information than a series of closed ended-questions.

Then she says, "This has been really helpful, Maya, thank you for telling me all of this. They sound like really good people and I don't understand why the department is so down on them. I will need to find out. I also heard you mention your sister, Jasmine. Next time we meet, maybe we can talk more about her. For now though, I bet you're getting ready to have a break from all of this talk, and we still need to decide how we will approach this tomorrow." She's right about that. I'm kind of glad I got to talk about all this stuff to someone who wasn't fussing at me but I'm worn out from it too. And I don't think I can take talking about Jasmine right now.

"Parking"

A client may mention something important in passing. Acknowledging that a subject deserves more attention helps to build rapport. However, time and your client's capacity to discuss emotional topics sometimes requires that you prioritize the immediate, simply note what you heard and suggest returning to it in another meeting. In interviewing parlance, this is called "parking." How would you handle Maya's mention of Jasmine?

"What the court is supposed to be deciding is whether you are in contempt, but the court will also have to start thinking about where you will go after you are done here in detention. What do you think about doing some therapy and taking good care of yourself, seeing all the doctors for you and the baby, while I try to work up a case for getting you placed with your aunt and uncle? It's going to take time for me to do that, I wish I could make it happen more quickly but that's just not the way it works. But that gives you time to get settled in with doctors and counselors and school. The more on top of your game you are, the more likely your social worker is to see that you can handle taking care of yourself while you are living with your family."

> ### Counseling
>
> *The traditional counseling model calls for the lawyer and the client to brainstorm options, with the lawyer helping the client generate the consequences of those options, thereby allowing the client to make an informed decision. For adolescents, this model can help them practice more advanced reasoning skills. Here, Julia doesn't follow the model.*
>
> * *What do you think of Julia's approach here?*
> * *What other ways might she have approached this?*

I interrupt her then partly because I'm not paying attention and partly because I'm still trying to tell her the whole messed up story, and partly because it sounds like she's telling me what to do and I just don't like that and I tell her, "I think it's because they are black and I am white. Well, my Aunt Hen is half-black but the white half doesn't count not when you look black, and my Uncle Marcus he's all black, and they have two little girls, my cousins Tasha and Sandra they look all black too. And sometimes I think all this shit about my mom is bogus and it's really about how they don't feel right letting me live with them."

She looks surprised. And confused a little, but also like something is starting to make sense to her, so I go on, "We have a lot of different daddies in my family going all the way back. But my mom is white and my grandma is white; and I am guessing my daddy is white, although sometimes people tell me I look a little like an Indian but I don't see it. I mean, I have red hair. I think Indians have black hair. Still, that would be kind of cool if it were true, but I am pretty sure I can't ever know who my daddy is, my mom is too strung out to know. Anyway, as far as I am concerned, Uncle Marcus is the only good guy I have ever been around, except for maybe my boyfriend. But, no, Uncle Marcus is even better than Di. He doesn't have a temper or nothing."

My lawyer just sits there quiet and finally says, "Well, they can't use the fact that your Aunt and Uncle are African American as a reason not to place you with them,[68]

---

68. *See* ch. 1, for a discussion of the Multi-ethnic Placement Act as amended by the Inter Ethnic Placement Act prohibiting state officials from relying on race when deciding upon particular foster care or adoptive home placements.

but—I hear you—it's hard to know what people think way down deep. Sometimes they don't even know themselves, but they wind up finding other excuses to do what they want. You know what I mean? Just because the law says that they aren't allowed to let race come into it doesn't mean that race doesn't sometimes sneak in."[69]

Implicit Bias

Research has shown that implicit bias impacts perception and decision-making in subtle yet profound ways.

- *One way to test your level of implicit bias is Project Implicit: https://implicit.harvard.edu/implicit/takeatest.html*

"Yeah, I guess so." This is all making my head hurt. All I know is that it seems like everyone thinks it's weird to have a white girl live with a black family. No one even seems to believe that they *are* my family.

"I promise to look at this real hard and see if I can come up with a strategy to show that your Aunt and Uncle are a good placement for you. There's a lot more I need to know. So please don't think I am promising that I can make it happen. I wish I could, but I can't, and I don't want to promise you anything I can't 100% be sure of. Ultimately, it's the judge who decides, but I can put the best case in front of her. You know what I mean? I can't wave a magic wand and make it happen but I can do my best to convince the judge she should make it happen."

"I get it. You don't get to decide. The judge does that. I been to these hearings before."

"That's right. You've probably been to a lot of them. Last time you saw a judge it was Judge Jackson, but this time you'll see Judge Harris. A lot of people say she likes to think of herself as a Mama Bear. She is really protective of the kids in her court. Sometimes that means that she acts like she thinks she's your mother and she winds up giving you a little bit of a lecture about the choices you have made. So you might want to be ready for that. On the plus side, she wants to see kids with family, if it's possible, and so she will also lecture the case worker about looking for your relatives. That's good for us, but the problem is that other case workers have looked into your Aunt Hen and there will be old notes in your file saying she isn't safe, which is why I don't think the court will place you with Aunt Hen and Uncle Marcus tomorrow."

She pauses and looks at me like she's waiting for me to say something, and when I don't she says, "I know that's a lot to take in. What questions do you have?"

All of that legal stuff makes no sense to me. Sounds like a lot of going around in circles or something. My face must be showing that because she asks me to tell her what I think the hearing is about tomorrow. She says she wants to make sure she did

---

69. For a discussion of the influence that implicit bias exerts on legal processes, see Herry Kang, et al., *Implicit Bias in the Courtroom*, 59 UCLA L. Rev. 1124 (2011–2012).

a good job explaining it to me. I try to make sense of it, "So the judge will want to know if Sarah has looked into me staying with my aunt but when she says they aren't safe, she will believe her?"

"Could be . . . unless I can convince her that Aunt Hen and Uncle Marcus are really safe after all. But, I need time to come up with that proof, and besides the only thing that's really supposed to be decided tomorrow is whether you should stay in detention for a while because you ran away from the Phoenix. But if they don't put you in detention, they have to decide where you will go."

"Oh, yeah, I remember that contempt thing."

"Got it!"

She keeps talking, planning things out, and I am getting tired of all of this, especially since none of it really matters, I'm not going to get what I want, and the judge will do whatever the judge wants to do, but then she asks, "So I will have to find a way to contact your Aunt and Uncle. We don't know for sure yet if they are able to take you and the baby; they don't even know you're pregnant, do they? Can I talk to them about that if I find them?"

> ### *Confidentiality*
>
> *Review Rule 1.6. of the Rules of Professional Conduct.*
>
> * *Julia might have assumed that disclosure about Maya's pregnancy was within her authority to achieve Maya's goals, but she asks for permission anyway.*
> * *Why might Julia have asked even if she weren't required to?*

I doubt that they know, and I let her tell them. It seems kind of weird letting my lawyer do that but in a way it's not so bad because then I don't have to tell them and I think that my Aunt Hen will be good about it but she might also be mad at me, and so maybe it will be okay for her to hear it from someone else first, especially since it seems like my lawyer won't talk trash about me like other people might. I don't know their address, but I tell her what bus you take to get to their house and where you get off and where you walk and what their house looks like. She takes it all down and says she will look into it.

Then she asks me whether my mother or anyone ever gave me any reason to believe that my father might be a Native American. She says it's important because it can make a real big difference in how my case is handled.[70] I tell her no; it's just that there are a lot of Indians in the homeless camps she hangs out in.

---

70. *See* Indian Child Welfare Act of 1978, 25 U.S.C. § 1901.

She also wants to know about whether there are any other relatives I want her to bring up. I tell her all I had was my grandma and my sister and my aunt, and that's all that I know about.

"Have you seen your grandma since you came back into foster care? Do you know how she is? Sounds like she got sick?"

"Yea, she got real sick. I haven't seen her since she went into the hospital."

"Would you like me to see if I can find out how she is?"

"Maybe . . . she might be dead." I say it and it sounds so real now that it is hanging out there. It makes me feel scared to know the answer. It seems like she can see how I'm feeling and she looks a little bit sad too.

"I am so sorry that no one ever checked on her for you. Do you want to know? It's ok if you feel like you can't handle this right now. You have a lot on your plate."

She doesn't try to make things sound better than they are. She knows grandma might be dead too. It hurts but I like that more than those people who try to make everything sound all happy when it's not.

"Yeah, I want to know. Either way, I want to know." When I say that, I feel sad but better somehow all at the same time.

"OK then, I will see what I can do to find out. How's that? I will put it on the list together with finding your Aunt and Uncle. And we will talk about your sister another day, ok?"

I tell her yes and for a moment there it's like I almost trust her. We'll see.

But then she asks me again what I think about her idea—that I wait at a group home until I can go stay with Aunt Hen. I shrug. I say I hate counseling. I am sick of talking about stuff I barely remember and want to forget.[71] She says she understands that. She doesn't try to convince me that it's good for me to go back and talk about all the bad stuff and I appreciate that. Most adults try to tell me that it's good for me to look at all that ugly shit.[72] She asks me if there are ever times when I feel like I could use

---

71. Careful assessment and referral to proper treatment for trauma exposure is critical. Indiscriminate targeting of those who have experienced a critical incident immediately after exposure to trauma can prove not only ineffective but also may be harmful because referrals to inappropriate treatments may "exacerbate trauma by interfering with the natural recovery process." Resilience studies make clear that those who benefit even from empirically validated interventions are a small minority; and, therefore, "appropriate assessment and diagnosis are perhaps the central task before referral." George A. Bonanno & Anthony D. Mancini, *The Human Capacity to Thrive in the Face of Potential Trauma*, 121(2) Pediatrics 6 (Feb. 2008). [https://perma.cc/6WTE-HTQQ].

72. A long-standing principle of trauma recovery is empowerment. The person who experienced the trauma "must be the author and arbiter of her own recovery. . . . Many benevolent and well-intentioned attempts to assist the survivor founder because this fundamental principle of empowerment is not observed. No intervention that takes power away from the survivor can possibly foster her recovery, no matter how much it appears to be in her immediate best interest." Judith Lewis Herman, Trauma and Recovery: The Aftermath of Violence—from Domestic Abuse to Political Terror 133 (1997).

help dealing with stuff that is happening right now not the stuff from a long time ago that I don't even want to remember.[73] I tell her, yes but that I feel like my Aunt could help me with that stuff just fine and that I wouldn't have as much stuff to deal with anyway if I could just stay there with her and my Uncle Marcus and my cousins.

I am not sure if we are getting anywhere but at least she is asking me what I want, not telling me. Still, she keeps bringing up that I should stay at some group home for a while. What choice do I have?

I think it's time for her to leave because she looks at the clock in the room and starts talking about tomorrow. "So tomorrow morning, they will bring you up to the court-room at about 8:30 in the morning."

"Shit, that's early."

"I know, right? But that's when it all gets started. We never know for sure when your case will be called but they will probably call your case pretty early. That's why I wanted to be sure to have some time to spend with you today. Your social worker will be there and she will have an attorney who will tell the court what she thinks should happen."

She must see that I am getting ready for her to leave because she asks, "Is it Ok if we talk a little bit more now about what might happen at the hearing tomorrow? I know I've been here for a while and you might want a break."

"I guess so. It's not like I have somewhere else to go or anything." Maybe she's almost done. I hope so.

"It's probably almost time for you to have something to eat and I don't want to keep you from that; so I will try not to keep you too much longer. Like I said before, tomorrow the judge will decide whether you are in contempt of the order requiring you to stay in the group home. So we should probably talk about that a little more. First of all, did you realize that there was a court order that said you had to stay at the Phoenix?"

"I don't know. I guess so. I mean I knew that was where I was supposed to be."

"I think you were at the hearing when the judge said that's where you would have to stay? That would have been a couple of months before you ran away?"

"I think I was there, yeah."

---

73. Trauma-Focused Cognitive-Behavioral Therapy (TF-CBT) is a three-stage therapeutic process in which the client first undergoes a stabilization phase in which they learn relaxation techniques, skills to address their maladaptive behaviors as well as information necessary for them to understand the dynamics that underlie what they experiencing in the here and now. It is only after stabilization is achieved that the skilled therapist invites discussion of the underlying trauma itself. The purpose of this trauma narrative is to process the underlying events in order to dissipate anxiety, fear and other suffering that arises as a result of being triggered by past trauma. The final phase of TF-CBT remains tied to skill-building around safety plans, social skills, and other needs that the particular young person might have. *See* Judith Cohen, *Trauma-Focused CBT for Children and Adolescents*, Nat. Child Traumatic Stress Network, [https://perma.cc/6FJF-5SJE].

She's paging through all of the papers in her file, and keeps talking, "So the judge is probably going to say you knew, I think, and I think that since you have run away before and you have been in detention, I think the judge is probably going to think that you realize that running away could get you in trouble, but you did it anyway. Do you see what I am saying? I am not trying to tell you that I think what you did *is* wrong. You probably had your reasons for leaving, but I am just saying that the judge is probably going to believe that you knew you weren't supposed to do that."

I tell her I get that the judge will probably want to make me stay in detention for a while. She is trying to explain something about the law, how the judge can't really keep me there if I do whatever assignment she gives me, unless they decide to charge me with shoplifting or something else and if that happens, then I'll have some other attorney handle that.

I am starting to get hungry and I am just starting to tune out when she asks, "So, tomorrow, I can tell the judge why you ran away or you can. If we don't, the judge will probably ask you anyway. How would you answer that?"

"Because I hated that group home. I was never even allowed outside the fenced-in yard. It was like being in prison or something."

Then she starts telling me about what the judge might do even if I say that. She says that the judge probably will tell me I have to spend seven days in detention unless I write an essay about what I did while I was on the streets and what I learned about how dangerous it is. Not that again!

And then she asks whether I will write the essay. And I ask her, "Why should I?"

"So you can get out sooner, that's the main reason really."[74]

I tell her I'd rather just stay here for the seven days unless they are going to let me go live with my Aunt. She asks me if I ran away to stay with my aunt. I tell her no, because the last time I did that my aunt told CPS that I was there, not because she didn't want me but because she wanted to do it right. But she shouldn't have done that because they still think she's a loser. So this time I just ran away and stayed wherever I could, at a lot of different places. I didn't want her to send me back again.

---

74. There are two types of contempt: civil and criminal. As Justice O'Connor explained in her dissent in *Hicks ex rel. Feiock v. Feiock*, 485 U.S. 624, 646 (1966), "Civil contempt proceedings are primarily coercive; criminal contempt proceedings are punitive." In other words, civil contempt seeks to coerce compliance with court orders by imposing a sanction the duration of which is terminable on compliance with the court's order. By contrast, criminal contempt seeks to preserve the authority of the court by punishing past misconduct with a finite sanction. Civil contempt is frequently used in family law matters, particularly in child support. In civil contempt, the contemnor can purge him or herself of the contempt sanction by complying with the court order. Gerard Glynn, *Contempt: The Untapped Power of the Juvenile Court*, 15 Fla. Coastal L. Rev. 197, 198-199 (2014). In this narrative, Maya's actions are the subject of civil contempt proceedings because by writing an essay she can end her period of detention.

She puts down her pen and stops writing. She looks at me then, and says, "That must have been rough. I mean, you were gone, how long? Six months? That's a long time to have to make it out there."

I can't tell whether this is a trick. Is she trying to get me to tell her something or is she just being nice. If everything I say is a secret, then what's the trick? What does she want? Why does she care?

"It was hard sometimes, but I made it work."

She says, "I bet it was hard. You must be a very strong person."

I look at her and shrug. I just don't know what to say. I don't know what she wants me to say.

After what seems like forever, she changes the subject.

Entering into Trauma Territory

- *Does Julia need to know about Maya's life on the streets to do her job as her lawyer?*

- *Do you think she should have commented on her experiences there? Why or why not?*

"Do you want to tell the court why you left the group home or do you want me to tell her?"

"You can tell her I guess."

"I will but just in case the court asks you before I get the chance to say, it's fine for you to say what you said about why you left. It's the truth and I can use it to say you will do better somewhere that's not a group home, somewhere that's more like family. We also want to say that it is your goal to live with your Aunt Hen and Uncle Marcus. Does that sound right?"

"Sure."

She tells me that she will see me tomorrow bright and early and that if the judge orders me to stay in detention she will stay in touch while she tries to work out a plan to get me with my Aunt and Uncle.

"One more thing," she says.

"Yeah?"

"I take it you don't like it that everybody seems to know your business?"

"Yeah, it sucks."

"Well, tomorrow I can at least ask the court to close the hearing so that no one except the people involved with your case can be in there.[75] Sometimes it gets crowded

---

75. Most states do not allow the public access to the court files of youth in dependency proceedings. However, states vary with respect to how they handle the hearings themselves. Some states require

in the courtroom with people waiting around for their turn or to get orders signed. Stuff like that. Would you like me to ask the judge to not let anybody else in except the people in your case?"

"Yes."

"Like I said before, it's up to the judge to make all of the decisions. I just do the asking, but I think she will agree that we should keep this hearing private."

The way she looks at me when she leaves, like she actually sees me, makes me feel a little weird but somehow good. She looks like she would give me a hug if she were allowed. But it's OK, I don't really want a hug anyway.

Maya's Social Worker Offers a Solution

It's almost dinnertime and my social worker is back again. *Doesn't this lady have any other kids to bother?* I am so tired of talking to people about this stuff, missing my meals, then puking up the food I eat too quickly. I just zone out while she talks on and on. I listen, kind of, but I don't say much. My own thoughts just rattle around in my head but I am too exhausted to even say them.

She says that she has found one "option for placement" for me and they accept pregnant and parenting girls and all of the "services" I need are real close by. She says that they have a "great program," including help with learning about my baby, public nurses to help with prenatal and postnatal care, and the school is "super cool" and there's childcare while you're in school. She says it's all girls, some of whom are pregnant or parenting and some aren't, and she thinks I would really like it. *How would she know?* She says the girls on her caseload who are there say it's the best.

There is a catch though. *Of course there is? What do I have to do—give them my baby?*

The program is for what she calls "commercially sexually exploited children." *Huh?*

I figure out what she means by that is girls who have been pimped out. What a weird way to say it, what a long way to say it, it's like they don't want to call it out for what it is. And I am not a child and neither were any of the rest of us. I bet they thought a long time before they came up with that one.

I don't say anything at all. I just look at her. She says she doesn't expect me to make a decision right this second, but by tomorrow morning I will need to tell her. She wants me to know there's a bed available now and they're only going to hold it for me until noon, which is why she is going to tell the judge she doesn't want me in detention for

that all courtrooms hearing dependency matters be closed. Others allow the courtrooms to be opened to the public, but allow for the closure of the hearing upon motion. *See, e.g.,* WASH. REV. CODE § 13.34.115; *Legal Research: Public Access to Abuse/Neglect Proceedings,* FIRST STAR [https://perma.cc/V2ED-KES7] (last updated June 2010). *See generally* ANITA HARBERT, JENNIFER TUCKER-TATLOW & BLAINE ABATE, LITERATURE REVIEW: OPEN JUVENILE DEPENDENCY COURTS (Feb. 2011) [https://perma.cc/57J3-5NPP] (providing background on open vs. closed courts in dependency and state specific overview of open vs. closed courts).

the week. We have to grab it while we can. She says I could stay there for up to four months at least and probably up to a whole year and after that, if I do well in the program, I would go to the head of the line for a teen parent home. She says that these folks really do understand how the street works and nothing I say or do will surprise them. *Wanna bet?* She says that if I say I will participate and not run away again, she will tell the judge tomorrow that she wants me to be released right away so that I can claim the bed. But otherwise, she says I'll have to stay in juvie until she can find another alternative.

She looks at me and waits like it's my decision or something. *Since when has it ever been my decision?* So I ask her, "What about my Aunt Hen and Uncle Marcus?"

She looks at me with that *haven't-we-talked-about-this-already* look and says that she can't get me released to them right away even if she wanted to because there would have to be clearance and lots of background stuff. She admits that she really doesn't know my Aunt and Uncle but that prior caseworkers have said that my Aunt has anger management issues and wouldn't keep me safe from my mom. I tell her that's bullshit.

She says, "Bullshit or not, given what's in your file already I will have to do some investigation and documentation to justify changing the agency's opinion on that subject." She doesn't seem mean when she says it. She seems almost like she's thinking about it.

She asks me to think about Safe Harbors. That's the name of the place for pimped out girls. Pretty lame, I know right? Then she says she'll see me tomorrow.

Maya's Contempt Hearing

The court is right next door to detention, so you just roll out of bed and you're there, which is pretty much what I did this morning. I see how the other kids and parents look at me as I get led past them. I am wearing orange and my hair is all messed up because I really didn't have time to do anything about it and, to make it look even more like I just got out of bed, I am wearing those ugly slippers and big white socks. I also have to have an officer with me all the time. The other kids look at me like I am either super bad ass or super scary. I don't feel like either one. I feel super queasy. I just hope I can hold down the little bit of breakfast I ate. My hands are cuffed behind my back and the idea of having to puke when you can't even use your arms for balance sounds like a mess waiting to happen.[76]

I see my lawyer coming down the hall and she asks the officer if she and I could have a moment in the interview room alone. The officer says yes, and before we go in, my lawyer asks if the officer would take my cuffs off.

---

76. For a deeper discussion of the use of shackles and handcuffs on juveniles in delinquency proceedings, *see* ch. 9, *Juvy*, n.12.

"Really. I think we'll be just fine." My lawyer looks at her all friendly, not hardly bossy at all, but still the officer listens to her.

As the officer goes around behind me to take the cuffs off, the she looks at me in the eye real serious and says, "I'll be standing right outside this door, peeking in the window."

It feels good to be able to move my arms again. I shake them out at my sides. You don't realize how much you use your arms to keep you steady until they are stuck behind your back.

We get in the room and I tell her thanks.

"Don't mention it."

Yesterday, she just had one little file. But here she is with two files—the same little one and another big fat file she pulls out of a big black brief case. "Holy shit! Is that all about me?"

She smiles a little and says, "Well, this is just part of your file actually; there are even more volumes back at my office. This is just the two most recent ones. Most of it is court stuff and reports from your different social workers. It's not all about you exactly, a lot of the older files are about your mom and the legal things that have happened in your case. Must be pretty weird, huh, to have all of this stuff that all your lawyers have read?"

"Yeah, that's a lot of paper. Do they talk about my baby in there?" I wonder whether the social worker and the lawyer have the same file because I know my social worker always talks about "my file" as though it's some kind of thing that's permanent and out there and standing in the way of everything I want to do. As in, *I would love to let you stay at your Aunt Hen's but the file won't let me because of something some ass-hat social worker said about her because she stood up to her and told her she was full of shit.* Or something like that.

"I want to see what's in that thing," I tell her.[77]

"There's no report from your social worker about your pregnancy yet, but that could come up in court today. Right now we need to talk about a few things to get ready for court. We can take some time to look at your file if you want on another day, OK?"

It's a little hard to pay attention but I say OK. All that stuff about me and I don't even know what it is. Some people put together all of that paper and don't none of them know me at all.

---

77. Under M.R. 1.4(a)(4), a lawyer is required to "promptly comply with reasonable requests for information." MODEL RULES OF PROF'L CONDUCT, R. 1.4.

> ### Client Files
>
> *Maya is curious about the all-powerful file and what it contains. Service providers, including lawyers, often accept what is in a file as accurate and complete. But a client may disagree with what is in her file or may feel it doesn't tell the whole story. Attorneys need to exercise good judgment in deciding how to use the reports and records of others.*
>
> - *We know that Maya's file fills a whole file cabinet drawer. What should Julia do about Maya's request to see it?*
>
> - *How should Julia regard the agency reports she receives?*

The lawyer says that she talked to my social worker already this morning, and the social worker said that she hadn't had a chance yet to make up her own mind about my Aunt Hen, but at least Sarah gave my lawyer Aunt Hen's phone number. The lawyer says that my social worker is real big on this place called Safe Harbors.

"I know. She told me all about it yesterday after you left."

"Wow. You had a lot going on yesterday, huh? What do you think about Safe Harbors as a place to start while I work on checking out things with your Aunt and Uncle like we talked about yesterday? I can call them when I get out of court today. I'll keep trying until I reach them. And then once I find them and talk to them and see what they think, I can start working on seeing what I can find to convince your social worker, and then if I can't convince your social worker, we can ask the court to change your placement."

> ### Interview Scope
>
> *Julia never asks Maya how she became pregnant. She does not ask her who the father is. She does not ask her whether her life experience fits with the client population that is served by Safe Harbors.*
>
> - *Should Julia have inquired further? Why or why not?*

It sounds good that at least she's starting to work on getting hold of them, but she acts as though she doesn't believe me that they'll say yes. They'll say yes. Maybe other kids don't have anybody who cares about them but I do. She thinks I'm one of those kids who talk about all the people who are going to be there for them but there is really nobody when it comes right down to it. I've met plenty of those kids in group homes. Kids who say *my mama's coming to visit me just as soon as she gets out of rehab* or *my auntie, she'll be here next Tuesday 'cause it's my birthday and she's going to bring a cake.* But then next Tuesday rolls around and there ain't no auntie and there ain't no cake except for the one the staff gets from Safeway and we all sit around the table and sing but the kid knows that it's just because we have to sing if we want to eat the cake. And that mom, she never gets out of rehab or never went in or if she did she never graduated or if she did graduate she didn't bother to come back and get her kid. That's why I don't talk about my business with anyone in a group home. It just sounds like another lie as in *my Aunt Hen would come get me if only my social worker would let her.* But it would be true for me. That's the difference. I want to tell the lawyer that this situation is different. I am not one of those sorry-ass kids, but I don't because just saying it makes me sound like one of those sorry-ass kids.

Instead, I ask her what this Safe Harbors place is really like and if I have any other choice. She says she's heard good things but she doesn't really know; it's a pretty new program and she's never had a client there, so she can't tell me what it's like. She also says that even if I don't want to go, they could still put me there.

Just like I thought, I really don't have a say.

She says that it's true that there are fewer licensed places that are allowed to have pregnant or parenting teens and so it is possible that the social worker will wind up having a challenge finding a place to put me.

"Good! Then she'll *have* to let me go live with Aunt Hen, right?"

She says, "It could work that way, which would be good right? But it also could be that if the social worker is really out of options locally, and doesn't think she should place you with Aunt Hen, she could look into other places anywhere in the state and sometimes they even look in other states when they are really stuck."

I don't want that. It's hard enough to get used to a new group home, let alone living out in the middle of nowhere. We agree that she will still say that I want to live with my aunt and uncle but that in the in-between time, I will give this place a try. Because really, what choice do I have?

Helping Clients Assess Risk

Lawyers in dependency proceedings often have to help their clients understand the possible outcomes that they are facing in order to fully inform their decision-making, including the risks that they will not get what they want.

- *Do you think Julia adequately informed Maya of the likely outcomes?*

- *What might you have done differently?*

About then, some other lady knocks on the door's window, opens the door and says, "You're up."

We all hurry out of the interview room and head into the courtroom.

The courtroom looks vaguely familiar. It's been awhile since I've been to court. It's small, not like on those murder TV shows where the courtroom looks like a rich person's living room with lots of big dark wood and fancy leather chairs. Even Judge Judy got it better than this. The judge sits behind a fake wood desk and we sit at a fake wood table in plastic chairs and the fluorescent lights buzz like mosquitoes. The tables are all connected like a big U, and in the back of room there are a few folding chairs along the wall for people who want to watch, but the only people there are a few other lawyers and social workers, I guess, waiting their turn. They must be next, I guess. I hope the lawyer remembers what she said about getting everybody out. I don't want all those people, whoever they are, listening to my stuff.

The judge is a black lady, which I think might be good. The lawyer didn't tell me that. Maybe she will let me stay at Aunt Hen's after all. She looks at me and nods, but she doesn't smile. It's like she wants me to know that she does not approve of what I've done, but she doesn't even know what I did yet or does she?

Some other lady sitting at a small desk next to the judge's bigger one says, "In the Dependency of Maya Phillips, case number 10-7-6581."

Then everybody starts introducing themselves, but not really. They all know each other it seems like, and they say their names like they are robots.

"Samuel Green for the State, together with social worker Sarah Prince, BRS Unit, seated to my right."

"Julia Yasko, attorney for the youth, Maya Phillips, seated to my right. Your honor, at this time I move to close the courtroom. Certain matters may come up today which involve a discussion of the youth's medical condition and having the courtroom open will violate her privacy. Closing the courtroom is in the best interest of the child."

"Is there any objection?" The judge asks and looks at the man attorney who says, "None here your honor."

"Alright then. The courtroom will be closed. Will all those not involved in this matter please exit the courtroom?"

I turn around and watch as all the people leave. At least they won't be hearing all about my business.

Then the judge looks at the man attorney and gives him a nod as though she knows already what he is going to say but she needs him to say it anyway, and so he starts talking.

"Your honor, we're here today on a motion to show cause why the youth Maya Phillips should not be held in contempt of court for refusing to obey the court's order of placement. As the record reflects, Maya left the grounds of her last group home approximately seven months ago and failed to return. A pick-up order was issued and pursuant to that order she was held in detention this weekend after having been detained by a store security officer for suspected shoplifting. That charge has not been filed, and the merchandise, a pregnancy test, has been returned."

The judge looks at me then with her one eyebrow arched, like she understands why we closed the courtroom. I think I hear her sigh.

He goes on, "As the record will also reflect, this is the second time that Maya has run from placement and has been subject to contempt proceedings. If she didn't know the last time what the consequences would be, she certainly knew this time. The first time she was held in contempt, she refused to purge and was held in detention for the full seven days while the department worked hard to find her a suitable placement at the Phoenix House. Ordinarily in a case like this, we would ask that she be held in contempt in detention until she purged herself of that contempt, and we might even explore the filing of a criminal contempt with the prosecutor so that she begins to take this court's orders more seriously. However, her social worker, Ms. Prince, has really scrambled and has been able to find a placement for her at Safe Harbors. We are concerned that if we wait the seven days, the bed may be taken. Therefore, we ask that the court find Maya in contempt, but allow her to purge that contempt by agreeing to successfully remain in this placement until otherwise ordered by the court."

The judge starts talking, asking the lawyer questions about whether she can do what he wants her to do. Sounds like she kind of wants to lock me up anyway, but after he talks some more she seems kind of satisfied. I think he's winning.

It's all just so much lawyer talk to me but I think I get it. I need to go to Safe Harbors or I'll be in trouble.

Finally, the judge looks at my lawyer and says, "Counsel?"

"Your honor, the issue noted for hearing today is whether Maya Phillips should be held in contempt of court. Placement was not noted. However, this matter is evolving into a placement hearing because of the Department's decision to forego a request for detention, which we of course do not oppose. However, given the placement issues that this raises, I would like to provide the court with some context. This is the second dependency for Maya Phillips. Her first dependency involved a stable placement with her grandmother. While placed with a relative, Maya never ran from care. She went to school and thrived. According to her GAL's reports from her first dependency, Maya showed a strong, early aptitude for math. Maya only came back into care because her grandmother suffered a stroke."

She looks at me then and I can't help but feel sad remembering that but I try not to show it. My feelings aren't nobody's business but my own. My grandmother did the best she could and so did I. I called 911 and the medic said she might be dead if it weren't for me. I wonder if the lawyer remembers she promised to find out whether she's still alive.

"Your honor, this youth has suffered a lot of losses. The loss of her grandmother was very hard on her. She was suddenly and completely cut off from her family. The grief over the loss of her grandmother has been compounded by her disappointment that the department has continually refused to place her with her Aunt Henrietta and Uncle Marcus, who appear to have been willing relative placements. This lack of family connection has led to a series of failed placements and two runs, all of which has resulted in her having lost ground educationally.[78] It appears that she only has one

---

78. *See* Mark E. Courtney et al., Chapin Hall, The Educational Status of Foster Children (2004), http://www.chapinhall.org/sites/default/files/publications/152.pdf [https://perma.cc/UV8H -LRM9].

high school credit. Her last placement, in a semi-secure, highly structured group home, was about as different from a family placement as can be had. This youth wants and needs to be with family."

I look at my lawyer as she talks. Not sure I understand all of what she is saying but I can tell she is trying hard to let the judge know I am smart and that I do good when I am with my family. I like that. I wonder how she knew I did good in math. I guess that's part of that huge file about me. So not all of it's bad. It feels like she found that one good thing to say about me, which makes me feel like maybe the judge will listen to her. The judge's head is tilted to one side and she seems like she is listening. So that's good, I think. My lawyer keeps talking.

"I have spoken to Maya and she has expressed to me that her strongest desire continues to be to live with Henrietta and Marcus Clark, her aunt and her uncle. I understand that, several years ago, a prior social worker objected to Maya's placement with her aunt and uncle and that the state's position has remained the same ever since. I have spoken to her current social worker about placement with Maya's aunt and uncle and she has indicated that she is at least willing to consider looking into it again for the future, and this morning Ms. Prince provided me with their contact information so that I might reach out to them. In the meantime, Maya has agreed that she will enter Safe Harbors, but she wants the court to know that she wants to be with her family. This seems reasonable since, as I understand it, Safe Harbors is a time-limited program and for Maya to obtain stability the department will need to look elsewhere. I am sure that we can all agree that Maya needs some form of permanency as she moves toward adulthood as a parent."

"Finally, your honor, given how quickly this placement issue has arisen, none of us have really had an opportunity to learn about the full range of services that may be provided or required for Maya to engage in while she is there. Maya has expressed to me some reluctance to engage in the type of mental health treatment she has received in the past, but is interested in services that will help her with her day-to-day stressors, with her need to take good care of herself while she is pregnant, and with learning what she will need to know to be a good parent in the future. We ask that she not be ordered to participate in mental health treatment at this time but that she be permitted to make that decision on her own based on whether she believes the services offered to her will meet her needs at the time that they are offered.[79] According to

---

79. Research has shown that while the number or variety of court-ordered services in which a young person participates is not correlated with resilience and positive functioning, the level of reported user satisfaction with any of the services ordered does bear a positive correlation. In other words, if the adolescent perceives the service to have met his or her needs, then positive results accrue. Simply complying with ill-fitting, unwanted services would appear to be a waste of time and resources. *See* Michael Ungar et al., *Patterns of Service Use, Individual and Contextual Risk Factors, and Resilience Among Adolescents Using Multiple Psychosocial Services*, 37 Child Abuse & Neglect 150 (2013).

state law, Maya is of an age to refuse consent to mental health treatment, and only an involuntary commitment can force her to engage in treatment she does not want."[80]

Minor Consent/Privacy in Your Jurisdiction

Maya's rights, as a minor, to consent or refuse treatment, are at issue here. In addition to the question of consent, the problem of privacy arises, particularly for foster youth.

• *What is your state's approach to a minor's right to consent or refuse consent for the types of treatment involved in Maya's case?*

• *Who has the right to access a minor's medical information?*

The judge says, "Don't tempt me." But I think maybe she is joking because she is smiling a weird smile and she thanks my lawyer. She looks all serious when she asks the social worker what the story is with my aunt and uncle. My social worker answers.

"Your honor, I know that Maya wants to live with her aunt and her uncle, and it is true that I personally have not had much interaction with these family members. I believe that once her aunt did call but that I was not able to provide her with the information that she sought concerning Maya. My notes reflect that her aunt was disappointed with my answer, perhaps a bit argumentative, but not unreasonably so. However, the notes in my file also indicate that there have been serious concerns in the past because the aunt maintains a relationship with Maya's mother whose rights have been terminated and that the aunt has defended her sister's behavior to the former social worker. The file also indicates that Maya's mother poses a serious danger to Maya. Maya's mother appears to suffer from co-occurring mental health and chronic substance abuse issues. The records indicate that when Maya and her sister were living with their mother, she may have allowed sexual exploitation of her children in order to supply her drug addiction.[81] With all due respect to Ms. Yasko, I can't help but think that it was this exposure from Maya's own family that laid the foundation for the behavior that Maya has engaged in while on the run. The former social worker was rightfully concerned that any exposure to Maya's mother presents a serious risk and therefore placement with the aunt was ruled out. The file notes also indicate that the aunt had anger management issues. Given all of this and the fact that Maya is now pregnant and presently wants to carry her pregnancy to term and

---

80. Age of consent for mental health, substance abuse and reproductive health treatment varies from state to state. For a compilation of state statutes related to minors and consent to medical treatment, *see* Nat'l Dist. Attorneys Ass'n, Minor Consent to Medical Treatment Laws (2013), [https://perma.cc/CSM5-C6KT]; *see also* Guttmacher Institute, Minors' Access to Prenatal Care (2014), [https://perma.cc/ZD9M-4KE5]; Guttmacher Institute, An Overview of Minors' Consent Law (2014), [https://perma.cc/Y5N-NCQH].

81. See, *supra*, note 53.

parent her child, we believe that it is critical that she have wraparound services[82] that will put her in the best position to parent her own child successfully. Safe Harbors does just that."

"As for whether Maya should be court-ordered to participate in all of these services, I understand that she may find therapy to be painful, given what she has been through, and it looks like she has not had the opportunity to engage in any sustained therapy in the past due to her run history. However, Safe Harbors employs evidence-based treatment[83] for trauma and they are very experienced with working with youth who have lived experiences like Maya's. While I understand the problems with forcing anyone to participate in therapy, I would really encourage Maya to keep an open mind as to all services and at least allow the staff to offer her the widest range of help that is available to her."

The judge looks at me again and says, "Yes — this is indeed important news that Maya is having a baby, and yes, she should want to take advantage of all of the help she can get to make herself ready to be a parent, and that includes addressing her own mental health." She turns to my social worker and continues, "And I agree with you, Ms. Prince, it sounds like this child needs to deal with her own problems before she tries to parent. But we all know that family can help with that, too, right? So . . . what about family? It's been a while since anyone put fresh eyes on this Aunt and Uncle. Maybe things have changed for them. And what about other family members? When was the last time the department performed a relative search for this child?[84]

I am not liking the way she is talking about me, like I am a child with problems or something, and I can't tell whether she is giving my aunt a second chance or telling her to look for someone else. Aunt Hen's the only one who's really stood by me. I don't know about anybody else.

My social worker answers, "Your honor, I understand, and it appears that since the termination of parental rights, no relative search has been done."

---

82. "Wraparound services" generally refers to holistic and individualized services that are designed by a team of professionals seeking to meet all of the needs of the child or family needing support. Ideally these services are provided in an easily accessible setting, such as the home. *See* Alyssa E. Scaparotti, *Serious Emotional Disturbances: Children's Fight for Community-Based Services Through Medicaid Litigation*, 41 Suffolk U. L. Rev. 193, 197–198 (2007).

83. "Evidence-based treatment" refers to those treatments that have been proven effective for treating children and youth for the specific mental health issue identified. These lists change over time as treatments are subject to more rigorous testing. For a list of evidence-based treatments for children that have been evaluated according to the criteria proposed by the Division of Clinical Psychology of the American Psychological Association, see Leyla Stambaugh et al., *Evidence-Based Treatment for Children in Child Welfare*, 27 Child L. Prac. 97, 102 (2008).

84. "Relative search" refers to the identification and location of relatives that fall within the state's definition of relative. Sometimes referred to as "family finding," these search methods vary from state to state. For a discussion of the duty to engage in the search for relatives and what a thorough relative search would include, see Rose Marie Wentz & Kelly Lynn Beck, *Maintaining Family Relationships for Children in the Child Welfare System*, 31 Child L. Prac. 97 (2012).

"Well, I understand that the department seems to think when *parental* rights are terminated, whole families disappear, but you and I, we know that isn't true, now don't we? Hop on that, will you? By our next review hearing, I want to hear about the results of your relative search. This child is going to need help for a lot longer than Safe Harbors, or any of us for that matter, is going to be able to give her."

"Yes, your honor." My social worker makes some notes in her file.

The judge nods towards my lawyer again, like it's her turn.

My lawyer repeats how she appreciates that my social worker is at least willing to consider looking into my aunt and uncle again and that a thorough relative search will be done. She also tells the judge that, if the past is any indicator, I will do best when given the support of my own committed family. She sounds so nice, like she's trying to figure out a way to agree with everybody. I am tired of nice. I want her to not sound so nice after what the social worker said about my aunt and about my mom and how the judge talked about me like I was a child. Why do we have to be so nice when they aren't?

> ### Collaboration, Advocacy and Adolescent Perceptions
>
> *Julia may have believed that thanking the social worker nudged her closer to an eventual agreement, but Maya was not pleased.*
>
> • *Did Julia adequately prepare Maya for her approach in court?*
> • *How does one maintain an advocacy role within a collaborative context?*

I feel anger rise up from inside me like a nasty burp beginning to form and that churning mixes with my sick stomach and I swear I might just puke all over them. Anger barfed up all over their fat files and their fake wood and their boring suits. All this stuff inside me makes my brain so noisy I can't really hear what's going on but I see that the judge is looking at me and talking. I really don't know what she is saying, something about the difference between what's best for me and what I want, which of course does *not* help me feel any less mad at all. When she's done, she looks at me as though she expects me to say something too.

I forget what my lawyer said I could say. None of it seems right anymore anyway. I look at my social worker and say, "She's lying on my Aunt Hen. She acts like my Aunt Hen is some kind of crazy. . . ."

Then the judge puts up her hand, like a traffic cop. I almost expect her to blow a whistle. She looks at me down her nose and says, "I hear that you are upset that today you aren't getting what you want, but it's my job to protect you, and so I am going to do that. You put me in a tough spot because I don't want you to run away again just because you aren't getting what you want, but I also cannot let you have what you want if what you want will put you at risk. I also hear that you are willing to stay at Safe Harbors, according to what your attorney said here. Is that right?"

"Yes, but she said she would get me with my aunt if I did good there."

The judge looks at my lawyer and me, like maybe she thinks either I am lying on my lawyer or my lawyer needs to straighten me out. She sighs again and makes her lips into a straight line that cuts across her face. She folds her hands in front of her and leans forward. She is so looking down on me right now.

Then she says she is the one who makes the decisions here and she wants to be straight with me. She says that she won't promise that I will get to stay with my aunt because she doesn't know anything about what is going on with my aunt right now but she will promise that it's more likely she will believe me about what's best for me if I act right, take care of myself and don't run away again.

That's kind of what my lawyer said she'd say. The judge looks me hard in the eye and she says, "Listen up. You have to show me that you know what you are talking about when you say you know what is good for you. I can't believe you about much of anything if you keep running off, because you know and I know and everyone in this courtroom with any sense knows that running away and living on the streets is definitely not what's good for you; it never was but it's especially not good for you *now*."

She sits back in her seat and scoots it back like she's almost about ready to stand up and leave, but she doesn't. She keeps on talking at me, "But that's what you have chosen to do so far. So you need to show me that you have good sense and *then* I will listen to you. You have to give me a reason to trust you. Do you understand, young lady?"

I want to shout at her and tell her that I hate her and I hate the way that she is talking to me like I am stupid because I am not, and the fact that she is talking to me about trust is a joke. She wants to trust me? What about her promises or the promises of any of these people? Hell, she may not even be here the next time I go to court. Why should *I* trust *her* or *any* of them?

But I don't say any of that because right then, the way she is looking at me, it tells me that I am stuck. I don't have any say. And if I fight, it will be worse. But I don't answer. She can't make me answer.

The judge looks at my lawyer and says, "Make sure she understands what I am saying. She can't keep running off like this. If she really wants to keep this baby, she should stay put, even if she doesn't care about herself."

"Yes your honor."

There she goes being all polite again. Just once I'd like to see somebody really fight. Like that time that my Aunt Hen got into it with one of my social workers in the hall after one of the first hearings I was at. She was so mad. I had never seen her like that before. She was all up in her face shouting, "How dare you?" and "That's *my* child, not *your* child!" and she even said a few curse words at her too. I guess my lawyer is being all polite so she won't be written off like my Aunt Hen. But I gotta say, I felt loved right then. I felt sad and scared, but proud right then when I heard her shrieking in the hallway at that social worker who said she was not good for me and I needed to go live with strangers instead. She was shouting and no one could make her shut up, until one of the sheriffs came and took her outside.

The judge then says a bunch of stuff in the same robot voice that everyone used to introduce themselves to start with. Basically, I think she is telling everyone that I have to go to Safe Harbors and if I run away again I won't ever get to stay with my aunt because then she will know for sure I'm a stupid fuck. Except she doesn't say it like that. But I know that's what she means.

And just like that, they are calling out the name of the next kid's case "*In re* dependency of Rachelle Peters, Case number blah blah blah."

Storytelling and Advocacy

Samuel Green, Sarah Prince, and Julia Yasko each offered stories depicting Maya and her family during the course of this contempt hearing.

- *How does each person characterize Maya?*
- *What is the theme of Maya's story in each?*

Maya after the Hearing

The officer is about to take me back downstairs when my attorney comes racing out of the courtroom. She calls out to the officer to hold on a minute while she finishes up with the order, that she still needs to talk to me. I need to pee, and I tell the officer and she hollers back to my lawyer that we'll be in the restroom and then back in the lobby. It feels like everyone in the lobby looks up to see who the girl is that has to go to the bathroom. They been waiting so long for their turn that just about anything is interesting.

As I head off to the bathroom with the officer, I see my lawyer walk down the hallway with the guy attorney. They are looking at a piece of paper and talking. He takes it from her and they lean against a counter while he writes.

Maya's Attorney after the Hearing

The outcome of this hearing is not quite standard. There is a form order that recites the usual elements for a finding of contempt and those blanks can be completed easily. The trickier part arises when we try to complete the blanks provided to explain how contempt will be purged. Usually, we would simply fill in the blank on the form with "the youth may purge contempt by writing a _____-word essay on the dangers of running away from her placement." But that won't work here. So Sam and I have to negotiate the language.

I tell him that I think that my client has already purged contempt by agreeing to placement and that the language should simply reflect that.

He thinks that she purges her contempt by agreeing to placement, to obey the house rules, and to consider all services offered.

I point out that the judge never mentioned anything about "house rules" and that including it is like putting a red cape out in front of a bull. You don't do that to a teen with a run history. You let the experts who are staffing the place work with her and let them tell her what the rules are. It's not necessary and is just daring her to misbehave. Besides, the judge never said anything like that. I tell him I might be able to get my client to be on board with his language about considering services but I don't even want to talk to her about the "house rules." And I tell him I also want the order to reflect that the department is being ordered to do a relative search, to include the maternal aunt.

He says he doesn't want Maya to be misled that they are considering the maternal aunt for placement and so he says he prefers that the order say "a complete relative search." He says he also needs her to understand she can't break the rules, get kicked out and then think that's her free pass to go live with her aunt.

I promise to make that clear to her. But that I have to talk to her before I can agree to any language in the order that deals with services.

He says I will have to be quick unless I want to wait through a couple more hearings to get the order signed. He's got another case or two this morning.

I say I have to be back for the afternoon shelter care hearings; so it's OK with me to take the time to make sure my client is on board.

Contingent on my client's approval, we settle on language that reads "the youth has purged contempt by agreeing to: placement at Safe Harbors and to consider all services offered. The Department is ordered to conduct a complete relative search."

Client Consent and Negotiations

Rule 1.2 of the Rules of Professional Conduct require that an attorney abide by a client's decision whether to settle a matter.

- *Does this rule apply to this circumstance?*
- *Why else might Julia want to consult with her client before agreeing to the language of the order?*

When Maya comes out of the bathroom, I ask the officer to give us a little space while I discuss the order. We don't have time to wait for one of the interview rooms right now and so we head for a couple of chairs off in the far end of the lobby.

"So, Maya, I know we've just been through a tough morning. It can be rough to have everyone talking about you and your family like that."

"Whatever." She is slumped in her chair and her eyes are almost closed. I can tell she is very done with this process, probably done with me too for now at least, but I want her to understand what just happened and that, as crummy as it feels, there were some positive signs.

So, I forge ahead, "So what just happened was that the judge found that you are in contempt because you did walk away from the Phoenix when you knew you weren't supposed to. But rather than have you spend any time in detention, she is finding that you aren't in contempt anymore because you are agreeing to go to Safe Harbors."

"Yeah, I get that."

"I want to read this language to you though because it is a little more specific about what it means for you to go to Safe Harbors and because it also makes Sarah have to do some things too. You aren't the only one. This order says that they can't force you to do any services and that it's up to you to decide to do what you think works for you. We don't know what this place is like and so it could be that you love what they offer, it could be that you don't."

"Whatever."

I am losing her, but I read her the language anyway. "And it also says that Sarah has to look for your relatives. All of your relatives. I don't know if you heard the judge in there but she also told her to look into Aunt Hen and Uncle Marcus too."

After I am done, she asks, "Yeah. That's good I guess. Can I go back now?"

"If that's what you want, sure, but after this order is signed they will be releasing you and you will be going over to Safe Harbors. Is it OK if I check on you once you're there maybe after I have had a chance to check in with your Aunt?"

"Whatever. Yeah, I do want to know what Aunt Hen says. I don't want to be in no group home long."

"I understand. Hey . . . at least Sarah has to do a relative search and they are relatives and so is your grandmother and your sister. It will give me an opening to find out how everyone is doing."

"Sure. I gotta go." And she looks at the officer. It seems like she's hoping she says *time's up.*

"One more thing. . . ." I am going to make one last run at this and this is probably not the best topic for me to bring up right now, but if I don't and she blows out of this placement thinking it's her ticket to her Aunt Hen's, I will be kicking myself.

"What?" She looks angry, like she is so very done with this conversation.

"I just want to make sure that you heard what the judge said. I know you are pissed right now and you have every right to be. But if you run away or do something to get kicked out of here, that will set us back in terms of getting you to be able to stay where you want to stay. I am only saying this because I want to help you get what you want. So I have a question for you."

"What is it?" she asks through her teeth.

"I know you've had a lot of experience with being angry. What do you do to help yourself calm down when it gets like that?"

She looks at me like I am crazy.

"Mostly everybody has something they do that helps. I bet you do too. And you don't have to tell me what it is. That's ok. But I just want you to treat yourself special right now. If you can do something for yourself that won't get you in trouble but that will make you feel better, do it."

She turns away to leave with the correctional officer, but as she does, I could swear she says, "I count."

Not sure what she means by that. Is she blowing me off, letting me know that she knows she matters? And then I remember the notes about her strengths in math. Could it be that she actually counts to calm down? Before I can say anything else, she's gone.

I hurry back to Sam who is already heading in on his next hearing. Before they start, we present the order to the judge and get it signed. Then I quickly and quietly leave the courtroom to wait in the hallway near the clerk's office for my copy.

As I am waiting, I meet a new attorney who is saying goodbye to her client. Katie something. I have seen her in the hallways before but we've never really met. She says she saw me at one of the CLEs. She was in the back of the courtroom when I moved to close. She didn't realize you could do that. She asks if we could have coffee sometime, that she'd like to "pick my brain."

Reaching Out to Mentors

Here, Katie reaches out to Julia to make a connection for mentorship.

- *How comfortable are you in reaching out to mentors?*
- *Do you think that having a mentor is important?*

I am happy to do that. Everyone needs to bounce ideas off of someone. I give her my card and she says she'll email me.

Before I head out, I pull out Maya's file and write in the memo section:

TO DO:
Contact Aunt and Uncle re: placement
Ask Aunt and Uncle for update on grandmother
Talk to Sarah about client's sister
Schedule time to meet with client at Safe Harbors

Reflections and Exercises

1. *What? So What? Now What? A Five-Minute Reflection Opportunity.* Take just five minutes to write and reflect on the following questions:

   a. What did you feel as you read the stories of the legal systems' interactions with Maya?

b. How is what you recorded feeling relevant to your learning and/or practice?

c. Now what do you do with these insights as you move forward in your learning and/or practice?

2. *Imagining a Different Story for Maya:*

a. In Part I, we learned that Maya has experienced a lot of turnover in the professionals who have control over her life. The impermanence and brevity of the relationships she has with those paid to help her further deepens her distrust and inability to seek help when she needs it.

   i. Put yourself in Maya's shoes. What would a better system of advocacy look like to her?

   ii. Dream big. Describe your ideal advocacy practice. What would standard practice look like?

   iii. Now assume that you have been witness to the changes that wrought the system of your dreams. You are being invited to speak at a gathering twenty years from now and the topic is "Change in the Making: How A System of Meaningful Advocacy Came to Be." You are going to tell the audience what happened to move your system of advocacy to the one of your dreams. Write bullet points for your speech.

b. In Part II, we see Maya placed in detention and held as a runaway from the foster care system. But for her social worker's need to claim a coveted placement for her, she could have been held in detention for seven more days.

   i. What factors determined how long Maya spent in detention?

   ii. What interests are served by keeping Maya in detention?

   iii. What are the negative consequences of holding Maya in detention?

   iv. Imagine a better intervention that could have taken place after Maya was picked up for running away.

Chapter Six

Lawyers Helping Lawyers

In this chapter, you will learn about the importance of forging relationships within the community of professionals who do the challenging work of representing children and youth. Attorneys whose practices focus upon advocacy in the dependency system need to be able to ask for and provide support within their practice communities. For a junior attorney, like Katie, this often means finding someone who can serve as a mentor, who will help her learn strategies for navigating both the legal system and the stresses that too often lead to burnout and high turnover rates. For a more senior attorney, like Julia, the need for community is no less great, and serving as a mentor with the opportunity it provides for reflection can provide its own sense of satisfaction.

But first, you will catch a glimpse of their busy professional lives as they try to make sure that they carve out time for these important relationships.

A Very Hectic Morning

Katie Almost Cancels: Client Emergency

Katie starts the day feeling behind. Zach had decided to take a mental health day, which throws her off. Usually, he is up and literally running before she even opens her eyes. Then he comes back from his run and brings her coffee in bed, but today no running, no coffee, just a happy warm snoozing Zach cuddling up next to her. If it wasn't for the text she heard coming in from her brother, Austin, she probably would have dozed even longer. Austin was asking whether she had heard from their dad. But when Katie sees the time, she jumps out of bed so fast she doesn't even respond. She doesn't know what is up with that, and she doesn't really want to know. The way she sees it, she has been through therapy; her brother clearly hasn't. He seems to have taken over where she left off: Family Caretaker in Chief. Katie, on the other hand, now refuses to be drawn in. Her dad is grown. Her mom is grown. They are all grown. And it's time to let go of trying to make sure everyone is sober, not mad at anyone else, and managing to hold down their respective jobs.

Katie feels that her own job is more than enough for her to manage. Sometimes, she wishes she could be Zach. He gets to design things that actually come into being. He goes to work. He works with a team. They have projects. And when the projects are over, they all go out for a beer and celebrate. And then he takes a mental health day and sleeps like a baby. By contrast, Katie's cases often take years to close and even the small victories she has along the way feel overshadowed by the crises and relapses of struggling families.

When Katie finally makes it into the office, her original plans for a catch-up day are set aside after she sees her first email. A social worker from one of her cases wants to set an emergency hearing tomorrow for a client who has just "busted out of placement."[1] The client was now in the CRC,[2] a temporary shelter for young people between placements, and so Katie needs to run over there and see what has happened.

The CRC is a noisy and chaotic place. No one stays there very long and everyone is in some sort of crisis. Katie's client is angry and pacing when she meets her in the visitation room. She can't or won't stay still. She keeps saying it's not fair. Her foster parent kicked her out and it just isn't fair. She's talking about how her brother and sister are still back there, probably wondering what happened to her. They are still allowed to be there because they are "cute and little and haven't done anything wrong yet," but eventually they will break the rules too and then what? Will they all be kicked out, one by one, and wind up in different places? That would be horrible. They need each other to make it through this.[3]

Katie feels overwhelmed by this outpouring of emotion. She wishes there were a way she could ask her client what happened and just get an explanation of the events of the evening, but that's not possible. She's too upset. Katie nonetheless asks her to back up and tell her about last night, but she just can't stay tracked on a story. Something about how the foster mom says she is a bad influence just because she stayed out past curfew. Her client admits she was out with her friends but now they won't be her friends because she will probably have to change schools again[4] and she might as

---

1. Research has shown that roughly 95% of foster children experience at least one placement disruption during their time in out-of-home care. Philip A. Fisher et al., Michael Stoolmiller, Anne M. Mannering, Aiko Takashani, Patricia Chamberlain, *Foster Placement Disruptions Associated with Problem Behavior: Mitigating a Threshold Effect,* 79(4) J. Consult. Clin. Psych. 481–487 (Aug. 2011). Placement disruption has been defined as "an unplanned change in foster placement made in response to a demand for a replacement by a child's caregiver." Sigrid James, *Why Do Foster Care Placements Disrupt? An Investigation of Reasons for Placement Change in Foster Care,* 78(4) Social Science Rev. 601 (Dec. 2004).

2. "CRC," as used here, stands for "Crisis Residential Center." Different jurisdictions may refer to these programs differently. When a young person has to leave a placement without a planned transition, they often have to go to temporary crisis shelters like this one while their social worker seeks an alternative placement.

3. Research indicates that the risk of placement disruption increases with age and externalizing behaviors for youth in foster care. *See* James, *supra* note 1. While it is true that joint sibling placement is associated with better placement stability, it is also true that siblings are often separated when older sibling behavior becomes problematic. *See* S.J.Leathers, *Separation from Siblings: Associations with Placement Adaptations and Outcomes Among Adolescents in Long-Term Foster Care,* 27 Child. and Youth Serv. Rev. 793 (2005).

4. In addition to the challenges frequent school changes pose to normal adolescent social development, frequent school change also impacts educational attainment. Research has shown that the students with four or more school moves during their elementary school years are on a trajectory to be a full year behind their educationally stable peers by the time they finish elementary school. *See,* David Kerbow, Patterns of Urban Student Mobility and Local School Reform 20 (1996).

well just give up if she is going to get sent away every time she finally makes friends and gets asked to hang out with them.

In some ways, this girl reminds Katie of what she was like as a teenager. Katie was angry most of the time too. She stayed in her room with the door closed for hours, pounding on her pillow, tearing up pieces of paper, Kleenex, even her clothes at times, ripping things into tiny little shreds just to be able to destroy something. She told her dad to go to hell once when he staggered in drunk after work yelling at her and her brother because her mom wasn't there to yell at. A fight ensued that got pretty ugly, even physical. Still, Katie feels sure it would never have occurred to her dad to send her away, to just give up and say she was a bad influence and put her in a strange place away from Austin, with a bunch of other rejected teenage girls and boys. And yet, this is what this client is going through. It *is* unfair.

Katie looks at her client pacing and wishes she could do something, but what? She doesn't know what to say or do. After her client tires herself out and there's a small break in her tirade, Katie tells her what she thinks she would have wanted to hear when she was her age, "That sucks, that really, really sucks."

Then her client cries. She cries loud and angry tears. Until she cries quiet tears and there are no more Kleenex in the strategically placed box. Katie doesn't know what to do with a client who has come undone in this way. It feels wrong to take notes. It feels wrong to hug her. It feels wrong to say, "I know how you feel." It feels dismissive to change the subject. So she just sits there with her, feeling really uncomfortable and guilty for possibly making things worse by acknowledging how bad the situation was and "making" her cry.

Eventually, when the silence gets too long, Katie tries to shift gears; she asks her client whether she thinks she could try to patch things up with her foster parent. She doesn't think so. Katie asks her whether she has any place else she would like to go. She doesn't think so. When Katie asks her about friends and family, the client suggests a friend's house and perks up a little with the idea that she could stay in the same school. But then she talks herself out of her optimism by worrying that because the friend she has in mind is one of the friends she was out late with last night, her social worker won't let her stay with his family. Katie sees bigger threshold questions—like, is this boy a boyfriend? How would that boy's parents feel about this idea? Would they be approved as a placement? Could they be licensed?[5] She doesn't ask her client about any of that. It feels like that would be more than she can handle right now. So, instead she asks her for all of the information she has about these parents and any of her other friends from the school she would want to stay with. Katie tells her client she will see what her caseworker has in mind, whether it's possible to get her back in with the foster

---

5. States define "relative" differently. Federal policy guidance allows state agencies to define "relatives" narrowly, based on biology or legal ties, or more broadly to include "Tribal kin, extended family and friends, or other 'fictive kin.'" CHILDREN'S BUREAU, ADMINISTRATION FOR CHILDREN AND FAMILIES, U.S. DEPARTMENT OF HEALTH AND HUMAN SERVICES, LOG NO. ACYF-CB-PI-10-11 14 (July 9, 2010) [https://perma.cc/5V8V-AX35].

parent or to stay with a friend so she can stay in the same school. Katie tells her she will also see about arranging visits for her with her brother and sister in the meantime.

The mention of her brother and sister makes tears well up in her client's eyes again and Katie feels bad leaving her there on that note, distraught and alone. She wants to tell her that everything will be alright, that sometimes foster parents just need to cool down, that she will repair what has been broken, but she feels that would be over-promising and then what would happen if she can't fix it? Her client would never trust her then. So she says nothing except she will do her best. Poor kid. She has to rely on the best that an attorney just out of law school can offer.

So much for playing catch-up. Whoever has the biggest emergency or the next hearing, that's what seems to occupy Katie's time at any given moment.

She gets back to her office and the reminder pops up letting her know that she's already ten minutes late for her lunch with Julia. She thinks about trying to call her to cancel, but she doesn't. She feels guilty for leaving her waiting. She hopes Julia will understand. She tells herself that Julia must know how these things happen, right?

Julia Almost Forgets

An Important Phone Call

When she started this latest stage of her career, Julia thought that maybe she should just work out of her home because the pay per case was not that good, but she soon decided that she needed to have at least a physical separation between her work life and her home life. So, she rents some space in an office-sharing building near her house.

She is glad that she has an office to walk to in the mornings and to shut the door behind in the evenings. She doesn't mind that she has to get up earlier or that her return home is delayed. She finds that she gets her best ideas when she is not thinking so hard, when she can be distracted by something that is *not* the problem at hand. It's either on her walks in or when she's hiking or kayaking or gardening that the fog clears long enough for that little bit of insight to emerge or for something to reappear that has fallen off the checklist.[6]

As Julia leaves the house this morning, her wife, Jill, tells her that Aurora called yesterday hoping they would come to visit her for Mothers' Day this year. It used to be, after Aurora was first married, that she would take Julia and Jill out somewhere special to celebrate her two moms, but now that Aurora has her own little one, it's harder for her to get away with Theo in tow. Now Mother's Day is about Aurora as a mother. Julia promises Jill she will look at her calendar once she gets to work; she is looking forward to seeing Aurora and her little family again. Julia hopes she and Jill

---

6. For an exploration of how the brain generates creativity when the conscious mind is not watching, see David Eagleman, Incognito: The Secret Lives of the Brain (2012).

can visit for the weekend and get some good grandma time in. Aurora and Steve could go out on a date in the evening and maybe Aurora could even have a full day to herself. Julia knows that is the best Mothers' Day gift ever—to luxuriate in the simple pleasures of walking down a sidewalk with both arms free while heading off to a destination of one's own choosing.

Julia is thinking about seeing Aurora again as she walks, remembering what it was like when Aurora first came to live with them. Aurora was a wild one, so wild Julia remembers telling Jill that maybe they shouldn't do this. Julia knows all too well how children who have been neglected because of their mothers' addictions have trouble attaching to their caregivers,[7] but Aurora's mother was Jill's sister, and Jill was determined that her niece would not wind up in the child welfare system. Jill had heard way too much from Julia about the failings of foster care. So Aurora came to live with them when she was six years old. At first they were her Aunt Jill and Aunt Julia but, gradually, when it became clear that Aurora's mom wasn't coming back, they both shifted to momma J and mommy J. Then the J's just fell off, and they became her parents as far as Aurora was concerned. But because the father, whoever he was, never surfaced and because Aurora's mom just disappeared, they never really went through the trouble of a legal adoption. Jill felt that she could not give up on her sister by filing some kind of lawsuit against her, even if the chances were that her sister would never even know or show up. Julia at times worried that they did not have the security of a legal family, but the years flew by and before they knew it Aurora had grown up and was on her own. Before they were able to get married,[8] Jill and Julia were used to doing work-arounds to ensure that they got at least some of the protections traditional families were able to take for granted. They had wills and in them they made sure that Aurora was treated just as they would have treated their own daughter. They had also been able to work with the schools[9] and doctors[10] to make it clear that they were the caregivers in charge.

---

7. *See*, ch. 1, *The Impact of Child Maltreatment on Children and Youth.*

8. It is now unconstitutional for states to deny marriage to same-sex couples. *See* Obergefell v. Hodges, 135 S.Ct. 2071 (2015).

9. While typically it is parents who assert the rights for their children in the educational context, the law recognizes the fact that often children are cared for informally for by relatives or others in the absence of their parents. For example, the Individuals with Disabilities Education Act (IDEA) defines "parent" to include "an individual acting in the place of a natural or adoptive parent (including a grandparent, stepparent, or other relative with whom the child lives." 20 U.S.C. § 1401(23). *See also*, Cal. Fam. Code § 6550; Ohio Rev. Code § 3109.69; Tex. Educ. Code Ann. § 25.001.

10. Many states have enacted statutes permitting non-parental caregivers to provide consent to medical treatment for the children in their care. The approaches taken are not uniform. Some of these statutes require written permission from the parent unless legal custody has been determined while others provide for the possibility of allowing a caregiver without written consent from the parent to act. Some only apply to certain classes of relatives while others apply to any individual who is caring for a child. *See for example*, Cal. Fam. Code § 6550; D.C. Code § 16-4901; Fla. Stat. Ann. § 743.0645; Ga. Code Ann. § 19-9-124, et seq.; Nev. Rev. Stat. Ann. § 129.040; Tex. Fam. Code Ann. § 32.001; Wash. Rev. Code. Ann. § 7.70.065(2)(a).

The fact that Aurora is for all intents and purposes their daughter does not mean that Jill has forgotten her sister. Julia often finds Jill's searches on the computer—she will always be looking for her sister in the criminal dockets or the obituaries. Searching at homeless shelters evolved into internet searching long ago. Jill's experience with her sister helps her to have patience and respect for what Julia does. She understands why it is so important that kids have someone in their corner when they are separated from family. She loves that Julia has the heart to do her job; for her, it would be too close to home. She would be taking in all of her clients if she were Julia. Jill is always reminding Julia to keep looking for a family member somewhere for all of the kids she represents; one of her favorite expressions is "Every family tree has at least one healthy branch." And Julia almost always replies—"Yes, but it's not always easy to get the Department to go out on that limb!"

With the exception of Jill's quietly persistent search for her sister, the drama in Jill and Julia's lives has dissipated. They watch with amazement as Aurora—all settled down—turns into the mom that she wanted to have. Happily married, staying at home, having a schedule, being consistent. Jill and Julia were not exactly the best for having consistent schedules—they came into her life with their own busy careers and without much thought as to what it would mean to be parents—but they were consistently patient and unconditionally committed, which was called for when Aurora was a teenager. They were both afraid to say it out loud back then, but they both thought it—*what if she turns out like her mom? What if she takes off and never comes back?* In the middle of those fits and tantrums, the wild nights when she didn't come home when she was supposed to, they could never have imagined this calm girl, this happy young woman, this great mom who was calling to invite them over to celebrate her own Mother's Day at her house.

So, as Julia walks into her office, noticing the whirring metallic chirp of a hummingbird nearby, somehow the dots between her role as aunt/mommy and Maya's Aunt Hen connect, and Julia makes a mental note to follow up with Hen for Maya. Maybe Hen will be that patient adult who will tolerate Maya's teenage drama no matter what. Julia tried calling her once since the hearing and left a message but they have not connected yet.

Once she gets settled in at her office, checks her schedule and texts Jill with a thumbs up for a long weekend visit with Aurora, Julia calls Henrietta Phillips. After she explains who she is and her role, Hen warms up to her pretty quickly. She's excited and eager to know how Maya is and when Julia breaks the news about Maya's pregnancy, her reaction is what Julia would expect from the parent of a teenager. She's upset, concerned, and wants to know more. When Julia tells her that Maya wants to carry her pregnancy full term and raise the child herself, Julia can almost hear her shaking her head.

"Dear Lord, how does she think she is going to raise a baby all on her own? That sounds like a disaster waiting to happen right there." After a bit of a pause, she sighs and says, "Well, I guess now that she's got herself into this mess, she is going to need some help to keep from making a bigger mess of it, but not *too* much help. We can't let her think being a mom is an easy job she can just put off on somebody else. Then we'll have a houseful of babies."

Julia tells her that Maya wants to be placed with family but that right now the court has ordered that she stay at a group home. Julia explains that she will either need to get the social worker to agree or persuade the court over the social worker's objection that placement with family is the right thing to do. But first things first—would Hen consider the possibility of Maya and eventually her baby staying with her?

"I've been wanting Maya to come stay with us for the longest time. But Maya *and* a baby? I will have to talk to Marcus about this. We were kind of thinking our baby-raising days were over. Of course, once they're here, you have to love 'em, don't you? They have a way of stealing your heart." Already, she's moved past being upset with Maya and is reluctantly chuckling about the idea of having a baby in the house. "It's a good thing they're so damn cute."

Julia likes her. She can tell she wants to say yes. But it's a big thing to agree to without talking it over with her husband. Hen seems so reasonable; Julia remains curious about why the department kept her out of the running as a placement for a girl who has so few options and has cost the state so much money in semi-secure group care settings. Hen must have really pissed someone off somewhere along the line.

They talk for a while about the logistics—whether they have room (it will be very tight), where Maya would go to school (there is a high school not far from their house but she would be further behind her peers in credits), what their work schedules are like (they had worked it so one of them was always home when the girls were home, which meant they didn't see much of each other but the kids were well taken care of), how to handle child care (she doesn't know what would happen when Maya is in school but she could look at re-adjusting their schedules again), how old her girls are (8 and 10) and how she thinks they would get along with Maya and possibly a baby (they would be excited about a baby but Maya would have to behave because they aren't used to a lot of nonsense and she won't let Maya lead her girls astray). Mostly Hen worries about taking care of the baby during the school day and how they will all fit into their two-bedroom apartment. Rents are doing nothing but going up, even though neither she nor Marcus have had a raise in a long time;[11] they can't afford a bigger place.

Julia explains that if they go to the trouble of becoming licensed they would receive more money for a high needs child with a child of her own, which will likely cover the increase in the rent, but licensure will involve a time investment. Plus, their actual apartment will need to be approved, which means they will need the bigger place before they actually go for the final license, which means they will need to do some pretty creative problem-solving. If they go with a relative placement, the licensing

---

11. The American economy has been experiencing widening income inequality as wages have remained stagnant while the cost of living has been on the rise. *See,* PEW RESEARCH CENTER, Drew Desilver, *For Most Workers, Real Wages Have Barely Budged in Decades,* PEW RESEARCH (Oct. 9, 2014) [https://perma.cc/QS5V-MH25].

requirements will be waived. They will still need to undergo a basic background check, but if they pass that, they might be permitted to have Maya stay with them. But, they will only get a small child-only welfare benefit[12] for Maya and possibly the baby, which may not cover the increase in the rent for a bigger place. And of course this will require the department to be on board—either willingly or by court order.

> ### The Impact of Licensing Requirements on Relatives
>
> *If licensing requirements are not waived for relatives, it can sometimes be challenging to deal with basic issues like available housing, criminal history, and employment.*
>
> * *Locate the licensing requirements in your state.*
>
> * *What challenges, if any, would Aunt Hen have in being licensed to serve as a placement for Maya in your jurisdiction?*

Which brings the conversation around to the big question—will the social worker agree and if not will Julia be able to persuade the judge to order placement with them rather than the licensed group home? Hen worries about investing a lot of time and emotional energy into even thinking about changing their living situations and persuading her husband to go along if they will just be disappointed again.

Julia asks Hen to explain what happened back when Maya was removed from her mom and then later from her grandmother. The first time, the state placed Maya with her grandmother, Katherine Phillips, and that was fine because Hen, Katherine's daughter, still got to see Maya and help Katherine out a lot. It was easier to get Maya placed there because Katherine had more room and lived closer to the elementary school. Katherine also had more time to spend looking out for Maya because she wasn't working. The social worker was willing to waive the licensing requirement for Katherine to have just Maya but she wasn't sure Katherine was able to handle both girls, given that Jazz was heading to middle school. The social worker said she wanted the girls to be separated anyway because Jazz had taken on too many parenting responsibilities. Finally, Hen said that no matter how much she disagreed with the social worker about separating Maya and Jazz, the social worker insisted that Katherine should have Maya and that Jazz would need to be in a special kind of foster care to deal with everything she'd been through.

---

12. "Welfare" is the common term used to refer to benefits received through Temporary Assistance to Need Families (TANF). The typical TANF benefit is provided to families that are income eligible and the amount of the benefit is calculated based upon the number of children and adults in the household. However, in certain limited circumstances, a TANF benefit may be provided because of the status of the child in the home, rather than the income of the household. Nonparent relative caregivers are entitled to receive this "child-only" TANF payment. *See*, Gene Faulk, Temporary Assistance for Needy Families (TANF): Eligibility and Benefit Amounts in State TANF Cash Assistance Programs 2 (2014), Congressional Research Service [https://perma.cc/TVG7-TLJA].

Then, just when Maya had settled in and was starting to catch up in school, the stroke happened and poor Maya had to find a new place to be. Hen assumed that she would come live with her and Marcus, and she was more than willing to have that happen. But after her mother's stroke, Hen was "not in a good place." She was exhausted because she was pregnant with her second child, she had a young one at home, Marcus had a long-distance truck driving job and was gone a lot. Meanwhile, she was trying to divide her time between her child who was in pre-school and her mother in the hospital. On top of that, she had gone searching for Maya's mom to let her know that their mother was in the hospital, but she wasn't able to find her anywhere and was worried about her too. She had a lot on her plate.

Nevertheless, even with all of that going on, Hen says she was more than willing to take Maya, and it looked like it might work out until the social worker asked Hen about whether she felt that Maya should ever see her mother again. She didn't lie. She wishes now that she would have, but instead she said she felt that Maya should see her mother if she wanted to because, no matter what, Chicken would always be Maya's mother.

The social worker didn't ask many questions after that, and it seemed like the things that Hen told her to try to make her soften towards Chicken only made things worse. So when she went to the hearing about where Maya should stay, all prepared to take Maya home with her, the social worker surprised her by saying she was recommending foster care because the only known relatives wouldn't protect Maya from her mother who was known to prostitute her children to support her drug habit. Hen says she lost it then. She says it would have been hard for her to hear that kind of talk in the best of circumstances but, given how worn out she was, she acted "pretty crazy" both in the courtroom and out in the hallway and she wound up being kicked out of the courthouse. She explains to Julia that ever since then it seems like nobody will consider her.

Julia tells her that it made perfect sense that she would have been stretched so thin at a time like that and asks her whether Sarah, Maya's current social worker, has called her yet to talk. Hen says that this call is the first she has heard any news about Maya in a long time.

Julia explains that because Maya has been on the run for a while she has not had a chance to find out what direction she should be taking with the case. Julia apologizes to Aunt Hen for leaving her out of the loop for so long.

Looking at her notes one last time, Julia is reminded to ask about Maya's grandmother. There is a silence and Hen sighs deeply, "My mother is still alive but not herself. She's an amazing woman, how she's made it through everything. She was just beginning to recover from the stroke when she got her Alzheimer's diagnosis. She is in a nursing home now. She doesn't seem to know who anyone is anymore."

Julia says she is so sorry to hear that, how hard that must be after all they have been through together.

"Yes," is all that Hen can say.

Julia says that she will need to deliver that news to Maya. She also promises to talk to Sarah if Hen decides that she wants to be considered as a placement. She explains that while there are no guarantees and while the state seems to think that Maya needs to be in a structured non-family setting right now, Maya's current social worker is not unreasonable and may be persuaded to reconsider, especially since Maya's options are narrowing now that she is pregnant and the judge wants a renewed relative search. They agree that Hen will talk to Marcus and let Julia know something soon.

Getting off the phone, Julia wishes she could just wave a magic wand and give Hen and Marcus a new three-bedroom apartment, get them licensed for foster care, and, while she is at it, provide Maya and her soon-to-be little baby with a school that has a day care and all the support they both will need to get off to a good start. Instead, she knows she will need to persuade Sarah and get her on board enough to want to problem-solve the challenges that will make it possible for Maya and her baby to finally return to family.

Julia looks at her "to do" list and realizes that she still had lots "to do." She is immersed in drafting another client's "Report to Court" due for a review hearing next week when she hears the little reminder sound on her computer letting her know that it is time for lunch. She almost forgot! She'd better get going; it's a bit of a walk to Maxwell's.

A Mentoring Lunch

They find each other, coming in at about the same time, both looking ready to apologize to the other, if they could only remember what the other one looked like. They recognize each other in line as much by their confused, searching expressions as by their actual faces.

"I am so glad I'm not too late." Katie says as they sit down at an open table near the window. "I got behind this morning when I had to go see a client at the CRC."

"No problem. I got distracted, too, trying to get a client's aunt to consider taking her in and then writing a report for another client.[13] I get so sucked in that I forget to take lunch sometime."

"Yeah, my case this morning was a tough one. My client was kicked out of her placement after some sort of fight with her foster parent and now she's separated from her younger brother and sister. What a mess. I want to try and patch things up with her

---

13. RULE 1.6 of the ABA MODEL RULES OF PROFESSIONAL CONDUCT prohibits a lawyer from revealing information relating to the representation of a client without he client's informed consent unless it is "impliedly authorized in order to carry out the representation." RULE 1.14 provides that a "lawyer shall, as far as reasonably possible, maintain a normal client-lawyer relationship with the client" with diminished capacity to make adequately considered decisions. Specifically, RULE 1.14(c) provides that the client with diminished capacity is entitled to the protections of RULE 1.6, even if the lawyer feels the need to take protective action on the client's behalf.

foster parent but my client seems to think that's a losing proposition. I hope she's wrong. It just seems so unfair."

"Well, it *is* unfair. Sometimes you just have to let your client know you see the unfairness and then do the best you can."

Katie's relieved to hear Julia react in the same way she did, but she doesn't tell her how much she embraced her teenage self in the moment, with her "that sucks" comment. She isn't sure whether Julia would approve. She isn't sure whether she herself approves. She still isn't sure how to react to the emotional deluge that can happen with some teenagers. It seems like she always has to deal with one extreme or another—a great big shrug or a great big meltdown.

The waitress comes, and they are distracted by the menus. After they order their iced teas, Julia asks, "So how long have you been practicing?"

Is it that obvious? Katie thinks. "I am coming up on a year now. I started as a temp, filling in when Shauna went on maternity leave, and then Erin went on maternity leave, and somehow I got to stay on even after she came back. I keep waiting for them to notice I am still here," Katie says with a smile.

"Oh, I'm sure they're glad to have to you. They are really overloaded right now. It seems like the economy has made dependency filings go up.[14] Is dependency the rotation you wanted?"

"Yes, actually, either that or the juvenile defense division. I'd like to get over there at some point, too, but for now I am just trying to learn my way around these cases. I did a clinic when I was in law school and we represented kids but, man, the 'real thing' is a lot more intense than my clinic! I can't believe I had three cases then and felt overloaded."

"Yeah, you do have a lot going on. I have probably about half the cases that you do now because of the pilot, and I am still running from one thing to the next."

"That must be nice, to have half the cases. I look at my client list and I'm embarrassed to admit that I get some of them confused with each other, and I suspect that there are still some I haven't even met. Especially the runaways. They disappear and then they're off my radar and I'm embarrassed when it's the hearing date and either they show up and I have to introduce myself for the first time or they don't show up and I have nothing to say to the judge. There are a few clients I can't forget—the ones that are either amazingly resilient or amazingly sad."

---

14. Research has indicated that the incidence of child maltreatment rose as the economy declined during the most recent economic recession. *See*, R.P. Berger, J.B. Fromkin, H. Stutz, K. Makaroff, *Abusive Head Trauma During a Time of Increased Unemployment: A Multicenter Analysis,* 128 PEDIATRICS 637 (2011) [https://perma.cc/2W6P-D2R4]. At the same time, state and local governments were being impacted, sometimes having to lay off employees, due to dwindling resources caused by shrinking tax bases. *See*, CENTER ON BUDGET AND POLICY PRIORITIES, NICHOLAS JOHNSON, ET AL., AN UPDATE ON STATE BUDGET CUTS, (Feb. 9 2011) [https://perma.cc/RX33-XSGR]; Center for Economic and Policy Research, Matt Sherman and Nathan Lane, *Cut Loose: State and Local Layoffs of Public Employees in the Current Recession* (Sept. 2009) [https://perma.cc/R7JS-QKTH].

The waitress comes back and they both quickly study the menus and order. As she scurries off to the next table, Julia says, "It was so nice of you to reach out and set this lunch up. Now that I am on my own, I actually don't do this as much as I used to. When I was at the defenders, we would just all sort of travel from the office to court together and hang out. I do miss that."

"Are you kidding? I'm really glad *you* could do this. My supervisor is great, but honestly we have had so much turnover lately that she is busy covering for people who have left, or interviewing new people she hopes to hire. I think she's counting on me to take care of myself at this point. There are others who I can talk to, of course, but everyone is so busy, it seems like we get our questions answered and talk to each other more on the office listserv and by email than in person! So when I saw you at court that day and remembered you on that panel talking about how to do this work for a long time without burning out, I thought, *now that's somebody I have to get to know.*"

> ### Confidentiality & Listservs
>
> *Katie mentions seeking help through her office's listserv. Practitioners often join listservs as a way of creating supportive communities of practice. However, listservs that reach beyond the attorney's firm can pose ethical concerns.*
>
> - *What are some of the listservs that attorneys in your jurisdiction utilize?*
> - *How can attorneys participate without running afoul of the Rules of Professional Conduct?*

Julia is trying to remember what she must have said that had piqued Katie's interest, but she isn't even sure which panel it was. She is a regular for both the brown bag lunch talks that the dependency section of the bar did and for panels at any number of conferences. She has grown a bit tired of the sound of her own voice, but they keep asking her back. The fact that others had not yet grown tired of her was probably a testament to what Katie was talking about—the constant turnover in some of the offices.[15] If it wasn't the rotation system that did it, it was the stress of the work itself. So her voice would remain forever new, even if she and the conference organizers had heard it all before.

"So you think you want to make a career of this, do you?"

"I thought so. Or I mean, I *think* so."

"I hear a *but* in there."

---

15. For a study of the high attrition rate of attorneys serving children in dependency proceedings and the conditions that underlie it, see Public Advocate for the City of New York, Betsy Gotbaum, A Dangerous Cycle: Attorney Turnover at ACS Leaves Children Unprotected (Sept. 2006), [https://perma.cc/8BZ7-T7S2].

"Yes, I really do want to do this work, but I want to do it well. And I am just not sure how to do that. And of course it is discouraging when you have so many cases,[16] and not only because there's too much work, but because they start to all look the same and, well, kind of hopeless." Katie is grateful that the food arrives and interrupts her flow. She doesn't want to sound too negative.

> ### Caseloads
>
> *Attorneys for children often have to juggle large caseloads. Some states have standards; some states don't. Even those states that do have standards, may or may not follow them.*
>
> • *What is the practice in your jurisdiction with respect to caseloads?*

As they settle into eat their lunch, Katie shifts tone, "So how do you do it? I mean how long have you done it? And do you still really love it? Have you always loved it? What's your secret?"

Julia laughs. She looks at Katie's fresh face peering over her Caesar salad, her blue eyes looking back at her expectantly, as though she has all of the answers. "Well, I *have* been doing this for quite a while, now that you mention it. I haven't loved every minute of it, that's for sure, and I had a much needed break when I rotated through all of the other practice areas, but eventually I did decide that this was the work for me. Let's see, I have been doing some sort of appointed counsel work, either for kids or

---

16. The National Association of Counsel for Children (NACC), The American Bar Association and the Children's Bureau recommend that a full-time attorney represent no more than 100 individual clients as distinguished from cases. This standard assumes that attorneys will sometimes represent children in sibling groups who are involved in the same case as well as the fact that sometimes an individual child may have more than one case as in when a child has both an ongoing dependency and a termination of parental rights proceeding. See, National Association of Counsel for Children, David Katner, et al., NACC Recommendations for Representation of Children in Abuse and Neglect Cases 4 (2001). States are not bound by these recommendations and are free to develop or ignore caseload standards. See, AR Sup. Ct. Adm. Order No. 15 § 2(n) (full-time caseload of no more than 75 cases; part-time caseload of no more than 25); Judicial Council of California, Dependency Counsel Caseload Standards: A Report to the California Legislature (April 2008) (establishing standards setting the maximum caseload of an FTE dependency attorney at 188) [https://perma.cc/SJK9-Y9MM], *but see*, ACLU of California, System on the Brink: How Crushing Caseloads in the California Dependency Courts Undermine the Right to Counsel, Violate the Law, and Put Children and Families at Risk (2015) [https://perma.cc/L95V-UUEP] (finding that the actual caseloads of attorneys in some California counties ranged between 400–500 clients per attorney); Massachusetts Committee for Public Counsel Services Manual for Assigned Counsel at Ch. 5, No. 22 (2011) (setting a maximum of 75 open cases per attorney); NY CLS Standards & Admin Pol § 127.5 (providing that attorneys shall not represent more than 150 children but allowing for adjustments based on the policy's other provisions); Washington Administrative Office of the Courts, Statewide Children's Representation Workgroup, Meaningful Legal Representation for Children and Youth in Washington's Child Welfare System § 1.4 (2010), [https://perma.cc/S27J-T224] (setting a maximum of no more than sixty child clients with a total of no more than 80 cases per full-time attorney).

parents or folks on the offender side, for almost thirty years now. How did that happen?" Julia smiles with the surprise that comes from realizing rather suddenly that you are indeed at that age when people regard you as either wise or foolish, depending on how they view "old" people. Apparently, this one thinks her wise; so she savors the moment.

"So, why?" Katie asks rather simply.

"Why?"

"Yes, why? What makes it worth thirty years of your life?"

"Whoa. That's a big question. Let me think about that for a minute, and while I do, how about if I ask you a smaller question?"

"Sure."

"The client you saw this morning? The one at the CRC?"

"Yeah?"

"What do you like about her?"

Katie cocks her head, looks surprised, "I don't know if I know her well enough to know what I like about her."

"Well, how long did you talk to her?"

"About an hour maybe."

"Well, we've only been talking for fifteen minutes and there are things I could say that I like about you right now. So think about it. What did you like about her?"

Katie squints, leans back in her chair and answers slowly, "I like that she is concerned about her brother and sister and that she misses them already even though she has only been away from them for a day. I think it's pretty amazing that as a teenager she is able to also think about them while she is busy not knowing where she will be next."

"That's good. She has strong bonds. She's able to remember the people she loves when she's in more of a precarious place than they are. Anything else?"

"I don't know. She certainly isn't shy about saying how she feels. I've had clients who I can't get to tell me anything. She is not one of them. Why do you ask?"

"Well, I think that people who do this work and do it for a long time like their clients. And the cast of characters that comes with them. Some people say that they can't believe anyone could do this work, see all of this messy human stuff and not become judgmental and cynical. I am ok with turnover, I guess, if it means that the people who have become cynical are leaving to find something else to do where people live up to their expectations. You can't be like that and be happy or effective. You have to like people and be able to face the reality of their situation."

Katie smiles, looks Julia in the eyes playfully and adds, "And have low expectations?"

Julia laughs along with her, "Well, you should have high expectations for the state; but you have to have realistic expectations for the children and families who aren't even asking for the state's 'help.'"

"OK. Well, how do you not get to feeling hopeless or angry when the state doesn't live up to your expectations and it seems like between the parents' problems and the state's problems, the kids are lucky to get out of their childhoods alive?"

"Oh, I feel hopeless and angry with astounding regularity."

"And sad?"

"Yes, and sometimes sad. I learned a long time ago that a good cry in the privacy of my home is both necessary and actually quite beautiful. It reminds you that you are alive. That you are still human, that despite it all, you loved those people in your files. There is heart-break in the work we do and we have to acknowledge that if we want to resist becoming hard and bitter."

Katie didn't know what to say. A lifetime of beautiful heartbreak. Really, is that what she signed up for? "Thirty years of anger, hopelessness and tears?" she asked, sounding more weak and whiny than she wanted.

"Well, not every day for thirty years. You know what? The other day, I was thinking about this client I had way back when I first started doing this work. I remember when I first met her. She had come from a really crazy situation. Both of her parents were mentally ill. Her mother was schizophrenic and her father was paranoid and violent toward her mother. She had an older sister who helped to raise her, but her sister ran off and then my client essentially took care of herself while also trying to look after her mother. Eventually, she told a teacher about the situation and asked for help. This was one of those cases where the young person invited CPS into her life and asked to please be removed. She was. She had a lot of catching up to do in her life, in her school, and she moved around a lot in care because she had so many problems. I thought she might even wind up like her mother or father, struggling with mental illness and homelessness. She aged out and this was back before there even was extended foster care.[17] I wasn't sure where she would wind up. I was scared for her and whenever I would see young people living on the streets, I would look the girls straight in the eyes, expecting to see her there. But you know where I found her?"

"Where?"

"Years later I was at my neighborhood pool with my daughter, Aurora. Aurora was about seven at the time and I was there sitting at the edge of the pool watching her and I looked over and there she was, my client, sitting on the edge of the pool too, playing with her son who looked to be about three years old. She was happy and healthy and having fun being a mom. She had made it."[18]

---

17. *See*, ch. 5, *Maya's Social Worker's Story* for a discussion of extended foster care.

18. Dr. Emmy Werner is one of the earliest pioneers of resiliency studies and is responsible for the longest running longitudinal study of resiliency. For decades, she studied resiliency by tracking the experiences of all children born in 1955 on the island of Kauai. In 2012, she reflected upon her life's work

"Wow. Did she talk to you?"

"Yes, briefly, we talked. She told me she had gone back and gotten her GED, that she had gone to community college and got her associates degree. And that she was living with her boyfriend's family who helped her take care of the baby so she could work. All that to say, you don't always know. In fact, when we're in the middle of it, we never know. Sometimes our clients make it in spite of us, sometimes they make it in some small measure because of us, but mostly they make it just because of who they are, how resourceful they have had to become, and maybe because someone along the way saw who they could become. Maybe it was her sister she has to thank; maybe she got her off to a good start.[19] Or maybe there was a foster parent or a teacher[20] or even a friend.[21] Maybe I said something that let her know I saw her strengths. I don't remember. You just don't know. And some of those cases that you aren't hearing from? You aren't hearing from them because they are doing just fine without you. There is joy even in what we think must be the most miserable of situations; that's been a good lesson for me to remember. I can't always remember it when I need it, but I try."

Katie thinks about this. She wonders if it's true that someday, years from now, she would see her client from this morning out with her now grown siblings, all of them, watching their children play at the park. Taking the long view is hard from where she sits. She feels so new and steeped in emergency reaction mode. It's hard to imagine that her path would ever cross with any of her clients again; they seemed to live in a world apart from hers. Still, to know that the clients had a life and future apart from hers, that could be brighter than what she's seeing right now is helpful. After all, Katie, the teenager behind the shut door of her bedroom, could not have imagined that she would be where she is now—in a good relationship with a great guy, a lawyer doing the job she wants to do, able (on most days anyway) to distance herself from the drama of her family. So why should her clients be any different? They don't all end up homeless or in jail, right?[22]

---

by noting that "we cannot label a person as resilient; it is a process. Over time, young folks raised in adversity can adapt successfully to whatever demands are made of them. It is not that being resilient in the teen years means someone will be resilient at age 100, because there are changes. Most of the changes are in a positive direction." *See*, Emmy Werner, *Risk, Resilience, and Recovery, in* 21(1) Reclaiming Child. & Youth 18 (2012).

19. Early family relationships are particularly important in shaping long-term resilient trajectories. *See*, Suniya S. Luthar, *Resilience in Development: A Synthesis of Research Across Five Decades*, *in* Developmental Psychopathology, Vol. 3: Risk Disorder, and Adaption 756 (Dante Cicchetti & Donald J. Cohen, eds., 2d ed. 2006). Because we enter the lives of our clients when their families are in crisis, we are unaware of those who might have nurtured and strengthened the child in the past and we know little of those times when the parent who is now in crisis was better able to function and provide the basis for future resiliency.

20. Supportive relationships with adults, including with teachers, can generate resiliency. *Id.* at 769.

21. A supportive relationship with a single friend can serve as a buffer in times of family adversity. Supportive friends with well-functioning families can also serve as models for the future. *Id.* at 770.

22. While it is true that studies have shown higher rates of most negative life outcomes for young people who exit foster care (higher rates of homelessness, unemployment, poverty, mental health problems and criminal justice involvement) these statistics also show that not all young people

Katie asks more questions, seeking solutions for her specific to cases. Are there ways to deal with situations like the one she had this morning to keep the kids together when the placement for one has become a problem? What do you do when the department wants to require your client to engage in mental health treatment but your client doesn't want to? Is there a way to move a client into placement with a friend's family if they are unlicensed and not a relative? Should you try to repair a relationship with a foster parent or just take your client's word for it that it's over?

Seeking Help Ethically

Katie and Julia are not in the same law firm. What are the ethical constraints that they have in discussing their cases with each other?

Julia draws upon her experience as best as she can to answer, but she also knows that so much of the time, the answer depends upon who the players are, whether you have a social worker who is willing to work with you, what services are available, how committed the possible placement options were. They wind up talking about the importance of relationship building and being able to see the situation from multiple perspectives—this is key with other lawyers, service providers and social workers as well as with clients, with family, with caregivers, and with whomever else was important to your client. If you can get people to come together to solve a common problem, success is more likely. But then there are those times when you have to know when to stop trying to problem-solve and shift into advocacy mode, get the judge involved, do some research beyond the statute to get your client's goal accomplished. Even then, you have to figure out a way to do it respectfully because on some other case you will be working with many of the same players to reach agreement.

Problem-Solving in the Dependency Context

Problem-solving with other players can be an effective way to achieve solutions in the multi-disciplinary context.

- *What are some of the ethical challenges for lawyers in-out-of-court problem-solving mode when the client is not present?*

- *What are the advantages and disadvantages of having the client present while the lawyer is engaging on out-of-court problem-solving?*

---

experience these outcomes. For example, while it may be true that, in one study, 7% of those 23- and 24-year-olds who had exited foster care were incarcerated by the time of their final interview, this also means that 93% had escaped that fate, and while close to 24% had experienced at least one night of homelessness, 76% had not. *See* Mark E. Courtney et al., *Midwest Evaluation of the Adult Functioning of Former Foster Youth: Outcomes at Ages 23 and 24*, Chapin Hall U. Chi. 9 (2010), [https://perma.cc/FS8W-77KH]. This view is not to diminish the relatively poor outcomes of youth exiting care or the struggles that they face as young adults. Rather, it is meant to show that the vast majority of young people do escape these dire outcomes.

The hour flies by with no time for dessert. Katie needs to get back to talk to the social worker about whether her client can remain where she is, maybe the foster parent just needed respite,[23] with the client spending just a little time away with a suitable adult she knows who lives near the school, and afterwards the foster parent can see that the younger children need to be with their older sister, maybe she can be brought around, maybe somehow she can help them to see that they can choose to take a deep breath and try to realize that this is normal teenage behavior that needs limit-setting but not complete rejection.

And Julia needs to get back and finish that report. She also wants to try to get a call into Sarah to test the temperature on her willingness to consider Hen and Marcus. And she needs to check in with Maya and see how she is doing in the group home.

As they head out the door, Katie thanks Julia again. She sees her walk past the parking lot, and shouts out, "Hey, you need a ride?"

Julia answers, "No thanks! I'd rather walk."

Reflections and Exercises

1. *What? So what? Now what? A Five-Minute Reflection Opportunity.* Take just five minutes to write and reflect on the following questions:

   a. What did you feel as you read this chapter?

   b. How is what you recorded feeling relevant to your learning and/or practice?

   c. Now what do you do with these insights as you move forward in your learning and/or practice?

2. *What's Your Story?* Not every lawyer who practices mergers and acquisitions has personal experience with a deal gone wrong. Not every lawyer who practices entertainment law has sought his fifteen minutes of fame. However, every lawyer who practices law involving families has a family. And while some families have had a more privileged set of circumstances than others, no family is immune from heartache and challenge. In this chapter, we get a glimpse into the family stories of both Katie and Julia. Their stories bear some similarities with the experiences of their clients. Their stories are also different from those of their clients.

   a. How do you think these similarities and differences may impact their work—both positively and negatively?

   b. Is it important for lawyers who do this work to examine their own stories? Why or why not?

---

23. "Respite care" refers to a temporary placement that allows the foster parent or other caregiver short-term relief to engage in self-care and return to caregiving after having their own physical, mental and emotional needs met. Best practice would be that respite care is a regularly planned, naturally occurring part of a child and foster parent's service plan. All too often, it is engaged in an emergency when the placement is in danger of disruption. To learn more, see National Resource Center for Respite and Crisis Care Resources, Factsheet Number 51 (1998), [https://perma.cc/T686-BCXM].

    c. What aspects of your family history might come into play if you were to do this work?

3. ***Imagining a Different Story:*** This chapter highlights the challenges that attorneys in a busy practice have with seeking out the support they need from one another. Imagine a system that institutionalizes the kind of support that attorneys need to survive and thrive in this practice. What would such a system look like?

Chapter Seven

Michael's Childhood under State Supervision

At the initial shelter care hearing, the judge separated Michael and his sisters from their mother and each other pending a formal trial where a judge determines whether they meet the definition of "dependent children," i.e., whether they have parents capable of safely caring for them.[1] The shelter care order governs where children will live and how often they will have contact with their parents during the time period leading up to the dependency fact-finding or trial. It mirrors the concept of pre-trial detention in a criminal proceeding—where defendants are held in jail or released pending a finding of guilt by a jury or the entry of a guilty plea.

In Part 1 of this chapter, you will learn about the most common way that children are found dependent—through the entry of agreed findings. The State has to prove that a child meets the definition of dependency by a preponderance of the evidence standard for civil proceedings. This decision is made by a judge, not a jury. Very few cases go to trial.[2] Instead, often cases are negotiated and settled with the parents agreeing to the findings in exchange for an agreeable disposition order.[3] The disposition order sets forth the requirements that the parents will have to meet in order to have their children returned to their care and their case dismissed. Youth will also be bound by these orders, which often remain unchanged for months and set forth where youth will live, how they will visit with their parents and siblings and what services will be offered to the youth. You will be exposed in this chapter to how attorneys negotiate with the State and multiple parties to come to a resolution of the dependency petition.

You will also be introduced to Michael's grandmother and learn about the complexity of kinship care. And you will meet the Court Appointed Special Advocate (CASA), a volunteer who represents the best interests of Michael's siblings. This role was discussed in Chapter One, as one way that many states comply with federal

---

1. States have different definitions for determining whether children are dependents. *See* e.g. Washington RCW 13.34.030(6), California WELFARE AND INSTITUTIONS CODE SECTION 300, ARIZ. REV. STAT. § 8-201, OHIO REV. CODE 2151.04.

2. It is difficult to find any national data on dependency trial rates, or even general civil trial rates, although it is generally recognized that civil trials have become rare. *See* Margo Schlanger, *What We Know and What We Should Know About American Trial Trends*, 2006 J. DISP. RESOL. 35 (2006).

3. Many states have also implemented dependency mediation programs to resolve child welfare cases. *See generally,* Anne Elizabeth Rosenbaum, *Embracing the Strengths and Overcoming the Weaknesses of Child Protection Mediation*, 15 U.C. DAVIS J. JUV. L. & POL'Y 299 (2011).

requirements that all children in dependency proceedings have a guardian ad litem representing their best interests.

In Part 2 of this chapter, you will observe how Michael and his family live under the court's order. You will learn about what happens after dependency is established and how the court's orders are implemented. You will be introduced to some of the challenges that a lawyer can face representing a youth who has been found dependent, once the initial disposition plan has been entered and the legal issues are less well defined.

Part 1: Becoming a Dependent Child

Michael after the Shelter Care Hearing

After his first and only experience at juvenile court, Michael has no interest in going back.[4] It is a lot of stress. While he is pleased with himself for speaking up for his sisters in court, he has no idea whether it made any difference, despite the judge's assurances. Leaving the courthouse with Reggie he feels a pit in his stomach. The world is shifting, caving in around him. He feels untethered. He is relieved to be driving away from the courthouse but he has never felt so alone.

Katie meets with Michael briefly after the shelter care hearing and hands him a piece of paper. She may have tried to explain to him what happened in court and what was on the piece of paper, but at that point Michael is unable to absorb any more information. He does remember her saying that he may not have to come back to court if they are able to "work out an agreement." Sounds like a good idea to him. He takes the paper and looks for the door. He hears Katie say she would call him as he walks away.

Michael's Mother Michelle after the Shelter Care Hearing

Michelle almost goes back to the pipe one more time after the shelter care hearing. She is so close. After being lectured at by her attorney and the social worker in the juvenile court hallway, she has to fill out a whole bunch of forms with different government workers. "Screened" they call it—for a public defender, for treatment, for whatever. She is used to having to fill out forms and wait. She left with a stack of papers. One of the pieces of paper she is given had a phone number to call to get into treatment.[5] When she gets back to her empty apartment she stands in the kitchen and

---

4. Although Michael is reluctant to go to court, some states have surveyed youth who attend their dependency court proceedings and have found that many youth are interested in attending their court hearings and have a positive experience. *See, Engaging Youth in Court: A National Analysis*, ABA CENTER ON CHILDREN AND THE LAW (2015) [https://perma.cc/J3QL-FTBA]; *Dependent Youth Interviews Pilot Program*, WASHINGTON STATE CENTER FOR COURT RESEARCH, Final Report to the Legislature (2010), [https://perma.cc/6Z8Y-P3FE].

5. Many parents who could benefit from treatment do not receive adequate services. This is due to a combination of limited availability, a lack of funding, lack of coordination among providers, and

stares at that piece of paper. God, she needs a beer but her refrigerator is empty. She digs through some drawers looking for a cigarette. She doesn't smoke cigarettes much but she is desperate to calm her nerves. No cigarettes, but, hallelujah, she finds a small piece of folded up foil. Can it be? One very small rock inside. It must be DJ's secret stash. She holds it to her face and closes her eyes. She has a moment of calm. She starts to dig around the drawer for something to use to smoke it and her cell phone rings.

"What happened today?" Momma J. speaks loudly over the sound of her car engine. "I was going to come down there, but my car wouldn't start. Goddamn battery again. Anyway, do I gotta pick up your babies somewhere? I got the thing running and I am on my way to your apartment now."

Michelle is jolted back to reality. She looks at the foil pouch in her hand and before she can change her mind she goes to the toilet. She winces to see her opportunity for one last high flushed away.

"Can you hear me? Are you in the toilet or what?" Momma J. rattles on.

"Yeah, sorry. Yeah, you gotta call the social worker right now. You gotta tell her that you will take the kids."

Momma J. decides to drive directly to the CPS office and try to speak with Emily. Michelle is relieved not to have to deal with her mother's scorn and judgment. She dials the number on the piece of paper.

Michael's Maternal Grandmother's Story: Jacqueline Griffith or "Momma J."

"I am not a young woman anymore. I am tired. I can't take all those children without some help." Momma J. says this with resignation. Emily Peters is all business. She hands Momma J. the background check forms and applications for various public assistance benefits.[6]

---

the mismatch between the time needed to complete treatment and the time horizon of dependency proceedings. Child Welfare Information Gateway, U.S. Dep't of Health & Human Servs., Parental Substance Use and the Child Welfare System 5 (2014), [https://perma.cc/83R6-REY6].

6. As of 2013, 28 states and the District of Columbia include a criminal background check on relatives, and in some cases on other adults in their households, as part of the placement process. Child Welfare Information Gateway, U.S. Dep't of Health & Human Servs., Placement of Children with Relatives 3 (2013), [https://perma.cc/35RK-Y32S]. If relatives are deemed to be suitable placements, they can receive standard foster care payments if they are properly licensed, and are eligible for assistance through kinship care or relative caregiver programs available in thirteen states. Id. Relatives seeking placement generally must meet minimum requirements including passing criminal background checks and participating in a home study. Additionally, relatives who would otherwise not be eligible for their states' income assistance programs, may qualify for TANF as a result of the child's cost of care. See Correne Saunders et al., Children Without Parent in the TANF Caseload, 34 Child. & Youth Servs. Rev. 1024 (2012).

Momma J. is 57 years old. She was born Jacqueline Sykes, the daughter of Jeffrey and Margaret Sykes in Oakland, California. She has four adult children and 10 grandchildren. She has reason to be tired. She has been taking care of children — her own or her grandchildren — since she was 18 years old. She thinks she did a pretty good job, too, given the fact that she never had enough money and the men in her life were challenged when it came to providing for their families.[7]

There aren't men around anymore like her daddy, who migrated west from the segregated south in the 1950s. Her daddy undertook a perilous journey across the country so he could raise his children with some kind of opportunity. He got a city job in Oakland, as a janitor. He didn't get paid a lot of money, but it was enough to buy a modest home and take care of his wife and three children.[8] Unfortunately, he passed too early.[9] He had a heart attack at the age of 47 leaving his wife, Margie, with three children that weren't yet grown. Margie didn't have much earning potential but managed to make a little bit of money as a housekeeper. It was a struggle. They lost their home and moved into public housing. She became depressed and turned to alcohol, which drove her children away.

Once a talented athlete and good student, Jacqueline couldn't stay motivated after her father passed. Her dreams of college seemed to be just that — dreams. Unable to stand her mother's sorrowful drinking and confident in her ability to fend for herself, she left home at the first opportunity. When she got pregnant at 17, she didn't worry. She was sure that Willie Griffith was "the one." He was optimistic, funny and told her how much he loved her again and again. He had a job at a hotel and played music on the side. He was romantic and hopeful, not terribly unlike the Jeffrey Sykes who brought his family out west years before.

---

7. At almost any point during the past thirty years, the unemployment rate of black workers has been more than double the unemployment rate of white workers. Lawrence Mishel et al., The State of Working America 339 (12th ed. 2012). During recessions, this unemployment gap widens further. *Id.* These disparities have been associated with anti-black discrimination in hiring practices. *See* Marianne Bertrand and Sendhil Mullainathan, *Are Emily and Greg More Employable than Lakisha and Jamal? A Field Experiment on Labor Market Discrimination,* 94(4) The Am. Econ. Rev. 991 (Sept. 2004).

8. Between 1910–1970, millions of African Americans left the southern United States and moved to the north and west in what is known as the Great Migration. Suzanne C. Eichenlaub et al., *Moving Out But Not Up: Economic Outcomes in the Great Migration,* 75 Am. Soc. Rev. 101, 101 (2010). These migrants left the racial violence and lack of economic and educational opportunities that persisted under Jim Crow. *Id.* at 102. Conventional migration theory suggests they had improved economic outcomes; however, recent empirical research suggests that migrating blacks did not fare better economically than those who remained in the south. *Id.* at 118.

9. African Americans have a lower life expectancy than whites, and although the "life expectancy gap" has been shrinking nationally, from 8.1 years in 1990 to 5.4 years in 2009, state data suggests a significant variation by state. For example, the District of Columbia has the highest life expectancy gap for African Americans, nearly 15 years, and the gap remained unchanged from 1990-2009. Sam Harper et al., *Trends In The Black-White Life Expectancy Gap Among US States, 1990–2009,* 33(8) Health Affairs 1375–1382 (2014). Black males have the highest rate of avoidable deaths from heart disease, stroke and hypertensive disease. Centers for Disease Control and Prevention, *Vital Signs: Avoidable Deaths from Heart Disease, Stroke, and Hypertensive Disease — United States, 2001–2010,* 62 Morbidity & Mortality Wkly Rept. 721–27 (2013).

Jacqueline and Willie didn't need much to be happy their first few years together. But, when it was clear that Willie's career as a professional musician was not going to take off, Jacqueline did her best to find consistent work. She found mostly retail jobs— JC Penney's, Sears, and Macy's. She really wanted to work as a grocery store cashier, where the money was much better, but she could never break in. She never made much more than the minimum wage and sometimes had periods of unemployment where the family had to rely on public assistance. Those were rough times with Willie. Jacqueline never stopped loving him. But he could be such an asshole when he was forced to confront his shortcomings as a provider.

What Jacqueline really wanted more than anything was to own a house. A house with a fenced yard and a garage. But, that never happened on her minimum wage salary. She could barely pay the rent, much less have anything left to save for a down payment.[10] She and Willie lived hand to mouth. Food banks helped out and her children never went hungry.[11] Still, they lived mostly in apartment complexes in less desirable neighborhoods. She knew that her children were not introduced to the best parts of society and that they may not have had all the opportunities they deserved, but they were never on the street.[12]

> ### Poverty
> *Momma J. describes a life of financial struggle.*
> * *How do you think poverty impacted Michael's family's child welfare involvement?*

---

10. On average, African American women are paid 63 cents for every dollar paid to white, non-Hispanic men. In 2014, African American women had a median annual income of $33,772 while non-Hispanic white men had a median income of $53,267. THE AMERICAN ASSOCIATION OF UNIVERSITY WOMEN, THE SIMPLE TRUTH ABOUT THE GENDER PAY GAP 10–11 (Spring 2016 ed.), [https://perma.cc/MSM8-UYD2]. The low home ownership rate for African American families is not just a result of income disparities, but is also a result of persistent and historical racial discrimination practiced in the lending and housing markets. *See generally,* Ta-Nahesi Coates, *The Case for Reparations,* THE ATLANTIC, June 2014, [https://perma.cc/4Q22-YAC9].

11. The wealth gap between white families and African American families widened significantly during the three decades that preceded the Great Recession, and was further exacerbated by the economic downturn. In 2009, the median wealth of white households was 20 times that of black households and 18 times that of Hispanic households. RAKESH KOCHAR ET AL., PEW RESEARCH CTR., TWENTY-TO-ONE 14 (2011), [https://perma.cc/2M7U-ND5H].

12. Much research has been done on "neighborhood effects," i.e., the consequences of growing up or residing in a disadvantaged neighborhood. While studies link living in a poor neighborhood with lower cognitive skills and academic achievement, among other markers of inequality, the relationship between children and their families and neighborhoods is complex. For a review of the literature and a discussion of the importance of context in interpreting the research, see Patrick Sharkey & Jacob W. Faber, *Where, When, Why, and For Whom Do Residential Contexts Matter? Moving Away from the Dichotomous Understanding of Neighborhood Effects,* 40 ANN. REV. SOC. 559 (2014) [https://perma.cc/L8T5-YNFK].

Time flies when you are working and raising children. Jacqueline became "Momma J." when her first grandchild was born. By this time, Willie Sr. had left. After one particularly violent argument Jacqueline told Willie Sr. to leave and not come back. He followed her instructions. Mothering transitioned into grandmothering without a break. Her oldest, Willie Jr., became a father when he was 18. He and his girlfriend moved in with Momma J. for a year or so with that first grandbaby. They eventually moved on to the baby's mother's family, but she was always the go-to childcare provider—for a day shift or for a whole weekend. She didn't mind, she loved chubby little NeNe, the sweetest baby ever.[13]

Momma J.'s oldest daughter, Denise, who went by Dee, was her first child to struggle with drug addiction. She was the social one, couldn't miss a party. Dee had her first baby at 16 and two more children by the time she was 19. Momma J. did her very best to protect these innocents and Dee from CPS and the police, but it was an exhausting and losing battle. So when her third child, Michelle, started dropping her children off to go drugging with her friends, Momma J. did not have it in her to be the loving grandparent she once was. She felt herself hardening in ways she never expected. Saying things she never thought she would hear herself say.

At the time of the shelter care hearing for Michelle's four children, Momma J. has two grandchildren already in her custody. She had adopted Dee's oldest, Beatrice, who was now a sophomore in high school and causing her stress.[14] She also had Dee's youngest, four-year-old Anthony. The apple of her eye, really, but it was all she could do to keep up with him. He was with her informally; Dee agreed to leave Anthony with her during one of her jail stays and she never asked to have him back. Dee visits now and again when she needs something from Momma J., but mostly she stays away knowing it will be impossible to pry him away from his grandmother.

"No, I don't have a man living with me. Lord, I'm taking care of all these grandchildren, I don't need somebody else to take care of." Momma J. is responding to Emily's inquiry about additional criminal background checks that would need to be completed. Momma J. doesn't mention Roy, who occasionally stops in and keeps her company—he is none of their business. Besides he isn't like a boyfriend or anything. "And, what do you need to come look at my house again for? All those other times with Dee and Michelle you people seemed happy to just drop babies off at my house

---

13. Grandparents play an increasingly important role in raising children. A study examining the shift in multigenerational care found that more than 60% of grandparents provided grandchild care over a ten-year period from 1998–2008. *See* Ye Luo et al., *Grandparents Providing Care to Grandchildren*, 33 J. Fam. Issues 1143 (2012).

14. Thirty-three states provide for a streamlined adoption process in cases where children are placed directly with relatives. Child Welfare Information Gateway, U.S. Dep't of Health & Human Servs., Placement of Children with Relatives (2013), [https://perma.cc/R77W-SEUD]. In 2007, almost one-fourth of children adopted out of foster care were adopted by relatives. Sharon Vandivere et al., U.S. Dep't of Health & Human Servs., Adoption USA 56 tbl.1 (2009), [https://perma.cc/C6KD-3FJ4].

without so much as a 'thank you.' But I got nothing to hide so feel free to stop on by. Oh, and I need some beds for the girls."[15]

Momma J. does everything the Department asks begrudgingly, but satisfactorily. Angel and Michael came to stay with her about a week after the shelter care hearing. Aliyah went to stay with Tommy Sykes, which Momma J. was just fine with. "About time he took some responsibility for her," she tells Michael when he complains that they won't be able to see Aliyah.

The first week went fine. Angel and Beatrice moved into one bedroom with brand new bunk beds and Michael and Anthony shared the third bedroom. Momma J. got the kids back into school and had after-school child care arranged. She successfully hounded the social worker for food coupons. Angel almost lived up to her name. She sulked around a little but she was sweet with Anthony and Poochie, Momma J.'s little dog. Michael, on the other hand, was surly. Momma J. thought something had gone wrong inside that boy. So ungrateful. She felt it when he first walked into her house and she knew that there was going to be trouble. She couldn't have him causing disruption in her house, what with Beatrice getting on her last nerve and Anthony needing so much love. She could only do so much. She had to set boundaries. She warned Michael about his attitude and tried to teach him to be thankful for what he had.

The trouble that comes is actually worse than she expected. She has never seen Michael be violent, and when his anger turns physical Momma J. is actually afraid. She doesn't have the strength she once had. She feels vulnerable. Out of the clear blue one day Michael just got crazy and busts up a lamp. Like some kind of alien she doesn't know. After all she has done for him too. But, it could have been worse. Luckily, Momma J. still has some of her athletic ability and she is able to intervene before he hurts someone and wastes a pot of her delicious home cooked chili. Thanks to her swift response, Michael doesn't seriously burn someone.

Momma J. does not hesitate to call the social worker. "You come take this child immediately. After all I have done for him; I will not let him destroy my home and threaten my family. He needs to get some kind of help." She is convinced it is the best thing for everyone. She hugs him warmly goodbye, then waits for the call from her daughter.[16]

> ### *Placement Disruption*
>
> *There are many negative outcomes associated with multiple placements for youth in care. What, if anything, could the State have done to prevent placement instability for Michael?*

---

15. Nineteen states and the District of Columbia require relative caretakers to be certified as a foster care home. Roughly half of them, however, will temporarily approve placements during the licensing process. CHILD WELFARE INFORMATION GATEWAY, *supra* note 14, at 3.

16. Behavior related disruptions have been found more likely to occur amongst older children and shortly after entering out of home care. James, Sigrid, *Why Do Foster Care Placements Disrupt? An Investigation of Reasons for Placement Change in Foster Care*, 78(4) SOC. SERV. REV. 601 (2004).

"Momma how *could* you??" Michelle is crying on the other end of the phone. She is always crying these days.

Momma J. is resolute. "I told you I can't do it anymore. That boy is not right. He used to be so sweet, but he got violent. He isn't safe here. I'm not sayin' he is always gonna be that way, but I can't take it right now.[17] I gotta focus on my other responsibilities. I gotta protect the other kids. He's gonna be fine. You just gotta get your shit together and get him home with you. You can't be puttin' all this on me. You know it's about you. You know what you gotta do. You gotta stop just cryin' and get away from all that shit. When are you gonna do that? When?"[18]

The phone went dead.

The Dependency CASA Volunteer's Story: Ellen Anderson, CASA for Aliyah, Angel and Deja

At 58 years old, Ellen Anderson still thinks about getting her license to be a foster parent again but she knows that it isn't realistic. Ellen's two grown children are back home living with her — part of the "boomerang generation"[19] — and her elderly parents require a lot of her time. So she settles for her role as a volunteer Court Appointed Special Advocate ("CASA") representing the best interests of foster children in dependency court proceedings.[20]

Still, Ellen regrets not taking in foster children after she lost her husband. Charlie was not really up for caring for other people's children. She could have pushed him — he was a kind and generous man. But Charlie was fearful of becoming too attached to children who would be with them only temporarily. Ellen knew that pain and

---

17. A growing body of research on the adolescent brain has revealed the neurobiological changes that underlie the risky behaviors and emotional reactivity that characterize this developmental period. Adolescents are prone to suboptimal decision-making, particularly in emotionally charged situations. B.J. Casey et al., *The Adolescent Brain*, 1124 ANN. N Y ACAD. SCI. 111 (2008).

18. While federal policy has long encouraged relative placement, research is mixed on whether kinship care provides more placement stability. While some studies have found that children are less likely to disrupt from kinship care, particularly for behavioral reasons, a review of 26 studies on placement disruption found that kinship care was not a significant protective factor. Oosterman, et al., *Disruptions in Foster Care: A Review and Meta-analysis*, 29 CHILD. AND YOUTH SERV. REV. 53 (2007). There are studies that show children initially placed in kinship foster homes are more likely to remain in their initial placement than children placed in non-kinship foster homes. *See* Koh, Eun, *Permanency Outcomes of Children in Kinship and Non-kinship Foster Care: Testing the External Validity of Kinship Effects*, 32(3) CHILD. AND YOUTH SERV. REV. 389 (2010). Research on African American kinship caregivers show that they tend to be older and in poorer health, which may present obstacles to effective foster parenting. *See* Anne K. Rufa & Patrick J. Fowler, *Kinship Foster Care Among African American Youth: Interaction effects at Multiple Contextual Levels*, 42(1) J. SOC. SERV. RES., 26 (2016).

19. A 2012 report by the Pew Research Center found 29% of young adults lived with their parents, up from 11% in 1980. KIM PARKER, THE BOOMERANG GENERATION: FEELING OKAY ABOUT LIVING WITH MOM AND DAD, Pew Research Center (2012) [https://perma.cc/87KF-3UQ4].

20. For a discussion of the role of CASA, see ch. 1 — *CAPTA: Child Protective Services*; and *Counsel for Youth in Dependency*. *See About Us*, CASA: Court Appointed Special Advocates for Children, [https://perma.cc/9RDF-NBGU?type=image].

couldn't in good conscience bring it upon her partner. After he died too young from a heart attack, Ellen briefly entertained fostering children again, but she knew that it wasn't the answer to her immobilizing grief. Widowed at 55, she was unprepared for the rest of her life. Financially she would be fine. She would be more than fine with Charlie's substantial life insurance policy and several other investments. He was a planner. An aero-space engineer who loved his job and made a comfortable living which allowed her to quit her job as a nurse to devote her time to raising their children. That was more than 25 years ago now—she can hardly remember what she did when she worked in the intensive care unit.

Before Ellen began dating Charlie, she was a young nurse, working long days and happy to have only her cat to look after. She was naturally a caretaker, and she gave 100% to her career—caring for patients who were often suspended between life and death. Standing beside worried spouses, parents, sons and daughters she channeled a calm presence beyond her years. She will never forget meeting Clara, a three-year-old who came in to the ICU to see her mother who was in a coma. She came with a young woman who did not appear related to her. Ellen learned that this was her CPS worker. Clara's mother, who suffered from a tragic and unexpected amniotic embolus while giving birth to her second child, had no partner or family to care for Clara. Clara's dark eyes, tiny frame, hopeful voice, "Hi Mom," drew Ellen in immediately. As Ellen slowly answered Clara's questions about the machines and tubes that protruded from her mother, Clara grabbed Ellen's hand and held it tightly. That small hand, reaching for comfort in a strange and frightening place, attached Ellen to Clara forever.

Ellen asked the CPS worker what would become of Clara if her mother died, which she knew was likely imminent. The CPS worker said, sounding very tired, "We're looking for a foster parent who can care for her for at least 90 days while we search for family. Right now she is in a receiving home that will have to give her up after 30 days."[21]

Without thinking Ellen blurted, "How about me? Can I take her?" The CPS worker looked surprised, raising her eyebrows inquisitively. Ellen continued, "I mean, I don't know if you have to check my house or what, but I have a lot of experience taking care of kids and if I could figure out child care while I am at work I think we would get along really well." Ellen could barely believe what she was saying. Her words hung in the air and, strangely, she did not want to pull them back. Something about that delicate and vulnerable three-year-old hand wrapped around hers changed everything. Ellen did not want to let go.

As it turned out, back then nurses in her jurisdiction did not need to be licensed to have children temporarily placed in their care by the State so long as they agreed to

---

21. Some states have specific categories of foster care, such as "Receiving Care" or "Emergency Foster Care" that focus on short-term care at initial placement. *See e.g.*, Wash. St. Dep't Soc. & Health Serv., Washington State Children's Administration Practices and Procedures Guide, § 4528, [https://perma.cc/3S6Q-T9AX]; 55 Pa. Code § 3130.37.

go through the licensing process.[22] Two-and-a-half weeks after she impulsively offered her services, Clara came to live with Ellen and her cat in her two-bedroom apartment. The next five months were a blur. A joyful, poignant, exhausting, invigorating blur. And then it ended, almost as abruptly as it began. A caseworker called her one day and said, simply, "We found Clara's great aunt. She wants her to come live with her as soon as possible." And just like that, within a week, little Clara with a duffle bag of still-newish clothes and toys, was whisked away.

Licensing Requirements for Foster Parents

- *Does your jurisdiction have different criteria for licensing certain types of professionals for foster care?*

- *Should there be exceptions for non-state licensed individuals to care for children? Why or why not?*

Ellen's heart was broken, but she was not one to brood or to sit still. Having now been licensed as a foster parent, Ellen decided she would make herself available to take in another child. Her friends and family were baffled by her decision. They were unsuccessful in discouraging her. *You are young and single, you should be having fun! You will just get hurt again. You will never get a date, much less a boyfriend or husband.* Ignoring all the warnings, Ellen fostered four more children over the next year and a half, all infants with medical needs. The Department was thrilled to have a nurse who could care for this difficult-to-place group. Ellen liked caring for babies — she found infants did not leave a gaping hole in her heart like Clara had when it came time to turn them over to their parents, relatives or to foster parents interested in adoption.[23] She probably would have kept it up, but she decided to take a break after she began dating Charlie. She still laughs when she thinks about the look on his face when he was dropping her off after their second date and the babysitter opened the door and handed Ellen a crying infant.

---

22. States may grant waivers to licensing requirements for foster parents and vary considerably in how they do so. ANA BELTRAN & HEIDI REDLICH EPSTEIN, AMERICAN BAR ASSOCIATIONN CENTER ON CHILDREN, IMPROVING FOSTER CARE LICENSING STANDARDS AROUND THE UNITED STATES: USING RESEARCH FINDINGS TO EFFECT CHANGE (2012) [https://perma.cc/G7B5-WUTP].

23. In 2015, over 52,000 children in the United States were adopted from the foster care system. *See* U.S. DEP'T OF HEALTH AND HUMAN SERV., ADMINISTRATION FOR CHILDREN AND FAMILIES, ADMINISTRATION ON CHILDREN, YOUTH AND FAMILIES, CHILDREN'S BUREAU, ADOPTION AND FOSTER CARE ANALYSIS AND REPORTING SYSTEM, AFCARS REPORT (2016), [https://perma.cc/L8R2-JC96]. In an effort to eliminate delays in permanency for children in foster care, the concept of "concurrent planning" is used to pursue all possible options for a child while pursuing reunification. To that end, some states will place children whose parents have a "poor prognosis for reunification" with foster families who are willing to adopt should reunification efforts fail. *See* CHILD WELFARE INFORMATION GATEWAY, U.S. DEP'T OF HEALTH & HUMAN SERVS., CONCURRENT PLANNING: WHAT THE EVIDENCE SHOWS, CHILD WELFARE INFORMATION GATEWAY ISSUE BRIEF, April 2012, [https://perma.cc/6FBX-UAV6].

> ### *Foster Parents and Concurrent Planning*
>
> *Foster parents are put in the position of supporting reunification efforts while caring for foster children as their own. Sometimes they are asked to be willing and ready to adopt a foster child that cannot go home. How do you think foster parents balance these competing concerns?*

"Oh, gosh, I guess I forgot to tell you. I'm a foster parent. I take care of infants for the state. Just temporarily." Charlie, without meaning to, started to slowly back away. *Oh no, my friends were right.* Ellen knew right then that she was going to have to make a choice, and it was easy. Charlie. Three months after that awkward end to their second date, Ellen packed up a diaper bag with a few items and took her last foster child to the DCFS office. She didn't wait to meet the new foster parents. Charlie was outside in the car, which was packed with camping gear for their weekend in the mountains.

Three decades later, Ellen has a more complete understanding of the system that places children in her care. She was fairly oblivious back then—caseworkers brought babies to her home and picked them back up. She knew nothing about their mothers or fathers except what might be inferred from the descriptors "drug-addicted" or "mentally ill." Sometimes she heard about a sibling, but usually in the context of "can you take one more?" She never saw a courtroom or really had any clue about what took place there. Once, a State's attorney called to ask about her availability to testify in a trial. She was terrified by the prospect and, fortunately, the case settled the day before she was scheduled to appear in court.

Now, after two years as a CASA, Ellen is reasonably comfortable appearing in juvenile court. While she doesn't love it, she is no longer terrified of speaking to judges or lawyers. She prefers the part of her volunteer job where she talks to parents and children. Being a CASA is less time consuming than being a foster parent, but it actually seems harder. Listening to all the different stories, sifting through the often-contradictory evidence and then having to make a life altering recommendation that will likely be followed by a judge—weighs heavy on her.[24]

---

24. In a 2004 study, researchers found that in 71% of cases, judges followed all of the CASAs recommendations. Caliber Associates, Evaluation of CASA Representation Final Report, 30 (2004). The same study found CASA volunteers spent an average of 3.22 hours per case per month. *Id.* at 15. CASA volunteers spent one hour less per month on African American children's cases. *Id.* at 22.

> ### CASAs and Volunteer Guardians ad Litem
>
> * *Does your jurisdiction have a CASA program or a volunteer guardian ad litem ("GAL") program to represent the best interests of children in the dependency system?*
>
> * *How do they operate?*
>
> * *What are the pros and cons of your system of child representation?*

Another thing about being a CASA that differed from her foster parent experience all those years ago is the training she receives. Thirty years ago, the foster parent training was minimal. It was mostly around basic childcare, safety, and some cursory information about the legal processes.[25] As a CASA she is required to take a full week of training, which includes topics that are new to her. A half-day of training was dedicated to "cultural competence." She heard about the challenges that arise because of the differences between the race and backgrounds of CASAs and the children they serve.[26] An African American CPS worker spent an hour explaining the history of how black children and families have been treated by the State over the past century.[27] It is the first time that Ellen has been confronted with the racial disparities in the foster care system. She had actually never thought about it, even though three of the five children she had fostered were black. And she lives in a very white city.

Ellen isn't sure what to do with this information. She feels something. Is it guilt? It is uncomfortable. But why should she feel guilty? She is trying to help.[28] She doesn't care whether the children are black or white. She just wants them to be safe. Is it anger? She was taught to be colorblind. Why is there a woman now drawing attention to the color of the children that she is there to help? Why does it feel like the rules are

---

25. Today, states vary considerably in the amount of training they provide and/or require for licensed foster parents. Forty-seven states have laws or regulations that require pre-licensing training, but the minimum number of hours ranges from no minimum requirement (19 states) to 22–30 hours (8 states). Ana Beltran & Heidi Redlich Epstein, *Improving Foster Care Licensing Standards Around the United States*, 31(6) CHILD LAW PRACTICE NEWSLETTER 93 (March 2012), [https://perma.cc/T8HT-25PR].

26. CASA volunteers are overwhelmingly white and female. According to a 2012 report, nearly 82% of all CASA volunteers are white. A similar percentage of volunteers are women. They tend to be older individuals. About one quarter are retirees. Only 11% are in their twenties; 14% in their thirties; 18% in their forties; 23% in their fifties; and 34% were 60 or older. The most commonly held profession, whether currently employed or retired, is that of teacher, followed by medical professional. *See* THE NATIONAL CASA ASSOCIATION, NATIONAL CASA ANNUAL LOCAL PROGRAM SURVEY REPORT 2012 (2012), [https://perma.cc/W2GA-LXW7].

27. *See* ch. 1—*A Brief History of State Intervention*; GEOFF K. WARD, THE BLACK CHILD-SAVERS: RACIAL DEMOCRACY AND JUVENILE JUSTICE 52–54 (2012).

28. Group-based guilt, such as guilty feelings one might feel for being white, is considered a self-focused emotion that may be less useful than other-focused emotions, such as empathy, as a motivator to support efforts for racial equality. A. Iyer et al., *White Guilt and Racial Compensation: The Benefits and Limits of Self-focus*, 29(1) PERSONALITY AND SOC. PSYCH. BULL. 117 (2003).

changing, that she is now supposed to notice race? Why does she feel like she is being treated like she is doing something wrong?[29]

> ### *Racial Demographics of Courtroom Advocates for Children*
>
> - *If your jurisdiction has a CASA or volunteer GAL program, how are volunteers recruited and trained?*
>
> - *How do the racial demographics of the foster care children in your jurisdiction compare to the racial demographics of the CASAs or GALs?*
>
> - *Do these differences matter?*
>
> - *What might be done to address these differences?*

Ellen is immediately taken in by Aliyah and Angel Griffith. They are smart, funny and kind. Some of the children she represents are withdrawn and sullen—she assumes because of the abuse they endured. In contrast, Aliyah and Angel are shy at first, but warm up quickly, unveiling wit and poise. Ellen instinctively assumes this is a result of their being raised well. Aliyah's first question to Ellen is "Do you have kids? What are they like? Do you know where they are right now?" Angel is more interested in Ellen's pets and whether she thinks that all children should have their own dog that they could keep with them no matter where they live. Ellen assumes they had a parent that nurtures in them strength, curiosity and manners. How could an unfit parent impart such qualities? The dissonance is confusing.

As Ellen gets to know the girls through regular check-ins, she learns that Aliyah and Angel are deeply connected to their mother Michelle and their brother Michael. They each tell story after story of how well Michelle and Michael take care of them, make them go to school, do their homework, do the dishes and all of the other things that they understand would signal positive parenting. They are hesitant to speak of DJ, Michelle's most recent partner, but they speak candidly about their mother's drug problem. "We know what to do when she is using drugs. Please. Don't think we are

---

29. The term "color-blind" to describe opposition to race based discrimination dates back to U.S. Supreme Court Justice Harlan's dissent in *Plessy v. Ferguson*, 163 U.S. 597, (1896) ("Our Constitution is color-blind, and neither knows nor tolerates classes among citizens. All citizens are equal before the law.") Today many legal scholars criticize "color-blind constitutionalism" and sociologists criticize color-blind ideology as perpetuating racism by ignoring the lived experiences of those who are not white. *See* Neil Gotanda, *A Critique of "Our Constitution is Color-Blind,"* 44 STAN. L. REV. 1 (1991); Adia Harvey Wingfield, *Colorblindness is Counterproductive*, THE ATLANTIC, September 13, 2015, [https://perma.cc /63RR-9GGC]. One example of how color-blindness operates in a counterproductive way is when a white person says to a person of color, "I don't think of you as [Black, Latino, etc.] This well-meaning 'compliment' suggests that there is something negative about being [Black, Latino, etc.] and that it is preferable to ignore the person's racial identity and think of the person as white."

just little children." At 10, Aliyah is remarkably convincing. She seems to be an old soul—something that Ellen finds both admirable and troubling.[30]

Ellen struggles with what the best is for the children. She wants very much to help Aliyah and Angel achieve their stated desire to be back together as a family. Still, she remains concerned about the allegations in the dependency petition regarding Aliyah's complaints about her mother's "scary boyfriends" who may have touched her. Ellen knows not to directly ask her about this,[31] but she also feels like Aliyah's unwillingness to talk about DJ is a clear indicator that he is perhaps the perpetrator. Aliyah has no real complaints about living with her father, Tommy, but she is clear that ultimately she belongs with her mother, brother and sisters. She is able to clearly articulate how she feels at her father's home: "I love my dad, but I don't really fit with his family." She talks optimistically and confidently about her future: "I think that this has been a good chance to get to know my dad better. But I can't stay there all the time, my mom will need me when she gets out of treatment and I need to be with her too."

Angel is also clear with Ellen about what she wants—to be with her mother and siblings—although she is more cautious than Aliyah. "Momma J. is doing a good job taking care of me. I don't mind staying a little longer with her just to make sure everything is ok." Ellen tries to figure out why Angel might be hesitant to be returned to her mother—and she really can't tell whether Angel has concerns about her mother's drug use, fear stemming from possible sexual abuse by DJ or whether she is worried about leaving Poochie the dog. Angel also adds, "I want Michael to come back. I think Momma J. is done being mad at him. And Aliyah should also come visit more."

> ### *CASAs and Conflicts*
> *Ellen represents the best interests of three different siblings in different placements. If conflicts arise between the siblings as to their best interests, how should she resolve them?*

---

30. The concept of childhood in Western culture has changed over time. Today, it is generally accepted that children should be cared for and excused from adult responsibilities like employment and sibling care, but that has not always been the case and is not necessarily the norm in non-Western cultures. "Adultification" occurs when children take on adult–like roles, and happens in various contexts, for example where families are economically stressed. Ethnographic studies of disadvantaged families suggest that eldest boys tend to become primary or secondary breadwinners or become their mother's confidant while eldest girls tend to take on domestic caretaking roles. There are risks associated with adultification, such as poor academic achievement, but there are also assets, such as self-confidence and problem-solving skills. The consequences of adultification are highly contextual. *See* L. Burton, *Childhood Adultification in Economically Disadvantaged Families: A Conceptual Model*, 56(4) FAM. REL. 329 (Oct. 2007), [https://perma.cc/5T8E-MGER].

31. THE NATIONAL CASA ASSOCIATION VOLUNTEER TRAINING CURRICULUM, VOLUNTEER MANUAL 2007 REVISION, V-12 [https://perma.cc/RX4Z-3AMU] ("Please note that it is not your role as a CASA/GAL volunteer to interview a child about the allegations; many of the children have been interviewed many times and additional interviews may be harmful to the child and to any potential criminal prosecution.").

Ellen tries to remember being seven and 10 years old. It is so long ago, but she is sure that she was never asked who she wanted to live with or whether she felt safe with her parents. Her clearest memories are of playing hide and seek with her three older sisters in the vacant lot behind their large suburban home.

Michael's Attorney Katie Olson: From Shelter Care to Dependence

It is difficult for Katie when there do not seem to be any good options for her clients—but it is worse when she knows that there might be but everyone is moving too fast and missing them. That's what she thought when Michael spoke up in court for his sisters during the shelter care hearing. How can she possibly have known to bring that up when she had just met her client and was handed a pile of discovery just minutes before the hearing? Three fathers, four children and years of abuse and neglect can hardly be digested in the time she has to prepare. It is only supposed to be "shelter care"—not permanent—no one is found "guilty." But she knows the importance of the first 90 days of an out-of-home placement.[32] Often that first hearing will set the tone for the whole case. Or not.

As much as Katie thrives on the exhilaration, the shelter care hearing is exhausting, as usual. She feels badly when she says good-bye to Michael after trying to explain the court's order. He looked shell-shocked. And who is she to comfort him? A stranger he met just hours ago. She teeters on that familiar precipice of incompetence. *What am I doing here?*

Katie has not yet had a real trial. She has had some contested disposition hearings where she cross-examined witnesses and put on evidence, but never a full fact-finding where she challenged the state's case in its entirety. More than 90% of dependency cases in Baker County are settled through agreed orders. There is no right to a jury and the burden of proof is so low for the state, just a "preponderance of the evidence," making it almost impossible for a parent to win.[33] Termination of parental rights cases are more likely to go to trial, but Katie has not yet had to handle one.

---

32. The National Council of Juvenile and Family Court Judges recommends that adjudication take place within 60 days of removal, citing the traumatic effect of removal and the imperative to hold a hearing as soon as is practical. NAT'L COUNCIL OF JUVENILE & FAMILY COURT JUDGES, RESOURCE GUIDELINES 47 (1995), [https://perma.cc/E7ZW-PNWP].

33. Dependency proceedings are civil so the civil standard of proof applies. The exception is for Indian children who fall under the Indian Child Welfare Act ("ICWA") where the standard of proof is clear and convincing. *See* ch. 1—*The Indian Child Welfare Act.* In most states, parents and children do not have a right to a jury in dependency or termination of parental rights cases. LINDA A. SZYMANKSI, NCJJ SNAPSHOT: IS A JURY TRIAL EVER AVAILABLE IN A TERMINATION OF PARENTAL RIGHTS CASE?, Nat'l Ctr. for Juvenile Justice, (2011), [https://perma.cc/4KJU-NYGA].

Dependency Trials

- *How often are trials held in your jurisdiction?*
- *Who presides over these trials?*
- *What types of cases go to trial versus settle?*

Michael's case settles. With his mom in in-patient treatment, there is no way to fight the finding of dependency. Capable or not, Michelle is clearly unavailable to parent. It is awkward when a youth wants to fight to go home and a parent is not available. It happens more often than Katie thought it would. She naively assumed that she would be helping to save children from evil parents, but more likely than not the child wants to go home.[34] The most unpleasant part of her job is when she has to tell a young person that their mom or dad cannot or will not take them, no matter how hard they fight the social worker. She hasn't figured out an effective way to cushion that blow of abandonment and betrayal. It doesn't seem to help to say to her client "Just wait, this is just temporary." Her strategy is usually to find something else to fight about—something where she can get a "win." Like increased visitation or a plan for return home written into the disposition order. That will give her client something to look forward to. She also tries to argue for positive language about the youth to be included in the court's orders—and will beat back any "services" that are onerous or unnecessary.

In Michael's case, visitation becomes the focus of Katie's advocacy. Michael basically checks out after the shelter care hearing. She struggles to get him to engage with her, even in person, and the only time he looks alive is when she discusses the opportunity to see his father in prison and the possibility of placement with his sisters. Although Michael is unwavering in expressing his desire to live with his mother, Katie also knows he is doing OK in Mr. Jeffries' foster home. They talk a lot about what it is like at Mr. Jeffries' house, how Michael spends his time, what he eats, where he sleeps, how he gets to school, what Mr. Jeffries is like, etc. Katie gives Michael plenty of opportunities to complain and he does not. Of course, that doesn't mean he is ecstatic to be there, but she knows that it is as tolerable as foster care might get for him. At least for now. Besides, he blew out of his grandmother's house in less than two weeks and he really doesn't have any other options. She will explore other relatives for him, but he can't give her any names. She got the social worker to track down his mom's cousin, Porsche, whose name came up at the shelter care hearing, but it turns out she has her hands full with two children and a recent CPS history of her own.

---

34. A survey of maltreated children emerging from dependency proceedings found that 77% felt positive or somewhat positive about seeing their parents in court, and 64% indicated that they wanted to return home immediately. Stephanie D. Block et al., *Abused and Neglected Children in Court: Knowledge and Attitudes*, 34 CHILD ABUSE & NEGLECT 659, 665 (2010).

Katie figures out that she can't get any useful information by just asking an adolescent whether or not they like their placement. She used to do this and found out that even if a client says "yes" it usually means "It's not so terrible that I want to tell you anything right now, can we stop talking?" The other problem is that an adamant "No" will lead to the inevitable question "Is it bad enough that you want to risk going somewhere potentially worse?" She usually has to ask a whole bunch of questions about what goes on there to get an idea of just how good or bad a placement is and whether she thinks she can do better for her client. For Michael, with no relatives willing to take him in, even if he isn't crazy about Mr. Jeffries' house, it is the "devil he knows" and he could do a lot worse. Just a few weeks back Katie had visited a client who was placed in a mobile home park two hours away from the city with about nine cats and the stench that goes with them. Foster care is a crapshoot. Michael was lucky.

> ### Narrative Interviewing: Listening for Story
>
> *Narrative interviewing seeks to develop the settings, scenes and characters of the client's story. It recognizes the many stories that are sometimes embedded in a client's simple statement. It also seeks to draw out from your client what s/he knows about the competing stories that could arise.*
>
> * *How does Katie use narrative interviewing with Michael?*

Settling a case means signing off on an Agreed Order of Dependency and an Order of Disposition, which then must get approved by the court. It probably doesn't take as long as preparing for and going to trial, but Katie thinks it must come close. She came into this work because she wants to interact with more people and less paper. Turns out she gets a whole lot of both.

Katie feels pretty good at talking to people and figuring out what motivates the different system players. She even gets comfortable arguing in court. What she doesn't love is spending hours staring at a computer screen reading lengthy boilerplate documents filled with words that real people don't actually use. "Someday," she thinks, "If I have any extra time I am going to start a campaign to put all of these forms we use in and out of court into plain English."[35] She wonders how children and their parents can be expected to understand all the legal terms and unfamiliar language. She suspects that they aren't. The child welfare system is really just a mechanism to control

---

35. There has been a recent movement to put court forms into plain language. *See* Dyer, Charles et al., *Improving Access to Justice: Plain Language Family Court Forms in Washington State*, 11 Seattle J. for Soc. Just. 1065 (2013). A study conducted in California tested the benefits of plain language using a Proof of Service form. Only 23% of the participants tested on the original form were able to state what its purpose was—but 70% understood the purpose of the plain language form. "Since research shows us that readers who cannot determine a document's basic purpose typically abandon further reading, the original forms appear to be of little value." Mindlin, Maria, *Is Plain Language Better? A Comparative Readability Study of Court Forms*, 10 Scribes J. Legal Writing 55, 60–61 (2006).

the poor and to police their families.[36] *Does she really think that? So depressing and not even a year into her career. How can she be a part of this?*

One of Katie's least favorite reading assignments is a lengthy document entitled "Individual Service and Safety Plan" or "ISSP" for short. An ISSP is a multi-page fillable document social workers are required to complete prior to each dependency court hearing. If the child has been in the system a long time, it means that many different social workers have updated the document, which increases the likelihood that there are errors. Katie finds them impossible to read. She will page through until she gets to the "narrative" section — the only part that usually describes what is actually going on with the youth and the parents. Most of the document is boilerplate with checked boxes to meet federal reporting requirements.[37] She imagines that the social workers who labor over these tedious missives enjoy them about as much as she does.

The narrative section in Michael's ISSP submitted before the dependency pre-trial conference says:

> *Michael continues to reside at Mr. Jeffries' foster home after a short failed placement with his maternal grandmother. He attends Adams Middle School where he is in the 7th grade. He is struggling with math but will be provided an after-school tutor. He likes music and will hopefully be participating in the school band. He visits weekly with his mother and sisters. He has expressed an interest in visiting with his father, who is currently serving a sentence at Brannan Hills Correctional Facility.*

Reading this for the first time, Katie feels inadequate, again. She didn't know Michael likes music. Why didn't that ever come up? So much for her rapport-building skills, she decides she will try to bond with him about music next time. She loves music. Probably not the same music as Michael, but at least it is something.

Agency Reports

Federal law requires written case plans for dependent children.

- *What do agency reports look like in your jurisdiction?*
- *When and how do lawyers, parents and other parties receive them?*
- *Do caseworkers provide youth with copies of these reports?*

Similar to the book-length ISSP's, dependency court orders also ramble on for pages. The AAGs draft them and email them to the attorneys in advance of the

---

36. *See* Dorothy E. Roberts, *Prison, Foster Care, and the Systematic Punishment of Black Mothers*, 59 Ucla L. Rev. 1474 (2012).

37. Title IV-E of the Social Security Act (SSA) requires each state that receives funds for substitute-care services to establish a written case plan for each child in substitute care. 42 U.S.C. §671(a)(16). The act also requires each state to establish a case review system. *Id.* For more about the influence of Federal legislation on State dependency systems, see ch. 1 — *The Federal Statutes that Drive the State Systems.*

pre-trial conference. Like the ISSP, the dependency order is generally written in boilerplate language that is indecipherable to regular people. Katie is ethically obligated to make sure that her clients understand these orders before signing them. It is a pain. She has yet to get a child client to read through the entire order with her. She is pretty sure that adult clients don't read the orders either.

She does not make Michael read the entire draft dependency order and she also spares him the trip to court. She meets with him at his foster home where they talk generally about the order that will be entered and she points out sections while Michael glances at it from a distance. It is a little risky not to have Michael present at the pre-trial conference in case issues come up that need his approval, but she figures in this case she has a pretty good feel for what they will be able to get changed in the order — which is not much. She knows Michael wants to go home to his mother as soon as possible and wants as much contact with his sisters as possible if they cannot be placed together. She figures he does not have the interest or stamina to concern himself with the details of the dependency order, although her experience with him at the initial shelter care hearing showed her that he does care that his family is portrayed accurately.

> ### *Ethics, Client Authority and Communication*
>
> *Rule 1.2 of the Model Rules of Professional Conduct require a lawyer to abide by her client's decision to settle a matter and to consult with a client as to the means by which she pursues her client's objectives. Rule 1.4 requires a lawyer to keep her client "reasonably informed" about the status of a matter and to "explain a matter to the extent reasonably necessary to make informed decisions . . . ."*
>
> * *So far, has Katie complied with these Rules?*

Pre-trial conferences are held at the Baker County Juvenile and Family Justice Center every Thursday morning. Attorneys and social workers trickle in carrying thick files; prepared to negotiate more than one dependency order. These are hardly "conferences"—attorneys just crowd around outside of Courtroom 4 or 5 and shuttle orders around from party to party, negotiating while standing, or, if they were lucky, sitting in an interview room when they are able to snag one. The court's wishful thinking in establishing this procedure is that parties would negotiate over email or phone and show up at the pre-trial conference with signed orders ready to enter. If it is a particularly challenging case, or one that has been continued several times, an in-person meeting of the parties might take place at the AAG's office before the scheduled pre-trial conference date. This is exceedingly rare. More likely than not, attorneys are reviewing the draft orders with their clients for the first time that morning and madly crossing things out or scribbling in language in an effort to reach a resolution.

Katie hates this whole process. As a new attorney, she needs time to go over this unfamiliar language and she still feels uncomfortable, under any circumstances, signing court orders that will govern seemingly every aspect of her client's life for the next several months. *Who is she to do that?* Somehow, arguing in court and having the judge decide seems almost easier than having to painstakingly pour over and agree to pages of obscure language.

> ### Settlement Negotiations
>
> • *How are dependency cases resolved in your jurisdiction?*
>
> • *Many jurisdictions are using mediation to resolve dependency cases which can be very useful. Does this happen in your jurisdiction?*
>
> • *What is the role of the child's attorney?*

For the most part, Katie finds she has little negotiating power as the child's attorney with respect to the agreed "findings of fact" or any of the services that are being asked of the parents. She has some influence if her client is aligned with the State. Then the State might accommodate additional negative facts the child may want to add about the parents to support the finding of dependency. After all, children should have the most reliable evidence of their own victimization. But when a child wants to go home and the parent concedes unfitness, Katie has not figured out a way to bolster the parent up if her own attorney will not do it. She will always challenge facts in the findings that the child clearly states are not true. And, in Michael's case she is able to exclude some of the "lies" that he initially pointed out to her when they reviewed the dependency petition together before the shelter care hearing. She does not, however, manage to take out anything significant or get the findings to the short and innocuous format that she prefers. Why the AAGs insist on overdoing the factual findings she still can't grasp. They usually have the agreement of the parents and it often just seems like overkill — the equivalent of running up the score.[38]

> ### Dependency Findings
>
> • *In your jurisdiction, how detailed are the court's written findings?*
>
> • *Why might different parties want more or less specific findings?*

---

38. The National Council of Juvenile and Family Court Judges ("NCJFCJ") Enhanced Resource Guidelines for judges presiding over dependency proceedings addresses negotiated dependency findings: "Accepting pleas based on 'watered-down' facts compromises the court's ability to order appropriate services and ensure that the conditions that caused the child to come in to care have been ameliorated. . . . A clear record of the facts established at adjudication may be useful in later legal proceedings as it may foreclose later factual disputes or may provide important evidence which would otherwise be unavailable. *See* Sophie I. Gatowsk et al., Enhanced Resource Guideline: Improving Court Practice in Child Abuse and Neglect Cases 180, National Council of Juvenile and Family Court Judges, [https://perma.cc/5BSL-7AF7].

Katie is also not particularly effective in weighing in on what the parent needs to do to have the child returned. That is, unless the child clearly expresses a desire not to go home. In those cases, if the child asserts that she doesn't want to return home until the parent does "X" the State seems happy to oblige by piling on service requirements. Otherwise, Katie is rarely even asked about what services a parent might need before reuniting with her clients.

In Michael's case, his mom's parenting deficiency is straightforward and Katie hates to see additional hurdles put up after she completes treatment. She is able to negotiate language in the order that reunification with Michael will be contingent only upon Mom's successful completion of in-patient substance abuse treatment and not on any additional court-ordered services, such as parenting classes or individual counseling. While she doesn't doubt every parent could benefit from a parenting class, these types of requirements just seem to be reflexive barriers the Department puts up out of habit. Removing that requirement is a small win, as they often are in this business.

The real haggling in Michael's case comes around the language concerning placement and visitation. Katie wants to get Michael what he wants — to go home as soon as soon as possible. She argues for the following language.

Placement:

☐   ☐ father ☐ legal custodian ☐ legal custodian ☐ guardian.

☒   shall have the authority to place and maintain the child in: DSHS which shall have the authority to place and maintain the child in:

> ☐   Relative placement with _____ (name).
>
> ☐   Placement with a suitable person: _____ (name).
>
> ☐   The home of an adoptive parent or other person with whom the child's siblings or half-siblings live.

☒ Licensed care: Licensed care:

>> ☐ investigation of relative placement options. investigation of relative placement options.
>> ☒ because there is no relative or other suitable person with whom the child has a relationship and who is willing, appropriate and available to care for the child.
>> ☐ because there is reasonable cause to believe that relative placement would jeopardize the safety or welfare of the child; and/or hinder efforts to reunite the parent(s) and child.

☒ Continuation of the ordered placement is subject to the following placement conditions:
The Department *shall* return Michael to his mother's care upon successful completion of in-patient treatment.

It is a non-starter. Katie gets the usual: "We don't know where his mother will be living, what type of follow-up program she will be required to do . . . blah blah blah." She settles for:

*The Department **has authority to** return Michael to his mother's care upon successful completion of in-patient treatment and proof of suitable housing.*

At least they won't have to come back to court before Michael can go home. Katie will probably still have to pressure the social worker to exercise her "authority" but it can happen sooner rather than later. She rarely gets the state's attorney to agree to "shall" language but she keeps trying. She hates orders that give so much power to the Department. They seem almost meaningless. Why not just enter an order that states "The Department can do whatever it wants"? She is sure the AAGs would be really happy with that.

With respect to visitation, it seems ridiculous that Michael, at 13 years old, should have to be supervised when he visits with his mother. Her issues are neglect—she neglected Michael and her other children when she was high. How this creates a risk during a visit, particularly one that will likely take place at a treatment facility, makes no sense. Nevertheless, the proposed language looks like this:

Visitation:

☒   children) and mother shall be as follows:

Weekly for at least one hour, supervised by a DSHS-approved supervisor. The Department has authority to liberalize.

Seriously? The language is applicable to all of the children—not taking into account their different needs or the well-established fact that visitation is critical to promoting reunification.[39] For the Department, it is most efficient to provide one visit for the family per week—within the standard contract of a service provider that provides transportation and supervision. Sadly, the Department gets away with this all of the time because of its "lack of resources." Efficiency rules the day. That means in order to get more visits, parents and children have to propose some arrangement that won't cost the Department anything. Katie hears that it hasn't always been this way. It depends on the state budget and even what time of year. This is one of Katie's pet issues. It seems to her very clear in the law that the Department cannot deprive the parents or children of visitation unless it is harmful to the children.[40] It does not say anywhere in the statute anything about depriving children of visits with their parents because the state has run out of money. Nevertheless, when Katie argues this point to judges she often gets exasperated looks and an unwillingness to enforce the statute. She doesn't let it get to her. She is willing to keep setting hearings to make the judges turn her down, because she knows

---

39. *See, e.g.,* S.J. Leathers, *Parental Visiting and Family Reunification*, 81 CHILD WELFARE 595 (2002) (finding that visiting frequency is highly predictive of reunification).

40. *See, e.g.,* WASH. REV. CODE § 13.34.135(2)(b)(ii)(C) ("Visitation may be limited or denied only if the court determines that such limitation or denial is necessary to protect the child's health, safety, or welfare."); CAL. WELF. & INST. CODE § 362.1(a)(1)(A) ("Visitation shall be as frequent as possible, consistent with the well-being of the child."); TEX. FAM. CODE § 262.115(c) (ensuring parents who pose no risk of harm can visit their children within five days of their removal from the home).

she is right. However, in Michael's case, given his aversion to court, his willingness to take public transportation and his amenable foster parent, they settle on this language:

> *The Department shall provide transportation for Michael for weekly visits with his mother for at least one hour. Michael and his mother may arrange additional visits in consultation with the mother's treatment providers and Michael's foster parent and treatment providers (if any). The Department reserves the right to set a contested hearing regarding visitation should the mother become non-compliant with services.*

This allows Michael to take the bus to his mother's residential treatment facility after school or on weekends, so long as her counselors there say that it is OK. The visits have already been occurring there, and Michael indicates that they were going fine and he would go more often if he is allowed. This language also left things pretty open for when his mother completes in-patient treatment, so long as she remains compliant with services—which means staying drug free.

Katie is also able to get the Department to agree to set up monthly phone visits between Michael and his father in prison. A real victory would have been to get a face to face visit ordered, but given that it has been years since Michael has seen his father and it is a five-hour drive to the facility, it seems unlikely a judge will order it.[41] Katie will fight that battle in the future if she needs to. Since Michael has not yet even spoken with his father, she does not want to commit him to an in-person visit even though she suspects he might jump at the opportunity.

---

41. The location of a many prisons in rural areas contributes to the low rates of visits incarcerated parents have with the children. In 2004, over 60% of incarcerated parents were housed more than 100 miles from their home and less than half of all incarcerated parents had a personal visit with their children—a 10% decrease from 1997. SARAH SCHIRMER ET AL., INCARCERATED PARENTS AND THEIR CHILDREN: TRENDS 1991–2007, The Sentencing Project (2009) [https://perma.cc/E7HJ-FMXC]. Some states have statutes specifically addressing the services to be offered to incarcerated parents, including visitation. *See* CAL. WELF. & INST. CODE § 361.5(e)(1) (outlining reasonable services to incarcerated parents, including visitation). Courts have also addressed what services are reasonably required where a parent is incarcerated. *See, e.g.,* State in Interest of A.T., 353 P.3d 131, 135 (Utah 2015) (A juvenile court must order reasonable services for an incarcerated parent only when reunification is consistent with the primary permanency goal established by the court."); New Jersey Div. of Youth and Family Services v. R.G., 217 N.J. 527, 563, 217 A.3d 1258 (NJ 2014) (Where incarcerated father's release was imminent and he exhibited efforts and a willingness to reunify, the state's failure to do more than speak to the father on the phone and complete two psychological evaluations did not constitute reasonable efforts to provide reunification services, citing to several suggested services such as visitation, collect telephone calls and transportation to court proceedings.).

> ### *Parental Visitation*
>
> - *Are there laws or policies in your jurisdiction that govern the amount of visitation parents and children have in dependency proceedings?*
>
> - *Do these policies or laws take into consideration the child's age?*
>
> - *How does the court determine whether visits must be supervised?*
>
> - *Who provides supervision?*
>
> - *Are there laws, policies or practices that address visiting parents who are incarcerated?*

Last but certainly not least, Katie has to address sibling visitation.[42] She knows this is going to be a real problem with four children living in separate placements. Mom has the baby, Deja, staying with her in treatment. That visit will be fairly easy as long as Michael is visiting regularly with his mother. Visits with Aliyah can get tricky. She went to live with her father Tommy Sykes right after the shelter care hearing and now her lawyer is requesting a trial. The Department doesn't really have anything on Tommy as an unfit parent, but from what Katie can tell he does not have an order giving him custody of Aliyah except the shelter care order. If Aliyah's case is dismissed, Michelle will still have a right to parent unless Tommy has a custody order limiting her rights.[43] This is really complicated — Katie is concerned that if Tommy just goes away with Aliyah and her case is dismissed, Michael has no guarantee he can see her. Katie isn't sure she can do anything to stop that from happening. This must be why she hears some people call dependency proceedings "poor people's family court." Tommy will likely have to agree to remain in the dependency proceeding to protect Aliyah from her mother until he can get an order in family court giving him full custody. It is unclear to Katie how he will do that. She thinks that it is in Michael's interest that Aliyah be found dependent so that the Department would be on the hook for providing visits, but that doesn't strike her as quite right either.[44]

---

42. 42 U.S.C. § 671(31) (When siblings are placed separately the state must make reasonable efforts "to provide for frequent visitation or other ongoing interaction between the siblings, unless that State documents that frequent visitation or other ongoing interaction would be contrary to the safety or well-being of any of the siblings.").

43. *See* Unif. Child Abduction Prevention Act § 2 cmt. (Nat'l Conf. of Comm'rs on Unif. State Laws 2006) ("Generally both parents have the right to companionship and access to their child unless a court states otherwise.).

44. Dependency courts often have exclusive jurisdiction over dependent children, which usually means that custody determinations cannot be made by family courts without express authority. *See* Wash. Rev. Code § 13.04.030 (The juvenile court has exclusive jurisdiction to establish the custody of dependent children unless concurrent jurisdiction is granted by the court.) *See also* Leonard Edwards, *Moving Cases from Juvenile to Family Court: How Mediation Can Help,* 16 U.C. Davis J. of Juv. L. & Pol'y 536 (2012), [https://perma.cc/K85B-4C82] (Discussing how family courts modify juvenile court dependency orders regarding custody in California.).

> ### *Dependent Children and Parenting Plans*
> *Children often come into the child welfare system with informal custody arrangements between their parents and/or other guardians. The dependency proceeding often provides the first formal legal framework for custody and visitation between parents.*
> - *How are these types of cases handled in your jurisdiction?*
> - *How should they be handled?*

Finally there is Angel. She is still with grandma—but who knows how long that will last? Momma J. seems pretty volatile. She didn't hesitate to kick Michael out and Katie is convinced she could do the same to Angel. That whole episode is really frustrating. Katie didn't even get a call from the caseworker until several days later after there was nothing she could do.[45] Not that she could have stopped it. One time Katie did successfully mediate a dispute with a relative caregiver. That was one of her better moments—sitting down with her client and her client's aunt at their kitchen table until they reached an agreement that would allow the client to stay at her aunt's. They put together a written plan for what to do when they got into a fight. Katie wonders if she could have done that for Michael with Momma J.? Anyway, it seems to Katie like lawyers for the kids are the last to hear about things. She tells Michael to call her if there are any problems, but of course he didn't. A 13-year-old boy doesn't just naturally think, "Hey, I'm feeling upset and uncomfortable here living with my resentful grandmother, perhaps I should call my attorney." Katie figures she should just be thankful that the social worker doesn't trash on Michael in the ISSP by including unflattering details about the incident with Momma J. But now she wonders whether Momma J. will be an obstacle when it comes to facilitating visits between Michael and Angel. Katie thinks maybe she should have called Momma J. herself. She shudders at the thought.[46]

The AAG's proposed language on sibling visitation includes transportation for weekly visits for Michael and his sisters, which is probably the most that they can hope for. She is also able to get the AAG to agree to language which will encourage the children's caretakers to arrange for "additional visits whenever possible." It probably won't happen, but it will be good to have it in the order when, in the future, Katie will have to set a contested hearing to make the visits actually happen.[47]

---

45. Different jurisdictions have laws, regulations or policies with respect to whether and how lawyers receive notice about their child clients' placement. *Compare* Del. Code tit. 29, §9007A(c) (agency must give "reasonable notice" of changes in placement), *with* 42 Pa. Cons. Stat. §6311(b)(6) (agency must notify at "the earliest possible date" of any plan to relocate).

46. The ABA promulgated standards for representing youth discuss a lawyer's duty to investigate, which includes interviewing, among others, relatives. *Standards of Practice for Lawyers Who Represent Children in Abuse and Neglect Cases, Standard C-2(6) Investigate,* ABA (Feb. 5, 1996), [https://perma.cc/U7FX-XT3G].

47. The procedures for reviewing dependency court orders vary and are largely governed by local practice. Some local jurisdictions have developed procedural rules for bringing contested matters

> ### *Sibling Visitation*
>
> • *Does your state have laws giving siblings the right to visitation? What do the laws require?*
>
> • *How is sibling visitation facilitated in your jurisdiction?*
>
> • *Do children have the ability to enforce their right to sibling visitation? If so, how?*

In negotiating visits, Katie has to interact with the girls' CASA, Ellen Anderson. Katie is disappointed. She runs into her in the hallway as the proposed dependency and disposition orders are being shuffled from party to party. Granted, she has some biases against CASAs because she feels that they generally impose their white middle-class values inappropriately through their "best interests" recommendations to the court.[48] But why can't she find a CASA who is ready to take the State on with respect to the issue of sibling visitation? Why do CASAs buy into the resource excuse and not work hard to keep siblings' relationships in tact? At least that is her experience so far, which admittedly is limited. When Katie asks her about advocating for more family visits, Ellen Anderson actually says "I think it might be good for the girls to have a break from each other and the trauma that they experienced together living with their mother." *What kind of bullshit is that?* Siblings need each other to get through the trauma of separation from their families! What can she possibly be thinking? Katie holds her tongue and writes Ellen off, realizing that it isn't helpful to her client to get angry or engage on this issue at this time. She settles for the weekly visits between Michael and his sisters and goes on her way.

Katie is just wrapping up a conversation with mom's attorney, George, about when his client will be done with treatment, when the AAG, Mike Stevenson, pokes his head into the attorney room and says, "Are you guys ready yet? Jeez, what else could you possibly want?" His tone is joking—or so Katie thinks. They all want to be done. It is lunchtime.

Katie replies, "If George is ready, I am ready. I have to defer to his judgment on most of this stuff." Katie needs George to work hard for his client, so she is happy to suck up. "I just need to make a call to my client."

George is paging through the order and doesn't look up. He says, "If you sign, I will get my client's signature."

Katie sends a text to Michael: "Call me. Katie." She has pre-arranged this with Michael and his school so that Michael won't have to come to court. She isn't sure if it will really work. When Michael receives the text he is supposed to ask his teacher if

---

before the court. *See, e.g.,* KING COUNTY LJuCR 3.12, [https://perma.cc/8EXQ-BPLH]; 3 SNOHOMISH COUNTY LJuCR 3.9(c), [https://perma.cc/HH3P-55JW].

48. For a critique of CASA program from a critical race perspective, see Amy Mulzer & Tara Urs, *However Kindly Intended: Structural Racism and Volunteer CASA Programs*, 20 CUNY L. REV. 23 (2017).

he can make an important phone call and his teachers are supposed to have been advised by the school counselor that this is okay. Katie is not surprised when 15 minutes pass and there is no call. She knew it was a long shot.

She reviews the order again, with all of the changes and then reviews the notes from her meeting with Michael. She looks at her phone one last time—no message. She sighs.

Copy Received; Approved for Entry; Notice of Presentation Waived:

_____

Signature of **Child**
☒ Signature of Child's Lawyer
Katherine Olson
Print Name
Bar No.70652

_____

☐ **Mother** Mother
☐ Pro Se, Advised of Right to Counsel

_____

☒ Signature of Mother's Lawyer
George Bowman
Print Name
Bar No.10894

_____

☐ **Father** Father

_____

☐ Signature of Father's Lawyer
☐ Pro Se, Advised of Right to Counsel

_____

Print Name
Bar No.

Ethics and Client Authority (Again)

MR 1.2 allocates authority to clients to settle matters and MR 1.4 imposes a "reasonableness" standard with respect to communicating with clients in order to allow them to make decisions.

- *Did Katie comply with the Model Rules here?*
- *Did she make the right decision to allow Michael to skip the dependency hearing, given her concerns that the phone call wouldn't work?*

Part 2: Living as a Dependent Child

Michael: Dependent and in Foster Care (Again)

Michael wakes up to the smell of bacon. This no longer takes him by surprise. After more than three months of living with Mr. Jeffries, he has become accustomed to the smell of bacon signaling Saturday morning. Weekdays bring cold cereal for breakfast, but Saturdays mean bacon, eggs and pancakes. Usually at least two or three of Mr. Jeffries' grown children come by and fill the kitchen before Michael makes it downstairs.

The three months at Mr. Jeffries' house are not uninterrupted. About one week after the shelter care hearing, Michael carried a duffle bag full of his only belongings to his grandmother's where the court had ordered the Department to place him if she was "available." He had lived with Momma J. several times before, usually when his mother was on a crack binge or in an in-patient treatment program. Once they were just homeless—after his mother's clean and sober housing ran out and they didn't have enough money for first and last month's rent. Momma J's patience with her daughter's addiction wore thin over the years. Actually, Momma J never had much patience that Michael could remember. At the hospital just after Deja was born she announced clearly and loudly for Michael and all the world to hear, "You will not dump these kids on me one more time. I have my own life and I won't let you ruin it *again*!" Michael wondered how many times his mother had ruined Momma J's life already, but he knew better than to wonder about this out loud.

When Emily dropped Michael off at Momma J's, Angel was already there curled up on the couch with Poochie the terrier, watching cartoons. Emily had somehow talked Momma J into taking both of them, once Michelle entered a 90-day in-patient treatment program. "Three months," said Momma J to Emily as she hugged Michael. "And I need those food coupons. I can't afford to be feeding two more mouths with no help."[49] To Michael, Momma J was a complicated mix of love and hate. She had a big, warm embrace and always smelled like vanilla—but her words could cut you like a knife even as you leaned into her protective embrace. She did not hide her disdain for taking in her grandchildren, or her pleasure in being a rescuer. His stomach tightened even as he melted into her sturdy arms.

Less than two weeks later, Michael's duffle bag was packed again. When Reggie arrived in his Toyota, Michael was sitting on Momma J's front porch leaning on his

---

49. RTI INT'L & UNIV. OF N.C. AT CHAPEL HILL, CHILDREN IN TEMPORARY ASSISTANCE FOR NEEDY FAMILIES (TANF) CHILD-ONLY CASES WITH RELATIVE CAREGIVERS 3–18 (2004), [https://perma.cc/BFY2-RUGQ]. In the case of food assistance, however, relative caregivers eligible for child-only TANF might not qualify if they exceed the income limits. And whereas all states provided cash assistance as recently as the mid-2000s, recent studies have noted that some states—Arizona, Oregon, Nevada, and Washington—now limit their child-only grants to relative caregivers with very low incomes. OLIVIA GOLDEN & AMELIA HAWKINS, URBAN INST., TANF CHILD-ONLY CASES 3 (2012), [https://perma.cc/7NGF-GQW2]. For a broader look at the evolving politics of the food stamp program over time, including how it has been constrained by different methods of financing, see RONALD F. KING, BUDGETING ENTITLEMENTS: THE POLITICS OF FOOD STAMPS (2000).

belongings. The day before, Momma J was going off about Michelle, what a "horrible crack whore" she was and telling Angel that she better watch out or she might turn out the same as her "sorry ass mother." Michael snapped. He is angry at his mother, but he still misses her terribly and can not bear Momma J's hateful tirade. It is like something tore inside him. He watched his hands reach out and grab a lamp that stood next to the living room couch and he threw it full force against the wall. The light bulb exploded and went out. That explosion gave Michael a strange feeling of light-ness. Angel screamed. Michael watched, as if out of body, as his arms stretched out reaching for the pot of chili simmering on the stove. Momma J's thick forearm came down hard on Michael's wrist before he could grab the pot handle and pull it to the floor. "That's it." Momma J. shrieked. "You're done!" She grabbed Michael's elbow and twisted, pulling him toward the couch. She shoved him down next to Angel who was crying and sucking her thumb. She is surprisingly strong for a woman who com-plains frequently about her aging joints.

Michael does not have a lot of feelings when he got into Reggie's Toyota. He is numb. He definitely does not want to talk. He had spoken to his new caseworker, Jessica, on the phone the day before when Momma J handed him the phone and shouted, "You tell her what you did. You tell her why you gotta go." All he remembers Jessica saying was "Well, at least she didn't call the police."[50]

Reggie greets Michael, "Hey. Rough time at grandma's?"

Michael shrugs and makes eye contact briefly. "I turned 13. I guess I'm too old now for her shit."

"Man, you had a birthday? That's right. You a teenager now." Reggie whistles while he puts on his seatbelt and starts the car. Concern crosses Reggie's face as he put the pieces together—Michael's mounting disappointment capped by uncontain-able, understandable rage. He stays silent.

Michael does not know where Reggie is taking him. He assumes he will be sitting in the DSHS office for hours while Jessica makes phone calls and tries to find some-one willing to take an angry teenager. His spirits lifted cautiously when they pull up in front of Mr. Jeffries' house. Reggie detects Michael's surprise. "You didn't know you were coming back here?"

"Nah." Michael tries to sound disinterested. He isn't sure why he does not want Reg-gie to sense any relief on his part, but it is easy to maintain the blank expression he has perfected during his short life.

Now Michael lays in bed, no longer confused by his surroundings. He is thankful it is Saturday. The breakfast smells are familiar. Mr. Jeffries is not shouting at him to get downstairs so he would not miss his bus. He can stay in his nice warm bed. The

---

50. Michael's behavior could constitute a property crime, and in many states it would be consid-ered a crime of domestic violence. *See, e.g.,* Wash. Rev. Code § 9A.48.090 (malicious mischief in the third degree, a gross misdemeanor); Cal. Penal Code § 594 (malicious mischief); Ariz. Rev. Stat. § 13-602 (criminal damage).

downside is he has time to think about his family. He thinks of his sisters waking up in different places. He thinks of his mother and feels a wave of sadness and guilt, wishing she did not have to wake up by herself, without the smell of bacon, with no one but Deja for comfort. He remembers that today will be the last visit he would go to at New Beginnings, the treatment program his mother will soon complete.[51]

New Beginnings is located in a residential neighborhood on the outskirts of downtown. It looks like a nondescript aging two-story apartment building. There are a few residents and staff standing out front talking and smoking when Reggie and Michael pull up Saturday afternoon. Michael knows the drill. He waves away the smoke, enters the building and signs in at the front desk. He gets his visitor badge and heads to the family room. Angel and Aliyah are already there with their mom and Deja. Michelle is braiding Angel's hair and Aliyah is sitting close to her mother bouncing Deja on her lap. Michelle immediately stops braiding and jumps up to hug Michael. Michael takes a minute to hug back. His mother holds him patiently whispering 'I love you baby' repeatedly like a soothing mantra. Going from Mr. Jeffries' house to family visits is always disorienting for Michael. Of course he is happy to see his mother and sisters, but it will take him a few minutes to warm up and transition from Michael the foster child to Michael the oldest son and brother.

The 90 minutes fly by as they always do. Michael tells his mother about school and his new after-school program at the community center. He carefully avoids any mention of Mr. Jeffries. Angel and Aliyah argue over who can hold Deja. Aliyah talks too much about her "brothers" (Tommy Sykes' children) until Angel becomes sullen and announces she wants to go "home"—which causes Michael to angrily remind Angel that her foster mom's house is not her "home"' and she won't be home until they move back together with their mother. When Reggie arrives, Michelle greets him warmly, "Hey, I guess next week we'll be somewhere else." Reggie nods and tries to look hopeful. "Yes ma'am. I hear you are going to have your own place. Congratulations."

"I guess. I will believe it when I see it." Michelle throws her arm around Michael who stood head to head with her. A dark shadow passes between them. She speaks softly to him, "You know we will be together as soon as I can get a few things straightened out. Just give me a few more weeks. I'll get it all set up for us. Get your PlayStation ready alright?"

Reggie interrupts and says, "Sorry, gotta go," which really means "You know you aren't supposed to be talking like that during visits; don't make promises you can't

---

51. For many years states have funded residential treatment programs for pregnant or parenting women suffering from drug addiction. A review of these programs' efficacy found that they are associated with slight improvements in parenting skills, but that much more research is required because they have not been studied closely. *See* Alison Niccols et al., *Integrated Programs for Mothers with Substance Abuse Issues*, 9 Harm Reduction J. 14 (2012), [https://perma.cc/WDG4-MN3S]. The Affordable Care Act now (Jan. 2017) requires insurers to cover substance abuse treatment and also establishes incentives to address patients' needs in a more efficient and cost-effective ways, leading to expectations that addiction programs will be more heavily studied and will be integrated into traditional primary care services. Substance Abuse and Mental Health Serv. Admin., Dep't of Health and Human Serv., Innovations in Addictions Treatment (2013), [https://perma.cc/J5GS-EUXW].

keep."[52] He looks at Michelle and she looks down, fighting back a wave of emotion. Michael says, "I love you, Momma. I'll see you next week." Angel and Aliyah simultaneously rush him, holding on tight around his waist chirping "Don't go BB, stay a little longer." "BB" was an old nickname for "Big Brother" which has come back into regular usage after the family was split up. Michael kisses the tops of his sisters' heads and pulls away. For the second time that day, he feels the disturbing feeling that comes with shaking loose one identity to put on another. He rides back to Mr. Jeffries' house in silence, watching the streetlights pass by, putting distance between him and his blood.

When Michael gets out of Reggie's car, Reggie says, "Don't forget about Tuesday. Someone will be picking you up after school for your phone call with your dad. Not sure if it will be me, but don't mess around after class, be outside by 2:30. OK?" Michael had temporarily forgotten about Tuesday, but quickly shifts gears and braces himself for yet another wave of emotion that he is unable to identify. He sets his jaw, presses his lips together, nods and waves as the door slams shut and the Toyota drives off.

A Call from Prison: A Father Visits with His Son

Eric is on minimum security and is allowed to have three books in his cell in addition to his bible. He also has a stack of legal paperwork that has been growing since the news that his oldest son is in foster care. On top of the stack is the most recent communication from a public defender appointed to represent him in his son's dependency case.

LAW OFFICES OF THOMAS WOLF

ERIC GRAYSON
DOC# 23917
BRANNAN HILLS CORRECTIONAL FACILITY

CONFIDENTIAL LEGAL MAIL

RE: *The dependency of Michael Griffith, DOB 1/22/02*

Dear Mr. Grayson:

Enclosed please find a copy of the **AGREED ORDER OF DEPENDENCY AND DISPOSITIONAL ORDER** entered in the above referenced case. It is important that you read it carefully and comply with the requirements set forth.

The next hearing date is a **DEPENDENCY REVIEW HEARING**, scheduled for **6/12/15**. You will receive a report from the caseworker 2 weeks before that hearing. Please contact me when you receive the paperwork so that we can discuss your position for the hearing.

---

52. Research on how to manage parent-child contact in the dependency context is lacking and policies on supervised visits vary widely by jurisdiction. *See,* PEG MCCARTT HESS, VISITING BETWEEN CHILDREN IN CARE AND THEIR FAMILIES: A LOOK AT CURRENT POLICY ,13 (2003) (The National Resource Center for Family-Centered Practice and Permanency Planning, Hunter College School of Social Work), [https://perma.cc/4ASR-863B]("Policies regarding supervision of visits range broadly, from those that require that all visits be supervised initially and at periodic intervals to those that state that supervision should occur only when required for child protection or for other specific purposes."); Stephanie Taplina & Richard P. Mattick, *Supervised Contact Visits: Results from a Study of Women in Drug Treatment with Children in Care,* 39 CHILDREN & YOUTH SERVS. REV. 65 (2014). (Finding substance abusing mothers on psychiatric medication or cannabis had their visits supervised more frequently and kinship care reduced the likelihood of supervision.).

Please do not hesitate to call if you have any questions. I will accept collect calls whenever I am in my office.

SINCERELY,

THOMAS WOLF
ATTORNEY AT LAW

Followed by the same long list of events leading up to the last hearing. . . .

The forms all look the same. More boxes are checked, a few sentences typed in to a boilerplate form.

He scans the pages for new information pertaining to him and finally finds something very brief in paragraph 4.7. There it is. The court ordered visits.

SUPERIOR COURT OF WASHINGTON BAKER COUNTY JUVENILE COURT

Dependency of: MICHAEL GRIFFITH

D.O.B.: 12/22/02

No: 14-7-0234

Order of Dependency (OROD)

☒ Agreed as to ☒ mother ☒ father ☐ other
☐ Contested as to ☐ mother ☐ father ☐ other
☐ Default as to ☐ mother ☐ father ☐ other
☐ Dismissed (**ORDYMT**) 4.1
☒ Clerk's Action Required: Paragraphs 4.1, 4. 3, 4.6 (EDL), 4.7

The court will hear ☐ disposition ☐ interim review ☒ dependency review ☐ permanency planning
☐ _____ hearing on [date] ___June 12, 2015___ at ___9:00___ a.m.
at: _____Baker County Juvenile Court, Room/Department: ___Court 1L___.

I. Hearing

1.1   **Petition**: A petition was filed by ☒ DSHS ☐ Licensed Child Placement Agency _____
☐ Other _____ alleging that the above-named child is
dependent, and the court held a hearing on _____ [Date(s)].

1.2   **Appearance**: The following persons appeared at the hearing:

☐ Child
☒ Mother
☐ Father
☐ Guardian or Legal Custodian
☐ Child's GAL/CASA
☒ DSHS/Supervising Agency Worker
☐ Tribal Representative
☐ Interpreter for ☐ mother ☐ father
☐ other _____

☒ Child's Lawyer
☒ Mother's Lawyer
☒ Father's Lawyer
☐ Guardian's or Legal Custodian's Lawyer
☐ GAL/CASA's Lawyer
☒ Agency's Lawyer
☐ Current Caregiver
☐ Other _____

1.3   **Basis**: ☐ The court heard testimony ☒ The parties submitted an agreed order.

II. Findings

Except where otherwise indicated, the following facts have been established by a preponderance of evidence:

2.1   **Child's Indian status**:

The petitioner ☐ has ☐ has not made a good faith effort to determine whether the child is an Indian Child.

☒   Based upon the following, the child is not an Indian child as defined in RCW 13.38.040, and the federal and Washington State Indian Child Welfare Acts do not apply to these proceedings: The child was born to parents who were not enrolled or eligible to be enrolled in any tribe that is recognized under federal or state law.

2.3   **Statutory Basis:** ☒ The child is dependent according to RCW 13.34.030, in that the child:

☐   (a) has been abandoned, as defined in RCW 13.34.030;
☐   (b) is abused or neglected, as defined in Chapter 26.44 RCW, by a person legally
responsible for the care of the child; and/or
☒   (c) has no parent, guardian or custodian capable of adequately caring for the child, such
that the child is in circumstances which constitute a danger of substantial damage to the
child's psychological or physical development.

2.4   **Placement:**

☒   If the court schedules a separate disposition hearing, the child should remain in the
placement and care authority of DSHS/Supervising Agency pending further order of the
court.

☐   The child should be placed or remain in the home of the ☐ mother ☐ father ☐ legal
custodian ☐ guardian.

☒   It is currently contrary to the child's welfare to return home. The child should be placed or
remain in the custody, control and care of ☒ DSHS/Supervising Agency ☐ a relative
☐ an other suitable person for the following reasons:

☒   there is no parent or guardian available to care for the child; and/or
☐   the parent or guardian is unwilling to take custody of the child; and/or
☐   the court finds by clear, cogent and convincing evidence that a manifest danger
exists that the child will suffer serious abuse or neglect if the child is not removed
from the home, and an order under RCW 26.44.063 will not protect the child from
danger.

☒   The child should be placed or remain in:
☐   Relative placement.
☐   Placement with a suitable person and this placement is in the child's best
interests.
☐   Adoptive parent or other person with whom the child's siblings or half-siblings
live.
☒   Licensed care:
☐   pending completion of DSHS/Supervising Agency investigation of
relative placement options.
☒   because there is no relative or other suitable person who is willing,
appropriate, and available to care for the child, with whom the child has a
relationship and is comfortable.
☐   because there is reasonable cause to believe that relative placement
would jeopardize the safety or welfare of the child; and/or hinder efforts
to reunite the parent(s) and child.
☐   The child is an Indian child as defined in RCW 13.38.040, and this placement
complies with the placement priorities in RCW 13.38.180, and 25 U.S.C. § 1915.

2.5   **Reasonable Efforts:**

☒   DSHS/Supervising Agency made reasonable efforts to prevent or eliminate the need for
removal of the child from the child's home; but those efforts were unsuccessful because:

☒   The health, safety, and welfare of the child cannot be adequately protected in the
home.
☒   Specific services have been offered or provided to the parent(s), guardian or
legal custodian and have failed to prevent the need for out-of-home placement and
make it possible for the child to return home. The following services have been
offered or provided to the child and the child's parent(s), guardian or legal custodian:
☐   as listed in the social study (ISSP); and/or

4.7	**Visitation:**
☐	If disposition is heard separately, reserved pending dispositional hearing.
☒	The specific visitation plan between the child(ren) and mother shall be:

☐ as set forth in the visitation attachment.

☒ as follows:

The Department shall provide transportation for Michael for weekly visits with his mother for at least one hour. Michael and his mother may arrange additional visits in consultation with the mother's treatment providers and Michael's foster parent and treatment providers (if any). The Department reserves the right to set a contested hearing regarding visitation should the mother become non-compliant with services.

☒ The specific visitation plan between the child(ren) and father shall be:

☐ as set forth in the visitation attachment.

☒ as follows:

The Department shall arrange for monthly visits telephonically.

_____

_____

☐ Visitation between the parent/custodian _____ [name] and the child may be expanded upon agreement of the parties.

☒ The specific plan for visitation or contact between the child and child's siblings shall be:

☐ as set forth in the visitation attachment.

☒ as follows:

The Department shall arrange for weekly visits, including transportation, between Michael and his three sisters: Aliyah Griffith (DOB: 7/1/04), Angel Griffith (DOB: 3/31/07), and Deja Jones (DOB: 8/3/14). The children's respective caretakers are encouraged to arrange for additional visits whenever possible.

_____

It is getting close to 3:15 pm and Eric is beginning to feel agitated that a guard has not come to take him to Officer Jenkins' office. He paces his room in a familiar pattern and opens his Bible to calm himself. He remembers that he has asked for prayer from the men in his bible study and he feels a wave of peace. The heavy clunk of the lock releasing on his door signals that he is not forgotten.

Officer Jenkins' office is small and sparse. An old vintage looking telephone sits on his desk next to a pile of neatly stacked papers, and that is about it. Eric sits across from Mr. Jenkins with the desk and phone between them. Officer Jenkins says, "I will step outside once the call comes in." Eric thinks that is decent of Jenkins, but he knows that the phone call will be monitored by CPS and recorded by the Department of Corrections so he doesn't really expect a private conversation. Privacy is a foreign concept to him after years of lock up. The clock on the wall says 3:19. Eric bows his head and folds his hands, praying and waiting. The phone rings at 3:21. "Officer Jenkins. . . . Yes, ma'am. OK. 20 minutes? OK. Here he is."

"Hello?"

"Hello?"

"Hey, son, it is so good to hear your voice. I have been looking forward to this for a long time."

"Yeah."

"How are you doing?"

"Good."

Michael's voice does not sound familiar to Eric. He sounds much older than he expects. He hasn't spoken with him since he has been in prison, well, maybe it was a few years before that. Michael sounds distant. Eric remembers he is on speakerphone so maybe that makes Michael sound farther away than he really is. The conversation drags slowly at first, Eric asking questions and Michael responding with one-word answers. Things began to pick up when Eric starts talking about his own mother, Michael's grandmother, and how she has been out for a visit recently. He talks about what the visiting room is like and how much he appreciates it when someone makes the long trip to see him. Michael asks about his paternal grandmother, where she stays and with whom. Then he tells Eric he has had a few problems at Momma J's but she might be over it now. Eric chuckles softly at that, letting out a whistle "yeah, you don't wanna mess with Momma J. She can sure hold a grudge."

Eric rambles about his workout schedule, how he is able to work a little bit in the kitchen and how he feels confident about getting through the next couple of years with the support of God and some of his fellow inmates. Michael says that he is thinking about going out for football next year and that he will need to start lifting because he is probably too small. Eric mentions that he is sorry for what he has put Michael and his other children through and that he hopes that soon, God willing, he will be able to make it up to him. This is met with silence on the other end of the phone. Eric suddenly becomes worried that he violated some Department rule for phone visits with incarcerated parents, but he can't think of what one. After what seems like an endless pause, Michael says, "Yeah, it's cool," which is followed quickly by a female voice: "We need to wrap this up now." Eric hurries, "OK, yeah, well thank you for talking to me Michael . . . and please write if you can and I will write to you for sure. And maybe someday soon you can come out and visit me and we can get to know each other even better. Take care and be good and don't worry too much. I love you."

Michael says "I love you too, bye" and a woman cuts in.

"Thank you Mr. Grayson. We will schedule the next phone call through your counselor, Officer Jenkins, in about one month." The young woman's voice trails off as Eric's mind and heart fixate on Michael's parting words. Something feels warm running through his whole body. He may have hung up the phone without saying goodbye to the woman on the other end, but he doesn't care. He leans back in his chair, rubs his face and allows his huge toothy smile to fill the room as Officer Jenkins walks back in.

Michael's Attorney: Representing a Dependent Child

Katie usually feels relief once the dependency and disposition orders are entered on one of her cases. It gives her a feeling of finality, even though it is just the beginning of her client's legal relationship with the state. In her office, the practice is to close the file and re-open a new file for the review hearing, which will occur a few months later.[53] She is surprised when she receives a call from Mr. Jeffries about one month after Michael's dependency order has been entered. She feels a sense of dread. *This can't be good.*

In Katie's limited experience, she doesn't hear directly from her clients' foster parents very often. She will speak to them when she calls her clients or when she visits clients in their homes. She finds these relationships awkward. Are these paid caretakers allies or adversaries? The answer is different depending on the client or, more likely, depending on the day.

Katie feels warmly toward Mr. Jeffries based on her brief interactions with him. She knows Michael has mixed feelings about his placement — mostly because he remains fiercely loyal to his mother and siblings. Getting too close to Mr. Jeffries might chip away at his allegiance to his family, so it is difficult for Katie to get a good sense from Michael how he really feels about Mr. Jeffries. For the most part, Katie senses that Michael is as happy as he ever will be in the care of a stranger.[54]

When she returns Mr. Jeffries' call she is surprised to reach him and was preparing to leave a message when his bass voice picks up, "Jeffries here."

"Hi Mr. Jeffries. This is Katie Olson returning your call about Michael."

"Oh, thank you Ms. Olson. I appreciate you getting back to me so quick."

Mr. Jeffries pauses.

"Of course. What's up?" Katie cringes at her own informality. *Does she sound like a real attorney?*

Mr. Jeffries speaks slowly and deliberately, "Well, you see, Michael is struggling with something that you ought to know about and maybe you can do something."

Katie feels her stomach tighten. She hates these ethically fraught conversations that start out with someone speaking to her on behalf of one of her young clients. *Maybe she is just overthinking her ethical responsibilities.*[55]

---

53. The Adoption Assistance and Child Welfare Act of 1980 requires courts to review dependency cases six months from a child's initial removal. 42 U.S.C. § 675(5)(B).

54. In one of the only surveys of foster youth in which they were questioned directly about their experiences, almost 65% of youths reported that they felt very positive about their current placements. John Tamai & Rose Krebill-Prather, Soc. & Econ. Sci. Research Ctr., Wash. State Univ., Survey of Washington State Youth in Foster Care 16 (2008), [https://perma.cc/7W2Y -BCJ3] (full report available from link at the bottom of the article). But about 25% reported that they had ran away from their placements at one point, with the most common reasons given that they did not get along with their foster parents and/or did not like the placement. *Id.* at 17.

55. The Model Rules of Professional Conduct prohibit an attorney from implying that they are disinterested when communicating with an unrepresented person. If the lawyer "knows or reasonably should know" that the person misunderstands the lawyer's role in the matter, the lawyer must make "reasonable efforts" to correct their understanding. MR 4.3.

"OK." She knows this means "Go on . . ." without any mention that she may have a duty to later share whatever Mr. Jeffries' tells her with Michael. Sometimes foster parents do not completely understand her role. They might even say something like, "Don't tell your client, but . . ." to which she will then respond "I can't keep information from my client." But Mr. Jeffries doesn't say this and she decides to assume that he is an experienced foster parent who understands her role as Michael's attorney.

"Michael hasn't seen his mother or his sisters for three weeks, ever since she got out of the treatment program. His social worker has just left messages cancelling the visits and I haven't been able to reach her to find out why. I don't usually like getting in the middle of these things, but Michael is struggling and he should be able to see his mother. I don't know if you can do anything about this, but maybe you can call his social worker. Maybe you will have better luck."

"Thanks for letting me know. Is Michael there now? Can I talk to him?"

"No ma'am. He is out with one of my sons playing ball. He should be back in a bit. I don't really want him to know I am worried about him or that I'm interfering with his mother. It's not my place." *Uh-oh. Now he says it.*

"Well, since Michael is my client I really should get his permission before I contact his social worker about this. He's really the boss of me." She pauses realizing how ridiculous she just sounded. This whole conversation feels very unnatural. She believes Mr. Jeffries wants the best for Michael, why does she have to sound so patronizing? "Can you please tell him to call me?"

"I guess so. But can't you just get the state to follow the court order without having to get Michael agitated? He can get real worked up inside about his mother and sisters. He sometimes just stops talking and I come close to having to drag him out of bed to go to school." Mr. Jeffries speaks calmly and sounds eminently reasonable.

Katie hates this pickle she finds herself in. Mr. Jeffries is probably right about Michael getting agitated and she certainly doesn't want to participate in upsetting him further if she can avoid it. However, she can not work on his behalf without getting his authorization, or can she? Damn those Rules of Professional Conduct. Do they require her to consult with her client, even if he is a teenager suffering from the trauma of separation from his family?[56]

---

56. The Model Rules of Professional Conduct require an attorney to abide by her client's decisions concerning the objectives of representation and also require her to consult with clients on the "means by which they are to be pursued." MR 1.2. The rules also require an attorney to "reasonably consult with the client about the means by which the client's objectives are to be accomplished" and "keep the client reasonably informed about the status of the matter." MR 1.4. Where a client's decision-making capacity is diminished, which may be the case when representing youth, her attorney should maintain a normal-client lawyer relationship "as far as reasonably possible." MR 1.14.

> ### *The Lawyer's Relationship with a Youth's Caregivers*
>
> *Foster parents can be excellent advocates for the young people in their care. They are often in the position to encourage and counsel youth in their care. They may be the one person who encourages the youth to contact their attorney when things are not going well.*
>
> - *How should Katie relate to Mr. Jeffries?*
> - *Should she consult with Michael about her role and interaction with Mr. Jeffries?*
> - *What are the pros and cons of taking this approach?*

"Can you give me the contact information for his new social worker? I haven't spoken with her since she got the case. Perhaps I will just check in with her to see how things are going and that might get us some movement or at least more information." Katie is confident that she is within her authority to check in with the newly assigned social worker.[57] And she is also fairly confident that Michael wants visits with his family—a position he has clearly and consistently stated on many occasions. While it isn't necessarily Katie's job to see that the court order is followed, she thinks she can check in with the social worker without committing Michael one way or the other.

"Jessica Cole. Let me see if I can find that number." Mr. Jeffries leaves and returns with the number. He thanks Katie and ends their conversation by saying "Michael is a good boy." Katie agrees, but she feels uneasy, as if Mr. Jeffries feels compelled to say this in order to spur her into action on his behalf. As if Michael deserves her help like another child might not. She shakes it off. She needs to stop overthinking everything.

Katie is able to reach Jessica a few days later after leaving two or three messages. Jessica seems likable, knowledgeable and well-intentioned. She is young and not jaded, perhaps like Katie herself. She explains that Michael's mother is not able to find suitable housing after completing treatment and is still on a waitlist. She has moved back in with her boyfriend DJ and did not ask for visits during the transition. According to Jessica, Michelle wants to have things more together before she has a visit with all of her children. Jessica says she didn't push it; she didn't want to set Michelle up for failure. She even praises Michelle for thinking about how the visits might negatively impact her children. She says that she would be happy to move the visits forward if Michael wants them.

This makes sense to Katie, although she doesn't agree with Michelle's decision to not visit and she doesn't think that Michael would either. She doesn't say this to Jessica. All she says is, "Let me get back to you after I talk to Michael." She thinks to herself

---

57. Agencies that serve children differ in their approaches to assigning caseworkers to cases. In some jurisdictions, after dependency is established, a case will be transferred from CPS, the investigative branch, to a caseworker that is tasked with supervising dependent children and providing reunification services to families.

that she should also probably reach out to Michelle's attorney. It won't look good for Michael and his mother to be at odds at this early stage in the proceedings.

Before they hung up, Jessica says, "One more thing I should let you know, not that it will matter for visits with Michael in particular. DJ isn't doing anything: no services, no UAs, barely visited Deja when Michelle was in treatment. I'm not saying anything just yet about Michelle staying with him because I know that housing can take time, but if she really wants her other kids back she is going to have to get out on her own away from DJ. He isn't helpful. In fact, I'm afraid she won't be able to keep Deja with her much longer if this continues, but I'm trying to give her a little more time."

"OK, thanks for letting me know." Katie appreciates Jessica's providing this information, but feels frustrated because there is nothing she can really do with it. It is frustrating that this stepfather, or whatever he is to Michael, can ruin any chance that Michael, his mother and sisters will be together again as a family. As someone who likes to fix things, Katie is annoyed.

Katie hates talking to her teenage clients over the phone. Especially the boys. She briefly contemplates texting Michael—"How are visits going with your family?"—but she knows that will not get her any reliable information. So, despite her packed schedule she decides to drive to Mr. Jeffries' house and talk to Michael in person about the visitation issue. Face-to-face is always preferable for her, although she doesn't always have the time or energy to make this happen. She is partial to Michael and she likes Mr. Jeffries too. She is not this accommodating for all of her clients. For example, she almost always calls her client who is placed in the rural trailer park with too many cats. The long drive and smell of cat pee does not inspire in-person meetings.

> ### Methods for Communicating with Young Clients
>
> *When choosing a method for client communication, a lawyer must consider her ethical obligations of confidentiality, competence and keeping her client reasonably informed.*
>
> - *When should lawyers use email, text, telephone or in-person communication with young clients? What are the factors to consider?*
>
> - *Are there other methods of communication that lawyers might use with youth? What about social media or texting apps?*

When Katie arrives at Mr. Jeffries' house, she finds him in the yard, up to his elbows in dirt as he crouches over raised garden beds. He invites her to look at his work, rows of newly planted lettuce seedlings, next to rows of blossoming strawberry plants. "Come back in a week or two and I'll have a harvest ready for you. My berries are world renowned." Mr. Jeffries proud look turns suddenly sheepish when he invites her in—calling out Michael's name as he steps out of his plastic gardening shoes. "Well, look who's here! Michael, aren't you lucky to have an attorney who makes house calls?" Katie realizes then that Michael didn't know she was coming and Mr. Jeffries was awkwardly trying to play dumb.

Michael emerges from upstairs and looks a little confused but not unhappy to see her. He gives off the impression that he just woke up from a nap. Mr. Jeffries quickly exits so that they can have a private conversation at the dining room table.

Katie tries to act casual and upbeat so as to not cause Michael alarm. She doesn't expect him to be excited to see her. As much as she wants to believe that her clients like her, she knows she is often just a reminder to them of the system, the unpleasant-ness of court and their broken families.

Katie drops her brief case on the floor and sits across from Michael and jumps in, "So, how's it going?"

"Fine."

"OK. Well, I thought I would stop by and check in, see how things are going. It was pretty rushed after the last hearing and I just want to make sure that you are still doing OK here at Mr. Jeffries' house and that you have been getting regular visits with your mom and sisters." Katie thinks she probably talks too fast. There is a pause before Michael responds as if it took him a minute to catch up.

"If I don't like it here, then what would happen?" Michael does not waste time get-ting straight to the point. Katie appreciates the directness.

"Well, I'd try to help you figure out why you don't like it here and where you might like it better. And if there is a way to get you to a different place you like better I would try to do that." Vague enough to sound helpful, she thinks, without inviting trouble.

Michael looks at Katie with no emotion as he appears to absorb the information. "Nah, I can stay for now. It's alright. But when my mom gets her place I should go there." Michael's position hasn't changed, although Katie notes Michael's use of the word "should." Nothing she learned in law school helps her read the tone or facial expressions of a 13-year-old boy in foster care. Any expertise she has is likely derived from being an older sister to a brother who was once 13.

"Do you know how your mom is doing? When did you see her last?" Katie is glad that Michael brought this up so that she can get him to tell her about the lack of visits without having to let on that she already knows.

"I saw her a while ago. She's alright. She finished treatment. She's almost found a place I think." Michael speaks confidently.

Katie groans inside. *Oh crap. He isn't telling me what I think I already know.* She keeps at it. "Great. That's a big accomplishment. Sometimes it's rough to transition after treatment. You probably know that. Also, sometimes when people move, visits can get messed up, but it's the Department's job to make sure that you still get to see your mom and your sisters no matter where they are living. Are your sisters still doing OK?"

"Yeah, the same. They want to move back with our mom too." *Still nothing about the skipped visits.* Michael taps his fingers on the dining room table, which now seems to create a vast expanse between them. Katie wishes that she had chosen a less formal setting for their conversation. The dining room now feels like the conference room at her office — serious, un-inviting.

"Well then, I better find out when that can happen. I will check in with your social worker and maybe with your mom's attorney and make sure that things are moving forward. Does that sound OK?" She isn't prepared for Michael's lack of candor. She can't bring herself to ask him directly about the visits now, after acting like she knew nothing.

Candor with Clients

Model Rule 1.4 governs an attorney's ethical obligation to communicate with clients and keep them informed.

- *Did Katie follow MR 1.4 when she failed to reveal to Michael that she had spoken with Mr. Jeffries and heard that he was missing visits with his family?*

- *How should she have handled this situation?*

- *When, if ever, should an attorney withhold information from her client?*

Michael just looks at Katie. After a pause he says, "I guess so."

Michael's fingers tapping on the table remind Katie of their shared interest in music. "Hey, I hear you like you music. I do too. I play the drums."

Michael doesn't say anything, but his lips curve ever so slightly up. Katie thinks she is making some rapport points here.

"Yeah, I was actually in a band in high school and college. A girl band sort of thing." Now she knows she is going too far. She suddenly feels ridiculous. There was a long pause.

"Remember Michael, as your lawyer I am supposed to help you get what you want. So things like living with your mom, visits with your mom and sisters — I know those things are important to you and if those things don't happen the way you think they should then we can go to court and ask the judge to make them happen. I mean we don't have to go to court immediately, we can try other things. Like I could call your caseworker and see if she will do something without asking the judge to make her do it. Does that make sense?"

"So if I want to go live with my mom and the social worker says no then you can ask the judge to let me go there anyway?" Michael got it.[58]

---

58. Children are rarely empowered to challenge the decisions of adults so it can be difficult for them to understand or trust their lawyers' ability to advocate for what they want, even when their lawyers have told them that they will follow their direction. For a discussion of the challenges presented by the unfamiliar nature of the attorney–child client relationship, *See* Emily Buss, *You're My What? The Problem of Children's Misperceptions of their Lawyers' Roles*, 64 Fordham L. Rev. 1699 (1996).

"Exactly! I mean I can't guarantee what the judge will do, but we have a chance to tell the judge our side and all the reasons why it is best for you. I will do everything I can to convince the judge."

"What if I want to go live with my dad?"

"Oh, wow. Did your dad get out of prison?" Katie is caught off guard. She doesn't hide her surprise.

"No. Not yet. But I talked to him a couple of weeks ago."

"Oh yeah, I meant to ask about that! I'm sorry. How did that go?"

"It was alright. He sounds different than I remember." Michael's eyes light up ever so slightly and Katie can tell that he is pleased. She has a fleeting thought that Michael may very well end up with his dad, given what she knows about how difficult crack addictions are to overcome.[59] She tries to put that out of her mind.

"Did he tell you when he was getting out?"

"Nah. But I don't think it's too long."

"Well, that's something else I can check on. He should probably have a release date set by now. Have you met your new social worker? Jessica?"

"Yeah, she was here one time. She talked to Mr. Jeffries mostly."

"I haven't met her yet. What did you think?" Katie thinks it is important to get her clients' opinion about their caseworkers. She often finds her clients to be astute judges of character. Their perceptions of the people charged with "supervising" their lives is telling.

"She's nice, I guess." Katie thinks that is pretty good for a first impression.

Katie stays for a few more minutes talking about school, sports and inquiring whether the food is good at Mr. Jeffries' house. By the time she leaves she has almost forgotten Michael's unwillingness to share with her the fact he has not had recent visits with his mom or sisters. Katie feels confident that Michael understands that she will be talking to his social worker. She assumes that, for whatever reason, Michael prefers that Katie find out about his mom's troubles from the social worker and not from him.

---

59. As noted in previous chapters, research shows a weak to moderate association between receiving substance abuse treatment and sobriety. Pendergrast, et al., *The Effectiveness of Drug Abuse Treatment: A Meta-analysis of Comparison Group Studies*, 67(1) Drug and Alcohol Dependence 53–72 (June 2002) (finding a 57% success rate for the treatment groups compared with 42% for the comparison groups not receiving treatment.). Research also has shown that incarcerated fathers are one-third as likely as non-incarcerated fathers to be reunified with their children. Researchers theorize that this phenomenon is explainable due largely to incarcerated parents' inability to access and complete services. Amy C. D'Andrade & Melanie Valdez, *Reunifying from Behind Bars: A Quantitative Study of the Relationship Between Parental Incarceration, Service Use, and Foster Care Reunification*, 27(6) Soc. Work in Pub. Health 616 (2012).

> **Client Trust and Candor**
> - *Why might Michael withhold information from his attorney?*
> - *Is there anything that Katie should have done to encourage Michael to disclose more information?*

When Katie reaches Jessica a week later she asks again about whether visits are happening and whether Michael's mom has found a place to live. Jessica says that Michelle was just admitted to a transitional housing program and is on a waiting list to get a Section 8 housing voucher.[60] Michelle isn't very excited about the transitional housing program because she is only able to get a one-bedroom apartment located in a neighborhood she doesn't think is good for her children. In addition, the program is extremely structured. She has to attend a lot of meetings and report all of her efforts to seek employment. According to Jessica, Michelle doesn't want to try to move Michael or the other children in with her there.[61] She is hoping that her public housing will come through so they can have a place of their own, without a lot of rules and restrictions. Jessica says that Michelle still hasn't called her to set up visits with the children and she is just waiting to hear from her.

"What about Michael's father? Do you know when he will be getting out?" Katie asks hopefully.

Jessica finds notes from her conversation with Michael's corrections counselor. According to Officer Jenkins, Eric Grayson will be eligible for release in October 2016, assuming he continues to earn good time, which he seems to be on track to do.[62] This is almost a year and a half away.

---

60. The U.S. Department of Housing and Urban Development (HUD) oversees a federal voucher program to assist very poor families in obtaining housing on the private market. This program is often referred to as Section 8 housing—in reference to Section 8 of the Housing Act of 1937—and is administered by local public housing authorities. *See* 42 U.S.C. §1437f. Waiting times to receive a voucher can be long: a study commissioned by HUD revealed that 44% of all voucher holders waited at least a year before receiving one, and 20% waited over three years. Meryl Finkel & Larry Buron, Abt Associates, Study on Section 8 Voucher Success Rates: Volume 1 (2001), [https://perma.cc/YLP5-T9UP]. Some Public Housing Authorities participate in U.S. Housing and Urban Development's Family Unification Program ("FUP"), [https://perma.cc/BG7C-K99V], which prioritizes Housing Choice Vouchers for families involved in the child welfare system as well as youth who age out of the foster care system. *See also* Social Impact Research Center, Not Even a Place in Line: Housing Choice Voucher Capacity and Waiting Lists in Illinois (2015) [https://perma.cc/MF9E-VM77]; Alana Samuels, *How Housing Policy is Failing America's Poor*, The Atlantic (June 24, 2015) [https://perma.cc/GRF9-G4Z4].

61. Unsurprisingly, housing is frequently a barrier to reunification for families involved in the child welfare system. For a discussion of the relationship between housing and child welfare see Amy Dworsky, *Families at the Nexus of Housing and Child Welfare*, State Policy Advocacy & Reform Center (Nov. 2014), [https://perma.cc/R5ZV-4W4A].

62. Legislators seeking to get "tough on crime" in the 1980s and 1990s enacted criminal justice policies that placed limits on early release time in the federal prison system and nearly all fifty states. Joseph N. Parsons, *A Constitutional and Political High-Wire Act: The Role of* Brown v. Plata *in Solving*

"I hope Michael has something permanent before then. But who knows? We can't count his father out." Jessica acknowledges that the current court order requires phone visits for Michael and his father and it does not prohibit in-person visits. Jessica, however, is not particularly interested in facilitating visits for Michael at the prison. Besides being difficult to arrange and expensive, in her view, boys visiting their fathers in prison normalizes the prison experience, maybe even glamorizes it. She is familiar with research on "scared straight" programs, programs that bring youth into adult prisons to deter criminal behavior. Those programs were found to actually increase criminal offending.[63] It seems to her that boys visiting their fathers in prison can have similar affects.[64]

On both issues, Michael's visits with his mother and his father, Katie does not feel she has authority to pursue the issues further with Jessica without talking to Michael. She is satisfied she understands the options and will have to figure out what her client wants. Although she assumes Michael wants to visit both his mother and father — under the circumstances she can't be sure. She will have to check in with Michael. *Will he want to override his mother's wishes?* This whole process feels very inefficient, going back and forth between her client and the social worker. But she can't think of a better way to protect her client's interests that doesn't take so much time.

America's Prison Crisis, 75 U. Pitt. L. Rev. 99, 111–12 (2013). These policies have been blamed for prison overcrowding, which in turn has led to financial crises at the state level. W.C. Bunting, *The Regulation of Sentencing Decisions: Why Information Disclosure Is Not Sufficient, and What to Do About It*, 70 N.Y.U. Ann. Surv. Am. L. 41, 43–44 (2014). In a reversal of some of these earlier policies, many states and the federal government now do in fact allow inmates to earn early release time, or "good time credit," calculated through various formulas. *See, e.g.*, 18 U.S.C. § 3624 (allowing persons in federal prisons to reduce their sentences by 54 days of every year served in which they "displayed exemplary compliance with institutional disciplinary regulations"); Wash Rev. Code § 9.94A.729 (permitting persons to earn reductions of 10–50% of their sentences, depending on what crimes they were sentenced for); Cal. Const. art. I, § 32 (added by Prop. 57, passed Nov. 8, 2016) (among other criminal justice reforms, Prop. 57 increased availability for Good Conduct Credits).

63. Scott O. Lilienfeld et al., *Why Ineffective Psychotherapies Appear to Work*, 9 Persp. on Psychol. Sci. 355, 358 (2014) ("[C]ontrolled studies suggest that Scared Straight is not merely ineffective but probably harmful.").

64. Some social workers and caregivers resist the idea of children under their supervision visiting incarcerated parents because they believe the conditions are unpleasant or that visitation will negatively affect the children. Ross Parke & K. Allison Clarke-Stewart, Effects of Parental Incarceration on Young Children 7 (2002), [https://perma.cc/629U-AA89]. Research on the effect on children of visiting parents in jail or prison is limited and the findings are mixed. There are studies showing negative outcomes for children who visit their parents in prison, including insecure attachment, attention problems in school and negative school behavior following visits. There are also studies showing decreased feelings of alienation toward the parent and fewer school suspensions associated with visiting incarcerated parents. The studies are mostly small in size and differences may depend on whether there is a targeted intervention which tends to produce more positive outcomes (e.g. Girl Scouts Beyond Bars). Negative outcomes may be attributed to the particular visiting environment or policies, which can vary greatly from prison to prison and between prison and jail. J. Poehlmann et al., *Children's Contact with their Incarcerated Parents: Research Findings and Recommendations*, 65(6) Am. Psychologist 575 (2010).

Michael Goes Back to Court: The Dependency Review Hearing

Michael is feeling good. He is close to ending the school year passing all of his classes, maybe even getting an A and a couple of B's. He has settled in to a routine at Mr. Jeffries' house that helps him get his homework done. Twice a week he goes to the community center and meets with a tutor. On the other days, he does his homework as soon as he got home from school, and then he is allowed to hang out with James, Mr. Jeffries' 22-year-old son. James takes Michael to go shoot baskets at the school down the street. If the weather is bad they will play video games or listen to music. James lives with one of his cousins a few miles away, but he stops by almost every day — conveniently before dinnertime. When the days start getting longer, Michael and James can sometimes convince Mr. Jeffries to take them for a ride after dinner in his classic 1969 Camaro — windows down, old-school music turned up — a treat for all.

This rhythm is disrupted by the reality of Michael's court-supervised life. Reggie's reminder call that he will pick him up for court puts Michael in a dark mood. His lawyer called and met with him, so he didn't understand why she can't just go to court without him and then tell him what happened. Isn't that what she is paid for? She says she could, but then insists, "It would really help if you are there."[65]

Mr. Jeffries also tells him he should go. "It's your life. You need to make sure you know what's goin' on and that you don't have things done to you without having any say in the matter." Michael's social worker also came to see him before the court hearing and she piled on, "The judge needs to see you. She makes decisions about you and she needs to know who you are."

Michael understands that court is important, but he doesn't know what difference it makes if he shows up. In his experience, he feels the adults are just talking, talking, talking and it is both boring and stressful at the same time. He isn't convinced that he actually has a say in anything or that the judge's ability to look at him for a few minutes will bring his family back together. Nevertheless, he succumbs to the pressure. Mostly so he can see his mother and possibly his sisters. And, despite his skepticism, he does not enjoy the idea of things being said about him, about *them*, without him there.

---

65. The NACC and ABA Standards for Representing Children in Abuse and Neglect Proceedings provide that children should be present at significant court hearings, regardless of whether they will testify. Standard D-5, Standards of Practice, Nat'l Ass'n of Counsel for Children, [https://perma .cc/FU4Q-XRUY]. Jurisdictions vary on encouraging or requiring youth to attend their dependency court hearings. Some states require that children of a certain age be given notice of the hearings and their right to be present. *Compare* Conn. R. Sup. Ct. Juv. § 32a-5 (requiring consultation with youth who are the subject of any permanency hearing, but also allowing for their exclusion from the courtroom for good cause), *and* Md. Code Ann., Cts. & Jud. Proc. § 3-823(j)(1) (requiring consultation on the record with the child in an age-appropriate manner), *with* Wash. Rev. Code 13.34.070 (only requiring a summons to be issued to children twelve years or older). For a summary of state statutes regarding youth participation in dependency hearings *see Engaging Youth in Court*, ABA, [https://perma.cc /2GL7-F9DG].

The court lobby is full of families, lawyers and social workers. Some look listless and bored, others are racked with emotion — sadness, anger, anxiety or a combination of all three. The lawyers are easy to spot because they are wearing suits and are almost without exception white.[66] There are a handful of children around Michael's age, most of them not white. A few appeared a little younger, most looked older. Michael avoids eye contact, but takes every opportunity to discreetly check out the other young people who might be going through the same ordeal he is.

Michael scans the room for his mother and his sisters. He doesn't know for sure whether they will be here. He doesn't see them but he does see his attorney leaning against a wall, talking to a girl who looks to be about Michael's age. He takes a seat, resigning himself to a long wait. He wishes for a smart phone so he can play games or listen to music — but quickly remembers he is lucky to have a prepaid phone. He feels it in his pocket, comforted knowing that he still has at least 100 texts available this month.[67]

When Katie does finally greet Michael, she looks distracted. She leads Michael to an interview room where she eventually makes eye contact and asks him how he is doing. Michael gives his standard response, "Alright."

"So, Michael, are you visiting with your mom and sisters? Because if you aren't we need to bring that up today with the judge." She gets quickly to the point, which catches Michael off guard — but he likes it.

"I've seen them."

"Every week?"

"Something like that."

"Michael, I am sorry to have to press you on this, but my job is to make sure that your social worker follows the court orders if it helps you attain your goals. If you aren't getting visits with your mom or your sisters the judge can do something about that. Visits are really important if you are going to be returned to your mom."[68] Katie speaks slowly, like she is making an effort.

---

66. The 2010 U.S. Census documented that 88.1% of lawyers are white. AMERICAN BAR ASSOCIATION, LAWYER DEMOGRAPHICS (2012), [https://perma.cc/XP3Z-V5DX].

67. Generally, a foster youth's access to a mobile phone will be determined by the foster parent. There is a recent movement toward promoting foster youth normalcy. The Preventing Sex Trafficking and Strengthening Families Act of 2014 requires states to, among other things, provide "developmentally appropriate activities" to youth in care. Public Law 113-183, 42 U.S.C. 671(a)(24). Some states have already implemented the law. See WASH. REV. CODE § 74.13.710 (Foster parents have the authority to approve of their foster children's "normal childhood activities" based on a "reasonable and prudent parent standard."); CAL. WELF. & INST. CODE § 362.05; MINN. STAT. § 260C.212, subd. 14.

68. One study showed visitation to be the strongest predictor of reunification with children who were visited by their mother as recommended by the court's order ten times more likely to be reunified. Inger P. Davis et al, *Parental Visiting and Foster Care Reunification*, 18(4/5) CHILD. AND YOUTH SERV. REV. 363 (1996). *See also,* Sonya J. Leathers, *Parental Visiting and Family Reunification: How Inclusive Practice Makes a Difference*, 81(4) CHILD WELFARE 595 (2002). (maternal visitation a strong predictor for reunification with 12- and 13-year-old children).

If he was going to be returned to his mom? Michael hangs on this word, wondering why his attorney would suggest that there is a question as to whether he will go home. Shouldn't she have said *when*? *When* he is returned to his mom? He tries to wrap his brain around this new idea—that reuniting with his mother is contingent upon how often they visit. He understood only that she needs to stop using drugs and find a place for them to live. He now realizes that there might be all kinds of other requirements that he knows nothing about. He feels a growing sense of panic.

Michael decides he better give Katie more information. This might help her be more positive. "My mom and I talk on the phone and we've been meeting sometimes at the library by Mr. Jeffries' house. But not every week, and the social worker may not exactly know about it."

Katie tries to conceal her surprise. "What about your sisters?"

"She brings Deja. But I haven't seen Angel or Aliyah for a while. I think they are OK. They are with family."

Katie pauses, obviously thinking about her next move. Michael looks at her for a response, wondering if she is angry. He adds, "Don't tell my caseworker if it is going to get my mom in trouble. We'll stop if you think it hurts my chances of going home."

"Does Mr. Jeffries know?"

Michael doesn't answer. He is starting to feel very uncomfortable. He probably shouldn't have said anything.

"Don't worry, I won't tell anyone if you don't want me to. I am on your side, I am not trying to get anyone in trouble—especially you." Katie is now looking very intently at Michael and she seems genuinely concerned.

Attorney's Duty of Truthfulness to Others

Model Rule 4.1 governs an attorney's duty to be truthful in statements to others.

- *Is Katie being ethical when she promises not to tell anyone about Michael's visits with his mother?*

"Yeah, he kinda knows." Michael decides he has gone this far, he might as well keep going—what else could he do? Besides he is now confused about whether the visits are a good thing or a bad thing. *If he was going to be returned to his mom? If?*

Once the cat is out of the bag, Michael keeps going and tells Katie that he likes visiting with his mom at the library because no one is around to watch them and it feels more "normal." He also admits that he likes having time alone with her and Deja, without his sisters there. He feels like he and his mother can talk about more "real" things—like how his mom is doing in her recovery and what is happening with DJ. He is able, or he thinks he is able, to explain that he misses his sisters but he knows as long as they aren't in foster homes they don't need to see him as much. He figures that his mom thinks the same thing and that she will make it up to them when she finds a place to live where they can visit without social workers watching them.

Katie looks like she is trying to figure out what to do. She starts flipping through the file in front of her. Michael likes this better than her looking directly at him. "Wait a minute. The court order allows you to arrange visits with your mom 'in consultation with treatment providers' and Mr. Jeffries." Katie is reading from her file. "You haven't done anything wrong. It's totally OK under the court order."

Michael feels relieved. It is strange that he had been feeling guilty about visiting with his own mother and sister. Secretly meeting at the library. Like their laughter, the stories they share, are somehow criminal. Strange that he feels he has to protect his mother and Mr. Jeffries from some unknown trouble that could come from spending time with his family. Obviously the rules are unclear, even to his lawyer who had to look them up in the file. And apparently breaking these unclear rules can jeopardize his ability to go home. He is used to being careful about who he trusts with information about his family, but this is really messed up. He wishes all of these people would just go away and leave his family alone.

"Can you just tell me when I get to go back to my mom?" Michael wants this all to be over.

After a pause, Katie responds, "I wish I could tell you. It depends on your mom, when she gets situated, and ultimately what the judge decides. I would like to talk to your mom's attorney about the visits. Is that OK? We just need to make sure that we are on the same page. It's a good thing that you have been able to see her. We just need to figure out whether the social worker knows about it and what we should do about visits with your sisters."

Michael asks Katie if she can just talk to his mom directly because he isn't sure what she has told her attorney. It will be way less complicated.

"Unfortunately, no, I can't. The court rules say I can't talk to a party who is represented by a lawyer. If you want to talk to her, you can, and let me know if it is OK."[69]

Right about that moment someone knocks on the interview room door and it is Michael's mom's attorney, George. When Katie opens the door, he says "Can we talk about a few things?"

"Yes. Perfect timing. Come on in. Michael will want to hear this too." George's expression made it clear that he didn't intend to have this conversation with Michael present but in the interest of time he dives in.

"So my client hasn't been able to see her girls. She hasn't told the social worker that she has been seeing Michael on the sly, so she wants visits set up with all of the kids as soon as possible. She also thinks Michael should be visiting his sisters. Any objection?"

---

69. MODEL RULES OF PROF'L CONDUCT R. 4.2. A lawyer may speak to a represented party about the subject of the dispute only if the other lawyer consents or if a law or court order permits her to do so. *Id.*

George looks over at Michael and Michael tries to maintain eye contact. Acting like a man, he thinks.

"That would be great, but you know the court order allows for Michael and his mom to visit as long as her treatment providers and his foster dad are consulted." Katie has her finger on a piece of paper in her file.

George leans over and gets close to the piece of paper. "Well, I'll be. Oh, yeah. I did that. That's a good paragraph there." Michael rolls his eyes. What's the point of these attorneys writing all this stuff in their files if no one even remembers what it says?

"So I guess we just need to let the social worker know that Michelle and Michael have been visiting with the foster parent's permission, right? That's good. That's more compliance with services." Michael is glad that George doesn't look over at him when he says this. Michael is still processing that the visits he and his mom are hiding because they are supposedly prohibited are now a good thing.

Why Did This Happen?

Michael hid his visits with his mother from Katie, perhaps thinking that he was doing something wrong. Katie gets herself into a pickle when she doesn't ask Michael directly about what she already knew to be true. As it turns out, the visits were authorized by the dependency order.

- *Why did this happen? What were the ramifications of this misunderstanding? Could it have been avoided?*

- *What are ways that attorneys can ensure that their clients understand court orders and what is and is not permitted while they are under state supervision?*

"Right. But she should also set up visits with the girls. Michael would like that too, I think." Katie glances at Michael. He nods. "Also, can you tell us what's going on with Michelle's housing situation? Michael is just waiting for her to get a stable place to live so he can go home."

Michael wonders what she means by "stable place to live" because he never used those words before. Not that he would mind a "stable place to live" but whatever place his mom finds to stay that has room for him will be fine.

"Yeah, she's working on it. You know it sucks not to have money." George blurts this with apparently no regard for Michael. Michael thinks he likes George better at that moment.

George left the interview room without looking at Michael or Katie. Katie is scribbling notes in her file. Michael feels suddenly tired. He puts his head down on the table. Katie says, "Are you OK?" He shakes his head up and down without lifting it from the table. Katie says, "OK, I gotta go talk to your social worker and I'll find out when we will get into court. Maybe you can go find your mom and wait for a bit."

Michael lifts his head. He remembers he hasn't seen his mom yet and that is the whole reason he came. He follows Katie out of the interview room and quickly scans the court lobby. He finds his mom. She is sitting next to some strangers with Deja standing on her lap bouncing up and down. Michelle wore her best jeans, high heel sandals and a new shirt that Michael hasn't seen before. He feels proud of her. She looks really put together. She is exchanging words with the strangers next to her; they look like they are getting along. He sneaks up behind his mom and makes a face at Deja who squeals with delight. He ducks behind the chair when his mom turns around and then pops up quickly to startle her. Michelle laughs and pulls Michael toward her without getting up, hugging him and making a Deja sandwich. This makes Deja giggle and shake her bottom from side to side. Michael grabs his little sister under his arm like a football and takes off to do a lap around the lobby. He weaves between attorneys and parents and circles back to his mom who is shaking her head and laughing. Michelle says to the woman sitting next to her, "Deja sure loves her brother. I carry her like that and she cries but Michael can't do no wrong by her."

Michael takes a seat next to his mom, holding Deja high over his head, her pink t-shirt inching up exposing her brown belly, contagious baby laughter tumbling out and infecting everyone around her. A voice over the loudspeaker booms "All parties on the Griffith matter please go to Courtroom 4."

Michael files into the courtroom behind his mother; Deja is on his shoulders grabbing his short afro with one chubby fist and beating his head like a drum with the other. He wonders whether he will get in trouble for this, but the judge is not on the bench yet. He knows he isn't supposed to wear hats in the courtroom, but he isn't sure if he can wear his sister on his shoulders.

Michelle peels Deja off of her brother, tears erupting from the almost one-year-old. She sits down next to her attorney, holding Deja tightly on her lap and cutting her cries short with a bright green pacifier. Michael looks around while taking a seat next to Katie. He sees a few familiar looking lawyers. DJ and Tommy are noticeably absent.

When Judge Adams enters the courtroom and everyone is asked to stand up, Michael feels slightly less confused than when he first found himself there five months ago. Judge Adams acknowledges him with a faint smile and a nod before saying, "Please be seated." Michael feels his palms start to sweat.

Michael doesn't understand what is at stake today exactly.[70] He knows he isn't going to be able to go home. He understands now that he can continue visiting with his mom at the library and he is under the impression he may get visits with his sisters soon.

---

70. Federal law requires that states receiving Title IV funds for foster care provide court or administrative reviews of a dependent child's status at least every 6 months. This review should include "the safety of the child, the continuing necessity for and appropriateness of the placement, the extent of compliance with the case plan, and the extent of progress which has been made toward alleviating or mitigating the causes necessitating placement in foster care, and to project a likely date by which the child may be returned to and safely maintained in the home or placed for adoption or legal guardianship," 42 U.S.C. § 675(5)(B).

Katie hasn't really told him what is going to happen in court. Michael decides to try to get Deja's attention and see if he can get her to smile without squealing.

The judge askes the social worker to talk about the family's progress. Michael tries to listen to Jessica's speech to the judge and he thinks it sounds mostly positive. She reports that his mother has successfully completed treatment and is looking for housing. She reports that Michelle "maintains contact with Michael" following treatment and is scheduling visits with her daughters this week. Michael tries to pay close attention when Angel and Aliyah are mentioned. Nothing stands out—they are both "progressing well in their placements." The only thing she says about Michael is that he is doing well in his foster home and at school. *That's it?* Michael is amazed that the past five months of his family's separation can be summarized in just a few short minutes.

It isn't all good though. When mentioning DJ, Jessica states that he is not responding to her efforts to contact him and that he is "out of compliance" with the court's orders. Michael doesn't know exactly what that means, but he knows it can't be good. Jessica's mention of DJ seems to wake up the man in a suit sitting next to her who Michael assumes to be a lawyer. After Jessica finishes talking he says, "Your honor, actually, Mr. Jones has not established paternity and the State gives notice that it will move to dismiss him as a party if he does not take steps to do so by the next review hearing."[71]

"Dismiss him" sounds like a good idea to Michael. That's what he usually did. He takes note to ask Katie what this means later. He wonders why DJ didn't bother to show up. He knows from his mom that DJ isn't in jail and is supposedly looking for work, so why can't he get himself to court? Michael's face feels hot thinking about how Deja should have a father who can show up. He tries not to think about what is probably the case: DJ is either high, looking to get high or coming down from a high. Michael is ordinarily dismissive of DJ because Michael only had the bandwidth to concern himself with his own family. But he now has a sinking feeling that DJ might somehow be a real threat to them. He is trying to piece it together. Something about the way DJ is thrown into this mix, this complicated room filled with lawyers and a judge, makes Michael concerned. Anger starts to well up inside of him and he commits to making sure that Deja does not get hurt. He looks over at her and catches her gaze. His eyebrows go up and Deja grins and pumps her arms exuberantly.

After Jessica and her attorney stop talking, the judge turns to a middle-aged white woman that sits on the other side of them and smiles warmly at her. Michael has not seen this woman before. She looks more like a social worker than an attorney, but he has no way to tell. He tugs at Katie's sleeve. She leans her ear toward him and he whispers, "Who is that?" She tells him it is the "CASA" and she will explain her role later. She says something about his sisters and their interests, but he doesn't understand.

---

71. Jurisdictions differ as to how they treat parents who have not established paternity. For example, Florida law requires that a prospective parent claiming paternity be given an opportunity to become a party to the dependency case by executing an affidavit of parenthood which, if not contested by the known parent, affords the prospective parent the status of "parent." FLA. STAT. § 39.503(8).

"Good morning, your honor. Ellen Anderson, volunteer CASA for the girls Angel, Aliyah and Deja. I have had the pleasure of meeting with Angel and Aliyah in their placements and they are lovely girls. Angel is just finishing the 1st grade and she improved her skills considerably over last year. Her grandmother has done an excellent job providing a loving and stable environment. She is very involved in an after-school tutoring program that she likes very much."

There was that term "stable." Michael feels sick to his stomach.

"Aliyah is finishing the 3rd grade. She is also doing better this year in school and she is thriving in her father's home. She had a bit of an adjustment at first getting used to her half-siblings, but her father and step-mother have done a remarkable job integrating her into their family. She recently joined a community drill team that her step-mother coaches."

Their family? Michael feels sick again. "The girls both report enjoying time visiting with their mother and brother and sister and they would like more time if possible."

Reporting Child's Stated Interest to the Court

Ellen doesn't tell the court that the girls want to go home to their mother. Should she? Why or why not?

Whew. At least that is something. Michael brightens ever so slightly. He wonders who this lady is and who told her she could speak for his sisters like that. He is sure that Angel and Aliyah would never want their mother to think that they preferred being away from her. This CASA person makes it sound like this terrible situation they find themselves in is *better.*

Ellen Anderson also mentions Deja briefly. "Deja, as you can see, is a delightful and healthy 10-month-old who is clearly bonded to her mother and her brother. I met with Deja and her mother at the New Beginnings treatment program where they both seemed to do very well. Michelle should be commended for her hard work overcoming her addiction. I am hopeful that Michelle will continue in her sobriety so that she can have her other children returned soon." Ellen smiles at Michelle across the table. Michael is now perplexed. This Ellen person now sounds like she is on his mother's side, when seconds ago she was going on about Momma J. and Tommy being all that. His irritation turns to confusion. Maybe Katie can enlighten him later about what this stranger's job is supposed to be.

Just as before, the judge asks every lawyer if they want to speak. Every lawyer has something to say except DJ's lawyer who says "I have nothing to add at this time." Michael thinks that is lame. A lame lawyer for a lame father. When it is her turn, Katie says Michael is doing well and looking forward to returning to his mom when she gets settled. Michael prefers "settled" to "stable," a word she had used before when talking about what his mom needs to do before they can be together.

Finally, after all of the lawyers talk, the Judge looks at Michael and thanks him for coming. She smiles with her mouth, the rest of her face remains stern behind her glasses. She asks Michael how he is doing and whether there is anything he wants her to know that perhaps his lawyer has left out. Having spoken in court before, Michael is less afraid, but he keeps his responses very short. The judge says something about his schoolwork and having a good summer.

Talking to the Judge

Some research suggests that judges benefit from having youth appear in court.

- *How might judges make their interaction with youth in the courtroom meaningful?*
- *What are the barriers to meaningful communication between judges and youth who appear before them?*
- *What might the lawyer's role be?*

The judge then addresses Michelle directly. She starts out nice, commending her for completing treatment and taking good care of Deja, but then she shifts her tone to very serious, like teacher serious. Michael tries to listen carefully for a clue as to when their family might be back together. The judge says something about getting a place to stay "as soon as possible" for her children's sake. Michael likes the idea of "as soon as possible" and he mostly finds himself agreeing with the judge—but something doesn't sit quite right. There is something slightly foreboding in the judge's tone. There is a negative feeling that Michael can not understand or explain. He decides to brush it off.

When Michael leaves the courthouse, his spirits are lifted by time spent with his family and what appears to be a positive response from the Judge. He had a few rushed minutes with his lawyer in the hallway. She promises to come see him soon to answer questions if he has any. She says, "Keep doing what you are doing and don't worry too much." He isn't sure what she means, but she was kind and he knows that she is trying to help him.

Michael's Mother Michelle Tries to Put Everything Back Together

Shit. 4 p.m. Michelle is so tired of waiting in the public housing office. She has been there for two hours. She takes the Number 14 bus there the day after her dependency review hearing. The bus breaks down and she has to walk eight blocks to catch the Number 3, so she gets to the housing office much later than she has planned. She hears the judge loud and clear: "You must get a place for your children as soon as possible." And now the office is going to close before she even gets to talk to someone.

She didn't hear the "or else" part of the judge's directive exactly, but she knows what the judge was implying. She has heard plenty of stories of babies being "adopted out" to strangers. She sits through enough meetings with other addicts to hear the horror stories; mothers weeping uncontrollably as they continue to battle addiction and guilt years after losing their children.[72] Those stories often drive her to stay clean. They haunt her now. She has nightmares where addicted mothers from her past form a circle around her, taunting her and saying, "So now who is a bad mother?" These ghostly women in her dreams tear at her clothing and try to steal her shoes. Michelle often wakes up in a state of panic.

Now she sits and tries not to stress. She tries to believe that her family's entire future does not depend on the answer she will get when they call her number and she meets with a housing worker.

"How long?"

"About nine months. For a two-bedroom. Longer for three-bedrooms." The housing worker is looking at her computer while she delivers the news to Michelle. When she looks up, she sees Michelle walking out the door.

Reflections and Exercises

1. *What? So What? Now What? A Five-Minute Reflection Opportunity.* Take just five minutes to write and reflect on the following questions:

   a. What did you feel as you read about Michael's life as a dependent child?

   b. How is what you recorded feeling relevant to your learning and/or practice?

   c. Now what do you do with these insights as you move forward in your learning and/or practice?

2. *Mapping the System:* At the end of Chapter One, you mapped your state's dependency system. Where is Michael now on your map?

3. *Imagining a Different Story for Michael:* The court system is not designed for youth to navigate. Court orders and processes are inaccessible. Between court hearings, youth are going to school, visiting their families, interacting with foster families and otherwise living their lives. Meanwhile, lawyers are often negotiating with professionals over the terms of their client's lives.

   a. How might lawyers get information from or about their clients between court hearings? Are there ways that they can build and maintain trusting relationships with their clients outside of court?

   b. Can dependency court orders be developed, implemented and monitored to serve youth and their families more effectively? How?

---

72. In 2015, 62,378 children were waiting to be adopted after their parents' rights had been terminated. The AFCARS Report, Adoption and Foster Care Analysis & Reporting System, U.S. Dep't of Health and Human Serv., (FY 2015) [https://perma.cc/BL22-9N7B].

Chapter Eight

Maya in and out of Safe Harbors: From Group Care to Permanency

In this chapter, you will learn about the importance of the lawyer's role as counselor, out-of-court advocate and problem-solver in the context of shifting and shrinking options.

In order for lawyers to have a positive impact on the trajectory their clients' cases, they must participate in the decision-making that happens prior to hearings. Effective lawyering requires the attorney to have a working knowledge of the many different types of meetings held by agency social workers. Often, it is in these out-of-court meetings that the state agency develops the placement plan that the agency will put before the court. If the attorney for the youth participates actively in these out-of-court processes, the likelihood of influencing the agency's recommendation or reaching agreement increases.

In Part I, you learn about Maya in the context of her new placement, a group home designed to help youth who are leaving "the life" of what typically has been criminalized as juvenile prostitution. In this section, you will see Maya struggle with how difficult it can be to live in close quarters with others who have their own trauma histories. You will learn the story of Kai, who shares Maya's space and whose story sheds some light on the intersectionality of race, sexual orientation and gender identity. You will learn about the trauma-informed services that are built into the design of this model program and the important role that a caring adult or mentor can play in helping a young person recognize her own strengths.

In Part II, Julia, Sarah, and Maya grapple with what Maya's future placement will be in the context of her upcoming permanency planning hearing. Permanency planning hearings must be held at least once a year for the purpose of seeking the court's approval of a plan designed to find a permanent home outside of the system. The most sought after permanency plans, as prioritized by the statutes, are reunification with a parent or adoption. Reunification is not an option for Maya, given that her mother's rights have been terminated. It also would appear that the state has not positioned her for an adoption. Another permanency plan option is guardianship. In a typical guardianship, the dependency is dismissed and responsibility is given to an adult to care for the child until the age of eighteen. If the state has not been successful in finding someone to serve as a guardian for the child, alternatives include long-term relative care, long-term foster care, or independent living.[1] Here, you will see the importance of attorney engagement with social work processes to move the case in the direction of the client's permanency planning goals. You will also watch as Julia helps Maya understand what is happening in her legal case and what her options are going forward.

In Part III, you witness an extra-judicial decision-making process designed to empower and engage families—family group conferencing. Julia's familiarity with the different types of social work processes and her ability to navigate and advocate for one type of meeting over another helps to move the case closer to Maya's stated goals.

Finally, in Part IV, Judge Goodloe returns for the permanency planning hearing, in which the parties inform the court of Maya's permanency plan going forward.

Part I: Maya in Group Care: Safe Harbors

Maya Settles In

I was feeling pretty sorry for myself when I first got here. I was sick all the time and I was so bored. I just wanted something to happen, anything, even something bad would be better than this nothing. In the first month, I would think about Kiki and Diamond and even Hailey and remember all the fun stuff we did, how we could do whatever we wanted whenever we wanted and I didn't have to think about doctor appointments and counseling appointments and social worker appointments and lawyer appointments. I didn't really care what day it was then. It didn't matter. I was free.

Sometimes I just want to feel something. I even miss the fear, those times when I was with a date turned bad and I could watch myself turn from fear to numbness to nothingness and then fade back in again. There's nothing like that moment when you come back and you realize you are still alive and you didn't die even though you thought sure you would. You're still alive and you suddenly feel almost happy, kind of high, like *shit* that was a rush.[2]

And I do miss Diamond, the way he was in the beginning, the way we were together in the beginning, when he told me about when he was little and what he saw happen.

---

1. For a review of the dependency process and permanency planning, see ch. 1 — *The Federal Statutes that Drive the State Systems.*

2. Adolescents who experience trauma as a child are more likely to show a pattern of risky sexual behaviors. *Identifying and Addressing Trauma in Adolescents: A Conversation with David A. Wolfe*, 22(4) The Brown Univ. Child and Adolesc. Behav. Letter 1, 4–6 (2006, April). Even if the trauma is experienced during adolescence, risk-taking behavior often increases after the trauma exposure. Ann E. Norwood et al., *Disaster Psychiatry: Principles and Practice*, 71(3) Psychiatr. Q. 207 (2000). Research has also established a link between violence exposure in adolescence and sensation seeking through both substance abuse and sexual risk taking. Sonya S. Brady, et al., *Mechanisms Linking Violence Exposure to Health Risk Behavior in Adolescence: Motivation to Cope and Sensation Seeking*, 45 J. of the Am. Acad. of Child & Adolesc. Psychiatry 673 (June 2006).

And when I told him about what I remembered from when we were living in the squat, the shit that my mom did that I pretended I didn't see, the things that Jazz had to do because my mom turned away and let those guys do what they wanted. Di and me had our stories and we had each other. He held me tight, he kissed my hair, he told me that he was glad that we were safe together finally. I told him that it wasn't his fault that his mom got killed. He would even cry sometimes, but we would wind up smiling. Even though he wasn't the first guy I'd been with; the sex with him was the best ever because it was so real. I miss that.

But now, look at me, my ankles are all puffy, my belly is pooching out over my shorts and poking out from beneath my shirt. I hardly ever wear makeup anymore because where would I get the money for that? I try not to look at myself in the mirror because I don't recognize the girl there. Is that even me?

Probably about once a week I get my stuff together to walk out. You can do that here; there are no locked doors,[3] although if you have prostitution charges and you walk out they will send a warrant for you and then you're in twice as much trouble as you used to be,[4] but I don't have those charges; I'd probably just get seven more days in juvie for contempt.[5] But every time I get ready to go, I wind up feeling too sick or too tired or too hungry in a way that I have never felt sick or tired or hungry before and I kind of just don't have the energy. I do wish I could smoke some weed though. When I first got here, when I was so sick, I felt like it might stop me from puking and if all I was going to do was lay around and be tired, why not be stoned?

> ### Alternative Responses to Juvenile Prostitution
> * How does your state handle juvenile prostitution?
> * Are minors charged with crimes or treated as victims?

---

3. Whether to allow minors who have been commercially sexually exploited to leave group homes specifically designed for them is a policy and practice question that is often debated, with those arguing in favor of locked facilities in order to protect young people from their traffickers facing off against those who say that lock-down simply mimics the same coercive tactics that traffickers use. *See,* Garrett Therolf, *Plan for County Facility to Keep Pimps Away from Foster Youth Advances,* L.A. Times (May 13, 2015) [https://perma.cc/D5X8-EXAR].

4. For a report detailing different approaches taken by states seeking to shift the paradigm from one that punishes minors for juvenile prostitution to one that treats the minor as a victim in need of services, see Shared Hope International, JuST Response State System Mapping Report: A Review of Current Statutes, Systems, and Services Responses to Juvenile Sex Trafficking (2015) [https://perma.cc/AT9X-P8M4]. Among these approaches is the "diversion approach" described here. Under diversion, the young person is not immune from prostitution prosecution but is diverted to services in order to avoid a delinquency adjudication. In order to avoid the adjudication, the youth must successfully complete the services. *Id.* at 9. Ohio and Washington are identified as states following this model. *Id.* at 47–56.

5. For an exploration and critique of the use of contempt as a way of regulating girls as status offenders, see Cynthia Goodsoe, *Contempt, Status, and the Criminalization of Non-Conforming Girls,* 34 Cardozo L. Rev. 1091 (2014).

Then I'd remind myself that this baby is real, it's not just the flu, it's a real person, and if I want to do better than my mom did, if I want to show them that I can be good like Aunt Hen and do this, if I want to show them I should be with my family, I need to be here in this boring place just a little bit longer and not get stoned.

Julia, my lawyer, reminds me about this a lot. I have seen her a couple of times since I got here. She checks in to see how I am doing and to let me know what she's doing on my case. She told my Aunt Hen about me being pregnant and she said that Aunt Hen was more worried about me than mad. She said Aunt Hen talked to Uncle Marcus. They are good with me coming to live with them but there's lots to work out, like their apartment is kind of small. She's trying to figure out where I will go to school and what I will do with the baby when I am in school.

Julia also just wants to know how I'm doing with being pregnant and how school is, stuff like that. We've been trying to come up with a plan that she can try to sell to my social worker. Last time I saw her, she said there's some kind of hearing coming up soon and the social worker is going to have to explain why I should still be in a group home because the law says being with family is better. That's all good news, but she also says that we need to show that Aunt Hen and Uncle Marcus can take care of me. I think she's afraid the judge still might think I'm some kind of crazy person, like my mom.

The Importance of Frequent Client Contact

Brief and frequent check-ins with teenage clients ensure that lawyers are fulfilling their ethical responsibilities to keep their clients informed. Checking in frequently also helps to build trust and to give clients an opportunity to talk about problems and accomplishments as they arise.

* *At minimum, how often do you think a lawyer should make contact with a teenage client?*

I'm not sure whether I trust Sarah, though. She totally trash-talked my family at that last hearing. She came by the other day with a bunch of forms that I had to sign. One of them said I understood my right to go to school, see the doctor and be safe or something like that.[6] She also gave me a copy of a bunch of stuff like my birth certificate and told me to keep it in a safe place.[7] I don't exactly have a lot of "safe

---

6. The Preventing Sex Trafficking and Strengthening Families Act requires that any youth under the responsibility of the state who is 14 years of age or older must be informed of his or her "rights with respect to education, health, visitation, and court participation, the right to be provided with documents specified in section 675(5)(I) of this title . . . , and the right to stay safe and avoid exploitation." 42 U.S.C. § 675a(b). The documents referred to under section 675(5)(I) include a copy of a credit report, a social security card, birth certificate and state ID. An acknowledgement signed by the youth that she has received a written copy of her rights, explained in an age-appropriate way, and the required documents also must be included in the agency's case plan. 42 U.S.C. § 675a(c).

7. *Id.*

places," but whatever. She asked if I had any questions and I asked her what about my right to live with my family because my attorney said that she had to let me stay there if I am doing good and I am doing good, aren't I? So I should get to go live with my family, like my attorney said, right? She said that she was "very impressed" with me but she was working on still figuring out whether my relatives were "suitable." It sounded like a bunch of excuses to me.

> ### The Lawyer-Client-Social Worker Relationship
>
> *What the client hears the lawyer saying may sometime find its way into the client's conversation with the social worker.*
>
> - *What are the advantages and disadvantages of this dynamic?*

Sarah also asked me questions that weren't any of her business. She says she has to because of the rules. She tries to get me to talk about why I ran away and what I was doing while I was on the street.[8] I tell her my lawyer already said why I ran away — because I hated my group home that was like a jail and I was sick of not being listened to about wanting to live with my family. And I told her again that, no, I didn't stay with my Aunt Hen. It's bad enough I have to go over that same old story, but then Sarah starts asking me all these personal questions about whether I did sex things for money or food or whether I worked in a strip club or did porn. What do I look like? Some kind of fool? I mean for real? I seen enough TV to know I don't need to answer questions like that. I'm not a f-ing idiot. I told her it was none of her f-ing business.

After she leaves, I just want to bust up the place, like Di said he used to do whenever he was ready to move on.

It's not easy holding it all together. I think I need more props for that. I would just like for once for somebody to say, "Congratulations. You didn't punch anyone in the face today."

There are times that the other girls here get on my last nerve. I haven't exactly made any friends. There is this girl, Kai, who was my roommate when I first got here. So here's the thing, I know there are a lot of queer kids out on the street and they do whatever they need to do to make it. I get that. No judgment. But it's weird having to

---

8. 42 U.S.C. § 671(a)(9)(C)(I) requires state agencies receiving foster care funds to prove through agency records that it is identifying youth who are or at risk of being a sex trafficking victim. A sex trafficking victim in the context of minors is someone who is under 18 when induced by force, fraud, or coercion to perform a commercial sex act. 22 USC § 7102(9). "Commercial sex act" is broadly defined to include "any sex act on account of which anything of a value is given or received by any person." 22 U.S.C. § 7102(4). Under 42 U.S.C. § 671(a)(35)(A), states must gather information on the "primary factors that contributed to the child's running away or otherwise being absent from care, and to the extent possible and appropriate, responding to those factors in current and subsequent placements." States are also required to "determine the child's experiences while absent from care, including screening the child to determine if the child is a possible sex trafficking victim." *Id.*

live in the same small room with one, and get dressed and undressed around someone who you know could be into you. She didn't seem to give a damn about walking
around naked or whatever in our room. It's not like she tried to get with me; actually
she could be mean or just flat out ignore me. I didn't know if it was because she was
mad at me because I'm white or straight or whether she just stays mad at everybody
all the time. Now that I know her better I think she's just fucked up. She spends all
her time either acting crazy like she is going to lose her shit on anyone who looks at
her cross-wise or laying out on the floor just waiting for you to trip over her and not
even caring if you do. We fought all the time at first, over stupid stuff really; neither
of us wanted to be thrown together with someone we didn't know. Just seeing her
made me want to snap. We got into it good in the TV room one day, fighting over
what show to watch. I say she hit me first. She says I hit her first. Whatever. Johanna,
who runs the place, decided maybe we needed to keep our distance and have our own
rooms, which she could make happen, because apparently most of the girls here don't
stay very long[9] and so there was space for us to stop double-bunking. Me and Kai—
we are both pregnant and so we have a little bit more reason to stay on at least until
we find some place better to be, even though I am not sure that Kai is really wanting
to have that baby. Sometimes she talks about getting rid of it, which judging from the
way she acts most of the time, would not be the worst idea. I mean, you can't be a
mom if you're either losing your shit or staying in bed until the day's almost gone.
Still, I can put up with her much better now that she is not in my space all the time.

Before they gave us separate rooms, I sat on the couch in the living room a lot and
wouldn't do nothing. They would say it was time for me to meet with my teacher and
I would just not go. They would say it was time to eat and sometimes I would eat and
sometimes I wouldn't. They would say I should go see Anita and most of the time I
ignored them. I always went to the doctor, though, because my lawyer said I needed
to show everybody that I know how to take care of a baby and the first way to do that
is to take care of myself. And I signed up for the baby class, but it hasn't started yet.

But it ain't all bad. Miss Minnie is the best. She's the one who keeps me from going
crazy in this place, even though that's supposed to be Anita's job, I guess. Anita is my
counselor. And Robin is pretty good as a teacher, but honestly Minnie is the one I
learn easiest from.

I'll never forget that first day she talked to me. Miss Minnie is this tiny, funny-
looking little lady (who is so skinny you can kind of imagine what she'll look like

---

9. Service providers report that, while the most successful residential programs for sex trafficking
victims are those in which the young person is there voluntarily, it is not unusual for young people to
run away and relapse, in much the same way that those who are in treatment for substance abuse do.
Leaving the program is so common that many shelters report having specific protocols to work with
running as part of each girl's treatment plan, as well as intensive case management during typical
high risk run periods, such as intake and specific points in therapy. HEATHER J. CLAWSON, ET AL,
FINDING A PATH TO RECOVERY: RESIDENTIAL FACILITIES FOR MINOR VICTIMS OF DOMESTIC SEX
TRAFFICKING, U.S. DEP'T. OF HEALTH & HUMAN SERVICES, STUDY OF HHS PROGRAMS SERVING
HUMAN TRAFFICKING VICTIMS, (9/15/2007) available at: [https://perma.cc/NDT8-455S].

when she is dead and just a bunch of bones). She came out from the kitchen and saw me sitting on the couch. She has black hair that's so thin and soft and short and just a little bit curly, it looks like just a bunch of feathers sitting on top of her head. She puts all this white powder on her face like she thinks it's hiding the red blotches on her skin underneath but it doesn't really. She's always got some red lipstick on. All she's doing is cooking all day in the kitchen for a bunch of girls, so she doesn't have to look good, but she tries anyway.

She came out of the kitchen and saw me sitting on the couch and she says to me, "So what kind of food makes you really retch? I mean really puke your guts out? I been hearing you and it sounds pretty nasty." It's like the first thing she ever said to me.

I thought, *well, that's a strange question, like, is she planning the menu for tonight and does she want to make sure I have another chance to get sick all over the place?* She looked at me like she's waiting for an answer and won't go away until I give her one and so I told her that every time she cooks broccoli, just smelling it in the pot, makes me blow chunks, even if I am upstairs where the bedrooms are. I never thought that broccoli could smell so bad.

"Good to know," she said and after that she just stopped making broccoli, not just for me, but for everybody.

And then about a week later when I started feeling a little bit better, she caught me just sitting on the floor in the hallway doing nothing, and she asks, "What are you really hungry for?"

And I told her I didn't know why but the thing I wanted more than anything else in the whole world was watermelon.

Damn if that Miss Minnie didn't go and get some watermelon.

This baby is going to be made out of watermelon, I swear. I have eaten so much watermelon, thanks to her, and I am still not tired of it.

I was starting to get over feeling sick all the time, which the doctor says is natural because I am pretty deep into my "second trimester," and Minnie asks me if I would help her in the kitchen a little bit. At first I was thinking like, *hell no, so this is why she was being all nice to me. She just wanted somebody to do her work for her.* So I pretend to ignore her. But she keeps coming back around, asking me what else I had to do that was so important that I couldn't spend some time in the kitchen with her. I finally say ok, but I don't really know much about cooking. And she just says, "Well, looks like today is your lucky day then."

So I start helping Minnie in the kitchen because she was right, I really didn't have anything else to do. And it turns out I kind of like it. I like that she just handed me this big sharp knife and showed me how to chop real fast and smooth, rocking it with one hand on the handle and the other on top of the dull side of the blade. I learn to measure and how there are three teaspoons in a tablespoon and two cups in a pint.

Some of the time we are quiet and just work and other times we talk, nothing big. She just says things like, "I think this needs some more kick, don't you? What do you think, more pepper? Now taste it. Better, right?" And it just feels good, like I can do something right, and when people say good things about the food, Minnie always says, "That's right, Maya is the best cook we've had in this place in a long time."

It reminds me of a feeling that I had a long time ago, maybe when I was with my grandma, that feeling like I'm proud of myself and so is someone else. It feels homesick and happy at the same time.

I hate having those feelings. It messes me up. Some days it makes me want to punch her and I know that sounds really sick, because I really do like her, and I don't know how to explain why I get that way. Maybe it's like I think *what if I get to like you and then you quit your job or I finally get what I want and go to Aunt Hen's? What then? Will I have to stop cooking? Will I have to stop seeing your skinny ass every day?* But then I think, fuck it, I'll just get what I can right now because that's always the way it is.

One day in the kitchen I say to Minnie, like I don't care what the answer is going to be but really I do care more than I think I should and I feel nervous just asking, "How do I get to be a cook, like a real cook who people pay, like on those shows where the guy with the white shirt tells people to hurry up and do this and do that and make sure it tastes really good or else you're voted out of the kitchen?"

She shrugs, acts like it is no big deal I am asking, and says, "Well, you already cook good, and that's a good start but you need to have a diploma or something to get a good job like that; you probably need to get done with high school and then get a little extra school for cooking. No problem for someone smart as you."

I'm not so sure. I know I have like one high school credit, which is pretty bad. I don't know how many I'm supposed to have but probably I'm supposed to be in my second year of high school by now.

Minnie says school here is different, but I have been to plenty of "different" schools before. The Phoenix was supposed to have been "different" but it was just the same old school, only worse. A bunch of miserable pissed-off teenagers jammed into one small room, all of us trying to "move at our own pace" through what other kids our age learned two or three years before. Guess what? Our pace was pretty slow and we just fell further and further behind.

I know I can't read or spell very good but I'm not stupid. I just got behind when my grandma got sick and I wound up going to a new school right when they started getting serious about reading. And then between moving around to different foster homes and group homes and being on the streets I feel like I missed a couple more grades. I got pissed off a lot and some schools put me in the class for the bad kids.[10]

---

10. Children in foster care are more likely to exhibit oppositional and aggressive behaviors. This behavior appears as early as kindergarten and may persist and escalate if proper interventions aren't

Some schools put me in the grade that my age said I should be in and other schools put me in the grade where I left off. Wherever they put me, I was screwed.[11]

Minnie can probably tell I'm not so sure about it because she looks at me and just says, "I know you're smart enough, Maya. You should just tell Robin you want to figure out a way to get through school faster. That's her job. She's helped other kids here graduate. You can do it too. Until you get that diploma, we'll just keep cooking and you'll get lots of on-the-job training, alright?"

So I talked to Robin and she says I have two choices. I can wait until I'm sixteen and get a GED,[12] and that will probably be good enough to get me into the community college where I can take the classes I need to become a cook. But to do that, I will have to officially drop out of school[13] and study for each of the subjects and take the

---

tailored to their needs. See, K.C. Pears, et al., *Effects of a School Readiness Intervention for Children in Foster Care on Oppositional and Aggressive Behaviors in Kindergarten,* 34(12) Child. and Youth Serv. Rev. 2361–2366 (2012). Sometimes this behavior leads to school discipline that can result in further educational disruption. C.G. Smithgall, et al., Behavior Problems and Educational Disruptions Among Children in Out-of-Home Care in Chicago, Chapin Hall working paper (2005). Or the youth may be identified for special education interventions that can result in placement in "behavioral disordered" classrooms where students with similar aggressive or oppositional behaviors are placed. Aubyn C. Stahmer, et al., *Developmental and Behavioral Needs and Services Use for Young Children in Child Welfare,* 116(4) Pediatrics 891 (2005). One study showed that nearly half of California children in foster care who were placed in group homes or licensed children's institutions (LCI) had a special education classification, with "emotional disturbance" being among the most common. Thomas C. Parrish, et al., Policies, Procedures, and Practices Affecting the Education of Children Residing in Group Homes: Final Report (2001), American Institutes for Research.

11. Research shows that state-dependent youth are held back more than their non-dependent peers. National Working Group on Foster Care and Education, Fostering Success in Education: National Factsheet on the Educational Outcomes of Children in Foster Care 5, Res. Highlights on Educ. and Foster Care (Jan. 2014), [https://perma.cc/6VBW-3QVC].

12. Research indicates that youth in foster care are more likely to complete high school with a GED than with a high school diploma. Peter Pecora, et al., *Improving Family Foster Care: Findings from the Northwest Foster Care Alumni Study,* Casey Family Programs (2005); Peter Pecora, et al., *Assessing the Educational Achievements of Adults Who Formerly Were Placed in Foster Care,* 11 Child and Fam. Soc. Work 220 (2006). Research also suggests that the GED is not as valuable as a high school diploma for those who succeed in earning it. *See,* James Heckman, et al., The GED Working Paper 16064, National Bureau of Economic Research (2010); Thomas M. Smith. *Who Values the GED? An Examination of the Paradox Underlying the Demand for the General Education Development Credential.* 105(3) Tchr's College Rec. 349 (2003).

13. The GED test may be taken by anyone who is at least 16 years old and is not enrolled in high school. States vary and may restrict eligibility beyond what the testing service allows. *See,* GED Testing Service, *Frequently Asked Questions* [https://perma.cc/F7H3-UWC5]. *See, e.g.,* Wash. Rev. Stat. § 28A.305.190 (vesting the State Board of Education with the authority to promulgate regulations governing the eligibility of youth between the ages of sixteen to nineteen to take a GED test under limited circumstances, such as when the youth provides a "substantial and warranted reason for leaving the regular high school education program, if the child is home-schooled, or is . . . enrolled in a dropout reengagement program."); 19 Tex. Admin. Code § 89.43 (establishes requirements for 17-year-old applicants with parental permission; establishes requirements for 16-year-old applicants but only if under the supervision or custody of a public agency; applicants must not be enrolled in school unless in an approved high school equivalency program); Iowa Code §§ 259A.2, 259A.6 (Only youth who are residents of juvenile institution or under the supervision of a probation officer may

tests one-by-one so I can show that I know enough. I looked at some sample tests with her and I was good on some of the math. But then I saw the other stuff—the reading and the writing and the science and the social studies. It looked really hard.[14] I don't know any of that and I suck at reading so it will take me forever to study for it and get good enough at reading to even take the test.

> ### Your State's GED Eligibility Requirements
>
> *Foster youth often get far behind in school, making attainment of a high school education through a GED a viable option.*
>
> • *What are your state's eligibility requirements for a GED?*

I ask her what the other choice is and she says that I can "build my own curriculum" with her to catch up on my credits. She calls that "alternative school."[15] I can always switch from the "alternative school" to the GED when I feel ready.

> ### Alternative Education in Your School District
>
> *School districts vary widely with respect to the number and quality of alternative education options.*
>
> • *What programs, if any, are available in your jurisdiction?*
>
> • *What measures are available to assess their quality?*

Robin asks me what "lights my fire"—she always talks like that, all these expressions that make her sound kind of old-fashioned and silly, even though she's like the

---

apply to take the high school equivalency exam; otherwise applicants must be at least 18 years of age and the applicant's high school class must have graduated).

14. The GED test was revamped and the new version rolled out in 2014 is more difficult, more expensive, and only available online, leading to a decline in both the number of test takers and the percentage of those passing. *See* Kaitlin Mulhere, *GED Drop*, Inside Higher Ed. (Jan. 20, 2015), [https://perma.cc/UJC4-V83V]. Cory Turner and Anya Kamenetz, *A Sizeable Decrease in Those Passing the GED*, nprEd, (Jan. 9, 2015), [https://perma.cc/837F-TYZP] and *The GED Test: One Test, Eighteen Million Lives: The 2002 Series GED Test*, GED Testing Service, [https://perma.cc/EN7F-4LKD].

15. There is no one fixed definition of "alternative education," a fact that confounds researchers hoping to learn more about the efficacy of such programs. Often alternative education is defined more by the population of students it serves than the content of the program itself. The student population of many alternative schools consists of those who have either previously dropped out or been pushed out of traditional schools. The key characteristic of successful alternative schools is an awareness of the developmental needs of youth that looks to: physical and psychological safety; appropriate structure; supportive relationships; opportunities to belong; positive social norms; support for self-empowerment; opportunities for skill-building; integration of family, school and community efforts; and an attention to racial and cultural identities, as well as needs arising from disability. *See*, Laudan Y. Aron & Janine M. Zweig, Educational Alternatives for Vulnerable Youth: Student Needs, Program Types, and Research Directions, 20 (Nov. 2003), The Urban Institute [https://perma.cc/NZ64-NDMT] [hereinafter Aron & Zweig Educational Alternatives].

youngest staff person here—and then we can start using my "passion" to get better at my reading and other subjects.[16] I tell her I like to cook. She thinks that is a great place to start.

Then one day I'm in the kitchen with Minnie and she says to me, "Hey Maya, can you pull out one of those cookbooks over there?"

"Which one?" She has a whole shelf of them, some fat and some thin, lots in between.

"Whichever one you want. Let's cook up something new today, ok? I think we're all getting tired of the same old stuff."

"Not me," I say, "I still like as much watermelon as I can get."

She laughs, "Well, yeah, but not everybody can survive on watermelon like you do. And I think that pretty soon even you are going to need to eat something else if you hope to grow that baby any bigger." We both look at my baby bump. It's true. For almost six months, I don't look too pregnant. The doctor did say I should be gaining more weight now.[17]

I look at the row of cookbooks. I can't read what most of them say. The words are long and strange, but there is one that said *Down Home Food,* and I could read that easy enough. Not sure what all will be in it but still it sounds like maybe the kind of food Aunt Hen might cook. Aunt Hen had to learn about down home cooking from Uncle Marcus's mom, because Aunt Hen didn't grow up around that kind of food. Anyway, when I pull it out, I see that the black man on the cover is holding a big plate of greens and corn bread, just like Aunt Hen cooks. He's looking so pleased with himself, and I wonder if that could be me someday—getting paid to be happy.

Minnie says, "Good one!" and I put the book down on the counter. She tells me to pick out what we want to make. I page through and I find a picture of sweet potatoes all bubbling in a brown syrup with lemons on top and I can almost smell them cooking at Aunt Hen's house and I say, "This! This right here!"

"You do have a sweet tooth, don't you?" Minnie says, "But that's a good choice. I think we have all of the ingredients and who doesn't love sweet potatoes?"

---

16. Among the characteristics of a successful alternative school is that the curriculum is "compelling, challenging and inviting." In order to accomplish this, the alternative school must be freed from the strictures of the more uniform curriculum required by most school districts. *Id.* at 34.

17. Research indicates that teenage pregnancy increases the risk for a variety of negative birth outcomes, including low birth weight, preterm delivery and neonatal mortality. These risks are present even when the sample is controlled for socioeconomic status and access to prenatal care. *See* Xi-Kuan Chen, et al., *Teenage Pregnancy and Adverse Birth Outcomes: A Large Population Based Retrospective Cohort Study,* 36(2) Int. J. Epidemiol. 368 (2007). However, the risks of low birth weight are higher for black pregnant adolescents as compared to their white peers. This disparity appears to exist without regard to neighborhood risk factors. *See* Sheryl L. Coley, et al., *Does Neighborhood Risk Explain Racial Disparities in Low Birth Weight among Infants Born to Adolescent Mothers?,* 29(2) Gynecology 122 (April 2016).

"Well, maybe Kai. She's always got something to complain about." We both laugh because we know it's true but Minnie is always careful not to talk trash about any of the other girls.

"How many people is this recipe good for?" She makes me look for the word *servings* up near the top of the page, and it says 8–10 next to it. I realize that isn't enough, especially since some people will probably want seconds. I tell her we have to find another recipe.

Minnie says, "We're good; we just need to make this recipe bigger." Soon we're counting up how many people we have to serve and who will eat a whole bunch and who will pick through it like it's not good enough no matter how good it really is and we are laughing again. Then she asks me to do the math on the recipe and when I look at it that way, it gets super easy. We just need to make three times as much. I've always liked multiplication. But some of it is hard because it's fractions and I never learned those and so we have to actually just measure some things out three times to be safe.

They are so good. It's a good thing we made so much. Even Kai asked for seconds.

After dinner, I ask Minnie if I can take the cookbook with me to meet with Robin and she says sure. Robin is really excited. She says that we have enough right there in that book to get us started on all four subjects I have to learn.[18]

I ask her, "For real? It's just a cookbook."

"Yes, but you can learn math with it, right? I mean you had to figure out how to make the recipe big enough. We can also think about the math for how to make it smaller. Then you'd have to divide and learn how to divide fractions. And then there's the cost of the ingredients and working out the budget for a whole meal and the timing so that the meat and the vegetables are ready at the same time. There's plenty to work with here."

"I guess that's right, math is easy. I mean it's like in everything, but how are we going to get other subjects out of cooking?"

"Well, have you ever thought about where this food comes from, like what is the history of this food? Why do some people eat this food and other people eat other kinds of food?"

"Not really." I explain to her about Aunt Hen having to learn how to cook this kind of food for Uncle Marcus because she didn't grow up eating the same food.

---

18. Flexibility and individualized curriculum design are critical to the success of an alternative school. Preliminary research has shown that students who have had challenges succeeding in traditional schools flourish in alternative schools with non-authoritarian, flexible environments where they feel cared for and respected by staff. *See* Mary M. Quinn & Jeffrey M. Porrier, Study of Effective Alternative Education Programs: Final Grant Report 36, 38, 47, 55 (2006), American Institutes for Research, [https://perma.cc/564T-YH63].

"OK then, see there, right there. You've got a history and social studies course! Where did this food come from? How did it come to be that African Americans cooked one way and white people cooked another? And are there foods that white people eat and don't even know they wouldn't be eating if it weren't for the fact that African Americans or other people from other cultures made them first?"

"Like sweet potatoes?"

"Yes, like sweet potatoes."

I nod and smile just a little bit. She goes on to talk about how baking is just "chemistry in action." You mix this with that and suddenly you have something new. We can learn biology through studying about growing vegetables.

I kept thinking about reading. That's the problem. All this stuff sounds kind of interesting but if I can't read about it, I'll never get anywhere. She sees me looking worried I guess because she asks, "Hey, sorry, am I moving too fast? I just get excited.[19] We don't need to do all of this at once you know. I just want you to see that we can make this about what *you* want to learn. And I love that you have found something that makes you happy. That's the most important thing, that you are happy."

"No, it's not that. This is cool. I might want to . . ."

"Is there something that you're worried about, Maya?"

"Reading." That's all I could say.

"Oh, I see. Do you feel like you want to get better at reading?"

"Yeah, I wasn't in school when they taught it that much. I mean, I can read a little bit."

"OK. We'll work together on that. And there are videos that you can watch when you need a break and have to learn things that are above your current reading level. It's not your fault you missed so much school. You know, of course you have some catching up to do. We'll find out what you need so that you can do better, OK?"

I say ok, but after I get out of her office I just feel like I want to run out the door. And I do, but I don't really run. I walk. And I don't take any of my things with me and really all I do is go outside and feel the sun on my face. I walk about a block to the park and I sit there watching the kids play, their moms and babysitters pushing them on the swing. I sit there and think *is this what I'm going to do? School and a job and push my kid on a swing? How am I going to do all of that?* And I can't help notice I don't look like any of them moms. They're all older than me and dressed real nice and they have strollers that look like they cost a million dollars.

I watch a little girl playing all by herself in the sandbox. She doesn't look so rich. And I don't even see her mother anywhere. I feel strange all of a sudden. I watch her

---

19. Another distinguishing characteristic of a successful alternative school is teachers who are excited about their work and eager to connect with their students. Aron & Zweig Educational Alternatives, *supra* note 15, at 34.

dig and dig and dig like she is going to tunnel out of this world and into another one, I think *yeah, you go, you keep digging your way out, I feel you.*

And just then, for the first time, I feel my baby kick, not just on the inside. I feel a foot or elbow or something making my belly ripple on the outside where my hands are resting. And it is kind of ticklish. I wait for it to happen again, but it doesn't. So I take a deep breath in, hold it for just a quick second, and let it out slow, just like Anita said I should try when I get like this, when I feel too much.

Maya's Roommate: Kai's Story

I didn't choose to be here in this group home. I didn't choose to be on the streets neither. But once I was on the streets, I chose to be in the life. I chose to do it not just because of the money. I chose to do it because I got to be in charge. Ain't nobody can tell me what I do with my body except me; I don't mess with pimps and I do what I want.[20] And because I'm queer[21] I never have to deal with feeling one way or the other about the straight guys who want to pay me to be rough with them. Shit, if someone wants to pay me to put me in charge, I can get into that without getting too into that, if you know what I mean. Plus, there's something right about making money off the bat-shit crazy version of what my family thought I should want to do with "nice boys"

---

20. How those engaged in sex work view themselves in relationship to activities the law classifies as prostitution is subject to easy essentialism. Debate swirls around whether sex workers are autonomous actors capitalizing on their own agency or victims who are trapped and exploited through the nefarious schemes of others. This debate is reflected in the theoretical literature. *See* Shelly Cavalieri, *Between Victim and Agent: A Third-Way Feminist Account of Trafficking for Sex Work,* 86 Ind. L.J. 1409 (2011). Not surprisingly, when minors are involved, the debate is even more complex, given that minors are considered incapable of consenting to sexual activity, as evidenced by statutory rape laws. *See* ch. 5, n. 41. Attitudes are shifting, even among law enforcement, in how minors engaging in sex work are viewed. More law enforcement officers are viewing minors as victims rather than delinquents, but still often see arrest as the only way to protect them and provide access to services. *See* Stephanie Halter, *Factors that Influence Police Conceptualizations of Girls Involved in Prostitution in Six U.S. Cities: Child Sexual Exploitation Victims or Delinquents?,* 15 Child Maltreatment 151 (2010). How minors view themselves as they enter prostitution also varies. Research shows that more than half of those studied who entered prostitution as minors viewed prostitution as a means of re-asserting control over their bodies and sexuality. *See* Jennifer Cobbina & Sharon S. Oselin, *It's Not Only for the Money: An Analysis of Adolescent Versus Adult Entry into Street Prostitution,* 81(3) Soc. Inquiry 310 (Aug. 2011).

21. "Queer" is "used to refer to lesbian, gay, bisexual and/or transgender people or the LGBT community. For some, the term is useful to assert a strong sense of identity and community across sexual orientations and gender identities. . . . Used as a reclaimed epithet for empowerment by many, it is still considered by some to be a derogatory term." *See* Jaime M. Grant et al., Injustice at Every Turn: A Report of the National Transgender Discrimination Survey 180 (2011), National Center for Transgender Equality and National Gay and Lesbian Taskforce, [https://perma.cc/PX5H-XNS5] [hereinafter Grant et al., Injustice at Every Turn] In a recent national survey of 949 youth aged 13–24 engaged in the sex trade across six sites, 53% identified as heterosexual, 36% as bisexual, 9% gay, and 2% other sexual orientation. Four percent identified as trans female. *See* Rachel Swaner et al., Youth Involvement in the Sex Trade: A National Study viii (March 2016), Center For Court Innovation, [https://perma.cc/D4ZY-F65C] [hereinafter Swaner et al. Youth Involvement].

for free. "Yeah, Kai," I remember them saying, "Why don't you find yourself some nice boy to hang with? Why you kicking it with them dykes? That ain't you." Right.

I didn't exactly choose to be pregnant neither.[22] Shit happens. I go back and forth. I could use someone else, some family of my own, especially now that Mikayla's gone.

> ### Power, Agency and Choice[23]
>
> *Kai speaks of choice, the lack of it and her own power and agency. She is diverted to Safe Harbors after having been arrested for prostitution.*
>
> * *How is Kai's choice constrained by her identity and her circumstances?*
> * *If you were her attorney on her juvenile prostitution charge, how would you tell her story?*

The only reason I even stay here now though is to see what the baby will look like when it comes out. If it looks like it could belong to me and Mikayla, then I'll keep it and love it like nobody's business. If not, then they can have it. I don't need no light-skinned baby. I know that sounds cold; I can tell that Maya girl thinks I am a bitch for thinking that way. She thinks she's so much better than me, I can tell, talking all about how she's going to go stay with her aunt and be some kind of fucking happy family. Well, my family ain't got no use for me the way I am and I ain't going to change for them neither. She got her lawyer visiting her all the time too. Fuck, no lawyer I ever had comes to see me here, even the one who told me I could do this instead of sitting in juvie.

I tell myself my baby will be black, like me and Mikayla. I know. Not all babies come out the color they going to be and I probably will have to keep it a while even if it comes out all pink. I know from my cousins that babies get darker; their eyes even change color sometime. So I might have to wait. Which will be a mind fuck. But whatever. I'll deal.

Maybe it's a cop baby and I don't want to raise no cop baby.

---

22. Research over the past two decades shows that LGBTQ youth are between twice and ten times as likely to experience pregnancy than their heterosexual peers. The risks of unprotected sex are especially high for LGBTQ youth on the streets. *See* Elizabeth M. Saewyc, *Research on Adolescent Sexual Orientation: Development, Health Disparities, Stigma, and Resilience*, 21(1) J. Res. Adolesc. 256 (Feb. 2011). *See, also* Michele L. Ybarra et al., *Sexual Behaviors and Partner Characteristics by Sexual Identity Among Adolescent Girls*, 58(3) J. Adolesc. Health 310 (March 2016) (finding that lesbian girls were more likely to report infrequent condom use and discussion with partners about barrier methods of contraception than either heterosexual or bisexual girls).

23. For a critical race feminist analysis particular to prostitution exploring the notion of "choice" and the depiction of black women and prostitution *see*, Cheryl Nelson Butler, *A Critical Race Feminist Perspective on Prostitution and Sex Trafficking in America*, 27 Yale J.L. & Feminism 95 (2015). For intersectionality theory more generally, *see* Jennifer C. Nash, *'Home Truths' on Intersectionality*, 23 Yale J.L. & Feminism 445 (2011).

When I was little, I went to one of them daycares they put us in so our mama could look for a job, I learned that song, *Mary Had a Little Lamb*, but I heard the words all wrong and I used to sing, "Mary had a little lamb, little lamb, little lamb. Mary had a little lamb, po-lice was white as snow." My mom would laugh hard at that and say, "You got that right." I'd sing that shit over and over again for her and her friends and my aunties and uncles because I loved making them laugh. I didn't get the joke back then. I do now.

Mikayla though? She was dark and gorgeous. I'm dark too, not as gorgeous, but not bad-looking if I do say so myself. Or I used to be, before this baby blew me up like a fucking balloon. Now I look like one of them clown toys that pops back up every time you hit it, rocking on its fat ass to smile all up in your face and dare you to just try it again. Except I don't grin. I don't believe in grinning.

When I see myself in the mirror, or when I see those old videos from back in the day (you can still find them on the internet; someone's making bank there), I see the way I walk, how I take up all my space and act like I don't need to ask nobody's permission to be nowhere. I am for real in charge and not anything like one of them fake white lesbians that always be showing up in that vanilla porn that straight guys like. You know those "lesbians" that looks like Barbie dolls?

Don't get me wrong. I'm not real butch neither, just like if you see me coming you know not to mess with me. Still, I know how to work it, like my girl Missy.[24] Old school, I know, but she still workin' it.[25]

Talk about choices. I didn't choose to wind up with Mikayla neither. When I first met her, I fell hard. She was so fine, so femme, and so into me.[26] She smiled at me and I had never seen such a smile and such deep dark sparkling eyes smiling at me like that. I am not messing with you. I was like *damn girl, can I just stand next to you?* Pretty soon I found out that she was trans, and in desperate need of hormones to keep her right. But she couldn't get them except for on the streets.[27] She was

---

24. *See* Missy Elliott, *Work It, from* UNDER CONSTRUCTION (Elektra Records 2002).

25. *See* Missy Elliott, *WTF (Where They From)*, feat. Pharrell Williams (Atlantic Records 2015) [https://perma.cc/AH8A-L5MU].

26. Gender identity and sexuality are separate from one another. One's gender identity does not dictate one's sexuality, just as one's sexuality does not dictate one's gender identity. In a survey of 6,540 transgender and gender-nonconforming people, a wide range of sexualities were reported: 25% identified as bisexual; 23% identified as queer; 23% identified as gay/lesbian/same-gender, 23% identified as heterosexual; 4% identified as asexual; and 2% as other. *See*, GRANT ET AL., INJUSTICE AT EVERY TURN, *supra* note 21, at 28.

27. The lack of access to appropriate health care for transgender people, as well as the hurdles within transgender treatment protocols themselves, makes self-medication through a variety of black market sources common. *See* Gene de Haan et al., *Non-Prescribed Hormone Use and Barriers to Care for Transgender Women in San Francisco*, 2(4) LGBT HEALTH 313 (Dec. 1, 2015). Caitlin Dewey, *How the Internet Black Market Profits Off Trans Discrimination*, WASH. POST (Jan. 29, 2016) [https://perma.cc/J8B9-39XE]. For transgender minors, the problem of access to proper medical care is even greater, creating a heightened risk of medically unsupervised hormone replacement therapy. *See* Emily Ikuta, *Overcoming the Parental Veto: How Transgender Adolescents Can Access Puberty-Suppressing Hormone Treatment in the Absence of Parental Consent Under the Mature Minor Doctrine*, 25 S. CAL. ITERDISC.

doing sex work to survive and to keep all that shit stitched together as best she could.[28]

I gotta tell you the truth. At first, for just a second, I did wonder if I could make it work with Mikayla. I been with girls plenty. In case you haven't figured it out, that's what got me kicked out of my house.[29] And I have definitely known some girls who were bois.[30] I never met anyone like Mikayla, though. She was the most femme girl I'd ever been with.

> ### *Parental Rejection and Dependency*
>
> *Kai never made it into the dependency system but instead joined the ranks of the many queer youth who are homeless due to parental rejection.*
>
> - *Should parental rejection due to sexuality or gender identity be grounds for dependency?*
>
> - *What reasonable efforts should the state make to avoid removal or to reunify a child with her family in such situations?*

Mikayla was soft and sweet, like maybe she never had any facial hair to get over, like she probably been moving like a girl since she was three years old, more like a girl's supposed to move than I ever even knew how.

Still, even though I get paid to do shit with men, they've never done anything for me; their junk is just plain old funny looking. So I was a little worried, but it turned

---

L.J. 179 (2016). For an exploration of how youth are attempting to secure treatment for themselves, see Samantha Caiola, *Taking Charge: How Trans Youth Are Trumping the Medical System*, THE YOUTH PROJECT (Oct. 29, 2013).

28. Transgender people suffer high levels of employment discrimination. This, coupled with challenges of completing an education in the context of severe bullying and high dropout rates, means that income levels are extremely low. It should be noted, however, that educational attainment does not provide the same level of protection against poverty for those who are transgender and gender-nonconforming as it does for the general population. In a national survey of 6,540 transgender or gender-nonconforming individuals, 15% had incomes under $10,000, 12% earned between $10,000 and $20,000 per year, with some of the lowest earners having college degrees. By contrast, only 4% and 9%, respectively, of the general population had earnings at this level. A small percentage of the transgender community turns to the underground economy in order to survive. Eleven percent of this survey sample engaged in sex work. By contrast, only 1% of women in the general population are estimated to be engaging in sex work. The rate of sex work is highest among those who have experienced family rejection. *See* GRANT ET AL., INJUSTICE AT EVERY TURN, *supra* note 21, at 22–23, 33, 102; ERIN FITZGERALD ET AL., MEANINGFUL WORK: TRANSGENDER EXPERIENCE IN THE SEX TRADE 15–17 (Dec. 2015), [https://perma.cc/LWX8-SRJW] [hereinafter FITZGERALD ET AL. MEANINGFUL WORK].

29. Lesbian, gay and bisexual youth are over-represented in the homeless population. To learn more, see Margaret Rosario et al., *Risk Factors for Homelessness Among Lesbian, Gay and Bisexual Youths: A Developmental Milestone Approach,* 34(1) CHILD AND YOUTH SERV. REV. 186–193 (Jan. 2012).

30. "Boi" is one of many gender identities embraced by those in the gender non-conforming community. *See* GRANT ET AL., INJUSTICE AT EVERY TURN, *supra* note 21, at 24.

out I just loved Mikayla so much it didn't matter. It turned out I loved every bit of who she was, even the bits she didn't want any more but was still stuck with.

Being trans is rough no matter what.[31] Being black and trans and on the streets is not just dangerous.[32] It can be deadly.[33] She tried to be careful. And she was mostly good. She was upfront about her situation, put the word out in a way that she hoped would only bring in those who knew what to expect. Even that wasn't bullet proof. Some guys targeted her anyway, like they wanted to get rid of her, wipe her confusing beauty right off this planet.[34]

> ### *Intersectionality*
>
> *Intersectionality has been described as an institutionalized system of "multiple jeopardy,"[35] of oppression and domination based upon overlapping identities of race, gender, class, and sexuality.*
>
> * *Which multiple jeopardies has Mikayla experienced?*
> * *How can awareness of intersectionality influence your work as an attorney?*

31. For a thorough study of the myriad challenges faced by transgender people see GRANT ET AL., INJUSTICE AT EVERY TURN, *supra* note 21.

32. The rate of homelessness was highest among black transgender study participants, three times higher than the rest of the population. Couch surfing and being forced to have sex with someone in order to sleep in their bed were also reported at the highest rates for black transgender and gender non-conforming respondents. The challenges of being homeless and transgender are compounded by discrimination within shelters, many of which are sex-segregated, leading to frequent exclusion, forced housing that is contrary to their gender identity, and assaults in dangerous and hostile shelters. Transgender people of color experience higher rates of physical and sexual assault within the shelter setting than their white counterparts. Homelessness is associated with higher rates of incarceration and underground employment within the transgender and gender-nonconforming community. Fifty-five percent of those who reported being homeless were also engaging in sex work, as compared to only 10% of those who were not homeless. Black participants in this study also reported higher rates of physical assaults in public accommodations than their white counterparts, which means that even accessing a motel or hotel room for the night can be dangerous. *See* GRANT ET AL., INJUSTICE AT EVERY TURN, *supra* note 21, at 112–119, 127, 132. LGBTQ and HIV-affected black survivors of hate crimes were 1.4 times more likely to be injured and 2.0 times more likely to require medical attention than white survivors of hate violence., OSMAN AHMED & CHAI JINDASAURAT, LESBIAN, GAY, BISEXUAL, TRANSGENDER, QUEER, AND HIV-AFFECTED HATE VIOLENCE IN 2013 10 (2014 Release Edition), National Coalition of Anti-Violence Programs [https://perma.cc/46Y4-44JC] [Hereinafter AHMED & JINDASAURAT HATE VIOLENCE].

33. The National Coalition of Anti-Violence Programs (NCAVP) tracks hate crimes perpetrated based upon LGBTQ status. In 2013, 72% of the LGBTQ homicides targeted women who were transgender, with 67% being transgender women of color. This homicide rate gains even greater significance in light of the fact that violence against transgender victims only represent 13% of the total reports made to NCAVP. AHMED & JINDASAURAT HATE VIOLENCE, *supra* note 32, at 8.

34. Among the reasons advocates argue for the decriminalization of sex work is that, in those countries which have done so, sex workers are less likely to be victims of violence or subject to coercion. FITZGERALD ET AL. MEANINGFUL WORK, *supra* note 27, at. 9.

35. *See* Jennifer C. Nash, *'Home Truths' on Intersectionality,* 23 YALE J.L. & FEMINISM 445, 446 (2011).

But that isn't what killed her. It wasn't the streets.

The last time I saw Mikayla was when we were picked up by the police.[36] The cops felt us both up[37] — wanting to see if we were "real," saying they needed to know which lock-up to send us to. I told them me and Mikayla would stick together.[38] But the cops didn't want to hear what I had to say about it. One of them tazed me and then another one hit me for cussing at him and I blacked out.

We were taken away in separate cars. When I came to, there was cum dried on my legs. They all acted like, "Of course there is . . . you're a fucking whore."[39]

I didn't even get to say goodbye. They say she committed suicide in her cell.[40] Bull shit. Mikayla was beautiful and she knew it. Mikayla was into me. Mikayla would have waited to get back out and check on me. She knew she wouldn't be there long.[41]

---

36. Forty-one percent of all black transgender study participants reported having been arrested or held in a cell strictly due to bias of police officers on the basis of gender identity or expression. *See* Grant et al., Injustice at Every Turn, *supra* note 21, at 163.

37. Transgender survey participants reported more frequent inappropriate touching by police officers than other survey participants. Fitzgerald et al. Meaningful Work, *supra* note 27, at 10. In a New York study of LGBT youth engaging in survival sex, nearly all of whom were also youth of color, 63% described negative encounters with the police, including being called names such as "faggot" and "dyke" and being subject to invasive touching. *See* Meredith Dank, et al., Locked In: Interaction with the Criminal Justice and Child Welfare Systems for LGBTQ Youth, YMSM, and YWSW Who Engage in Survival Sex, *Overview* (Sept. 29, 2015), The Urban Institute, [https://perma.cc/WA5B-7J8U] [hereinafter Dank et al. Locked In]. Common among transgender youth are reports that they are unlawfully stripped searched to "assign" gender based on anatomical features. *Id.* at 15.

38. Law enforcement, judicial officers and transgender youth themselves report dangerous outcomes when a young person is misgendered and placed in the wrong facility for their gender identity. *See* Dank et al. Locked In, *supra* note 37, at 76.

39. LGBTQ youth report that throughout the process of arrest, booking and pre-arraignment detention, they feel unsafe due to police misconduct that includes verbal harassment, physical abuse, sexual assault and rape. Dank et al. Locked In, *supra* note 37, at 8. Seven percent of black gender non-conforming research participants reported having been sexually assaulted by the police, and 9.2% of sex workers reported sexual assault. *See* Fitzgerald et al. Meaningful Work, *supra* note 27, at 160. Once taken into custody, black gender non-conforming people are at the highest risk of physical and sexual assault, not only by inmates, but by correctional officers as well. Fitzgerald et al. Meaningful Work, *supra* note 27, at 167. Almost 11% of those arrested for sex work reported having been sexually assaulted by a correctional officer. *See* Fitzgerald et al. Meaningful Work, *supra* note 27.

40. Transgender sex workers have a suicide attempt rate that is 37 times higher than the general population. Sixty percent of those surveyed reported having attempted suicide at least once. Fitzgerald et al. Meaningful Work, *supra* note 27 at 24. Unfortunately given the rate of police violence against black men and women generally and the particular vulnerabilities of transgender sex workers, it may be difficult for a victim's loved ones to believe police explanations relying on suicide. *See* Daniel Funke and Tina Susman, *From Ferguson to Baton Rouge: Deaths of Black Men and Women at the Hands of Police*, L.A. Times (July 12, 2016) [https://perma.cc/FC9G-SM5Q]; For an exploration of a high profile case of a contested suicide of a young black woman detained after a brutal arrest, see Debbie Nathan, *What Happened to Sandra Bland?* The Nation (April 21, 2016) [https://perma.cc/X9DP-GHU9].

41. While it is true that the typical disposition for a prostitution charge rarely results in a sentence or disposition involving lengthy incarceration, research has shown that transgender and gender

Maya's Friend and Mentor: Minnie Water's Story

I would rather cook. Most of the girls here come to me not because I was once like them, but because I find the secret ingredient that makes them feel a little bit more like they are at home in this place. Not necessarily the home they grew up in because — believe me — I know that home is not always filled with the smells and tastes of safety, but maybe some home that they stumbled onto or that they wished for or let themselves imagine. I find out what they like and I make it for them and it helps to keep them here. I know that leaving the life is not easy.[42] Eating good makes this strange safety bearable.

And they know that I don't judge. They don't know why their lives don't shock me. They don't need to know why; a few have found out. Maya might someday figure it out; she might learn that I too once had a boyfriend I thought I loved, who *got* me, and who turned me out.[43] His street name was Fire Starter — yes, even back then we had street names — but his real name was Darrell. I only found that out when I went to his trial. It was odd seeing him sitting there, all cleaned up, with his lawyer, being *Darrell.* Back in those days, it was rare to charge a pimp, but he had so many young girls that they made an exception. Still, I was much more likely to be arrested than he was or than my johns were. And I was arrested. A lot.[44] When I was a kid, they'd release me and Fire Starter was usually right there in the parking lot to pick me up, warning me to be more careful next time. Even when I was too old for juvie, I didn't spend much time in lock up; I didn't know what my record would mean for me when I finally broke away from that life,[45] because I didn't ever think I would leave it.

I give this place credit. With my record, winding up in his kitchen cooking for teenage girls would seem like the last thing I would be hired to do and I am sure they probably had to go through some crazy paperwork to hire me *and* keep their license.

---

non-conforming individuals have spent considerable amounts of time incarcerated, with black survey participants having spent the most time deprived of their liberty. *See* GRANT ET AL., INJUSTICE AT EVERY TURN, *supra* note 21, at 164.

42. Linda M. Baker et al., *Exiting Prostitution: An Integrated Model,* 16(5) VIOLENCE AGAINST WOMEN 579 (2010), Sage, [https://perma.cc/3U8L-LJ36] (describing a six-stage model for exiting prostitution: 1) immersion; 2) visceral awareness; 3) conscious awareness; 4) deliberate planning; 5) initial exit (often followed by re-entry); 6) final exit.).

43. A Canadian study found that 16% of their survey sample of 44 women who had been prostituted stated that a boyfriend or a pimp to whom they had an emotional attachment first "turned them out," usually when they were minors. *See* M. Alexis Kennedy et al., *Routes of Recruitment: Pimps' Techniques and Other Circumstances That Lead to Street Prostitution,* 15:2 J. OF AGGRESSION, MALTREATMENT & TRAUMA 1, 7(2007).

44. A 2009 study combining both FBI and state data sources resulted in an estimated 1,130 young people under the age of 18 arrested for prostitution. Sixty-seven percent of these arrests came from five states: California, Nevada, New York, Texas, and Washington. By contrast, only 607 defendants were arrested on charges of commercial sexual exploitation of children during the same period. *See* SWANER ET AL. YOUTH INVOLVEMENT, *supra* note 21, at xii.

45. Barriers to exiting street-level prostitution include: 1) individual factors, such as the effects of trauma from adverse childhood events; 2) relational factors, such as strained family relationships; 3) societal factors, such as discrimination and stigma; and structural factors, such as a criminal record. SWANER ET AL. YOUTH INVOLVEMENT, *supra* note 21, at 588–590.

But these ladies don't just talk the talk that women who have been in the life deserve a break; they walk the walk.

Really, I wouldn't be here at all if it weren't for Reed. He isn't a social worker. He isn't a teacher. He isn't trained for any of that. He is this rich guy whose conscience got the best of him I guess. He'd go to his fancy architect office everyday where he built huge houses for one or two rich people and maybe their dogs to live in. He's a health nut; so he rides his bike to work every day, rain or shine, and every day he'd pass us all, waking up and falling asleep on the park benches by the bike trail, getting ready to go out and fly our signs on the highway entrance ramps.

One day, he just got off his bike. He sat down on the bench. He just said hello. And he started talking to us, learning our stories. He is some kind of geek and photographer too because he started a webpage and he asked us if it was ok if he made portraits of us, not like some people do, not like the people who look at us like we are animals in a zoo and take our pictures without asking, usually for some art project. He said he wanted to capture how beautifully unique each and every one of us was as people. We laughed at him and shook our heads. Not everyone agreed to do it, but I thought why the hell not? So a few of us let him take our pictures and then he asked us if it was OK if he told a little bit of our stories on the internet and let people know what we needed. Maybe people would help us out.[46]

Reed is a really nice guy; he respects us. And you know what else he did? He touched us, not in a creepy way. But, when you are homeless, people who aren't homeless avoid you literally like the plague. But not Reed. He'd pat us on the shoulder, shake hands, stuff like that. He looked us in the eye, unless we didn't want to be looked in the eye. Some of us can't stand it. You can tell from them photos that he did see the beauty in everyone. He saw us for who we are as people, even with our clothes and hair that isn't always clean, even with our black eyes and our wrecked smiles. He saw us.

I told him my story one day. I remember sitting on the bench with him and we shared a sandwich and we drank from his thermos of hot tea. He came back the next day and read my story back to me to see if it was ok and showed me the picture he took. I was just nodding and saying yes, that's right. When he asked me whether I needed him to change anything or leave anything out, I just shook my head no. I told him wasn't anyone ever said such nice things about me before, not since my grandmother. He hugged me then and said it was time for the world to see what a beautiful person I was.

He told my story of how I been on the streets since I was thirteen and how I been trying to get on my feet and he asked people if they had ideas about how they could help.

And people did have ideas, lots of them. One person helped me get some good interview clothes. A hairdresser came and fixed me up real nice. One person asked

---

46. "Reed" is loosely based upon Rex Hohlbein, the founder of *Facing Homelessness*, [https://perma.cc/P3YB-E4ZJ]. You can hear his story here: https://www.youtube.com/watch?v=_dpanM1yPbk.

me if I would be a cook for her at her house a couple of days a week so that she didn't have to rush home from work and do it. Word spread and I got more gigs like that. And here I am cooking at this job, still doing catering when I have the time, and I am inside now.

Getting housing was even harder than getting a job. Even with a job, it was hard to find something I could afford, but eventually I got a voucher. At first I was in one of those "podments"—a tiny studio with my own bed in it and a bathroom down the hall. About a year ago, I finally earned enough to move into a one-bedroom with its own kitchen, bathroom and a little living room with a fold-out couch.

I carry that story Reed wrote with me everywhere. And I mean I *literally* carry it with me in my purse because it reminds me that you never know what good people there might be out there waiting for you.

It's up to me now to be one of those people, to just say hello.

> ### *Disruptive Innovations*
>
> *"Disruptive innovations" refers to new approaches to old problems that sidestep the strictures that most assume apply. For example, one might assume that it takes a social worker to solve the problem of service delivery to those experiencing homelessness. The usual method of funding social services relies on established philanthropy or government. But here you see a model started by an architect with a passion for photography and social media who enlisted storytelling and crowd sourcing to address individualized needs. Think outside the box—can you imagine a disruptive innovation that would address a problem that you have identified while reading this text?*

A lot of the girls say no when I ask them to help in the kitchen. They have other things on their minds. Or cooking is boring to them. Or they really just want to hurry up and get out of this place and back to the streets. So you can see why it makes me happy that Maya decided to say yes. I need to be careful about showing her how much I like her or getting too excited about the fact that she wants to be a cook. A little bit of appreciation goes a long way. She doesn't trust any of it, I get that. She hasn't learned how to accept that someone sees her like Reed saw me. Not yet.

Notice I say *yet*. Because now I know people can turn the corner. I know Maya can turn the corner. And you know what? Even if she doesn't turn it today? Or this month? Or this year? I know it's a long life. And I would rather believe in her now; so that someday, hopefully sooner rather than later, she can remember that somebody saw her for who she wanted to be.

Maya's Therapist's Story: Anita Cunningham

Being in the life is not the most traumatic thing that's ever happened to most of my clients. It's just the most recent traumatic thing.[47] That's not to make light of their experiences on the streets, but usually there has been so much loss and abuse that has come before, that has made sex work seem like the best choice, that has made the relationship with the pimp, if there is one, seem so necessary and so natural. And for some, it is not just an act of survival; it is a coping mechanism, a way to take control of your body even as you put it at great risk.

Many of my clients come armored in extreme adolescent bravado; they don't present as victims. This doesn't mean that they haven't been exploited; it doesn't mean that they haven't been hurt. But it does mean that treating them like victims, making them see themselves that way, just so that they fit into the latest policy narrative, does not serve them. Spinning victim narratives may work for the legislators who control the purse strings and pass the laws, but it doesn't make for good therapy.

It's important to stay nimble and have more than one tool in your therapist's toolbox to do this work well because each young person is different and what will work for one, won't work for another. I try to stick with evidence-based practices but I always remember that what matters most in any therapeutic relationship is trust, and how to build that requires a certain amount of creativity when it comes to working with adolescents. They are in a middle ground, somewhere between play therapy and adult talk therapy. They are easily restless and bored and cognitively they fall along a wide spectrum of capacity, especially young people whose normal development has been interrupted in the ways that my clients' lives have been. Some clients need to express their stories through their bodies, not their words, because that is where the trauma is living. So sometimes we draw; sometimes we walk; sometimes we even jump up and down.[48]

But safety comes first. The first ingredient of a safe relationship is choice. A young person cannot feel safe if they are being forced to engage in a relationship; so we don't require participation but we explain what we do and offer the service. If the client expresses interest, we consistently let her know that she is the one who decides what direction the therapy will take. As a therapist, I also try to create a safe relationship in which the client knows that it's ok to share whatever she wants, that I won't be shocked

---

47. Dominique Roe-Sepowitz et al., *The Impact of Abuse History and Trauma Symptoms on Successful Completion of a Prostitution-Exiting Program*, 22(1) J. HUMAN BEH. SOC. ENV'T 65 (2012) (finding that the majority of the 49 women participants in a residential prostitution-exiting program reported childhood abuse, adult abusive relationships, and victimization, and concluding that in order to be successful residential programs must clinically address trauma-related sexual issues, concerns and behavior).

48. Sensory interventions for traumatized children, adolescents and parents (SITCAP) is a model of treatment in which children and adolescents are encouraged to externalize their areas of distress, to learn to tolerate and release affect, and to restore a sense of mastery and power. Different modalities are used depending on the developmental stage and individual interests of the client, but often they include play for younger children and drawing for children of all ages. WILLIAM A. STEELE & CATHY A. MALCHIODI, TRAUMA INFORMED PRACTICES WITH CHILDREN AND ADOLESCENTS 12–14 (2012).

or judge or crumble, that I see the strength in her endurance and that her vulnerability is not her weakness.[49] (OK—sometimes I do hear a story that makes me want to crumble, sometimes I do feel angry or hopeless myself,[50] but I need to save that reaction for my own time, with my own therapist who can help me take care of myself in the midst of these stories. My client doesn't need to feel like she has to take care of me.)

> ### *Creating Safety/Hearing Trauma Stories*
> *Anita describes the importance of safety and the attitude she brings to hearing her clients' stories.*
> * *How can attorneys create safety when hearing their clients' trauma stories?*

If and when my client is able to engage in something that looks a bit more like "talk therapy," the two main clinical techniques I fall back on are motivational interviewing[51] and trauma-focused cognitive-behavioral therapy—TF-CBT for short.[52] I use motivational interviewing to get and hopefully keep my clients engaged, to help them decide what goals they want to set for themselves[53] and I use TF-CBT to help them de-fang the trauma so that it can get out of the way of their reaching their goals.[54]

---

49. *Id.* at 144–147.

50. Among the warning signs of trauma exposure response are: 1) anger and cynicism; 2) chronic exhaustion; and 3) feeling helpless and hopeless. Others include: 1) a sense that one can never do enough; 2) hypervigilance; 3) diminished creativity; 4) the inability to embrace complexity; 5)minimizing; 6) inability to listen or deliberate avoidance; 7) dissociative moments; 8) sense of persecution; 9)guilt; 10) fear; 11) inability to empathize or numbing; 12) addictions; and13) an inflated sense of importance related to one's work. LAURA VAN DERNOOT LIPSKY WITH CONNIE BURK, TRAUMA STEWARDSHIP: AN EVERYDAY GUIDE TO CARING FOR SELF WHILE CARING FOR OTHERS, Ch. 4 (2009 Berrett-Koehler Publishers, Inc.).

51. "Motivational interviewing is characterized by an empathic relationship between therapist and client and avoidance of confrontation and persuasion. The therapist uses active listening skills to elicit motivation to change from the client, including discrepancies between belief, values and behavior, whilst also being mindful of the importance of self-efficacy if change is to be successful." Sarah A. Jones et al., *Client Experiences of Motivational Interviewing: An Interpersonal Process Recall Study,* 89(1) PSYCH. AND PSYCHOTHERAPY 97 (April 2015), [https://perma.cc/B4N6-J9PW].

52. When working with children and youth who have experienced trauma arising out of the family context, Trauma-Focused Cognitive-Behavioral Therapy (TF-CBT) is frequently recommended. This therapy integrates several approaches, primarily cognitive, behavioral and family therapy with non-offending family members or caregivers. TF-CBT is focused upon assisting the child with overcoming fear, anxiety and maladaptive coping behaviors. *See* Child Welfare Information Gateway, U.S. Dep't of Health & Human Servs., Trauma Focused Cognitive Behavioral Therapy for Children Affected by Sexual Abuse or Trauma, CHILD WELFARE INFO. GATEWAY (Aug. 2012), [https://perma.cc/RDG6-P8YL].

53. Motivational interviewing has been found to be an effective pretreatment intervention which enhances the likelihood that adolescents will engage in group cognitive behavioral therapy. *See* Sarah Dean et al., *Motivational Interviewing to Enhance Adolescent Mental Health Treatment Engagement: A Randomized Clinical Trial,* 46(9) PSYCHL. MED. 1961 (July 2016).

54. For a compendium of empirically supported and promising practices to assist clients who have experienced trauma, see *National Child Traumatic Stress Network Empirically Supported*

Motivational Interviewing works well for my clients because it's all about allowing the client to be in control of her own change agenda and making sure that she feels heard. My clients have all been lectured to before. They have all been told that what they are doing is dangerous or immoral or illegal. Those messages mostly serve to shame and they don't lead to change. Therapy should do at least this much — tell the client her future is hers to decide.

To make it all the way through this process takes time and consistency, which is sometimes a problem because my clients come and go a lot. Still, trauma work can't be rushed. Before clients can have meaningful opportunities to tell their trauma narratives, they literally have to learn to breathe. And after they have been able to retell their narratives in a way that helps them to understand why their bodies and brains have been reacting in the ways they have, then we work together to learn new skills that will help them feel safe but that won't get in the way of them living their lives.[55]

You hear a lot about "triggers" and many teachers and group therapists are conscientiously giving trigger warnings for those who may have experienced traumatic events.[56] While it's good to give people a heads-up that what they are about to hear or see may contain assaultive language, sexual or physical violence, I think this oversimplifies what a trigger is in the PTSD context. Triggers are an idiosyncratic thing. They aren't always what you might expect. Sometimes they are a smell or a sound. I had one client whose trigger was the smell of a certain kind of soap, because her stepfather always bathed her with it after he sexually abused her. A client may have more than one trigger from one event or the many events to which she's been exposed. So, unfortunately, trigger warnings can't protect my clients from their own unique reactions to their own uniquely experienced traumas.

It is hard to face your triggers in order to rid yourself of them, but it is harder still to live your life afraid to enter a bathroom. And that's just the flight response — the avoidance of things that threaten you. There's also the fight response. The need to lash out in order to protect oneself from a threat that feels real also gets some of my

---

Treatments and Promising Practices, The Nat'l Child Traumatic Stress Network, [https://perma.cc/W89V-NRYK].

55. TF-CBT is a three-stage therapeutic process in which the client first undergoes a stabilization phase in which they learn relaxation techniques, skills to address their maladaptive behaviors as well as information necessary for them to understand the dynamics that underlie what they are experiencing in the here and now. It is only after stabilization is achieved that the skilled therapist invites discussion of the underlying trauma itself. The purpose of this trauma narrative is to process the underlying events in order to dissipate anxiety, fear and other suffering that arises as a result of being triggered by past trauma. The final phase of TF-CBT remains tied to skill-building around safety plans, social skills, and other needs that the particular young person might have. *See* Judith Cohen, *Trauma-Focused CBT for Children and Adolescents*, The National Child Traumatic Stress Network, [https://perma.cc/Z2RH-TJGG].

56. The use of trigger warnings to let students know that material to be read or discussed may address subjects that could be difficult for some students has resulted in controversy across college campuses. *See* Sophie Downes, *Trigger Warnings, Safe Spaces and Free Speech, Too*, N.Y. Times (Sept. 10, 2016) [https://perma.cc/2SN3-A3ER].

clients in trouble—kicked out of schools, off of buses, out of group homes. Here, we don't call the cops as our first response, because we know that aggression is often a triggered reaction.

My job is to help my clients unravel the mysteries of their unique experiences. It takes a lot of courage for them to look at what their trauma has done to them.

Maya has been slow to approach therapy. This isn't unusual, especially given her experience in the child welfare system. Foster kids have been ordered to undergo therapy from a very young age, but the available mental health treatment does not always follow evidence-based practices. And because the youth themselves move around so much they have had to start over again many times with new providers.[57]

Mental Health Services for Youth in Foster Care

- *What is the practice in your jurisdiction when it comes to ordering youth to participate in therapy?*
- *What types of mental health services are available for youth in foster care who have experienced trauma?*

So I have to find the hook. What is that one thing they would like to change about how they feel and act in the world? The goals have to be real and concrete.

Given her big-picture goals of having her baby and living with family, Maya decides to work on managing her impulse to run away. She is learning some tricks she can use to help herself relax so it isn't so hard in those moments that she just wants to run out the door.

So for the last few sessions we have been practicing breathing. This technique is a "pattern-interrupt," but I call it "16 seconds" when I explain it to my clients because 16 seconds sounds totally do-able. You breathe in deeply through your nose counting 1-2-3-4, you hold that breath for 1-2-3-4 and then you breathe out 1-2-3-4 and hold that breath out for 1-2-3-4. And then you breathe normally. Just doing this simple exercise helps a lot of clients interrupt whatever pattern of flight or fight might be happening.[58] Maya seems to take to it right away. I don't expect this to work for her

---

57. Among the challenges identified by foster parents seeking to access mental health care for the children in their care is the lack of continuity of service provision caused by the scarcity of appropriate services, the multiple transitions that children have had to undergo through placement changes and the fact that their mental health records did not follow them from one placement to the next. *See* Eileen M. Pasztor et al., *Health and Mental Health Services for Children in Foster Care: The Central Role of Foster Parents,* 85(1) Child Welfare 33, 43–44 (2006) [https://perma.cc/85NS-AP5Z]. *Accord,* Cyndy Johnson et al., Raising the Bar for Health and Mental Health Services for Children in Foster Care: Developing a Model of Managed Care, (2013) Council of Family and Child Caring Agencies, [https://perma.cc/74E6-R7BB].

58. This exercise is an adaptation of a meditation exercise developed to achieve clarity in high stress moments. Introducing a pattern interrupt can stop the surge of stress hormones that escalate

more automatic reactions to her triggers, like when she lashes out in response to feeling threatened. We haven't gotten that far yet.

We are making progress. At some point, I hope she will talk more about what makes her want to run, what makes her want to fight. But I have been hearing rumors about funding troubles.[59] We may not be able to keep Maya for the full year. It will be awful if Maya shows willingness to go deep and then I have to say, "Never mind." So for now we are keeping it simple and concrete, so that if she has to leave she will have some tools to take with her.

Maya's Teacher's Story: Robin Fletcher

I love my job. I don't think I ever could have imagined that this would be where I would land, but I am glad for the detours I took from my original "five-year plan" that delivered me here. When I was in college, I wanted to go to law school, but I kept hearing from all of my mentors that I should have more life experience. And so I signed up for Teach for America for two years.[60] I thought I would go to law school after that and hopefully land a public interest law job.

Teach for America took me to a tiny town in the Arkansas Delta. It was there that I learned the expression, "making a way out of no way."[61] That should have been my school's motto. The children and their families did a lot with so very little and they taught me how to find and make meaning through being a teacher.

I had found my passion, but it wasn't in teaching a curriculum that forces everyone to move in unison through a series of tests that suck the life out of learning.

---

the flight or fight response. See DAVIDJI, DESTRESSIFYING: THE REAL-WORLD GUIDE TO PERSONAL EMPOWERMENT, LASTING FULFILLMENT, AND PEACE OF MIND 58–60 (2015).

59. Programs, like Safe Harbors, are often created as pilot projects, sometimes referred to as "demonstrations projects," and are intended to model best practices as a way of attracting ongoing sponsorship for and institutionalization of their innovative approaches to service delivery. Pilot projects bring with them a host of constraints and political challenges, not the least of which is being perceived by more mainstream organizations as syphoning needed resources. The typical trajectory of demonstration projects involves efforts expended in securing sponsorship, planning, initiation, institutionalization, stabilization and phase-out. FELICE DAVIDSON PERLMUTTER, HUMAN SERVICES AT RISK: ADMINISTRATIVE STRATEGIES FOR SURVIVAL, 123–125 (D.C Heath & Co. 1984). Furthermore, the often top-down approach as well as time-limited scope of pilot projects receiving insecure funding creates challenges in forging relationships with the community that the pilot project seeks to serve. Elizabeth Mulroy, *Community as a Factor in Implementing Inter-organizational Partnerships: Issues, Constraints and Adaptations,* 14 NONPROFIT MGMT. & LEADERSHIP 47, 57 (2003).

60. Teach for America seeks to recruit high performing college graduates to teach in high needs urban and rural schools. A Teach for America Corps member is placed in a school for a two-year period. *See Teach for America,* [https://perma.cc/8MJ5-JPBX].

61. As Lonnie Bunch, the founding director of Smithsonian's National Museum of African American History and Culture, has described, "The defining experience of African-American life has been the necessity of making a way out of no way, of mustering the nimbleness, ingenuity and perseverance to establish a place in this society." Lonnie Bunch, *The Definitive Story of How the National Museum of African American History and Culture Came to Be,* SMITHSONIAN.COM (Sept. 2016) [https://perma.cc/L5J8-M77U].

There has to be a more innovative approach that values the context and culture of each learning community.

I wound up here at Safe Harbors as an alternative school teacher, helping these girls find their way out of no way. There are precious few opportunities in public education to be creative with what and how we teach.[62] This is one place where we are given license to do whatever it takes to engage our students.[63] Do we always succeed? If success means that every girl who walks in the door walks out a high school graduate, then no. Are there some girls who are so distracted, disinterested or disturbed that they can't focus on or prioritize learning? Absolutely. But when a student lets me see who she is, what really interests her, like the other day when Maya brought that cook book in and plopped it on my desk, if that's success, then yes I do have a fair number of them.

Part II: Maya's Attorney Working Behind the Scenes: Preparing for a Permanency Planning Hearing

Maya's Attorney Receives the Agency's Case Plan

Maya's permanency planning hearing is set for two weeks from now, so I expected to receive an ISSP. I didn't expect it to say what it did. I scrolled through the many pages of boiler-plate. With no parents involved in Maya's case, the only relevant pieces are buried towards the end where the social worker summarizes how Maya has been doing, the services she recommends, and what her permanency plan should be. I am not surprised that the primary agency plan remained the same — "long-term foster care." The alternative plan at least is hopeful — "long-term relative care."[64]

"Long-term foster care" and "long-term relative care" are both frowned upon as "permanent plans" since neither results in the child leaving the system to live in a home with permanent legal responsibility.[65] But with an older teen like Maya who has run

---

62. For a discussion of the tension between the professed need for rigorous common educational standards and the challenges such standards pose to the instructional environment for students, see Diana Pullin, *Getting to the Core: Rewriting the No Child Left Behind Act for the 21st Century,* 39 Rutgers L. Rec. 1 (2011–2012).

63. Alternative schools, often the only opportunity to continue education for those students who have been expelled from other schools, are often exempted from the educational accountability standards in place at mainstream high schools. Deborah Gordon Klehr, *Addressing the Unintended Consequences of No Child Left Behind and Zero Tolerance: Better Strategies for Safe Schools and Successful Students,* 16 Geo. J. on Poverty L. & Pol'y 585, 595–596 (2009).

64. Concurrent planning (working on both a primary plan and an alternate plan to ensure that should the first plan fail, a second is waiting in the wings) is standard practice and is encouraged by federal legislation. *See* 42 U.S.C. § 673b(i); Child Welfare Information Gateway, U.S. Dep't of Health & Human Servs., Concurrent Planning for Permanency for Children (Nov. 2012) [https://perma.cc/Q3P7-V2S7]. To find statute information for a particular State see *State Statute Search,* Child Welfare Information Gateway, [https://perma.cc/DMX4-DQSN].

65. If the agency proposes "another planned permanent living arrangement," outside of adoption, guardianship or long-term relative care, additional burdens are placed upon the state to justify its reasons for doing so. 42 U.S.C. § 675a(a).

away from so many placements, just staying put probably sounds like an accomplishment to her social worker.

What does surprise me is the narrative at the end of the report:

> After a slow start at Safe Harbors, Maya has stabilized in and is benefitting from this placement. She has shown progress in service participation, including therapy and the development of a learning contract to further her education. She has attended her prenatal appointments and has expressed interest in an infant parenting class, which is scheduled to begin in the coming weeks.

> However, the funding that supports Maya's placement will be withdrawn and her placement will no longer be available after September 30th.

> Maya's due date is September 20th. Efforts are underway to find a licensed therapeutic foster care placement for Maya and her newborn as quickly as possible.

> After intensive, ongoing efforts to locate relatives,[66] the following relatives were found: 1) Henrietta and Marcus Clark and their two minor children (maternal aunt, uncle and cousins); 2) Jasmine Phillips (older half-sister in extended foster care); 3) Katherine Phillips (maternal grandmother in a long-term memory care facility); and 4) Lawrence Gordon, a minor half-sibling (Lawrence Gordon is Maya's nine-year-old, maternal half-brother who resides with his father Luke, his father's wife Shannon, and a younger half-brother, Nolan, the child of Luke and Shannon). All relatives, with the exception of Lawrence Gordon, live in the county. Lawrence Gordon lives out-of-state on the Umatilla Reservation. Criminal and CPS background checks have been run on all family with no disqualifying records.

> Plans are underway to hold an FTDM[67] as soon as practicable in order to explore an alternative plan of relative placement. Maya continues to express her desire to be placed with Henrietta and Marcus Clark.[68]

> There is no reason to believe that Maya is an Indian child[69] within the meaning of the Indian Child Welfare Act. Luke Gordon has denied paternity. The tribe's ICWA liaison finds, given the known facts, Maya is not eligible for enrollment.

---

66. If the agency proposes "another planned permanent living arrangement," the agency must document "intensive, ongoing, and unsuccessful efforts for family placement." 42 U.S.C. § 675a(a)(1).

67. Family Team Decision Meetings (FTDM) follow a model developed by Casey Family Programs in 1992 and replicated in many state child welfare agencies across the country. The model seeks to engage family members and other supportive adults with professionals in the decision-making process when a youth's case is at a critical juncture. A variety of professionals may also be involved. The meeting is led by a facilitator with no connection to the case. While consensus is sought, the agency holds the ultimate decision-making authority. See The Annie E. Casey Foundation, Four Approaches to Family Team Meetings 3 (2013), [https://perma.cc/Q923-XY27].

68. If the agency proposes "another planned permanent living arrangement," the agency must document the child's desired permanency outcome." 42 U.S.C. § 675a(a)(2).

69. An "Indian child" is defined for purposes of the Indian Child Welfare Act as "any unmarried person who is under age eighteen and is either (a) a member of an Indian tribe or (b) is eligible for

In conclusion, Maya's near-term best interest would be served by continuing in a therapeutic context and the agency seeks the authority to place her in a therapeutic foster home should one be available at the time her current placement ends. In the alternative, if no appropriate licensed therapeutic foster care placement exists, the agency requests authority to place with an appropriate and safe relative.

So many bombshells in this report. There's the fact that Maya will be leaving the group home sooner than planned. Will she see this as good news or bad? She has a half-brother? Does she have any clue he even exists? Her sister has been located and is right here, close at hand. Her grandmother too, in memory care, which confirms what I learned from Hen. Has Sarah shared any of this with Maya? How willing is Sarah to consider any of these people as placements now that Safe Harbors is no longer available?

I told Maya what I learned about her grandmother soon after I spoke with Hen. She took it in but revealed little of how it made her feel. She just stared at me and quickly changed the subject, asking me what else I had learned from her aunt. I answered her questions and never came back to the subject of her grandmother. I have seen that blank look from other clients. It's like she doesn't know how to feel about the news — happy her grandmother's not dead? Sad that her grandmother may not remember her? Angry that no one bothered to tell her about this before?

I will have to share the information in this report with Maya and prepare our response for the court. But before I reach out to Maya, I call Sarah, Maya's social worker, to learn more. After several rounds of phone tag, we finally connect.

> ### *When to Use Email, When to Pick Up the Phone*
> *Julia decides to call Sarah rather than email.*
>
> * *When is email the best way to communicate with another professional in the case?*
> * *When is a phone conversation the best way?*

"Sarah! Great to hear from you. Thanks for not giving up. Is this a good time to talk a little bit about Maya Phillips' case?"

"Sure. Have you met with her yet to tell her the news?" I see. Sarah's reserving that task for me.

"I wanted to talk to you first and get your take on all of this. I was really surprised to hear about her current placement going away like that."

---

membership in an Indian tribe and is the biological child of a member of an Indian tribe." 21 U.S.C. § 1903(4).

> **Ethical Concerns When Speaking with an Agency Social Worker**
> *Review the rules governing confidentiality.*
>
> - *Has Julia violated this rule by seeming to answer Sarah's question about whether she has talked to her client?*
> - *If you think she has, what should she have done instead?*

"Me too! I just found out last week. And it's not that Safe Harbors is going away. It's just that Maya's bed is privately funded. It's intended for youth coming off the streets voluntarily. The other beds have federal money from the VTA[70] appropriations and they are reserved for kids who are picked up for prostitution. She doesn't qualify for one of those and so when the director got word that the donor wasn't going to re-up, they told me, but only because I called to ask how things were going so I could prepare the ISSP. I mean, really? When were they going to let me know? I guess they kept hoping that somehow things would change and they would find another funder. I pressed them on it because I thought maybe they could just use Maya's state funds, but she says that they aren't licensed to provide services solely with IV-E[71] funding and that her bed with services exceeds the IV-E rate anyway."

"I wonder if Maya's therapist has prepped her for this?" I ask hoping Maya won't be completely unaware of the situation.

"I asked that question too and the director said that the therapist knows but that as far as she knows no one has talked to Maya about it yet. I think they don't want to tell her until they are absolutely sure that there's no money."

"Well, you know, I'm going to have to discuss this with her to do our responsive report. What are your thoughts on the placement issue? What about the relatives? It seems like you found a lot of key people, including a half-brother?"

"Yes, that brother was a surprise to me too. I thought I'd just do another search on the mother's name to see if there were any other dependencies involving her and there he was. After Lawrence was born, the tribe intervened pretty quickly and it became an Interstate Compact[72] case first and then jurisdiction was transferred to the tribe; so it wasn't on our radar for very long. Mom relinquished at birth, and dad and the tribe were interested from the start. So that was that."

---

70. The Justice for Victims of Trafficking Act provided supplemental funding to support trafficking victim programming. *See* 18 U.S.C. § 3014(e).

71. Title IV-E of the Social Security Act provides for the funding of foster care placements in every state and the District of Columbia. In order to qualify, placements have to be licensed to receive Title IV-E funding. *See Title IV-E Eligibility Reviews Fact Sheet*, CHILDREN'S BUREAU, (March 12, 2015) [https://perma.cc/B49A-4JCA].

72. The Interstate Compact on the Placement of Children governs the placement of dependent children across state lines. It is a uniform law adopted by all fifty states that establishes procedures for the interstate placement and determines the responsibilities for services and case supervision. *See ICPC FAQ*, ASS'N OF ADMIN. INTERSTATE COMPACT PLACEMENT OF CHILD. [https://perma.cc/J7XZ-MYBE].

"I bet they were surprised to hear from you."

"Yes, I'm sure Luke thought he had heard the last from us a long time ago. I talked to him, and he seems like a real sweet guy. He and his wife might even be willing to be a placement for Maya and the baby. But it would be complicated accessing case supervision with them being on the reservation and Maya not being a tribal member. I've never had a case like that before, but I figure we need to be looking everywhere, so I am going to do an FTDM to bring everybody up to speed and get a read on their interest. I thought I might be able to get Luke and Shannon to participate by phone and Maya could at least hear their voices."

I have been to many FTDMs with my clients; some are better than others. The idea is to try to get family members involved in the decision-making at key points in the case, like when a child is looking at a possible change in placement. It is a good sign that Sarah is thinking this way, but in an FTDM, the service providers often outnumber the family and the social workers drive the agenda.

"Have you thought about an FGC[73] instead?" I ask. FGCs allow the families to have more control over the decision-making because they get to have private meeting time to generate their own plan for the social worker to consider. FGC facilitators are usually committed to involving the youth in deciding who to invite, and the definition of "family" is stretched to fit important people in the child's life. I have just the facilitator in mind for this.

> ### *Agency Case Planning Meetings*
>
> *Agencies in different jurisdictions engage in different types of meetings that influence the direction of the case.*
>
> - *What types of meetings are used in your jurisdiction and for what purposes?*
> - *Who is invited to attend these meetings?*
> - *What role does or should the lawyer for the youth have in these meetings?*

---

73. FGC or Family Group Conference, sometimes referred to as a Family Group Decision Meeting (FGDM) is based on a model adapted from traditional Maori practices in New Zealand. In this meeting, the family is broadly defined to include a broader network of persons who have an interest in the child's well-being. While professionals are involved in the first part of the meeting to share their concerns and information, the family group is provided private family time to develop their own plan which they propose to the professionals after they are summoned to rejoin the meeting. The agency social worker can reject or seek modifications of the plan. A trained facilitator with no connection to the case shepherds the professionals and family through the process of information-sharing and final decision-making. However, even the facilitator is absent from the room during private family decision-making. *Supra* note 67, at 1.

"I don't know. . . . I mean, couldn't that be overwhelming for Maya? And what if I can't support the family's plan?" I can tell Sarah hasn't had much experience with FGC. I've yet to have a family's plan rejected.[74]

"We wouldn't do it if Maya didn't want it to happen, of course. I haven't talked to her about this, but I just want to be able to put it out there as an option. She may say no. And that's fine. But I have seen these work out pretty well. And sometimes for a young person like Maya who has lost connection with her family it can help her just to know that there are people pulling for her,[75] especially as she gets ready to have this baby. She's going to need all the help she can get. Have you seen Althea do one of these? She is so good."

"Althea Olloway? No I haven't, but I know a colleague who had a good outcome in an FGC she facilitated."

"I'm not surprised. She knows how to work a room. What do you think? Are you willing to consider it if Maya wants to do it? She can work with her therapist to get ready." I know I'm pushing her hard here, and there are some social workers I wouldn't do this with. I know they would get their backs up, thinking I'm telling them how to do their job, but I think Sarah can handle it. Her ego isn't in the way. We both just want to get to a solution that will work for Maya.

"I don't know Julia, maybe. But I still haven't had a chance to go out and see what Henrietta and Marcus's apartment looks like and have a real talk with them. I know their place is small. What if Maya gets all excited and then they can't do it? It's one thing for me to kill her dream, but to have family say no to her could be soul crushing."

"So you've talked to Hen?"

"Yes, I have, but just briefly and she seems pretty hesitant."

"She's had some unpleasant experiences with the system when she was under a lot of stress. You have to give her another chance. I think they want to come through for Maya. They just need help figuring out logistics."

---

74. In New Zealand's first eight months using the FGC method, approximately 2000 cases were referred. Ninety percent of those cases resulted in family-proposed plans. Only two of those family plans were rejected by the agency due to safety concerns for the child. John H. Angus, *Perspectives on The Children, Young Persons and Their Families Act of 1989: One Year On,* 3 Soc. Work Rev. 5 (ANZASW) (Winter 1991).

75. A study of the use of Family Group Conferences for children and youth ages 11 to 18 who were in group home placements in the state of Washington found that 36% of the youth moved to less restrictive foster-care placements, 37% returned home to their parents or were placed with relatives. In addition, interviews with the involved youth concluded that one of the main benefits of the FGC was that the youth felt connected and cared for as a result. Many youth were surprised at how many family members showed up. Common responses included, "I couldn't believe they were all there, mainly just to see how I was doing." *See* Angela Dawson & Briana Yancey, Youth Participants Speak Out About Their Family Group Conference 1–2, American Humane Association (2006) [https://perma.cc/G8CT-QARC].

"I hear you, but you know Maya is a high-needs case and I just need to make sure they aren't in over their heads with her and a baby."

"OK. But it couldn't hurt to have them at an FGC, could it? At this point, don't we need to be looking at someone who will be there for Maya for the long haul? I mean she's going on sixteen years old and in a little over two years she could be out on her own with a toddler. If she's going to run to them then anyway, it's probably better they get involved sooner rather than later."

"I get it. I get it. I will consider an FGC, but I want an opinion from Maya's therapist. Could you get that for me? I don't think Maya wants me talking to her therapist and I really don't want to interfere with that relationship."

"Well, let me talk to Maya. I'm not sure whether she even wants to do an FGC. But if she does I'll talk to her about getting her therapist's opinion."

"I just want to do what's best for her. I've seen kids run before, even after what we thought were very positive experiences with family. It's sometimes scary to take in that you do actually have people who care about you. She's still a teenager and a teenager with serious mental health issues."

"I hear what you're saying. But she has been doing well, going to therapy and school, working hard, and so I would like to have her get some reward for that—some acknowledgement of her ability to make good decisions. If she wants to have an FGC, I think we need to give her that one."

"Maybe. But we forced her into Safe Harbors and look how well she's doing. That's why I wanted to find her a good therapeutic foster home—a step-down from the group home into family living but with more trained support. I know this one placement who almost took her last time."

"Another placement?" I know that Sarah has to understand how bad it is for kids to bounce around from one placement to the next.

"Well, I don't know if the foster parent can do it. Let me get online and check to see if she still has a space." I hear the clatter of keys and I think to myself it's unlikely that Maya will want to do this, but better to know about it than be surprised. The keys stop clicking and Sarah says, "Yes, yes she does have a spot. But as I said, I am not sure whether she'll say yes. She has a great track record with girls who have been transitioning out of therapeutic group homes. She's also licensed for newborns."

"Where does she live in terms of distance from Safe Harbors? Just in case Maya wants to continue using those services and they are available to her there."

"Well, that's a problem. This foster parent is on the other side of town. It would take a while for Maya to get back to Safe Harbors from there and with our budget cutbacks I can't promise that we could get her transportation. She'd have to spend a lot of time on city buses. But I know that there are a lot of other services near this foster parent. Plus, the school there is pretty good, pretty accommodating for teen moms."

"It's going to be hard for her to have to start over again. I think if she were with her aunt she could probably just take one bus to Safe Harbors. Not a bad commute. Something to think about, assuming she really wants to stick with the services and school there. I'll need to ask her." I'm assuming that Maya still wants to stay with Hen and so I'm making as many good pitches as I can for why that would be a good thing.

> ### Advocating for Something Different (without Client's Permission)
>
> *Here Julia is advocating for a different sort of social work intervention that she hasn't even explained to Maya yet.*
>
> - *Is Julie acting ethically?*
> - *From a strategic perspective, what are the advantages and disadvantages of Julia talking to Sarah before she talks to Maya?*

"Yeah, but her aunt will have to get a bigger place if she expects to be licensed; so she could be moving too anyway," Sarah points out.

"Maybe you could just approve Hen for a non-licensed relative placement? I know the financial support isn't as good but they might take it.[76] I just think we need to keep all our options open, don't you?"

"Speaking of which, I hear that her half-brother lives in a bigger place with plenty of room."

I know Sarah is just being hopeful, but it sometimes seems that social workers are more willing to consider the relative they have no experience with than the relative they do. It's like the reverse of that old saying—they're more comfortable with the devil they don't know. Not that Luke is bad. Or good. The point is we just don't know.

"Hmmmm. She doesn't even know he exists. And living out in the country? In a different state? Of course, we'll talk about all of this but it seems like a pretty big change."

"Maybe a change is what she needs, get her totally away from the streets here. We have just a little over a month to get this worked out, so we have to keep everything in mind."

---

76. Unlicensed relative caregivers rely upon the public assistance programs like Temporary Assistance to Needy Families (TANF) for financial support. Even if their income is too high to qualify for the full TANF benefit, they almost certainly will receive the child-only portion of the benefit because eligibility for the child-only portion considers only the child's income. However, the child-only portion of TANF is fairly small. Licensed foster care payments are considerably higher. *See* Child Welfare Information Gateway, Kinship Caregivers and the Child Welfare System 10 (May 2016) [https://perma.cc/HEQ6-GEHD]; For a comprehensive look at the types of licensing requirements prospective foster parents face and when waiver is used, *see* A. Beltran, et al., *Improving Foster Care Licensing Standards Around the United States: Using Research Findings to Effect Change*, ABA Center on Children and the Law, (March 2012) [https://perma.cc/9JCJ-B5E3].

I sense that this conversation is getting just a bit strained, and so I need to wrap it up in a confident, but collaborative, way. I know neither one of us wants to end it in a tit-for-tat argument over whether Maya should get to stay with her Aunt Hen.

"Okay. Next steps. I'll meet with Maya and discuss all of this with her, and if she's interested in the FGC, I'll reach out to Althea and see if she's available. How does that sound?"

"Will you ask Maya about getting her therapist's opinion about an FGC? And I'll also check in with the director at Safe Harbors to see if it's even an option for her to continue services there after she leaves."

"Sounds good, but I'm still not sure how Maya feels about services. Still, it's good to check, just in case. And, yeah, I'll talk to her about her therapist."

"OK. I think the court will expect me to at least have an FTDM with some family members. So you can tell her that I would like her to participate if we go in that direction."

"Will do. Thanks, Sarah. I really appreciate being able to work with you on this case. Maya's come such a long way. We have a chance to make a difference for her, you know?"

And I hear her voice soften, "I sure hope so, Julia. That would be great, wouldn't it? Let's talk again soon."

A good note to close on. Now to find out what Maya thinks.

Maya and Her Attorney Walk and Talk

Sometimes Julia and I go for walks while we talk. I like it better that way because I don't always like looking people in the eye, especially about the stuff I have to talk to Julia about.

It's hot out. We head to the park, which is good. We can walk by the lake and be in the shade and watch the crazy dogs splash around and chase those bright green balls people throw in the water.

Meeting with Clients Outside of the Office

Until now, we have only seen Julia meet with Maya in the context of detention or the court.

- *What are some of the advantages of meeting with a client outside of an office?*
- *What are some of the concerns that could arise?*

Julia wants to know what's new. I catch her up on all my school stuff and the stuff me and Minnie's been doing in the kitchen. I just made the best biscuits the other day; they were so easy.

But then I tell her to get ready because I have some really big news about the baby.

She looks at me and I'm smiling a little and she smiles a little and she says all eager, "What's the news? Tell me!"

"You know how I told you before that I didn't want to know what the sex of my baby was? That I wanted to be surprised, even though I felt pretty sure that the baby was going to be girl?"

"Yeahhh? And?"

"Well, we were doing the ultrasound thing and I could hear the heartbeat and the doctor was showing me the screen. I could see my baby's face! His little nose and eyes. And his feet and his hands."

"His?" she asks all smiling because I'm all smiling.

"Uh-huh. His. The doctor was pointing out all the different things about him and she asked again because she said she wouldn't talk about the baby's sex if I didn't want her to. And then I just got so curious because, well, there he was like a real person and everything and I told her to tell me. So she did. . . . And I'm having a boy!"

"Wow! How does that feel?"

"I was surprised. I was so sure for some reason that it was a girl, but now I'm excited he's a boy. He feels real now. I can't wait for him to get out where I can see him. I'm tired of being pregnant, really tired. It feels like I've been pregnant forever."

"I bet. You're almost there! Just a few more weeks, right?"

"Yeah, the doctor says I'm still due on the 20th but because it's my first that's just a guess, could be earlier. I been getting these fake contractions[77] already."

"You seem like you're doing really well, Maya, taking good care of yourself, getting yourself ready for whatever comes next. That's what I wanted to talk to you about today — the what-comes-next part. Remember how I said you have a hearing coming up in a couple of weeks?"

"Yeah?"

"And remember how the judge told Sarah she had to look for your relatives last time?"

"Uh-huh. Has she done it? She told me she was 'looking into it,' but I never heard anymore from her about it."

"Yes, she has looked for your relatives and found quite a few. She did a report that she filed with the court. I got a copy of it. It has lots of news in it. I called her right

---

77. Braxton Hicks contractions frequently occur during the last few months of pregnancy. These contractions are caused by a tightening of the uterine muscles and are a precursor to the real labor. They are erratic, less painful and typically of shorter duration than actual labor. *See Labor and Delivery, Postpartum Care*, Mayo Clinic, [https://perma.cc/DD2V-RMD6].

away to talk about it because I wanted to make sure I understood what she was saying before we met. There's news about your relatives and news about Safe Harbors. What do you want to talk about first?"

"I want to know what she said about my family."

"She found your Aunt Hen and Uncle Marcus, of course. And she also found your sister Jazz. And your grandmother. . . . ."

"She found all them?" I can hardly believe it, "Where's Jazz?"

"She's right here in the county somewhere. She's in extended foster care, which means that she's getting money from the state still to help her out. I don't know all the details of what her living situation is, but it sounds like she's doing well."

"Wow, can I see her?"

"Would you like to?'

"Yeah! She needs to know she's going to be an aunt!"

"OK then, we will definitely tell the court that you want to see her."

For real? I might actually see her? What does she look like now? I still see her like she was when we were staying in that one lady's house, like forever ago. She was like, what? Maybe just nine or ten?

Julia says, "Your grandmother is in a nursing home, like I said before, and it seems like she may have some memory problems."

"I still want to see her," I blurt out before I have the chance to even think about it.

"OK, I will put that in our report too."

"Do you think the judge will let me?"

"Yes, I do. I can't promise but I know that this judge is very pro-family. Remember, she wanted Sarah to do this search."

"What about Aunt Hen and Uncle Marcus? Can I go live with them then?"

"I do want to talk to you about that, but before we get there, I want to finish telling you about all of the family that Sarah found."

"What do you mean? There's more? There isn't anybody else. Unless it's my mom and I thought they gave up caring about her."

"It's not your mom. They found someone else that I didn't know about."

"Who?" I start wondering if they figured out who my father is somehow.

"It turns out that your mother had another child, a boy named Lawrence. He's younger than you."

"What? No. What? You're kidding me," this makes no sense. When would that have happened? How come she never said nothing?

"Sarah says it turns out that your mother had a relationship with a man named Luke and they had a baby together, but your mom couldn't keep the baby because of her problems."

"Yeah. She's a mess." I want to say *but I love her anyway* but I don't say it, partly because it would feel weird to say that to my lawyer and partly because I'm just not sure how I feel about her anymore. Mostly I just don't want to turn out like her.

"It sounds like your mom has had a lot of problems for a pretty long time. But, it turns out that Luke, your younger brother's father is a member of a tribe in Oregon. Luke went back to the reservation there and eventually the baby, Lawrence, came to live with him. Luke got married to someone else and they have a little boy of their own too. They all live on the reservation with Lawrence, your half-brother."

"A little brother? Damn."

"Yeah, a little brother."

The dog I've been watching is swimming way out into the middle of the lake now. He sees some ball or stick I can't see. I just watch his yellow head moving out there above the water. All I'm doing is watching that head and then I hear myself say, "This Luke guy, he's an Indian?"

"Yes, he's a member of the Umatilla Confederated tribes."

We both just sit there for a while. I don't know what she's looking at. I'm not even sure what I'm looking at anymore.

"You think he might be my father too?" And I feel like it's somebody else asking these questions.

"Sarah had that question too. So she called him up. She says that he didn't meet your mother until years after you were born. But if you want to, I could see if he would be willing to take a paternity test or maybe even look into bringing a paternity case, just to be sure he's telling the truth."

"Naah, if he says he's not my father, then he's probably not my father. I never heard of him before anyway." I think I must be talking quiet because Julia scoots over closer on the bench to hear me.

"Well, you let me know if you want me to find out anything else about him. Sarah seems to think it would be good for you to meet him and your brother. She says she'd be willing to try to arrange that."

"What, so now some guy we never heard of is good enough for me but my Aunt and Uncle who been there for me forever aren't?"

"Let's talk about what she said about Aunt Hen and Uncle Marcus. Is that OK with you?"

"Yeah, sure, why not? Let's hear it."

"The good news is she ran a background check on them and she says that no problems showed up."

"No shit. I could have told her that."

"She's also moving a little bit towards being willing to consider them. The way that social workers do these reports — they have to have a Plan A and a Plan B. Plan A is what they say they want to have happen and Plan B is what they will go with if Plan A doesn't work out. Do you get what I'm saying?"

"Kind of," but actually, I'm still thinking about the fact that somewhere I have a little brother and how weird that is. Everybody always thought I was an Indian. Maybe he *is* my dad.

"So, what do you want to hear about first—her Plan A or her Plan B?"

"What are you talking about?"

"I thought so. I could tell your mind's off somewhere else. I don't blame you. Where were you? In your head I mean?"

"I was just thinking about this whole little brother thing and how people always say they think I'm an Indian. I mean, don't you think that's weird? I mean, I never thought I looked like an Indian. I'm guessing there's some red-haired drug dealer out there that's probably my father. So none of it matters, but still . . . it's just weird."

"It is weird. All of a sudden you have a brother."

"Yeah . . . I'd like to know if he has red hair though. If he has red hair, I want a test!"

"That would be just too much of a coincidence, wouldn't it?"

"Yeah." We sit there a little while and my back is starting to hurt and so I say, "Can we walk? I can't sit no more."

We walk near the lake, under the shade trees and then Julia asks, "So you ready to hear about Safe Harbors? Then we can circle back to what Sarah recommends."

"Sure," I do feel better now, like I left that little brother and his Indian daddy sitting on the bench over there.

"It's pretty big news too actually. It sounds as though the program has some budget problems and so come September 30th, you probably won't be able to stay there anymore."

I stop walking and just look at her, "What? Why?" I feel like all this news is just flying at me, whipping past me like bullets that almost hit me. Your sister's practically your neighbor. Your social worker thinks your aunt and uncle aren't so bad. You got a brother who's an Indian. And now … you don't have a place to stay no more.

"Well, you know how you've told me that most of the girls who are staying there have prostitution charges, but you don't?"

"Yeah, what's that got to do with it?"

"It turns out that they had two different kinds of money that they use to pay their bills—one is from the government that pays for the girls who have prostitution charges or who are witnesses against their pimps."

"That ain't me. No way would I turn on Di," I don't even think about it when I say it, but she just keeps rolling with it, like it's no big deal.

"And nobody is asking you to. The money that funds you to stay at Safe Harbors comes from a different place, not the government. It's somebody who just gave the money as a gift to Safe Harbors and said, 'Use this for kids who don't have any charges against them, who just need to be off the streets so that they don't get charges against them.'"

"That makes more sense to me. You shouldn't have to get in trouble to have a place to stay."

"Yeah, that's probably what this person thought, and I'm sure that they hoped that other people would agree and give their own money, but now the money is about to run out and they haven't found any new money to replace it."

"Well, that sort of sucks. I mean, I want to go live with my Aunt Hen, but for a group home, Safe Harbors is pretty good and if they won't let me stay with Aunt Hen, I want to stay."

"That's good for me to know. Tell me more—what do you like about Safe Harbors?"

"Why should we talk about that if I'm going to have to leave?" I'm feeling grumpy and I'm not sure why. I mean, this could be my big break. They might *have* to let me stay with Aunt Hen now. But still I feel angry, like this is why I should never have let myself like anything or anyone because if I do then you know they will switch it up on me.

"That's a good question and we don't have to talk about Safe Harbors if you don't want to. I just want to know in case there is a way we could still try to take advantage of some of the things that Safe Harbors has to offer even if you aren't living there anymore."

I take a deep breath and I say, "I don't know. I like how I do my school there and I like that I get to cook and sometimes I like some of the things that Anita helps me with. I just started my baby classes and I was getting all excited about them, and I have all my doctor appointments all lined up."

"That's a lot. You've done everything that Sarah wanted you to do and then some really."

"I know. But does that mean that after September 30th, I get to stay with Aunt Hen and Uncle Marcus?"

"So, first let me tell you what she says she wants to have happen in her report and then let me tell you about the phone conversation she and I had because I think we might be able to do better than what she says in her report."

"I'm so sick of Sarah. Why do we always have to work so hard to get on her good side?"

"I know this is frustrating. It's really hard to believe, but I do think we are making some progress. Not saying she's all the way there, but almost."

"Well, she better fucking say it's OK. I mean where else am I going to go?"

"So, like I said before—she has to have a Plan A and a Plan B. Her Plan A in the report is that you go to a licensed therapeutic foster home, which means that you would not be in a group home anymore but you would be living out in the community with foster parents who have special training to help with the sorts of things that Anita is working on with you. Her Plan B is that you will be with relatives. She doesn't say which relatives, but really there's only two sets that she's turned up—your Aunt Hen and Uncle Marcus or Luke and his wife, Shannon."

"Hell no to Plan A. Hell yes to Plan B—if it's Aunt Hen."

"I thought you might say that. I asked her about her Plan A and she told me she has a particular foster parent in mind who does have room for you but she admits that it's not perfect because it's pretty far away from Safe Harbors. She agrees that it would be better to keep you closer to Safe Harbors if you could still go to school and counseling there. And, as it turns out, your Aunt Hen and Uncle Marcus's place is closer to Safe Harbors than this other foster parent is. So I think we actually have her much further along than we did before when she was unwilling to even consider them."

"Yeah, but she still says she wants me to do this other thing more, right?"

"That's what her report says."

"Well, I'm not doing it. I swear. What the fuck else does she want me to do to prove that I can live with who I want to live with?" If they only knew how many times I almost left, how many fucking times I got up when I didn't want to get up to go see the doctor or the teacher or the therapist or even goddamn Minnie who wants me to help her make the breakfast now too. Shit, I don't know why I don't just run. What the fuck good does any of this do? I don't want to breathe and count my breaths. I don't want to even have this baby right now. I just want them all to stop with changing up the rules all the fucking time.

And then I hear Julia say the nicer version of what is rattling around in my head. Always the nicer version.

"I talked to her about that. I didn't say it quite like that, but I told her you had done what you needed to do to prove that you know what's best."

"And what's her problem then with Aunt Hen and Uncle Marcus?" I take those deep breaths anyway.

"Mostly I think she's worried they don't have room for you."

"I don't give a flying fuck if I have to sleep on the couch. Hell, I've slept on the sidewalk. A couch sounds fucking good to me." I'm so mad I'm crying now, and I hate crying.

"OK, Maya, I hear you. It is crazy that sleeping on a couch should stop you from staying with your family." She moves away a little, giving me some space, but the look on her face is that look she gets, like she wants to give me a hug or something. But I think if she touched me now, I might pound her.

"Damn straight." I sniffle and wipe my eyes, pulling myself together.

When a Client Gets Angry

Here, Maya lets Julia see how angry she is.

- *Does Julia respond well? Why or why not?*
- *How would you respond?*

"I am not really sure how solid Sarah is with the foster parent idea anyway. On the one hand, she seems to like this foster parent, but she also said that she wants to have a meeting with you and your family members."

"A meeting? What kind of meeting? Why?"

"I told her I would talk to you about what kind of meeting we wanted to have. She has one idea about what it should be and I'm trying to get her to consider another kind."

"When? What are you talking about?" My heart is still racing but I'm trying to hear what she's saying.

"We would need to have it pretty soon, in the next couple of weeks. And we would do it so that we could have everybody sitting down together to hammer out a plan. In the kind of meeting that I am suggesting, usually more family members are there and the family, including you of course, has private time to come up with your own plan, rather than having the social worker tell you what the plan will be. The social worker can still turn down the family's plan but, honestly, the social workers are almost always surprised by how much they like the family's plans."

I am imagining being alone in a room with my Aunt Hen and Uncle Marcus and maybe my sister Jazz and my grandma when Julia explains the other kind of meeting that Sarah wants, where I wouldn't be alone with my family and then she asks, "What do you think? Sarah is going to have a meeting; it's just a matter of what kind of meeting it's going to be. You don't have to go to either one if you don't want to. But if you are there, you can help to say what you want and what you don't."

"I need to be there. It's just weird, you know. I haven't seen everybody all together in a really long time." I feel exhausted all of a sudden, like I'm done shouting and just want to sleep.

"I bet it is weird. And then there's these new members of your family that you didn't even know about."

"Do they have to be there? It's not like I am going to go and live with them."

"I think Sarah wants to try to get them on the phone at least so you can hear their voices, but if it's too much I could ask her not to do that."

"Maybe . . . if he came I could see what he looks like I guess. But I wouldn't be able to tell that over the phone. Tell her he can come but only if he comes in person."

"Let me see if you and I can figure out which kind of meeting you want, because that might help a little with figuring out who gets invited."

"I want the one where I get to do the inviting."

Julia smiles and says, "That makes sense. Neither of these meetings give us perfect control over that, but if we go with the one that I'm thinking about, we might have a little more control over who gets asked."

"I want that one then."

"Alright, well let me make sure you understand what that one looks like first before we settle into it because I don't want you to agree to it just because I suggested it. If you don't want to do it, it doesn't happen, OK?"

"I get it. I'll tell you if I don't want to do it." Then she launches into this explanation about how sometimes in an FGC everybody's in the same room together and sometimes they're not. And Sarah wouldn't run the meeting, but she would still be there for part of it. Some other lady would be in charge.

I tell her I like that idea better than the one where we all have to sit and listen to what Sarah wants to do. She asks who I would like to have come.

"Well, Uncle Marcus and Aunt Hen. I'd like to invite Jazz because she's part of my family too."

"Sounds good. It's important that you think of this as being not just about where you will live, but also about who you want to have in your life. People can help out in all kinds of ways. Just knowing you can call someone up on the phone when you need help might be nice."

"I guess so. I never done that before though."

"Well, that's what we'd like to try to change with this. So who else would you like in the room?"

"My grandma, if she can come."

We go to a picnic table in one of them shelter areas where people have picnics, but nobody's there so I can rest and Julia can take notes. She gets out her yellow pad of paper and starts writing. Why do lawyers always write on yellow paper?

"OK—So your aunt and uncle, your sister, your grandma. Now the other thing to know about these kinds of meetings is that you can have other people there who may not be relatives by blood but who may have become important to you. And they can sit in during the family time and they can be part of the plan. Is there anybody like that who you'd like to invite?"

I think about it and it seems strange, but only one person comes to my mind, "Minnie."

"Minnie?"

"Yeah, she's the cook at Safe Harbors."

"Oh right! That's a great idea. She seems like someone who has made a big difference for you. Anyone else?"

"Nah. That's it. Minnie and the rest."

"And what about Luke and his wife?"

"Well, I don't know, but maybe. Maybe, if they show up in person. If they want to do that. They probably won't show up."

"OK, you don't have to decide on everybody right now. There's one other thing. Sarah would like me to ask you to get a note from your therapist saying that it will be ok for you to be involved in an FGC. She's concerned that an FGC might be overwhelming for you."

"Why wouldn't *her* meeting be overwhelming?"

"I guess because she thinks that in her meeting it's not just you alone with your family having to come up with a plan. In her meeting, everyone is there all the time including her. And there may not be quite as many family members there."

"She thinks it would be a good thing for her to be in the room the whole time? I wish she didn't have to be there at all."

> ### *Neutrality When Offering Options*
> *Attorneys provide their clients information about options and let them choose which one they want. Often that means that options have to be compared so that the client understands the differences between them.*
> - *Is Julia being neutral in the description of the two meeting options?*
> - *Should she be?*

"I like the idea of letting my family and me come up with our own ideas without Sarah in the room. It might be good because I don't want Aunt Hen going off on Sarah and messing it up. She can get mad at social workers sometimes."

"Is it OK if I talk to Anita about this and see if she's willing to sign something saying it's OK for you to do this?"

"I guess."

She takes out a piece of paper and explains to me that if I sign it, then Anita is allowed to talk to her and she says she won't ask her about anything except the note for Sarah.[78] I sign it.

---

78. States vary as to when minors are considered old enough to consent to mental health treatment. *see* Nat'l Dist. Attorneys Ass'n, Minor Consent to Medical Treatment Laws (2013), [https://perma.cc/CSM5-C6KT]; *see also* Guttmacher Inst., Minors' Access to Prenatal Care (2014), [https://perma.cc/ZD9M-4KE5]; Guttmacher Inst., An Overview of Minors' Consent Law (2014), [https://perma.cc/Y5N-NCQH]) The Health Insurance Portability and Accountability Act (HIPAA) protects the privacy rights of patients and forbids the release of information without proper permission. *Your Rights Under HIPAA*, U.S. Dep't of Health and Human Servs., [https://perma.cc/BXW4-5VF2]. Permission is to be sought from the person who has the authority to consent to the treatment. *Id.* For young children, these permissions are typically given by the

> ### Age of Consent for Mental Health Treatment
> *Different states have different rules about whether and when a minor can refuse or consent to mental health treatment. What is the law in your jurisdiction?*

Then Julia asks me if I have any other questions and even though I feel like my whole life right now is one big question, I tell her no.

Maya's Attorney and Social Worker Agree to a Continuance

It's not always easy to move quickly when there are so many moving parts. Trying to balance the work on my other cases with the multiple efforts it takes to touch base with Anita, tee up Althea to do an FGC on short notice, call Hen to see how she is feeling about all of this and then finally get back on the phone with Sarah takes persistence, but the days are winding down until the hearing and even more importantly until Maya either loses her placement or has a baby. Shortly after our last meeting, Maya was admitted for what looked like early labor, only to be released. I would really like for her to not have to adjust to being a mom in the midst of uncertainty about where she will live.

Finally, Sarah and I connect. I think Maya's admission into the hospital scared her too. She's much more flexible.

In the end, we agree to an FGC. Anita is in support and that seems to satisfy Sarah. I have been able to get Althea lined up. But she couldn't do it until after the permanency planning hearing is scheduled. Sarah and I agree that asking for a continuance makes sense.

---

parent. *Does the HIPAA Privacy Rule Allow Parents to See Their Children's Medical Records,* U.S. Dep't of Health and Human Servs., [https://perma.cc/7H58-BW6S]. For young children in foster care, permission may need to be sought instead from the social worker or perhaps the court-ordered caregiver, especially if the parents' rights have been terminated. However, because HIPAA defers to state law in determining who has authority to consent to treatment and hence has access to records, 45 C.F.R. § 164.502(g)(3), practices for foster youth vary from state to state. *See, e.g.,* Cal. Civ. Code § 56.103 (health care provider may disclose medical information to a county social worker or probation officer for the purpose of coordinating health and medical care to a minor); 55 Pa. Code § 3130.91 (distinguishing between routine and non-routine medical care for purposes of determining authority to consent to treatment). For older children, like Maya, if the state law allows for her to consent to or refuse mental health treatment, then her permission will be required before her therapist can discuss her work with her. *See HIPAA Privacy Rule and Sharing Information Related to Mental Health,* U.S. Dep't of Health and Human Servs., [https://perma.cc/QSH9-RY9W]. In addition to HIPAA requirements, therapists are also governed by their own codes of ethics requiring confidentiality. *See* Am. Counseling Ass'n, 2014 ACA Code of Ethics, Section B (2014) [https://perma.cc/ZRA4-JJCP]; Clinical Soc. Worker Ass'n, Code of Ethics sec. III (2016), [https://perma.cc/9MZX-5WK4].

> ### *Out-of-Court Advocacy*
> *Through persistence, Julia was able to move the case outcome closer to her client's goal of being placed with family.*
> - *What skills did Julia exercise to advocate for her client?*
> - *What strategies did she deploy?*
> - *What substantive knowledge did she have to have in order to be successful?*

After I get off the phone, I give Maya a quick call before I head to court for a full docket. It's hard to tell how she feels. She is quiet. I tell her that I have to run, but that I just wanted her to know that the FGC is going to happen, that Anita came through for her and Sarah agrees. I promise to check in with her tomorrow.

Part III: Maya's Family Group Conference

Stage 1: Introductions and Information Sharing

Even before I open the door to the meeting room, I can smell something good, something familiar. I smell food—the sweet potatoes from Minnie's cookbook; the biscuits my Aunt Hen used to make; something sweet like my grandma's cinnamon apple cake. Then, I remember that lady, Althea, who is going to be in charge of this; she told me that I shouldn't think of this like a big scary meeting, more like a "potluck." I think I know just from the smell of it, even before I open the door, who is going to be there, but I don't want to get my hopes up. I can't.

And now it's happening. When I peek into the room, it's pretty overwhelming. There are so many people in there. I shut the door and I look at Julia. I probably look pretty scared. I think maybe even Jazz is in there. I should be happy but my heart is racing and I feel dizzy, like I might fall right over.

Julia says to me, "You got this. Remember, I will be there for the first part with you but then you get to have your time alone with your family. I will be right outside nearby the whole time, just in case you have any questions or need an excuse to just take a break. I will be here for as long as it takes."

"All day?"

"All day if that's how long it takes. I brought my knitting and a good book." Julia knits? I wouldn't have guessed that. She looks toward the door and puts her hand on my shoulder in an almost hug.

I open the door just a little bit again and I see that Aunt Hen and Uncle Marcus are for sure both there. I am so pregnant, I am about to burst. What will they say when they see me? What will they think? I close the door real quick again. I hear Uncle Marcus chuckle a little bit.

Julia says, "Let's try that counting thing you told me you practice with Anita."

"I can't remember how it goes." I think I might pass out. I'm serious. I can't remember anything.

"OK. What is it? Deep breath in, right?"

I take a deep breath in.

"Breathe out slowly."

I breathe out slow.

Julia counts, "1-2-3-4," while I breathe out until there ain't nothing left.

We do it two more times.

Althea pokes her head through the door and smiles at me and says, "You ready, sweetheart? There's some people in here who can't wait to see you." She's a happy lady, with a warm smile and twinkly hazel eyes. There's no room for sad when you see her.

I nod my head. I feel one foot go out in front of the other and before I know it I'm on the other side of the door.

They did the conference room up all nice, with decorations and a table cloth on the folding table and the food, so much food, and lemonade and iced tea. And presents too, all wrapped up in paper with baby stuff on it. Rattles and storks and umbrellas and giraffes. They are for me; for me and my baby.

And then I look at the people around the table and I can't believe my eyes. There's people I know, people I think I know, and people I swear I have never seen before in my life. I'm frozen in place. Aunt Hen finally gets up from her chair and comes over to me, she grabs my hands, and she says, "Well, just look at you!" Then, she pulls me close and laughs, "I can barely get my arms around you! I guess you *are* going to make me a great aunt!"

Uncle Marcus gets up and hugs me too. And then the one I think is Jazz, now all grown, looking really good in a nice outfit, gets out of her chair and she helps me to sit down at my place at the table. Julia sits down next to me. I think Julia's crying a little bit, sniffling but she's pretending it's just a cold.

When Jazz sits back down I see that she is sitting next to a skinny old lady. I look at her and think, *Is that grandma?* It kind of looks like her but it kind of doesn't; she is looking at me the same way, like she knows me, but she doesn't.

Althea tells everybody to introduce themselves and she says the people who know me are supposed to share a memory about me and those who don't know me yet can explain how they are a part of my family. She asks Aunt Hen to go first.

Aunt Hen looks at me and smiles like she's got it all under control. She takes her own deep breath in and out and talks not just to me but to everyone in the room, "Good afternoon, everybody. I am Maya's Aunt Hen and I am just so happy to be here today and to see you, baby. I have so many good memories of Maya. She was such a fun and busy little girl." She tilts her head like she's watching a little movie in her brain, and says, "Here's one. When Maya and Jazz were little, when you were maybe only three years old Maya, before my little girls were even born, I remember taking you to see the fireworks down by the lake. Jazz, I mean Jasmine, you spent most of the time covering up your ears on the blanket. But Maya, you were busy ooh-ing and aah-ing the whole time, right along with all the grown-ups. You were having such a great time, Maya, and when the grand finale started, you got up and danced around, throwing your fists up into the air with each boom. You were such a joy to watch, just exploding with excitement."

I don't remember that but Jazz — who I guess is Jasmine now — is nodding along, smiling and saying, "Yeah that was Maya alright. So much energy."

Then Uncle Marcus said, "You used to always call me Uncle Barkus, remember that, Maya?"

I do kind of remember that. Or at least I remember my favorite stuffed animal, Barkus, that I had when I was little. I took that puppy with me everywhere. I lost it when Jazz and me got taken away. But that's probably why I called it Barkus, 'cause of Uncle Marcus. Maybe they gave him to me? Yeah, I think they did.

Jazz looks at me and says, "Maya, first I want to say that I have thought about you every day, wondering *where* you were and *how* you were. We have so much catching up to do. I can't believe I'm here today with you and all of these people."

Me either.

"Anyway, what I remember most was how mom used to always take us to grandma's when we were little and grandma always made that cake for us, and so I made one just like it for today because it was your favorite. Isn't that right, grandma? Apple cinnamon crumble cake was Maya's favorite?"

And then the skinny old lady looks at me and she nods like she's thinking real hard. One side of her mouth is turned down like it's frowning, but the other side looks almost like it's smiling. She says, "That's right?" more like it's a question than an answer.

I say, "Hello grandma?" I can't believe she's still alive. Just barely, it looks like.

Jazz is patting her arm and looking at me like I shouldn't expect too much and just then grandma bursts out, "13 times 13!"

Everyone looks like they are all embarrassed for her but I am not. I know exactly what she is saying. I know that grandma remembers even if they think she doesn't, "169!" I say back at her just like I used to.

"That's right!" she says. That's a memory we both have. It comes back to us both, how in third grade when everyone thought I was dumb and everyone thought I was too behind and would never catch up, Grandma said *we'll show them in that math bee, Maya, we'll show them you know all of them times tables. Even the thirteens!* And grandma came to school just to see me do it. Said she wouldn't miss it for the world.

I feel like crying and running and laughing and maybe even dancing all at once, like them crazy fireworks that Aunt Hen says I used to like, but I can't even move.

Grandma probably gets it. She can't show it either, how all these feelings feel, how it's hard to always believe that these lost memories are real, that they are still there, buried down deep somewhere.

Next, it's this guy's turn. He has dark wavy hair and a round tan face. He is slow talking and his voice has a sing-songy sound to it. He says, "Hello Maya. My name is Luke Gordon and this here's my wife, Shannon."

He nods to the lady next to him. She's pretty. Her hair is long and thick and dark too. He keeps talking, "I know you don't know who I am but I'm glad to meet you because your mother used to tell me about you. I have a boy who is your brother. His name is Lawrence and he's younger than you are, about half your age. He would like to meet you some day. Your mama and I, we had Lawrence, and your mom, she couldn't keep him because she was sick. I never met you before so I don't have any memories of my own but your mother, she loved you and she talked about you all the time, how much she missed you, how much she wanted to do right. But it was hard for her. She had a struggle, you know?"

Aunt Hen looks at grandma and Jazz; Aunt Hen looks like she might cry, but grandma and Jazz are just staring.

Shannon pats Luke's arm, maybe to get him to be done or maybe to let him know he's doing a good job. I don't know which, and she just says, "Very glad to meet you, Maya. Thank you for letting us be here today."

I just look at them. I really can't say anything. I don't know what to say. I don't want to hear about my mom and her being sick right now. I don't want him to make everybody sad.

Aunt Hen says, "I know Maya. I was surprised too. I didn't know anything about Luke. Your mom tried to tell me about him, I think, but I didn't get it; I thought she was the one who was mixed up, but it was me who got it wrong."

That's when Minnie speaks up, and I am so glad to finally have somebody who knows what I'm like now say something. She says, "Hi everybody. I feel really special that Maya asked me to be here today. My name is Minnie Dawson and I like to think of myself as Maya's friend. I just want to say this girl here is strong and smart and tough. And she can sure cook!" She shoots me a smile and sees how nervous I am, and says, "I really think we should take a break from all this talking and start eating before everything gets cold, don't you Maya?"

Uncle Marcus says, "I hear that!" And we all get up, and head to the table to fill our plates.

I am glad for a break from all of the talk about me. I look at Julia and she gives me a little hug as we stand in line at the food table. I let her.

While we're all eating, everybody is talking and asking questions and it's like how I guess family reunions must be. I learn that Jazz is some kind of nurse now and I figure out that Umatilla is a reservation or a tribe or something in Oregon and that Luke lives there. I also see Sarah, my social worker, going around introducing herself to people. I even hear her talking like a normal person to my Aunt Hen.

After our plates are all cleared, Althea asks whether everyone is ready to get back to business; this pretend easy life is over and we all quiet down so she can explain what will happen next.

"I am so pleased that all of you could make it here for Maya. You all have offered so much love this afternoon for her and for each other. I can just feel it. Can't you?"

Uncle Marcus says, "Amen."

Althea smiles and keeps going, "What we are going to do next is a little bit of sharing about what Sarah, Maya's caseworker, sees as the situation right now, and give you all an opportunity to ask her any questions you might have so that when Sarah, Julia and I leave the room, you all will have what you need from us to come up with your own plan. Julia is Maya's lawyer and she's here to support Maya and to speak for Maya if she wants her to. So it's OK, Maya, if you want to ask Julia to come back into the room at any time. After we leave the room, you will have the chance to work together to come up with your own plan. Then when you're finished, you'll let us know and we'll come back and you can tell us what you've worked out. Sarah will ask you questions to make sure she understands what you're proposing and then she'll have a chance to respond. I don't want you to feel rushed to come up with something today; if it takes longer than one afternoon, that's OK too. That happens sometime." She looks at everyone, "Any questions about what we're going to do next?"

It's quiet and most people are shaking their heads no.

"Sounds like we're ready to get started, then?"

Julia is sitting on one side of me and Minnie is on the other side. The rest of my family is all gathered around the table looking more serious now than before. Except for grandma. She looks the same. Half smiling. Half frowning.

"Alright then. Everyone, I would like to introduce you to Sarah. She is Maya's social worker. Sarah?"

"Good afternoon everyone. It's been such a pleasure getting to know all of you. I'm hoping to be a resource for you. We all understand what Maya's basic situation is. She is due to have a baby any day now, and Safe Harbors' budget has been cut and they won't be able to offer her housing after September 30th. Unfortunately, this means Maya needs a new place to start her life as a mother. Maya has been taking good care of herself, has gotten back on track with school, has been going to counseling and obviously has been inspired by Minnie. She has been learning about how to take care of a baby and she's signed up for services that will help her when she's a new mom. If she stays local, she can continue to work with her schooling through Safe Harbors. Let me just stop there. Are there any questions I can answer for you?"

There is a little moment of silence while everybody looks at everybody else and then Aunt Hen asks, "Do we have to be licensed as foster parents to have Maya and her baby come live with us? I don't think any of us is licensed."

"Good question. Usually, the Department prefers that you go through licensure but that does take time, possibly more time than we have. So we have a couple of options.

First, I could ask for a waiver of licensure—either a temporary waiver to give you time to get licensed so that Maya can be placed as soon as she needs to be or a permanent waiver if you don't intend to get licensed ever. It's also possible that if there are some requirements that you can't meet to become licensed I might be able to get the department to agree to overlook them and let you be licensed anyway.[79] If you are licensed, you will receive a monthly foster care payment that is more than what you would get if you don't get licensed.[80] But you will also have more requirements that you will have to meet or have waived."

"What requirements?" Uncle Marcus wants to know.

"Well, most of them are not too much of a problem and we can help you get through them, but the biggest challenges are finding the time for the training and having the required amount of space or bedrooms for the number of children you have. For example, if you are licensed, you can't have children sleeping in common living areas.[81] If you don't go for licensure, we could probably overlook that if the home otherwise passes a very basic safety inspection."

Aunt Hen seems determined not to lose her temper or give up, "Is there any way we could get help to get a bigger place so that we could get licensed?"

"It's hard to say. We could help with a one-time security deposit for a new place and with moving costs from our emergency funds, but you would have to be able to afford the ongoing rent based on your earnings and the projected foster care payment."

"How much would the foster care payment be?" Uncle Marcus asks.

Aunt Hen looks at me and adds, "This isn't about the money, Maya. We are fine with being poor. We know what it's like to just have enough to get by. It's about doing the best we can to make sure we can have you stay with us, if that's where you want to be."

---

79. In 2008, The Fostering Connections to Success and Increasing Adoptions Act allowed states to waive non-safety-related licensing requirements for relatives in order to deepen the capacity of relative care providers to take children into their care. *See*, Children's Bureau, Administration on Children, Youth and Families, U.S. Dept. of Health and Human Services, Report to Congress on States' Use of Waivers of Non-Safety Licensing Standards for Relative Foster Family Homes (2011), [https://perma.cc/V6HJ-9BM9].

80. For example, in Arizona, the basic daily rate paid to a licensed foster parent of a child Maya's age in 2015 was $28.89. Unlicensed relative caregivers, on the other hand would receive daily support of $1.74. *See* Arizona Dep't of Child Safety, CSO-1109A, Family Foster Home Care Rates and Fee Schedules (2015), [https://perma.cc/N6F7-8MRD]. The unlicensed relative caregiver could also apply for child-only Temporary Assistance for Needy Families (TANF), which would provide for an additional $164.00 per month. *See* Elissa Cohen et. al., The Urban Inst., Welfare Rules Databook: State TANF Policies as of July 2015 111 (2016) [https://perma.cc/M9XY-EFLA]. Therefore, the unlicensed relative would receive total support of $216.20 per month while the licensed foster parent would receive $866.70 per month. For a comprehensive look at the types of licensing requirements prospective foster parents face, *see* Beltran, *supra* note 76.

81. *See, e.g.*, Wash. Admin. Code §388-148-1470(3) (setting general requirements for the child's bedroom and prohibiting the use of hallways, kitchens, living rooms, dining rooms and unfinished basements as bedrooms); Mo. 13 C.S.R. 35-60.040(2)(A) (prohibiting allowing a foster child to sleep in a hall or any other room which is ordinarily used for other than sleeping arrangements); Mich. R. 400.9306(2) (prohibiting the use of any room as a bedroom that is primarily used for purposes other than sleeping).

I am glad she said it. I don't want nobody thinking they're in it for the money.

"Again, that's hard to say for sure, we would need to look at the tables and the current rates, but based on Maya's current situation including the fact that she will have a baby,[82] it would probably be close to $1000 a month."

"And would we get any help for Maya and her baby if we're not licensed?" Aunt Hen wonders.

"That gets tricky too. You would be able to receive a TANF benefit for taking care of Maya; that would run about $300 per month.[83] Whether Maya would qualify for help from TANF for her baby depends, in part, on your income, so it's hard to say at this point whether she would qualify, but given that you both work it seems unlikely."[84]

Uncle Marcus says, "Well, if we're just looking at $300.00, that isn't going to cut it for a bigger place, not here in this town."

"I know," Sarah says, "That's one big reason why getting licensed might be best."

Foster Care and TANF Rates

States vary as to their rates for both foster care and Temporary Assistance for Needy Families (TANF).

- *What would the foster care payment be for Maya in your state?*
- *How much TANF would her family receive if they cared for her without licensure?*

---

82. When a foster youth is also a parent, that youth has parental rights with respect to her child, and federal law provides that the foster care maintenance payments for the mother should be increased to ensure support of the minor's child. 42 U.S.C. § 675(4)(B); 45 C.F.R. 1356.21(j). The foster youth's child is also categorically eligible for Medicaid so that health care needs will be met. *See* Child Welfare Information Gateway, Health Care Coverage for Youth in Foster Care and After 3 (2015) [https://perma.cc/5M8Q-UW6U]. The amount projected here is based upon Washington state's per diem foster care payment for a foster youth with a minor child. *See* Child Trends, Casey Child Welfare Financing Survey: Family Foster Care Provider Classification and Rates: Washington Profile [https://perma.cc/94JT-LP9R].

83. Relative caregivers are eligible for a child-only benefit under the Temporary Assistance for Needy Families (TANF) program. 42 U.S.C. § 672 (a)(3). The amount of this benefit fluctuates widely among the states. The amount provided here is based upon Washington State's child-only benefit for non-parental caregivers. *See* Elissa Cohen et. al., The Urban Inst., Welfare Rules Databook: State TANF Policies as of July 2015 111–12 (2016) [https://perma.cc/M9XY-EFLA].

84. States impose a variety of conditions upon minor parents seeking to take advantage of TANF benefits. While the time that they receive TANF during their minority does not count against their 5-year lifetime limit, 42 U.S.C. § 608(a)(7)(B), they may be subject to a host of other requirements, such as living with an adult and attending school. Furthermore, in determining eligibility, most states consider at least a portion of the income of the minor parents' other household members. *See* Elissa Cohen et. al., The Urban Inst., Welfare Rules Databook: State TANF Policies as of July 2015 46–48, 75–76, 123–124 (2016) [https://perma.cc/M9XY-EFLA].

Uncle Marcus says, "And what if we just want to get her out of foster care completely? What if we just want to take care of her ourselves without any help or courts or social workers or anything?"

You go, Uncle Marcus.

"There are ways that Maya could exit the system completely for sure. Maya can be adopted or you can do a guardianship. Either way, her case would be dismissed. But there might be benefits for Maya if she stays in the system past her eighteenth birthday."

Hold up. Stay in the system after I'm eighteen? I've been waiting to get out from under this long enough. Why would I want to do that? I am itching to say *hell no*, but I keep it to myself.

This is where Althea pipes up, "Sorry, Sarah, I don't want to interrupt, but could I just make a suggestion?"

"Sure — I know we're really getting into the weeds here. It gets complicated, and I don't know how much to explain."

"No, no — you're doing great. The family has questions and they are important, and you are doing your best to answer them. But what I am going to say is that there are a lot of consequences that flow from these different legal choices, for Maya and for the family she lives with. I want to make sure that Maya understands them all before she says what she wants, and I think there's a lot that you all need to discuss before you figure out the legal stuff — whether it's long-term care, guardianship or adoption. Maya should have a chance to really talk out those details with Julia here before she makes decisions about that. What I would like to ask the family to do is keep your eyes on the prize — which is coming up with a plan that works for Maya. If you all could have what you wanted for Maya and her baby, what would that be? And what, if anything, would you need from Sarah? What I am hearing is that there's a lot of interest in helping Maya. Sarah — can you speak to where the Department is right now with respect to its willingness to consider family members who might want to be a part of Maya's life?"

"Sure. I'd be happy to speak to that. I have spoken to my supervisors before coming here today and they are supportive of integrating family back into Maya's life. I have had a chance to speak with some of you and with your permission I have run the background checks that my supervisors wanted from me, and there are no problems on that front. We do think that Maya should continue with more services — counseling, ongoing help with school, help with parenting, independent living skills and the like. But we also know that the Department is not always going to be in Maya's life, but hopefully, you will. I'm ready to listen to what you have to say about how this should happen. I can't promise miracles. The resources we have to offer are never enough, but I'll do my best."

"Perfect, Sarah, thank you," Althea says, "Does anyone else have any other questions that they feel they need answered about what it is we are asking you to do?"

Luke surprises me by piping up, "Does Maya have to stay in this state? Can she come to Oregon to live if she wants to?"

Sarah answers, "Maya does not have to stay here. She can go to another state. There's a special process for that[85] and it takes longer[86] to get it all finalized but yes, she could go out of state if that's part of the plan."

"What if she just wants to visit? Is that OK?"

"That would probably be OK, we would just need to know about it and plan ahead a little."

I keep thinking, *for real?*

Althea looks to me and asks, "Do you have any questions, Maya? I know Julia explained to you what we were going to be doing today but I know that this is a lot for you to take in. Have you ever had this much family in one room before?"

I shake my head, "Never."

"Well, they're all here for you. And they know that whatever is going to happen here has to be something that *you* want, so you be sure and let them know what that is, OK? And if you aren't comfortable with something, can you tell them?"

Nobody has ever asked me what I want, except for Julia. No social worker has ever told me I could say no. I look at Julia like *is this for real.*

Julia says, "I just want you all to know that this is a really big day for Maya. I think she won't mind my saying that this is a bit hard for her to believe. So if she is speechless sometimes, please know it's not because she has nothing to say. She just might need to take her time in being able to think it through. She might need some breaks."

The Lawyer's Role in the FGC

Julia has been relatively quiet during the first part of the FGC.

- *What should the lawyer's role be during the information sharing portion of an FGC?*
- *Could Julia ethically provide the family with information about legal permanency options, like relative guardianship or adoption?*

Jazz speaks up, "It's OK. We got your back, Maya."

---

85. *See supra* note 72.

86. The length of time it takes to initiate the Interstate Compact on the Placement of Children (ICPC) process depends upon the expertise, efficiency and workload of the sending state agency. Once the process is started, the time to completion in the receiving state is also variable. Wait times range from less than a month to nine months. ICPC STATE PAGES, THE ASSOCIATION OF ADMINIS-TRATORS OF THE INTERSTATE COMPACT ON THE PLACEMENT OF CHILDREN, [https://perma.cc/U7WA -YBKU].

And there's this small bit inside me, this tiniest bit that believes this is the start of something new and better and different, but that tiniest bit is fighting with other bigger bits that can't believe that any of this will matter in the end.

As I watch Julia and the others go out the door, I take a deep, deep breath in and quietly, to myself, count as I let go.

Stage 2: Private Family Time

When Julia, Althea and Sarah leave, the seats on the other side of me open up. Jazz helps grandma get up and they move to be next to me so that Jazz is where Julia used to be and now grandma is sitting in Althea's seat, like the queen of the meeting. Grandma deserves that seat, but she can't really say much of anything. And without Althea here, we are all alone together and we don't know how to start.

There's a white board on the one side of the room facing us and Jazz breaks the silence and says, "Oh! I know! How about we write all the ideas we have on the board? We can erase stuff if you don't like it, Maya. And you can put your ideas up there too. What do you think?"

I shrug. I don't know what to do. What if now that there's nobody here to boss us around, we don't even know how to act? It's almost like we don't know how to be without them watching us. When they were here, we were "the family," but now that they are gone it feels like we aren't sure who we are. We are more than strangers, that's for sure, but we've never all sat together like this. Even though they know things about me that I don't know, there's still so much about who I am now and who I have been that they don't know and probably won't understand or even like. And there's tons of things I don't know about them.

Uncle Marcus takes another run at it, "How about Aunt Hen and I just throw our idea out there first, and you all can tell us what you think? And if you want to, Jasmine, you can write it on the board and then we can just see where it goes from there."

"OK," I agree because I want somebody to please come up with something.

"Alright, then. Hen and me have been thinking. We've talked about this a lot, not just now, but for years. You have no idea how many times she's tried to talk a social worker into this and we've gotten nowhere."

"That's for sure. It is hard to trust that they will say *yes* after all these *nos*. It could be that they finally ran out of ideas or it could be that this Sarah is just a different kind of social worker. She does seem less judgy. I don't know, but whatever it is, we have to take advantage of it while we got the chance," Aunt Hen says.

"I know," Marcus says, "It's like this Althea has some kind of magic or something. What's her deal? She just smiles and suddenly all of us appear here in this room together, and she smiles again and that Sarah rolls over like a dog wanting her belly scratched. Whatever that Althea's got, I sure want to get me some."

I'm smiling now and we're all talking again about how weird that all was. And we imagine Althea casting spells on everyone and everything we want to change. Uncle Marcus is taking her to work with him and having her say *abracadabra* to his boss and now he has a raise and we don't need any help from anybody. Luke has her sprinkling fairy dust over Lawrence and Nolan so that they'll always do their chores, love school, *and* become famous basketball players. Minnie says she'll just ask Althea to wiggle her nose and we could all just go *poof* and be in a plane heading some place fancy, like Hawaii. After we are done rubbing lamps, riding magic carpets, and laughing like a bunch of people who have known each other for longer than the last hour, we start to find our way back to the subject.

"Alright, listen up, this is what we been thinking," Aunt Hen says all hushed and quiet, like she's whispering a secret, but then grandma tells her to speak up, she can't hear so well, and so Aunt Hen says it again, more loud this time, "This is what we're thinking. We would love to have you, Maya, and your little baby come live with us. We have a lot of baby stuff still left over from the girls. I can't seem to let go of that stuff, and now I'm glad I didn't."

"I just found out he's going to be a boy," I tell her, almost like I'm apologizing, which sounds weird.

"Oh, that's wonderful! It will be great to finally have a boy in our family." Aunt Hen says.

"You got that right!" says Uncle Marcus, "I love my little girls and this woman here, but I am definitely out-numbered."

"Honestly, Maya, a crib is a crib and a baby don't care what color his sheets and sleepers are," Aunt Hen says.

Then Shannon chimes in, all happy to be thinking about baby stuff, "We'd be glad to share Nolan's old baby clothes. They grow out of them so fast. They never wear them out."

"Thank you," I finally say, and I realize I don't remember the last time I said thank you. I know I wanted to say it to Minnie before. I know I wanted to say it to Julia before. But I never could make myself, "And yes, I want to come live with you Aunt Hen and Uncle Marcus."

"I don't know how we're going to make it work in the apartment we're in right now, but we'll figure it out and hold Sarah to her word about helping us get into a new place. If we have to get a license, we can do it. It seems silly, but we can do it. What is it? A bunch of classes? We'll find the time somehow. We only have two bedrooms and one bathroom right now, and so I do think it would be tight once the baby comes, but you know we were thinking about getting a bigger place anyway because the girls are outgrowing that one bedroom. We might have to have you on the couch until we figure it out, but we'll be OK."

Minnie says, "I been thinking, listening to all of this talk. It's only me in my apartment. If Maya would want to live with me for a while just until you get a bigger place

I'd be glad to do that. It's not a huge place; it's a one-bedroom with a little den that has a fold out couch. Maya and her baby could stay in the den. And I live pretty close, so for a while at least, she could still go to school here at Safe Harbors. There's a day care that they use for our moms, maybe you can have your little boy there," and then she asks Aunt Hen, "Where do you all live, by the way?"

Aunt Hen says, "About 20 minutes away from here on the bus. There's a chance we might be able to get a bigger apartment in our complex but that's assuming there's an opening."

And all the while Jazz is just drawing stuff on the board. A small house with M on it for Minnie and then arrows pointing to a larger house with H&M for Hen and Marcus and then a little baby outfit with L&S for Lawrence and Shannon. And then a big bag with dollar signs on it and an SW, for social worker, written above it, sitting on top of the chimney of the bigger H&M house.

"What if there's not a bigger place in your apartment complex?" I ask.

"Well, then we might have to move further south to afford a bigger place."

"How far south?" I bet my cousins won't like moving. I know what it's like to have to leave your school and everything you know. They aren't as used to that.

"Probably about another 30 minutes by bus from here. So it could take over an hour for you to get here once you figure in the bus transfers. Are you worried about having to change schools? "

"I'm more worried about Tasha and Sandra having to change schools because of me. I don't want them to be mad."

"That's sweet of you, but we have been thinking about doing this for awhile, we are outgrowing that place. Better now than when they are older and in middle school or high school. It's too bad that the school year has already started, but we'll figure it out, if we need to. But what about you? You need to finish school. How will you do that if we have to move away from Safe Harbors?" Aunt Hen has her serious face on now. "You'll have a lot on your plate with a new little baby, going to school and all that."

It's scary to think about going to a regular high school. I can't imagine that, but I don't want them to think that I want to dropout, then I remember what Robin said and I tell them, "Robin — she's my teacher here — she says I could maybe go to community college to take chef classes and have that count some towards both college and high school. I could do that maybe instead. Either that or start studying for my GED. I like going to school here but I'm almost ready to do something else."

Jazz pipes up, "I did Running Start![87] That's a great idea. That's how I got started on my LPN even before I graduated high school. There's one in the south end.

---

87. "Running Start" is the name given to this jurisdiction's dual-credit program. Such programs permit eleventh and twelfth grade students to take college courses, typically at community colleges, allowing those students to simultaneously earn high and college credits. *See, e.g.,* WASH. ADMIN.

That's where I went." Jazz is busy drawing CC on an even bigger building near the house with the H&M on it.

Minnie looks over at me; maybe she sees how scared I look because she says, "It will be a lot to get used to, being a mom, changing schools, living with family, all of it. And I know that sometimes when things get tough you might want to run away. Guess what? Sometimes we all just want to run away. I bet even your Aunt Hen and Uncle Marcus feel that way some time."

Aunt Hen says, "Why sure we all feel overwhelmed sometimes. It's just a part of life. But we aren't going anywhere."

Minnie goes on, "They aren't going anywhere, but they have a lot more practice at staying put. What I'm thinking is that we need a plan to help you, for when the going gets tough. I want you all to think of me as that safety plan. If you need a break, if things get tense or too hard, you just need to let your Aunt Hen know you're going to Minnie's. Because you know what happens in families sometimes? Sometimes they get on each other's nerves. But it doesn't mean it's all over. It doesn't mean you need to bolt. It just means you need a little time away from each other."

"So true. So true," Uncle Marcus says.

"And that goes for us too," says Luke, "If you want to have a little break and get away from the city, let that little guy have some boy time with his little uncles, you can come and visit us. You heard what the lady said. You can leave the state if you need to. Just pick up the phone, yeah? You can get on the bus and be down with us in a few hours, and get some nice fresh air. Maybe in the summer, when you don't have any school or something?"

It's hard to imagine but I nod like it might be something to think about.

Jazz draws a teepee way down in the corner of the white board. Luke laughs and says, "We don't live in teepees. We have a three-bedroom house with running water and everything, you know? Plenty of room. Not fancy but we have the bedrooms. That's why I asked the lady about whether you could come live in another state, because we could have you stay with us. But I know you know your aunt and uncle here better than us, and it sounds like you have some good school plans. Still, it would be fine for you to come and visit any time."

Jazz is embarrassed and erases the teepee and draws a regular house. "Sorry!"

"Oh, it's OK. Some Indians lived in teepees. There's nothing wrong with them. But our people never really did. Wouldn't expect you to know that though. It's fine. You're a really good artist. I like what you're doing there."

"What do you think Maya, do you like this plan?" Aunt Hen asks.

Code § 392-169-015; Joanne Jacobs, *Some Teens Start College Work Early Via Dual Enrollment*, U.S. News & World Rep. (March 9, 2012), [https://perma.cc/P6ML-3Z7H].

I look at the white board filled with pictures of what my life could look like. I feel like I want to say something, be more excited, more happy but I can't get the words out.

"Are we missing anything?" Uncle Marcus asks.

Just then grandma starts to make a humming sound like she can't quite get out what she wants to say. She finally asks, "Come see me?"

"Yes!" I say, "If they'll let me."

"We'll put it in the plan and then they'll have to, right?" says Aunt Hen.

Jazz chimes in, "I know where she's at. Her nursing home is not too far from the community college I was talking about. I could take you."

"Thank you," both grandma and me say.

"Of course, grandma. I also wanted to say that I can babysit so you can just go out and have fun sometime. You can't just work all the time. I know you'll have a lot going on but, you still need to make friends and enjoy yourself, right? I mean you are still just 15 after all. You could also come and just hang out with me sometimes."

I seem to be saying thank you a lot now, but I say it again. And each time it gets easier.

"Is it time for us to take a break and maybe call them back in? Looks like we filled up that chalk board," Aunt Hen suggests.

"Sounds good to me!" I say, and as I walk out the door to head to the bathroom, I see Julia and she's knitting a tiny green sweater.

She looks up at me and says, "Well, don't you look radiant!"

Not sure what she means, but I realize that my face is actually tired from smiling.

Stage 3: The Family Presents the Plan

When we come back into the room, we all rearrange ourselves to make room for Althea, Sarah, and Julia.

Althea looks at the board and says, "My goodness! It looks like we have ourselves a big plan here. Who wants to tell me about this? Maya, would you like to do it yourself? Or would you like to pick someone else to explain it for you?"

I almost tell Jazz to do it, but then I change my mind and say, "I'll do it." And I think I surprise everyone when I stand up and go to the board. I point to each picture along the way, and say, "This is what we want to do. Aunt Hen and Uncle Marcus want me to live with them and I want to do that too. But they need a bigger place. So we need your big bag of money to make that happen," and I look straight at Sarah.

Everybody laughs, even Sarah, and Uncle Marcus says, "You tell it, Maya. You tell it."

I feel even bolder. "Well, we know it's going take some time for you to get all that money together and for Aunt Hen and Uncle Marcus to find a bigger place, and that's why Minnie says I can live with her until they get all licensed or whatever. She lives kind of close to Safe Harbors and so me and the baby can stay with her and I can go to school here until all that gets settled up. Then they'll either get a place in the building they're in now or move somewhere South near the community college I'll go to and grandma's nursing home, where they can get a bigger place for cheaper. If they move South, I'll go to Running Start and start my chef school. Jazz can show me around cause that's where she went. And I'll visit grandma, 'cause well she's my grandma and I want to visit my grandma."

And then grandma says, "That's right!" and there's more laughing.

"And once I get all moved in with Aunt Hen and Uncle Marcus, Minnie says that whenever we get on each other's nerves over here," I point to the H&M house, "and I feel like busting out, I can go to her house and stay for a while. And Luke and Shannon say I can go visit them too over here and run around out in the country with my boy and his boys, and they're going to send me their boy baby clothes," and I point to the house that used to be a teepee.

"And Jazz says I need to have fun too, which I agree with very much because I have not had any fun in a very, very, very long time and so she says that when I make friends or whatever and want to go do stuff because I am 15, she'll babysit," and I look at the board one more time just to be sure and I say, "And that's it!"

I sit down in my seat and they're all clapping and hooting for me and saying, "You got it, girl," and "Maya's not so quiet now, is she?" I sit down in my seat and even Minnie gives me a high five.

Althea says, "That was beautiful Maya," and she smiles that magical smile at Sarah, which makes us all bust out laughing, and she says, while she's still smiling, "What? What did I do?"

Uncle Marcus says, "Oh nothing, nothing Miss Althea. We just all were talking about how we do love your smile."

"Well, that's very sweet of you. I was just about to ask Sarah here what she thought of this plan."

We kind of want to laugh again but we also realize that this is not the time to mess with the situation and so we hold it back, and wait to hear from Sarah.

"I think this all sounds amazing. I am blown away, actually. This is a great plan. It has it all—placement, education, built-in respite care,[88] some child-care help, family connections and visitation. Of course, the big bag of money is key here and the bag

---

88. "Respite care" refers to short-term child- or youth-care services designed to provide temporary relief to the caregiver. Surveys of the post-placement needs of families caring for children and youth in the child welfare system rank respite care as among the most essential support services needed. Respite care may be formal, provided by a licensed foster parent or informal, involving other supports within the family or community. One study found that caregivers who used a mixture of formal and informal respite care reported positive experiences more often than those who utilized solely formal or solely informal respite care. E. Madden, et.al., *The Impact of Formal and Informal Respite*

may not be as big as you would like, but if we can talk about getting you licensed, that would help a lot."

Aunt Hen agrees that she will work with her on that.

"I do have one question—it looks like you will be working with Safe Harbors for at least as long as you are staying at Minnie's, is that right Maya?"

"That's the plan."

"Good. We can think about what other services you might want or need but I think that in terms of what we need for now, this works."

Julia has been writing it all down and taking pictures of the board with her phone. She says, "What I would like to do, if it's OK with you Sarah, is write this all up as our agreed permanency plan and route it to you and your AAG. We can work on some of the legal details, talking among ourselves, as to what we call these placements for now. If you will sign it, then we can get it in front of the court. Will that work?"

"Sounds good to me. I appreciate that. I'm sure that the AAG will too, since you were here for all of this. You and he can work out the details."

And just like that, it seems like it's done, Althea is putting together her folder and saying, "Thank you everyone so much for this wonderful afternoon. We are so glad you came, and you can stay and talk more if you have the time. Open up presents, visit some more. Sarah, Julia and I will be heading out now."

Part IV: Maya's Permanency Planning Hearing

I woke up this morning feeling like the baby might be getting ready to come, but I want to go this hearing. I never thought I'd say that. But I do. I want to prove to myself that this is real. Anita and Minnie are almost as excited as I am as we pile into Anita's little car and head out.

When we get there, I see that Aunt Hen and Uncle Marcus are already there, sitting in the waiting area on those black plastic chairs. They look tired and worried, but as soon as they see me, their faces light up and they come rushing over to give me a hug.

I see Julia walking out from one of the offices where all of the attorneys hang out. She's talking to this other girl. She must be an attorney too but she looks so much younger than Julia. They are laughing and smiling like they know each other, like this is some regular thing they do. And then I remind myself that this *is* the regular thing that Julia does, that I am not the only one who she has to go to court for. I resist saying to myself that Julia only does this because she gets paid to shuffle papers and us

---

Care on Foster, Adoptive, and Kinship Parents Caring for Children in the Child Welfare System, 33(6) CHILD & ADOLESC. SOC. WORK J. 523 (Dec. 2016).

around. Because today is different; I'm glad that I have an attorney who gets paid to make shit happen for me.

Julia heads over to see us, all excited to see us ready to go. I tell her that I really hope I can have my hearing first because I am not sure I should wait. I've been having more of them fake contractions. Everyone looks worried again and my Aunt Hen says, "Should you even be here?" Julia snaps to it, hurries off, disappearing into the courtroom, getting and dragging Sarah along with her.

A bunch of other attorneys are rushing into the courtroom too. Julia told me about this before. She says that before any of the hearings start all of the attorneys and social workers meet with the judge to check in and get a number for when their case will be called. If you're number one, you go first.

In a few minutes, all of the lawyers are coming out of the courtroom with their files and brief cases. They all have this look on their faces like they are searching for someone. Julia is searching for me.

She sees me and motions for us to all come follow her. We're number one!

I sit in the middle of the U-shaped table, looking straight up at where the judge will sit when she gets there. Julia is sitting next to me. Sarah is sitting off to the left with her lawyer, that skinny guy who was here last time. They have a lot of files piled up all around them. Aunt Hen, Uncle Marcus, Minnie and Anita are all sitting behind me in the folding chairs for the people who watch.

There are two ladies sitting below where the judge will sit. One is wearing a frilly shirt and lots of jewelry and makeup. The other one is wearing a uniform, kind of like a sheriff or something. She looks serious. They are both looking at computer screens at their desks. The fancy lady is stacking files carefully to get them in order. We know it's time to get started when the one in the uniform says, "All rise."

We all stand up like we are in church or something. I went to church with Aunt Hen and Uncle Marcus once. I wonder if I'll go to church all the time now. I hope not. Does Minnie go to church?

Everyone sits down before I even have a chance to finish standing up.

The same judge from before who looked at me over her glasses comes in and sits down. She smiles real big at me, which seems so different from last time. She nods to the fancy lady who pushes a button.

The judge starts talking, all the same stuff as always, saying my name, a lot of numbers and a lot of legal talk about the hearing. The skinny lawyer says his name. Sarah says hers.

And then Julia stands up and says, "Julia Yasko, here today for Maya Phillips who is seated to my left. I would also like to take this opportunity to introduce some important people who are in the courtroom today."

She turns around and looks at everyone. The courtroom is full to bursting, just like me. Aunt Hen, Uncle Marcus, Anita and Minnie, they all stand up as she tells the judge who they are and why they are important.

The judge looks so happy to meet them all, and she starts talking, "I have read the jointly filed permanency plan which reflects the results of your FGC, and I want to commend Maya's family and friends who are here today. I also want to acknowledge the excellent work that Ms. Prince did in performing her relative search and gathering this group together."

Sarah looks at Julia says, "Thank you, your honor. It was a team effort."

"I'm sure that is true. Some of the best work we do, we do together." Then she looks at me and I get nervous, even though she is smiling, "Maya, I also want to congratulate you for all of the good work you have done over these last months. You have been doing very well indeed. I see here that you are interested in the culinary arts?"

I'm not sure what that means, but I figure I had better go along with it, "Yeah."

"And it seems like you are making excellent progress with your other subjects. And you plan to continue to do that, even after the baby comes and you are not living so close to your teacher?"

She looks at me as though we are having a conversation and so I nod.

"Can I hear you say 'Yes, ma'am, I will.' The machine here has to record what we are doing and it can't hear your head nodding." She is smiling at me as she points to the button that the fancy lady pushed before.

"Yes, ma'am, I will."

"Thank you. And you plan to keep on seeing your doctor for yourself and your new baby even though it might be harder to get to just like you have been doing so well at Safe Harbors?"

"Yes ma'am."

"Wonderful, and how about Ms. Anita here? Will you keep seeing her to help you out? Being a parent can be stressful; it's not always easy."

"Yes ma'am I will." She is smiling and giving the side-eye to the recording machine to coax me on.

"Great, and do you still plan to help Ms. Minnie out in the kitchen, when you can, to keep learning more cooking skills?"

I turn around and look at Minnie and she gives me the thumbs up sign, and so I say, "Yes, ma'am, I sure hope I can."

"OK, I am not requiring you to go to counseling or to keep cooking with Ms. Minnie but it seems like both of these things have been good for you. Speaking of which, counsel, I see that there was a snag of some sort with approving Minnie as a temporary home for Maya. Has that been resolved?"

Sarah whispers something to the skinny lawyer who says, "Yes, your honor. We have resolved the issues arising from the background checks. The Department has determined that, given the level of clearance required for her position at Safe Harbors, we are comfortable with her serving as a temporary unlicensed placement[89] for Maya and as a respite care provider. She has been a good mentor for Maya and we feel that it would be better for Maya to remain close to Safe Harbors while her aunt and uncle work towards a move."

"That is good news. While Maya is staying with Minnie, what kind of support will she have as a new mother?"

The skinny lawyer nods to Sarah and she answers, "Your honor, the Department has made arrangements for her to have access to all of the services that she would have had if she had remained at Safe Harbors. The plan also provides for her to have the freedom to spend weekends with her Aunt and Uncle if she can work it out with them and wants to do so during the time she is staying with Minnie. The family thought, and we agree, that staying with Minnie at first provides a good opportunity for a gradual transition from Safe Harbors to a family setting."

"That sounds sensible." And then the judge looks back at me again.

"So, young lady, by the looks of it, you are about to have your baby any day now. It sounds like you have an opportunity here for a lot of help from Safe Harbors, Minnie and your family. Do you plan to take advantage of all of that help?"

"Yes, I do."

"And follow their rules?"

I nod.

She looks at the machine.

"Yes, ma'am, I will."

"Alright then. I will enter the proposed order approving the terms of the jointly proposed permanency plan, including visitation with family members, respite care, and the permanency plan of 'other suitable adult placement with Minnie Waters' to be followed by 'long-term licensed foster care with relatives.' I also approve an alternative plan of guardianship should that be something Maya and her relatives want to approach. No need to wait for court authority to make that move. I will set our next review hearing six months out. Congratulations, Maya, and thank you Mr. and Mrs. Clark and Ms. Waters. The court appreciates your commitment to Maya and her baby."

> **_Looking Ahead: Granting Provisional Authority_**
>
> _Judge Goodloe approves the family plan but takes an additional step of explicitly approving relative guardianship as an alternative._
>
> • _What is the significance of this move?_

---

89. For a discussion of the practice of temporary unlicensed placements, *see* Beltran, *supra* note 76.

Everyone says, "Thank you, your honor." The lawyers and Sarah say it first like they've said it a hundred times before. But then Aunt Hen and Uncle Marcus say it like they mean it. Minnie says it. Even I say it.

Reflections and Exercises

1. *What? So What? Now What? A Five-Minute Reflection Opportunity.* Take just five minutes to write and reflect on the following questions:

    a. What did you feel as you read about the various non-legal interventions involved in this chapter?

    b. How is what you recorded feeling relevant to your learning and/or practice?

    c. Now what do you do with these insights as you move forward in your learning and/or practice?

2. *Imagining a Different Story for Maya:*

    This chapter provides you with a glimpse of alternative processes for addressing the needs of dependent youth. Non-judicial proceedings have benefits and drawbacks.

    a. What are the benefits of non judicial processes like FGC?

    b. What are the risks of non-judicial processes?

    c. Could the dependency process be reformed to incorporate more non-judicial processes at various stages of the proceeding? How?

    d. How might Maya's story have been different under the alternative system you imagine?

Chapter Nine

Michael's Very Secure Placement

In this chapter you will learn about how youth in the child welfare system wind up in the juvenile justice system and how they survive in both systems at the same time. By entering the juvenile justice system, Michael becomes what is sometimes called a "dual status youth" or a "crossover youth." While there are different pathways for young people to become involved in both systems, Michael takes a common path: a foster youth who is arrested and adjudicated in the juvenile justice system.

Studies have shown that youth in the child welfare system are more likely to be processed formally in the juvenile justice system,[1] begin their juvenile justice involvement earlier than non-child welfare involved youth and experience a greater number of out-of-home placements.[2] There is a growing movement by courts to address the particular needs of these youth by emphasizing system coordination. Some of these initiatives show promise in reducing formal processing and recidivism.[3] Michael does not benefit from one of these initiatives. However, you will be introduced to Michael's delinquency attorney, Roger, who informally collaborates with Katie.

In this chapter, you will also be introduced to the "School to Prison Pipeline," a term used by some to describe how schools have increasingly come to rely on punitive discipline policies, law enforcement and the juvenile justice system to address misbehavior.[4]

---

1. J.P. Ryan et al., Knowledge Brief: Is There a Link between Child Welfare and Disproportionate Minority Contact in Juvenile Justice? (2011), Models for Change: Systems Reform in Juvenile Justice, John D. and Catherine T. MacArthur Foundation.

2. Gregory Halemba & Gene Siegel, Doorways to Delinquency: Multi-system Involvement of Delinquent Youth in King County (Seattle, WA) (2011), Models for Change: Systems Reform in Juvenile Justice [https://perma.cc/XK2Q-EZP7].

3. In Hampden County, MA, an initiative to use pre-trial multi-disciplinary teams for dual system youth resulted in decreased use of detention and decreased recidivism. Robert F. Kennedy Children's Action Corps, Dual Status Youth Initiative Report, First Edition: Early Gains and Lessons Learned, [https://perma.cc/XJ5B-GAHR].

4. This "pipeline" disproportionately impacts children of color, beginning with suspensions in elementary and middle school. See Judith Scully, Examining and Dismantling the School-to-Prison Pipeline: Strategies for a Better Future, 68 Ark. L. Rev. 959 (2016). In 2014, the U.S. Departments of Justice and Education worked together to provide resources to schools to address this problem. U.S. Departments of Education and Justice Release School Discipline Guidance Package to Enhance School Climate and Improve School Discipline Policies/Practices, U.S. Dept. of Education (Jan. 8, 2014), [https://perma.cc/579L-4494].

Michael's Foster Brother's Story: James Jeffries

James blows into the house and everything gets louder, urgent. "Dad. We have to do something. We can't just sit back and watch. How can you just pretend like this isn't happening? Aren't you fuckin' tired of this shit?"

Michael stays still, trying to blend into the furniture, not wanting to disrupt the flow of energy pouring out of James. At first Michael's stomach tightens — a reflexive response to angry voices. Angry voices are usually followed by violence of some sort. Broken glass. Swollen faces. But sitting there frozen on the couch, Michael quickly senses this is a different sort of conflict. He doesn't understand, but he wants to. It feels important.

Mr. Jeffries stays silent, as James' voice rises. Michael has never heard James swear in front of Mr. Jeffries before. He expects Mr. Jeffries to be angry, but he just looks tired. He shuts his eyes and rubs his brow like he has a headache. Finally, he says calmly, "Can you please watch your language. We aren't alone here."

Michael immediately realizes that he isn't invisible and he tries to sink deeper into the couch. James just gets more excited. "Yeah, well Michael should get prepared for what could happen to him. He's got no one to tell him. And you think giving him a roof over his head and feeding him is good enough? You just playin' along with the system. You keep thinkin' you're gonna save one child at a time, and they are killing us."

James turns on Michael, "You don't need nothin'. You understand? You feel me? You don't need no one, nobody to save you. You aren't some sad poor black boy the system gon' save. You watch out for yourself. You watch out for your own. Don't let them break you." James looks at his father, shakes his head and leaves. The door slams behind him. Michael can hear his car pull out of the driveway and speed down the street. Michael thinks James even drives like he's angry. Michael doesn't know that the next time he sees James, Michael will be the angry one.

After a few minutes of awkward silence, Mr. Jeffries sits down next to Michael on the couch. "I apologize for my son's behavior. He means well."

Michael feels lost. He likes James, looks up to him. He has never seen him acting this way. It is confusing.

"What's he so mad about?"

Mr. Jeffries looks at Michael and raises his eyebrows ever so slightly. He realizes for the first time that Michael has no idea what they were talking about. He pauses. "James is upset by what happened last night." Mr. Jeffries stands up, looking blankly out the window. "The police shot someone. A boy James knew from high school. We don't really know what happened yet. Just what the news reported. He's suspected of robbing the 7–11 store on 26th. The news says he didn't have a gun."

"Is he dead?" Michael asks.

"Yeah." Michael thinks he hears Mr. Jeffries' voice crack ever so slightly, but he isn't sure.

Michael and Mr. Jeffries sit together on the couch in silence. Michael does not feel much of anything. He knows people get shot by the police.[5] His friend Donte stopped coming to school after his dad was killed by a police officer. He hears Donte and his mom moved to another state.

Michael understands why losing his friend this way makes James angry. But he can't figure out why James is mad at Mr. Jeffries. What is Mr. Jeffries supposed to do about it? What is anyone supposed to do about it? Isn't this just the way it is? And what does James mean saying Michael doesn't need anyone to save him?

Michael wants James to come back. He wants an explanation. He doesn't expect answers from Mr. Jeffries. He somehow knows that Mr. Jeffries doesn't have any that will be satisfying. He decides to go to bed early. He puts on his headphones, an old habit used to drown out the sounds of chaos and sadness that penetrated the walls when his mom was not well. He turns the music up as loud as his ears can take it, "N****, we gon' be alright." . . . Kendrick Lamar sang him to sleep.

Michael's Teacher's Story: Mrs. Carter

Sometimes she fantasizes about leaving her job and realizing her dream of owning an organic farm. On other days she dreams about retiring to a life of travel. She allows herself to imagine days filled with nothing and no one to worry about, save for an occasional call home to her husband to make sure her garden is watered and the bills are paid on time.

Mrs. Carter usually finds these little journeys of the mind useful to counteract the challenges of teaching English and Science to 7th and 8th graders in an under-resourced middle school. But today, as she stares out the window of her classroom she is not able to distract herself with images of Mont Saint-Michel. She cannot stop thinking about Michael Griffith — a beautiful young man in her 6th period class. She glances down at his writing assignment, and resists the impulse to read it again, for a fifth time.

---

5. According to a database created by the *Washington Post*, police in the U.S. fatally shot 990 people in 2015. One in ten were unarmed. Unarmed black men were seven times more likely than unarmed white men to be shot. *See* Kimberly Kindy & Kennedy Elliott, *990 People Were Shot by Police this Year: Here's What We Learned*, WASH. POST, Dec. 26, 2015, [https://perma.cc/BL9C-5GBX]. Another database created by the GUARDIAN, *The Counted: People Killed by Police in the U.S.*, https://www.theguardian.com/us-news/ng-interactive/2015/jun/01/the-counted-police-killings-us-database, identified 1140 people killed by police in 2015. Both databases were created in response to the lack of comprehensive federal data on police use of force, which came to light after a series of widely publicized incidents where unarmed African Americans were killed during police encounters in 2014, including Michael Brown, Tamir Rice, and Eric Garner. In 2016, the U.S. Justice Department announced a plan to enable the collection of "use of force" data nationwide following the recommendations of the President's Task Force on 21st Century Policing. *Justice Department Takes Steps to Create National Use-of-Force Database,* WASH. POST, October 13, 2016. [https://perma.cc/J5NN-RCPN].

The writing prompt for the week's in-class assignment is one she used frequently at the beginning of the school year: "Write about a person who has had a significant impact on your life." She must have read thousands of these over the years. The essays were often moving, sometimes funny, occasionally surprising. Once in a while she reads a story that clings to her. The young author's voice will break into her thoughts as she falls asleep at night or when she tries futilely to imagine her forthcoming life of leisure. How will she nurture the gifted children who are entrusted to her with so little support from the system that these children beat against all odds?

This one clings.

> My mother Michelle is my inspiration. She has a sense of humor like nobody else. She gave me my intelligence and my love for taking care of people. All people. She doesn't care if you are old or rich or poor or black or white. She taught me to respect everyone. My mother has not always been treated with this respect. She has been judged wrongly. She has been judged because of her disease: drug addiction. This judgment has hurt me and my sisters a lot. This judgment ripped our family apart. This judgment will probably rip me apart.

It is that last line: "This judgment will probably rip me apart" that Mrs. Carter cannot shake. It encompasses all that so many of her students struggle with every day. Michael is perhaps referring to the judgment of his mother or where he came from, but he could just as well be referring to so many other ways that young African American boys are "judged" at school and elsewhere.[6] And the idea of Michael being "ripped apart" by the world around him — is there hope in the "probably"? Surely the odds are against him as he begins to understand the weight of oppression, which for many compounds generation after generation.

Janice Carter became a teacher because she wanted to make a difference in her own community. She knows the grim national statistics on educational outcomes for African American children. But she also knows that African American children can learn just as well as white children.[7] She wants to be the teacher that believes in them, engages them, fights for them and models intellectual strength. Her interests as a middle school student, in both literature and science, had kept her buoyed in a

---

6. Data collected by the U.S. Department of Education Office of Civil Rights reveals that as early as pre-school, African American children are suspended at disproportionate rates. *See* Civil Rights Data Collection, Data Snapshot: School Discipline (March 2014), [https://perma.cc/VD9X-PYQH]. Research also shows Black boys are viewed as older and more responsible for their actions than their white peers, thereby receiving fewer protections that are afforded to children. Phillip A. Goff et al., *The Essence of Innocence: Consequences of Dehumanizing Black Children*, 106(4) J. Pers. Soc. Psychol. 526 (2014), [https://perma.cc/YWB3-G5V4].

7. The achievement gap between black and white children has narrowed substantially since the 1970's; however, progress has been inconsistent and significant disparities remain. Researchers have pointed to school poverty and segregation as significant contributors. Racial and Ethnic Achievement Gaps, The Educational Opportunity Monitoring Project, Stanford Center for Education Policy Analysis, [https://perma.cc/GPL7-HYKT]; Sean F. Reardon, *School Segregation and Racial Achievement Gaps*, 2(5) Russell Sage Found. J. Soc. Sci. 34 (Oct. 4, 2016).

school system that predicted failure for her. Encouraged by her father, a college professor, she read voraciously: Octavia Butler, James Baldwin, Zora Neale Hurston,
W.E.B. Du Bois. Her mother, also an educator, instilled in her a fascination with plant
science. As a little girl, she planted and tended a garden with her mother and became
hooked on horticulture. She excelled in science classes, particularly those that touched
on plant life.

A few years ago, she got permission from her principal to start a garden on the
middle school campus. She recruited a small group of students who joined her in the
first Organic Gardening Club. She is troubled that her students know so little about
where their food comes from, but she manages to find a handful of youth who join
her after school once a week to get their hands dirty and learn about how vegetables
grow.

Mrs. Carter decides to reach out to Michael and ask him to join the gardening club.
At first he is suspect, "Who goes?" She doesn't want to tell him that it is a handful of
girls, mostly the studious type, so she avoids the question and says that she just thinks
it would be fun to spend more time together. He agrees to give it a try. The club meets
weekly during the year after school. They plan for spring planting season by choosing
the plants and starting indoor seedlings. During planting season, Michael is in the garden
at least three days per week. He becomes one of her most dedicated gardeners. Mrs.
Carter is delighted when Michael tells her he wants to continue during the summer
on the maintenance and harvest team. It will give her a chance to keep tabs on him
during break when she sometimes loses her students to the streets. It also will give
Michael a chance to earn a little bit of money when they start selling some of their
produce at the local farmers' market. She is acutely aware that kids with no pocket
money are at risk for all kinds of trouble.

When Mrs. Carter hears that Michael has been arrested at school, she is devas-
tated. She is used to her students getting into trouble, and knows that Michael is no
stranger to the principal's office. Still, she cannot get used to how quickly the school
administrators seemed to involve law enforcement these days.[8] The fight is serious
enough that it gets the attention of several teachers, but Mrs. Carter is not one of
them at the scene. When she hears from a student that Michael was involved she
heads to the office to see if she can help, but he is already gone. The assistant principal says casually, "I guess you'll have to visit him at juvy." Her face burns and her eyes
fill with angry tears. She spins around and leaves the office before doing something
she might regret. *Who are these people and how can they despise the children they are
paid to serve?*

---

8. Police presence in schools increased dramatically in the first decades of the 21st century in
response to tragic school shootings and federal funding for school based law enforcement programs.
Law enforcement in schools takes various forms including commissioned police officers, School
Resource Officers and security guards. This increased police presence has been criticized for contrib-
uting to the "school-to-prison pipeline." Catherine Y. Kim, *Policing School Discipline*, 77 BROOK. L.
REV. 861 (2012).

Mrs. Carter goes home that evening and looks up visiting information on the juvenile detention center's website. Only parents and guardians are allowed to visit without pre-approval. After about 20 more minutes of on-line research and listening to pre-recorded messages she locates the name of a real person she can call during business hours.

It takes two weeks and at least a dozen phone calls and email messages for Mrs. Carter to get permission to visit Michael in detention. She is shocked by how difficult it is. Why does the system work so hard to keep supportive community members, *teachers* for Christ sake, from visiting detained youth? She dreads seeing Michael in jail, an *inmate*, but she perseveres hoping all the while that he will be released before she clears the bureaucratic hurdles. She is not so lucky. When she finally makes it in, her best organic gardener is waiting for her in the drab visiting room wrapped in an orange jumpsuit and sporting plastic slippers. Her stomach churns and she thinks she might pass out.

Juvenile Detention Policies

Juvenile detention facilities often have strict visiting policies, but they vary based on local practice.

- *What are the rules in your local detention facility?*
- *What are the reasons for restricting visitors for detained youth?*
- *Do you agree with these policies?*

Juvy

It doesn't seem too bad. It is sort of what he expected. The food isn't great. The cement cell is difficult to sleep in at first. Michael gets used to it. The people are actually nicer than he expected. Some of the guards seem to like the young "inmates." He sees his friend Anthony. They nod casually when they recognize each other, lips closed tight to reign in the muted smiles that might connote relief or pleasure.[9]

Michael lands in juvenile detention for the first time shortly after his 14th birthday. The police handcuff him in the principal's office and walk him out of the building about 30 minutes after school lets out. There are still other students around, but

---

9. High incarceration rates tend to cluster in certain communities, which can have the adverse effect of normalizing jail or prison. Studies suggest that when prison is over-utilized and becomes normalized it acts as less of a deterrent. *See* BOSTON FOUNDATION, THE GEOGRAPHY OF INCARCERATION: A SPECIAL REPORT FROM THE BOSTON INDICATORS PROJECT IN PARTNERSHIP WITH MASSINC AND THE MASSACHUSETTS CRIMINAL JUSTICE REFORM COALITION, Oct. 2016. [https://perma.cc/NB3R-DLLU]. For a personal account about the effects of incarceration on families see, Dominique Matti, *My Dad Spent Years of My Childhood in Prison: His Incarceration Punished Me Too*, VOX (Sept. 28, 2016), [https://perma.cc/P28Y-FX4L]. The young author describes her experience having a father incarcerated, and what it meant to her as a child: "I knew he was gone, and I knew that for people like me, jail was a place that daddies and brothers and sisters and cousins and girlfriends went."

luckily no one that he recognizes. He isn't sure why this incident calls for handcuffs and police. He has been in fights before at school, and they didn't end like this.

Michael figures that it was the bloody nose. Michael is surprised that his punch landed so hard, he had never given anyone a bloody nose before. He figures this guy, Jay was his name, must have a really sensitive nose. How could Michael know about Jay's propensity to bleed? Michael is led to the principal's office by Ms. Jones, a teacher he usually likes. She speaks gently to him as his breathing slowly returns to normal. Once he is in the principal's office being questioned, Ms. Jones is nowhere to be found. It feels like he is asked the same questions over and over. This is familiar. Usually he just agrees with what the adults are saying, admits he has an "anger problem" and is sent home to face the wrath of Mr. Jeffries. He has been suspended before for a day, or two or maybe three. But this time, something is different. The principal is particularly angry and he brings in Officer Lenny.[10]

Michael doesn't have any problems with Officer Lenny. Some of Michael's friends who like to smoke weed behind the school gym complain about him, but Michael keeps a safe distance and has no complaints.[11] So Michael is surprised to find Officer Lenny nodding along with the principal, Mr. Peralta, whose face is getting redder and redder as Michael tries to answer their questions. Michael tries to explain that Jay started the fight. He tells them that Jay used a racial slur he shouldn't have used. He tries to ask them, "What would you do if someone called you a n***** orphan? What if they called your mom a crack head?" The adults can't hear him. Or maybe he doesn't say it right. Or maybe he doesn't really say it out loud—he just says it in his head.

When Michael is led into court for the first time from detention, he is a little relieved to see that it looks a lot like the courtrooms he has been in before. He glances around to see if he might recognize the judge or the attorneys or maybe his caseworker. He doesn't see any familiar faces. He sits down at the table facing the judge as the guard removes his handcuffs.[12] He sits there, alone. The judge is looking at a computer screen, a woman sitting at the other table is looking down at her file. Michael waits.

---

10. School officials are generally free to question students about criminal conduct and constitutional protections do not apply. Some school administrators take this role seriously and are being trained in interrogation tactics similar to those used by law enforcement. Douglas Starr, *Why Are Educators Learning How to Interrogate their Students*, New Yorker, March 25, 2016, [https://perma.cc/ZGU3-DDRR]. Police officers, however, are required to provide *Miranda* warnings to students if they are "in custody," i.e., if they do not feel free to leave, a determination that must include consideration of the student's age, if known to the officer or objectively apparent. State v. J.D.B. 564 U.S. 261 (2011).

11. Research regarding the relationship between students and police in schools shows student safety or perceived safety depends on the student's level of interaction with a school resource officer—more interaction leads to a greater feeling of safety but a lower feeling of school connectedness. Matthew T. Theriot, *The Impact of School Resource Officer Interaction on Students' Feelings About School and School Police*, 62(4) Crime & Delinq. 446 (Sept. 16, 2013).

12. The indeterminate shackling of youth in juvenile court has been restricted in some states by case law, statute and/or court rule. In 2015, the American Bar Association adopted a resolution urging governments to adopt a presumption against shackling juveniles in court and allowing restraints only

After what feels like a long time, a man in a suit bursts into the courtroom carrying a file. He sits down next to Michael, leans in and whispers, "Hey, I'm Roger. I'm your attorney today. Sorry I didn't get to meet you earlier. I had a couple of things going on, but I'm going to try to get you out of here today. You want to go back to Mr. Jeffries' house?"

Michael is taken aback. Roger is African American, younger than Mr. Jeffries but older than James. He is dressed stylishly, in what looks like a very expensive suit. Michael's only other experience with an attorney is with Katie. He realizes at this moment that lawyers do not all look the same. He responds, "Um, yeah. Like, now?"

"I've got this," Roger whispers and opens up his file, quickly scanning papers in the file in front of him. All of a sudden, the room comes to life. A woman sitting next to the judge calls out "This is the matter of Michael Griffith, case number 1-5-3-7-0." The judge looks up and at Michael and Roger. The woman at the other table comes to life and says, "Your honor, Jamie Storms here for the first appearance hearing on behalf of the State. We are asking the court to find probable cause based on the certificate signed by Officer Lenny Williams which you have before you."[13]

Michael is disoriented. He has never seen this Roger person before, so why does Roger act like he knows him and knows he lives with Mr. Jeffries? He seems cool, but where is Katie? Shouldn't she be here? Michael sees his caseworker Jessica appear in the back of the courtroom. He wonders what she will say. He wonders where his mother is and where Mr. Jeffries' is. Maybe his mom doesn't know. But Mr. Jeffries obviously knows he didn't come home from school yesterday.

Everything goes very quickly. Michael doesn't make out what the other lawyers say until he hears Roger say, "Your honor, Michael would like to return to his foster home. I know that his DSHS worker is here in the courtroom, but before you listen to her tell you she needs more time to find a placement, I want to tell you that I just got off the phone with Michael's foster father, Mr. Jeffries, and he is now willing to take Michael home."

---

after the juvenile has an opportunity to be heard and a finding that restraints are the least restrictive means necessary. Lorelei Laird, *Should Juveniles be Shackled in Court or Sentenced to Life Without Parole? ABA Leaders Weigh In*, ABA JOURNAL, Feb. 9, 2015, [https://perma.cc/87JD-Z54F]. For a map of states that ban juvenile shackling, *see* Anne Teigen, *States That Limit Or Prohibit Juvenile Shackling and Solitary Confinement*, NATIONAL CONFERENCE OF STATE LEGISLATURES, (Jan. 6, 2017), [https://perma.cc/M6TZ-J3ZQ].

13. The U.S. Supreme Court has held that the Fourth Amendment requires a determination of probable cause before a defendant is detained pre-trial. Gerstein v. Pugh, 420 U.S. 103, 95 S.Ct. 854, 43 L.Ed.2d 54 (1975). Most state and federal courts addressing the issue have applied this requirement to juveniles, although with some leeway. *See* Alfredo A. v. Superior Court, 6 Cal.4th 1212, 26 Cal.Rptr.2d 623, 865 P.2d 56 (1994) (Juveniles are entitled to a probable cause hearing, but not within 48 hours as proscribed for adult defendants in *County of Riverside v. McLaughlin*, 500 U.S. 44, 111 S.Ct. 1661 (1991)).

Michael is really confused now. *Now* willing? Does this mean that Mr. Jeffries does or does not want him? It crosses his mind that Roger may be bluffing, the way he is trying to get a jump on Jessica, but this is news that Mr. Jeffries may not want him to come back.

Jessica gets up from her seat in the back of the courtroom and waits for the judge to ask her to speak. "Your honor, I spoke with Mr. Jeffries last night and that is not what he told me. If Mr. Harris has new information, I am happy to check into it."

It sinks in. Mr. Jeffries does not want him back. Michael shouldn't be surprised. The last time Michael was sent home from school, Mr. Jeffries said, "You are on borrowed time." Michael didn't know exactly what that meant, but he knew that Mr. Jeffries was not happy with him. Mr. Jeffries' expectations were too much, Michael thought. Not everyone could be perfect like him.

Roger continues, "Mr. Jeffries says that he has some conditions that he would like to discuss with Michael, but I'm sure that they will be able to work it out. We are asking the court to release Michael to DSHS today to return to his foster home."

Michael feels a surge of anger. Conditions? What conditions? If Mr. Jeffries doesn't want him then no conditions are going to help. Michael turns to Roger and shakes his head. Roger looks at him with surprise. Michael whispers, "I don't want to go back there." Roger gets close, "Where do you want to go?"

"I need to go back to my mom."

Roger frowns. It isn't an angry frown. It is more of a confused frown. His face then relaxes and he just looks tired. "OK, can we talk about this after the hearing? I'll come down to meet with you. I can get Katie there too. For now, we just need the judge to release you to your caseworker. Where she takes you—we can discuss. OK?"

Michael nods. What are his choices? He is slightly reassured by the fact that Roger at least knows Katie. He hopes Katie can tell Roger his whole story so Michael doesn't have to explain it all over again.

The judge looks away from his computer screen and says, "Mr. Harris, does your client want to be released today?"

"Of course, your honor. We ask that he be released to his caseworker today and trust that we will work out an appropriate placement. This is Michael's first time in detention, he has no prior history of any kind, much less warrant history and he poses no threat to community safety if released to the custody of DSHS."[14]

---

14. States have different requirements for holding juveniles pre-filing or pre-adjudication. *See,* *e.g.,* RCW 13.40.040(2) (requiring probable cause that a crime has been committed and one of eight other reasons to detain, including likely failure to appear or "threat to community safety"); W.S.A. 938.205 (requiring probable cause that the "juvenile will commit injury to the person or property of others if not held," the parent is refusing or unable to provide adequate supervision, or the juvenile "will run away or be taken away" so as to be unavailable for the proceedings.). In *Schall v. Martin*, the US Supreme Court upheld a New York statute that allowed for pre-filing preventative detention for juveniles who presented a "serious risk" of committing a crime before they were returned to court.

The judge looks at Jessica again. "Is the Department in support of this?" Jessica pauses, looks at Michael and then his attorney. She looks a little stunned and conflicted. "Yes, your honor."

The judge says "Ms. Storms?" The attorney on the other side of room looks up from her file, uninterested, and says, "The State defers to the court."

The judge looks at Michael directly, "Young man, this is a very serious incident. You have not been charged yet, but I anticipate that you will be very soon and it will probably be a felony. Do you know what a felony is?"

Michael shakes his head. He thinks he knows, but he isn't going to say anything out loud.

"Well, if I release you, you are not going to be able to have any contact with the victim. He's a boy from school, right? And, you will need to obey a curfew of 7 pm. You will have to obey all the rules of your placement. If you don't, or if you get into any other trouble, I can make sure that you come back here and stay for a while. Got that?" The judge is like an old white grandpa. He appears serious, but Michael finds it difficult to take him seriously. He is like a character he might see on TV.

Michael nods. The judge says, "Speak up. I need you to answer out loud for the record."

"Yes. Sir." Michael speaks quietly, as usual.

At that point things move quickly again. The guard stands up and tells him to get up and put his hands behind his back. He is handcuffed and led away. Roger follows him out of the courtroom. As he is led away to his cell, Roger says, "I'll be down to see you shortly. I'm going to talk to your caseworker and see what is going on. You sure about Mr. Jeffries?" Roger looks genuinely surprised and concerned.

> ### Restraining Youth in the Courtroom
>
> • *Does your jurisdiction shackle or otherwise restrain youth in the courtroom?*
>
> • *How and under what circumstances?*
>
> • *What are the risks of shackling or not restraining youth who appear in juvenile court?*

---

467 U.S. 253 (1984). With limited due process protections for youth at this stage, concern about the overuse of pre-trial detention has grown, with particular concern for youth of color who are disproportionately impacted. Perry Moriarty, *Combatting the Color-Coded Confinement of Kids: An Equal Protection Remedy*, 32 N.Y.U. REV. L. & SOC. CHANGE 285 (2008). In an effort to reduce the use of secure detention, the Annie E. Casey Foundation's Juvenile Detention Alternatives Initiative has created and promoted a Detention Risk Assessment Tool to assist juvenile courts in making pre-trial detention determinations. *See* DAVID STEINHART, JUVENILE DETENTION RISK ASSESSMENT: A PRACTICE GUIDE TO JUVENILE DETENTION REFORM, [https://perma.cc/ZNT8-SJGL].

"Yeah." Michael has a hardened look. He feels that familiar chest pain. Like someone is squeezing his heart. Squeezing his whole chest. He can't take a full breath. He wonders if maybe he is having a heart attack or something.

About an hour later, Michael is summoned from his cage and taken down a maze of hallways until he is placed in an open room with tables. The room is mostly empty, except for one other inmate sitting at a table with what Michael figures is a lawyer. A white adult wearing a suit.

There is a small closet-sized room off to the side and out pops Katie. She waves him in. Roger is seated inside at a small table, he stands up and shakes Michael's hand.

Michael does not really feel like talking to Katie. He is irritated. Where was she when he was dragged into court in handcuffs? She might have been able to explain to the judge about his situation. He doesn't care anymore. The past 24 hours wearing detention attire and sleeping in a cement block told him exactly who he is. He isn't a poor "orphan" anymore. He is something else. He remembers James' tirade. He remembers "nobody can save you."

Roger speaks first. "Hey Michael. I just want to apologize for what happened in court."

This is unexpected. At first, Michael thinks he misheard. He makes eye contact with Roger and holds on to it. Roger does the same.

"I should have spoken with you earlier about what was going to happen and I shouldn't have assumed anything about Mr. Jeffries and you. I read notes that our social worker wrote from this morning and it said you wanted to go back to Mr. Jeffries' house. The notes also suggested that maybe he was not in agreement with that plan, so I called him. I know Jeffries because we used to go to the same church. I wanted to try to get you back there because I thought that was what you wanted. I was pressed for time so I didn't check with you first and I had something else blow up and, well, that isn't a good excuse. I'm sorry and I hope that Katie and I can work with you to come up with a better plan."

Ethical Concerns When Time Is Short

- *Did Roger violate any ethical rules by calling Mr. Jeffries and discussing Michael's case without his permission?*
- *How does Roger's lack of time impact his ethical obligations?*

Michael isn't prepared for this apology. Was it for real? No adults ever apologize to him for anything. Who is this guy? He is unlike any human he has encountered.

Michael says nothing.

Katie jumps in, trying to sound positive. "And I'm sorry too. I should have been at that hearing. We don't always get notice in time and I found out when Roger came back to the office after the hearing. I guess your caseworker left me a message, but I was in court all morning. But Roger is right. These are not good excuses and now we need to figure out where you want to go so that we can get you out of here."[15]

"I want to go to my mom's." Michael says this half-heartedly. He isn't sure he really means it. He feels a rage at the thought of his mother. It is a new feeling. And it is a tired feeling.

"Yeah, I know you do." Katie looks very serious now. "Michael, we talked about this before and it is a really difficult situation. Your mom doesn't have a place where you can stay. The judge won't let you go to a shelter with her, or go stay with her and DJ."

Michael looks intently at Katie as she speaks, but he can feel Roger's gaze on him.

"Yeah, but now I got nowhere else to go. So why can't I just go with her?"

Michael catches Katie and Roger looking at each other. There is a pause.

Roger takes a deep breath. He sighs and starts in. "Michael, what's going on right now is not your fault. You don't deserve your situation, but you still have decisions to make. You do have somewhere to go, even though I understand you might not want to go there right now."

"Nah. It ain't gonna work."

"Can you explain why?" Roger seems genuinely curious.

"Look, he doesn't want me there. His rules are crazy sometimes. He might mean well, but it's just a set up if I go back there." Michael leans back from the table while he speaks. He pushes his chair back like he is ready to get up and leave. He is pretty sure now that these people don't have anything new to offer him.

"For real? That's not what I heard. When I called Mr. Jeffries he sounded really concerned about you, like he cares a lot and wants you back. He is upset about the school situation but that's how parents get. He wants you to do well in school, it's a big deal to him." Michael is curious about what Mr. Jeffries said to Roger. But this doesn't change his mind. He knows deep down he is going to fail with Mr. Jeffries.

They sit in silence for a minute. Katie is the first to speak. "OK, then. We need to talk to Jessica about getting you another placement and getting you out of here. Do you have any ideas? It might take her until tomorrow, but I will call her as soon as I leave here."

"I'll just stay." Michael is dead serious.

---

15. Katie is identifying one of the issues plaguing cross-system youth: coordination between the juvenile delinquency and dependency systems. Models to better serve youth such as Michael have been developed, emphasizing cross-system coordination. *See* Lorrie Lutz & Macon Stewart, The Crossover Youth Practice Model (CYPM), Georgetown University McCourt School of Public Policy Center for Juvenile Justice Reform, (2015) [https://perma.cc/UAV3-HMB8].

Roger frowns. "I don't think that is a good idea. You haven't been charged with any-thing yet and if you are charged, your chances at having a fair trial or a reasonable sentence go way down when you are sitting in here."[16]

Michael looks at him blankly. He doesn't understand what Roger just said, but he doesn't really care and he tells him so. He gets up indicating his desire to end the inter-view. He waits to be taken back to his cell. Roger shakes his hand again and Katie looks at him sadly.

> ### Lawyer as Advisor
> - *How did Roger do advising his client?*
> - *Was he too pushy?*
> - *Should he have done more to help Michael understand what was happening?*
> - *What could he have done?*

One Child, Two Lawyers: A Tale of Two Systems

Walking back to the office, Katie learns about the juvenile delinquency system. When will Michael get charged? What will happen after that? Will he stay in deten-tion until a trial? Can he change his mind and get out? What type of a sentence will he be facing? Her lack of knowledge in this area is embarrassing, but Roger is patient and knowledgeable.

Roger admits that he is concerned about the charges. There is some mention of a possible broken nose in the arresting police officer's statement. He explains that this could mean Michael will be charged with a felony.

Katie is out of her comfort zone. She does not have an interest in the criminal side of things. It scares her. Dealing with police and jails and prisons gives her a pit in her stomach. She isn't sure why this makes her more uncomfortable than abused and neglected children being ripped away from their parents by state social workers, but it does.

"Will you keep his case?" She is hopeful that Roger will stick with Michael. She knows his reputation as a skilled and caring attorney.

"I'll try. I've been over caseload, so they may not let me have it. But I'll talk to Nancy."

---

16. Studies of adult defendants find that pre-trial detention significantly increases the probability of a conviction. Will Dobbie et al., The Effects of Pre-Trial Detention on Conviction, Future Crime, and Employment: Evidence from Randomly Assigned Judges, Princeton University, (2016) [https://perma.cc/7BEA-QYBG]. Defendants detained before trial are also more likely to be sentenced to jail or prison and for longer periods of time, CHRISTOPHER T. LOWENKAMP ET AL., INVESTIGATING THE IMPACT OF PRETRIAL DETENTION ON SENTENCING OUTCOMES (Nov. 2013), [https://perma.cc/NC7R-VATU].

Katie explains to Roger about Michael's dependency proceeding. Roger knows a little bit about how that system works, but not much. He has only recently started handling juvenile cases. He has spent most of his career handling adult felony cases. Juries. Drugs. Guns. People's lives on the line.

"So what's up with his mom?" Roger seems intent on solving Michael's immediate problem.

"Well, it's pretty heartbreaking. She is an addict. She completed treatment right after the dependency was established and was on a waitlist to get into housing and get all of her kids back. The waitlist is so long. She relapsed last summer and lost her youngest who was still placed with her. She actually got back on track quickly, but then had a dirty UA for marijuana. Which, honestly, for a crack addict doesn't seem too bad. She got kicked out of her clean and sober transitional housing and went back to a partner that uses and is not a good influence. I guess I shouldn't be surprised that Michael has been having trouble at school or at his foster home. They say 'relapse is a part of recovery' but when you have four kids in foster care you don't really get a lot of chances." Katie is putting all this together as she fills Roger in.

"So what does that mean for Michael?" Roger's concern is thinly veiled by his lawyer-like demeanor.

"Unfortunately, the caseworker for the younger sisters recently filed a termination petition. They have been in out-of-home care for more than fifteen months and so the law requires it." As she says this, Katie thinks to herself this may not be exactly right. Deja hasn't actually been out of the home for fifteen months yet. And aren't there some exceptions?[17]

"Termination of parental rights. Like the death penalty for parents, huh?" It is painful to hear Roger say this out loud.

"The good news is they didn't include Michael in that petition. His caseworker knows that he would fight it and, besides, it isn't like he is going to be adopted. But the bummer is Michael's relationship with his sisters will change. He knows this."

"So, is there a trial date set?"

"Yeah, it is in November. Which is a drag because I will not be around. I mean, he isn't really a party to that trial but if his mother relinquishes, someone needs to make sure that his sibling rights are protected."[18] Katie's heart sinks just thinking about it.

---

17. ASFA requires state agencies to file termination petitions when children are in foster care for 15 of the most recent 22 months, with limited exceptions. 42 U.S.C. §675(5)(E). Thirty-two states and the District of Columbia have codified those exceptions and do not require filing a termination petition when children are in the care of a relative, a termination is contrary to the child's best interest, or the parent has not been provided with reasonable services for family reunification. CHILD WELFARE INFORMATION GATEWAY, U.S. DEP'T OF HEALTH & HUMAN SERVS., GROUNDS FOR INVOLUNTARY TERMINATION OF PARENTAL RIGHTS, (2013) [https://perma.cc/RY67-GJN2].

18. When the termination of parental rights results in an unrelated adoption, sibling relationships are also legally severed. However, some states have provided mechanisms to encourage sibling contact

"Well, I might be able to fill in. I should learn this stuff anyway. You can coach me, right?" Katie is flattered by the suggestion that this seasoned attorney could learn something from her.

"I'm a rookie, so coaching is a stretch, but of course I will help any way that I can. That would be so great, Roger. Thank you."

"Where are you going?" Roger asks casually.

"I don't know for sure, but somewhere warm I hope. It's a honeymoon kind of thing." Katie doesn't talk a lot about her personal life at work, except with a few close friends. She assumed her engagement is not particularly interesting to most of her colleagues, including Roger.

Roger surprises her with a huge grin and an enthusiastic side hug. "You are getting married? For real? That's great news. Marriage is great." Suddenly, he looks like he is the one getting married. His face glows as he recounts his own wedding and honeymoon that took place almost 15 years earlier. Katie is pleasantly surprised. As they arrive at the office, Roger is finishing up a story about his honeymoon, which involves a trip to the emergency room for a broken toe. He is laughing from his gut as he pats her on the back, "I'm truly happy for you, Katie. Don't worry about Michael. I've got him covered. We'll be a team."

Coordinated Advocacy

- *How is representation handled in your jurisdiction when a client is involved in both dependency and juvenile delinquency matters?*
- *Does the same attorney represent the client in both?*
- *Do two different attorneys coordinate their representation?*

Katie goes to visit Michael the next morning after getting in touch with Jessica. Jessica says that she will look for another placement, but "don't hold your breath." Jessica is not shy about her frustration with Michael's refusal to return to Mr. Jeffries. "Michael is lucky to have an option like Mr. Jeffries."

Lucky? Katie can't see much luck coming Michael's way. How quickly a child goes from being a victim in need of saving to a bad kid in need of fixing. A sympathetic

---

through open-adoption agreements. *See e.g.*, CHILD WELFARE INFORMATION GATEWAY, U.S. DEP'T OF HEALTH & HUMAN SERVS., POSTADOPTION CONTACT AGREEMENTS BETWEEN BIRTH AND ADOPTIVE FAMILIES (2014), [https://perma.cc/NGB9-6WT3]. For a discussion of the challenges faced by siblings post-termination and adoption see Rebecca Scharf, *Separated at Adoption: Addressing the Challenges of Maintaining Sibling-Of-Origin Bonds in Post-Adoption Families*, 19 U.C. DAVIS J. JUV. L. & POL'Y 84 (2015). For an argument construing the language of the Fostering Connections Act to mandate states put in place statutes favoring post-adoption contracts between siblings see, Randi Mandelbaum, *Delicate Balances: Assessing the Needs and Rights of Siblings in Foster Care to Maintain Their Relationships Post-Adoption*, 41 NEW MEX. L. REV. 1 (2011).

deserving foster child becomes an ungrateful and difficult adolescent almost overnight.[19]

Katie runs into Roger on her way down to detention. He wishes he could join her but he has a hearing. She is relieved. She is excited about working with Roger and pleased that Michael has a competent attorney for his criminal case, but she thinks some time alone with her client might reveal what is underlying his decision to remain in detention. She is wrong.

Michael barely speaks during their meeting. Katie can't get him to give her much of anything. She tries open-ended questions about his last few weeks at Mr. Jeffries'. She is met with a glare. It isn't really an angry glare. It is vacant. Empty. He doesn't budge. Michael will stay in detention unless and until the Department finds a placement for him—not at Mr. Jeffries. Katie asks Michael whether he has seen his mom or his sisters. Nothing. She acknowledges how "messed up" the termination petition is. Nothing. She had spoken with him previously about what the petition means—it seems unhelpful to belabor it now. But she knows it is underlying everything. Does he? Does it matter?

When a Client Makes a "Bad" Decision

Michael decides to stay in detention.

- *Should Katie, as his advisor, do more to explain to him the negative consequences of his decision?*
- *Should she have done more to understand the basis for his decision?*

Katie finds one very faint crack in Michael's armor. Or at least she thinks she does. Roger. Michael brightens ever so slightly when she mentions him. Maybe she imagines it—it doesn't make much sense given Roger's connection to the criminal incident that brought Michael to detention. Yet, Michael makes eye contact and shrugs when she asks him what he thinks about Roger. A shrug seems non-committal, but it is communication. Following the shrug, Michael engages briefly to say Roger seems like a good attorney. Katie feels a tiny reprieve. She is not alone anymore.

Michael's Criminal Attorney's Story: Roger Harris, J.D.

Roger Harris Jr. became an attorney because he wanted to make a good living and make his parents proud. His parents worked hard to put him through college—his father as a salesman and his mother, a nurse. They were solidly in the middle class, however, and Roger wants more. He dreams of buying his parents a vacation home in the sun, where they can retire as snowbirds going back and forth from their Midwest home.

---

19. Youth of color are particularly susceptible to more punitive attitudes and may not benefit from the protections reserved for children. *See* Kristin Henning, *Criminalizing Normal Adolescent Behavior in Communities of Color: The Role of Prosecutors in Juvenile Justice Reform*, 98 CORNELL L. REV. 383 (2013).

Roger got into a decent law school. He spent the summer after his first year working in a big law firm—an opportunity he landed with good grades and excellent people skills, which he displayed at a diversity recruitment event. He loved working downtown, the beautiful office, the smart and successful people he worked alongside. He enjoyed going out to lunch at expensive restaurants with partners and associates. The legal work was interesting, but not riveting. He figured that he would have plenty of time to find a niche and land one of those fantastic view offices. He was offered a job for his second summer, which he enthusiastically accepted.[20]

His second summer was not quite as enjoyable. He still loved the big firm atmosphere but the newness wore off. And although the work was challenging it was also concerning. It seemed the role of the lawyer was moving money from one party to another—without necessarily solving some of the underlying problems. The lawyers he saw seemed removed from the individuals and companies they represented.

Roger worked mainly in the litigation section of the firm, which was his preference. He was a natural advocate. He started winning debates and mock trials beginning in middle school. He longed to go to court and hone his skills at oral advocacy, but quickly learned that civil litigation would provide few opportunities to argue in court, at least not for a very long while. For him, civil litigation meant a lot of pouring through discovery and researching legal issues for motions that would often not be filed or would be settled without argument. Still, Roger worked hard and tried to find the best in every assignment and in everyone he met at the firm. He was surprised when he did not receive an offer at the end of the summer. The economy was not great, but he was disappointed to not be one of the three summer associates out of a class of six to receive an offer. Nevertheless, Roger is a man of great faith and optimism— surely he would find his place as a lawyer.[21]

The beginning of his third year of law school, Roger joined his fellow Black Law Student Association members in a moot court competition sponsored by the National Bar Association. He always enjoyed competing, so he was pleased to participate and travel with his classmates. The case was a criminal one and although Roger had not been drawn to criminal law, he found the issue—racial profiling by the police during a traffic stop—fascinating. Having been stopped numerous times by the police for "driving while black" he felt a personal connection to the issue.[22]

---

20. Law firms have historically used summer programs for recruitment of new attorneys. According to the National Association for Law Placement (NALP), the median number of summer associates has fallen slightly from eight in 1993 to six in 2015. Perspectives on 2015 Law Student Recruiting, Nat. Ass'n of L. Placement (2015), [https://perma.cc/X7UM-Q63T].

21. Trends in the legal job market vary by sector. Hiring by big and medium law firms grew steadily from 1994–2008 and then collapsed. Big law firm hiring bottomed out in 2011 while medium law firms continue to decline. In contrast, government jobs have remained relatively stable over this period and public interest jobs increased after 2008 following the recession. *The Stories Behind the Numbers: Jobs for New Grads Over More Than Two Decades*, Nat. Ass'n L. Placement, NALP Bulletin, Dec. 2016, [https://perma.cc/KS38-4Q75].

22. According to data reported by the Bureau of Justice Statistics, a higher percentage of black drivers (13%) than white (10%) and Hispanic (10%) drivers were stopped by police during 2011. A

Roger's team made it to the finals where they were judged by a panel that included some of the best criminal lawyers in the country. His team did not ultimately win, but Roger spent a life-changing evening after the event socializing with the judges. He spoke with both prosecutors and criminal defense attorneys. More than one of them insisted that he consider a career in criminal law. Roger was flattered. He liked being in the company of these talented lawyers. He felt comfortable. He fit in. He gravitated toward the criminal defense attorneys. He asked questions about the financial strain and what the path would be moving forward. Did he have to be a public defender? Would he make a livable wage? He was told that public defense was an excellent way to get trial experience and there were many excellent public defenders to learn from. Some public defense offices paid a livable wage.[23] In addition to the practical questions, Roger had intense conversations about the state of the criminal justice system: mass incarceration, deep racial disparities, targeting of African Americans, the excessive use of force by police. He was completely drawn in.

Roger returned to school ready to shift his career path. He began by setting up informational meetings with every public defender or criminal defense attorney he could find. His determination paid off and he landed a job with the public defender's office after graduation. He never looked back.

When Roger finally finds himself working in juvenile court, he is surprised by how much he likes the cases and clients. He grew up in an office that privileged felony attorneys. Lawyers who did murder trials are "real lawyers." Capital cases are the pinnacle of accomplishment and being certified by the court as "death qualified" is the ultimate achievement.[24] Roger made it to the "top" and it is his experience co-counseling a capital case that brings him to juvenile court, which is considered a well-deserved break. The irony is he feels a heavy weight on his shoulders representing young clients. At times he feels desperate to get through to them so they won't find themselves where his client Jerome had been—facing the death penalty at 24 for killing a police officer.[25] He knows that this is not rational—most kids don't go on to commit murder. But the trauma of holding a client's life in his hands left an indelible mark.

---

lower percentage of white drivers stopped by police in 2011 were searched (2%) than black (6%) or Hispanic (7%) drivers. *Traffic Stops*, BUREAU OF JUSTICE STATISTICS, [https://perma.cc/7RNQ-AYVB]. *See, also,* Sharon LaFraniere & Andrew W. Lehren, *The Disproportionate Risks of Driving While Black*, N.Y TIMES, Oct. 24, 2015, [https://perma.cc/RT4D-VGBW] (Examining the wide racial differences in traffic stops and arrests in Greensboro, N.C.).

23. According to the National Association for Law Placement (NALP), in 2014 the median entry-level salary for public defenders was $50,400. *See, NALP's Public Sector & Public Interest Salary Report Turns Ten!*, NALP, [https://perma.cc/D3M9-NNBS].

24. *See e.g.,* CAL. CT. RULE 4.117, WASH. SPRC 2, FLA. RULE OF CRIM. PROC. 3.112.

25. According to data collected by the Law Enforcement Officers Memorial Fund, 521 police officers were shot between 2006 and 2015. *See Causes of Law Enforcement Death*, NATIONAL LAW ENFORCEMENT OFFICERS MEMORIAL FUND (2006–2015), [https://perma.cc/3RCL-ERNB]. Most states that impose the death penalty, allow for its imposition when the victim of murder is a police officer. Jeffrey L. Kirchmeier, *Aggravating and Mitigating Factors: The Paradox of Today's Arbitrary and Mandatory Capital Punishment Scheme*, 6 WM. & MARY BILL RTS. J. 345, 421 (1998).

Michael gets under Roger's skin. Not because Roger thinks Michael will become a serious offender, but because Roger is a parent and cannot stop himself from reflexively wanting to protect and care for his young African American clients. When Michael wants to go to trial for the school fight, Roger is ready to mount a defense like he might for any adult facing years in the state penitentiary. He rides his investigator to find every possible witness, he requests all of Michael's school records, sets up interviews with the school administrators, and explores expert witnesses to evaluate how trauma and bullying bear on Michael's ability to control his behavior. Unfortunately, Michael's blow to his classmate's face results in a small but clearly documented fracture to the student's nose. A broken bone equals a felony assault and it is risky to go to trial.

> ### *Identifying with Your Client and His Community*
> *Roger has an affinity for Michael based on their shared identity.*
> * *What are the pros and cons of this type of lawyer–client relationship?*

The meeting in detention about whether to proceed to trial or take a plea deal could be like hundreds of other meetings Roger had with defendants over the years. Except this client is just 14 years old and has no one, *no one*, besides Roger available to advise him about his decision. At least no one that Roger knows about.

"Do you want to talk to your mom or someone about this decision?" Roger treats Michael as respectfully as he possibly can and strains to not sound paternalistic.

"How would I do that?" Michael asks, disbelieving.

"There has to be some way we can arrange it. I'll find your mom and bring her here myself. What's stopping me?"

Michael stares at Roger, in disbelief.

"Seriously, you have the right to talk to your momma if you want to. Say the word and I'll make it happen." Roger knows Michael doesn't really have a *legal right* to talk to his mother and he is blustering about actually being able to find her, but he can't stand the thought of Michael being alone. Or maybe he can't stand the responsibility he feels as the only adult on his side.

"Nah, you just tell me what you think I should do."

"I can't do that. It's your decision. I can tell you about the pros and cons and help you decide, but I can't make the decision." That is the simplest explanation Roger can give regarding his ethical obligations.[26]

After forty-five minutes of back and forth, Michael decides to take the State's offer, give up his constitutional right to a trial and plead guilty to a misdemeanor assault. If

---

26. MODEL RULE 1.2(a) requires lawyers to abide by their "client's decisions concerning the objectives of representation" and "consult with" clients "as to the means by which they are to be pursued." In criminal cases, the rule specifically requires a lawyer to abide by his client's decision whether to plead guilty.

Michael pleads he will be sentenced and released immediately and he will not have a felony on his record.[27] Roger is satisfied this a good result, although he knows that Michael's future placement is still uncertain.

Client Decision-Making

Michael wants Roger to make a decision for him.

- *Can Roger do that? Did he properly advise Michael?*
- *How can lawyers be sure that their young clients are making knowing and voluntary decisions?*

Roger tells Michael he will come back the next day with the plea forms and he will try to set the hearing for tomorrow afternoon. Michael has already spent more time in detention than he should have on a first misdemeanor and Roger wants him freed as soon as possible. Leaving the attorney visiting room Roger is troubled by the question of where Michael will go when released. He walks through the visitor's waiting room, trying to ignore the overwhelming number of black faces—family members waiting to visit their children.

A middle-aged woman in braids approaches him. "You aren't Roger are you?"

"Who wants to know?" Roger smiles as he jokes with the stranger.

"I'm Janice Carter. I am Michael Griffith's teacher."

Roger doesn't hide his surprise. It is a good surprise. "Well, I just came from talking to Mr. Griffith. Smart kid, right?" Roger has a habit of referring to his young clients as "Mr." or "Ms."—similar to how he addressed his adult clients.

"Absolutely. But can you please tell me when he will get out of here?" Mrs. Carter cuts straight to the point. Roger likes her.

---

27. States vary widely on how juvenile criminal history records are made accessible to the public. Despite popular belief, only a small number of states keep juvenile records confidential or remove them from public disclosure when a youth turns 18. As a result, juvenile records can impact negatively education, employment, and housing opportunities. Most states have a process for removing a juvenile record from public disclosure through sealing or expungement. Only a few states treat juvenile adjudications exactly the same as adult convictions. (IOWA ADMIN. CODE r.491-6.5(c); IDAHO ADMIN. CODE r. 16.05.06.010; COLO. REV. STAT § 19-1-103(2).) For a review of state laws on juvenile records see RIYA SAHA SHAH ET AL., JUVENILE RECORDS: A NATIONAL REVIEW OF STATE LAWS ON CONFIDENTIALITY, SEALING AND EXPUNGEMENT (2014), Juvenile Law Center, [https://perma.cc/T9JK-F5FS]. For an overview of the harms caused by the public release of juvenile records, see RIYA SHAH & JEAN STROUT, FUTURE INTERRUPTED: THE COLLATERAL DAMAGE CAUSED BY PROLIFERATION OF JUVENILE RECORDS (2016), Juvenile Law Center [https://perma.cc/P5XP-E579]. Advising clients on the consequences of juvenile records presents ethical challenges for lawyers whose clients' developmental immaturity may make it challenging for them to weigh future costs of their decisions. *See* Michael Pinard, *The Logistical and Ethical Difficulties of Informing Juveniles About the Collateral Consequences of Adjudications,* 6 NEV. L.J. 1111, 1119 (2006).

> ### Facilitating Resilience
>
> *Research shows youth acquire resilience through relationships with adults who validate their strengths.*
>
> - *What is the lawyer's role, if any, in facilitating these types of relationships?*

"Actually, I'd prefer Michael tells you himself if you are going in to see him right now. You know, confidentiality and all. But I'm sure glad to know you. Do you have a business card or something so I can reach you later?" Roger isn't sure whether Michael wants him to give this person information. *So he isn't completely alone. Why didn't Michael mention this teacher? Why didn't Roger think to ask?*

Michael Moves Through the "School-to-Prison Pipeline"

Michael spends a month in detention awaiting his trial. It is not necessary. It is his first offense and he should have been released, but his caseworker is unable to locate a suitable placement, or at least one that is suitable to Michael.[28]

Detention grows monotonous but the predictability is not all bad. Michael starts to feel at home with staff and the other detainees. The monotony is punctuated by a few notable visits.

James is the first. He comes about a week after Michael is admitted to detention. Michael is surprised. He hears from other kids that only immediate family members are allowed in to visit. When he lays eyes on James in the visiting room he can see that James is not happy. Michael mirrors James' mood.

"How you doin'?" James doesn't smile. He looks dead serious.

"Alright. You?" Michael is telling the truth. He wasn't expecting to see James but he is un-phased.

"Well, I'm trying to figure out why you sitting in here when you could be at home." James is agitated and gets right to it.

"Home? I ain't got no home. Remember? Nobody gon' save me. Nobody gonna give me no 'home.'" Michael feels old listening to his own voice spitting back James' words to him.

---

28. Between 1997 and 2013, 97,093 children were detained in juvenile detention facilities while they awaited adjudication. Of these 97,093 children, the vast majority were detained for less than one month, but 18,826 were detained for one to six months, and 1,581 children were detained for six months or more awaiting adjudication. *Easy Access to the Census of Juveniles in Residential Placement 1997–2013*, NATIONAL CENTER FOR JUVENILE JUSTICE (NCJJ) (the research division of the National Council of Juvenile and Family Court Judges), http://www.ojjdp.gov/ojstatbb/ezacjrp/ (updated 2015). Michael's experience is consistent with studies showing that youth who have been in foster care spend longer periods in detention. HALEMBA & GENE SIEGEL, DOORWAYS TO DELINQUENCY, *supra* note 2.

"Look, the old man don't mean nothing. He's trying his best and you gotta get out of this place. You don't belong here."

"Yeah? Where do I belong?" Michael hates his own harsh jaded tone.

"Man. Who are you? Why you all like this? You stay here and you gon' be like the rest of them. Why you want to be that?"

"I don't wanna be nothing. I wanna be with my family, just like you wanna be with yours."

James proceeds to try to convince Michael to just say he is sorry to Mr. Jeffries and tell him that he will do right. That's all he has to do and things can go back to how they were. Doesn't he want to hang out anymore? Play some hoops?

Michael is irritated. Who does James think he is acting like he has all the answers now? James hasn't even seen him but once since his "no one gon' save you" speech. He doesn't even know about his mom's troubles. How Michael is on the brink of losing his sisters. He doesn't know about why he popped that kid's nose and why he would do it again.

James' mood turns dark and angry. "You know why so many kids look like you in here?"

Michael glances around and waits.

"Cuz they don't know who they are. They been told they're nothing. You been told you are nothing. Your momma tells herself she ain't nothing. Now you gonna go along and do the same. You gonna be what they say you are." James is shaking his head. Michael is getting confused. His head starts to throb. He hates James talking about his mom this way.

"I don't want to save you Michael. I want you to save yourself. I want *us* to save *ourselves*. I want you out here with me. I want you to fight, like I fight. You are not nothing. Can you see for yourself? You are a strong black man. You and me, we got work to do. It's a movement."[29] James' voice starts to trail off in intensity. He begins to look distracted.

Michael has no words. His head feels full like it did that day he heard James yelling at Mr. Jeffries. He wants to say yes to James. He wants James' approval. He wants to fight with him, even though he doesn't know what they are fighting. But James doesn't know him. James doesn't have to worry about his mother or siblings. James isn't waiting for his father to get released from prison. How can Michael join whatever fight James is waging when he has his own?

---

29. Although not specifically referenced by James, one movement that has mobilized numerous groups and individuals "in response to the sustained and increasingly visible violence against Black communities in the U.S." is the Movement for Black Lives. *See About Us*, The Movement for Black Lives Matter [https://perma.cc/795D-XTVM]. In 2016, the Movement released a platform. The Movement for Black Lives Matter, A Vision for Black Lives: Policy Demands for Black Power, Freedom & Justice (2016), [https://perma.cc/AG2M-MDDN].

James leaves unsatisfied. He doesn't return. Michael is disappointed but draws strength from knowing that he stood his ground. He stood up for his family. He stood up against whatever James was putting on him.

The only other visitor Michael has, besides his lawyers, is Mrs. Carter. When she first comes in, he is embarrassed. She represents the school where he was put out. He knows she isn't responsible for that, but he can't help but associate her with the place where he has failed. She makes it clear that she came to see him as "a friend." But friends don't bring schoolwork. She acts like he will be back in class with her any day. Michael can't tell her one way or the other.

Mrs. Carter comes the first time about a week after James' tumultuous visit. Michael finds himself opening up to her about James and asking if she understands why he is so angry. Why does he say such confusing things?

Mrs. Carter responds like a teacher. The next time she visits she brings books from "her home shelf": *Assata: An Autobiography*,[30] *The Autobiography of Malcolm X*,[31] and *Soledad Brother: The Prison Letters of George Jackson*.[32] She explains that the books are older but the themes are current and Michael may find it interesting how many upstanding people have been right where he is—locked up. She checks with the detention staff and they approve her leaving the books with him, but three books is the maximum number he can keep in his cell at any one time.

Mrs. Carter visits four times total before Michael is released. It is the best part of his detention stay by far. They discuss the books she brought. She treats him like a capable student—in stark contrast to how he is treated as a juvenile inmate. Their time together is spent entirely delving into the readings, questioning if and how they apply today. His eyes are opened to what James is talking about. Michael makes other friends that would stick with him outside—Jamal, Ricky and Marshall—but the minutes with Mrs. Carter fill him with, well, he guesses it might be something like love. Not like his mother's love or his sisters' love. But some kind of love that transcends the jail suit and the heavy metal doors that lock behind him when the visits are over.

Mrs. Carter's fourth and last visit is on the heels of Michael's meeting with Roger about the plea deal. Michael wants to tell her about the plea deal. He wants Mrs. Carter to tell him that it's a good decision. That it will be ok. She gives him an opening.

"I just met Roger outside. He says that you can tell me when you are getting out of here."

"As soon as I plead guilty. Then they have to let me out." Michael sounds more confident than he actually is.

"How do you feel about your decision?" Mrs. Carter has a teacher's voice.

---

30. Assata Shakur, Assata: An Autobiography (1987).
31. Malcolm X & Alex Haley, The Autobiography of Malcolm X (1965).
32. George Jackson, Soledad Brother: The Prison Letters of George Jackson (1970).

"I won't have a felony on my record."

> ### *Juvenile Criminal History*
> * *Are juvenile criminal history records public in your jurisdiction?*
> * *What are the impacts of a juvenile record?*
> * *Can juvenile records be expunged or sealed? What is the process?*

"That sounds good." She leaves some space. She looks like she might say something, but stays quiet. Michael feels her approval. The space Mrs. Carter leaves usually draws him out. He wants to say something about how it doesn't matter if he gets out because he doesn't have a place to go. He stays quiet. He doesn't want his family problems to diminish what they have.

Their last visit ends with Mrs. Carter making sure that Michael has her mobile number and promises to call. Michael waits for her to ask him where he will go, but she never does ask. Her last words to him, "I will see you soon." *If only.*

At the plea hearing, Michael sits next to Roger. There is no one else in the courtroom except for the prosecutor, judge and the lady who sits next to the judge. Roger has prepared him for this time, he has painstakingly gone through pages and pages of forms that Roger has filled out and Michael signed.

Judge: "Michael, do you understand that you have a right to have a trial and make the state prove the allegations in the information beyond a reasonable doubt?"

Michael: "Yes."

Judge: "Do you understand that you have the right to call witnesses and present evidence to challenge the state's evidence against you?"

Michael: "Yes."

Judge: "Do you understand that by pleading guilty today you are giving up these constitutional rights?"

Michael: "Yes."

Judge: "Has anyone made any promises to you, other than any agreed-upon recommendation by the prosecution in order to get you to plead guilty today?"

Michael: "Yes."

Judge: "Really? Someone made you promises?"

Michael looks at Roger for help. Roger shakes his head.

Michael: "No."

Michael makes it through the rest of the questioning without messing up. The judge says that Michael's plea is "knowing and voluntary" and then pauses and asks, "Are the parties ready to proceed to disposition?"[33]

---

33. Research indicates that youths possess limited understanding of the plea process, are "not fully aware of their legal options," and are "overly influenced by the short-term benefits associated with

Michael looks at Roger again. Roger leans in and whispers to Michael, "Sentencing" and then looks at the judge and says, "Yes, your honor."

The prosecutor says something quickly. Roger talks a little bit longer. He says a few nice things about Michael. The judge looks at Michael, "Michael, is there anything you would like me to know?" Michael is prepared. Roger told him that the judge will ask him if he wants to say something.

"No."

Michael pays close attention as the judge announces that Michael will get 30 days, with credit for time served. Michael does the math in his head and wonders what will happen to the extra days he has served. Michael struggles to focus as the judge reads a list of "probation conditions" Michael must follow.[34] Just minutes ago he was nervous about responding to questions and now he is bored and restless.

The hearing ends and Roger gets up and shakes Michael's hand before the guard puts the handcuffs on and leads Michael away. Michael wants to ask Roger when he will see him again, but instead just says, "Thanks."[35]

Juvenile Plea and Sentencing Hearings

The procedures in juvenile criminal or delinquency proceedings often mirror adult hearings.

- *In your jurisdiction, what happens during these hearings?*
- *Are they meaningful for the youth?*
- *Do other community members attend?*

Michael's Re-Entry

Michael is released with 34 days of credit for time served. He sees Jessica waiting for him as he passes through the heavy metal doors wearing the clothes he wore to

---

accepting their plea deals." Tarika Daftary-Kapur & Tina Zottoli, *A First Look at the Plea-Deal Experiences of Juveniles Tried in Adult Court*, 13 INT'L J. OF FORENSIC HEALTH 4, (2014).

34. Youth often do not understand the conditions of their probation after listening to them being read to them in court. To that end, juvenile justice reform efforts have focused on improving understanding and compliance through creating developmentally appropriate colloquies. ROSA PERALTA & GEORGE YEANNAKIS, JUDICIAL COLLOQUIES: COMMUNICATING WITH KIDS IN COURT, MODELS FOR CHANGE: SYSTEMS REFORM IN JUVENILE JUSTICE (Dec. 2013) (John D. & Catherine T. MacArthur Foundation), [https://perma.cc/CS2K-3NG9].

35. A public defender's relationship with his or her client usually ends after disposition. The National Juvenile Defense Standards, promulgated through the MacArthur Foundation's Models for Change initiative to give guidance to juvenile defenders, provide in Standard 1.4(c): "When possible, counsel should represent a client at post-disposition hearings, including probation and parole violation hearings, institutional disciplinary hearings, and extension of incarceration determinations." *See* NATIONAL JUVENILE DEFENSE STANDARDS, MODELS FOR CHANGE: SYSTEMS REFORM IN JUVENILE JUSTICE 23 (2013) [https://perma.cc/C5WH-GHS5].

school more than a month ago. Jessica is warm when she greets him and takes him directly to McDonald's (his choice) on the way to his new placement. It's June so Jessica says it doesn't make sense to enroll him in school for such a short time. She says she will work on getting him into summer school so he can get caught up on credits. Michael's mind goes to Mrs. Carter and he smiles to himself thinking he should get credit for their visits. He forgets about the gardening club. It seems so long ago.[36]

During the summer Michael hangs out with Jamal and Ricky, the friends he made in detention. They smoke a lot of weed and occasionally go for rides in other people's cars. Jamal and Ricky understand him. They each have at least one parent who is incarcerated or battling drug addiction. Neither Jamal nor Ricky has been in foster care; they stay around with different family members and friends. They are also on probation so they needed to be careful not to get caught—they have an unspoken agreement to hold back on taking big risks.[37]

Ricky is the only one to get "violated" all summer. He had a dirty UA for marijuana. He did not time it right and was caught off-guard when his probation officer called early one morning. He spent three days in detention. When he bounces he tells Michael his probation officer is "trippin.'" "How come you and Jamal never got to pee in a cup?"[38]

Juvenile Probation as a Rehabilitative Tool

- *How does your jurisdiction use probation for juvenile offenders?*
- *Is it effective?*
- *What are the common conditions the court imposes?*
- *What are the penalties imposed when youth violate the conditions of probation?*

At the group home, run by a non-profit that doesn't seem to have much money to pay their staff, Michael decides to keep his head down and not give them a reason to kick him out. The better he is at following the rules, the less likely they are to suspect what he is out doing with his friends. James finds him there.

---

36. Detention disrupts a youth's education resulting in higher dropout rates for youth who have been incarcerated. One study showed that those incarcerated as a juvenile are 39 percentage points less likely to graduate from high school and are 41 percentage points more likely to have entered adult prison by age 25 compared with other public school students from the same neighborhood. Anna Aizer & Joseph J. Doyle, Jr., Juvenile Incarceration, Human Capital and Future Crime: Evidence from Randomly-Assigned Judges, Niber Working Papers Series, [https://perma.cc/D85A-H8TH].

37. For a discussion of risk-taking behavior in adolescence, see ch. 1 — *Adolescent Brain and other Contributors to Delinquent Behavior and Juvenile Justice Involvement.*

38. The use of probation to monitor juvenile and adult offenders has a long history, but there is little research to support its effectiveness in reducing recidivism. *See* Dick Mendel, *Case Now Strong for Ending Probation's Place As Default Disposition in Juvenile Justice*, JUVENILE JUSTICE EXCHANGE (Apr. 14, 2016), [https://perma.cc/AJE2-ZRRF].

Michael is surprised to see James sitting on the stoop waiting for him one late-summer afternoon. James is reading a paperback. He is wearing new glasses—Michael thinks they are ridiculous. James smiles like Michael hasn't seen in a while. "Hey Little Man. What's up?" James called Michael "little man" when he was first at Mr. Jeffries' house. It seemed endearing then. Now it is awkward. Michael doesn't feel little anymore.

"Not much." Their hands clap together and shake. James leans in for a hug. Michael stiffens.

"Yeah. I know. I haven't been around much and I should have come back to juvy to see you again." James is apologetic. "I found out from your caseworker you were here and I've been by a few times but I guess I keep missing you. Anyway, we're having a party at the house for dad's birthday tomorrow. A big barbecue—ribs, chicken, you know. He'd be really happy if you came. I would too. Can I pick you up?"

Michael feels something like happiness. It is like he is just some kid getting invited to a family birthday party. *This is how other people live.* Michael agrees to go. Just like that. All is not forgiven and he can still back out, but for that moment he is going to act like everything is cool. And then it is. He eats ribs. Listens to stories. Laughs. Eats chocolate cake. Helps clean up and finally takes a ride in the Camaro back to the group home. Getting out of the car he says "Thanks" making eye contact for the first time with Mr. Jeffries. He thinks he sees regret in Mr. Jeffries' eyes when Mr. Jeffries says, "See you around." James crawls out of the tight back seat and echoes his dad. "Yeah, we'll see you around. For sure." He jumps in the front seat and they speed off.

Mr. Jeffries' birthday party is not the most memorable part of the summer. Michael's first in-person visit with his father at the penitentiary is. Michael isn't nervous about going there. He knows what it is like now to be locked up. He also has had weekly video calls with his dad, paid for by the Department per the "reunification plan."[39] His dad is no longer a stranger. He is, well, a father.

Eric Grayson, DOC # 23917, was transferred to a minimum-security facility about an hour and a half drive away. The move came in anticipation of his release date, which is a few months out. The facility is sprawling cement in a rural suburb. Michael has never been this far from the city where he has always lived. The drive is like watching a movie.

His dad is smaller than he imagined. He is solid, bulked up from years of lifting weights, but he is shorter than Michael thought he would be. Michael is almost as tall as he is when they stand face to face. His dad seems nervous. He can't stop smiling. He keeps calling him "Son," which is both pleasant and unsettling to Michael.

---

39. Prisons and jails are increasingly contracting with private companies to provide video visits, for a fee, to inmates and their families. While these services can be beneficial, particularly for those incarcerated in rural areas far from their family, critics are concerned about the cost and the drawbacks of replacing in-person visits. Bernadette Rabuy & Peter Wagner, Screening Out Family Time: The For-Profit Video Visitation Industry in Prisons and Jails, Prison Policy Initiative (Jan. 2015) [https://perma.cc/B6J5-NXY6].

Jessica, who drove Michael to the visit, gives them space and sits at an empty table near the door of the cafeteria that serves as a visiting room. Michael wonders why Jessica decides she doesn't need to closely monitor the visit — what makes his dad "safe" now? Is it because she has listened in on enough phone and video calls?

The hour goes by quickly. Michael's dad does most of the talking, telling Michael about his plans when he is released. He says he will be on work release within a month and that will give him the chance to demonstrate skills that will lead to a permanent job. He says he looks forward to the chance to show Michael that he wants to be a real dad. He also talks hopefully about his other children. He admits that the mothers of Michael's half-siblings have not been overly receptive to his attempts to re-establish himself as a father, but he says that he will not give up. He talks about wanting Michael to know these other children who are his family.

Michael takes it all in. It is not exactly new information. Jessica has been talking to him about "permanency" for a while now. She said that one of Michael's options could be to live with his father when he is released. During one of their check in meetings at the group home, Jessica asks Michael how he feels about the idea of living with his dad. Michael does not give her an answer.[40] How can he be expected to know when there are still so many unanswered questions in his life? What about his mom? What about his sisters? What about James and Mr. Jeffries? How is this all supposed to fit together?

Seeing his dad and listening to him talk about a job, a home and his other children makes Michael feel hopeful. He tries to imagine what living with him might be like, but he can't. His mind wanders to his mother and he wonders what she would think. She doesn't even know he is there now with his father. She has been mostly absent since her relapse, although she calls and checks in now and then. He tries to visualize what they looked like as a couple. He thinks of Deja, Aliyah and Angel. He has been visiting with them pretty much every other week since their mom went back to the drugs. He pictures his sisters with him there talking to his dad. Michael thinks they would get along.

The visit ends with Michael and his dad talking about books. During their video visits Michael told his dad about the books Mrs. Carter had given him to read. His dad was impressed and would bring it up every time they talked. It's the only part of Michael's detention experience that they discuss.

> ### *Visiting Incarcerated Parents*
>
> - *In your jurisdiction are children provided in-person visits with their incarcerated parents?*
> - *Is there a Department policy addressing such visits?*
> - *If not, what should the policy be?*

---

40. Federal law requires states that receive Title IV funding under the Social Security Act ensure that children in foster care are visited monthly by their caseworkers. 42 U.S.C. 624(f)(1).

"Hey, before you go, you seen Mrs. Carter since you been out? Did you tell her what I told you to tell her?"

"Nah. It's summer."

"I bet she wants to hear from you anyway. Teachers want to know how their students are getting along. She took an interest in you and you should show her you appreciate it." Michael's father sounds like a father. Michael feels guilty for not reaching out to Mrs. Carter but happy his father knows who she is and that she is somebody that matters in his life.

Jessica and Michael drive in silence most of the way back from the penitentiary. As the city draws closer, Jessica asks quietly, "Any more thoughts about living with your dad?"

"What?" Michael hears her, but buys time to digest the question.

"Your dad is getting released in less than six months. It may take him a while to get settled but he has been clear that he would like you to move in with him as soon as he has a place."

"So I get to decide?" Michael has been to court enough times where he is told "it's up to the judge" or "the judge will decide." Is he now in control? He doesn't think so.

"Well, the judge will have to approve it," Jessica says. *Of course, Michael knew it!* "But I won't even ask the judge to do that if you aren't interested in the plan. If you are, I don't think it will be a problem. I mean, assuming your dad gets settled."

She means *doesn't screw up.* Michael gets it. He has been asking to live with his mother for months. He doesn't get to decide that because she screwed up by relapsing and moving back in with DJ, who doesn't do shit. He gets that his dad is pretty much his only option. He can't stay in a group home forever. It has to cost a lot of money for the State. He hates it anyway. *But what will his mom do? What about his sisters?*

Michael manages to avoid answering Jessica's question directly. He says something like, "I guess it could work." The hopefulness he felt while talking to his dad seems to gradually wear off as they get farther away from the prison and closer to the group home.

Summer ends and school starts. Michael has to enroll in "Westside Academy" a re-entry high school for youth who have been in jail and are on probation. They put "academy" in the name to make people think it isn't just an alternative school for bad kids. He is ambivalent. He can't go back to middle school and organic gardening anyway. He is a freshman now. Or at least he should be.[41]

----

41. Education is a key component to successful development for all children, but children involved in the child welfare and/or juvenile justice systems face significant barriers to accessing quality education, particularly when they are released from secure facilities. *See* Peter Leone & Lois Weinberg, Addressing the Unmet Educational Needs of Children and Youth in the Juvenile Justice and Child Welfare Systems (2012), Center for Juvenile Justice Reform, [https://perma.cc/Z5P7 -TP4K]. School districts have increasingly relied on alternative schools to serve youth who have been

Westside Academy feels a little like detention. The students are all black or brown. Michael recognizes a few of them from detention. The teachers are a mixed bag. Some are like the jail guards who seem to like kids and others seem like they got stuck there, maybe because they did something wrong in life. Michael tries to stay motivated and keeps reading and writing. He knows that this school is not giving him a great education, but no one gives him a hard time about living in a group home or being on probation. Everyone has a family member who is locked up. Everyone knows there are some things that don't get talked about.

> ### *Educational Advocacy*
>
> *Michael's school is suboptimal.*
>
> * *Whose job is it to advocate for an improved educational experience? Katie? Roger? His social worker?*

Michael reads now for fun. James is his inspiration. James comes by Michael's group home almost every week with a new book. He brings everything from super hero graphic novels to old books written by black authors who have been dead for a long time. At first Michael suspects that James is just getting too old for basketball and video games. He feels kind of bad for him, which provides further motivation for maintaining a shared interest in reading.

Michael finds himself staying up late reading about the Harlem Hellfighters,[42] or fantasy by Octavia Butler. He reads the biographies of Malcolm X and Miles Davis. He dives deep into James Baldwin and Langston Hughes. He can't keep up with his literature mentor, James, but he sure tries. It takes his mind off his mother. Off of his failing school. Off of his criminal record. He feels less alone. He keeps his own journal. Some original writing, but mostly quotes from authors he has read:

> *For while the tale of how we suffer, and how we are delighted, and how we may triumph is never new, it always must be heard. There isn't any other tale to tell, it's the only light we've got in all this darkness.*
>
> —James Baldwin, *Sonny's Blues*[43]

---

identified with behavior problems. Research shows that alternative schools can result in tracking, stigmatizing and criminalizing youth of color. Judi Vanderhaar et al., *Reconsidering the Alternatives: The Relationship Between Suspension, Disciplinary Alternative School Placement, Subsequent Juvenile Detention, and the Salience of Race*, 5(2) J. OF APPLIED RES. CHILD.: INFORMING POL'Y CHILD. AT RISK Art. 14 (2014), [https://perma.cc/Q5GV-9XNC].

42. The "Harlem Hellfighters" was a nickname given to the 369th Infantry Regiment of the U.S. Army, which fought in World War I and consisted mostly of African American soldiers. *See* WALTER DEAN MYERS & BILL MILES, THE HARLEM HELLFIGHTERS: WHEN PRIDE MET COURAGE (2006).

43. JAMES BALDWIN, SONNY'S BLUES (1957) (originally published in *The Partisan Review*; collected in *Going to Meet the Man* (1985)).

Reflections and Exercises

1. *What? So What? Now What? A Five-Minute Reflection Opportunity.* Take just five minutes to write and reflect on the following questions:

   a. What did you feel as you read about the ways that the two different systems impacted Michael?

   b. How is what you recorded feeling relevant to your learning and/or practice?

   c. Now what do you do with these insights as you move forward in your learning and/or practice?

2. *Imagining a Different Story for Michael*:

   This chapter discusses how youth in foster care face challenges at school that can lead to juvenile justice involvement. Once foster youth find themselves in both systems, there can be competing narratives about how they should be served. Different lawyers and professionals enter in and may work at cross purposes.

   a. How should Michael's school have responded to the incident that led him to detention?

   b. What might the barriers be for schools that seek non-criminal responses to student misbehavior? How might those barriers be overcome?

   c. Should courts treat youth who are in both the child welfare and juvenile justice system differently than they treat youth who are only in the juvenile justice system? If your answer is yes, how should they should they be treated? Should court processes be different?

   d. Should legal representation for "dual status" or "crossover" youth be handled differently? For example, should there be one lawyer or two?

   e. What should the scope of representation be for a lawyer representing youth who are involved in multiple systems and may also have legal issues outside of those systems, like education or housing issues?

Chapter Ten

Maya Leaves the System

In Part I of this chapter, you will watch Maya, as a young mother and dependent child, navigate the challenges of finding her place in her family while still under state supervision. You will also witness how her family members struggle, under the watchful eyes of the state, to maintain their commitment to her as they attempt to integrate her into their already established patterns and expectations. You will consider the lawyer's role amidst the challenges that families face as they seek to implement the plans that they have crafted.

In Part II, you will also learn about the choices that youth and families must make around whether, when, and how to exit the child welfare system. These decisions often require the youth's attorney to not only understand the options that are available through the dependency system, such as extended foster care and relative guardianship, but also the benefits that would be available from other government programs. As a young mother of an infant who will straddle the legal boundaries of minority while still in high school, Maya's attorney needs to learn what help is available to her, both within and outside of the child welfare system. You will see the ways in which these considerations come into the counseling session in which Julia seeks to help Maya decide whether to exit the system before or after her eighteenth birthday.

Part I: Becoming a Family

Maya and Her Son, Will

I had trouble deciding on a name for him when I was still pregnant. I was at Safe Harbors then, not with Minnie yet, not with my family. And then, the day after that hearing, after all those fake contractions, he finally decided it was time to be born. He was just waiting for us to get it all sorted out. So I could relax and do like they said in that class . . . . breathe.

I was glad my doctor was able to be there. I was afraid that I would get somebody else who would treat me bad. They think you can't tell the difference. But you can tell. Some nurses and doctors, they talk down to you like you're a baby or ask you questions about whether you have thought about how you will manage to take care of a baby all by yourself. I don't say anything but I want to tell them that I am not all by myself. I got people who are going to help me and besides taking care of this baby is just about all I been thinking about. If one of them had been there instead of my doctor, and I started having real labor pains, I wouldn't have been able to be so quiet. But my doctor isn't like them. She's just the opposite; she tells me how proud she is of me and how good I am doing.[1]

It hurt like hell. I'm not going to lie. But you know what? It wasn't as bad as all that, and I am glad I made it through without hardly any pain meds. Hell, I been through other kinds of pain that did me no good.[2] As soon as they let me hold him, I put my face down to kiss the top of his head, with all that smooth black hair, and he smelled so good. And I saw his tiny, balled fists, and I watched how they opened when he cried, his little fingers fanning out like he was looking for help, looking for a hand to hold. And I said to him, "Here I am, little man. I'm here." And all five of his fingers curled around my one. He turned his face to my chest and the nurse helped me to understand that he was looking to breastfeed, something that only I could do for him. When she said that, I realized it wasn't weird but a special thing between just him and me.[3]

When I look at him, I know right away he isn't Di's. Di is white, and this little guy is not. He isn't black neither. He is kind of almost brown but it is his eyes that give him away. He came from that time we were down in the International District, when Di got the shit kicked out of him. Which makes sense, timing-wise. I look at him and he looks at me with those black eyes. I know right then how much I love him and that I will always love him.[4] No matter where he came from, no matter where he goes, he will always be mine.

And then I know that his name should be Will. Not named after anybody in particular. But named after the promise I am making him. I will always love him and he will always be mine. And when I told the nurse what to put on his birth certificate, she says, "You mean William?"

------

1. Lisa Kane Low et al., *Adolescents' Experience of Childbirth: Contrasts with Adults*, 48 J. Midwifery & Women's Health 192 (2003)(qualitative study of pregnant adolescents in a southeastern alternative school finding typical reports of health care providers being "a jerk," "rude" or "having an attitude," but, by contrast, when treated with respect they felt more willing to ask for more information and assistance; also finding that pregnant adolescents tended to expend more emotional energy thinking about taking care of a baby than developing a birth plan, as compared to adults).

2. *Id.* (qualitative research study finding that many young mothers reported that having endured the birth experience without intense medical or pain interventions provided them with confidence in challenging situations going forward).

3. Although adolescent mothers are less likely to breastfeed than older mothers, *see* KS Scanlon et. al., *Racial and Ethnic Differences in Breastfeeding Initiation and Duration, by State — National Immunization Survey, United States 2004–2008*, 59 Morbidity & Mortality Wkly. Rept. 327 (March 26, 2010) [https://perma.cc/2VL9-8SK6], the role of nurses in early postpartum moments can make a significant difference in initiation of breastfeeding. Adolescents require more intensive social supports to initiate and maintain breastfeeding; primary among these social supports is building esteem around the important role of breastfeeding in infant health. *See* Jane S. Grassley, *Adolescent Mothers' Breastfeeding Social Support Needs*, 39 J. Obstetric, Gynecologic & Neonatal Nursing 713 (2010).

4. Qualitative research confirms that among the emotions that run high for teenage mothers in foster care is that of falling deeply in love with their newborns. Elizabeth M. Aparicio et al., *"I Can Get Through This and I Will Get Through This"*: *The Unfolding Journey of Teenage Motherhood In and Beyond Foster Care*, 0 (vol.) Qualitative Soc. Work 1, 8 (2016), [https://perma.cc/96JD-EJKX].

And I said, "No, just Will." I double-checked the paper to make sure she got it right.

She wanted to know if I had a middle name for him and I hadn't thought of one yet, so I told her "M."

"Just the letter 'M'?"

"Yeah, just the letter M." M for Marcus maybe, or Minnie, or Maya, for Mine. Because that is who he is—Mine. The lady looked at me a little funny, like *maybe* she got the joke I was trying to make, but it wasn't a joke. Maybe he can decide what he wants it to stand for later on when he knows better who he is.

It wasn't long after that, we moved in with Minnie. And I am just happy and tired most of the time now. I sleep so easy when I hold him. He sleeps so easy too as long as he's in my arms. I've even got the hang of breast-feeding, which I never thought I'd do, but it's worked out ok. I carry him with me to Safe Harbors when Minnie goes to work and I meet with Robin and Anita.[5] I go from there to all the doctor appointments. It's a busy life just trying to keep it all together, staying on track with my schoolwork and all the appointments. Everyone keeps telling me how lucky I am, that he's such an easy-going baby;[6] he even sleeps pretty good at night and when he wakes up, I just nurse him real quick and he goes right back to sleep.[7]

The good thing about living with Minnie is she never had any babies before herself; so she doesn't try to tell me what to do.[8] She doesn't freak out when I sleep with him. Aunt Hen's all the time worried I am going to smash him or spoil him or make

---

5. Maya's ability to take to Will with her to school no doubt assisted in her maintaining her breast-feeding routine. Among the challenges that adolescent mothers face in breastfeeding is the pressure they receive to return to school and the perceived obstacle that breastfeeding poses to achieving educational goals. *See* Antonia M. Nelson, *Adolescent Attitudes, Beliefs and Concerns Regarding Breastfeeding,* 34 MCN Am. J. Maternal Child Nursing 249 (2009).

6. Most new parents struggle to deal with the stressors of parenting a newborn. An adolescent mother's capacity to handle these stressors is influenced by a number of factors ranging from their own personal abuse and neglect histories to the level of current support they experience in their new role. An important variable in the successful establishment of a positive mother-infant bond, particularly for adolescents who may have fewer coping skills, is the characteristics of the infant him or herself, including the child's temperament. John G. Borkowski et al., Risk and Resilience: Adolescent Mothers and Their Children Grow Up 14 (2007).

7. Bed-sharing is practiced worldwide and is thought to have been practiced widely historically. While the practice is not as common in western cultures as elsewhere, it appears to be on the rise in the U.S. and U.K., with between 50–75% of all new parents reporting that they bring their infants to bed with them during some or all of the night. Bed-sharing persists despite prominent U.S. medical and health organizations' recommendations against it. Bed-sharing is particularly common for those mothers who breastfeed. Research indicates that mother-infant bed-sharing results in a significantly greater number of feedings per night compared to those mother-infant dyads sleeping separately, thereby strengthening the mother-infant breastfeeding bond. *See* Lee T. Gettler & James J. McKenna, *Evolutionary Perspectives on Mother-Infant Sleep Proximity and Breastfeeding in a Laboratory Setting,* 144 Am. J. Phys. Anthropol. 454 (2011).

8. Teenage mothers in foster care report a wide variety of experiences with parenting in the context of a relationship with a court-ordered caregiver—from meddlesome to supportive to absent. Aparicio, *supra* note 4, at 8.

it so that he never will want to sleep by himself. She has her ideas about how it should go, raising a baby, and every time I visit her with the baby on the weekends, like the judge said I could do, she lets me know what I should be doing different. She's so proud of the crib that she got for him. She keeps wanting me to put him in it but all he does in there is cry and cry; she says he just needs to get used to it, that it will be better for him and me when he does because then I can have some rest on my own. But I always just pick him up. Because hearing him cry is way harder than holding him. Don't tell her, but there are times I am happy to get back to Minnie's where Will and me can just be ourselves.

When Thanksgiving rolls around, we are invited to Hen and Marcus's for the big dinner. And everybody is so excited to see the baby. There are so many relatives there that I hadn't ever met before. Jazz is there too, but she is the only person I know besides Aunt Hen, Uncle Marcus and my cousins. They are mostly all Marcus's family and there are a lot of them. And they all knew each other and are laughing and telling stories and it gets pretty loud and I feel lost in it all. Will keeps getting passed around and that is nice because I got to eat a whole dinner without having to hold him but it also feels weird because it is like they all know what to do with my baby but they don't quite know what to do with me. Not only am I the only white girl in the family, with a little half-Vietnamese baby, but I am somehow also *Henrietta's* long lost niece. That's what most of them call her, especially the older people. One lady, she is pretty nice, I think she is one of Uncle Marcus's sisters, she keeps saying how good the biscuits that I brought are and how lucky Aunt Hen is to have such a good cook moving in with her, but everyone else is just busy talking about all these other people I don't know. Jazz keeps introducing herself as *Jasmine*, and she isn't as shy as me, so she is talking to everybody. I feel like I don't really know her either. Afterwards, when I go back to Minnie's, she isn't there because she is still over at Safe Harbors, cleaning up after their big dinner, and I feel kind of lonely and scared that I might never fit in anywhere.

That's when I email Kiki my number. She messages me. It feels good to talk to someone my own age again. Someone who gets it. She tells me all about the crazy stuff that has happened since I left. When I tell her about Will, she wants to see a picture.[9] She thinks he's so cute. She says Di has turned into a serious pimp and I need to stay clear of him because he is mean for real, but then she texts me a photo of him, thinking she is showing me how mean he is, but all I see is Di talking to another girl and maybe he looks mad, I don't know. He does have his hand wrapped around her wrist like he isn't going to let her go, but I just find myself getting jealous.

---

9. Youth report that using social media helps them to feel connected to their friends' lives and feelings. Many youth also reported that they get support on social media during rough times, a finding that was stronger for girls than it was for boys. *See* Amanda Lenhart et. al., Pew Research Center, Teens, Technology and Friendships, Ch. 4: *Social Media and Friendships* (2015), [https://perma.cc/T6J3-LZ7P].

> ### The Importance of Friendships for Adolescents
>
> *As a developmental matter, peer relationships are never more important than they are in adolescence.*[10] *Put simply, teenagers need and will seek out friends.*
>
> - *How should lawyers for youth in dependency proceedings take this aspect of adolescence into account?*
> - *What does this important developmental fact mean in the context of advocating for youth whose daily lives are heavily regulated by the state?*

I haven't told anybody about talking with Kiki. I know that Aunt Hen will flip her shit and I'm pretty sure that no one else will like it neither. I can't have Minnie mad at me; she's the one person in my life who always thinks I'm doing good. So I haven't told her neither. And Jazz seems like she never does anything wrong. And Julia doesn't need to know all my business, even though she's checking in on me all the time. But really, talking to Kiki helps me to stay put in a weird sort of way. I look at those photos of the street and then I look at Will and I know that there is no way in hell I'll take him out there.[11] But still I need to know that I have a friend. And Kiki has always been cool with me. So she's my secret slipped in between all the grown up things that I have to do.

And there's plenty of grown up things to do. Robin has helped me a lot with my reading. It's still not my favorite thing, but I am getting good enough to knock out more of the credits I need to almost catch up with where I'm supposed to be in high school. That feels good. I went from having like one credit in my freshman year to finishing up my sophomore year. It's been harder to work with Minnie in the kitchen, though, because of Will. They keep saying I should put him in the daycare but he just turned three months old, and I'd have to pump so he would have something to eat. The thought of doing that makes me feel strange, like I'm some kind of cow or something, and so I just keep saying I'm not ready yet to put him in daycare. Besides, sometimes I can put him down in the carrier and he watches me work in the kitchen; it's just not the kind of thing I can count on lasting for real long.

This Christmas is different than any other Christmas I've had. Not just because of Will. We are getting to spend tonight, Christmas Eve, with Aunt Hen and Uncle Marcus, so that we can wake up tomorrow morning and be together as a family. I'm glad that all the other relatives aren't here. Just me and Will, Uncle Marcus and Aunt Hen,

---

10. *See* D. Albert et al., *Peer Influences on Adolescent Decision Making,* 22 Current Directions Psychol. Sci. 114–120 (2013).

11. Many teenage mothers in foster care report being unable to cope with their living situations when parenting their infants and report that they either wanted to or did run away from their foster placements. Aparacio, *supra* note 4, at 8.

Tasha and Sandra. We're doing all this stuff that they do every Christmas Eve, all this make believe stuff that Tasha and Sandra probably don't believe in anymore, they pretend they do. Aunt Hen says that she wants me and Will to start out on his first Christmas with some "family traditions." She says she's really sorry that I had to miss out on so many, but them days are gone. They put out cookies and milk for Santa Claus and they leave him letters saying what they want for Christmas. Tasha and Sandra make me write one for myself and another for Will. I don't even know what I want for Christmas. I never had to think about that before. When I was on the streets, I didn't have Christmas, except maybe a special dinner at the drop-in shelter. When I was in group homes, we all just did a gift exchange and sometimes we would get a gift card. Shirley got me slippers once.

Before we go to bed, Uncle Marcus reads the story from the Bible about Jesus being born[12] and he reminds us that this is what Christmas is about—how good things can come from really poor people. He looks at me for a second and smiles when he points out that Mary was a teenager when she had Jesus and that, even though he was so poor he had to sleep in a crib made out of hay, Jesus turned out to be the savior of the whole world who loved everyone, no matter what. And because of that, we now all get to love each other no matter what. I've never been much for church or Bible stories, but I like it the way that Uncle Marcus tells it.

Will gets up in the middle of the night and we both sit for a while and just look at the tree with its red, yellow, and green lights. It's got all these ornaments on it that Tasha and Sandra made. I wonder if Will will have his on there someday. Or if I will have my own tree for him by the time he's big enough to make an ornament. I don't remember my mom ever being with me like this in front of a Christmas tree, but maybe she was when I was this tiny. I promise to do better, to be there not just for this Christmas, but for all Will's Christmases so he can remember me when he is grown.[13] I rock him until we both fall back to sleep on the couch.

When we wake up again, Aunt Hen doesn't even fuss that Will isn't in his crib. Somehow, they managed to sneak all the presents under the tree while we were sleeping. Tasha and Sandra come running out in their red nightgowns. I watch as they tear into everything, shrieking so loud that Aunt Hen has to tell them to shush because they're scaring the baby. But Will isn't scared; he's just startled and wide-eyed, his arms and legs flailing all around like he wants to help unwrap everything too. They must have got what they wrote about in their letters. I got more than I asked for. I got makeup and nail polish and clothes that were mostly all the right size and looked good. This could be my life now, having a family that knows what I want. Sandra and Tasha help me to open up Will's presents—mostly diapers and cute clothes and a fluffy stuffed dog like the one I used to have that I called Barkus. Sandra and Tasha come running out from their room with a small box for Will and tell me to open it. They're really

---

12. *Luke* 2:1–20 (King James).

13. Teenage mothers in foster care frequently report that they both struggle with and are motivated by the complicated histories they have with their own mothers. Aparicio, *supra* note 4, at 9.

excited about this one. It's an ornament that they made themselves, a big shiny red one with "Will's First Christmas" painted on one side in white letters that look all sparkly like snow and on the other side is his birthday, September 18, 2016. The girls want to put it on the tree themselves but Aunt Hen makes them let me and Will put it on. I find a bare space near the top and hang it there.

"Wait, wait" Aunt Hen says and she runs and gets her phone so she can take a picture of me holding Will in front of the tree right near the ornament. Then she makes the girls stand with us and she takes another picture.

And then Uncle Marcus makes her stand there with us and he says, "There they are, all my girls," and then he says to Will, "Little man, we have *got* to stick together!"

Which means, of course, Aunt Hen has to take a picture of Uncle Marcus holding Will in front of the tree too.

I think we must be all done when I see Tasha and Sandra bringing out this really big box that they say is for both Will and me. I open it up, and inside it is another box and inside that is another box and inside that is another box and they are all laughing as I keep having to open up another box and another, until I get to this jewelry box but when I open it up, there's no jewelry in it. Inside, there's a piece of paper and when I unfold it, it looks like a form or a diploma or something.

Uncle Marcus laughs and says, "You know what that is?'

I shake my head. I have no idea.

"It's our foster care license. We're good now. And guess what else?"

"What?"

"We got us a new place to stay, with three bedrooms. Starting the New Year, you and Will can move in with us!" And then Sandra and Tasha come running to hug me, and Aunt Hen is crying she's so happy.

So it's official.

Maya's Very New Year

When we first moved, there was so much newness for us all to get used to. Aunt Hen, Uncle Marcus, Tasha and Sandra, me and Will, we were all in a new place. Tasha and Sandra and me had new schools. It turned out there was a Voc-Tech High School near us that had a cooking program and so I got signed up to go there, but I couldn't take Will with me no more and so that part was hard. There was a daycare that Sarah found for me nearby that she is paying for while I go to school. It was rough at first because I decided to give Will formula for daycare and he didn't like the bottle. Aunt Hen thought I should pump but she didn't push it. I think we all knew we had a lot to get used to without getting into fights about that. Still, the formula made him get tummy aches and so he wasn't sleeping as well at night and he was always wanting to nurse when I was around. So I was pretty tired.[14]

> ### *Teenage Parenting and the Realities of School*
>
> *Returning to school is challenging for teenage mothers. Breastfeeding rates are lower among teenage mothers than they are for adults, in part, because of the challenges posed at school.*
>
> * *Do school districts in your jurisdiction have policies and practices that encourage, discourage or simply ignore this reality for teenage mothers?*

School was super hard at first. I have to get up way early because I have to get Will to daycare. And I started in the middle of the school year, so I didn't know what was going on. The only thing good was that when it comes to the cooking classes, I was way ahead of everyone else. And I'm better at math than just about everyone too. But the English class was hard, and everyone was working on writing a paper about a book that I hadn't read. I had to take a history class and the textbook was big and thick and was so boring. Aunt Hen signed me up for free tutoring after school two nights a week but I hated it.

Things have gotten better now. My teacher worked with me and Aunt Hen[15] to change the assignment for English so I could get it done this semester. I still worry about whether I'll be able to keep up next semester, though.

The best thing is Lamar. Yes, I met someone a couple weeks ago. Lamar is a senior and we been texting and, yes, some of it has gotten pretty hot.[16] Because he's hot and I'm not some old lady just because I'm a mom. I mean I got to live too, don't I? I also know some other seniors who hang out with him now; so I'm making friends. I been hanging out with them on weekends. Sometimes I take Will to Jazz's because I don't really think that Hen and Marcus approve. They say Lamar is too old for me, cause

---

14. Qualitative research indicates that breastfeeding teenage mothers may switch to formula during the school day because, as one young mother reported, "It is a problem for the school. Like sometimes it get really, you know, wet and hurt and there's no pump at the school." Mothers reported that not nursing during the day also meant being up for more feedings at night, leading to challenges with being tired and keeping up with schoolwork. Paige Hall Smith et al., *Early Breastfeeding Experiences of Adolescent Mothers: A Qualitative Prospective Study*, 7 Int'l Breastfeeding J. art.13 (2012), [https://perma.cc/36R3-EFWV].

15. Research indicates that returning to school after the birth of a child is one of the positive markers of adaptation to teen parenting and was more likely to occur with the assistance of parents. Frank Furstenberg, *Reconsidering Teenage Pregnancy and Parenthood*, 6 Societies art. 33 (2016).

16. *See* Christopher D. Houck et.al., *Sexting and Sexual Behavior in At-Risk Adolescents*, 133 Pediatrics e276 (2014) (research reporting that 22% of at-risk early adolescents reported sexting (the sending of sexual explicit text messages or pictures) within the previous six months and that those who sexted engaged in co-occurring risky sexual behaviors).

he's kind of a "returning senior," which means he's almost twenty. They don't like the way he wears his clothes either. He sags. They see him when he comes by in his car to pick me up. It's nice to not have to be going places on the bus all the time. Aunt Hen shakes her head every time he comes to get me. She really hates it when he picks me up for school in the morning because then Will is with me too so we can drop him off at the day care. I always make sure he's in a car seat, so I don't get what the big deal is.

> ### Statutory Rape
>
> *Maya is almost, but not quite sixteen, when she meets Lamar. Lamar is almost twenty. If they were to engage in sexual intercourse in your state, would Lamar be committing a crime?*

Jazz is always asking me lots of questions about Lamar too. I know what she's getting at. She's worried he's bad for me; she doesn't want me to get pregnant again either.[17] One day, she just took me to Planned Parenthood. I didn't think I could get pregnant because I was breastfeeding but they told me that only works if I'm not using any formula and he's nursing all the time.[18] They said I need to be careful about diseases too. So I got this thing in my arm that's supposed to keep me from getting pregnant for three whole years.[19] They say I can get it out if I want to have kids sooner. They also told me I still needed to use condoms to stay safe from diseases, but I know Lamar isn't into that and he says he's been tested and he's clean. I don't tell Jazz or the lady at Planned Parenthood that though. I just take all the condoms she gives me and put them in my backpack. They offer to test me too, but I tell them I don't have enough time that day, maybe later.

> ### Access to Birth Control for Youth in Foster Care
>
> *State laws vary with respect to whether a minor may access contraceptives without parental involvement. Maya is nearly sixteen when Jasmine takes her to Planned Parenthood.*
>
> - *Would she be able to access birth control in your state?*
> - *Do attorneys for foster youth have a responsibility to discuss birth control access with their clients?*

---

17. Longitudinal research shows that, within eight years after birth during adolescence, approximately 86% of study participants reported having more than one child, with 29.8% reporting two children, 33.3% reporting three children, and 20.2% reporting having four. BOROWSKI, *supra* note 6, at 20.

18. Breastfeeding can be an effective method of birth control in the first six months after delivery but only if done correctly, meaning that the infant is fed at least once every four hours during the day and once every six hours during the night and no other type of food is supplied. Once menstruation resumes, breastfeeding should no longer be relied upon as a birth control method. *Breastfeeding as Birth Control*, PLANNED PARENTHOOD, [https://perma.cc/KP8B-GXL2].

19. *See Birth Control Implant (Implanon and Nexplanon)*, PLANNED PARENTHOOD, [https://perma.cc/5XGH-DSN7].

I've been so busy that I haven't really seen Minnie or Anita or Robin. I saw Minnie a couple of times right after we moved but it's kind of hard to get to her. Sometime I miss her, especially when Aunt Hen and I get cross-wise.

I sent Kiki a pic of Lamar and me. She says we should come party with her some time and I been thinking about it but I don't know. I can't tell Aunt Hen that I am going to do that. Not Jazz or Minnie either.

Family Self-Protection: Act I — Aunt Hen

I feel like such a fool. Just yesterday, I told Marcus how proud I was of her. The tension has been building between us over that sorry boy, Lamar. I mean, I get that she is going to want to have friends and be a normal teenager, but she has other responsibilities and she has to make other choices if she hopes to keep her life turned around and keep herself and this baby out of trouble. I mean we all been making sacrifices here, trying to do right by her and Will. We picked up and moved, Tasha and Sandra changed schools, we spent all that time in those classes to get licensed, we put up with having a social worker come and check on us every goddamn month, sometimes twice a month, and now, she does this.

I was just saying to Marcus how good it is that she remembered about the family plan we came up with. Because it's true that we were all needing a break from each other. She came in after school on Friday with this story about how she felt that maybe it was time for us to use that part of the plan that talked about what to do when we get on each other's nerves. She wanted to give me a break, she said. She's talked to Minnie, she said. She'll spend the weekend with her, she said. She was going to take Will to Jazz's so that me and Marcus would have a real break from all of our responsibilities and she could have a break from being a mom. She hadn't ever let herself have a whole weekend away from him. It was such a mature thing. I thought then and there that we would make it through all this.

Well, here it is Sunday night and neither of them are back yet, not Maya and not Will. I call Minnie because I am thinking they'd be back for dinner and I just want to know if she has left yet. Of course, Minnie is confused. She hasn't seen Maya since back in January after we first moved. I panic and hang up, my heart racing with worry. I tell Marcus and he tries to calm me down because that's what he does but he looks worried too and he says, "You just sit down. I'll call Jasmine and see if she has Will."

So Marcus calls Jasmine and, thank Jesus, she does have the baby. But she is confused too because she says that Maya told her the same story about wanting to go to Minnie's.

So now the question is . . . where is that girl? I'm sure it has something to do with that no good Lamar. Lamar this and Lamar that. I'm so sick of hearing about him. Can't she see what he is? He wears them gang colors and his pants are about to fall off and I'm like, girl, we take you to church. There are nice boys at church. Why can't you just give one of them a chance? Phillip, he's a good-looking boy, and he's been nice to you. Why can't you at least say something to him? But she won't listen and now she's who-knows-where doing who-knows-what with someone who she doesn't even real-ize is bad news.

Jasmine comes over with Will and she brings her "Grandma Ruth" with her. She says it's cause she needs her to drive while she keeps the baby company in the back-seat of the car, but I think it's because she wants back-up to talk to me.

Will is fine, totally unaware of everything that's going on. She fixes him a bottle of formula and Grandma Ruth feeds him while Jasmine tries to calm me down. She says she's worried about Maya too. But when I start going off, wishing Maya had better sense like her, she smiles just a little at Grandma Ruth. They look at each other and nod like they have some secret and I say, "What?"

"Well, if you think this one here has *always* had this good head on her shoulders, you are very mistaken," Ruth says, giving Jasmine the side-eye.

"That's for sure. I was a handful wasn't I? Way worse than Maya even."

"I don't believe you," I say and Marcus comes and sits down next to me. He's already got the girls eating their dinner in the kitchen, away from all his drama.

"Well it's true," says Ruth, "This one ran away, for . . . ? How long was it that first time?"

"The *first* time?"

"Oh, yeah, I think she ran away like maybe three times in the first two months she was staying with me."

"Uh-huh. It's true. I did. The first time I think it was about four days and then it was only three and then two, and then when I figured out she was always going to be there for me to come home to, I just stopped and said the hell with it."[20]

"Oh, yeah, and the running wasn't the only thing. She had a mouth on her. And she would hang out with some of the nastiest boys too."

Jasmine looks pained and says, "Yes, it's true. I think I probably still owe you a bunch of apologies. I was pretty awful."

"You were a pill then alright. But I knew what you were doing. I could see you were smarter than how you were acting, if you'd just let yourself settle down." She looks at

---

20. Qualitative research seeking to unearth the secrets to success for those long-term foster care arrangements with adolescents has uncovered common themes characterizing successful placements that seem to have succeeded against the odds. Foster parents who are successful "start where the child is," with the understanding that the child may have challenges to overcome from their previous care experiences. In addition to this realistic appraisal of the circumstances, successful foster parents also adopt attitudes of tenacity and hopefulness that enables them to remain committed to the youth in their care despite the challenges that the youth may present. Nicholas Oke et al., *Against the Odds: Foster Carers' Perceptions of Family, Commitment and Belonging in Successful Placements*, 18 Clinical Child Psychol. & Psychiatry 7 (2011).

me and Marcus and continues, "And now look at her. Got herself a nursing assistant job and almost got herself an LPN. And she's *finally*, thank the Lord, dating sensible young men. *Good-looking* sensible young men, I might add."

"Well, just because I'm smart, doesn't mean I'm blind," says Jasmine, laughing.

I'm taking it all in. "I don't think that's it. I don't think she's testing us. I think she's being disobedient because she's been taken in by this Lamar."

"Well, she might not know she's testing you, and she does have a serious thing for Lamar but that's how I was too. I didn't know I was testing. I was just reacting the way I'd always learned to react. Go for what makes you feel good because you never know what pain lies around the corner. And if you don't like something, you just leave because there is no talking it out. There is only you're there or you're not. When I ran away I was in control and it felt good. I get that Lamar is a bad influence. I'm sure he is. But I bet she'll be back soon."

Will's sitting on Ruth's lap and she's patting him on his back. He lets out a nice burp and Ruth says, "At least she had the good sense to leave this one here behind."

"So what do we do? What if she's in some kind of trouble?"

Ruth says, "It's scary, I know. Raising teenagers is scary no matter what. With Jasmine, I always called the social worker after she was gone past when she said she'd be back.[21] I been a foster parent for them for so long that I could just work it out, they trusted me and didn't over-react every single time something didn't go as planned. But I know you're new. How will your social worker react?"

"I have no idea. I mean Sarah's not as bad as some I've had to deal with over the years, but I don't know how she would think about this," and then the thought of Maya having Will taken away shakes my heart. I know it's not just me that loves him beyond measure; Maya does too. That would break her. There would be no turning back for her. I don't want her to end up like Chicken with Will growing up with a long string of strangers.

And then there's all of the fights I've had with social workers over the years, how I've lost my temper and how Sarah keeps saying that Maya has special needs and that's why she wants her to be in a more "structured placement" and I say, "Maybe they won't let me keep Maya if they think she's running away again."

"I can't tell you what to do. I probably said more than I should already about it. I'm probably supposed to tell you to call her in right now. Some social workers are good and they understand that this kind of thing is just all part of the process. But other social workers are worried about things going wrong and they think if they just

---

21. Foster parents typically are required to report to their assigned social worker and/or to law enforcement when a child is missing from their care. *See, e.g.*, Wash. Admin. Code § 388-148-1425 (requiring foster parents to report as soon as there is reason to believe a child is missing or is refusing to return or remain in the foster parent's care; and requiring that law enforcement be contacted within six hours of the child being missing from care); 22 Cal. Code Regs. tit. 21, § 89361 (requiring that a foster parent report any unusual absence of a child within 24 hours).

find the perfect place then the teenager will behave perfectly. Well, guess what? No teenager behaves perfectly! I don't care whether you're in foster care or not. But I can't tell you what to do. But if they find out you didn't report, then you could be in even bigger trouble.[22] Do you have a lawyer you could talk to?"

"A lawyer! Lord, no, of course I don't. I don't know. I can call Maya's lawyer maybe. She seems like she would know what to do."

And so I decide to wait until the next day because it's too late on a Sunday to call a lawyer. She won't be in her office anyway.

I call in sick for work on Monday morning and call Maya in sick from school. And I'm sick. She's not back yet. Of course when I call Julia's office, she's not there and so I leave a message. And then I email her. And then I call her again. And she picks up.

"Julia, this is Henrietta Clark, Maya's aunt?"

"Oh yes, Hen, how are you? Is everything ok?"

"Not exactly, Maya's missing."

She sounds calm but concerned when she asks me to tell her more. And I tell her the whole terrible story all over again, how Maya made me out to be a fool, and even though I had told myself before I got on the phone that I was going to remain calm because this is somehow normal, I know I am starting to sound angry and loud.

"OK, Hen, I hear that you are really worried about Maya," she says.

"And I don't know what to do, you know? I know that having Will taken away would break her heart and I know that if they took her away from me after we worked so hard to get her here and we moved and everything, that would be awful."

"Wait up. Can you tell me why you are concerned that either of those things is going to happen?"

"Well, I haven't called Sarah yet because I am afraid that they will take Maya away from me because they were worried we can't handle her. And what if they decide that she can't be trusted with Will? That will be terrible. And if I don't tell Sarah and she finds out that I didn't report it, I could be in even bigger trouble, couldn't I? I mean I'm supposed to call and report if she's not here, aren't I? Will they take our license away?"

There is a long pause on the phone and then Julia says, "This is a challenging situation Hen. I represent Maya and I can't really give you legal advice but . . ."

---

22. States may suspend or revoke foster parent licenses for violating licensing requirements. *See, e.g.,* WASH. ADMIN. CODE § 388-148-1625; CAL. HEALTH & SAFETY CODE § 1550 (West).

> ### *Answering Caregivers' Questions*
>
> *Aunt Hen is an unrepresented person who is reaching out to Julia for help to decide whether to call the social worker and report Maya missing. Review your Rules of Professional Conduct.*
>
> - *To whom does Julia owe her primary duty?*
> - *What is her duty when speaking to unrepresented parties?*
> - *What more, if anything, should Julia say?*

"Hold on a second, Julia. Will is waking up." As I go to pick Will up from his crib, I hear a key in the front door.

Maya walks in. She is looking down, like she is ashamed, but when she looks up, I see that she has a black eye and a bruise on the side of her face. I pick up the phone, "Julia, I'm going to have to call you back. Maya's here now."

Maya's Very Long Weekend

None of it was supposed to go down the way it did. I just wanted to go with Lamar to see Kiki and maybe go to some parties. I had turned sixteen a few weeks ago and the party I had with Aunt Hen and Uncle Marcus, Tasha and Sandra was nice, but pretty boring. I was ready to have some real fun. I kind of wanted to show Lamar off too. To Kiki of course, but I think it also wouldn't hurt to have Di see me with him, for him to know that he's not the only one who's moved on.

And we did party, especially on Friday night. It was a blast. Kiki hooked us up and we even did some E[23] at a rave. I have never done that before but I think what the hell, it's my first time to get out in so long and I just want to bust out. And we do. Lamar isn't so much into the music there but he likes what the drugs do to us and the sex is intense.

Apparently word got out that I was back on the streets with someone else as my pimp. Never mind that it isn't true. Diamond is out to find me then and eventually he does. He winds up dragging me off and Lamar just stands back and says, "Hey man, I didn't know she was yours."

And I was like, "What the fuck? Is that how it is?"

There is all kind of shit that went down after that and my whole plan went to hell when I couldn't get away on Sunday because Di has me stuck in this motel room and won't let me go until I promise to pay him back. For what I don't know. He acts like he has spent all kinds of money on me a way long time ago, like I left him with some

---

23. "E," Ecstasy or Molly are the street names for MDMA, "a synthetic drug that alters mood and perception." It produces " feelings of increased energy, pleasure, emotional warmth, and distorted sensory and time perception," lasting three to six hours per dose. *See MDMA (Ecstasy/Molly)*, Nat'l Inst. on Drug Abuse [https://perma.cc/JXV2-Q3KJ] (last updated Oct. 2016).

big bills to pay or something. I tell him he is full of shit and that's when he hits me. So then I decide I'd better just do what he wants until I can get out. So he brings me a date and then another one and I do what they need. When the last date left and Di fell asleep, I was outta there.

And I ain't never going back. And Lamar can go fuck himself too. But now I have to face Aunt Hen and the rest. It wasn't supposed to happen this way; I wasn't supposed to get caught.

Maya's Lawyer Follows Up

The irony is that when Hen called I was just reviewing Sarah's ISSP for Maya's upcoming review hearing.[24] The report is glowing, and the indications are there that Sarah wants to move in the direction of a relative guardianship.[25] According to Sarah's report, Maya had done well with Minnie, used her remaining time wisely accessing services at Safe Harbors, had transitioned smoothly in the move to her aunt and uncle's home, was settling in at her new high school, was establishing a relationship with her sister, and was juggling her responsibilities as a young mother well. It couldn't sound any better. I had it on my to-do list to call Maya and see if there was anything else she wants to add to the report. After the dropped call from Hen, it seems that a call with Maya might not be enough; maybe I should set up a time to check in with her.

Hen didn't call back right away, which was just as well. It's Maya I really need to talk to. I call and Hen makes Maya come to the phone.

"Yeah?"

"Hi Maya. It's Julia. How are you?"

"OK."

"Can you talk right now?"

"I guess."

I can tell Maya doesn't want to talk. I suspect it has something to do with whatever it is that caused Hen to call me in a panic. But you never know, she may have just gotten up or been doing something else that she didn't want to be dragged away from. I'm

---

24. Federal law requires that a child's case plan be reviewed periodically but no less often than once every six months. Either a court or an administrative body may conduct the review. 42 U.S.C. §675(5)(B).

25. The Fostering Connections to Success and Increasing Adoptions Act was passed. This Act provided for financial and other services support for kinship (sometimes referred to as "relative") guardianships. 42 U.S.C. §§673(d)(1), 674(a)(5). One of the goals of the Act was to establish permanency for children in the care of relatives where termination of parental rights was not appropriate by providing some level of parity with the support provided for adoptions. However, there has not been a marked increase in the number of children exiting the system through kinship guardianships. *See* Josh Gupta-Kagan, *The New Permanency,* 19 U.C. Davis J. Juv. L. & Pol'y 1 (2015).

sure she would like to be done with lawyers and social workers calling her at home. So I just get to the point.

"I need to file a report for a review hearing that's coming up in your case next week. Can I set up a time to come see you, maybe tomorrow?"

"I don't think that's going to work. Can we talk on the phone instead? We could do it now."

"You're sure you don't want to meet in person?"

"Yeah, I'm sure."

I pause a moment, hoping she'll tell me what's going on. I can tell that somehow she is distracted, unable or unwilling to talk to me. I try to ask yes or no questions in case she can't talk freely, but it seems that this is one of those situations where yes and no likely won't tell me much.

"Is everything OK, Maya? Your aunt called yesterday and she sounded pretty worried."

"She's always worried, you know, but I'm back. No big deal."

"You and she are working things out?"

"Yeah, we're working things out. We're having some kind of family thing coming up. That's why I can't get with you right now."

"OK, well can I read you what Sarah wrote in her report and you can let me know if there's anything you disagree with or want me to add?"

"Sure."

I read her the report. I hear her sighing, especially at the parts about how she's adjusting to living with her relatives.

When I finish reading, she says, "Yeah, that sounds good."

When You Suspect the Client Is Not Telling the Full Story

Here Julia does not press Maya to tell her what she is feeling or what happened that caused Aunt Hen to call in such a panic.

- *Do you think she should?*
- *If so, how and why? If not, why not?*

I ask her how Will is doing, if there's anything new with him that I can add to the report.

"He's doing good. It's been a little hard because he has to have formula now and he's teething, so he don't sleep much, but it's all just normal baby stuff."

"OK, I'll say that he is healthy and growing and doing just what he should for his age. Does that sound right?"

"Yeah, sure."

"So Maya, this hearing is next Friday morning. If you want to be there, you can. I think the judge is going to be very pleased and so I'm sure it will be a good hearing."

"Do I have to go? I mean, I hate to miss school if I don't have to be there. I'm trying hard to keep up, you know?"

"No, you don't have to go. Nothing much is going to happen. I can let the judge know you want to be in school instead. It's just a check-in so that the court knows how you're doing."

"OK, well then, I'd rather not, if I don't have to."

"You don't have to."

> ### The Client's Decision Not to Come to Court
> *Here Julia does not try to persuade Maya to come to court, but takes her desire and reasoning at face value.*
> - *Do you agree with her approach? Why or why not?*

I ask her one last time if she would like to meet maybe later this week but she says no. I tell her I'll check in after the hearing, then, just to see how she's doing.

After I hang up, I draft my responsive report, saying that we agree with the agency's report, adding only that Maya is doing an excellent job as a parent, that her son is on track in terms of developmental milestones. It's important to make a record as to how she's doing as a parent. You never know what might come up in the future. I also sign off on the agency's proposed order finding that the "child" is in compliance with all services and the agency has met its responsibilities under the court's last order. When I send it all back to Sarah I let her know that she doesn't need to arrange for Maya to be at the hearing; she wants to be in school instead.

> ### Candor to the Tribunal
> *Julia has indications that not everything is going as well as Sarah thinks. Review your Rules of Professional Conduct.*
> - *Do you think that Julia has acted appropriately in filing this report? Why or why not?*

Family Self-Protection: Act II — Maya

Jazz says we should all meet at her Grandma Ruth's house because it is what she calls "neutral territory." I haven't ever been in that house before. I've been to Jazz's apartment above the garage in the backyard, but I haven't ever met her "Grandma Ruth" and honestly I'm not a fan because she *isn't* her grandma and it makes me mad to hear her talk about her like she is. But when I look grumpy about having to go there,

Uncle Marcus looks at me all stern and says he doesn't care because I am going, whether I want to or not.

I don't know what to expect at this meeting. Even in the car on the way over there, Aunt Hen keeps going back and forth between saying she has half a mind to give me a whooping herself and fretting over whether she needs to take me to see a doctor for the whooping that I already got. I'm not saying much of anything because the whole thing confuses me. Maybe they're getting ready to kick me out.

I haven't been back to school yet. I don't want nobody to see my face and I am so mad at Lamar I can't stand the thought of running into him. Uncle Marcus says it's OK for me to sit out a few more days but only if I am doing all my homework. I keep thinking maybe they don't care if I'm going to school because they plan on making me move out.

The house that I guess Jazz grew up in has all these pictures of Jesus everywhere. What it is it with everyone who is a foster parent and Jesus?[26] There are lots of kids in this house, but once we all get here, Ruth shoos them all upstairs to their rooms and we have the dining room all to ourselves — me, Aunt Hen, Uncle Marcus, Jazz and even Minnie, because, as Uncle Marcus points out, I made her part of this too. I hate that this is the first time I see her in weeks. She doesn't look mad, but she's not her usual friendly self either. Ruth excuses herself, she's got lots of laundry to do, and heads for the basement.

Uncle Marcus is in charge and he sounds serious. He talks about how I need to understand three things: first, that what I did is really wrong in lots of ways; second, that they are glad I trusted them enough to know I had a home to come back to even though I must have known how mad they'd be; and third that I have some hell to pay.

It seems like they aren't going to kick me out after all.

But then they make me tell them what I did. I can't tell them the whole story. I don't think they need to hear all the details about the rave and everything that went down in the motel with Di, but I think they get the picture pretty good anyway, especially Minnie. She's seen it all before, I'm sure. Something in Aunt Hen's face tells me she knows too, but she can't stand to hear no more.

I also don't tell them about the bag of weed that I still have from Kiki. I know I should have thrown it away and part of me wishes I could but the truth is that since that whole thing with Di happened the nightmares have come back and I'm all jumpy again. The bad feelings that I used to get, that I had forgotten about when I thought about how much fun it was to be on my own on the streets, they've started all over again. I don't want to lose it on Will when he cries too much. So I've been

---

26. Very little demographic information is maintained with respect to foster parents. However, one study in the nineties found that 77% of its sample foster parents identified with a Christian denomination. None identified as Jewish and only 4% stated they had no religious identification. *See* Kathleen M. Kirby, *Foster Parent Demographics: A Research Note*, 24 J. Soc. & Soc. Welfare 135 (1997), [https://perma.cc/J7VM-QW5C].

smoking. Just a little bit. Just in the middle of the night when everybody's asleep and I need to relax. I go outside so they can't smell it and I'm real quick. The bag's about half gone and I'm feeling better. I think once I use it up I'll be back to normal again.

Then Uncle Marcus asks me if I know what I done wrong.

"Everything." But he won't let me get away that easy. He makes me say it all out loud—from lying to Aunt Hen and Jasmine to using Minnie, to putting myself in a dangerous place with drugs and people who are bad for me. I feel bad talking about drugs like it's in the past, but is weed a drug, really? I mean it's natural, organic even, not some pill or powder. It's legal a lot of places now[27] and lots of people use it for medicine.[28] I kind of use it for medicine, but I'll stop when this bag's used up. Hopefully, I'll be calmed down by then.[29]

> ### *Marijuana Legalization and Minors*
> * *Is marijuana legal in your jurisdiction?*
> * *If so, how old do you have to be to purchase it?*

Then he makes me say I am sorry. To everyone. Individually. I even have to say sorry to Will who could have been taken away from me if the social worker found out I had left him to go back to the streets.

And everyone says they forgive me. Except Will, of course, because he can't. I'm holding him and he's asleep.

Then they tell me that I am grounded for the next month and that I have to do a bunch of chores. And they're taking my phone back too for a month.

Before we leave, Aunt Hen explains why she was really scared about having to tell Sarah that I was missing. She says that she doesn't want to lose me because it took me so long to get here. And she doesn't want Will to be stuck in foster care like I was.

I know that she's still mad but she's mad in that same way she was mad at the social worker who refused to let me stay with them way back after grandma's stroke. She's that same kind of "nobody's going to mess with my family" mad, but it's at me this time. I didn't know that she could get mad at me like that and still not kick me out.

But she can.

---

27. A total of 27 states allow the sale and use of marijuana either for recreational or medicinal purposes or both. *See* Melia Robinson & Skye Gold, *This Map Shows Every State that Legalized Marijuana on Election Day*, Bus. Insider (Nov. 9, 2016), [https://perma.cc/LGC4-T7NG].

28. Nineteen states have legalized marijuana for medicinal purposes only. *Id.*

29. Adolescent marijuana use is positively predicted by both parental maltreatment and peer marijuana use. *See* W. Alex Mason et al., *Parent and Peer Pathways Linking Childhood Experiences of Abuse with Marijuana Use in Adolescence and Adulthood*, 66 Addictive Behavs. 70 (2017).

Maya and Her Sister

After the big sit down at Ruth's, Jasmine—I've been working on calling her Jasmine more now—has been checking in on me more. Since I've been grounded she is like the only person I am allowed to hang out with who doesn't live with me. Her and Minnie. But Minnie has been keeping her distance. I don't know if she's mad or what. She says she isn't. She says she thinks I need time to be at home and make things right but that she will be around later if I need her. Still, it's hard for me to face Minnie because she's the one person who believed in me when no one from my family really even knew me yet.

Jasmine, though, she's easier to talk to than I thought because, as it turns out, she hasn't always been so on top of her game. Since I've been grounded she's been coming over and getting me because she has a car now.[30] Me and her sometimes just drive around and talk, with Will asleep in his car seat. It's easier to talk when you don't have to look somebody in the face. That's when she told me about how she busted out of even more foster homes and group homes than me and that she used to be mad because she thought our real grandma didn't want her and that everybody had forgotten all about her or was mad at her.

Driving Clients in Cars

Here, Maya notes how easy it is to talk in a car, which is not unusual for teenagers. Clients often need rides to court or to meetings.

- *Should a lawyer ever drive a client to court or other meetings? Why or why not?*

She even tells me about how it was her that put us in foster care and that she's spent a lot of time not knowing how to feel about it. It kind of messed her up. She's afraid I'll be mad, but she thinks she needs to tell me now because she doesn't like having that secret. For real, I'm surprised at first and kind of angry, but then when she tells me the story step-by-step I know that she was just ten years old and all she wanted was for us to go to school. She didn't know what all would happen after she talked to that principal. It isn't her fault.

---

30. Obtaining a driver's license and having access to a car is challenging for youth in foster care. One study of foster care alumni in independent living programs (median age 20) reported that only 39% of participants had a driver's license. The study also found that those who entered foster care at a younger age were less likely to have a driver's license and those who had informal life skills training from a caregiver were more likely to have a driver's license. *See* Melissa Nicole Smith, A Short-Term Longitudinal Study of the Adjustment of Foster Youth Across the Aging Out Transition and the Benefits of Life Skill Training 38–39, 42, 45 (2014) (unpublished Ph.D. dissertation, Catholic University of America) [https://perma.cc/VY53-FTCJ]). By comparison, a study of driver's license attainment across the United States noted that for the 20- to 24-year-old age group, 76.7% had a driver's license. Michael Sivak & Brandon Schoettle, U. Mich. Transp. Res. Inst., Recent Decreases in the Proportion of Persons with a Driver's License Across All Age Groups (2016), [https://perma.cc/57PY-6HBL].

It's good to have her to talk to because it isn't easy going back to school. I can't believe Lamar wants to act like none of that happened. I tell his friends what he did and they just laugh, like it's some kind of joke. They're on his side. So I am back to not having any friends again. And with the new semester, school's even harder with more reading.

I can tell Jasmine about how I'm lonely and how the friends that Aunt Hen and Uncle Marcus want me to hang out with are all from church and none of them understand what it's like to not have a normal family. She says that there's probably some kids at church whose families aren't all that normal, but she gets it; she knows how it feels to think you're the only kid in foster care in your class. She remembers having to do that stupid family tree assignment in fifth grade, the one where everyone turns in their nice neat family trees and ours is just a bunch of question marks and sawed-off branches.

She says that what got her through high school was this group called Youth in Action.[31] I say it sounds like an exercise class and I'm not into that. She laughs and explains it's actually a group of teenagers and twenty-some-year-olds who are in foster care or who used to be. She says she'll go with me if I want to try it out. Maybe . . . . after my month of being grounded is up.

Maya Joins Youth in Action

I leave Will with Aunt Hen and Uncle Marcus, and Jasmine picks me up to go to the Youth in Action meeting.

I'm pretty tired of meetings but this one isn't so bad. Mostly, it's everybody sitting around in a circle eating pizza and talking about what their weeks were like. Some of it's kind of like complaining but everyone's real nice to everyone else about it.

They ask me about my week and I don't know what to say but I tell them that school is rough and that my baby is almost seven months old and so he's teething which means I'm not getting any sleep. He's eating baby food now,[32] which helps to keep his belly full at night, but he still gets up crying. I find out there's this girl, Courtney, who has a little boy of her own. She had him when she was 15 and in foster care, just like me; her boy is four now. I can't imagine that someday Will's going to be four years old. Her son's name is Adam. He's in preschool and everything.

---

31. Foster youth and foster alumni organizations provide youth with a voice and an opportunity to learn how to use it to advocate on behalf of the issues that they identify. This particular organization is patterned after The Mockingbird Society. *See* Mockingbird Soc., [https://perma.cc/P8G2 -NCC6]. *See also* California's Foster Youth in Action [https://perma.cc/FCD9-JWRG]; Foster Care Alumni of America, [https://perma.cc/3VHL-R27T].

32. Babies are typically ready to be introduced to solid foods between four and six months of age. *Solid Foods: How to Get Your Baby Started*, Mayo Clinic [https://perma.cc/A47T-FZW7].

After everybody's done talking about their week, they talk about the different things they're doing to try to change the foster care system. Some of them write articles for this newspaper they have,[33] some of them get up in front of big groups of people and talk about what foster care is really like,[34] some of them even go to the state capitol and talk to people about changing the laws.[35] Courtney talks about how she's been working with this group of moms in foster care to come up with some ideas about how things need to change so we don't get pressure to have abortions or give up our babies once they're born. I wince remembering Shirley, but when Courtney asks whether I would want to join, I say maybe.

On our way out of the meeting, we get to talking—me, Courtney and Jazz—about school. Courtney tells me about how she's in Running Start, just like Jazz was. You get college credit while you're still in high school by taking community college classes. Courtney got behind in school too because of foster care and having Adam, but she's almost done now, and she'll have a whole year of college by the time she gets her high school diploma. She says I could maybe have two years of college credit if I start next year when I'm a junior. Plus, the school district pays for the tuition; so it's like you're getting to go to college for free. I've been scared I wouldn't pass the tests that you need to take to get in, but Courtney says the tests aren't too hard and that it can't hurt to try. Maybe I should look into it. I'd love it if I didn't have to go back to that high school.

> ### Youth-Led Advocacy Organizations
>
> *Adolescents are influenced by their peer group. Organizations like Youth in Action can provide youth in foster care with an empowering context to make friends.*
>
> - *Do the foster youth in your community have access to an organization like the one described here?*

Courtney also tells me about how when she first had Adam her social worker tried to take him away, saying that she couldn't have a baby because she smoked cigarettes[36] and she was too young. So maybe Aunt Hen was right to be afraid

---

33. The Mockingbird Society, for example, has a hard copy newspaper as well as a blog and news site and their webpage with articles written by Mockingbird Youth. *Blog*, Mockingbird Soc. [https://perma.cc/KQW7-W5JN].

34. Youth in the Mockingbird Society build leadership and advocacy skills by learning how to tell their stories effectively for purposes of training and systems change. *See Youth Speakers*, Mockingbird Soc. [https://perma.cc/WW48-M4PL].

35. The Mockingbird Society also prepares youth to advocate for legislative and policy change at the state and national level. *See Public Policy*, Mockingbird Soc. [https://perma.cc/76RB-QSBU].

36. Research has shown that exposure to secondhand smoke from cigarettes can cause Sudden Infant Death Syndrome (SIDS), respiratory infections, ear infections, and asthma attacks in infants and children. Secondhand smoke has been identified as the cause of 400 infant deaths per year. *See* David M. Homa, et al., *Vital Signs: Disparities in Nonsmokers' Exposure to Secondhand Smoke—United States 1999–2012*, 64 Morbidity and Mortality Weekly Report 103 (2015).

about me losing Will. But Courtney was lucky because she had a lawyer who really fought for her and taught her how to fight for herself too. So she got to keep him. She says she did quit smoking cigarettes later but that it wasn't right for them to try to take her son away. They wouldn't take away a rich mom's baby for that. She says that she is trying to get the state to change how they think about moms in foster care, to treat us like everybody else. Courtney has a lot of strong opinions and she isn't afraid to say them; she really loves her little boy, you can tell. Just like I feel about Will.

Part II. Options: Choosing Between Relative Guardianship and Extended Foster Care

Maya's Lawyer and Social Worker Face Budget Cuts

Julia heard the rumors but now the state budget reconciliation process is under-way and it seems that what she feared is coming true. Fewer federal dollars are making their way to the states because of the new block grant approach to just about everything. She has tried to be optimistic, focusing on the aspect of the block grant philosophy that professes to give greater freedom to the states to experiment, to keep only those programs that work, to save money by not having to be encumbered by bothersome and ill-fitting federal directives.[37] But it seems that really all this new approach does is fix the "unfunded mandate" problem by removing mandates in exchange for sending fewer funds.[38] Given the shrinking federal dollars, the state budget seems to focus on what it perceives to be the bare essentials of child welfare—answering the phones, doing investigations, and trying to deal with the severe foster parent shortage.

Services are shrinking, even funds that support transportation for visitation are being reduced, the kinds of emergency funds that social workers used to be able to draw upon at least in the beginning of the fiscal year are not being re-allocated. Lawyers for kids are barely on the table, despite the fact that the last administration had made strong statements encouraging states to appoint lawyers for children.[39] And certainly lawyers in pilot programs like Julia's, those with low caseloads that

---

37. *See* Robert Jay Dilger & Eugene Boyd, Cong. Research Serv., R40486, Block Grants: Perspectives and Controversies, *Summary* (2014), [https://perma.cc/4M29-P85U].

38. *Id.*

39. The Administration for Children and Families issued guidance emphasizing the importance of legal representation for children in dependency proceedings. The guidance highlights the empirical research that links quality legal representation to "improved case planning, expedited permanency and cost savings to state government." Info. Memorandum 17-02 from the Children's Bureau, U.S. Dep't of Health and Human Serv., to State, Tribal and Territorial Agencies Administering or Supervising the Administration of Title IV-E and IV-B of the Social Security Act, Indian Tribes and Indian Tribal Organizations, State Courts, and State and Tribal Court Improvement Programs, on High Quality Legal Representation for All Parties in Child Welfare Proceedings (Jan. 17, 2017), [https://perma.cc/VL8B-FNR5].

enable them to make things happen for the children and youth they represent, are
seen as luxuries. Julia watches as she sees her program eliminated in a simple budget
strikethrough. She is still funded through the end of the current fiscal year but there
is nothing in the new budget for the next biennial. She isn't even sure she can get her
old job back with the defender agency. She talked to Katie and she said that they
aren't hiring, even though people are leaving. Katie's caseload is going up. Julia isn't
sure she would want to work there, even if she could.

Sarah too is struggling with the news. While the money is going away, it seems that
the obligation to provide visitation, to make reasonable efforts, to find safe and appropriate placements, to fulfill the service plans that have been court ordered, all of it, is
still there. And her caseload is growing too because as staff leaves (and they are leaving
even more quickly now) they are not filling the new positions. The administration is in
another reorganization mode. People like Althea who used to do innovative programs
designed to work on the hardest cases are being given regular caseloads like everyone
else, just so everyone can try to keep up. The Governor is considering a complete over-
haul of child protection and child welfare services. No one seems to know what to do.

And so the imperative for the state to close cases that can be closed is stronger
than ever.

Reasonable Efforts When Resources Are Limited

*The state has the duty to engage in "reasonable efforts" to reunify fami-
lies once children are removed. Statutes also require that services be
provided to support the youth.*

- *Is the lawyer's duty to advocate for services for the client any different when funding is restricted?*

Maya's Social Worker Meets with Her Proposed Guardian

When I look down my list of cases, there aren't that many that look like they can be
closed. Truth is, working in the BRS unit,[40] I've grown accustomed to defining success
as not having a mentally ill child age out at eighteen into homelessness. A good ending
is when I can help a young person become eligible and choose to go into extended
foster care. At least then, there is a reprieve, one that allows for some maturation and
skill development before they are set loose to fend for themselves at 21. The cases are
transferred into a different office when youth enter extended foster care, and the social
workers there hopefully see their clients leave the system with more skills and a better
plan for where to go next.[41] That's what I like to imagine anyway.

---

40. "BRS" refers to this jurisdiction's "Behavioral Rehabilitative Services," a specialized service
designed to address the intensive mental health needs of youth in foster care.

41. *See* Clark M. Peters et al., *Extending Foster Care to Age 21: Weighing the Costs to Government
Against the Benefits to Youth,* CHAPIN HALL U. CHI. (2009) [https://perma.cc/S6H6-YTT6] (finding

Maya's is one of my cases that might be able to be closed. She can move out of the system fairly quickly through a relative guardianship. I've been to see them monthly and each visit is the same. Her relatives report she is doing well, and so does she. Will is healthy and happy. Maya is in school. She's even talking about signing up for Running Start classes. She sees her sister Jasmine frequently. The family supports are all in place. She isn't seeing a therapist anymore, but considering everything she has going on and how well she's handling everything, I can see why she might want to take a break from that. She can come back to it later if she needs or wants to. She'll still be entitled to Medicaid if she is in a relative guardianship;[42] so her mental and physical health needs will be covered. This case doesn't really need my supervision, so why not let them move on?

I double-check the records to see if we ever got Maya on SSI, a federal program that provides financial payments for people with disabilities.[43] Most of the kids on my caseload qualify because of their mental health diagnoses. Once eligibility is established, all of the benefits are handled by central administration because the benefits actually go to reimburse the state for the kids' care,[44] which seems wrong if you ask me. I mean, isn't it like asking poor kids to pay for their own foster care?[45] But, no one asked me. Still, it's good for me to know when I am considering a guardianship for a family because if the amount of the disability payment is higher than what the guardianship payment would be, then the family is better off taking the disability benefit instead. But when I check the records, it seems like she slipped through the cracks on this one too. Probably because she was missing from care so much, her application just never got worked up. So it looks like the guardianship subsidy is the best bet, if they want to do it.

Eligibility for SSI

It sounds like Maya might be eligible for SSI.

- *Does anyone have a duty to explain this to her?*
- *Is this part of Julia's job?*
- *Is it something Sarah should do?*

---

that youth in Illinois who took advantage of the opportunity for extended foster care were better positioned in terms of educational attainment than their peers in Wisconsin and Iowa who, at the time of the study, had no extended foster care programs in which to enroll).

42. *See* 42 U.S.C. § 673(b)(3)(C).

43. *See* 42 U.S.C. § 1381.

44. For an explanation of the relationship between the federal Supplemental Security Income (SSI) program and the federal foster care program, *see* Soc. Security Admin., Social Security Advisory Board Statement on the Supplemental Security Income Program (2014), [https://perma.cc/Z6S3-N7X2].

45. For a similar critique with accompanying legal analysis, *see* Daniel Hatcher, *Foster Children Paying for Foster Care*, 27 Cardozo L. Rev. 1797 (2006).

And maybe they won't want to do it because they will miss out on extended foster care benefits if they go with the guardianship. Hen and Marcus are licensed foster parents, so Maya can take advantage of extended foster care when she turns 18 and stay in foster care until she is 21,[46] a benefit she will lose if she goes into guardianship now.[47] But she won't turn 18 for almost two years, and is extended foster care really necessary? Shouldn't those funds be reserved for youth who don't have anyone to support them when they turn 18? I know that Hen and Marcus have come to rely on foster care payments to help afford the larger apartment they are in, but will they really not keep Maya if that money goes away when she turns 18? Or will they, as Hen said in the FGC, find a way to be poor with Maya, just like they were poor without her? I know this sounds harsh, but if you saw who else is on my caseload, you would understand. And I do need to be able to have more time to spend with them.

> ### *Eligibility for Extended Foster Care*
>
> *Federal law permits states, at their option, to offer extended foster care to children who become subject to guardianships after their 16th birthdays. Maya's state has not elected to offer this benefit.*
>
> *   *What are your state's eligibility criteria for extended foster care?*
> *   *Would Maya be eligible in your state if she were to elect to go into a guardianship with her Aunt Hen and Uncle Marcus at 16?*

So when I show up at Hen's to discuss this possibility, she already has the place cleared on the kitchen table for us to sit down. She's gotten used to me needing a place to spread out with Maya's file and the paperwork that each visit entails. Marcus is at work, Will is at daycare, and everyone else, including Maya, is at school, so it's just the two of us. I ask her how things are going, if there's anything new, and she assures me that everything is fine, that Maya has even become involved in Youth in Action working on issues involving teen moms in foster care, which is great news, a sign that she is finding a community of positive peers.

"You and Marcus have been doing such a wonderful job with Maya, really. It's amazing how far she's come in such a short time, without any blowups or anything. What's your secret?"

---

46. The federal government provides funding to the states to assist those youth who are in foster care on their eighteenth birthday. 42 U.S.C. § 677(a)(1). These funds may be used by the states to provide financial assistance for those youth who wish to remain in foster care until their twenty-first birthday. 42 U.S.C. § 677(a)(5).

47. Federal law allows states to opt to provide extended foster care payments to youth who become the subjects of guardianships or adoptions after they reach the age of sixteen. *See* 42 U.S.C. § 675(8)(B). A few states have elected to make extended foster care available under these circumstances, sometimes with other specific qualifiers. *See, e.g.*, CAL. DEP'T OF FAM. & CHILD. SERVS., HANDBOOK 24: EXTENDED FOSTER CARE PROGRAM, YOUTH RECEIVING KINSHIP GUARDIANSHIP ASSISTANCE PAYMENTS(KINGAP) OR ADOPTION ASSISTANCE PAYMENTS (AAP), (last updated June 2013), [https:// perma.cc/TGE4-K2EC].

"Oh, we have our ups and downs, you know. She's still a teenager after all. But we all make it work, just like the family plan says. Jasmine has been a blessing too. Maya can talk to her about things she can't talk to us about."

"That FGC did seem to do the trick.[48] I'm glad Julia talked me into that one."

"Oh, that was her idea? That Julia does a good job, so I guess I'm not surprised. She stays on top of things with Maya. There are some things from the plan we haven't done yet though. Like we haven't been to see my mother as often as we should; we been by once, to show her Will, you know. But she didn't know us; so it was hard. And we been so busy with the baby and everything."

"How about Luke and Shannon. Have you heard from them?"

"No, not really. But I have been thinking about maybe catching up with them again once school starts winding down for everybody. I don't know if Maya is going to want to take any summer classes but if she's free I could see if she might want to go with Will to visit them and meet her brother. It's been a lot of change so I haven't pushed it, but maybe once school is out she'll be looking for something like that to do. I don't want her with too much time on her hands. Will keeps her busy, no doubt, but she's got to do something else too — visit them, take classes or maybe get a job now that she's 16. If she goes to visit them for a few weeks or something, would I need to get your permission first?"

"Yes, you'll need to let me know your plans. I'll approve it, no problem.[49] It's just a formality really. I trust you to do the right thing for Maya and Will. That's something I want to talk to you about actually. Remember at the last hearing how the judge said that she was going to make relative guardianship your alternative plan?"

"Maybe. I guess so. Not sure."

"It's OK; there was a lot going on that morning. The judge thought it was likely that things would go well and that you and Marcus might want to just get out from under the system and have Maya's court case dismissed. You can be her guardians and

---

48. Research indicates that both the long-term and immediate outcomes of family group conferencing are positive, with stability and safety in the placements and plans devised by families. *See* Katharine Cahn et al., *Long Term and Immediate Outcomes of Family Group Conferencing in Washington State*, Int'l Inst. for Restorative Pracs. (June 30, 2001), [https://perma.cc/J24H-HKRJ].

49. Federal law now requires that states establish the "reasonable and prudent parent" standard, which cedes more authority to foster parents to allow the youth in their care to engage in developmentally appropriate activities without first seeking agency approval. *See* 42 U.S.C. §671(a)(10). However, some states may continue to impose requirements for permission to travel for lengthy periods and/or outside of the court's jurisdiction. *See, e.g.,* Wash. Admin. Code § 388-148-1435 (requires written agency approval if trip is for longer than 72 hours or is outside the country); Mich Dep't of Health & Hum. Servs, FOM 722-11, Children's Foster Care Manual, Prudent Parent Standard and Delegation of Parental Consent (2015) [https://perma.cc/6WYZ-VETC] (requires consent from parent or legal guardian for out of state travel and if parents whereabouts are unknown, then the court is petitioned for consent).

still get financial support until she's 18.[50] You just won't have to have these visits from me and she won't have a court case anymore. I think it's time to ask whether you'd like to do that. You can do a guardianship or really even an adoption[51] if you want to."

"We can adopt Maya?"

"Yes, you can. Her mother's rights have been terminated[52] and her father's rights have never been established because no one knows who he is. We could terminate them just to be safe."[53]

"I know you all have terminated her mother's rights, but that's my sister."

"I understand, and you don't have to adopt. I just thought I would mention it in case. At this point, you get the same government benefits either way. The main difference is that if you adopt it's like legally she is your child, just as if she'd been born to you and Marcus."[54]

"Well, that's just not true. I can't do that to my sister, take her child away from her like that."

"That's perfectly OK. A lot of relatives feel that way. That's one reason why relative guardianships came about. A guardianship just says that you are responsible for her until she becomes an adult at 18, instead of the state. We can get out of your hair."

"But we would still get the foster care payments?"

"Yes, it would be called a guardianship subsidy. It might not be as high as it is now because Maya has been 'high needs' for a while now, which means your payments have been higher than the basic rate. I can see my supervisor saying that since her behaviors have settled down your rate shouldn't be as high.[55] But that review would likely have happened soon anyway. The main thing is, if you did the guardianship, the payments would stop once she turns 18."

"Well, I guess they weren't going to go on forever anyways."

---

50. Federal law assumes that the amount of the guardianship assistance payment will be negotiated but will in no case be more than the foster care payment which would have been paid on behalf of the child had she remained in foster care. 42 U.S.C. § 673(d)(2).

51. Adoption results in the creation of a legal parent-child relationship that supplants any preexisting parent-child relationships. *See* Ann M. Haralambie, Handling Child Custody, Abuse and Adoption Cases, § 14:1 (Dec. 2016 Update). A prerequisite to adoption is either parental consent or the legal termination of parental rights. *See* Ann M. Haralambie, Handling Child Custody, Abuse and Adoption Cases, § 14:5 (Dec. 2016 Update).

52. *Id.*

53. States vary in their approaches to the rights of unnamed fathers. Best practice is to notify the John Doe father by publication and terminate his rights. *See* Ann M. Haralambie, Handling Child Custody, Abuse and Adoption Cases, § 14:7 (Dec. 2016 Update).

54. Haralambie, *supra* note 53 at § 14:1.

55. The amount of the guardianship subsidy is to be geared to the circumstances of the guardian and the needs of the child. 42 U.S.C. § 673(d)(1)(B)(i).

Tying the Amount of Foster Care Payments to Child Mental Health Needs

If Aunt Hen were honest with Sarah about Maya's behavior, it's possible that her foster care payments would continue to be high.

• *What are some of the unintended consequences that flow from policies tying the amount of foster care payments to the behavior or mental health needs of children?*

"That's true, but I should tell you, to be fair, that if Maya were to stay in foster care with you, she could be eligible for extended foster care when she turns 18. That means that if she's in school or working part-time, she could continue to be in foster care until she's 21.[56] Of course, then the department would still be involved in your lives and she would still have to go to court for review hearings.[57] I don't know if she would even want to do extended foster care though. She has to want it. It's her choice then."[58]

"But, if she wanted to, we can get the payments until she's twenty-one?"

"Well, it will either be you or whatever her living situation is, assuming that where she's living is court approved. It's more likely that the court will approve her living situation if the state agency approves it. So it means that we will still be checking up on where she is and what she wants to do.[59] So, for example, if she goes off to college, the payments can go towards paying for her dorm.[60] But you know, she can't decide

---

56. *Supra* note 41.

57. Federal law requires that youth who receive extended foster care must maintain eligibility for extended foster care by: 1) completing secondary education or a program leading to an equivalent credential; 2) being enrolled in an institution which provides post-secondary or vocational education; 3) participating in a program or activity designed to promote, or remove barriers to, employment; 4) employed for at least 80 hours per month; or 5) being incapable of doing any of the activities described above due to a medical condition, which incapability is supported by regularly updated information in the case plan. 42 U.S.C. § 675(8)(B). Not all states provide extended foster care for all eligibility categories allowed by the federal statute, and a few end coverage before 21, while others extend benefits beyond 21. Some allow youth to leave foster care at 18 but re-enter if they choose before a certain age. *See* Bruce A. Boyer, *Foster Care Re-Entry Laws: Mending the Safety Net for Emerging Adults in the Transition to Independence*, 88 TEMP. L. REV. 837 (2016). Whatever the requirements, it is expected that regular review hearings will continue to assure that the youth continues to meet them. 42 U.S.C. § 671(a)(16).

58. Eligible youth can and do elect not to remain in foster care when they reach age eighteen. *See* Boyer, *supra* note 57.

59. For a review of the various housing options available for approval and requirements of various state programs, *see* LISA COY ET AL., CTR. FOR CHILD WELFARE, U. S. FLA., EXTENDED FOSTER CARE HOUSING, SERVICES AND SUPPORTS (2013), [https://perma.cc/8R26-CRXC].

60. Some state programs particularly call out college dormitories as agency-approved placements. *Id.* at 9–10, 12, 14, 17, 19–20, 22–23, 26–27, 29–30 (Arkansas, California, District of Columbia, Illinois, Maine, Michigan, Minnesota, New York, North Dakota, Tennessee, Texas, Washington, Arizona specifically note that college dormitories are approved extended foster care placements).

she wants to go back to the streets and still get the foster care payments for herself, because no court will approve that and someone will be checking in to make sure she's where she's supposed to be, you know what I mean?"

"Well, sure. The state won't pay her to live on the streets."

"Exactly, and of course if she's running away and not staying in her approved place-ment, eventually she'll lose that benefit, if the extended foster care social worker finds out. Not to scare you though; it seems like we don't have to worry about that at all."

"No . . ." Hen trails off, and then comes back. She looks like she's thinking it through, "So we won't have you as our social worker if she got extended foster care?"

"Probably not, unless they change the way things are arranged, which is always pos-sible, that's for sure. But right now, there's a different office that handles extended foster care cases and one of the main things those social workers do is make sure that the young people who are getting extended foster care are doing what they're sup-posed to be doing so that they still qualify."

"I see."

"I know this is a lot to think about and I'm sure you want to talk to Marcus and Maya about it before you make a decision, but really I just wanted to let you know that if you want to get Maya out of this system and be her guardian, which means you could make all the decisions together with her, without involving me or any other social worker, then I would support you on that. I can make that happen. Like that decision to go see Luke and Shannon and to meet Lawrence? That will be yours. You won't have to tell me your plans."

"No offense, but that sounds pretty good."

"No worries. I understand. It's my goal for kids to get to the place where they can just have a normal family life. Still, Maya may want to talk to her lawyer about all this before you make a decision. I just want to let you know that I believe in you and I trust you, and I know that you don't need me in your lives anymore."

Hen takes it all in thoughtfully, says she doesn't have any more questions, and that she'll get back with me. I tell her that the next hearing in Maya's case is sched-uled in September for permanency planning, and with any luck we could have the guardianship done in time for that, maybe even before.

Maya's Family Makes a Decision

Tasha and Sandra are both at different friends' houses and Will is taking a nap when Aunt Hen and Uncle Marcus stop me from doing my homework, saying they want to talk. Which makes me nervous and I wonder whether they figured out about the weed, even though I smoked my last blunt last week. Or is it some bad thing that has hap-pened that they have to tell me. Has grandma finally died? Could it be my mom? Did Aunt Hen find her somewhere? She says she doesn't have time to go looking for her these days but I have heard her calling the different shelters, letting them know that if she shows up they should tell her our new address.

"No, no, it's nothing like that," Uncle Marcus says, "We just want to have some time to talk to you about some things, legal stuff about your case mostly. It doesn't change anything about how things are or will be when it comes to the day-to-day. We just wanted to let you know what Sarah talked about with Aunt Hen last time she was here visiting."

That doesn't necessarily make me feel that much less nervous. I'm hoping Aunt Hen doesn't tell Sarah about me sneaking out. I know she doesn't want to but I also know she's a really bad liar.

"Did you tell her about what happened?"

"No, I didn't," Aunt Hen says, like it's not something she is proud of and I should be thankful for, "I hope she never finds out about that either because she thinks we've been doing such a perfect job raising you."

I want to tell her that she is doing a perfect job raising me. But I also want to tell her that I'm too old to be raised by anybody. But I don't say any of that. I just say, "Thanks for not telling her."

"You're welcome. What she came to say," Aunt Hen continues, "is that she thinks we're doing such a good job that she wants to make us your guardians and have the judge say you don't need to be in foster care anymore."

"What? What do you mean? Like no more social workers? Ever?"

"Yeah, like no more social workers." Uncle Marcus says with a smile.

"And no more lawyers, and no more of you having to go to court, except to get the guardianship set up," says Aunt Hen.

"For real?"

"For real." Uncle Marcus says.

"And you'll do that?" I ask them, almost in shock.

"Yes, we'll most certainly do that," says Aunt Hen and Uncle Marcus is nodding too, saying, "Of course we will."

"We want to know what you say to that idea before we say anything else to Sarah," says Uncle Marcus.

"I say yes!"

And then they're both giving me a hug. Hugs don't freak me out anymore. I still don't hug back. I'd like to someday.

But then Uncle Marcus says, "Before we tell Sarah, though, we want you to talk to Julia about it."

"Why? You said no more lawyers." I just want this to be over. What can there be to talk about?

"Well, Sarah says that if you stay in foster care with us until you are 18, you can be in extended foster care," Aunt Hen says.

"Like Jasmine?"

"Yeah, like Jasmine," Aunt Hen says.

"Well, I don't care about none of that. I mean she needs it because she has to pay rent to Ruth. But Ruth's not real family."

"We know, but we still think you should hear it out from Julia because she can explain it all to you better than we can and besides there may be other things that you're missing out on that Sarah just isn't telling us about. I mean that's Julia's job — to tell you about all this legal stuff, to have your back on that, right?" Uncle Marcus says.

"Yeah, but I already know what I want."

"We hear you. But there are things to think about. I mean, what if you want to go get an apartment on your own or with Jasmine when you're older? Apartments are expensive. We want to have you and Will stay with us for as long as you want to, but we know that you probably will want to get out on your own someday. We don't want you walking away from something that you might want later, you know?" says Uncle Marcus.

"I guess so, but I would like to just be normal, to not have any of that stuff. I don't want any more *help*, not from them."

"We don't blame you, but we want you to talk to Julia first."

I've never called Julia myself. The only time I ever thought about calling her was when I was stuck with Diamond, but I didn't. Aunt Hen and Uncle Marcus have her number. And Uncle Marcus dials it and hands me the phone. It goes to voicemail. I get nervous and hang up. We practice what I will say and then I call again.

I leave her a voicemail, "Hello Julia, this is Maya. Call me back, OK?"

Maya's Attorney Counsels Maya and Her Family

I am surprised to hear from Maya. And a little concerned. Very few clients call me, which is why I make it a point to check in with them by phone at least twice a month, something I didn't use to be able to do before the pilot and my caseload was lowered.

I did call Hen back before that last review hearing to ask whether she had planned to file a caregiver's report. The social worker is supposed to tell them before each hearing that they have the right to attend and that they can file a report if they want to.[61] Sometimes they file a report with the court but don't realize they're supposed to give me a copy too. I don't like surprises. Hen said she wasn't planning on filing a report or coming to court and that she and Marcus had handled the situation with Maya. She didn't want to talk about it any more than Maya did.

---

61. Federal law requires that foster parents and other caregivers be provided with "notice of, and the right to be heard in, any proceeding to be held with respect to the child." 42 U.S.C. § 675(5)(G).

I used to get more involved in the family lives of my clients, but more and more I realize that families shouldn't depend on me or social workers to resolve all of their differences. Every family struggles with teenagers testing limits. Micro-managing those dramas is not a terribly good use of my time. I won't always be there and most families can work things out without my help. I sense that Hen and Marcus can handle Maya. They are one of those couples with mutual strengths. Marcus is calm and level-headed, but firm when he needs to be. Hen is a bit hot-headed but loving; it's not the worst thing for Maya to see both of these temperaments working together as parents.

Still, when I get the phone call, I wonder if I have misjudged the situation. Have things gone south? Should I have stepped in to mediate the situation? I have done that in other cases when it's really necessary to avoid having a client kicked out of a placement she wants to be in.

I call Maya back, and I learn I have nothing to fear, that she is calling me because her Aunt Hen and Uncle Marcus insisted. As I thought might happen, Sarah is interested in moving forward with a relative guardianship but had mentioned that Maya would lose out on extended foster care. Even though they seemed to want to move forward, they also want Maya to talk to me about extended foster care first. I suggest that we meet at their apartment in case she wants me to talk to her aunt and uncle too. She says that's fine since this meeting is really their idea anyway. I let her know that I want to talk to her alone first and then we can invite them to join if she wants them to. She agrees.

Involving Caregivers in Conversations with Clients

Julia admits to having brokered conversations between unhappy caregivers and her clients, and here she suggests having Aunt Hen and Uncle Marcus involved in the conversation about extended foster care.

- *What are the ethical constraints on conversations like these?*
- *What are the risks and benefits of involving caregivers in client counseling sessions?*

When I get to the apartment, Will is really fussy, Tasha and Sandra are fighting over what to watch on TV, and Hen is making them both mad by turning off the TV and telling them they have to go to their room and do homework. I always try to make my appointments with clients after school but one of the downsides is the chaos of after-school activity in a small apartment. The weather isn't bad, a little cool, but it's one of those sunny late spring days and I ask whether taking Will for a walk in the stroller I see parked near the door would be a good idea. Hen is getting ready to strap him in and head out with him herself when I suggest that it would be fine if Maya and I go; that way she can keep her eye on Tasha and Sandra.

Meeting in Client's Placements

Julia suggests meeting with Maya at the apartment she shares with Hen, Marcus, Tasha, Sandra and Will.

- *What are the benefits and risks of setting a meeting in a client's home?*

She's fine with that. Marcus should be home in a half hour and then there will be more hands on deck to help out.

Will stops crying almost immediately once we are outside moving. He's suddenly and totally happy. I have to resist being distracted by his babbling. He's nine months old and he doesn't miss a thing. It seems like he's even starting to talk a little bit, bouncing and reaching out to a dog passing by, saying, "Bar, Bar, Bar!"

"He sure has a lot to say!" I say to Maya.

"Yes, he does. He's trying to say *Barkus* because he thinks all dogs are named Barkus. He's a talker and a crawler, and he's always getting into trouble these days, wanting to put things in outlets, get into cabinets. We are constantly baby-proofing and have to keep all the little things up off the floors and coffee table. He pulls himself up sometimes too. He's just . . . . a lot." She looks both proud and weary.

"Well, it looks like you're doing a great job with him — he seems like he's ahead of himself developmentally?"

"Yeah, that's what the doctor says. He's not supposed to be pulling up until next month, so he might be walking before too long."

"Wow, then you'll really be busy. How are you keeping up with it all?"

"Yeah, it's a lot but I have a lot of help. Tasha and Sandra even. They love to play with him now."

"I'm sure your aunt and uncle are proud."

"I think so. I don't know. Sometimes they get mad, you know. I'm not perfect."

"Who is?"

"Nobody I guess, but I messed up pretty bad a while back and we had to have a big family meeting and it was kind of a mess . . . . but I think we're over that now."

"Sounds like you must be, if they're interested in the relative guardianship."

Conversational Interviewing

Julia and Maya have an established relationship now. The "interviews" they are having seem more like conversations and less like fact gathering.

- *What is Julia learning from these conversations that is relevant to Maya's case?*

"Yeah, that's why they want me to talk to you. I want to do it, but they act like I'm giving up something big if I do."

"Well, you will be giving up being able to do extended foster care, which means you could have money from the state until you are 21."

"But I've been waiting to turn 18 to get out from under foster care my whole life, why would I decide to stay in after I turn 18?"

We make it to the park and she puts Will in the baby swing. There are other moms with their babies nearby so I don't answer her question just yet. Maya's pushing Will. One minute he's laughing and the next minute he's asleep, "I knew that would happen," she looks at me and smiles. "Here, let me see if I can get him back in the stroller without waking him up. Then we can talk without him interrupting us so much." It's obvious she knows how to handle this baby, and it's just as obvious that she's proud to show me.

We stroll on a paved path that takes us away from all of the playground equipment and other moms, and — sure enough — Will is out like a light.

"OK, so let me explain this step by step and since Hen and Marcus want you to understand it, I am going to check and make sure I am explaining it well as we go, OK?"

"OK."

"First of all, you are only eligible for extended foster care if you are actually in foster care when you turn 18."[62]

"So that means if we do the relative guardianship I can't get extended foster care later."

"That's right. It's always possible that they can change the law later to make it so you can,[63] but as the law stands right now, if you leave foster care before you are 18, you can't ever be in extended foster care."

"I don't really care because I want to be done with foster care."

"OK. But just so I understand, can you tell me what that means for you, to be done with foster care?"

"It means I don't have to have social workers come and see me or Aunt Hen. It means I don't have to worry about them deciding I'm not a good mom and taking Will away. It means I don't have to keep going to court. It means if my mom shows up it's not the worst thing in the world. We can decide how to handle that ourselves.

---

62. *Supra* note 41.

63. Some states do provide for extended foster care for those who entered guardianships after their sixteenth birthday. *Supra* note 41. California also allows youth whose guardianship or adoptions disrupt, thereby resulting in a lack of support, to request extended foster care. *See* Cal. Welf. & Inst. Code § 388.1.

It means I can just be a regular person in a regular family. I don't have to ask anybody's permission to just be me."

"You've thought about this a lot."

"Yeah, I have. No offense, but I'm so ready be done with all of this."

"None taken. So what are your thoughts, then, about what will happen when you turn 18? That probably seems a long way down the road when you just turned 16 a few months ago but it will sneak up on you. How far in high school will you be?"

We have to work it out together; Maya will be midway through either her junior or senior year when she turns eighteen, depending on whether she takes courses during the summer and how the Running Start program goes.

"If you do the relative guardianship, what that means is that the payments your aunt and uncle receive will stop in March of either your junior or senior year. Do you know if they will be able to make ends meet in this apartment?"

"Not really."

"Do you want to talk to them about that before you make a final decision?"

"Well, I know that they said the decision was up to me; so they must not need the money, right?"

"Maybe. I don't know. Maybe they can afford it or maybe they were thinking you all would move again."

"I don't really want to move in the middle of school again."

"OK, well, there's something we should find out then. The second thing I want you to understand is that even if you don't do the relative guardianship and take extended foster care, you don't have to stay in extended foster care all the way until you are 21. You can stop being in it any time you want to be."

"So I could do it just until I graduate high school?"

"Yes, you can stop any time you want to because when you are 18 you are legally an adult and the state can't force you to be in foster care. You are old enough to make your own decisions."

"Well, if they realize that, then why do I have to still have a social worker and go to court and all of that?

"That's a great question. I guess the law works in the same way that some families work, which is that they will continue to support you so long as you are following their rules. You can decide not to follow their rules, but then you have to figure out how to support yourself."

"Well, I'm sick of that. I think Aunt Hen is sick of it too. She gets tired of having to see Sarah all the time."

"You mentioned that you are all tired of social workers and that you're worried that they'll decide Will shouldn't be with you. Can you tell me why you say that?"

"Well, it's like you said a long time ago, we have more people watching us. And I know from my Youth in Action meetings that kids in foster care have had their babies taken away from them for stuff that regular moms wouldn't even be reported for, like smoking cigarettes and stuff. And even though Sarah seems OK, they change social workers all the time and who knows? She might quit and then I'll get some crazy one who thinks it's wrong that we all live in a small apartment and that I'm the only white person in there. Besides I'm not perfect you know. I make mistakes sometimes. You people think I'm perfect because I'm better than I was but I still do things that make people mad, and somebody else who doesn't know how I used to be could see how I am now and think it's not good enough and suddenly decide Will would be better off with somebody else."

I'm surprised that she remembers that comment I made before Will was even born and I am surprised that she's as aware as she is of the dynamic of having different social workers. I guess she's been living with it a long time. Even though I think she's probably inflating her risk, I can't argue with her reasoning, and the fact is that I suspect that there is more to what happened when she failed to come home on time than I know. I don't want her to make too much of whatever happened there, but I also don't want to minimize what might be valid concerns.

"Maya, first of all, you're absolutely right that Sarah may not be your social worker forever. In fact, it's very likely that if you were to go into extended foster care, that you would have a different social worker assigned to you. That social worker would want to make sure that you are staying where they have approved your placement to be. That social worker is also a mandatory reporter, which means that if she saw anything that seemed to be putting Will at risk of child abuse or neglect she would have to report it. But what I see here is a baby who is very well cared for."

"I know but Aunt Hen says . . . . Never mind."

"Maybe we should talk about it, Maya. It seems like there is something you're not telling me. Remember I won't tell anybody anything you tell me unless you want me to. Not Sarah and not even your Aunt Hen. I just want to make sure that you have a clear understanding of what your real risks are when it comes to Will."

Then she tells me the story of what happened that weekend; she even tells me some things she said she didn't tell her aunt and uncle, things she wants me to know just in case someone were to find out, like that she took ecstasy at the rave and did a trick in the motel in order to get out of there. She said she didn't want to see me right away because she had a bruise on her face and she was also just feeling really bad about everything.

"That sounds like a really frightening weekend and that you acted very bravely to get out of it."

"Yes, but Aunt Hen almost called the social worker to let her know I ran away and, if she had, and if they had sent the police out into that mess to find me before I got home, she says I might not have gotten to stay here anymore and they might have taken Will away from all of us."

"I like to think that wouldn't have happened. They probably would have let Will stay with your aunt and uncle."

"But not with me maybe? You don't know for sure what would have happened, do you?"

"No, I can't say for sure."

"See, that's what I mean. How would you like it if you didn't know something like that?"

"I'm sure I wouldn't like it one bit." Will stirs and she puts a pacifier in his mouth. "Have you done anything like that since?"

"No, I haven't been late coming home. Not once and I haven't seen Kiki or Diamond or any of them. I even stopped texting her. I've been too busy. I do know this guy now at Youth in Action, though, Johnathan. I think we might start going out, but he's nothing like Diamond or Lamar. He's one of the leaders at Youth in Action and he's got a job and is finishing high school and everything. He's saving up to go to college someday. I think Aunt Hen and Uncle Marcus still might think he's too old for me because he's 18, but he does go to church, so that's something. But mostly we just been hanging out after the meetings, you know?"

"Maya, there's nothing wrong with having a boyfriend. I can't say whether Aunt Hen and Uncle Marcus will think that someone who is 18 years old is too old for you. But it doesn't sound like you are going to be running off or doing drugs again anytime soon, am I right?"

"No, I'm not doing E again and I don't even want to hit the streets again. That messed me up bad. But you know, I hate having to watch our backs all the time."

"You don't like the feeling that Sarah is always paying attention to what you're doing."

"Yeah. It's bad enough that Aunt Hen and Uncle Marcus are watching me all the time."

"That makes sense. Have you thought about what you might want to do after you graduate high school?"

"A little bit. If I have my AA in culinary arts I may just try to get a job and then I won't need all that state money anyways. I can just help pay rent wherever I am, you know? Whether it's with Aunt Hen and Uncle Marcus or with Jasmine or wherever."

"That sounds good. Have you talked to them about that?"

"Not really. A little bit, because Aunt Hen and I were talking about how I need to get a job this summer maybe. She says I need to get a job and take a class so I'll stay busy. She's always wanting me to stay busy."

"Do you think maybe you should talk to Aunt Hen and Uncle Marcus more about your plan to work after you graduate from high school and get your AA before you make this decision?"

"Maybe."

"OK, one other question I have for you is this—what about Will's daycare? Right now, that's getting paid through the state. It's possible that that can change anyway because there's lots of cutbacks happening right now, but have you thought about how you will handle childcare if that goes away?"

"No, not really."

"OK, so it seems like there's a lot of unanswered questions. Let me throw out one possibility."

"OK."

"I will need to talk to Sarah to find out about whether you will still get the daycare benefits until you turn 18 under the relative guardianship.[64] She may be able to make that happen. If that's true, then we can look into seeing if you can get TANF while you're in high school after you turn 18[65] and maybe some daycare through TANF to keep you in school."[66]

"What's that?"

"TANF stands for Temporary Assistance for Needy Families. It's what most people call welfare. I don't know for sure if you will qualify for it or not if you are living with Hen and Marcus, but I think you will. It's not as much money as what Aunt Hen and Uncle Marcus are receiving now, but it could be enough to cover the difference in rent. I don't know because I don't know what their budget is like. The thing about TANF is that you only want to use it when you really have to because you are only allowed to get it for five years.[67] And you never know, you could need it more later. Sometimes, they'll let you get it for more than five years but you have to kind of fight for it and it's not guaranteed."[68]

"Sounds like we need to talk to Aunt Hen and Uncle Marcus, huh?"

---

64. *Supra* note 43.

65. States vary as to how they treat the income of non-caretaker adults in the household when calculating household income for purposes of eligibility. Most states do not include that income in the calculation. *See* Erika Huber et. al., The Urban Inst., Welfare Rules Databook: State TANF Policies as of July 2014 25 (2015) [https://perma.cc/74ZL-P23G].

66. The federal government provides the states block grants that can be used for the purpose of providing childcare for TANF recipients to enable them to attend school or work. *See* 42 U.S.C. § 9858c (c)(2)(A); Office of Family Assistance, U.S. Dep't. of Health & Human Services, TANF-ACF-IM-2016-03, 2014 Child Care Reauthorization and Opportunities for TANF and CCDF (2016), [https://perma.cc/T8MB-3YC6].

67. Federal law prohibits states from using federal money to "provide assistance to a family that includes an adult who has received assistance under any State program funded under this part . . . for 60 months (whether or not consecutive). 42 U.S.C. § 608(a)(7)(A).

68. Federal law does include a hardship exception to the five-year lifetime limit, but state agencies must be circumspect in granting it in the individual case, given that no more than 20% of the number of families receiving federal support may be doing so in excess of the five-year limit. 42 U.S.C. § 608(a) (7)(C).

"Yes, that's why I thought we might want to meet with them too. We can do that today if they have time and you want to. They may not know all the answers to these questions either until they sit down and look at their budget, but it's good to get all the answers first before you make up your mind. And there's one other thing I should mention before we head back to talk with them."

"What's that?"

"Well, I don't want you to make you worried unnecessarily. It's just that lawyers are always supposed to think about any bad things that *could* happen before you make a big decision like this one."

She sighs and looks at me like, "Really?"

"Well, I just want you to know that if you make the decision to go with the relative guardianship and your case is dismissed before you turn 18 and then something happens with Aunt Hen and Uncle Marcus so that they can't take care of you, then you have given up your extended foster care payments. I just want to make sure you understand that."

"I understand that. They aren't going to kick me out, I don't think."

"I don't have any reason to think they will, but it's just my job to say that."

We stroll back to the apartment. Maya is quiet. Maybe I pushed too hard to have her think about the worst-case scenario. Maybe I pushed too hard because I have seen too many homeless youth on my city streets and I never want to see Maya back there again. I believe in this family, but I also know they are bucking the odds. I understand why they want out but I also wish they could have more financial help longer.

> ### When Lawyers Have Agendas
> - *Does Julia push her agenda too much in this counseling session?*
> - *Does she strike the right balance between counselor and advisor?*

Will wakes up almost as soon as he is back in the busy apartment, but Hen plops him in the high chair. He gets all excited when he hears the baby food jar lid pop open. Hen sends Tasha and Sandra to their rooms to do their homework "for real this time." Maya says she'll feed Will while I explain to Hen what we were talking about in the park. Marcus joins us so we can all be on the same page.

I explain to them that Maya remains interested in the relative guardianship but that as Maya and I were talking about what happens when she turns 18 we realized we need to have a little more information from them and that I have some ideas I want to share as well. I remind them again that I represent Maya here but Maya has given me permission to speak with them freely as to her thoughts.

I tell them that they can also get a lawyer to help them with this if they want. They say they are fine without a lawyer, they trust I understand what is going on and they can't afford one anyway. I tell them that my duty is to Maya but it seems like everyone is wanting the same thing—to move ahead with the relative guardianship if possible and to understand what benefits will be available to help out financially.

> ### *Speaking with Unrepresented Parties*
> - *What constraints do the Model Rules impose on the conversation here between Julia, Maya, Aunt Hen, and Uncle Marcus?*
> - *Does Julia comply with those constraints?*
> - *What, if anything, would you do differently?*

We talk about budget and the TANF idea. Marcus and Hen say that they can both work some extra hours if Maya will agree to be at home with the kids on the weekends. And they also expect her to work part-time during the summers at least. They agree that the daycare issue is a problem during the school year and if Maya works summers, and that we need to find out what Sarah has to say about that. They agree that, if necessary, Maya should get whatever benefits she can after she turns 18 in order to make sure Will can be taken care of when she's in school. They agree that having the money in extended foster care would make it easier but that they understand why Maya doesn't want to mess with foster care anymore. They seem committed to make it work somehow.

They don't seem worried. They just look at me and nod. They say they get it. They know they are passing up benefits in the future. They say if daycare is a problem, they will look at re-arranging their work schedules. They've done it before.

They've been poor without Maya. They can be poor with Maya. What matters is that they are with Maya. And Will, too.

Maya's Lawyer Negotiates Relative Guardianship

It takes almost two months to get all the answers on the benefits questions and to negotiate the amount of the relative guardianship subsidy, but eventually Sarah and I work out the details. I have to stay in close contact with Maya because her sign-off is required, too.[69] We have a few more "family meetings" to make sure that the amount of payment[70] and the services that they'll be receiving will be fair and sufficient. I let Hen and Marcus know that they can hire their own attorney and get reimbursed for the attorney's help up to $2,000[71] but they decide to rely on my negotiating

---

69. Federal law requires consultation with youth fourteen years of age or older with respect to a kinship guardianship assistance agreement. 42 U.S.C. § 673(d)(3)(A)(iv).

70. Federal law assumes that the amount of the guardianship assistance payment will be negotiated but will in no case be more than the foster care payment which would have been paid on behalf of the child had she remained in foster care. 42 U.S.C. § 673(d)(2).

71. Federal law requires that the state pay up to $2,000 in nonrecurring costs associated with establishing a guardianship. 42 U.S.C. § 673(d)(1)(B)(iv).

with the state. They say that what is best for Maya is also best for them. I understand they don't have the money to pay an attorney up front and wait on the state for reimbursement, and so with Maya's permission, we forge ahead together as a team to get as much as we can from the state.

> ### *Negotiating Guardianship Agreements for Youth*
>
> *Given Maya's age, federal law requires her involvement in the decision to enter into a guardianship. However, the benefits that are being negotiated here flow directly to her guardians and not to her. Hen and Marcus are unable to afford their own attorney.*
>
> * *Who is Julia representing in this negotiation?*
> * *What Model Rules are implicated here?*
> * *Does Julia comply with them?*

Sarah is thrilled that Hen and Marcus are interested despite having to give up extended foster care. We work it out so that daycare is part of the kinship support package,[72] together with a monthly monetary supplement. It is less than what they have been receiving but not quite as low as the base monthly foster care benefit. And Maya and Will both will continue to be covered for their medical. We also make sure that there is a provision in the agreement that reminds Hen and Marcus that they have the right to apply for additional services in the future if they become necessary as well as information about how to apply for those services.[73]

Sarah has a harder time guaranteeing what benefits will be in place after Maya turns 18. In this budget climate, everything is up for grabs. She does confirm that if all things remain the same, Maya will qualify for TANF for her and Will,[74] which will help cover rent for Marcus and Hen. She'll also qualify for daycare if she remains in school.[75] This half-hearted set of assurances seems to be enough for them to move forward.

I work with Sam, the AAG, to get the guardianship petition filed. We agree to use the September permanency planning hearing date for the hearing.

Maya's Last Hearing

Aunt Hen says it's time I get a "Sunday Best" outfit. She says she always hears that when you go to court you should wear your Sunday Best. Never mind that I been going

---

72. Under federal statute, a kinship guardianship assistance agreement must specify "the additional services and assistance that the child and relative guardian will be eligible for under the agreement." 42 U.S.C. § 673(d)(1)(B)(ii).

73. Federal law requires that all kinship guardianship assistance agreements describe the process for requesting additional service. 42 U.S.C. § 673(d)(1)(B)(iii).

74. *Supra* note 57.

75. *Supra* note 59.

to court forever, wearing whatever I had, and nobody seemed to mind. Today is a special day, because it's my last hearing.

So we all show up — me, Will, Uncle Marcus, Aunt Hen, Tasha and Sandra — looking a little out of place for the kind of court we are in. Uncle Marcus in his suit. The girls with their hair all braided and beaded. Aunt Hen wearing high heels. And me in a dress that's cute, but not too cute. Even Will has a little bow tie on.

Jasmine is going to try to come but at the last minute she has to go to work. I didn't tell Minnie about it because I want it to be just us, just family. It's true she is a big part of how I managed to stay put at Safe Harbors and if I hadn't stayed put at Safe Harbors I wouldn't be in court for this now. But I don't want this day to be about Safe Harbors; I want it to be about my family. Not that I won't still call Minnie sometime. I probably will. I imagine someday, when I get my first real job in a restaurant, I will track her down and send her an invitation for dinner, on-the-house. I will have flowers at her table and tell everyone that if it weren't for her I wouldn't be where I am today.

But for now, I want it to just be about the Phillips-Clark family. We are the family that makes everyone look twice because we don't *look* like we belong together but we *act* like we do — a light-skinned black lady with a husband who is dark and handsome, two little black girls in that awkward stage of almost-middle school, a vaguely Asian baby, and me, a red-headed white girl. All of us with our polished shoes, and scrubbed faces.

Julia is here too. This time, though, it's not just me at the table in front of the judge. I'm holding Will who keeps throwing Barkus on the floor and laughing every time I pick him up. Uncle Marcus and Aunt Hen are also at the table. Of course, Sarah and that same skinny-man lawyer are here — as always. Tasha and Sandra are sitting close behind us on folding chairs.

There are some other people sitting in the chairs beside and behind them. Lawyers and some sad-looking parents, social workers, sleepy teenagers and a couple of little squirmy kids with adults. I don't know them, but when Julia asks me if I want to close the hearing so no one else will be there, I say no. I think about all those times I never saw anything happy happen in this court and I think about all the kids who probably think they'll never get out of the system, and all of the social workers who need to know that families can take care of each other, and I think, no, let them see this.

The lady in the uniform says, "All rise," and we all get up and sit down again real quick. I hear Sandra giggle a little bit because I told her that would happen. Aunt Hen shoots her a look and she gets quiet real fast.

The same lady wearing a different fancy shirt this time, one with polka dots, pushes the button, and I think, *this is the last time they're going to have to make a recording about who my family is and isn't, the very last time.*

The Judge looks up, smiling bigger than even last time, and she doesn't seem like she's going to holler at anyone, not today, and not at me, not ever again. She says, "We are here today on two matters: *In re* Guardianship of Maya Phillips, Case no. 16-0478 and *In re* Dependency of Maya Phillips, Case No.10-7-6581. Will the parties please introduce themselves?"

And everyone goes around and introduces themselves and even Will blurts out something, which makes everyone laugh and the judge says, "Yes, you want to be introduced too, don't you? Ms. Phillips, would you like to introduce your son?"

And it takes me a second to realize she's talking to me, and I say, "This is Will Phillips."

"And how old is little Mr. Phillips?"

"He's going to be a year old next week."

"Well, he's looking quite dapper today. Welcome, Mr. Phillips. OK counsel, let's proceed with the guardianship petition first."

"Yes, your honor," says Sarah's lawyer, "The state has filed the petition for relative guardianship in this case. The mother's rights have been terminated and the father is unknown. So notice is not required. The state asks this court to order that Henrietta and Marcus Clark be appointed as guardians for Maya Phillips, with all the rights and duties attendant thereto. The Clarks are Maya's maternal aunt and uncle. You will recall, your honor, that Maya was placed with the Clarks as a part of the permanency plan that was approved by the court back in September of last year. Maya is doing very well and she and her son have fully integrated into the household. Maya has a strong bond with her aunt and uncle and they in turn have demonstrated a strong commitment to caring for her on a permanent basis.[76] Although the Clarks could adopt Maya, they have determined that guardianship is the more appropriate arrangement given the respect that Henrietta Clark wishes to accord her sister, Maya's mother, who is unable to care for Maya.[77] The Clarks are aware of the availability and amount of the guardianship subsidy, and other benefits, which they will be receiving upon entry of the order. And Maya has been consulted with regarding the guardianship and agrees.[78] In fact, we have an agreed order for the court. We ask that it be entered."

---

76. Federal law governing kinship guardianships requires that it be shown that the child has a strong attachment to the relative guardian and that the guardian has demonstrated a strong commitment to caring for the child permanently. 42 U.S.C. §673(d)(3)(A)(iii).

77. Federal law governing kinship guardianships requires that it be shown that neither being returned home nor being adopted are appropriate permanency options for the child. 42 U.S.C. §673(d)(3)(A)(ii).

78. Federal law governing kinship guardianships requires that it be shown that if the subject child is 14 years of age or older that she has been consulted with respect to the guardianship. 42 U.S.C. §673(d)(3)(A)(iv).

Proving Relative Guardianship

The state's attorney makes an offer of proof in support of the relative guardianship in Maya's case. This offer relies on the minimum federal requirements. States may vary on the specific proof required.

- *Does your state permit relative or kinship guardianships?*
- *What are the elements of proof required in your state?*

"Thank you. Does counsel for the youth have anything she wishes to put on the record?"

"Yes your honor. First, I would like to take a moment to introduce Tasha and Sandra Clark, Maya's cousins, who are seated behind me. They took the morning off from school today to be here." The judge smiles and nods, and Julia continues, "Maya is very happy to move forward with this guardianship today. She has been advised that by choosing this option she is foregoing the opportunity to remain in extended foster care beyond her 18th birthday. The family, too, is aware of this fact. However, Maya and her family are fully prepared to forge ahead together. She and Will have their full and loving support now and into the future."

"Thank you, counsel. And welcome Tasha and Sandra. I'm glad you can be here today. I know that this is an agreed order but I would like to have Mr. and Mrs. Clark sworn in, together with Maya."

Julia whispers for me to stand up and raise my right hand. I hand Will to her and he doesn't like it because he doesn't know her. Aunt Hen and Uncle Marcus stand up with their hands raised too. And the judge says, "Do you swear or affirm that you will tell the truth, the whole truth, and nothing but the truth?"

We all say yes and I get a little nervous. This is like real court now. She isn't playing. Julia hands Will back to me and holding him makes us both feel better, more calm.

"Thank you. You may be seated. Mr. Clark?"

"Yes, your honor," Uncle Marcus says.

"Are you willing and prepared to assume all responsibility for Maya Phillips until she turns 18?"

"Yes, your honor, and then some. I love her and that little boy like they were my own."

"Mrs. Clark?"

"Yes, your honor?" Aunt Hen says, her voice cracking a little.

"Are you willing and prepared to assume all responsibility for Maya Phillips until she turns 18?"

"With all my heart, your honor, yes."

"Maya—do you agree to have Henrietta and Marcus Clark serve as your guardians?"

"Yes, ma'am, I do." I remember to say *ma'am* like last time.

"Alright then. Mr. and Mrs. Clark, the court acknowledges and appreciates what wonderful caregivers you have already been for your niece and I know that she is very lucky to have you. The order for guardianship is entered." She signs a paper and hands it to the polka-dot shirt lady. "Now, Ms. Yasko, would you like to move for dismissal?"

"Yes, your honor, I am very happy to move for the dismissal of the dependency of Maya Phillips. The entry of this court's order of guardianship makes unnecessary any further state intervention."

"Any objection?"

The skinny lawyer stands up, "None your honor."

"Maya—your lawyer has asked that your dependency be dismissed. This means you will no longer be in foster care. Do you understand that?"

"Yes, ma'am." I'am sure that I must be grinning pretty big right about now.

"Do you have anything at all you would like to say?"

Will lets out a happy squeal. Even the skinny lawyer smiles.

I wish I had some big speech planned. I wish I could say everything that is trapped inside. Someday it might come out. Someday I might make sense of what happened, why it happened, and what made it all stop at last.

I look at Aunt Hen and Uncle Marcus sitting there proud, at Will who is trying to get down off my lap, and all I have to say is, "No, ma'am. We're all just ready to go home."

Reflections and Exercises

1. *What? So What? Now What? A Five-Minute Reflection Opportunity.* Take just five minutes to write and reflect on the following questions:

    a. What did you feel as you read this final chapter of Maya's story?

    b. How is what you recorded feeling relevant to your learning and/or practice?

    c. Now what do you do with these insights as you move forward in your learning and/or practice?

2. *Achieving Maya's Goals:* Maya and her relatives finally achieved the goals of being together and being free from state intervention.

    a. Why did it take so long? What were the barriers?

    b. Why did it finally happen? What factors contributed to her ability to achieve her goals?

3. *Imagining a Different Story for Maya*: Knowing everything you know now about Maya and her family's journey as well as the challenges that the child welfare system faces, how would you change the way that the state intervenes in the lives of families?

Chapter Eleven

Michael Goes Home

In this chapter you will learn about how Michael and his sisters begin the process of exiting the system. You will learn about the complex legal relationships of siblings when they have different permanent plans that may result in legal barriers to their ongoing relationships. For example, when the state terminates a parent's rights as to one child, what does it mean for that child's siblings? Do they still retain any rights as to their siblings?

In this final chapter about Michael's journey through the child welfare and juvenile justice systems, you will see how Michael's two attorneys work together on his behalf. These attorneys have their own stories that collide with Michael's in different ways. In the end, a permanent plan is implemented but much remains to be told about what the future holds for Michael and his family.

Michael's Lawyer Prepares for Vacation and Termination

Katie is unavoidably distracted. Planning a wedding, even a "simple" one, is a ton of work. Her grandparents are generous and help out financially, but Katie and Zach have no other family interested in pitching in with the details. Aren't mothers of the bride supposed to take care of some of the minutiae? Oh right, not her mother. Her mother is currently residing in Costa Rica with her latest boy crush. Katie secretly hopes her mother will not show up and save them all from the awkwardness of her parents being in the same room. Although between her mother and her father, Katie feels her mom is less of a risk. Her father will get drunk and embarrass her. It is inevitable. It cannot be stopped. She seriously considered not inviting him, but after weighing the pros and cons she decided she could not live with the guilt that her father would heap upon her when he discovered that he was excluded. The wedding will be over soon, but she is stuck with her father for the foreseeable future.

As the wedding date approaches, Katie does her best to stay on top of her caseload. She starts early preparing coverage memos for the three weeks that she will be out of the office. She does her best to make sure that she doesn't have any trials or significant hearings set while she is away. She talks to her supervisor months in advance and asks her to not assign new cases that will need attention during the month of November. Katie prides herself in being organized. It is her way of maintaining control in the out-of-control world of the dependency system. She loves neat and tidy files. She loves color-coded post-it notes. She loves having an email inbox with less than a dozen emails. She holds tightly to these habits. They keep her sane in an insane world.

Michael's file is on top of her "coverage" pile. She types a memo.[1]

Coverage Memorandum

TO: Roger Harris
FROM: Katie Olson
RE: Michael Griffith—siblings' TPR, Deja and Angel Griffith, 11/16/16

Thank you Roger for agreeing to cover Michael's case while I am gone!!

Prelim Hearing: 11/9/16 (Court 5)
TPR: 11/16/16
AAG: Taylor

Mother—Michelle Griffith (Atty-George Bowman)
Deja (2)—pre-adopt foster home
Angel (8)—maternal grandmother (willing to adopt)

Background

Client, Michael (14 yo), resides in a group home (ph.# in file). The PP for him is Return Home to his father. (Note this is a misnomer, since Michael isn't "returning"—he has never lived with his father.) As you know, he is close to his mother and sisters—and very concerned about staying connected to them.

Mom is out of compliance with dependency orders and a termination trial is set for her two youngest children, Deja and Angel Griffith (CASA=Ellen Anderson). There is one more sister (Aliyah), but her father recently obtained custody of her in family court and her dependency will be dismissed.[2] Michael knows about this.

Mom's attorney emailed 10/30 -still no decision by mom on whether she will proceed to trial. She could voluntarily relinquish and enter into open adoption agreements.[3] She could

---

1. Note: Footnotes appearing in the memorandum do not appear in the original memorandum. The notes are to facilitate the understanding of the issues for the users of this book.

2. Some dependent children exit the system through family orders that place them with a fit parent or family member. For a discussion of how this process plays out in California, *See* Judge Leonard Edwards, *Moving Cases from Juvenile to Family Court: How Mediation Can Help*, 16 U.C. Davis J. Juv. L. & Pol'y 535 (2012).

3. Once a child is adopted, the adoptive parents are generally the sole decision-makers with respect to who may have contact with their adoptive child. Open adoption agreements, allowing some ongoing contact between biological parents and children, have been created by state statute and are sometimes negotiated in exchange for a parent's voluntary relinquishment when facing involuntary termination of their parental rights. As of 2014, approximately 28 states had statutes that created written and enforceable open adoption agreements. *See* Children's Bureau, U.S. Dep't of Health & Human Servs., Postadoption Contact Agreements Between Birth and Adoptive Families (2014), [https://perma.cc/W8SH-FBTH]. A handful of states provide explicitly that mutual agreements for post-adoption contact are nonbinding and unenforceable. *See* Ohio Rev. Code Ann. § 3107.39(3)(b); S.C. Code Ann. § 63-9-760(D); S.D. Codified Laws § 25-6-17. In other states, courts have held open adoption agreements are unenforceable without a state statute explicitly authorizing them. *See, e.g.*, Birth Mother v. Adoptive Parents, 59 P.3d 1233 (Nev. 2002) (finding that a post-adoption contact agreement was unenforceable without specific statute providing for enforceability); Matter of Welfare

also work out a relative guardianship with the grandmother for Angel. She is reportedly using again and back together with the father of her youngest, Deja. That father (DJ) has not participated in services and has unresolved issues around possible sexual abuse of Angel. Not sure how to assess the likelihood of trial. 50-50?

Sibling visitation order

Last February I set a motion for sibling visitation to get regular visits for Michael with his sisters. They were all in separate placements and the Department dropped the ball. The court ordered bi-monthly visits with Aliyah, Angel and Deja. The court also allowed Michael to have liberal visits with Aliyah and Angel "as arranged by caretakers."[4]

Per my last contact with client (10/27), sibling visits have been consistent and are still important to Michael.

Coverage Needed

Attend trial or negotiate sibling contact in agreed orders of relinquishment/open adoption/ guardianship.

Michael's goal is to protect his relationship with his siblings and make sure that his sisters aren't getting railroaded and aren't being forced to give up on their mom. I have talked with him extensively about how/whether this can be done. I don't think Michael has legal standing at his sisters' trial. I researched whether he is a party to his sisters' cases and he isn't.[5]

If trial goes forward—argue it isn't in the best interest of the children to have their mother's rights terminated.

Michael does not want his mom's rights to parent Deja and Angel terminated—so he wants to do what he can to stop that from happening. However, he knows that if mom decides not to fight the petition he can't do anything about it on his own. If the case goes to trial, his ability to influence the decision is also limited.

Mom's attorney said he doesn't need him as a witness if they go to trial. I think this is because parents who call their children as witnesses may not be looked favorably upon by the judge. Michael asked if he can go and observe and say something on his own. Caseworker said she did not have an objection but thought his attorney should be present with him. I don't think Michael really wants to sit through a 2–3 day trial—I told him that you could go for

---

of D.D.G., 558 N.W.2d 481, 485 (Minn. 1997) ("We again emphasize that there is no legal impediment to informal open adoption arrangements made at the time of adoption. *C.H.*, 554 N.W.2d at 741. But whether open adoption arrangements may be enforced in court is a different issue.... [T]he termination of parental rights statute indicates that the legislature intended a clean break in the parent-child relationship at the time of termination. See MINN.STAT. § 260.241, subd. 1").

4. The federal Fostering Connections to Success Act (2008) encouraged states to ensure frequent visitation for siblings in foster care. Pub. L. No. 110-351, 122 Stat. 3949 (codified as amended at 42 U.S.C. § 671(a)(31)). Some states have statutes that require the State to provide sibling visitation for children in care. *See e.g.,* CAL. WELF. & INST. CODE § 16002; GA. CODE ANN. § 15-11-135(e); IND. CODE § 31-28-5-2; IOWA CODE § 232.108; MD. CODE ANN. FAM. LAW § 5-525.2; NEB. REV. STAT. § 43-1311.02; N.J. ADMIN. CODE § 10:46B-3.4; 40 TEX. ADMIN. CODE § 700.1327; WASH. REV. CODE § 13.34.130.

5. A few state legislatures and courts have established rights for siblings to assert themselves in each other's dependency or termination cases. Randi Mandelbaum, *Delicate Balances: Assessing The Needs And Rights Of Siblings In Foster Care To Maintain Their Relationships Post-Adoption,* 41 N.M. L. REV. 1, 13 (2011). For example, California has a statute allowing siblings to petition to assert sibling rights 388(b) and California also has an exception to termination if there would be "substantial interference with a child's sibling relationship" CAL. WELF. & INST. CODE § 366.26(c)(1)(B)(v); *In re* Hector, 23 Cal. Rptr. 3d 104, 108 (Cal. Ct. App. 2005).

him—although you couldn't testify for him. I know this is unusual to appear at a trial where our client is not a party, but it makes sense in this case since Michael's relationship with his siblings is important and the issue of sibling contact will or should come up.

If Michael wants to testify he can offer evidence that it is not in the best interest of the children to terminate based on (1) his knowledge of their relationship with their mother and (2) based on the risk termination will be to their sibling relationships. Even though there are statutes that suggest this relationship should be given consideration at adoption (see below) it isn't guaranteed.

RCW 26.33.420, the adoption statute provides that "law and science" recognize the importance of the sibling bond and mom's attorney Bowman should be encouraged to argue this and get evidence in through the caseworker or otherwise about this.[6] I emailed him this publication: _Sibling Issues in Foster Care and Adoption_, Child Welfare Info. Gateway (Jan. 2013)[7] citing social science supporting the sibling bond. Michael's arguments will be stronger with Angel than Deja because of the amount of time they have spent together. This is too bad, because he is most at risk of losing Deja who is in foster care. Frankly, Michael will probably get access to Angel as long as she remains with the grandmother and Michael can stay on the grandmother's good side.[8]

I'm not sure what else Michael could try to do/argue; feel free to think of something!

Sibling Rights

- In your jurisdiction, what rights do siblings have to participate in each other's proceedings?

- Can they petition for contact post-adoption? How?

If mom relinquishes—negotiate sibling contact in open adoption agreement: [9]

Unfortunately there is nothing that requires the state to consider Michael's relationship with his siblings at relinquishment; however, at adoption the court is supposed to consider

---

6. WASH. REV. CODE § 26.33.420 ("The legislature finds that the importance of children's relationships with their siblings is well recognized in law and science. The bonds between siblings are often irreplaceable, leading some experts to believe that sibling relationships can be longer lasting and more influential than any other over a person's lifetime.")

7. CHILD WELFARE INFORMATION GATEWAY, U.S. DEP'T OF HEALTH & HUMAN SERVS., SIBLING ISSUES IN FOSTER CARE AND ADOPTION (2013) [https://perma.cc/AYS2-SWEC].

8. In most states, siblings have very limited rights with respect to post-adoption contact. Jill Elaine Hasday, _Siblings in Law,_ 65 VAND. L. REV. 897, 904–912 (2012). In an unusual case, the New Jersey Supreme Court, in _In the Matter of D.C.,_ held that siblings can petition for visitation with their brothers and sisters who have been adopted by non-relatives, subject to the avoidance of harm standard pursuant to the state's third-party visitation statute. 203 N.J. 545, 573, 574 (N.J. 2010) ("the analysis is a fact-intensive one in which the sibling "bear[s] the burden of establishing by a preponderance of the evidence that visitation is necessary to avoid harm to the child." Citing _Moriarty, supra,_ 177 N.J. at 117, 827 A.2d 203.).

9. Less than half of the states that have statutes regarding post-adoption contact specifically address post-adoption sibling contact. Mandelbaum, _supra_ note 5, at 18. A few state statutes provide for some limited rights to sibling visitation for formerly dependent children post-adoption. _See e.g.,_ ARK. CODE ANN. § 9-9-215 (c)("Sibling visitation shall not terminate if the adopted child was in the custody of the Department of Human Services and had a sibling who was not adopted by the same family and before adoption the circuit court in the juvenile dependency-neglect or families-in-need-of-services case has determined that it is in the best interests of the siblings to visit and has ordered

sibling contact. *See* RCW.26.33.430. I think the mom would be open to including sibling contact in any open adoption agreement she negotiates with the Department if she relinquishes. The tricky part is knowing that this is happening—so if AAG or mom's attorney says the trial is not going forward try to get with mom's attorney as soon as possible to make sure she negotiates for sibling contact in addition to her own contact with the girls. AAG may support this but it will depend on the foster parents and whether they want to maintain contact.

I have gone over all of this with Michael already—of course he may not remember or understand it. I told him that you will be getting in touch with him and I think he was very excited to get to talk to you/see you again.

ONE MORE THING: If you want to talk about the sibling issues or anything procedural, attorney Julia Yasko (jyasko@jyasko.net) has been a great resource and is always willing to talk through issues. She is the most experienced dependency attorney out there.

THANK YOU!

Katie is concerned that the memo is too long. Roger knows Michael and they have discussed the case quite a bit. She doesn't want to offend Roger by telling him things he may already know, but she wants him to feel prepared and she wants to make sure he knows that this is an important case. And, there is always the chance that another attorney from her office will have to step in if Roger has something come up. Writing a lengthy memo also helps relieve her guilt about leaving Michael during this critical stage in his case.

> ### *Work-Life Balance*
>
> *Katie struggles with how thorough she needs to be when she prepares to leave her caseload to go on vacation.*
>
> - *Can she write lengthy memos for all of her cases?*
> - *How else can she be sure that her clients will be competently represented in her absence?*

Katie stays late in the office finishing her coverage memos and tidying up her office. This is the longest vacation she has taken and she is worried that something will come up that she hasn't anticipated. She dreads the thought of her colleagues being irritated or her clients not being served. She can hear Zach's voice in her head, "Let it go. We're getting married!" It has been his mantra for everything the past few months. She heeds his advice. Leaving the office she feels lighter than usual, her brief case has no files.

---

visitation between the siblings to occur after the adoption."); Fl. Stat. § 63.0427 (A child's whose parents' rights have been terminated has the right to have the court consider postadoption contact with the agreement of the adoptive parents.); Mass. Gen. Laws ch. 119, § 26B (The court or department shall ensure post-adoption sibling visitation "whenever reasonable and practical and based upon a determination of the best interests of the child.").

Michael's Criminal Defense Attorney Crosses Over to Dependency Practice

Roger is a seasoned public defender. He is caught off guard by how much the termination of parental rights proceeding bothers him. How is it the court can sever a parent-child relationship permanently? Or a sibling relationship? It does not make sense to him. He cannot imagine what could undo his relationship with his children, short of death. A court order declaring that he is not Sanya's father and Samuel is not her brother? Impossible. A court has no power to change his flesh and blood. Termination of parental rights is a death sentence in spirit but not in truth.[10]

> ### *Reinstatement of Parental Rights*
> - *Does your state have a statute that permits reinstatement of parental rights post-termination?*
> - *If so, what are the criteria? If not, should there be such a statute?*

Roger can't stop thinking about his own children as he reviews Michael's coverage memo. Sanya is just a year older than Michael. Roger's heart swells up inside his chest when he thinks about his teenage daughter. People warned him that teenage girls were trouble, but his girl is perfect. She is also an exceptional sister to her younger brother. Roger is blessed. He looks at her photo on his desk and then focuses again on the memo before him. He notes to himself that he is not cut out for dependency practice. The stakes are too high, the issues too emotional.

On the way to the courthouse for the termination hearing, Roger mulls over what he will say to Michael and tries to imagine how Michael will respond. They had a long discussion a few days ago, when it was still unclear exactly what might happen. Roger feels heavy and, as is his habit, says a short prayer asking God for help.

Roger shakes Michael's hand as he sits down next to him on the bench outside of the courtroom. "So, it looks like your mother has decided not to go to trial." Roger looks serious and gets right to the point.

"What does that mean?" Michael asks.

"It means that she is agreeing that Deja and Angel can stay where they are — permanently." Roger feels sick as he says this out loud.

---

10. While termination of parental rights is generally a final decision, in response to high numbers of legal orphans some states have implemented legislation that permits the reinstatement of parental rights under certain circumstances. Lashanda Taylor, *Resurrecting Parents of Legal Orphans: Unterminating Parental Rights*, 17 Va. J. Soc. Pol'y & L. 318,331 (2010); *see, e.g.,* Cal. Welf. & Inst. Code § 366.26(i)(2); Wash. Rev. Code. § 13.34.215.

"She's giving up." Michael looks down. Roger says nothing. They sit quietly for a few minutes.

Michael gets up and looks toward the door, "I don't care."

"Your mother's attorney negotiated an agreement so that you can still have regular contact with Angel and some contact with Deja as well." Roger tries to sound confident without glossing over how painful this is for Michael.

Termination of Parental Rights and Open Adoption Agreements

- *How many cases in your jurisdiction resolve through relinquishment and open adoption agreements? Is there data available?*
- *Are these agreements enforceable in your state and how?*

"She didn't even show up today?" Roger hears contempt in Michael's voice.

"I don't think so." Roger does not know for sure, but he had seen Michelle's attorney alone talking to the Assistant Attorney General.

"Fuck this." Michael heads for the door.

Roger does not know whether to follow him. It happens so quickly. Michael's caseworker heads him off before he gets to the door. Roger watches the caseworker touch Michael's arm and say something to him. He can't make out what she is saying, words of comfort? Michael stands still for a moment then shakes his head and walks out the door. Roger sits frozen on the bench. He watches the caseworker follow Michael outside. Roger has no idea what to do. He reaches in his pocket for his phone. He types, "Love you sweetie" and hits send. He looks down as his phone vibrates, "Thx Daddy, Luv u 2."

Michael's Last Hearing?

It's been several months since Michael went to court for his sisters' hearing. That was rough. His mom's rights to his sisters "terminated." He hates thinking about it. Michael hopes this is the last time he has to come to court.

Michael passes through security and the first person he recognizes is Katie. She is standing against a wall talking to someone who looks like a lawyer. She is holding a stack of files and Michael thinks her arms must get tired. He glances around, sees no other familiar faces and takes a seat in the lobby to begin the familiar waiting game. He chooses a seat where he can see the entrance. He is anxious to see who shows up today.

His father is the first to show. Michael notes his dad's attire—a suit? Michael is impressed. He has never seen his father dressed this way—never seen anyone related to him dressed this way—and he feels pride. Michael's dad could almost be mistaken for one of the attorneys. The suit his dad is wearing isn't quite the quality of one that Roger would wear, but nevertheless it is a very nice suit.

Michael catches his dad's eye as he enters the lobby. Eric makes his way toward his son. He smiles nervously. He does not look relaxed. Michael gets up and hugs his dad awkwardly. They are getting used to each other. Michael remembers that his dad is not accustomed to juvenile court. Michael suddenly feels like he should do something to make his father more comfortable. Maybe he can help him relax. This is old hat for Michael.

After a few minutes, Katie comes over and Michael introduces her to his father. Eric smiles, still nervous, and shakes Katie's hand. Michael follows Katie to an interview room one last time.

"So, this is it. You OK?" Katie seems different. Michael isn't sure why, but something is different.

"Yeah." Michael feels different too. He feels old.

"We've talked about what is going to happen today in court, but do you have any questions? Anything new to tell me?" Katie is cheerful. Michael wonders if it has to do with him or with some other case she is handling this morning.

"I'm good." Michael wants to ask Katie if she knows whether his mother will be here today, but he doesn't. Best just to leave it alone and see what happens.

"OK. I don't think that there will be any problems with getting the plan approved. And, as we discussed, once the judge signs the order placing you with your dad, assuming everything goes well you can have your case dismissed in six months. You probably don't even have to come back to court again." Michael nods in agreement.[11]

"I hope, I mean I believe, things will go well, but if they don't, you can call any time. This is a big change for both of you, so it's important that you get support." Michael listens carefully to his attorney. He can see that she is trying to be positive.

"Do I have to talk in court?" Michael cannot guess—it seems like each time it is a little different.

"You may. I bet the judge will want to hear something from you. Even if it is just about school."

"Will my mom be here?" Michael blurts it without really thinking. It is nagging at him, so it will be better just to know rather than wait to see who is actually seated in the courtroom.

"I don't know, Michael. She could be. How do you feel about seeing her?" Katie's face gets soft and Michael feels some relief.

---

11. Some States require a period of supervision after a child is returned home prior to dismissal of the dependency petition. *See, e.g.,* Wash. Rev. Code § 13.34.145(11) (casework supervision must continue for at least six months after child is returned home).

"Doesn't really matter." Michael lies. He doesn't mean to lie but it seems like the right thing to say.

"Her attorney didn't file anything for this hearing, so I'm pretty sure that she doesn't have an objection. Even if she does, the judge is unlikely to give it too much weight at this point. Have you talked to her? Do you know if she is OK with this?"

Michael hesitates. It is a habit now to think before revealing information, even though he knows Katie can be trusted. He is still angry with his mom. How can she have given up on his sisters? She loves drugs and her stupid boyfriend more than her children. "I haven't talked to her for a while. Seems like she shouldn't really have a say."

"That's true."

"I don't think she cares," Michael adds.

"That's probably not true," Katie responds quickly looking up from her file directly at Michael. Michael looks away. He is not interested in getting emotional right now.

The familiar run-up to court proceeds. The face of a court bailiff peers through the window of the interview room and mouths "Ready?" to Katie. Katie nods and closes her file. She turns to Michael "Ready?" Michael lets this question hang. There is no way to know.

Michael sits in his usual seat centered in the courtroom in front of the judge. His father is to his right next to his attorney, a short middle-aged white man that Michael has seen a number of times before. It feels good to see his dad there for the first time. Michael glances over his shoulder to see if there is anyone else in the courtroom and he sees Roger slip in and take a seat behind him. They nod to one another. A few seconds later, the door swings open again. Michael braces as he anticipates his mother, and is instead surprised to see James followed by Mr. Jeffries. They pat Roger on the back and shake his hand. James leans forward and pats Michael on the shoulder before taking a seat next to Roger. Mr. Jeffries nods to Michael.

The bailiff calls out Michael's name in court. "Before the court is the matter of Michael Griffith, Case Number 15-7-0234. Will the parties introduce themselves?" The people sitting at the tables go around, as usual, and put their names on the record.

Michael holds his breath when he sees the judge look up and take note that someone has entered the courtroom. It is, of course, his mother. He turns to look. She is much thinner than the last time. She has dark circles under her eyes. In his memory she is much prettier than she appears today. He is used to seeing her high, but this isn't that look. She looks at Michael apologetically and moves quickly to take a seat next to her attorney. She says, "I'm sorry judge. I'm really sorry for being late."

Michael's face gets warm. He is angry and embarrassed by his mother's late entrance. Once again she shows that she doesn't care about him enough to even show up on time. Yet, she shows up. Despite his anger, Michael is relieved. He hadn't been sure whether he really wanted her here or not today. Now he knows. He wants her here.

The hearing continues. Michael is familiar now with how the lawyers each talk, the judge asks questions and eventually she turns to Michael's father. He pays attention, curious to hear what his dad might say in court. He feels nervous for him, although he isn't sure why. Michael's dad is always confident when they visit, but today he looks less so. Michael thinks it's probably the suit. It probably is uncomfortable.

"Mr. Grayson, is there anything you would like me to know that your attorney has not already covered?" Here it comes, Michael braces for his father's voice.

"Thank you, your honor. It's a privilege to be here today in your courtroom. I really didn't think I would have this chance to be in my son's life in this way. I know that I have not been there for him, for a while, and I am anxious to make it up to him. I know it won't be easy.[12] But I believe in our abilities to help each other and to contribute to each other's spiritual, intellectual and emotional growth. I am so proud of Michael and the young man that he is becoming. I want to do whatever I can to ensure that he continues to develop in a positive way." Eric looks at Michael as he finishes talking. Michael is glued to his father's words, his big, beautiful words.

Eric's attorney nods approvingly. The judge also nods and then looks at someone in the back of the courtroom. "Mr. Harris, is there something you would like to say?"

Michael is still digesting his father's words. It takes him a few seconds to understand that the judge is talking to Roger who has stood up apparently signaling to the judge that he wants to say something.

"Yes, your honor. Well, actually, I want to introduce Mr. Jeffries and his son James Jeffries. I know that this is a little out of the ordinary, but these two men are also very committed to the plan that you are approving today. Mr. Jeffries was Michael's foster parent and James is his son. They were hoping to say something briefly on the record, if no one objects."

Katie leans in immediately to Michael and whispers, "Are you ok with this? I'm sorry I didn't know they were coming and I don't know what they plan on saying." The other lawyers also whisper to their clients.

Michael looks over his shoulder at Roger, Mr. Jeffries and James. He nods approval. No one objects.

---

12. The Adoption and Foster Care Analysis and Reporting System (AFCARS) collects national data on the number of children who return to foster care within 12 months after they are reunited with a parent. The national median reentry rate for 2013 was 12%, *i.e.*, 12% of children reentered foster care in less than twelve months following reunification. The rates vary by state from 3.1% to 28%. There is a moderate correlation between the age of children entering foster care and the reentry rate. States with a relatively high percentage of children entering foster care age at age 12 years or older also had a relatively high reentry rate. Children's Bureau, U.S. Dep't of Health & Human Servs., Child Welfare Outcomes 2010 — 2013: Report to Congress 20–21 (2016), [https://perma.cc/S9BH-SUHZ].

> ### *Ethical Obligations When Presenting Evidence*
> - *Does Roger behave ethically by presenting Mr. Jeffries' and James to the court without his client's permission?*

Mr. Jeffries stands up. He is holding a hat and a pair of gloves in his hands. He speaks slowly, "Your honor, I just want Michael and both of his parents to know that he is a good boy, a special boy, and I am here to support them in any way I can. I had him for a short while, but I feel like he is family. And his family is family. I won't get in the way, but I am happy to be here for support. Thank you."

"Thank you, Mr. Jeffries. It is wonderful to have you in my courtroom. I appreciate the work you do on behalf of so many youth and I hope that Michael and his family will take you up on your generous offer of support." Judge Adams is as close to beaming as Michael has ever seen.

James jumps up next to his father. James is holding a book in his hand. "Your honor, can I say something?"

Judge Adams says, "Yes. Please state your name for the record."

"My name is James Jeffries. This is my father. I have been able to spend quite a bit of time with Michael, like a brother. I just want Michael's father, Mr. Grayson, to know that we want to stay part of Michael's life. Part of both of your lives. We are the same community and we need to stick together and help one another. That's all. Thank you." Michael feels pride at being called a brother to James. This is unexpected and welcome.

Michael tunes out after this, letting it soak in. He hears the judge thank James and Mr. Jeffries again and then lecture his father. Michael jerks quickly to attention at the sound of his mother's voice.

"Can I say something?" Michael looks at his mother as she asks the judge this question. He feels dread. Can't she just be present and not say anything?

Judge Adams looks up from her desk and looks at Michelle and then at her attorney. She pauses to give the lawyer a chance to weigh in. Michelle and her lawyer whisper back and forth and then the lawyer says, "Your honor, Ms. Griffith supports Michael's desire to live with his father and would like to address the court briefly."

The judge looks at Michelle with an expression that Michael cannot read. "Ms. Griffith. Go ahead. What would you like me to know?"

Michelle pauses, swallowing hard. "Your honor, I actually really want Michael to know that by agreeing to this it doesn't mean that I don't love him as much or that I will not keep working to get better, get healthy, so that I can be a better mother." She is trying hard to not cry.

The judge looks at her intently. Waits. "Thank you, Ms. Griffith. Is there anything else?"

Michelle closes her eyes. Michael can't look at her. "And I'm so sorry about his baby sisters, it hurts me every day too. That's all. Thank you." Michelle wipes her eyes and grabs a tissue from the box on the table.

"Thank you, Ms. Griffith. I see that the order continues to allow you visits with your son. I hope that you can work with the Department and Mr. Grayson to keep up your relationship with Michael." Judge Adams' speaks softly now. Michael doesn't look up to see her face.

The judge goes on, "This is not the end for you and Michael. It is a beginning."[13]

The judge then turns to Michael and starts her speech. "Michael, it is good to see you today."

Michael does not look up from the table for a while. He does not hear anything that the judge says to him. He feels eyes on him, but only the judge is looking at him. His mother's eyes are shut. His father is looking intently at the judge, as if to avoid looking elsewhere. Katie glances toward him. He looks at her quickly wondering if she knows how he feels. Have other youth been here? Done this? When the judge finally gets to "Michael, is there anything you would like me to know today?" Michael feels exhausted.

"No."

The judge does not persist. Michael is surprised, but thinks maybe she is giving him a break because it might be the last time she will see him. She ends with something about how "lucky" Michael is to have so many people supporting him today. She is confident that everything will go well for him and he will have a successful life.

As they file out of the courtroom, Michael feels a sense of relief and confusion. He's not sure what comes next, who he should talk to, what he should say. His caseworker is following him and wants to move his luggage from her car to his father's. His father is shaking hands with Mr. Jeffries. Roger and Katie are smiling, sharing a joke. His mother's presence is the strongest. He doesn't have anything to say to her, but he feels her next to him. She moves close and stuffs a folded piece of paper into his hand.

"I know you like reading and writing. I found this in a book and I copied it down for you. Maybe you've seen it. I love you, Michael. I'm not gonna give up, I promise." Michael watches his mother leave the courthouse. Through the doors he gets a glimpse of DJ in the parking lot smoking a cigarette, waiting for his mother. He unfolds the paper and reads.

---

13. Michael's mother's contact will continue pursuant to the dependency order. Once the dependency is dismissed, contact would be governed by a parenting plan or family court order, if any.

Mother to Son[14]

By Langston Hughes

Well, son, I'll tell you:
Life for me ain't been no crystal stair.
It's had tacks in it,
And splinters,
And boards torn up,
And places with no carpet on the floor—Bare.
But all the time
I'se been a-climbin' on,
And reachin' landin's,
And turnin' corners,
And sometimes goin' in the dark
Where there ain't been no light.
So, boy, don't you turn back.
Don't you set down on the steps.
'Cause you finds it's kinder hard.
Don't you fall now—
For I'se still goin', honey,
I'se still climbin',
And life for me ain't been no crystal stair.

Reflections and Exercises

1. *What? So What? Now What? A Five-Minute Reflection Opportunity.* Take just five minutes to write and reflect on the following questions:

   a. What did you feel as you read about the ways that the legal systems impacted Michael?

   b. How is what you recorded feeling relevant to your learning and/or practice?

   c. Now what do you do with these insights as you move forward in your learning and/or practice?

2. *The Rights of Siblings.* Sibling rights are very underdeveloped in the law and vary widely from state to state. In the child welfare context, if you believe that adoptive parents should have the ultimate authority to make decisions over their adopted children without interference, it may make sense to weigh in favor of giving fewer rights to siblings. In *Troxel v. Granville*, 530 U.S. 57 (2000), the U.S. Supreme Court held that fit parents have a constitutional right to decide with whom their children should visit in the context of grandparents seeking

---

14. Langston Hughes, Langston Hughes: Poetry for Young People 14 (Arnold Rampersad & David Roessel eds., 2006).

visitation with their grandchildren. How do you think statutes that grant rights to siblings for post-adoption contact would fare under *Troxel?*

3. ***Imagining a Different Story for Michael:*** In Chapter One you were asked to think about the stated purposes of the child welfare and juvenile offender systems and whether you thought that there were other purposes that these systems serve. Now, having considered Michael's journey through both systems, consider those stated or other purposes again as you consider how Michael fared.

   a. What purposes were served by the state's intervention in Michael's life?

   b. Did the systems that intervened achieve their intended goals?

   c. Are there other interventions that may have achieved the same goals? What would those be? Can lawyers advocate for the types of interventions that you suggest?

   d. What if there had been no state intervention?

Epilogue

Your Last Imaginings

I. Clients, Their Families and Friends

We enter our clients' stories for a season, but those stories continue long after the clients have exited our lives. In five years, Michael will be nineteen and Maya will be twenty-one. They are free to decide which relationships to establish and maintain and which they will sever and ignore. Just as clients grow and change so too, their family members and friends move forward with their own trajectories. All of the characters in these chapters undoubtedly will have setbacks and then move ahead. People will die and some may be born, all without Katie or Julia ever knowing.

Where will Michael and Maya be in five years? Who will they be connected to and disconnected from? Write your epilogue for them. You can narrate a day in their life five years from now. You can write a short story that brings us into the arc of a key relationship. You can write a series of poems that shows where they are with their key friends and family. You can write a song. A play. Whatever your preferred mode of expression, indulge your imagination. And feel free to do research and footnote, supporting your imaginings.

II. The Professionals, Community and the System

The lawyers, social workers and service providers in this book are perched at the brink of certain system de-funding and possible system collapse. As was foreshadowed by James Jeffries, community movements have bubbled up as those affected lose patience with state systems that intervene in harmful, even deadly, ways. Think about the many people involved in Michael's and Maya's lives. Who will remain within the faltering systems and why? Who will leave and why? What will happen to the systems themselves? Will change finally come? How? Tell the story of change through the eyes of one of the lawyers, professionals or community members looking back five years from now. And feel free to do research and footnote, supporting your imaginings.

Index*

---

* The references indexed here can be found in the supporting footnotes at the pages noted.